Frommer's®

W9-BMT-983

Walt Disney World® & Orlando with Kids

2nd Edition

by Laura Lea Miller

Here's what the critics say about Frommer's:

"Amazingly easy to use. Very portable, very complete."

—*Booklist*

"Detailed, accurate, and easy-to-read information for all price ranges."
—*Glamour Magazine*

"Hotel information is close to encyclopedic."

—*Des Moines Sunday Register*

"Frommer's Guides have a way of giving you a real feel for a place."
—*Knight Ridder Newspapers*

WILEY

Wiley Publishing, Inc.

Published by:

Wiley Publishing, Inc.
111 River St.
Hoboken, NJ 07030-5774

ISBN-13: 978-0-471-77343-6
ISBN-10: 0-471-77343-3

Editor: Naomi P. Kraus
Production Editor: Eric T. Schroeder
Cartographer: Roberta Stockwell
Photo Editor: Richard Fox
Production by Wiley Indianapolis Composition Services

For information on our other products and services or to obtain technical support, please contact our Customer Care Department within the U.S. at 800/762-2974, outside the U.S. at 317/572-3993 or fax 317/572-4002.

Wiley also publishes its books in a variety of electronic formats. Some content that appears in print may not be available in electronic formats.

Manufactured in the United States of America

5 4 3 2 1

Contents

List of Maps

Acknowledgments

Thanks to Amy Voss of the Orlando/Orange County Convention & Visitors Bureau; Gary Buchanan, Dave Herbst, Charles Stovall, and Lisa Boisvert over at Walt Disney World; Michael McLean and Jennifer Hodges at Universal Orlando; Jackie Wilson at SeaWorld, Nadine DeGenova of DeGenova Public Relations, not to mention all of the managers, sales reps, and PR reps at the countless hotels and resorts who have all been so incredibly helpful in answering my many questions and making my travels—and my life—so very much easier.

Big thanks to my five children—Ryan, Austin, Nicolas, Hailey, and Davis—who happily offer their opinions on just about everything. Their endless energy and enthusiasm is invaluable when touring the theme parks time after time. And deepest appreciation to my sister, who, instead of taking a few well deserved days off, often heads south to tour Orlando's many offerings and pound the pavement right alongside me.

My agent, Julie Hill, whose encouragement and enthusiasm are more appreciated than she'll ever know, is a blessing. And thanks to Naomi Kraus, my editor, for the time and effort she put into helping me with this project, not to mention her advice and guidance, which is always greatly appreciated.

—Laura Lea Miller

An Invitation to the Reader

In researching this book, we discovered many wonderful places—hotels, restaurants, shops, and more. We're sure you'll find others. Please tell us about them, so we can share the information with your fellow travelers in upcoming editions. If you were disappointed with a recommendation, we'd love to know that, too. Please write to:

Frommer's Walt Disney World & Orlando with Kids, 2nd Edition
Wiley Publishing, Inc. • 111 River St. • Hoboken, NJ 07030-5774

An Additional Note

Please be advised that travel information is subject to change at any time—and this is especially true of prices. We therefore suggest that you write or call ahead for confirmation when making your travel plans. The author, editors, and publisher cannot be held responsible for the experiences of readers while traveling. Your safety is important to us, however, so we encourage you to stay alert and be aware of your surroundings. Keep a close eye on cameras, purses, and wallets, all favorite targets of thieves and pickpockets.

About the Author

Laura Lea Miller is a freelance writer based in Orchard Park, New York. This snowbird has gladly flown south to warmer weather to spend countless hours scouring Central Florida's many theme parks, hotels, resorts, and restaurants over the years—both with and without her five children. A family-travel expert who focuses on Central Florida, Laura continues to religiously make an annual pilgrimage (or four or five) to the Land the Mouse Built, to ensure she can check out all of Orlando's latest and greatest offerings and provide you with the most up-to-date insider information. She's written several other Orlando and Florida books, including *Frommer's Walt Disney World & Orlando* and *Walt Disney World & Orlando For Dummies,* and has contributed to *Frommer's Florida.*

Other Great Guides for Your Trip:

Frommer's Florida
Frommer's Walt Disney World & Orlando
Frommer's Irreverent Guide to Walt Disney World
The Unofficial Guide to Walt Disney World
The Unofficial Disney Companion
Beyond Disney: The Unofficial Guide

Frommer's Star Ratings, Icons & Abbreviations

Every hotel, restaurant, and attraction listing in this guide has been ranked for quality, value, service, amenities, and special features using a **star-rating system.** In country, state, and regional guides, we also rate towns and regions to help you narrow down your choices and budget your time accordingly. Hotels and restaurants are rated on a scale of zero (recommended) to three stars (exceptional). Attractions, shopping, nightlife, towns, and regions are rated according to the following scale: zero stars (recommended), one star (highly recommended), two stars (very highly recommended), and three stars (must-see).

In addition to the star-rating system, we also use **six feature icons** that point you to the great deals, in-the-know advice, and unique experiences that separate travelers from tourists. Throughout the book, look for:

Finds	Special finds—those places only insiders know about
Fun Fact	Fun facts—details that make travelers more informed and their trips more fun
Moments	Special moments—those experiences that memories are made of
Overrated	Places or experiences not worth your time or money
Tips	Insider tips—great ways to save time and money
Value	Great values—where to get the best deals

The following **abbreviations** are used for credit cards:

AE	American Express	DISC	Discover	V	Visa
DC	Diners Club	MC	MasterCard		

Frommers.com

Now that you have the guidebook to a great trip, visit our website at **www.frommers.com** for travel information on more than 3,000 destinations. With features updated regularly, we give you instant access to the most current trip-planning information available. At Frommers.com, you'll also find the best prices on airfares, accommodations, and car rentals—and you can even book travel online through our travel booking partners. At Frommers.com, you'll also find the following:

- Online updates to our most popular guidebooks
- Vacation sweepstakes and contest giveaways
- Newsletter highlighting the hottest travel trends
- Online travel message boards with featured travel discussions

How to Feel Like an Orlando Family

In my house, and undoubtedly in many others, the mere mention of Walt Disney World and Orlando can cause little eyes to sparkle and smiles to appear, a phenomenon often accompanied by the spontaneous outbreak of jumping and dancing about the room. If there is any doubt at all that a trip to Orlando is worth the effort, I need only see the wonder, amazement, and excitement in the faces of my five kids, not to mention the tens of thousands of other kids I see when visiting Orlando. It simply confirms what I've known for a long time: that this is truly a magical place where children and families are the real VIPs.

For every business that caters to adult travelers, there are three or four others that roll out the red carpet to children of all ages and their families. The city tempts you with special child check-in desks, kid-friendly menus, character meet-and-greets, and slightly lower admission prices for those 3 to 9 years old. Some hotels and motels have special programs for youngsters—and, in a few cases, teenagers—giving them their own space to hang around with their peers. A handful of landing zones offer rooms themed to cartoon characters or action heroes. And almost every one of them lets kids ages 17 and under stay free with paying adults.

Thank Walter Elias Disney and his wannabes for that.

Uncle Walt laid the foundation for what in the past 3 decades has become America's *No. 1 vacation destination* for the young and young at heart.

Until Disney's heirs opened the Magic Kingdom in 1971, water-skiing and alligator wrestling shows were the only attractions, and central Florida's motels and restaurants had to make most of their living off business travelers or those who came to visit relatives at a high-and-dry naval training center.

Nowadays, The Kingdom That Walt Built tempts you with four major theme parks; two water parks; a dozen smaller attractions; two nightclub districts for when Mom and Dad need a rest; tens of thousands of hotel rooms, including timeshares or what they call the vacation club; scores of restaurants; and two cruise ships. Universal Orlando adds two theme parks to the mix, while SeaWorld tosses in two (soon to be three) more, and the smaller fry ante up 80 or so lesser attractions, an avalanche of restaurants, and enough hotel rooms to boost central Florida's total population to more than 114,000.

Of course, all of that comes with a price, and you're the one paying.

Amusement Business, a trade journal that charts theme-park attendance, says a typical family of four spends about $300 a day for admission, parking, a fast-food lunch, and two small souvenirs. That's without a room, other meals, transportation to and from Orlando, and other expenses.

Orlando Area Theme Parks

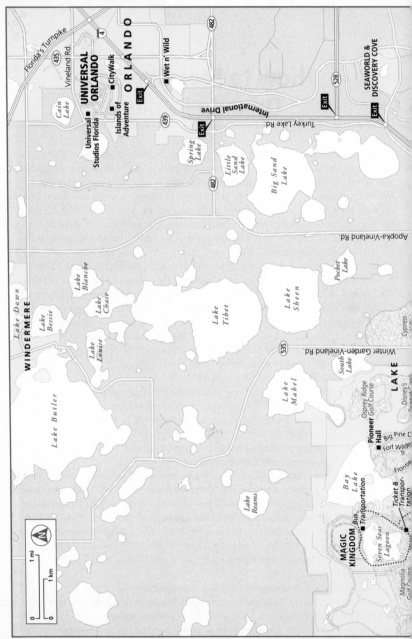

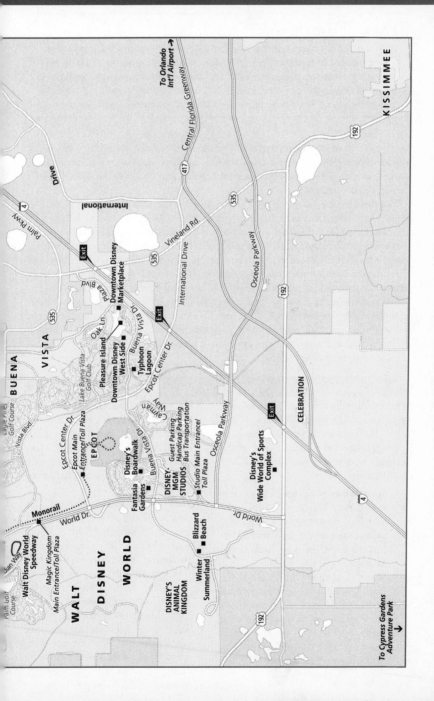

Fun Fact **By the Numbers**

With tourism once again on the rise, Central Florida finds itself hosting a staggering number of tourists. While individual parks don't release specific figures, *Amusement Business* magazine estimates theme-park attendance. Its figures show the Disney parks welcome around 45 million visitors annually; Universal's two parks, about 13 million; and SeaWorld chips in another 5½ million.

There's also an intangible price to pay: anxiety. There are so many things to see and do that even a 2-week stay and deep pockets won't allow you the time to hit all of the parks and attractions. That unravels some travelers and can leave the unwary family feeling slightly frazzled.

But don't panic—not yet, anyway. The solution to the situation is simple. Over the years, I've explored and re-explored the parks with (and without) my five kids in tow, dined at Orlando's restaurants, and scoped out the area's best resorts and hotels just so I can give you the inside track. With this book, you'll have the tools to plan ahead and make sure all members of your family have a good time. There's more than enough information here to make you a savvy shopper. My job: to make your family vacation easy to arrange and as enjoyable as possible, so you'll be able to relax and have fun while you're here. At the same time, I give you plenty of options to make your vacation affordable. I've noted some of the best deals around, along with a handful of ways to maximize your fun while keeping your expenses to a minimum. And Orlando tourism gurus will make sure your family has a steady stream of new things to see and do each and every time you visit.

1 Frommer's Favorite Orlando Family Experiences

From Cinderella Castle to Space Mountain, everybody loves the Magic Kingdom, but here are some other things to try at Disney and Universal, and in the greater Orlando area (see chapters 6 and 7 for details):

- **Spend a day at Epcot.** This is a great stop if your kids are old enough to have inquiring minds. You can travel around the world at the World Showcase pavilions; get your thrills riding Mission: Space, Test Track, and Soarin'; and then glimpse the future from ground level at Innoventions, where space-age products and interactive games await you. And what better way to cap your day than watching the **IllumiNations** fireworks show? For more details, see "Epcot," in chapter 6.

- **Star-gaze at the Orlando Science Center.** The center's planetarium is only part of the fun. Your heirs can dabble in Weird Science, 123 Math Avenue, KidsTown, and lots more at this popular downtown attraction. See p. 286.

- **Visit Disney–MGM Studios.** This park has plenty to offer both tots and teens. Ariel, Belle, and Bear in the Big Blue House come alive on stage, entrancing the younger set, while kids over 8 won't want to miss Tower of Terror and Rock 'n' Roller Coaster. The whole family should see the Light, Motors, Action! Extreme Stunt Show, where chilling chase scenes take center stage and stunt-car secrets are revealed, and then end the day with Fantasmic!—the after-dark fireworks, live-action, and laser-lights show.

⎛Moments⎠ Chills & Thrills

For parents and older children (who meet the mandatory height requirements) looking for the ups and downs of a good ride, here are the top
stomach-churners and G-force generators in Orlando (see chapter 6, "What
Kids Like to See & Do in Walt Disney World," and chapter 7, "What Kids Like
to See & Do Beyond Disney," for more information):

- **Incredible Hulk Coaster** (Islands of Adventure). You'll blast from 0 to 40
  mph in 2 seconds, spin upside down, and endure seven rollovers and two
  plummets on this glow-in-the-dark roller coaster. See p. 264.
- **Rock 'n' Roller Coaster** (Disney–MGM Studios). You'll launch from 0 to 60
  mph in 2.8 seconds and go into the first inversion as 120 speakers in your
  "stretch limo" mainline Aerosmith at (yeeeow!) 32,000 watts. See p. 222.
- **Dueling Dragons** (Islands of Adventure). Your legs dangle as you ride
  through five inversions at 55 to 60 mph and—get this—come within 12
  inches of the other roller coaster three times. See p. 267.
- **Summit Plummet** (Disney's Blizzard Beach). This one starts from a 120-
  foot-high perch and turns into the world's fastest body slide—a test of
  your courage and swimsuit, as it has you moving sans vehicle at 60 mph.
  See p. 237.
- **Twilight Zone Tower of Terror** (Disney–MGM Studios). The free-fall experiences (there are several scenarios) are more than thrilling—they're also
  scary (one of the ride's designers is too scared to get on it). Once your legs
  stop shaking, *some of you* will want to ride again. See p. 223.
- **The Amazing Adventures of Spider-Man** (Islands of Adventure). 3D doesn't
  get any better than this ride, which has you twisting, spinning, and soaring
  before a simulated 400-foot drop that feels awfully real. See p. 263.
- **Mission: Space** (Epcot). If you're claustrophobic or prone to motion sickness, stay clear of this ride, which simulates an actual liftoff (and the
  accompanying G-force) and gets the seal of approval from the NASA
  astronauts who helped design it. See p. 205.
- **Kraken** (SeaWorld). This floorless, open-sided coaster uses speed (up to 65
  mph), steep climbs, deep drops, and seven loops to create a stomach-
  churning ride that lasts far too long for some folks. See p. 276.
- **Revenge of the Mummy** (Universal Studios): In shadowy darkness, you'll
  plunge forward, propel backward, twist and turn, start and stop without
  warning—all while flames and fireballs are flying past you and creepy
  skeletal creatures give chase. See p. 254.

- **Check out Gatorland.** Located
between Orlando and Kissimmee,
this throwback park is a great way to
spend a half day at less than half the
price of the major theme parks. Make
sure to see Gator Jumparoo, which
has been the signature show since the
park opened in 1949. If you have
deep pockets, and your kids are over
12, they (or you) can be a Trainer for
a Day. And don't forget a visit to the
gift shop if the boys (and some girls)

want to take home an offbeat gator gift. See p. 282.

- **Experience Universal Orlando.** Universal Studios Florida and its sister, Islands of Adventure, combine cutting-edge, high-tech special effects with amazing creativity. Not-to-be-missed attractions: Back to the Future . . . The Ride; Fear Factor Live; Terminator 2: 3-D Battle Across Time; Revenge of the Mummy; Men in Black Alien Attack; Jimmy Neutron's Nicktoon Blast; Shrek 4-D; Dueling Dragons; the Incredible Hulk Coaster; The Amazing Adventures of Spider-Man; and Dudley Do-Right's Ripsaw Falls. You'll have a tough time tearing the younger ones away from A Day in the Park with Barney, Curious George Goes to Town, Fievel's Playland, Caro-Seuss-El, and Camp Jurassic.

- **Explore eco-edutainment at Sea-World and Discovery Cove.** Journey to Atlantis and Kraken give SeaWorld a little zip, but it's the hands-on encounters with sea critters, spectacular shows, and up-close viewing of the animals from polar bears to killer whales (kids of all ages will be entranced) that you should come for here. Its younger sister, Discovery Cove, gives you a chance to swim with dolphins and other undersea inhabitants (alas, currently at a cost of $259) as part of its package. At press time SeaWorld announced plans for a third park, a water park, set to open sometime in 2007. As with its predecessors, the slides and rides here will feature up-close animal encounters and aquatic edutainment.

- **Catch a wave at Disney's Typhoon Lagoon and Blizzard Beach.** Sandy beaches to sink your toes in and waterslides that range from terrifying to toddler-friendly—the entire family will find something fun to do at these water parks. You can hang ten and learn to surf before park opening at Typhoon Lagoon. Lessons are offered twice weekly for those with cash to spare.

- **Become a monorail co-pilot.** If there's no one but the pilot aboard, ask to sit up front, and you and your kids can pretend to drive Disney's monorail. Your best chance is if you board at the Grand Floridian, Contemporary, or Polynesian resorts, where the crowds are thinner than at the transportation center. And don't try this at park opening and closing times.

2 The Best Hotel Bets

Get all of the information you'll need on these and other area hotels and motels in chapter 4, "Family-Friendly Accommodations." But here are the high points:

- **Most Family-Friendly Hotels:** All Disney properties cater to families, with special menus for kids; videogame arcades; free transportation to the parks; extensive recreational facilities; and, in some cases, character meals and kids clubs. Camping at woodsy **Fort Wilderness** (© 407/934-7639) makes for a unique and fun-filled family experience. If bunk beds, bubbling springs in the lobby, and a gushing geyser sound good, check into the **Wilderness Lodge** (© 407/934-7639). Set sail for **The Yacht and Beach Club** (© 407/934-7639), where the sand-bottom pool and pirate-ship play area are just part of its seaside charm. The African Savannah serves as a backdrop for the **Animal Kingdom Lodge** (© 407/934-7369). Beyond the House of Mouse, the **Nickelodeon**

Family Suites by Holiday Inn (© 877/387-5437 or 407/387-5437), Holiday Inn Nikki Bird Resort (© 800/206-2747 or 407/396-7300), Holiday Inn Sunspree Resort Lake Buena Vista (© 800/366-6299 or 407/239-4500), and Seralago Hotel & Suites Main Gate East (© 407/396-4488) offer Kid Suites, kids' clubs, activities, and more. See chapter 4 for more family-friendly accommodations.

- **Best Moderately Priced Hotels:** Disney's **Port Orleans Resort** (© 407/934-7639) has Southern charm in its French Quarter and Riverside areas, and the pool in the French Quarter has a water slide that curves out of a dragon's mouth. See p. 89. In the free world, the **Hawthorn Suites Lake Buena Vista** (© 800/936-9417 or 407/597-5000) is near but sheltered from Disney, and has large rooms, free breakfasts, and weekday social hours. See p. 103. Nearby, the **Staybridge Suites** (© 407/238-0777; p. 105) has room to spare, with oversize 1- and 2-bedroom suites. Full kitchens, free breakfast, weekday receptions, and helpful services, including grocery delivery, are all part of the deal here. A second location on International Drive (© 407/352-2400, p. 115) offers much the same. The **Homewood Suites,** located near Downtown Disney (© 407/465-8200; p. 104), in Kissimmee (© 407/396-2229), and by Universal Orlando © 407/226-0669 all have full kitchens, free breakfast, and weekday-evening social hours.
- **Best Value/Deal:** That's easy: Disney's **All-Star Movies Resort** (© 407/934-7639; p. 92), **All-Star Music Resort** (© 407/934-7639; p. 93), **All-Star Sports Resort** (© 407/934-7639; p. 93), and **Pop Century**

Resort (© 407/934-7639; p. 94). If you're going to stay on WDW property, you can't beat them, though they would be significantly overpriced outside the realm. **La Quinta Inn Lakeside** (© 407/396-2222; p. 109) has 3 pools, putt putt, and an onsite convenience store. Extras include free shuttle service to all area theme parks and a kids-eat-free program. Plenty of restaurants are right nearby, and Disney's only 2 miles away. The **Comfort Suites Main Gate East** (© 407/397-7848; p. 106) offers plenty of freebies including breakfast, shuttles to the theme parks—all of them—and high-speed Internet access. From this all-suite hotel it's only a short walk to shops, restaurants, and minigolf, plus Disney's only minutes away.

- **Best Budget Motel:** The **Comfort Suites Maingate at Formosa** (© 407/390-9888; p. 109) is clean and comfortable, with a location and price that are hard to beat. Nearby restaurants and shops are steps away and Disney's just 2 miles down the road. Kids can check in at a treehouse at the **Howard Johnson Enchanted Land Hotel** (© 407/396/4343), where you'll find themed rooms, a kids' club, an onsite market, movies, and more. Little kids love the sleepy-bear-themed rooms at the **Travelodge Maingate East** (© 407/396-4222). Parents will love the free shuttles to the theme parks.
- **Best Spa for Kids:** That's not a typo. The **Nickelodeon Family Suites by Holiday Inn** (© 877/387-5437 or 407/387-5437) started something good with its **Kids Spa,** with services priced from $10 to $40 and packages costing up to $99. The resort also has a lounge where parents can spend a little time on their own. See p. 104.

- **Best Kids' Programs:** The Wizard of Diz has dandy kids' clubs at select resorts, but some really good ones can be found beyond Disney's doorstep too. The top five picks beyond Mickey's boundaries include Camp Hyatt at the **Hyatt Regency Grand Cypress** (© 800/233-1234 or 407/239-1234), Ritz Kids at the **Ritz-Carlton** (© 800/241-3333 or 407/206-2400), Camp Nikki at **Holiday Inn Nikki Bird** (© 800/206-2747 or 407/396-7300), La Petite Academy at **Gaylord Palms** (© 877/677-9352 or 407/586-0000), and Camp Holiday at **Holiday Inn Sunspree** (© 800/366-6299 or 407/239-4500). You can find more details in chapter 4, "Family-Friendly Accommodations."

- **Tops for Toddlers:** Watch your kids' faces light up when larger-than-life raccoon mascots Max and Maxine show up to tuck them in at **Holiday Inn Sunspree Resort Lake Buena Vista** (© 800/366-6299). See p. 103. Of course, it's hard to beat the **Nickelodeon Family Suites** (© 407/387-5437; p. 104), with its water park–style pools, themed KidSuites, and character breakfast. Kids from tots to tweens will go crazy for this one.

- **Tops for Teens:** I've yet to find a mainstream hotel that comes close to the activities offered in Common Grounds, the teen clubs aboard the **Disney Cruise Line**'s *Wonder* and *Magic* (© 800/951-3532). Activities for 13- to 17-year-olds include karaoke, a Hawaiian pool party, and improv. See p. 52.

- **Best Location: Disney's Grand Floridian Resort & Spa** (© 407/934-7639; p. 82), **Polynesian Resort** (© 407/934-7639; p. 84), and **Contemporary Resort** (© 407/934-7639; p. 81) not only offer waterfront access to Seven Seas Lagoon and Bay Lake, but also, they're right on the WDW monorail route, providing quick and easy access to the parks. The **Portofino Bay Hotel** (© 888/322-5541 or 407/503-1000; p. 113), **Hard Rock Hotel** (© 800/232-7827 or 407/503-7625; p. 113), and **Royal Pacific** (© 800/232-7827 or 407/503-3000; p. 115) are within walking distance of Universal's parks and CityWalk, with boat service available as well.

- **Best Views:** The whole family can watch the Magic Kingdom's Wishes fireworks display from the comfort of your room if you book one on an upper floor on the west side of the **Contemporary Resort** (© 407/934-7639; p. 81). And you have a front-row seat for the action at SeaWorld from the upper-east-side floors at the **Renaissance Orlando Resort at Sea-World** (© 800/327-6677; p. 114).

- **Best Family Pools:** Arguably the best pool in O-Town is at the **Hyatt Regency Grand Cypress Resort** (© 800/233-1234 or 407/239-1234). It's a half-acre, lagoonlike pool that flows through rock grottoes, is spanned by a rope bridge, and has 12 waterfalls and two steep water slides. See p. 100. The **JW Marriott's Lazy River** (© 800/241-3333 or

---

Fun Fact **Room Roulette**

If you wanted to stay one night in every guest room at the hotels and resorts currently on Walt Disney World property, it would take you over 72 years to get the job done.

407/206-2300) finishes a very close second. It's a 24,000-square-foot stream winding through small waterfalls and rock formations. See p. 102. The newest edition to the list is the **Nickelodeon Family Suites by Holiday Inn** (© 407/387-5437, p. 104).

Thanks to its two water park–style pools, complete with slides, flumes, squirters, fountains, and more, the action here is almost unending. Most Walt Disney World resorts have terrific pools, too.

3 The Best Dining Bets

While Orlando can't compete with U.S. destinations such as New York or San Francisco in the dining department, it has everything on the restaurant front, from fast-fooderies that will satisfy your kids to 5-star fine dining for a more adult palate. Look for more details on these and other eateries in chapter 5, "Family-Friendly Dining."

- **Best Character Meal:** Hands down, it doesn't get any better than **Chef Mickey's** (© 407/939-3463) breakfasts and dinners at Disney's Contemporary Resort. These "events" feature their respective namesake and other characters, but a word of warning: They draw *up to 1,600 guests* at each meal. See p. 161.

- **Best Kids' Menu Variety:** When it comes to the deepest menu for young tastebuds, **Pastamore Ristorante** at Universal CityWalk (© 407/363-8000) gives kids a choice of nine entrees. See p. 151.

- **Best Offbeat Kids' Menu:** With a menu that offers beef or chicken teriyaki, shrimp tempura, pork dumplings, and sushi, it's hard to beat **Ran-Getsu of Tokyo** (© 407/345-0044) in this category.

- **Best Burgers:** From Cheeseburgers in Paradise to Cuban Meatloaf Survival Sandwiches, **Jimmy Buffett's Margaritaville** at Universal CityWalk (© 407/224-2155) has some of the juiciest and most unusual burgers in town. See p. 151.

- **Best Outdoor Eating:** Kids can get into the festive jungle atmosphere while digging into their own wild menu at the **Rainforest Cafe** in Downtown Disney West Side, which offers indoor as well as patio dining (© 407/827-8500). See p. 137. The terrace at **Artist Point** (© 407/939-3463), the premier restaurant at Disney's Wilderness Lodge, overlooks a lake, waterfall, and scenery evocative of America's national parks. See p. 140. And the **Rose & Crown** at Epcot (© 407/939-3463) delivers a front-row seat for the IllumiNations fireworks display. See p. 129.

- **Best Value:** At **Romano's Macaroni Grill** (© 407/239-6676), the ambience and northern Italian cuisine score very high, and prices are low, low, low. See p. 148.

- **Best Spot for a Parent's Night Out:** Dinners don't get much more romantic than those at the Victorian-style **Victoria & Albert's** (© 407/939-3463). The meal is comprised of six courses served by a maid and butler. See p. 139.

- **Best Ice Cream:** Go for the splurge (you may need to let out your belt) at **Ghirardelli Soda Fountain and Chocolate Shop** (© 407/934-8855) in Downtown Disney West Side. See p. 307.

- **Best Barbecue:** Hands down, follow your nose to **Bubbalou's Bodacious BBQ** (© 407/628-1212) after catching a whiff of the tangy hickory

Tips   Orlando's Best Online Sites

Given Orlando's enormous popularity, it should come as no surprise that hundreds of websites are devoted to it. These sites have a lot of information about everything from Walt Disney World history to getting around town.

There are several sites written by Disney fans, employees, and self-proclaimed experts. A favorite (**www.hiddenmickeys.org**) is about **Hidden Mickeys,** a park tradition (see chapter 6, "What Kids Like to See & Do in Walt Disney World"). These subtle Disney images can be found scattered throughout the realm, though they sometimes are in the eye, or imagination, of the beholder. **Deb's Unofficial Walt Disney World Information Guide** (www.allearsnet.com) is another pleaser for Disney fans and offers tons of family info on hotels, restaurants, attractions, and more. And you should definitely take a look at Disney's official site, **www.disneyworld.com,** if you're planning a pilgrimage to the Land of the Mouse. The newest addition to the wireless waves, **www.travelinsights.com,** is filled with information for families, including the best hotels, hot spots, restaurants, recreation, and attractions in and around Orlando.

If a trip to one of Universal Orlando's theme parks or CityWalk is on your dance card, stop at **www.universalorlando.com**. You can check out the attractions, order tickets, make reservations, and find out about special events, among other things on the site. And fish fans can get in the know about Sea-World at **www.seaworld.com** and Discovery Cove at **www.discovery cove.com**.

If you're seeking general information about the city, accommodations, dining, nightlife, or special events, head over to the Orlando/Orange County Convention & Visitors Bureau site at **www.orlandoinfo.com**. *Orlando Weekly* (**www.orlandoweekly.com**) offers cutting-edge reviews and recommendations for arts, movies, music, restaurants, and much more from Orlando's premier alternative weekly. Links at the site include dining, arts and culture, shopping, and news. Other great options include the online version of the local newspaper, the *Orlando Sentinel,* at **www.orlando sentinal.com,** as well as the Sentinel-produced site **www.go2orlando.com**. Both feature information on upcoming events, area attractions, restaurant reviews, and local nightlife.

smoke. It tastes as good as it smells. See p. 159.

- **Best Italian Cuisine:** I have to give the nod to **Pacino's Italian Ristorante** in Kissimmee (© **407/396-8022**). It has great food and a moderately priced menu. See p. 156.

- **Most Entertaining Restaurant:** It's hard to contain yourself when the corny jokes and lively music kick into gear at the **Hoop-Dee-Doo Musical Revue** at Disney's Fort Wilderness Resort and Campground (© **407/939-3463**). See p. 120.

- **Best Steak House:** At the **Yachtsman Steakhouse** at Disney's Yacht Club Resort (© **407/939-3463**), the aged steaks, chops, and seafood are grilled over a wood fire. See p. 139.

- **Best Breakfast:** Disney character breakfasts certainly get the nod if you have children under 10 in tow. But it's hard to beat the buffet at **Boma** in the Animal Kingdom Lodge (© **407/ 938-3000**). See p. 140.

- **Most Kid-Friendly Service:** The "kids eat free with a paying adult" program, at the fun, all-you-can-stuff breakfast buffet at **Nickelodeon Family Suites by Holiday Inn** (© **877/387-5437**), makes it a winner. As a bonus, kids 12 and under (the real VIPs at this hotel) also eat lunch and dinner here for free when accompanied by paying adults. See p. 104.

- **Best Late-Night Dining:** The trendy **B-Line Diner** (© **407/345-4460**) at the Peabody Orlando is open around the clock for eclectic fare ranging from steaks to falafel sandwiches to grits and eggs. You and your kids won't be able to resist the desserts. See p. 154.

- **Best Spot to Celebrate: Emeril's** at Universal's CityWalk (© **407/224- 2424**) is a great choice for a high-end special occasion. See p. 149. The chefs at **Mikado Japanese Steak House** (© **407/239-4200**), located in the Orlando World Center Marriott, entertain you by slicing and dicing your meal. It makes for a fun evening out. For the pure party factor, you can't beat **Jimmy Buffett's Margaritaville** (© **407/224-2155**) at City-Walk. See p. 151.

- **Best Special Sunday Brunch:** The **House of Blues** (© **407/934-2583**), at Disney's West Side, has a down-home gospel brunch featuring live foot-stomping music and an array of Southern/Creole vittles that includes greens, red beans and rice, jambalaya, catfish, shrimp, and beef. The entertainment makes it a certifiable winner. Reservations aren't accepted for parties under six, so arrive early for the 10:30am or 1pm show. See p. 146.

2

Planning a Family Trip to Walt Disney World & Orlando

Within minutes of choosing Orlando as your vacation destination, panic might set in as you confront a seemingly endless selection of hotels, restaurants, attractions, and package plans to choose among. Talk about overload! An anxiety attack is inevitable if you don't do a little advance planning, with so much information to sift through. That's why I've filled this chapter with things travelers with kids in tow need to know before they go. In addition to the information you'll find in the following pages, plenty more helpful tips can be found in chapters 4 through 6—those covering the area's best hotels, restaurants, theme parks, and smaller attractions.

1 Visitor Information

As soon as you decide your destination is Orlando, immediately contact the **Orlando/Orange County Convention & Visitors Bureau** (aka the Orlando CVB) and its visitor center, 8723 International Dr., Suite 101, Orlando, FL 32819 (© **407/363-5872** or 800/551-0181; www.orlandoinfo.com). Staffers can answer questions; assist you with reservations; help you find discounts; and send maps and brochures, such as the *Official Destination Guide, African-American Travel Guide, Area Guide to Restaurants, Unexpected Orlando,* and *Official Accommodations Guide.* The free packet should arrive within 3 weeks and include the Orlando "Magicard," which is good for $500 in discounts on rooms, car rentals, attractions, and more. By calling the Official Travel Counselors (© **800/972-3304**), available Monday through Friday from 8am to 5pm, you can book vacation packages, buy discounted attraction tickets, and get plenty of planning tips.

The Orlando CVB's website also includes information on special vacation packages specifically designed for families and has a list of hundreds of family-appropriate things to see and do in Orlando.

For general information about **Walt Disney World,** including brochures and DVDs, write to Walt Disney World, Box 10000, Lake Buena Vista, FL 32830-1000; call © **407/934-7639** or 407/824-4321; or go online to **www.disneyworld.com.** You can view the planning kit online or have one sent to your home that also includes a planning DVD and a CD-ROM filled with planning information.

For information about **Universal Studios Florida, CityWalk,** and **Islands of Adventure,** call © **800/837-2273** or 407/363-8000, or write to **Universal Orlando,** 1000 Universal Studios Plaza, Orlando, FL 32819. On the Internet, visit **www.universalorlando.com.**

For information about **SeaWorld,** call © **407/351-3600** or visit online at **www. seaworld.com.** For **Discovery Cove** information and reservations, call © **877/4-DISCOVERY** or 407/370-1280. For online information, visit **www.discovery cove.com**.

You can also ask the **Kissimmee– St. Cloud Convention & Visitors Bureau,** P.O. Box 422007, Kissimmee, FL 34742-2007 (© **800/333-5477** or 407/ 847-5000; www.floridakiss.com), for maps, brochures, coupon books, and a vacation-planning kit, which details accommodations and attractions.

For information on Orlando's **International Drive** area, call © **866/243-7483** or on the Internet go to **www.InternationalDriveOrlando.com**. The staff has information about rooms, restaurants, attractions, shops, and the I-Ride Trolley. The website features 50 fun things to do in the area, many of them suitable for families with kids of all ages.

For information on all of Florida's family-friendly offerings, go online to **www.visitflorida.com**, the state's official vacation-planning site. There's tons of great information online, but if you order planning materials, you can customize your order to include only the publications you're interested in. Just a few of the choices include *The Official Florida Vacation Guide, Florida's Map, Undiscovered Florida, Worth the Drive,* and *Florida Family Getaways.*

ONLINE INFORMATION

The websites we listed above are good for a ton of other information too. Disney's recently revamped site, **www.disney world.com**, is not only filled with photos, but also has theme-park maps; current ticket prices; customized driving directions; park hours on specific days; ride and show information, including scheduled rehab dates; detailed descriptions of WDW dining options; information about special events; indoor and outdoor recreation options; the Disney Cruise Line; an online booking service; and much, much more.

Deb's Unofficial Walt Disney World Information Guide (www.allearsnet.com) is an excellent source of family fun and arguably the best unofficial Disney guide on the Internet, though it's one that at times isn't entirely objective. Disney doesn't own it, but it's run and written mainly by diehard Disney fans, so you have to factor out (or in, if you prefer) their exuberance while digesting the many tips this site offers. The no-nonsense, text-driven site includes comprehensive insider information on tickets, detailed restaurant menus, the scoop on the Disney Cruise Line, and other valuable tips. There are pages specifically aimed at parents of infants and toddlers, 5- to 11-year-olds, expectant moms, and families bringing one or more of their children's friends.

The sites built by Universal Orlando, **www.universalorlando.com**, and SeaWorld, **www.seaworld.com**, offer ride descriptions; ticket prices; some restaurant menus; and more, including information beyond the theme parks. While greatly improved to include far more information over the last few years, they still lack the thoroughness of Deb's and the Disney sites.

If you're looking for the best tips and insider information on saving some cash on your Disney vacation, go to **www. mousesavers.com**; the website includes a list of discount and reservation codes for the Disney resorts, as well as special discounts and offers of their own.

Another site chock full of information on Central Florida, reaching from the Gulf Coast to the Space Coast, is **www. travelinsights.com**. Written specifically with families in mind, it includes tons of insider tips, details on dining, and the inside track on all the area's best attractions and accommodations, with plenty more, including how to survive a family vacation in Central Florida.

The city's newspaper, the *Orlando Sentinel,* produces an online site at **www.orlandosentinel.com**. It has a variety of entertainment information. And if you go to **www.go2orlando.com**, you'll find the focus on attractions, accommodations, restaurants, discounts, and more.

Walt Disney World & Orlando—Red-Alert Checklist

- Along with The Mouse, Orlando's biggest draw is its warm and sunny climate. Though it may seem obvious, a word of caution is warranted regarding Florida's most natural and abundant commodity: the sun. The Florida sun is hotter and stronger than in many other parts of the country and, as such, requires that you, and especially your kids, take some extra precautions if you plan on enjoying it—and your vacation. One of the most important survival rules of an Orlando vacation: **Use sunscreen!** Pour on one with an SPF rating of at least 30 or higher, especially on kids, who need protection even more than you do. Florida's sun can deliver a dangerous burn (even sun poisoning) year-round—a souvenir I guarantee you do not want to take home with you. The sun can pack a powerful punch even on a cloudy day, so don't leave the sunscreen and hats behind. Also, don't forget to reapply sunscreen throughout the day; one application when you're sweating in the parks or playing in the pools will not protect you and your kids for very long. You can also protect yourself and your kids by wearing wide-brimmed hats, airy clothes, and sunglasses. If you have a child in a stroller, a light blanket will help protect infants or sleeping toddlers from the sun's rays. Also remember to drink plenty of fluids throughout the day to prevent dehydration, and have your kids do the same, even if they say they aren't thirsty. And remember—*children need protection* as much as or more than you do, and they may not recognize the symptoms of a burn, or of dehydration, until it's too late, so it's up to you to do it for them. Last but certainly not least, don't forget to pack a pair of comfortable walking shoes for those days spent pounding the theme-park pavement.
- Don't miss out on one of Orlando's great dining experiences. You can make same-day or day-before reservations in most Orlando eateries, but there are some exceptions to the rule; any Disney restaurant—especially those serving character meals or a dinner show—can have a waiting list a mile long. To avoid disappointment, be sure to use Walt Disney World's **Advanced Dining Reservations** (© 407/939-3463), which lets you stake a claim to a table up to 180 days in advance (even 2 years ahead of time, in some cases). Call as soon as possible to make your Advanced Dining Reservations, as some of the more popular restaurants and dinner shows get booked within hours—sometimes even minutes (no kidding)—of the time they start booking seating times.
- Many families come with their hearts set on (and days planned around) specific attractions, hotels, or restaurants. But some dreams don't come true, even at Disney. Disney has reduced park hours; limited the days certain shows are staged; and continues to temporarily close some hotel

rooms, restaurants, and attractions for rehab or to simply cut expenses. Universal Orlando, SeaWorld, and smaller players have taken similar steps. Before you promise your kids or yourself anything, make sure your dreams can come true by calling or checking the websites provided in this book. Also note that in the best of times, theme-park rides break down or have to be shut down for routine maintenance (though you don't get a break on ticket prices when your favorite rides or shows are dark). Some of the websites listed earlier in this chapter have **"rehab"** schedules and update them almost daily. The parks can change their hours not only seasonally, but also weekly—even daily—so check the week's schedule when you arrive so you'll know if you have to adjust your itinerary because of a last-minute schedule change or closing.

- If you purchased traveler's checks, make sure to record the check numbers, and store the documentation separately from the checks.
- Pack your camera, an extra set of batteries (and a charger, if they're rechargeable), and purchase enough film or memory cards before you go. If you packed film in your checked baggage, consider investing in protective pouches to shield film from airport X-rays. If you must buy film or other supplies, try a local discount store like Wal-Mart or a drugstore such as Walgreens for better prices (and selection) than you'll find at the parks and resorts.
- Bring along your ID cards, including AAA and AARP cards, student IDs, the Orlando "Magicard," and so on, as producing them will help save a few dollars along the way.
- Speaking of identification, did you bring a photo ID? That's a necessity at the airports, among other places, so keep it handy.
- Make sure to bring along emergency drug prescriptions; any prescription medicine you are currently using; and the phone numbers of your doctor, pediatrician, and insurance company (and your insurance card), along with an extra pair of glasses and/or contact lenses.
- Leave a copy of your itinerary with someone at home, and keep an extra copy yourself. Be sure it includes your hotel, car, and airplane information, as well as any reservation numbers for shows or restaurants.
- Find a safe place to stash your cash, credit cards, and other financial information (like credit-card PINs and so on).
- Be sure you've brought all your E-ticket information as well as other confirmation and reservation information. Write everything down on a separate paper as a backup if you accidentally misplace any official printed paperwork.

2 Money

ATMS

The easiest and best way to get cash away from home is from an ATM (automated teller machine). The **Cirrus** (© **800/424-7787;** www.mastercard.com) and **PLUS** (© **800/843-7587;** www.visa.com) networks span the globe; see the back of your card to learn which network you're on and then call or check online for ATM locations in Orlando. Be sure you know your personal identification number (PIN) and your daily withdrawal limit before departing.

ATMs inside the Disney theme parks are on Main Street in the Magic Kingdom and at the entrances to Epcot, Disney–MGM Studios, and Animal Kingdom. They're also at Pleasure Island, in Downtown Disney Marketplace, at Disney resorts, and at the Crossroads Shopping Center.

There also are ATMs near Guest Services at Universal Studios Florida, Islands of Adventure, and SeaWorld.

Inside the entrances of most of the parks, you'll find maps listing all ATMs. If this isn't the case when you visit, look for them at Guest Relations or Guest Services near the entrances or at most shops.

Outside the parks, most malls have at least one ATM, and they're in some convenience stores, such as 7-Elevens and Circle Ks, as well as in grocery stores and drugstores. But there often is an extra charge for using nonbank ATMs. Depending on your institution, those charges can range from $1 to $3.50 per transaction—the average is $2.75 across

Florida—when you're using an ATM not affiliated with your bank.

Be *very* careful when using ATMs; the Land of Mickey can lull you into a false sense of security. Goofy and Pluto won't mug you, but some of their estranged neighbors might. Cuddly critters aside, this is a big city, and its crime rate is the same as that of others. Even in seemingly safe places, when entering your ATM PIN, make sure you shield the keyboard from others in line. And if you're using a drive-through, keep your doors locked.

Note: You can also buy **Disney dollars** (currency with cute images of Mickey, Minnie, and so on) in $1, $5, and $10 denominations. They're good at WDW shops, restaurants, and resorts, as well as Disney stores everywhere. But I don't recommend buying them because you'll have to cash in leftover bills for real currency upon leaving WDW, which means still another line, or keep them as a souvenir (a rather expensive souvenir at that). Also, watch out if you have a refund coming. Some things, such as strollers, wheelchairs, and lockers, require a security deposit, and Disney staffers will frequently use Mickey money for refunds instead of the cash. If you don't want it, just let them know, and they'll be happy to give you real cash.

CREDIT CARDS

Credit cards are a safe way to carry money and provide a convenient record of all your expenses. You can also withdraw cash advances from your credit cards at

---

Tips Online Ticketing

The Big Three offer online booking of tickets, hotel rooms, vacation packages, and more. Disney's site is **www.disneyworld.com**. Universal Orlando's is **www.universalorlando.com**. SeaWorld's site is **www.seaworld.com**. All offer online-only discounts and specials with special savings if you purchase ahead of time online.

What Things Cost in Orlando	**U.S.$**
Taxi from airport to Walt Disney World (up to 4 people)	50
Shuttle from the airport to Walt Disney World (2 adults, 2 kids)	86–102
Double room at Disney's Grand Floridian Resort & Spa (very expensive)	359–890
Double room at Disney's Caribbean Resort (moderate)	139–215
Double Room at the Staybridge Suites Lake Buena Vista (moderate)	129–299
Double room at Disney's All-Star Music Resort (inexpensive)	79–137
All-you-can-eat dinner buffet at a Disney theme park restaurant	
Adult	27
Child	12
Child's meal at most theme park restaurants	5
Chef Mickey's character breakfast at Disney's Contemporary Resort	
Adults	18
Child	10
Huggies Pull-Ups, 21 count, at Walgreen's	15
2.5-ounce jar of baby-food entree at Publix	1.20
Tube of sunblock in the theme parks	10
Evening movie tickets at AMC, Pleasure Island	
Adult	8.50
Child	5.50
4-Day Magic Your Way Hopper ticket to Walt Disney World	
Adult	235
Child	183
1-day, 1-park ticket to Walt Disney World	
Adult	63
Child	52
1-day, 1-park ticket to Universal Orlando or SeaWorld	
Adult	63
Child	52
Admission to Orlando Science Center	
Adult	15
Child	9.95

banks or ATMs, provided that you know your PIN. If you've forgotten yours or didn't even know you had one, call the number on the back of your credit card, and ask the bank to send it to you. It usually takes 5 to 7 business days, though some banks may provide the number over the phone if you tell them your mother's maiden name or some other personal information.

Disney parks, resorts, shops, and restaurants (but not most fast-food outlets) accept five major credit cards: American Express, Diners Club, Discover, Master-Card, and Visa. Additionally, the WDW and Universal resorts will let you charge purchases made in their respective park shops and restaurants to your hotel room, but you must settle up when you check out. Be sure, however, to keep track of your spending as you go along so you won't be surprised when you get the total bill.

> **(Tips** **Dear Visa: I'm Off to Visit Mickey!**
>
> Some credit card companies recommend that you notify them of any impending trip so that they don't become suspicious of transactions and block your charges. If you don't call your credit card company in advance, you can still call the card's toll-free emergency number (see "Fast Facts," p. 66) if a charge is refused—provided that you remember to carry the phone number with you. Perhaps the most important lesson here is to carry more than one card, so you have a backup.

TRAVELER'S CHECKS

Traveler's checks are something of an anachronism from the days before the ATM made cash accessible 24/7. But remember that you will likely be charged an ATM withdrawal fee if the bank is not your own, so if you're withdrawing money every day, you might be better off with traveler's checks—provided that you don't mind showing identification every time you want to cash one. (Keep in mind that some places won't take traveler's checks at all, though that's rare in tourist-friendly Orlando.)

You can buy traveler's checks at most banks. **American Express** offers denominations of $20, $50, $100, $500, and (for cardholders only) $1,000. You'll pay a service charge ranging from 1% to 4%. By phone, you can buy traveler's checks by calling ℂ **800/807-6233.** American Express card holders should dial ℂ **800/ 221-7282;** this number accepts collect calls, offers service in several foreign languages, and exempts Amex gold and platinum cardholders from the 1% fee.

Visa offers traveler's checks at Citibank locations nationwide, as well as at several other banks. The service charge ranges between 1.5% and 2%; checks come in denominations of $20, $50, $100, $500, and $1,000. Call ℂ **800/732-1322** for information. AAA members can obtain Visa checks for a $9.95 fee (for checks up to $1,500) at most AAA offices or by calling ℂ **866/339-3378. MasterCard** also offers traveler's checks. Call ℂ **800/ 223-9920** for a location near you.

You can cash traveler's or personal checks of $25 or less (drawn on U.S. banks, if you have a driver's license and major credit card) and exchange foreign currency at **SunTrust Bank,** 1675 Buena Vista Dr., across from Downtown Disney Marketplace. The bank also has an ATM. It's open weekdays from 9am to 4pm and until 6pm on Thursday (ℂ **407/828-6106**).

3 When to Go

Orlando is the theme-park capital of the world, and you could almost argue that there really is no off season here, though the busiest seasons are whenever kids are out of school. Late May to just past Labor Day, long holiday weekends, winter holidays (mid-Dec–early Jan), and especially spring break (late Mar–Apr). Do, however, keep in mind that kids in other hemispheres follow a completely different schedule. Obviously, an Orlando—and most especially a Disney—vacation, is most enjoyed when the crowds are at the thinnest and the weather is the most temperate. Hotel rooms (likely the largest chunk of your vacation bill) are also priced lower (albeit slightly) during the off season, though don't expect that period to follow the traditional winter/ summer patterns of most areas.

Peak-season rates can go into effect during large conventions and special

Tips Weather Wise

It's not uncommon for the skies to open up on Orlando, even when the day began with the sun ablaze. Florida is well known for its afternoon downpours, so don't be too concerned; storms don't usually last too long. Most people simply run for temporary cover and then resume their activities when the rain slows to a drizzle or stops all together. It is wise, however, to bring along some type of rain gear ,as storms can spring up rather quickly. A small fold-up umbrella can protect you until you can get to shelter. If you forget your gear, rain ponchos can be purchased throughout the parks for about $6 for a child-size poncho or $8 for an adult size. The child-size poncho also happens to cover the average stroller quite well, protecting camera equipment and souvenirs—not to mention the child sitting inside it.

Don't let a rainy afternoon spoil your fun. Crowds are dramatically thinner on these days, and there are plenty of indoor attractions to enjoy, particularly at Epcot; Disney-MGM Studios; Universal Studios Florida; and even SeaWorld, where many of the attractions are actually indoors. The flip side, of course, is that many of the outdoor rides at Disney, Universal, and Sea-World are temporarily closed during downpours and lightning storms.

events. Even something as remote as Bike Week in Daytona Beach (about an hour by car northeast) can raise prices, including during the off season. These kinds of events will especially affect the moderately priced hotels and resorts located off Walt Disney World.

Best times: The week after Labor Day until the week before Thanksgiving when the kids have just returned to school, the week after Thanksgiving until mid-December, and the 6 weeks before and after school spring vacations (which generally occur around Easter).

Worst times: The absolute worst time of year to visit is during spring break—usually the 2 weeks prior to and after Easter. The crowds are unbelievable; the lines are unbearable (my kids have waited upward of 2 hours to hop on some of the most popular attractions); waiting times at local restaurants can lead to starvation; and traffic—particularly on International Drive—will give you a headache. The December holidays and summer, when

out-of-state visitors take advantage of school breaks and many locals bring their families to the parks (taking advantage of Florida resident discount months, which usually fall in May and Nov), can also prove a challenge. Packed parking lots are the norm during the week before and after Christmas, and the summer brings with it oppressive heat and humidity. You may have noticed that the best times to avoid crowds happen to coincide with the times your kids will likely be in class. While I don't usually advocate skipping school, I *strongly advise you to seriously consider pulling your kids out* for a few days around an off-season weekend to avoid long lines. (You may be able to keep them in their schools' good graces by asking teachers to let them write a report on an educational element of the vacation. Epcot, SeaWorld, and the Orlando Museum of Science offer the most in the way of educational exhibits.) Even during these periods, though, the number of international visitors guarantees you won't be alone.

Central Florida Average Temperatures

	Jan	Feb	Mar	Apr	May	June	July	Aug	Sept	Oct	Nov	Dec
High °F	71.7	72.9	78.3	83.6	88.3	90.6	91.7	91.6	89.7	84.4	78.2	73.1
°C	22.0	22.7	25.7	28.7	31.3	32.5	33.2	33.1	32.0	29.1	25.7	22.8
Low °F	49.3	50.0	55.3	60.3	66.2	71.2	73.0	73.4	72.5	65.4	56.8	50.9
°C	9.6	10.0	12.5	15.7	19.0	21.8	22.7	23.0	22.5	18.6	13.8	10.5

Note: If you're taking advantage of a land/cruise package (see "Disney Cruise Packages," later in this chapter), make sure you take into account the Florida hurricane season, which runs from around June 1 to November 30 (when the majority of Central Florida's afternoon downpours tend to occur). Inland, the worst is usually only sheets of rain and enough wind to wipe the smile right off your face. That said, the summer of 2004 (when 3 hurricanes passed through the area) was a noticeable reminder that worse can happen. If you are on the coastal areas or at sea, you will likely be at the point where the storms hit their hardest, making them extremely dangerous. Also, don't take tornadoes and lightning—two particularly active summer curses—too lightly. Central Florida is the lightning capital of the United States, and short but intense electrical storms aren't uncommon in summer (young kids may be frightened, but I've seen teens absolutely enthralled by the natural electric show). Just make sure all observing is done from a safe place.

KIDS' FAVORITE ORLANDO EVENTS

January

Capital One Florida Citrus Bowl. New Year's kicks off with this football game in downtown Orlando. It pits the second-ranked teams from the Southeastern and Big Ten conferences against each other. If your family's sports-crazy, this is a good place to go. Tickets run $60 before November 1, $70 thereafter. Call (C) **800/297-2695** or 407/423-2476 for information, or **Ticketmaster** at (C) **877/803-7073** or 407/839-3900 for tickets (on the Internet, visit **www.fcsports.com**). A free downtown parade is held a few days before the game and features marching bands and floats. Most kids will find it entertaining. January 2.

Walt Disney World Marathon. About 90% of the 16,000 runners finish this 26.2-mile "sprint" through the resort area and parks. It's open to anyone over 18 years of age, including runners with disabilities as long as they are able to maintain the pacing requirements. If you are unable to do so, you'll be picked up and transported to the finish line. The registration fee is $95 and includes a medal, cap, and other extras for those who finish—along with souvenirs for all who enter. The registration deadline is usually in early November, and preregistration is required. There's also a half-marathon ($85) and a Family Fun Run that includes shorter races for adults and kids ($25 if postmarked by Dec 26, 2006, $30 after that; $5 per child for the kids' races). Call (C) **407/939-7810** or go to **www.disneysports.com**. January 5–8.

February

Silver Spurs Rodeo. Real yippee-I-O cowboys compete in calf roping, bull riding, barrel racing, and more. The rodeo is a celebration of the area's rural roots and a nice escape from the more typical tourist traps. If you've got a little cowboy (or girl), it's sure to be a treat. For a root'n toot'n good time, head to the Silver Spurs Arena, 1875 E. Irlo

Bronson Memorial Hwy. (U.S. 192), Kissimmee. Call © **407/847-4052** or visit **www.silverspursrodeo.com** for details. Tickets run $10 to $25 if purchased in advance, $12 to $30 the day of the show. Third weekend in February (again for 3 days in October).

March

Atlanta Braves. The Braves have been holding spring training at Disney's Wide World of Sports Complex since 1998. There are 15 games during the 1-month season, and they usually offer a much more up-close experience than your young fans will get at a major-league ballpark. Tickets run $13 to $21. For information, call © **407/939-GAME (4326)** or check out **www.disney sports.com**. To purchase tickets, call Ticketmaster © **877/803-7073** or 407/ 839-3900. The games begin in late February.

Houston Astros. Here's another event for the sports-minded family. The Astros train at Osceola County Stadium, 1000 Bill Beck Blvd., Kissimmee. Tickets are $14 and $17. Get them through Ticketmaster at © **877/ 803-7073** or 407/839-3900. For information, check the Astros' website at **www.astros.com**.

Florida Film Festival. The Enzian Theater has been showcasing American independent and foreign films for more than a decade. This 10-day festival, sponsored in part by Universal Orlando, usually features a selection of family-friendly films that you and your kids might not otherwise get a chance to see, and some of the films presented are made by teenage students. If your child is a budding director, it's worth attending. The event was named 1 of the top 10 such events in the world by *The Ultimate Film Festival Survival Guide,* 2nd edition. Call © **407/629-8587** or look up **www.floridafilmfestival.com**.

April

World's Fair for Kids. The first-ever World's Fair for Kids will be held at the Orange County Convention Center on I-Drive in 2006. Themed pavilions will fill the center, highlighting the latest developments in sports, health, science and technology, communications, travel, learning, toys and games, and entertainment. Events, activities, and entertainment will all be geared to kids ranging from tots to teens. It's all part of the city's Family Spring Break event—a family-friendly version of spring break. Single-day tickets run $30, 2-day $50, and event-long $60. Kids 3 and under are free. Call © **407/363-5872** or go to **www.wfkids.com** for information and tickets. April 13–23, 2006.

Epcot International Flower and Garden Festival. This 6-week-long event showcases gardens, topiary characters, floral displays, speakers, and seminars. Children will likely be entertained by the topiaries in the Kids Garden, a family-friendly hedge-style maze; Kids Day; and animal and insect demonstrations (where ladybugs and butterflies get released). The festival is free with regular park admission ($63 adults, $52 kids 3–9). For more information, call © **407/934-7639** or visit **www.disneyworld.com**. The festival kicks off in late April and goes through early June.

May

Disney's All-Star Kids Classic Inline Marathon. Everyone's a winner when children ages 3 to 12 race on inline skates in several age-limited races at Walt Disney World's Wide World of Sports. All children get an award and goodie bag for participating. Proper skating safety equipment is required. It costs $5 to enter your child. For more information, call © **407/828-3267** or surf the Web to **www.disneysports.com**.

Orlando International Fringe Festival.
Over 100 diverse acts from around the world participate in this eclectic event, held for 10 days in May at various venues in downtown Orlando. Everything performed on outdoor stages, from sword swallowing to *Hamlet,* is available free to Fringe attendees after they purchase a festival button for about $10. There's also a special **Kids Fringe** during the festival's two weekends. Events include storytelling, theater performances, and a live cartoon band. Tickets for indoor events vary, but most are under $10. Call ✆ **407/648-0077** or visit **www.orlandofringe.com**.

Viva La Musica. This celebration of Latin culture and music is held annually at SeaWorld. Festivities include concerts, and crafts and food displays throughout the park. There is no extra charge to join in the fun, which happens on two successive weekends in the beginning of May. For more information and exact dates, head online to **www.seaworld.com**.

Star Wars Weekends. Every year, Disney features a fan-fest full of activities for *Star Wars* fanatics. Characters, as well as a handful of *Star Wars* actors, are on hand for up-close meet-and-greets. Games, parades, and special entertainment top off the festivities. Go to **www.disneyworld.com** to find out more. The celebrations run for five consecutive weekends beginning in May.

July

Independence Day. There's a free fireworks display in downtown Orlando at Lake Eola Park. For information, call ✆ **407/246-2827.** Disney and Universal both put on fireworks extravaganzas at their theme parks. Other fireworks events are listed in the local newspaper, the *Orlando Sentinel.* July 4.

Tampa Bay Bucs. The NFL Tampa Bay Buccaneers run their training camp at the Wide World of Sports Complex from late July through August. For information, call ✆ **407/939-GAME (4236)** or go to **www.buccaneers.com** for more information.

September

Night of Joy. The first weekend (Thurs–Sun) in September, the Magic Kingdom hosts a festival of contemporary-Christian music featuring top artists. This is a very popular event, so obtain tickets early. Performers also make an appearance at Long's Christian Bookstore in College Park, about 20 minutes north of Disney. Admission to the concert is $38 for 1 night (7:30pm–12:30am), $62 for 2 nights. Use of Magic Kingdom attractions is included. Call ✆ **407/934-7639** for concert details; for information about the free appearance at Long's, call ✆ **407/422-6934.** Universal has gone head to head with Disney on this one, scheduling its **Rock the Universe** concert the same weekend (✆ **866/788-4636**). Big-name Christian bands and speakers headline the event. Tickets (which include admission to the parks after 4pm) cost $38 for 1 night or $62 for both nights of the event. A package including both nights of celebration, as well as 3 full days of admission to the parks (Fri–Sun), runs $90.

October

Orlando Magic Basketball. The local NBA team plays half of its 82-game regular season between October and April at the TD Waterhouse Centre, 600 W. Amelia St. Ticket prices range from $10 to $100. Single-game tickets can be hard to come by the day of the game. Call ✆ **407/896-2442** for details, ✆ 877/803-7073 or ✆ 407/839-3900 for tickets. Online, go to **www.nba.com/magic**.

Halloween Horror Nights. Universal Orlando's Islands of Adventure

(© **800/837-2273** or 407/363-8000; www.universalorlando.com) transforms its grounds for 20 or more nights into haunted attractions with live bands, a psychopath's maze, special shows, and hundreds of ghouls and goblins roaming the streets. (*Note:* This event is too intense for most children but will probably appeal to some older teens.) The parks essentially close at dusk, reopening in a new, macabre form from 7pm to midnight or later. Adult admission ($63) is charged for this event, where liquor flows freely. In 2005, for the first time since the event's inception, guests were permitted to wear costumes (regulated) on some evenings (they were originally prohibited so that Universal employees could spot their peers). There's no word on whether this policy will remain in effect for future Horror Nights, so call and ask in advance if you plan to attend.

Mickey's Not-So-Scary Halloween Party. The Magic Kingdom (© **407/934-7639;** www.disneyworld.com) invites you to join Mickey and his pals for a far-from-frightening time. In this one, you can come in costume and trick-or-treat through the Magic Kingdom from 7pm to midnight on any of 15 or so nights in October (you'll get bags and can collect candy from characters in set areas in the park). The alcohol-free party includes parades, live music, and storytelling. The climax is a bewitching fireworks spectacular. This is your best Halloween bet if you have young kids. A separate admission fee is charged ($35 adults, $28 kids 3–9, add $5 if purchased the day of the event); tickets go on sale at the end of April and nearly always sell out.

Silver Spurs Rodeo. See the entry under "February," above.

Shamu's Halloween Spooktacular. Halloween festivities, all part of your regular park admission, include parades, special not-so-spooky shows, costumed characters, and tricks and treats. A special trick-or-treat family sleepover ($75 per person) is available on 4 select nights. See **www.sea world.com** for more details. Weekends throughout October.

Epcot International Food & Wine Festival. Here's your chance to sip and savor the food and beverages of 25 cultures. More than 60 wineries from across the United States participate. Events include wine tastings for adults, seminars, food, dinners, concerts, and celebrity-chef cooking demonstrations. Tickets for the dinner-and-concert series or wine tastings are $79 to $125, including gratuity. The party's not just for adults; kids get their own activities as well. In 2005, kid-friendly options at the festival included "The Buzz About Honey," where kids could (safely) observe honeybee-filled hives; the chance for children ages 4 to 10 to bake their own Toll House cookies at The Land through the Junior Chef Program; a "Bountiful Harvest celebration where kids could see how giant pumpkins grow; and "Nuts About Peanuts," where kids could attend "Peanut University" and learn about one of their favorite foods. The event also features 25 food-and-wine marketplaces where appetizer-size portions of dishes ranging from pizza to octopus on purple potato salad sell for under $5 each (it's a fun way to introduce older kids to exotic cuisines). Entrance to the festival is included in park admission. Call © **407/939-3378** for details or check out **www.disney world.com**. Dates generally run from around Mid-September to early November.

November

ABC Super Soap Weekend. For fans of ABC's daytime soaps, this is one don't-miss event. Soap celebs are on hand for parades, parties, Q&As, music, and more in this weekend catering to fans and fanatics alike. If you and your older kids are soap-happy, you'll be in heaven. The events are included with Disney–MGM Studios admission ($63 adults, $52 kids 3–9). Call ✆ **407/397-6808** or check out **www.disneyworld.com** for details.

Walt Disney World Festival of the Masters. One of the largest art shows in the South takes place at Downtown Disney Marketplace for 3 days during the second weekend in November. The exhibition features over 150 top artists, photographers, and craftspeople, all winners of juried shows throughout the country. You can listen to the music of the jazz festival or enjoy one of the many family activities, all for free. Call ✆ **407/934-7639** or visit **www.disneyworld.com**.

The Osborne Family Spectacle of Lights. This attraction has returned by popular demand after being closed for renovations in 2004 and 2005. Lighting up the nights at the Disney–MGM Studios are millions of sparkling bulbs acquired from a family whose Christmas-lights collection got a bit too bright for their neighbors (see "Star Light, Star Bright," in this section). The holiday display runs from November to early January.

Jack Hanna Animal Adventure at SeaWorld. For one weekend, renowned animal expert and TV host Jack Hanna shows off some of his unusual animals in a special show that's included in park admission ($63 adult, $52 kids 3–9).

December

Christmas at Walt Disney World. During the holiday festivities, Main Street in the Magic Kingdom is lavishly decked out with twinkling lights and Christmas holly; all the while, carolers are greeting visitors throughout the park. Epcot, Disney–MGM Studios, and Animal Kingdom also offer special embellishments and entertainment throughout the holiday season, and the Disney resorts are decked out with towering Christmas trees, wreaths, boughs, and bows.

Some holiday highlights include **Mickey's Very Merry Christmas Party,** an after-dark (7pm–midnight) ticketed event ($39 adults, $30 kids 3–9, add $5 if purchased the day of the event). This takes place on select nights at the Magic Kingdom and offers a parade, fireworks, special shows, and admission to certain rides. You also get cookies, cocoa, and a souvenir photo.

Holidays Around the World and the **Candlelight Procession** at Epcot feature hundreds of carolers, storytellers

---

Fun Fact Star Light, Star Bright

The Osborne family of Arkansas built a collection of 3 million-plus Christmas lights. It was so bright that neighbors complained and eventually went to court in what became a nationally known battle. Disney came to the rescue and, in 1995, moved the entire thing to Orlando, adding another 2 million or so bulbs. The show was canceled for the 2003 holiday season while Disney–MGM Studios built a new stunt show, but the December extravaganza has returned at a new location. This awesome family favorite is a must-see; there are few displays (if any) on the planet like it.

> **Fun Fact   Disney in December**
>
> No snow? No problem. While there may be a lack of the white stuff in Orlando during the month of December (or any other month, for that matter), WDW more that makes up for it by decking the halls as only Disney can: 11 miles of garlands, 3,000 wreaths, and 1,500 Christmas trees in all decorate Walt Disney World during the holiday season.

---

from a host of international countries, celebrity narrators telling the Christmas story, a 450-voice choir, and a 50-piece orchestra in a very moving display. Fireworks are included. One other cool item that kids love: the world's largest gingerbread house, which is appropriately decorated with cookies and frosting. Admission to the event is included in your park admission fee. Call © **407/824-4321** for details on all of the above or go to **www.disneyworld. com**. The holiday fun lasts from mid-December to early January.

Macy's Holiday Parade at Universal Studios Florida. *That's not a typo!* Universal and Macy's (the latter a tenant at the Mall at Millenia, p. 304) teamed up for the first time in December 2002 to offer a smaller version of **Macy's Thanksgiving Day Parade,** held at Universal Studios Florida. It runs from mid-December to early January, featuring several of the floats and gigantic balloons from the original New York City parade (© **407/363-8000;** www. universalorlando.com). Park admission is required.

Grinchmas at Islands of Adventure. The famous Seussian Scrooge, The Grinch, spreads his own brand of grumpy holiday cheer at Islands from late November through early January. Seuss Landing is transformed to Whoville for the holidays, with "Whos" running all about to create a festive mood. Families can explore his lair, see a holiday-themed show, and attend a tree-lighting ceremony. All the fun is included in your park admission ($63 for adults, $52 for kids 3–9).

Walt Disney World New Year's Eve Celebration. For 1 night a year, the Magic Kingdom is open until the wee hours for a massive fireworks explosion, a very kid-friendly event. Other New Year's festivities in WDW include a big (and pricey) bash at Pleasure Island (geared to older teens and young adults) featuring music headliners, a special Hoop-Dee-Doo Musical Revue at Fort Wilderness, and guest performances by well-known musical groups at Disney–MGM Studios and Epcot. Call © **407/ 934-7639** for details or visit **www. disneyworld.com**. December 31.

4 What to Pack

You're going to be spending a lot of time on your feet and most likely in the heat, so it's important to pack comfortable clothes and footwear. Brand-new shoes may look great, but chances are that if they're not worn in, your feet will pay the price. You won't need anything dressy unless you are going to an upscale restaurant or attending

a special event that requires it. Assume that the weather will be warm to downright hot, so make shorts and lightweight clothing a priority, but also remember to bring layers if you're coming December through February; it can get downright cold at times. Check the local weather forecast just before you go to see if jackets, or even

Tips   Leave That Baby Gear at Home

There's no reason to schlep like a Sherpa when you can rent nearly anything you'll need right in Orlando. Gear for tiny tots and toddlers—including strollers and cribs, swings and car seats, and even gear for a day at the beach—are all available by the day or by the week through a handful of area companies. Two personal favorites are **Babies Away** (© 888/923-9030 or 407/932-0189; www.babiesaway.com) and **All About Kids** (© 800/728-6506 or 407/812-9300; www.all-about-kids.com). Sound familiar? They're one of the area's better in-room babysitters, too. The bonus: Both companies deliver your gear right to your hotel and pick it up before you leave.

If it's supplies such as diapers and wipes that you're in need of, and you just can't stomach the thought of heading to the grocery store on your vacation, **Babies Bottom** (© 877/693-1670; www.babiesbottom.com) is the place to contact. The company sells a variety of name-brand diapers (sizes 1–6), swim diapers, wipes, travel-size shampoos and lotions (sunscreen and diaper rash), powders, hand sanitizers, a travel-size first-aid kit, and band-aids. The best part: They deliver it all right to your door. Babies Bottom offers package pricing based on your length of stay, or you can create your own package. Admittedly, the prices are slightly higher than at the stores, but the convenience will likely outweigh the extra few dollars—especially if you don't have a car.

---

mittens, may be necessary. Bring a sweater or sweatshirt no matter what the time of year, as the air-conditioning inside can be brutal—especially on the kids.

Don't forget to bring sunglasses, a hat, a bathing suit, and cover-up if you're coming in spring, summer, or fall; plenty of socks (Band-Aids and moleskin, too, to prevent blisters); and your camera.

Pack a small tote bag filled with toys, puzzles, games, and activities to keep your kids busy on the plane or in the car. If you're flying, be sure to pack a supply of hard candies or chewing gum for older kids, a bottle or sippy cup for tinier tots, to help them deal with the pressure they may feel in their ears during takeoff and landing.

If you're traveling with a toddler or baby, a lightweight and reasonably priced stroller, with a hood and storage space, is a good way to keep little ones from pooping out at the parks, keep them dry in the rain, and shaded from the sun. You can rent them at the parks if you don't want to schlep yours from home. Be aware, however, that the park version isn't appropriate for infants or even particularly good for kids under 2. They're constructed of hard plastic, making them uncomfortable; they don't recline (a necessary function, if you have younger children); and storage space is at a minimum. Nearly every hotel will have cribs (though of varying quality) on hand. Most restaurants can supply a highchair or booster seat, but this is where having your own stroller may come in handy. **www.babyage.com** and **www.amazon.com** both offer a good selection of travel-related gear if you can't find what you need at your local baby store, Target, or Wal-Mart. You won't need to cart your entire supply of diapers, wipes, formula, and food; there are Walgreen's drug stores, as well as Publix and Goodings grocery stores throughout the area, that carry familiar brands. Just remember to bring enough to tide you over until you can get to a store. Powder and rash creams should be added to the list as well. Orlando's heat and humidity can wreak havoc on baby bottoms, even if your kids aren't generally susceptible to problems. And don't forget the sunscreen and hats!

As for older kids, keep them to one bag apiece, and invest in suitcases or duffle bags with wheels; you don't want to be lugging their luggage in addition to your own. Kids are usually happy with one or two pairs of shoes (sneakers or hiking boots and sandals), jeans, shorts, and T-shirts, or whatever's fashionable at the moment. Pack a sweatshirt or sweater no matter when you're traveling, and include a jacket in cooler months. Backpacks for all kids over 5 are great for stowing unused jackets, books, pens, paper, souvenirs, suntan lotion, a baseball cap, water bottle, map, and sunglasses.

5 Insurance, Health & Safety

TRAVEL INSURANCE AT A GLANCE

Check your existing insurance policies and credit card coverage before you buy travel insurance. You may already be covered for lost luggage, canceled tickets, or medical expenses.

The cost of travel insurance varies widely, depending on the cost and length of your trip, your age and health, and the type of trip you're taking, but expect to pay between 5% and 8% of the vacation itself. You can get estimates from various providers through **InsureMyTrip.com**. Enter your trip cost and dates, your age, and other information for prices from more than a dozen companies.

TRIP-CANCELLATION INSURANCE

Trip-cancellation insurance helps you get your money back if you have to back out of a trip, if you have to go home early, or if your travel supplier goes bankrupt. Allowed reasons for cancellation can range from sickness to natural disasters to the State Department declaring your destination unsafe for travel, which isn't likely to happen in Orlando. (Insurers usually won't cover vague fears, as many travelers discovered who tried to cancel their trips in Oct 2001 because they were wary of flying.) In this unstable world, trip-cancellation insurance is a good buy if you're getting tickets well in advance; who knows what the state of the world, or of your airline, will be in 9 months? Insurance policy details vary, so read the fine print—and especially make sure that your airline or cruise line is on the list of carriers covered in case of bankruptcy. A good resource is **"Travel Guard Alerts,"** a list of companies considered high-risk by Travel Guard International (see website below). Protect yourself further by paying for the insurance with a credit card; by law, consumers can get their money back on goods and services not received if they report the loss within 60 days after the charge is listed on their credit card statement.

For more information, contact one of the following recommended insurers: **Access America** (© 866/807-3982; www.accessamerica.com), **Travel Guard International** (© 800/826-4919; www.travelguard.com), **Travel Insured International** (© 800/243-3174; www.travelinsured.com), and **Travelex Insurance Services** (© 888/457-4602; www.travelex-insurance.com).

MEDICAL INSURANCE

Most health insurance policies cover you if you get sick away from home—but verify that you're covered before you depart, particularly if you're insured by an HMO. You should also call your own physician prior to receiving any treatment (or as soon as possible thereafter); many insurers require some type of notification if you expect emergency expenses to be covered. If you fail to inform them of your predicament, you may find yourself stuck with the bill.

If you require additional medical insurance, try **MEDEX Assistance** (© 410/453-6300; www.medexassist. com) or **Travel Assistance International** (© 800/821-2828; www.travelassistance. com; for general information on services, call the company's Worldwide Assistance Services, Inc., at © 800/777-8710).

LOST-LUGGAGE INSURANCE

On domestic flights, checked baggage is covered up to $2,500 per ticketed passenger. On international flights (including U.S. portions of international trips), baggage coverage is limited to approximately $9.07 per pound, up to approximately $635 per checked bag. If you plan to check items more valuable than what's covered by the standard liability, see if your homeowner's policy covers your valuables, get baggage insurance as part of your comprehensive travel-insurance package, or buy Travel Guard's "BagTrak" product. Don't buy insurance at the airport, where it's usually overpriced. Be sure to take any valuables or irreplaceable items with you in your carry-on luggage, because many valuables (including books, money, and electronics) aren't covered by airline policies.

If your luggage is lost, immediately file a lost-luggage claim at the airport, detailing the luggage contents. Most airlines require that you report delayed, damaged, or lost baggage within 4 hours of arrival.

The airlines are required to deliver luggage, once found, directly to your house or destination free of charge.

CAR-RENTAL INSURANCE

Car-rental insurance costs around $25 a day. If you hold a private auto insurance policy, you are **probably** covered in the United States for loss or damage to the car, as well as liability in case a passenger is injured. The credit card you used to rent the car also may provide some coverage. Double-check with your insurance company as well as the car-rental company regarding what may or may not be covered on both ends. *Note:* Many car-rental companies now charge steep out-of-service fees if the car is out of commission for any reason after its return.

Car-rental insurance probably does not cover liability if you caused the accident. Check your own auto insurance policy, the rental company policy, and your credit card coverage for the extent of coverage: Is your destination covered? Are other drivers covered? How much liability is covered if a passenger is injured? (If you rely on your credit card for coverage, you may want to bring a second credit card with you. Damages may be charged to your card, and you may find yourself stranded with no money.) You don't need any surprises spoiling your vacation, so look at your coverage before reaching the rental counter.

For more on car-rental insurance, see "Getting Around," in chapter 3.

Tips **Quick ID**

Tie a yellow ribbon "round the old suitcase? Putting a colorful ribbon, bright neon baggage tag, or a sticker that stands out on your luggage makes it much easier to pick it out of the sea of suitcases making their way around the conveyor belt. It's also less likely that someone will mistakenly grab it, and if your luggage gets lost, it will be far easier to find.

THE HEALTHY TRAVELER

Limit your family's exposure to Florida's strong sun, especially during the first few days of your trip and, thereafter, during the hours of 11am to 2pm, when the sun is at its strongest. Use a sunscreen with the highest sun-protection factor (SPF) available (especially for children), and apply it liberally. If you have children under a year old, check with your pediatrician before applying a sunscreen; some ingredients may not be appropriate for infants.

You should also bring along some moleskin and plenty of band-aids. This will help with the inevitable blisters brought on by the day's activities.

WHAT TO DO IF YOU GET SICK AWAY FROM HOME

If you worry about getting sick away from home, consider purchasing **medical travel insurance,** and carry your ID card in your purse or wallet. In most cases, your existing health plan will provide the coverage you need. See "Travel Insurance at a Glance," earlier in this chapter, for more information.

If you suffer from a chronic illness, consult your doctor before your departure. For conditions like epilepsy, diabetes, or heart problems, wear a **MedicAlert identification tag** (© 888/ 633-4298; www.medicalert.org), which will immediately alert doctors to your condition and give them access to your records through MedicAlert's 24-hour hotline.

Pack **prescription medications** in your carry-on luggage, and carry prescription medications in their original containers, with pharmacy labels; otherwise, they won't make it through airport security. Also carry copies of your prescriptions in case you lose your pills or run out. Don't forget an extra pair of contact lenses or prescription glasses.

TRAVELING SAFELY WITH YOUR CHILD

There is one major safety issue when traveling with kids that usually comes up a lot more frequently in Orlando than it does in other destinations (though it's fortunately not common): The Lost Child.

Theme parks are hives of activity, and it's easy for you or your child to get distracted or confused; the next thing you know, Junior is missing. The good news is that the theme parks know this, and if it has to happen, better it happen here than in a lot of other places. So do not panic, no matter how inclined you may be to do so.

If a child turns up missing, report it immediately to the closest park employee. They are all trained to deal with lost kids—and to spot little lambs who've apparently gone astray from their flock. After making your report, find out where lost children are brought (there are usually one or two central locations in each park), and head directly there. Odds are your little wanderers are either already there or will arrive there shortly.

The best way to prevent any of this from happening is to take a few preventive steps:

- Dress your young children in something that's easily identifiable so you don't lose them in a crowd.
- Always set up a central, specific, and easily located spot for your kids to meet you, should you all get separated. Saying "I'll meet you at Cinderella Castle" rather than "I'll meet you at the entrance to Cinderella's Royal Table" is a recipe for disaster.
- Hold on tight to young kids when exiting the park at closing time, at parades, and when exiting shows. It's very easy to get separated when you're smack in the middle of a massive wave of people. I'm not a huge fan of toddler harnesses, but in this case, I make an exception.

- Either sew or affix a name tag to your child's clothing (though not in a place it can be read casually) with your child's first name; your cell-phone number, if you are carrying one; and a contact number at home. The minute you get into the park, show your kids the distinctive name tags that the theme park employees wear, and tell them to report to one of them if they get lost.
- Don't assume that rides or restrooms have a single exit, so always give a specific place for your child to meet you. Otherwise, you may end up in two different spots . . . and at least one of you will panic.

6 Words of Wisdom & Helpful Resources

SPECIAL FAMILY ADVICE

If you have trouble getting your kids out of the house in the morning, dragging them thousands of miles away may seem like an insurmountable challenge. But family travel can be immensely reward-ing, giving you new ways of seeing the world through smaller pairs of eyes.

No city in the world is geared more to family travel than Orlando. In addition to theme parks, its recreational facilities pro-vide loads of opportunities for family fun. Most restaurants have low-priced ($4–$7) children's menus (if not, the appetizer menu works well), plus fun distractions such as placemats to color or games to play while younger diners wait for their food. Many hotels have children's activity centers (see chapter 4, "Family-Friendly Accommodations," for details).

Keep an eye out for coupons discount-ing meals and attractions. The Calendar section in Friday's *Orlando Sentinel* news-paper often contains coupons and good deals. Many restaurants, especially those in tourist areas, offer great discounts that are yours for the clipping. Check the information you receive from the Orlando/Orange County Convention & Visitors Bureau (see "Visitor Informa-tion," earlier in this chapter), including free or cheap things to do. Also, many hotel lobbies have free coupon books available.

Most major theme parks offer parent-swap programs in which one parent rides while the other waits in a designated area along with the kids too young or too afraid to ride. Then parents switch places, and the parent who was waiting can ride without having to return to the end of the line. Inquire at Guest Services or Guest Relations, near the park entrances, or with the ride attendant.

Here are more suggestions for making traveling with children easier:

- **Are your kids old enough?** Do you really want to bring an infant or toddler to the parks? If you plan on visiting Disney several times as your children grow, the best age for a first visit to Disney is just about 3 years old. Why? Because the kids are old enough to walk around and enjoy the sights and sounds, and a good deal of the rides and shows as well. The thrill rides would most likely frighten them, but most inappropriate rides for the tiny-tot set have height restric-tions that prevent any unfortunate mistakes. If, however, this trip is going to be a one-time trip, I recom-mend waiting until your child is between 7 and 10. He still be able to appreciate the magic and wonder of the experience but won't have reached the stage where all he'll want is chills and thrills.

  Some of the characters walking about may make young kids a bit nervous, though most will run right up to Donald or Mickey and give them a big hug. Younger kids may need a nap just when you want to see

ⓘ Tips   The Royal Treatment

Geared to those who have no time to plan but plenty of money to spend, **Michael's VIPs (www.michaelsvips.com)** is a personal and professional tour-guide service that will take care of all of the tedious itinerary planning, but also provides personalized and private tours through all the attractions in and around Orlando that you wish to experience. The price tag hovers around $100 per hour (plus gratuity), with the average guest paying roughly $3,500 per vacation for their VIP experience. Every detail is pre-arranged, and your private tour guide ensures that you'll never have to think or make decisions as you tour the attractions. Due to Michael's extensive background knowledge of the area's attractions (he's a former WDW VIP host, where he was in charge of selecting and planning every attraction, dining, and activity choice while escorting world-famous celebs, athletes, execs, and their families throughout the resort), you'll experience minimal waiting times and maximum fun!

Don't have time to plan your vacation itinerary or your days at the parks? The **TourGuideMike Automated Vacation Planner** may be just what you need. Simply fill out the detailed questionnaire (**www.tourguidemike.com**; a charge of $22 applies); then, based on the information you provide, you'll get your own customized website to use to plan and tailor your itinerary. The best part: The site offers sample park tours and seasonal crowd charts to help you out.

a show or hop on an attraction, but if you have kids, this is nothing new to you. When you plan your day's activities, be sure to account for necessary breaks and naps. Will your whole family be able to enjoy the experiences that Disney, along with the other parks, have to offer? This is something you will have to decide. My five kids range in age from 4 to 12, and we have traveled with just about every age combination you can think of. On our first family trip, my oldest was 4, and his two younger siblings were ages 3 and 1. While the 1-year-old has absolutely no recollection of the trip, he was thoroughly amused by the sights and sounds everywhere we went. The 3-year-old (now 10) still remembers plenty. You'll need to take into account your kids' stamina, interest, and tolerance levels before you decide whether to make the trip and when planning your daily itineraries. My kids could go well into the evening inside the parks, but many other children can't, so it may take you longer to cover a park (it took me 2–3 days to tour Magic Kingdom when my youngest was 2). My 8-year-old nephew was petrified by some of the rides in the parks, and even my own kids, who'll try anything once and have never been wary of rides, freak out at attractions involving sensory effects. It may be repetitious, but I'll say it again: Know your own child before deciding whether he or she's ready for this sort of trip. Not every child will fall in love with Disney World at first sight, and it's a rather large expense to incur if Junior's going to be frightened, sleepy, or cranky the whole trip.

- **Planning ahead** Make reservations for "character breakfasts" at Disney (see chapter 5, "Family-Friendly Dining") as soon as possible. Disney now accepts them up to 180 days in advance, and many are booked minutes after the 180-day window opens, so mark your calendar to call (it can be as early as 4am PST). Also, in any park, check the daily schedule for character appearances (all the major ones post them on maps or boards near the entrances), and make sure the kids know when they're going to get to meet their heroes. It's often the highlight of their day. (Be wary, however, of promising specific characters, as schedules and character lineups can change.) Advance planning will help you avoid running after every character you see. The "in" thing of late is getting character autographs. The lines can be quite long, so you may want to pick and choose just a couple of favorite characters to do this with. Take my advice: Buy an autograph book and some Disney stickers (to decorate it) at home instead of paying theme-park prices.

- **Packing** Although your home may be toddlerproof, hotel accommodations aren't. Bring blank plugs to cover outlets and whatever else is necessary to prevent an accident from occurring in your room. Most hotels have some type of cribs available; however, they are usually limited in number and sometimes of questionable quality. Some hotels have bedrails available as well, though not as readily available as cribs are. Locals can spot tourists by their bright-red, just-toasted sunburns. Both parents and children should heed this reminder: *Don't forget to bring and use sunscreen with an SPF rating of at least 30.* If you do forget it, it's available at convenience stores, drugstores, some theme-park shops, and the resorts. Young children should be slathered, even if they're in a stroller, and be sure to pack a wide-brim hat for infants and toddlers. Adults and children alike should drink plenty of water to avoid dehydration.

- **Accommodations** Kids under 12 and, in many cases, those as old as 17 stay free in their parent's room in most hotels, but to be certain, ask when you book your room. Most hotels have pools and other recreational facilities that will give you a little no-extra-cost downtime. If you want to skip a rental car and aren't staying at Disney, International Drive and Lake Buena Vista are the places to stay. Hotels often offer family discounts; some offer "kids eat free" programs; and some provide free or moderate-cost shuttle service to the major attractions. International Drive also has the I-Drive Trolley, which travels the length of the road, making numerous stops along the way.

- **Ground rules** Set firm rules before leaving home regarding things such as bedtime and souvenirs. It's easy to get off track as you get caught up in the excitement of Orlando, but don't allow your vacation to seize control of your better judgment. Having the kids earn their own money or at least allotting a specific prearranged amount for them to spend works wonders. Making them part of your decisions also works wonders. They're far more accommodating and cooperative when they understand that everyone in the family gets a say in the plan for the day and that they will eventually get to do something or go somewhere that they want to.

- **At the parks** Getting lost is unfortunately all too easy in a place as strange and overwhelming as the theme parks. Toss in the crowds, and it's amazing it doesn't happen more often. For adults (yes, they get lost too) and older kids, arrange a lost-and-found meeting place before you arrive in the parks, and if you become separated, head there immediately. Make sure your kids know to find a staff member (point out the special name tags staff members wear) to help them. Attach a name tag with the child's first name and your cell-phone (or hotel) number to the inside of younger kids' T-shirts, and tell them to find a park employee (and only a park employee) immediately and show them the tag if they become lost.

- **Read the signs** Most rides post signs that explain **height restrictions,** if any, or identify those that may unsettle youngsters. Save yourself and your kids some grief before you get in line and are disappointed. (The ride listings in chapter 6, "What Kids Like to See & Do in Walt Disney World," and chapter 7, "What Kids Like to See & Do Beyond Disney," note any minimum heights, as do the guide maps you can get at the parks.) A bad experience—whether it be a dark, scary section of a ride; the loop-de-loop of a roller coaster; or too dramatic a drop—can cause your child long-lasting anxiety. It can also put a damper on things for the rest of your day (and possibly even your vacation).

I've explained to my older boys that if they hear adults screaming, that's a pretty good indication that a ride is not the best choice for them. With younger kids, you have to be steadfast in your decisions, though most height restrictions will keep those who really shouldn't be riding at bay. With the older ones . . . well, you may have to indulge them a bit and

let them ride just one; they likely won't make the same mistake twice. Note that once you get past the height restriction, age is not always as much of a deciding factor when it comes to rides as one might think. It really depends on your children's experiences and their personalities. I've seen 5-year-olds squeal with glee on rides that I can't even stomach; on the other hand, I've observed kids as old as 8 or 10 walk out of some of the attractions with those "touchy feely" sensory effects practically in tears.

- **Take a break** The Disney parks, Universal Orlando, and SeaWorld have fabulous interactive play areas, offering both parents and young kids a break. By all means take advantage of them. They allow kids to expend some of their pent-up energy after having to wait in lines and not wander far from Mom and Dad all day long. They offer a nice break for you, too (if you can sit down to watch them, that is). Note that many of these kid zones are filled with water squirters and shallow pools, and most of the parks feature a fair number of water-related attractions, so getting wet is practically inevitable—at least for the kids. It's advisable to bring along a change of clothes or even a bathing suit. You can rent a locker ($7 or less) for storing the spares until you need them. During the summer, the Florida humidity is enough to keep you feeling soggy, so you may appreciate the change of clothing even if you don't go near any water.

- **Show Time** Schedule an inside air-conditioned show two or three times a day, especially midafternoons in the summer. You may even get your littlest tykes to nap in the darkened theater. For all shows, arrive at least 20 minutes early to get the better seats, but not so early that the kids are tired of waiting (most waits are outside in the heat at Disney, while Universal has covered queue areas at most attractions).

- **Snack times** When dreaming of your vacation, you probably don't envision hours spent standing in lines, waiting and waiting (unless you have done this before, that is). It helps to store some lightweight snacks in a backpack, or in the stroller if you have one, especially when traveling with small children. This may save you some headaches, as kids get hungriest just when you are farthest from food. It will also be much healthier and will certainly save you money, as the parks' prices are quite high.

- **Bring your own?** While you will have to haul it to and from the car and on and off trams, trains, or monorails at Disney, having your own stroller can be a tremendous help. It will be with you when you need it—say, back in the hotel room as a highchair or for an infant in a restaurant when a highchair is inappropriate. Remember to bring the right stroller, too. It should be lightweight, easy to fold and unfold with one hand, have a canopy, be able to recline for naps, and have plenty of storage space. The parks offer stroller rentals for around $10, but these are hard and uncomfortable. They do not recline and have little or no storage space for the inevitable gear that

goes along with bringing the kids. And they are absolutely inappropriate for infants and young toddlers. They are good, however, if you have older kids who may just need an occasional break from walking. For infants and small toddlers, you may want to bring a snuggly sling or backpack-type carrier for use in traveling to and from parking lots and while you're standing in line for attractions.

- **Recommended reading** *The Unofficial Guide to Walt Disney World* is another good source of additional information, as is *Frommer's Walt Disney World.*

You can find good family-oriented vacation advice on the Internet from sites such as **Family Travel Forum** (www.familytravelforum.com), a comprehensive site that offers customized trip planning; **Family Travel Network** (www.familytravelnetwork.com), an award-winning site that offers travel features, deals, and tips; **Traveling Internationally with Your Kids** (www.travelwithyourkids.com), a comprehensive site offering sound advice for long-distance and international travel with children; and **Family Travel Files** (www.thefamilytravelfiles.com), which offers an online magazine and a directory of off-the-beaten-path tours and tour operators for families.

I've listed some additional tips for tackling the theme parks in chapter 6, "What Kids Like to See & Do in Walt Disney World."

Tips Kids Come First—or Do They?

Delta, Walt Disney World's official airline, has stopped allowing families with children to board first on its Orlando flights. It's more fair to the other passengers and often better for the kids, who won't be cooped up as long. Most other airlines, however, still allow preboarding for those traveling with tinier tots (usually under the age of 3) in tow.

FOR TRAVELERS WITH SPECIAL NEEDS

There's no reason for anyone with disabilities to miss most of the fun that Orlando and the theme parks have to offer—as long as you engage in a little advance planning. Autistic children, wheelchair-bound adults, and hearing-impaired teens all come to Orlando, and all of them are accommodated to the best of each park's ability.

ACCOMMODATIONS Every hotel and motel in Florida is required by law to have a special room or rooms equipped for wheelchairs. A few have wheel-in showers. Walt Disney World's **Coronado Springs Resort** (© **407/934-7639** or 407/939-1000; www.disneyworld.com) has 99 rooms designed to accommodate guests with disabilities. **Disney's Polynesian** and the **Grand Floridian** resorts are both particularly well suited to guests who use wheelchairs, as their location on the monorail system makes travel to the Magic Kingdom and Epcot a bit easier. Make your special needs known when making reservations. For other information about special Disney rooms, call © **407/939-7807.**

If you don't mind staying 15 minutes from Disney, **Yvonne's Property Management** (© **877/714-1144** or 863/424-0795; www.villasinorlando.com) is a rental agent for, among other things, some handicapped-accessible homes that have multiple bedrooms, multiple baths with accessible showers, full kitchens, and pools outfitted with lifts. Most cost less than $250 a night and are located in Davenport.

Medical Travel Inc. (© **800/778-7953;** www.medicaltravel.org) is another source of rentals, scooters and vans, and medical equipment, and can satisfy other needs of disabled travelers (including those with terminal illnesses) and their families.

Some hotels also have special "hypoallergenic" rooms for those with severe allergies or asthma. These rooms usually offer special ventilation systems, pillows, toiletries, and so on. Ask about this when booking your hotel if this is an issue for you or your child.

TRANSPORTATION

Public buses in Orlando have hydraulic lifts and restraining belts for wheelchairs. They serve Universal Orlando, SeaWorld, the shopping areas, and downtown Orlando. If you're staying at Disney, most shuttle buses on the Disney transportation system can accommodate wheelchairs.

If you need to rent a wheelchair or electric scooter for your visit, **Walker Medical & Mobility Products** offers delivery to your room, and there's a model for guests who weigh up to 375 pounds. These products fit into Disney's transports and monorails, as well as rental cars. Get more information by calling © **888/726-6837** or 407/518-6000, or on the Internet, go to **www.walker mobility.com. CARE Medical Equipment** (© **800/741-2282** or 407/856-2273; www.caremedicalequipment.com) offers similar services.

Amtrak (© **800/872-7245;** www.amtrak.com) provides redcap service, wheelchair assistance, and special seats if you give 72 hours' notice. Travelers with disabilities are entitled to a 15% discount off the lowest available adult coach fare. Documentation from a doctor or an ID card proving your disability is required. Amtrak also provides wheelchair-accessible sleeping accommodations on long-distance trains. Service dogs are permitted aboard and travel free. TDD/TTY service is also available at © **800/523-6590,** or you can write to P.O. Box 7717, Itasca, IL 60143.

INSIDE THE THEME PARKS

Many attractions at the parks, especially the newer ones, are designed to be accessible to a wide variety of guests. People with wheelchairs and their parties are

---

Tips Don't Forget the 407

Local calls in Orlando require that you dial the area code **(407)** followed by the 7-digit local number, even when you're calling just across the street.

---

often given preferential treatment so they can avoid lines.

The available assistance is outlined in the guide maps you get as you enter the parks. All the theme parks offer parking close to the entrances for those with disabilities. Let the parking-booth attendant know your needs, and you'll be directed to the appropriate spot. Wheelchair and electric-cart rentals are available at most major attractions. If you bring your own, keep in mind that wheelchairs wider than 24½ inches may be difficult to navigate through some attractions. And crowds may make it tough for any guest.

At Walt Disney World: Disney's many services are detailed in each theme park's *Guidebook for Guests with Disabilities.* You can pick one up at Guest Relations near the front entrances of each of the parks. Also, you can call ✆ **407/ 934-7639** or 407/824-2222 for answers to any questions regarding special needs. The guide is also available online at Disney's website, **www.disneyworld.com**. Examples of services are as follows:

- Almost all Disney resorts have rooms for those with disabilities.
- Braille guidebooks, cassette tapes, and portable tape players are available at City Hall in the Magic Kingdom and Guest Relations in the other parks (a $25 refundable deposit is required).
- Service animals are allowed in all parks and on some rides.
- All parks have special parking lots near the entrances.
- Assisted-listening devices are available to amplify the audio at selected attractions at WDW parks. Also, at some attractions, hearing-impaired

guests can use handheld wireless receivers that allow them to read captions about the attractions. Both services are free but require a $25 refundable deposit.

- Wheelchairs and electric carts can be rented at all the parks.
- Downtown Disney West Side, with crowded shops and bars, may be a bit difficult to navigate in a wheelchair. The movie theater is, however, wheelchair accessible.
- For information about Telecommunications Devices for the Deaf (TDDs) or sign-language interpreters at Disney World live shows, call ✆ **407/827- 5141** (TDD/TTY). You can usually get an ASL interpreter at several events and attractions if you call no later than 2 weeks in advance.

On a final note, if you or your child has a life-threatening food allergy (or even just a bad one), Disney will try to accommodate your needs so your family can have a meal at the park. Your best bet is to do this at a sit-down restaurant. When making your Advanced Dining Reservations (see p. 119 for more info), inform the reservations agent that the allergy is an issue. When you get to the restaurant, ask to speak to a chef about your particular concerns. You may end up having to pay a full adult price for your child if the dish she requires doesn't appear on the kids' menu, but you won't pay extra to have it specially prepared. *Warning:* If your child has a peanut allergy, forget about eating any Asian food in the parks; it's made with peanut oil. If you have doubts about what's in a dish, just ask; most restaurants carry an ingredient list.

At Universal Orlando parks: Guests with disabilities should go to Guest Services, located just inside the main entrances, for a *Disabled Guest Guidebook,* a TDD, or other special assistance. Wheelchair and electric-cart rentals are available in the concourse area of the parking garage. Universal also provides audio descriptions on cassette for visually impaired guests and has sign-language guides and scripts for its shows (advance notice of 1–2 weeks is required; call © **888/519-4899** [TTY] or 407/224-5929 [voice] for details). You can also get additional information online at **www.universalorlando.com**. From the main page, click either Islands of Adventure or Universal Studios Florida, and scroll down the left side to the ADA page.

Note: All Universal Orlando resorts offer rooms for those with mobility impairments. Note, however, that if you or your child has severe pet allergies, pets are accepted at all the Universal resorts.

At SeaWorld: The park has a guide for guests with disabilities, although most of its attractions are easily accessible to those in wheelchairs. SeaWorld also provides a Braille guide for the visually impaired and a very brief synopsis of its shows for the hearing impaired. Sign-language interpreting services are available at no charge but must be reserved by calling © **407-363-2414** at least a week in advance of your visit. Assisted-listening devices are available at select attractions for a $20 refundable deposit. For information, call © **407/351-3600** or check out the park's website at **www.seaworld.com** to see the park's accessibility guide.

OTHER RESOURCES   You can get information online at the **Orlando/ Orange County Convention & Visitors Bureau's (CVB)** website, **www.orlando info.com**.

WheelchairsOnTheGo.com is a comprehensive website that lists information on accessibility in Florida, from ground transportation to medical equipment rentals, accommodations, and attractions (and plenty more).

Many travel agencies offer customized tours and itineraries for travelers with disabilities. **Flying Wheels Travel** (© **507/ 451-5005;** www.flyingwheelstravel.com) offers escorted tours and cruises that emphasize sports and private tours in minivans with lifts. **Access-Able Travel Source** (© **303/232-2979;** www.access-able.com) offers extensive access information and advice for traveling around the world with disabilities. **Accessible Journeys** (© **800/846-4537** or 610/521-0339; www.disabilitytravel.com) caters specifically to slow walkers and wheelchair travelers and to their families and friends.

Organizations that offer assistance to disabled travelers include **MossRehab** (www.mossresourcenet.org), which provides a library of accessible-travel resources online; the **American Foundation for the Blind (AFB)** (© **800/232-5463;** www.afb.org), a referral resource for the blind or visually impaired that includes information on traveling with Seeing Eye dogs; and **SATH (Society for Accessible Travel & Hospitality)** (© **212/447-7284;** www.sath.org; annual membership fees: $45 adults, $30 seniors and students), which offers a wealth of travel resources for all types of disabilities and informed recommendations on destinations, access guides, travel agents, tour operators, vehicle rentals, and companion services.

For more information specifically targeted to travelers with disabilities, the community website **iCan** (www.ican online.net/channels/travel) has destination guides and several regular columns on accessible travel. Also check out the quarterly magazine *Emerging Horizons* (www.emerginghorizons.com; $15 per year, $20 outside the U.S.) and *Open World* magazine, published by SATH (see above; subscription: $13 per year, $21 outside the U.S.).

FOR GRANDPARENTS

Many family vacations now include several generations, and traveling with the grandkids to Orlando will provide a host of memorable experiences at both ends of the age spectrum.

Mention you're a senior when you make reservations. Although all the major U.S. airlines except America West have canceled senior-discount and coupon-book programs, many hotels offer discounts for seniors (Loews Hotels, which runs Universal Orlando's resorts, even offers a special package to grandparents traveling with their grandkids). In most cities, people over 60 qualify for reduced admission to theaters, museums, and other attractions, as well as discount fares on public buses.

You can order a copy of the *Mature Traveler Guide,* which contains local discounts mainly on rooms but also on attractions and activities, from the **Orlando/Orange County Convention & Visitors Bureau,** 8723 International Dr., Suite 101 (southeast corner of I-Dr. and Austrian Row), Orlando, FL 32819 (*©* **800/643-9492** or 800/551-0181; www.orlandoinfo.com).

Members of **AARP** (formerly known as the American Association of Retired Persons), 601 E St. NW, Washington, DC 20049 (*©* **800/424-3410** or 202/434-2277 weekdays; www.aarp.org), get discounts on hotels, airfares, and car rentals. AARP offers members a wide range of benefits, including *Modern Maturity* magazine and a monthly newsletter. Anyone over 50 can join.

Recommended publications offering travel resources and discounts for seniors include: the quarterly magazine *Travel 50 & Beyond* (www.travel50andbeyond. com); *Travel Unlimited: Uncommon Adventures for the Mature Traveler* (Avalon); *101 Tips for Mature Travelers,* available from Grand Circle Travel (*©* **800/221-2610** or 617/350-7500; www.gct.com); and *Unbelievably Good*

Deals and Great Adventures That You Absolutely Can't Get Unless You're Over 50 (McGraw-Hill), by Joann Rattner Heilman.

FOR SINGLE PARENTS

Single parents face special, unique challenges when they travel with their children. **Parents Without Partners** (*©* **561/391-8833;** www.parentswithoutpartners.org) provides links to numerous single-parent resources.

Single mom Brenda Elwell's website (**www.singleparenttravel.net**) is full of advice garnered from traveling around the world with her two children.

FOR GAY & LESBIAN FAMILIES

The popularity of Orlando with gay and lesbian travelers, including families, parallels the growing number of same-sex households in the area. **Gay, Lesbian & Bisexual Community Services of Central Florida,** 934 N. Mills Ave., Orlando, FL 32803 (*©* **407/228-8272;** www.glbcc. org), is a great source of information on Central Florida. Welcome packets usually include the latest issue of the *Triangle,* a quarterly newsletter dedicated to gay and lesbian issues, and a calendar of events pertaining to the gay and lesbian community. Though not a tourist-specific packet, it includes information and ads for local gay and lesbian clubs. **In the Company of Women** (*©* **407/331-3466;** www.companyofwomen.com) and **Gay Orlando Network** (www.gayorlando.com) are two other planning resources for travelers.

TRAVELING WITH PETS

Many of us wouldn't dream of going on a family vacation without our pets. And more and more lodgings and restaurants are pet-friendly. Policies vary, however, so call ahead to find out the rules.

None of the Disney resorts except Fort Wilderness allows animals to stay on the premises (service dogs are the exception) or have their own kennels, but resort

Tips The Peripatetic Pet

It is illegal in Florida to leave your pet inside a parked car, windows rolled down or not. The sweltering heat can easily kill an animal in only a few minutes. All the major theme parks have kennel facilities; use them.

Make sure your pet is wearing a name tag with the name and phone number of a contact person who can take the call if your pet gets lost while you're away from home. Better yet, the American Kennel Club has an affiliated non-profit **Companion Animal Recovery** service, where a veterinarian embeds a microchip in your pet, so that it can be identified—collar or not—should it get lost and end up in a shelter or veterinary office. The service is open to all pets, not just dogs, and has an excellent track record. For more information, check out the organization's website at **www.akccar.org**.

guests are welcome to board their animals overnight in kennel facilities at the Ticket & Transportation Center. If you require boarding only during the day, kennels are located at all four Disney parks. Universal Orlando & SeaWorld will board small animals during the day only.

Universal's three Loews-run resorts do allow pets on site. In fact, "Loews Loves Pets" is a program that caters to pets and their families by offering such pet-friendly amenities as food, leashes, bedding, toys, and more. Pet walking, pet pagers, and door hangers to let the resort staff know that there is a pet in the room are also available.

An excellent resource is **www.pets welcome.com**, which dispenses medical tips, names of animal-friendly lodgings and campgrounds, and lists of kennels and veterinarians. Also check out **www.dogfriendly.com**, which features links to Orlando accommodations, eateries, attractions, and parks that welcome canine companions.

If you plan to fly with your pet, the FAA has compiled a list of all requirements for transporting live animals at **airconsumer.ost.dot.gov**. Click the Travel Tips & Publications link on the home page; then select Traveling with Animals. You may be able to carry your pet on board a plane if it's small enough to put inside a carrier that can slip under the seat. Pets usually count as one piece of carry-on luggage. Note that summer may not be the best time to fly with your pet: Many airlines will not check pets as baggage in the hot summer months. The ASPCA discourages travelers from checking pets as luggage at any time, as storage conditions on planes are loosely monitored, and fatal accidents are not unprecedented. Your other option is to ship your pet with a professional carrier, which can be expensive. Ask your veterinarian whether you should sedate your pet on a plane ride or give it antinausea medication. Never give your pet sedatives used by humans.

7 Planning Your Trip Online

SURFING FOR AIRFARES

The "big three" online travel agencies, **Expedia.com**, **Travelocity.com**, and **Orbitz.com**, sell most of the air tickets bought on the Internet. (Canadian travelers should try expedia.ca and Travelocity.ca; U.K. residents can go for expedia.co.uk and opodo.co.uk.) **Kayak.com** is also gaining popularity and uses a sophisticated search engine (developed at MIT). Each has different business deals with the airlines and may offer different fares on the same flights, so it's wise to shop around. Expedia, Kayak, and Travelocity will also send you **e-mail notification** when a cheap fare becomes available to your favorite destination. Of the smaller travel-agency websites, **SideStep** (www.sidestep.com) has gotten the best reviews from Frommer's authors. The website (with optional browser add-on) purports to "search 140 sites at once" but in reality beats competitors' fares only as often as other sites do.

Also remember to check **airline websites,** especially those for low-fare carriers such as Southwest, JetBlue, and AirTran, whose fares are often misreported or simply missing from travel agency websites. Even with major airlines, you can often shave a few bucks from a fare by booking directly through the airline and avoiding a travel agency's transaction fee. But you'll get these discounts only by **booking online:** Most airlines now offer online-only fares that even their phone agents know nothing about. For the websites of airlines that fly to and from your destination, go to "Getting There," later in this chapter.

Great **last-minute deals** are available through free weekly e-mail services provided directly by the airlines. Most of these are announced on Tuesday or Wednesday and must be purchased online. Most are only valid for travel that weekend, but some (such as Southwest's) can be booked weeks or months in advance. Sign up for weekly e-mail alerts at airline websites or check megasites that compile comprehensive lists of last-minute specials, such as **Smarter Travel** (www.smartertravel.com). For last-minute trips, **site59.com** and **lastminutetravel.com** often have better air-and-hotel package deals than the major-label sites.

If you're willing to give up some control over your flight details, use what is called an **"opaque" fare service** like **Priceline** (www.priceline.com; www.priceline.co.uk for Europeans) or its smaller competitor **Hotwire** (www.hotwire.com). Both offer rock-bottom prices in exchange for travel on a "mystery airline" at a mysterious time of day, often with a mysterious change of planes en route. The mystery airlines are all major, well-known carriers—and the possibility of being sent from Philadelphia to Orlando via Phoenix is remote; the airlines' routing computers have gotten a lot better than they used to be. Your chances of getting a 6am or 11pm flight, however, are still pretty high. Hotwire tells you flight prices before you buy; Priceline usually has better deals than Hotwire, but you have to play its "name our price" game. If you're new at this, the helpful folks at **Bidding-ForTravel** (www.biddingfortravel.com) do a good job of demystifying Priceline's prices and strategies. Priceline and Hotwire are great for flights within North America and between the United States and Europe. But for flights to other parts of the world, consolidators will almost always beat their fares. *Note:* In 2004, Priceline added nonopaque service to its roster. You now have the option to pick exact flights, times, and airlines from a list of offers—or opt to bid on opaque fares as before.

SURFING FOR HOTELS

Shopping online for hotels is much easier in the United States, Canada, and certain parts of Europe than it is in the rest of the world. If you try to book a Chinese hotel online, for instance, you'll probably overpay. Also, many smaller hotels and B&Bs—especially outside the United States—don't show up on websites at all. Of the "big three" sites, **Expedia** may be the best choice, thanks to its long list of special deals. **Travelocity** runs a close second. Hotel-specialist sites **hotels.com** and **hoteldiscounts.com** are also reliable. An excellent free program, **TravelAxe** (www.travelaxe.net), can help you search multiple hotel sites at once, even ones you haven't heard of. It has an immense number of Orlando hotels in its database, and best of all, it almost always shows you the price you'll pay for your room, including the hotel taxes! (It doesn't include resort fees, however, and it doesn't monitor Disney Resort hotels either.) **Trip Advisor** (www.tripadvisor.com) is another excellent source of unbiased user reviews of hotels around the world. While even the finest hotels can occasionally inspire a misleading poor review from a picky or crabby traveler, the body of user opinions, when taken as a whole, is usually a reliable indicator.

In the opaque-website category, Priceline and Hotwire are even better for hotels than for airfares; with both, you're allowed to pick the neighborhood and quality level of your hotel before offering up your money. That said, *I don't recommend you use them unless you have older kids and are willing to opt for a second room.* Here's why: The sites guarantee only double occupancy and won't guarantee bed types, crib space, rollaways, or even that the hotel you get will have lots of child-friendly amenities. They also won't book a Disney resort. So unless

you're willing to get two rooms (you can request adjoining ones once your bid is accepted, though that's not guaranteed either), you could end up in a small room that won't fit all of you very comfortably.

For information on the hotel rooms Priceline uses in Orlando, check out **BiddingForTravel** (www.biddingfortravel.com). This must-see site should always be your first stop before bidding on a room through Priceline. The site not only lists the hotels the service uses, but also can tell you the amounts of recent winning bids. One recent winning bid got a rate of $70 a night at the Wyndham Palace Resort & Spa (p. 95)—more than $100 off the rack rate.

Note that Priceline is much better at getting five-star lodging for three-star prices than at finding anything at the bottom of the scale. *Note:* Hotwire overrates its hotels by one star; what Hotwire calls a four-star is a three-star anywhere else.

SURFING FOR RENTAL CARS

For booking rental cars online, the best deals are usually found at rental-car company websites (see appendix B, "Useful

---

Frommers.com: The Complete Travel Resource

For an excellent travel-planning resource, I highly recommend **Frommers.com** (www.frommers.com), voted Best Travel Site by *PC Magazine*. I'm a little biased, of course, but I guarantee that you'll find the travel tips, reviews, monthly vacation giveaways, bookstore, and online-booking capabilities thoroughly indispensable. Among the special features are our popular **Destinations** section, where you'll get expert travel tips, hotel and dining recommendations, and advice on the sights to see for more than 3,500 destinations around the globe; the **Frommers.com Newsletter,** with the latest deals, travel trends, and money-saving secrets; our **Community** area, featuring **Message Boards,** where Frommer's readers post queries and share advice; and our **Photo Center,** where you can post and share vacation tips. When your research is finished, the **Online Reservations System** (www.frommers.com/book_a_trip) takes you to Frommer's preferred online partners for booking your vacation at affordable prices.

Online Traveler's Toolbox

- **Airplane Seating and Food.** Find out which seats to reserve and which to avoid (and more) on all major domestic airlines at www.seatguru.com. And check out the type of meal (with photos) you'll likely be served on airlines around the world at www.airlinemeals.net.
- **Visa ATM Locator** (www.visa.com), for locations of PLUS ATMs worldwide, or **MasterCard ATM Locator** (www.mastercard.com), for locations of Cirrus ATMs worldwide.
- **Intellicast** (www.intellicast.com) and **Weather.com** (www.weather.com). Gives weather forecasts for all 50 states and for cities around the world.
- **Mapquest** (www.mapquest.com). This best of the mapping sites lets you choose a specific address or destination, and in seconds, it returns a map and detailed directions.
- **Universal Currency Converter** (www.xe.com/ucc). See what your dollar or pound is worth in more than 100 other countries.

Toll-Free Numbers & Websites"), although all the major online travel agencies also offer rental-car reservations services. I prefer **Travelocity,** because its rental page actually shows you what your car will cost you after including taxes and surcharges (though not including any rental fees for car seats). **Orbitz** comes in a close second. Priceline and Hotwire work well for rental cars, too; the only "mystery" is which major rental company you get, and for most travelers, the difference among Hertz, Avis, and Budget is negligible.

8 Getting There

BY PLANE
THE MAJOR AIRLINES
THE MAJOR AIRLINES There are over 37 scheduled airlines and several more charter companies serving the more than 31 million passengers who land in Orlando each year. **Delta** (© **800/221-1212;** www.delta.com) provides nearly 20% of the flights to and from Orlando International Airport, offering service from roughly 150 cities.

Other carriers include **Air Canada** (© 888/247-2262; www.aircanada.ca), **America West** (© 800/235-9292; www.americawest.com), **American** (© 800/433-7300; www.americanair.com), **British Airways** (© 800/247-9297; www.britishairways.com), **Continental** (© 800/525-0280; www.continental.com), **Northwest** (© 800/225-2525; www.nwa.com), **United Airlines** (© 800-241-6522; www.united.com), and **US Airways** (© 800/428-4322; www.usairways.com), to name a few.

Several so-called no-frills airlines (those offering lower fares but providing few or no amenities) fly to Orlando as well. The biggest is **Southwest Airlines** (© **800/435-9792;** www.southwest.com), which has flights from many U.S. cities to Orlando and Tampa. **Spirit Air** (© **800/772-7117;** www.spiritair.com) is another no-frills choice. **JetBlue Airways** (© **800/538-2583;** www.jetblue.com) is a low-cost carrier that operates out of a number of U.S. cities and offers direct flights to Orlando out of New York City. The latter has video screens offering 24 TV channels—a big plus for those traveling with kids—and is a huge favorite with From-mer's editors.

For a more comprehensive list of major airlines that fly into Orlando and their websites, see appendix B, "Useful Toll-Free Numbers & Websites."

ORLANDO'S AIRPORT

Orlando International Airport (© 407/825-2001; www.state.fl.us/goaa) offers direct or nonstop service from 60 U.S. cities and two dozen international destinations, serving more than 30 million passengers most years. Rated one of the top airports in the country, it's a thoroughly modern and user-friendly facility with tons of restaurants, shops, a 446-room on-premises Hyatt Regency Hotel, and centrally located information kiosks.

All major car-rental companies are located at or near the airport; see "Getting Around," in chapter 3 and appendix B, "Useful Toll-Free Numbers & Websites," for more information about car rentals.

AIRPORT   TRANSPORTATION

Orlando International is 25 miles east of Walt Disney World and 20 miles south of downtown. At rush hour (7–9am and 4–6pm), the drive can be a torturous hour or more; at other times, it's about 30 to 40 minutes, depending on your destination. **Mears Transportation Group** (© 407/423-5566; www.mearstransportation.com) has vans that shuttle passengers from the airport (you catch them at ground level) to the Disney resorts and official hotels, as well as most other Orlando properties. Their air-conditioned vehicles operate around the clock, departing every 15 to 25 minutes in either direction. Rates vary by destination. Round-trip fare for adults is $25 ($18 for kids 4–11) between the airport and downtown Orlando or International Drive; $29 ($21 for kids 4–11) for Walt Disney World/Lake Buena Vista or West U.S. 192. Children 3 and under ride free.

Quicksilver Tours & Transportation (© 888/GOTOWDW or 407/299-1434; www.quicksilver-tours.com) is more personal. Their folks greet you at baggage claim with a sign bearing your name. They're only slightly more expensive than Mears, but they're coming for you. And they're going only to *your* resort. The big bonus is a free 30-minute grocery stop, and there's no extra charge for car seats and boosters. Rates run from $95 to $115, depending on whether you want a town car or a van and, of course, on where you're going.

Tiffany Towncar (© 888/838-2161 or 407/370-2196; www.tiffanytowncar.com) offers a $95 round-trip rate for up to five people in a van from Orlando International to Disney ($70 to International Dr. or Universal).

Disney's **Magical Express** is a new service that began operating in May 2005 and will run throughout the 18-month-long "Happiest Celebration on Earth"

(Tips Stuck on You

Your tween or teen just got his or her first set of contact lenses and is probably very attached to them. But if your kids wear those lenses on a plane, they could possibly become too attached. The air in an airplane cabin is especially dry and depletes the moisture in the eyes. If your kids aren't careful, their contact lenses (or yours, for that matter) could get vacuum-sealed onto their eyes. And I doubt you want your first sightseeing experience in Orlando to be an emergency room. Your best bet is for everyone to ditch the lenses for the plane ride, but if that isn't possible, make sure all lens wearers put in lots of rewetting drops over the course of the plane ride.

Travel in the Age of Bankruptcy

Airlines go bankrupt, so protect yourself by **buying your tickets with a credit card**, as the Fair Credit Billing Act guarantees that you can get your money back from the credit card company if a travel supplier goes under (and if you request the refund within 60 days of the bankruptcy). **Travel insurance** can also help, but make sure it covers against "carrier default" for your specific travel provider. And be aware that if a U.S. airline goes bust midtrip, a 2001 federal law requires other carriers to take you to your destination (albeit on a space-available basis) for a fee of no more than $25, provided that you rebook within 60 days of the cancellation.

event at WDW. It's offered to WDW resort guests flying on select airlines to Orlando International Airport. If you use it, Disney will get your bags from the airport to your room without your having to lift a finger. Attach special luggage tags Disney will send you ahead of time, and check your bags at your departure city, and when you get to Orlando, check in at the special Disney desk before boarding a Disney bus that will transport you to your resort. Your luggage will be waiting for you in your room when you arrive. The service will save you both time and money; it must be booked at least 10 days in advance of your arrival through your travel agent or through Disney (© **407/ 934-7639;** www.disneyworld.com).

DRIVING TO WALT DISNEY WORLD   To get from the airport to the attractions, take the **North** exit out of the airport to **Highway 528 West.** Follow signs to **I-4;** it takes about 30 to 40 minutes to get to Walt Disney World if the traffic isn't too heavy (double or worse in rush hour or when there's an accident). When you get to I-4, follow the signs **west** toward the attractions.

Note: It's always a good idea when you make reservations to ask about transportation options between the airport and your hotel. Also be sure to ask how far you have to travel to pick up and drop off a rental car. Some lots are miles from the

airport, adding to the time you'll spend waiting in line and catching shuttles.

GETTING THROUGH THE AIRPORT

With the federalization of airport security, screening procedures at U.S. airports are more stable and consistent than ever. Generally, you'll be fine if you arrive at the airport **1 hour** before a domestic flight and **2 hours** before an international flight; if you show up late, tell an airline employee, and she'll probably whisk you to the front of the line.

Bring a **current, government-issued photo ID** such as a driver's license or passport. Keep your ID at the ready to present at check-in, the security checkpoint, and sometimes even the gate. (Children under 18 do not need government-issued photo IDs for domestic flights, but they do for international flights to most countries.)

In 2003, the TSA phased out **gate check-in** at all U.S. airports. Passengers with e-tickets, which have made paper tickets nearly obsolete, can beat the ticket-counter lines by using airport **electronic kiosks** or even **online check-in** from their home computers. Online check-in involves logging on to your airlines' website, accessing your reservation, and printing out your boarding pass— and the airline may even offer you bonus miles to do so! If you're using a kiosk at the airport, bring the credit card you used to book the ticket or your frequent-flier card. Print out your boarding pass from the kiosk, and simply proceed to the security checkpoint with your pass and a photo ID. If you're checking bags or looking to snag an exit-row seat, you will be able to do so using most airline kiosks. Even the smaller airlines are employing the kiosk system, but always call your airline to make sure these alternatives are available. **Curbside check-in** is also a good way to avoid lines, although a few airlines still don't allow it; call for your airline's policy before you go.

Security checkpoint lines are getting shorter than they were during 2001 and 2002, but an orange alert, suspicious passenger, or high passenger volume can still make for a long wait. If you have trouble standing for long periods of time, tell an airline employee; the airline will provide a wheelchair. Speed security by **not wearing metal objects** such as big belt buckles. If you've got metallic body parts, a note from your doctor can prevent a long chat with the security screeners. Keep in mind that only **ticketed passengers** are allowed past security, except for people escorting disabled passengers or children.

Federalization has stabilized **what you can carry on** and **what you can't.** The general rule is that sharp things are out, nail clippers are okay, and food and beverages must pass through the X-ray machine—but security screeners can't make you drink from your coffee cup. Bring food in your carry-on rather than checking it, as explosive-detection machines used on checked luggage have been known to mistake food (especially chocolate, for some reason) for bombs. Travelers in the United States are allowed one carry-on bag, plus a "personal item" such as a purse, briefcase, or laptop bag. Carry-on hoarders can stuff all sorts of things into a laptop bag; as long as it has a laptop in it, it's still considered a personal item. The Transportation Security Administration (TSA) has issued a list of restricted items; check its website (**www.tsa.gov/public/index.jsp**) for details.

Airport screeners may decide that your checked luggage warrants a hand search. You can now purchase luggage locks that allow screeners to open and relock a checked bag if hand-searching is necessary. Look for Travel Sentry certified locks at luggage or travel shops and Brookstone stores (you can buy them online at **www.brookstone.com**). Luggage inspectors can open these TSA-approved locks with a special code or key—rather than having to cut them off the suitcase, as they normally do to conduct a hand search. For more information on the locks, visit **www.travelsentry.org**.

Tips **Unplugged**

If you or your kids are flying with a cold or sinus problems, use a decongestant an hour before takeoff and landing to minimize pressure buildup in the inner ear. It's difficult for kids to make their ears pop, and they can have an especially tough time with pressure in their ears. Takeoff and landing can be especially painful—even dangerous—for a child with congested sinuses. Nursing and/or sucking on a bottle or pacifier, or a sippy cup of their favorite drink, will help alleviate pressure in your infant or toddler. A cough drop or hard candy should work for older kids (don't give these to younger ones, who might choke on them if there's turbulence).

FLYING FOR LESS: TIPS FOR GETTING THE BEST AIRFARE

There's no shortage of discounted and promotional fares to Florida. November, December, and January (excluding holidays) often bring fare wars that can result in savings of 50% or more, but in a slower economy, specials may be available more often. Watch for ads in your local newspaper and on TV; call the airlines or check out their websites. Here are some ways to keep your airfare costs down:

- Passengers who can book their ticket either **long in advance or at the last minute,** or who **fly midweek** or **at less-trafficked hours** may pay a fraction of the full fare. If your schedule is flexible, say so, and ask if you can secure a cheaper fare by changing your flight plans.

- No-frills airlines have reduced their price advantage, but some **charter** flights still go to Florida, especially during the winter season and particularly from Canada. They often cost less than regularly scheduled flights, but they're very complicated. It's best to go to a good travel agent and ask him or her to find one for you.

- Search **the Internet** for cheap fares (see "Planning Your Trip Online," earlier in this chapter).

- Join **frequent-flier clubs.** Accrue enough miles, and you'll be rewarded with free flights. It's free, and you'll get the best choice of seats; faster response to phone inquiries; and prompter service if your luggage is stolen, your flight is canceled or delayed, or if you want to change seats. You don't need to fly to build frequent-flier miles; **frequent-flier credit cards** provide thousands of miles for doing your everyday shopping. To play the frequent-flier game to your best advantage, consult Randy Petersen's **Inside Flyer** (www.inside flyer.com). Petersen and friends review all the programs in detail and post regular updates on changes in policies and trends. Petersen will also field direct questions (via e-mail) if a partner airline refuses to redeem points, for instance, or if you're still not sure after researching the various programs which one is right for you. It's well worth the $12 online subscription fee, good for 1 year.

9 Tips on Flying with Children

SAFE SEATS FOR KIDS

Note: Most airlines require that an infant be 2 weeks old to travel; bring a birth certificate. American and Continental require only that the child be 7 days old. Alaska lets babies fly as soon as they're born.

The practice of allowing children younger than 2 to ride for free on a parent's lap is still in effect; however, a new rule proposed by the FAA would require all children under 40 pounds to have their own tickets and be secured in a child safety seat, so be sure to double-check the rules when you book your flights.

Most major American airlines offer discounted infant tickets for children 2 years of age or younger, to make it more affordable for you to reserve a separate adjacent seat for your baby (and his safety seat).

If a seat adjacent to yours is available, your lap child can sit there free of charge. When you check in, ask if the flight is crowded. If it isn't, explain your situation to the agent, and ask if you can reserve two seats—or simply move to two empty adjacent seats once the plane is boarded. You might want to shop around before you buy your ticket and deliberately book a flight that's not very busy (though that's often difficult, given the destination). Ask the reservationist which flights tend to be

---

Tips **Don't Schlep It—Ship It**

If ease of travel is your main concern, and money is no object, consider shipping your luggage and sports equipment with one of the growing number of luggage-service companies that pick up, track, and deliver travel bags (often through couriers such as Federal Express). Traveling luggage free, however convenient, isn't cheap: One-way overnight shipping can cost $100 to $200, depending on what you're sending. Still, for some people, especially the elderly or the infirm, it's a sensible option. Specialists in door-to-door luggage delivery include **Virtual Bellhop** (www.virtualbellhop.com), **SkyCap International** (www.skycapinternational.com), **Luggage Express** (www.usxpluggageexpress.com), and **Sports Express** (www.sportsexpress.com).

The same advice follows for souvenirs. Why drag them back in an overstuffed bag, which may cause you to exceed the airlines' size or weight limits and pay a penalty fee? Many a UPS store can be found throughout Orlando, or if that's not convenient, most resorts will help with shipping arrangements for a fee. Rates are more reasonable to ship via FedEx, DHL, or UPS then to pay the airline's excessive overage fees.

---

most full, and avoid those if possible. Only one extra child is allowed in each row, however, due to the limited number of oxygen masks.

On international journeys, children can't ride free on parents' laps. On flights overseas, a lap fare usually costs 10% of the parent's ticket. Children under the airline's age limit (which ranges from 11–15 years old) can purchase international fares at 50% to 75% of the lowest coach fare in certain markets. Some of the foreign carriers make even greater allowances for children.

Note: Children riding for free will usually not be granted any baggage allowance.

Very few airlines offer child meals anymore, so come prepared with formula, juice, snacks, and sandwiches if you're flying around mealtime. Another option is to eat at one of the airport's fast-fooderies—or get a meal to go ,and bring it along for the ride. If your kids drink only milk, grab a few extra cartons at the airport, as oftentimes, I've found the airlines run out in flight. All major airlines except Alaska and Southwest will warm bottles on request.

CHILD SEATS: THEY'RE A MUST

According to *Consumer Reports Travel Letter,* the National Transportation Safety Board says that since 1991, the deaths of five children and injuries to four could have been prevented had the children been sitting in restraint systems during their flights. Even in the event of moderate turbulence, children sitting on a parent's lap can be thrust forward and injured. When you consider that a commercial aircraft hits a significant amount of turbulence at least once a day on average, you'd do well to think about investing a few extra dollars for a separate airline ticket and safety seat for your child.

The FAA recommends that children under 20 pounds ride in a rear-facing child-restraint system and says children who weigh 20 to 40 pounds should sit in a forward-facing child-restraint system. Children over 40 pounds should sit in a regular seat and wear a seat belt.

All child seats manufactured after 1985 are certified for airline use, but make sure your car seat will fit in an airline seat; it must be less than 16 inches wide. You may not use booster seats, seatless vests, or harness systems. Safety seats must be placed in window seats—except in exit rows, where they are prohibited, so as not to block the passage of other travelers in the case of an emergency.

The airlines themselves should carry child safety seats on board. Unfortunately, most don't. To make matters worse, overzealous flight attendants have been known to try to keep safety seats off planes. One traveler recounts in the November 2001 issue of *Consumer Reports Travel Letter* how a Southwest attendant attempted to block use of a seat because the red label certifying it as safe for airline use had flaked off. That traveler won her case by bringing the owner's manual and appealing to the pilot; you should do the same.

If you can't afford the expense of a separate ticket, book a ticket toward the back of the plane at a time when air travel is likely to be slowest—and the seat next to you is most likely to be empty. The reservationist should also be able to recommend the best (meaning the least busy) time for you to fly.

In-Flight Fun for Kids

With one of these children's game books on board, even the longest plane ride will go faster.

Great Games for Kids on the Go: Over 240 Travel Games to Play on Trains, Planes, and Automobiles
by Penny Warner
Retail price: $13
Ages 4 to 8
This book is full of entertaining educational games to help your kids while away the miles. Each game is highly engaging and entertaining, and requires few materials and very little space.

Brain Quest for the Car: 1100 Questions and Answers All About America
by Sharon Gold
Retail price: $11
Ages 7 to 12
This book features cards with questions about American geography, culture, and customs.

Vacation Fun Mad Libs: World's Greatest Party Game
by Roger Price
Retail price: $4
Ages 8 and up
As suggested by the title, this book is chock-full of Mad Libs. Your kids will want to keep playing even after you've touched down.

Additional sanity savers include **Boredom Busters!: the Curious Kids Activity Book** (Williamson Publishing Company, $13); **The Everything Kids' Activity Book: Games to Play, Songs to Sing, Fun Stuff to Do—Guaranteed to Keep You Busy the Whole Ride!** (Adams Media Corporation, $6.95); and **Kids Travel: A Backseat Survival Guide** (Klutz, $20). This last one's even endorsed by the Save the Parent's Sanity foundation.

EASING TRAVEL WITH THE TOTS IN TOW

Several books on the market offer tips to help you travel with kids. Most concentrate on the United States, but one in particular, *Trouble-Free Travel with Children— Over 700 Helpful Hints for Parents on the Go* (Book Peddlers, $9.95), is full of good general advice that can apply to travel anywhere. Other reliable tomes, with a worldwide focus, are *Adventuring with Children* (Avalon House Travel Series; $15) and *Lonely Planet Travel with Children* (Lonely Planet Publications, $10).

If you plan carefully, you can actually make it fun to travel with kids:

- If you're traveling with children, you'll save yourself a good bit of aggravation by **reserving a seat in the bulkhead** row. You'll have more legroom, and your children will be able to spread out and play on the floor underfoot.

- **Check your luggage,** and limit family members to one backpack or bag for which they are responsible. This will make life much simpler.

- Have **a long talk with your children** before you depart for your trip. If they've never flown before, explain to them what to expect. If they're old enough, you may even want to describe how flight works, assuring them if necessary that air travel is safe. Explain to your kids the importance of good behavior in the air (and in the airport)—how the crew depends upon their being quiet and staying in their seats during the trip to fly safely.

- Ask the flight attendant **if the plane has any special safety equipment for children.** Make a member of the crew aware of any medical problems your children have that could manifest during flight.

- **Be sure you've slept sufficiently** for your trip. If you fall asleep in the air, and your child manages to break away, there are all sorts of perilous predicaments they could get into. It's dangerous for a child to be crawling or walking around the cabin unaccompanied by an adult.

- **Be sure your child's seat belt remains fastened properly,** and try to reserve the seat closest to the aisle for yourself. This will make it harder for your children to wander off—in case, for instance, you're taking the red-eye or a long flight overseas, and you do happen to nod off. You will also protect your child from jostling passersby and falling objects—in the rare but entirely possible instance that an overhead bin pops open.

- **Try to sit near the lavatory,** though not so close that your children are jostled by the crowds that tend to gather there.

- Each child's bag should contain **clean, self-containing compact toys.** Electronic games can interfere with the aircraft navigational system, and their noisiness, however lulling to children's ears, will surely not win the favor of your adult neighbors. That said, if you're clear about the rules with regard to their use ahead of time, they can easily keep kids busy for hours. Magnetic checker sets and other such travel games are a great distraction, as are coloring books, crayons, and card games such as Go Fish.

  By all means, don't leave home without a favorite blanket or stuffed animal— especially if it's your child's best friend at bedtime. It might also come in handy if the going gets rough, and kids need something comforting to cuddle.

- The responsible adult (you, for example) will need a bag as well, filled with **age-appropriate extras** such as a deck of cards, postcards, pens, an address book, extra bottles, bibs, pacifiers, diapers, and chewing gum to help relieve any ear-pressure problems. A package of wipes is also handy. With an infant on board, you'll likely need a change of clothes for him or her and quite possibly for yourself.

- You'll certainly be grateful to yourself for **packing a few snacks** like rolled dried fruit, graham crackers, fishy crackers, and pretzels. Gingersnaps actually help curb mild cases of motion sickness. If you have a mini collapsible cooler, you can bring along yogurt (drinkable or in tubes) and cheese cubes, too. And don't forget to stash a few resealable plastic bags in your bag. They'll prove invaluable for storing everything from half-eaten crackers and fruit to checker pieces and Matchbox cars (not to mention the occasional dirty diaper).

- **Juice or cookies** will not only keep kids distracted during takeoff and landing—often the scariest parts of flight for a child—but will also help their little ears pop as cabin air pressure shifts rapidly. Juice (paper cartons travel best) will also keep them swallowing and help them stay properly hydrated.

- If your children are very young, don't forget to **pack bottles and extra milk or formula** (bottled water, too, if you use the powdered type), as these are unavailable on most aircraft. Many airlines prohibit flight attendants from preparing formula, so plan on mixing it yourself unless you bring along a travel-size can of ready-to-feed formula.

BY CAR

Orlando is 436 miles from Atlanta, 1,312 miles from Boston, 1,120 miles from Chicago, 1,009 miles from Cleveland, 1,170 miles from Dallas, 1,114 miles from Detroit, 1,088 miles from New York City, and 1,282 miles from Toronto.

- From Atlanta, take I-75 south to the Florida Turnpike to I-4 west.
- From points northeast, take I-95 south to Daytona Beach and I-4 west.
- From Chicago, take I-65 south to Nashville, I-24 south to I-75, and then south on the Florida Turnpike to I-4 west.
- From Cleveland, take I-77 south to Columbia, South Carolina, and then I-26 east to I-95 south to I-4 west.
- From Dallas, take I-20 east to I-49, south to I-10, east to I-75, and then south on the Florida Turnpike to I-4 west.
- From Detroit, take I-75 south to the Florida Turnpike and then exit on I-4 west.
- From Toronto, take Canadian Route 401 south to Queen Elizabeth Way and then south to I-90 (New York State Thruway), east to I-87 (New York State Thruway), south to I-95 over the George Washington Bridge, and then south on I-95 to I-4 west.

AAA (© 800/222-1134; www.aaa. com) and some other auto-club members should call their local offices for maps and optimum driving directions.

BY TRAIN

Amtrak trains (© 800/872-7245; www. amtrak.com) pull into stations at 1400 Sligh Blvd. in downtown Orlando (23 miles from Walt Disney World) and 111 Dakin Ave. in Kissimmee (15 miles from WDW). There are also stops in Winter Park, 10 miles north of downtown Orlando, at 150 W. Morse Blvd.; and in Sanford, 23 miles northeast of Orlando, 800 Persimmon Ave., which is also the end terminal for the Auto Train (see later in this section).

FARES As with airline fares, you sometimes can get discounts if you book far in advance. There may be some restrictions on travel dates for discounted fares, mostly around very busy holiday times. Amtrak also offers money-saving packages—including accommodations (some at WDW resorts), car rentals, tours, and train fare (© 800/321-8684).

The good news for families is that up to two children ages 2 to 15 can ride for half fare with a paying adult; one child under 2 rides for free with an accompanying adult. The discounts apply year-round and on all trains except Amtrak's Acela train.

AMTRAK'S AUTO TRAIN This option offers the convenience of bringing your car to Florida without having to drive it all the way. It begins in Lorton, Virginia—about a 4-hour drive from New York, 2 hours from Philadelphia—and ends at Sanford, 23 miles northeast of Orlando. (There are no stops in between.) Reserve early for the lowest prices. Fares average $530 ($1,100 with a berth) for two passengers and an auto. Call ✆ **800/872-7245** for details.

10 Package Deals for Families

The number and diversity of package tours to Orlando is staggering. But you can save money if you're willing to do the research. Start by looking in the travel section of your local Sunday newspaper and checking the ads in the back of travel magazines such as *Travel & Leisure* and *Condé Nast Traveler.* Also, stop at a sizable travel agency, and pick up brochures from several companies. Go over them at home, and compare offerings to find the optimum package for your trip.

You should also obtain the *Walt Disney World Vacations* brochure from Disney (see contact details at the beginning of this chapter), which lists WDW packages. Disney's array of choices can include airfare; accommodations on or off Disney property; theme-park passes; a rental car; meals; a Disney cruise; and/or a stay at Disney's beach resorts in Vero Beach or Hilton Head, South Carolina. And unlike the main Disney number, the number to call for a Disney vacation package is *free:* ✆ **800/828-0228** (the alternative number, 407/828-8101, is a toll call). Some packages are tied to a season, while others are for special-interest vacationers, including golfers, honeymooners, and spa aficionados.

Just make sure to press Disney reservation agents or your travel agent for the best deal they can find.

Although not on the same scale as Disney's options, Universal Orlando packages have improved greatly with the addition of the Islands of Adventure theme park, the CityWalk food-and-club district, and Universal's Loews-run hotels. The options include lodging, VIP access to Universal's theme parks, and discounts to other non-Disney attractions. Some include round-trip airfare. Contact **Universal Studios Vacations** at ✆ **800/711-0080** or go online to **www.universalstudiosvacations.com**.

SeaWorld also offers 2- and 3-night packages that include rooms from a choice of SeaWorld area hotels, car rental, and tickets to SeaWorld. Call ✆ **800/557-4268** or surf the Internet to **www.seaworldvacations.com**.

Another good source of package deals is the airlines themselves. Major airlines offering Orlando packages include **American Airlines Vacations** (✆ 800/321-2121; www.aavacations.com), **Delta Vacations** (✆ 800/221-6666; www.deltavacations.com), **Continental Airlines Vacations** (✆ 800/301-3800; www.covacations.com), and **United Vacations** (✆ 888/854-3899; www.unitedvacations.com). Packages can include round-trip airfare, accommodations, rental car or round-trip airport transfers, unlimited admission to Disney (or other) parks, and other special features. In packages that feature WDW and Universal Studios resorts, you will receive all the advantages given to guests of these properties. Prices vary widely, depending on the resort you choose, your departure point, and the time of year.

Tips **A Magical Gathering**

If you have a large family or are traveling with others, Disney launched a new program in 2003 that might work for you. The **Magical Gatherings** program caters to groups traveling together to Walt Disney World and offers online trip-planning tools to help you put together a vacation for the extended family.

Large groups of eight or more people (ages 3 or above) traveling together to Walt Disney World—**Grand Gatherings,** as Disney calls them—also get free assistance from a Disney trip planner, who will help you get hotel rooms, make dining reservations, recreation, schedule golf tee times, and put together special event and attractions options (these extras will cost you) that appeal to all age groups and that are not available to individuals and smaller families. Options (which can be reserved up to 90 days in advance) include special character breakfasts, safari outings at Animal Kingdom, and a fireworks cruise on the Seven Seas Lagoon.

If you're interested in this option, call Disney at © **407/934-7639,** or go to **www.disneyworld.com/magicalgatherings** and request a Magical Gathering Vacation Planning Kit or an interactive DVD. When you make the request, ask for specialized planning brochures for groups that include preschoolers, including information about favorite attractions for younger children, child-care options, and tips for a well-planned vacation with preschool-age children.

Several big **online travel agencies**—Expedia, Travelocity, Orbitz, Site59, and Lastminute.com—also do a brisk business in packages. If you're unsure about the pedigree of a smaller packager, check with the Better Business Bureau in the city where the company is based, or go online at **www.bbb.org**. If a packager won't tell you where it's based, don't fly with that company.

Before you invest in a package tour, get some answers. Ask about the various **accommodations** and prices for each. Then look up the hotels' reviews in a Frommer's guide, and check their rates for your specific dates of travel online.

Finally, look for **hidden expenses.** Ask if airport departure fees and taxes, for example, are included in the cost.

11 Disney Cruise Packages

There's hardly a Florida tourist market that WDW hasn't tried to tap. Oceangoing vacations are no exception. The **Disney Cruise Line** (© **800/951-3532;** www.disneycruise.com) launched the *Magic* and *Wonder* in 1998 and 1999, respectively.

The *Magic* is Art Deco in style, with Mickey in the three-level lobby and a *Beauty and the Beast* mural in its top restaurant, Lumiere's. The *Wonder*'s decor is Art Nouveau. Ariel commands its lobby, and its featured eatery, Triton's, sports a mural from *The Little Mermaid.*

Subtle differences aside, these are nearly identical twins. Both are 83,000 tons, with 12 decks, 875 cabins, and room for 2,400 guests. There are some adults-only areas, including **Palo,** an intimate and romantic Italian restaurant; however, both ships have extensive kids' and teens' programs that take up almost an entire deck. They're broken into four age groups: the **Flounder's Reef Nursery,** for ages 3 months to 3 years; **Disney's Oceaneer Club,** for ages 3 to 7; **Disney's Oceaneer Lab** ,for ages 8 to 12; and **Common Grounds** (on the *Wonder*) or **The Stack** (on the *Magic*), for ages 13 to 17.

Restaurants, shows, and other onboard activities are extremely family-oriented. One of the line's unique features is a dine-around option that lets you move among main restaurants (each ship has four) from night to night while keeping the same servers.

Something new: Visitors to Castaway Cay get the chance to participate in a hands-on stingray encounter, which includes a brief history and biology lesson, in addition to an in-the-water interaction with the stingrays.

The 3-night voyages visit Nassau and Castaway Cay, Disney's own private island; 4-day voyages add Freeport. There also are 7-night Eastern Caribbean (St. Thomas, St. Maarten, St. John, and Castaway Cay) and 7-night Western Caribbean (Key West, Grand Cayman, Cozumel, and Castaway Cay) itineraries. Special 10-day and 14-day Caribbean cruises are offered as well; call for details and rates.

Seven-night land–sea packages include 3 or 4 days afloat, with the rest of the week at a WDW resort. Prices at press time ranged from $799 to $5,199 adults, $399 to $2,199 kids 3 to 12, and $139 kids under 3 (*Note:* Infants under 12 weeks are not allowed aboard ship), depending on your choice of stateroom and resort. Packages are available that add round-trip air and unlimited admission to the WDW parks, Pleasure Island, and other Disney attractions. Cruise-only options for 3 nights are $399 to $2,849 adults, $229 to $1,099 kids 3 to 12, and $99 those under 3; 4-night cruises are $499 to $3,249 adults, $329 to $1,199 kids 3 to 12, and $99 kids under 3. Disney's 7-night cruises sell for $799 to $5,199 adults, $399 to $2,199 kids 3 to 12, and $139 kids under 3.

All cruises depart from Port Canaveral, which is about an hour east of Orlando by car. If you buy a Land and Sea package, transportation to and from Orlando is included. You can get discounted fares if you book well in advance and go during nonpeak periods, and specials or "Magic Rates" run periodically. For more information, call Disney Cruise Line or check out its very informative website, which also allows you to plan and reserve shore excursions before you go.

Tips **Avoid the Ups and Downs**

Nothing spoils a cruise like a storm—or worse. In the first case, consider avoiding hurricane season altogether (June 1 to Nov 30, though the peak is July to mid-Oct). These unpredictable storms can both spoil your fun and upset the strongest of stomachs. Avoiding the stormy seasons aside, pack a few motion-sickness pills or patches, just in case.

Speaking of spoiling a cruise, several cruise ships, including the Disney *Magic,* have had outbreaks of a virus that caused stomach flu–like symptoms in the past. This is no ill reflection on any one line: Cruise ships are closed environments, and sometimes, a passenger brings the illness on board. For an Internet rating by the **Centers for Disease Control,** go to **www.cdc.gov/travel/cruiships.htm.** Note, however, that the site is often weeks out of date.

12 Show & Tell: Getting the Kids Interested in Orlando

In most cases, you really won't have to do all that much to get your child interested in Orlando. It will be more a case of trying to restrain the obvious enthusiasm your youngsters will display at the idea of meeting Mickey and the gang or riding the Hulk Coaster. That said, involving your kids in the planning of your vacation will certainly help prevent any disappointments and will make them feel as though they're contributing to the experience.

Before you leave (I recommend at least 3–4 months), ask the folks at Disney to send you one of their vacation videos, which should be of interest to most of the family. You can get it by writing to Walt Disney World, Box 10000, Lake Buena Vista, FL 32830-1000; calling $\textcircled{C}$ **407/ 934-7639** or 407/824-4321; or going to **www.disneyworld.com**. Your little ones will no doubt enjoy watching the video, and you can gauge their reactions to certain rides, the characters, and attractions. This is also a good time to explain to young kids about height and weight restrictions that may keep them from riding a few attractions so you can avoid disappointment later on.

You might want to buy your younger children an autograph book before leaving so they can get character autographs in the parks. This is a wildly popular activity and a good souvenir for your children to bring back from Orlando.

Break out some Disney classic films before you go to get your kids in the mood. No matter what your child's age, you'll find something that Disney put out appropriate for them, be it the 2003 hit film *Pirates of the Caribbean* for your tweens and teens or the enchanting *Cinderella* for your little ones. *Disneyland*

Sing Along Songs is another good choice (even if it was filmed at Disneyland instead of Disney World), as it introduces tinier tots to the parks, rides, and characters they'll encounter on your trip.

On the book front, kids (and even adults) will enjoy **Popping Up Around Walt Disney World** (Disney Editions, 2004). This colorful and detailed pop-up book offers an illustrative tour through the world of Disney. It takes readers through the parks, details some of the attractions, and tosses in a bit of trivia too. **Hidden Mickeys, 2nd Edition: A Field Guide to Walt Disney World's Best Kept Secrets** (The Intrepid Traveler, 2005) is filled with trivia and, of course, those Hidden Mickeys—including tips on where and how to look for them.

Videos and documentaries on African animals and aquatic life, as well as age-appropriate books, will prepare your kids for the sights and sounds they'll experience at Animal Kingdom and SeaWorld. Similarly, books and videos on the different cultures represented in the World Showcase will give your kids a rudimentary introduction to the countries that they'll walk though at Epcot.

If you're visiting Universal's parks, you can watch Nickelodeon with your young kids and read them *The Cat in the Hat*. They'll be charmed when they actually get to ride through the story at Islands of Adventure. Older kids and teens might appreciate a selection of classic Marvel comic books or could be induced to watch some of the films that many of Universal's rides are based on, including *Shrek, The Mummy Returns, Back to the Future, Men in Black, Twister,* and *Jurassic Park.*

3

Getting to Know
Walt Disney World & Orlando

Orlando didn't become a favorite destination for families until just over 30 or so years ago. It was only after a magical man and a mouse named Mickey moved to town, after the Magic Kingdom opened its gates for the first time, that families first took notice.

Walt Disney started something back then—something big. He blazed a pioneering trail that over the last 35 years or so has spawned a deluge of development. I don't think even he could have predicted what was to come. Disney may not be the exact center of the Orlando universe, but it's a close call. Walt Disney World has grown to include 4 major theme parks; a large 3-part shopping, dining, and entertainment district; 22 resorts and timeshare properties; 9 partner hotels; 2 full-fledged water parks; a cruise line; and loads more. Those are Disney's ways of trying to keep you, your kids, and your tourist dollars from straying to Universal Orlando, Sea-World, or its other competitors. They are good at it, too. Although WDW is easy enough to navigate once you get your bearings, it's so sprawled out, you might just hesitate to leave.

But all that unrelenting cheerfulness, days of $2.50 sodas, and the solar-fried musk of sweaty patrons make it a small world, after all. Besides, you're cheating yourself if you don't spend some time away from Walt Disney's world, especially

if you have tweens and teens, for whom Universal Orlando (and its thrill rides) is a major mecca, or aquarium-lovers of any age, who will find SeaWorld a wonderfully relaxed place to visit. And don't overlook some of the less frazzling things to do in O-Town with your kids, including, among others, the Orlando Science Center. I'll let you know all about the area's layout and what's where in the first section of this chapter.

The good news is that getting around the major tourist areas of Orlando is relatively easy if you have a car, if you're a decent navigator, and if traffic is cooperating. If you plan on staying only in Walt Disney World, you can even make do without the car (the pros and cons of using Disney's own transportation network are listed later on). The major attractions are all centered on large interstates or highways, and the city has done its utmost best to make sure that your family (and its tourist dollars) won't get lost on the way to your chosen destination. Disney's taken efficiency a step further, creating a new private roadway that should result in less congestion along I-4 and offer a direct route to WDW. Construction's set to be completed just as this book hits the stands. And if you do get lost, you'll find a ton of roadside billboards on most major thoroughfares that will lead you right to the city's biggest attractions.

1 Orientation

VISITOR INFRMATION

Once you're in town, you can stop at the **Orlando/Orange County Visitors Center,** 8723 International Dr., Suite 101, Orlando (© **407/363-5872;** www.orlandoinfo.com). Folks working at the bureau will answer questions and give you maps, brochures, and coupons good for discounts or freebies. It's worth a visit even if you take my advice in chapter 2 and send for them before arriving. The bureau sells discount tickets to several attractions (savings on single-day passes to Universal and SeaWorld are $3 or less; Disney's 3-day or longer passes are discounted $4 to $15, and savings on passes to Cirque du Soleil, DisneyQuest, and Pleasure Island run $3 to $7). Its multilingual staff will also make dinner reservations and hotel referrals for you. The bureau is open daily 8am to 7pm except on Christmas. From I-4, take Exit 74A east 2 blocks, turn south on International Drive, and go 1 mile. The center is on the left, at I-Drive and Austrian Row.

The **Kissimmee–St. Cloud Convention & Visitors Bureau** is located at 1925 E. Irlo Bronson Memorial Hwy./U.S. 192, Kissimmee (© **800/333-5477,** 800/327-9159, or 407/847-5000; www.floridakiss.com). It's open Monday to Friday 8am to 5pm and offers maps, brochures, and coupons, too. From I-4, take Exit 64A/U.S. 192 east about 12 miles to Bill Beck Boulevard; then go left into the bureau's parking lot.

If you're driving into town from the north on I-75 and looking for the **Disney Welcome Center** in Ocala, Florida, the center has recently closed. You'll have to wait until you get to Orlando and head to the visitor centers listed above; your hotel concierge; or guest-services desk for tickets, maps, and other area information.

Finally, nearly all hotel lobbies and many restaurants, highway rest stops, and attractions have racks containing brochures for various activities. The brochures often include discount coupons.

INFORMATION (& MORE) AT THE AIRPORT

Orlando's theme-park fun starts almost from the minute you get off the plane.

Orlando International Airport has two Disney shops. The **Magic of Disney** (© **407/ 825-2370** or 407/825-2360) is in the main terminal, third level, right behind the Northwest Airlines ticket desk. **Disney Earport** (© **407/825-2339**) is in the main terminal, across from the Hyatt Regency. They sell WDW multiday tickets, make dinner show and hotel reservations at Disney resorts, and provide brochures and assistance. They're open daily, usually 7am to 10pm, but don't plan on making many purchases at the airport stores unless you're on your way home and find you've forgotten to buy that must-have Mickey for the kid who's watering your plants while you're gone. Chances are you'll find a far better selection and (possibly) cheaper prices elsewhere in town.

The **Universal Studios Stores** (© **407/825-2473**), usually open daily from 7am to 9pm, sell park tickets at two locations: Airside A, main terminal, and Airside B, Delta-side before security, both on the third level. **SeaWorld** stores, at Airside A and B, are open from 7am to 10pm (© **407/825-2642** or 407/825 2414). Kennedy Space Center (© **407/825-3170** or 407/825-3245), open from 6am to 9pm, has locations in both the East and West halls. For a complete list of airport stores and services, including hours and phone numbers, check out the website at **www.orlandoairports.net/goaa/main.htm;** click passenger terminal and then click shops and services.

Orlando Neighborhoods

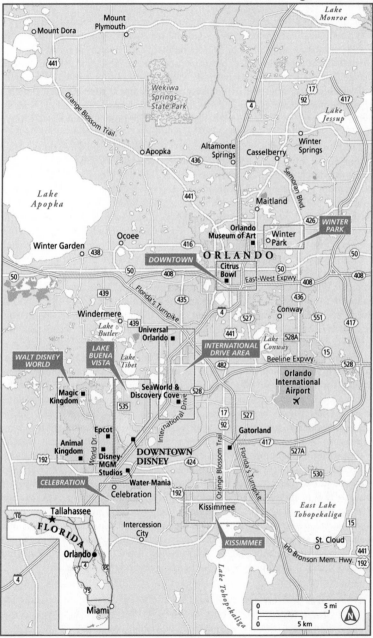

CITY LAYOUT

Orlando's major artery is Interstate 4, or **I-4.** This runs across Florida from Tampa to Daytona Beach. Exits from I-4 take you to all the Disney properties, Universal, Sea-World, International Drive, U.S. 192, Kissimmee, Lake Buena Vista, and downtown Orlando. Most are well marked, but construction is common, and exit numbers can change. For the latest exit numbers, see **www.myflorida.com**; for additional traffic and construction information, see **www.expresswayauthority.com**. If you get directions by exit number, always ask the name of the road, too, to avoid getting lost. Note that the road in question is often a traffic-laden nightmare loathed by locals. (Cellphone users can dial *C* **511** to get a report of I-4 delays.)

The **Florida Turnpike,** a toll road, crosses I-4 and links with I-75 to the north and Miami to the south. **U.S. 192/Irlo Bronson Memorial Highway** is an east–west artery that reaches from Kissimmee to U.S. 27, crossing I-4 near World Drive, the main Disney entrance road. Construction in and around where U.S. 192 and I-4 cross creates backups as bad as the ones on I-4 during rush hour (7–9am and 4–6pm daily). Farther north, the **BeeLine Expressway** (Hwy. 528), also a toll road, goes east from I-4 past Orlando International Airport to Cape Canaveral and Kennedy Space Center. The **East–West Expressway** (also known as Hwy. 408) is a toll road that can be helpful in bypassing surface traffic in the downtown area.

If you're jockeying between Disney and Universal, one of the lesser traffic evils is **Apopka–Vineland Road.** It tends to be less cluttered than I-4 or International Drive. Follow it north from Lake Buena Vista and the northeast side of WDW to Sand Lake Road; then go right to Turkey Lake Road and left to Universal. Another option would be to take Apopka–Vineland Road; turn right onto Palm Parkway, which then turns into Turkey Lake Road; and follow it to the Universal entrance.

I-4 and Highway 535 border **Walt Disney World** to the east (the latter is also a northern boundary), and U.S. 192/Irlo Bronson Memorial Highway borders it to the south. World Drive is WDW's main north–south artery. Epcot Center Drive (Hwy. 536/the south end of International Dr.) and Buena Vista Drive cut across the complex in a more or less east–west direction; the two roads cross at Bonnet Creek Parkway. Despite a reasonably good highway system and explicit signs, **it's easy to get lost** or miss a turn here. Don't panic or pull across several lanes of traffic to make an exit, especially once you're on Disney property. All roads lead to the parks, and you'll soon find another sign directing you to the same place. It may take a bit longer, but Goofy will still be there. Be sure to pick up a copy of the "Handy Guide to all the Magic," a map of the entire WDW road system; a guide to the WDW transportation system is in the back.

Note: If you're going to be driving around town, we highly recommend that you get a good, detailed map of the area. The map the Orlando/Orange County Visitors Bureau sends in its visitor packet (p. 12) and offers at its visitor center is one of the best. Tourist magazines such as *See Orlando, Travelhost, Where Orlando, and I ♥ Orlando,* many of which you'll find right at your hotel, have good maps as well.

ORLANDO NEIGHBORHOODS IN BRIEF

Walt Disney World The empire, its big and little parks, resorts, restaurants, shops, and assorted trimmings, are scattered across 30,500 acres. To put it in better perspective, it's roughly the size of San Francisco. The surprising thing to some folks: WDW isn't really in Orlando at all. It's actually southwest of the city proper, off I-4, in Lake Buena Vista. The convenience of staying here, however, comes at a price, with rooms running almost twice what they do in nearby Kissimmee. For kids (and some adults), however, this is the Promised Land.

Lake Buena Vista This is Disney's next-door neighbor. It's where you'll find the "official" (though not Disney-owned) hotels situated along Hotel Plaza Boulevard. It's close to Down-town Disney and Pleasure Island, and is a good spot for families who appreciate the perks of staying at an official Disney hotel but not the hefty prices of staying on the parks' doorstep. This charming area has manicured lawns, tree-lined thoroughfares, and free transportation throughout the realm.

Downtown Disney This is more Disney dessert than an actual neighborhood, though it's certainly large enough to be distinguished as one. Simply put, it's what WDW has taken to calling its two nighttime entertainment areas, Pleasure Island and Disney's West Side, as well as its shopping district, the Downtown Disney Marketplace. The area's filled with clubs, entertainment venues, uniquely themed restaurants, and interesting shops. Here, you can celebrate New Year's Eve every night, shop till you drop, or tempt your tastebuds—all in the space of a single afternoon or evening. It's best suited to older kids, teens, and parents. If you have tinier tots in tow, the afternoon may be a better time to survey this territory.

Celebration Driving through this quaint little town, filled with gingerbread-trimmed houses and apartments, some with white picket fences and shade trees in the front yard, you may find yourself musing about the Disneyesque perfection found throughout this 4,900-acre community. It should come as no surprise that Disney had a hand in its creation—experts as they are at creating the perfect version

of almost anything. The Market Street area's charming collection of shops, restaurants, even its own small hotel, is reminiscent of a bygone era—and a perfectly upscale version at that.

Kissimmee This once-sleepy city is closer to Disney than Orlando. It's just a few miles from Mickey and has some of the least expensive offerings in the area. Brought back to life by a multi-million dollar "Rebeautivacation" project, U.S. 192, Kissimmee's main tourist strip, now sports extrawide sidewalks, colorful (and plentiful) streetlamps, landscaping, and location markers. Even the roadway itself has been improved to handle traffic more easily and safely. Kissimmee is lined practically end to end with a variety of budget and moderate resorts and hotels, most of which cater to families (though a few more upscale options have started to spring up), a plentitude of casual restaurants, and a handful of minor attractions.

International Drive Area (Hwy. 536) Known as **I-Drive,** this busy tourist zone is home to more than 100 resorts and hotels, countless restaurants, attractions both big and small, shopping, entertainment, and even its own transportation system—the I-Ride Trolley. It's home to the Orange County Convention Center, host of the first-ever World's Fair for Kids, and offers easy access to Universal Orlando and SeaWorld. The areas north of Sand Lake Road are by far the most congested, filled to capacity with T-shirt shops, tourist traps, resorts, restaurants, and attractions. If you head south, toward the intersection at S.R. 528 (aka the Beeline Expressway), it's still chock full of restaurants and hotels, but the landscaping is far more appealing, and tree-lined walkways offer a more pleasant place to walk. The driving, however, is still slow going at best.

Downtown Orlando Orlando is actually much smaller than most major U.S. cities but has a charm all its own. The downtown area is actually northeast of Walt Disney World on I-4. It's far less congested with tourists than the theme-park zones. Parents in need of a night off will appreciate the array of upscale restaurants and nightclubs, along with theaters, museums, and more. Families will find the very visitor-friendly Orlando Science Center a fun and unique place to spend an afternoon. Shopping is plentiful, but it's the adults in the family who will appreciate the dozens of antiques shops that line "Antique Row."

Winter Park Those who make the effort to get up to Winter Park, located just north of downtown (Orlando, that is), will enjoy its upscale ambience and quaint southern charm. The town's biggest draw is Park Avenue, with its collection of upscale shops and restaurants set along tree-lined cobblestone streets. This part of the suburbs is a great adult getaway and a good place to relax and escape the WDW, Universal, and I-Drive crowds. It's not, however, a good place to take the kids.

2 Getting Around

In a city that thrives on its attractions, you won't find it difficult to get around—especially if you have a car. Don't count on public transportation to get you where you want to go—not quickly or efficiently, anyway. If you're traveling outside the tourist areas, avoid the 7-to-9am and 4-to-6pm rush whenever possible. Commuter traffic creates difficulties in any city, but here it's further complicated (and congested) by tourist traffic. And don't expect weekends to be any better; the locals who run the hotels, restaurants, and attractions still have to get to work, making commuter traffic a 7-days-a-week dilemma. Most of the parks don't open until 9am or so, and they usually stay open at least until dusk, so you won't miss much by leaving a little later. (The exception is Animal Kingdom, where the animals move around early in the day and then seek shelter and shade when the sun comes out; see "Animal Kingdom" in chapter 6, "What Kids Like to See & Do in Walt Disney World.")

International Drive has two alternative means of transportation: pedestrian and the I-Drive Trolley, though I don't at all recommend the former with kids in tow. Even with plenty of sidewalks, crossing this extremely busy road is a dangerous proposition. Drivers are often more interested in getting to where they're going than to any pedestrian daring to cross in front of them. The **I-Ride Trolley** (© **407/248-9590** or 407/354-5656; www.iridetrolley.com) is a much safer bet. It makes 85 stops between the Belz Factory Outlets on the north end of the drive and the Premium Outlets to the south. The main line trolley runs every 20 minutes, from 8am to 10:30pm, and costs $1 for adults and 25¢ for seniors; kids under 12 ride free with a paying adult; *exact change is required.* There's an unlimited 1-day pass available for $3 per person. For those of you staying on I-Drive, 3-, 5-, 7-, and 14-day passes are also available at a substantial savings. This is a great way to avoid I-Drive's bumper-to-bumper driving.

The good news if you are driving is that road signs have become more accurate than they were a few years back. But to make sure you're heading the right way, follow the directions I supply for the various attractions and hotels later in this book. Also, call your destination before leaving, and ask whether new construction or other temporary roadblocks might be in your way.

Some hotels offer transportation to and from the theme parks and other tourist destinations; however, you'll need to check with your hotel to find out just which parks they go to and whether they charge for the service. If your hotel does charge for shuttle service, by the time you add up the cost of transporting your family (and consider that you'll be at the mercy of your shuttle's schedule—not always the one your kids will adhere to), you're often better off renting a car.

BY DISNEY TRANSPORTATION SYSTEM

If you're going to stay at Disney and spend a majority of your time visiting its parks and attractions, using Disney's own, rather extensive transportation network is an option you should consider.

Guests at Disney resorts and "official" hotels get unlimited transportation via bus, monorail, ferry, and water taxi to all Disney's major parks throughout the day until well into the evening. There's also service to other Disney and official hotels, Downtown Disney, Typhoon Lagoon, Blizzard Beach, Pleasure Island, and other resort areas. If, however, you want to venture beyond Disney boundaries (say, to Universal or SeaWorld), you'll have to pay extra.

The system has several advantages—the biggest of which is that it's free. This can save you on car rental, insurance, and gas (which nowadays can mean big bucks). The cost of parking at the theme parks ($89 a day at the bigger parks) doesn't count as real savings because Disney resort guests can park for free, but you can avoid the lines at the lots. Another big advantage is the ability to split up and head off in different directions. One parent can head back to the room with younger kids in need of a nap, while the other can hang back with the older kids (unless they're old enough to strike out on their own) and play at the parks.

The disadvantages? There are some serious ones. The system can be slow as molasses, and you're at the mercy of Disney's schedule. Sometimes, you have to take a ferry to catch a bus to get on the monorail to reach your hotel. The system makes a complete circuit, but it's not necessarily the most direct path to your destination. It can take an hour or more to get somewhere that's right across the lagoon from you. This is especially true if you stay at the outlying Disney resorts, such as Fort Wilderness.

Another problem: If you're staying at Disney's Value and Moderate resorts, and you've got little kids in tow, be advised that you're going to have to hike quite a bit from the theme-park exit to the bus stops that will get you back to your hotel. Even exhausted adults won't relish the walk at the end of a tiring day, and it'll be that much worse if you're carrying a day's worth of souvenirs, a diaper bag, a camera bag, and a tired toddler. Buses to these and other resorts can also get crowded, and the last thing tired and cranky kids will want to do is get packed in like sardines and remain standing for what could be a long ride.

Fun Fact **Crash & Burn**

Talk about culture clash. The Race Rock Café on International Drive, known for parking NASCAR racers in its lobby and having mini-racers streaking across the ceiling, was once the home of an opera-theme restaurant. It lasted until . . . well, the fat lady sang (ouch).

And finally, without a car, you may find yourself at Mickey's mercy, spending all your time (and money) in Mickeyville.

If you have time before locking in your trip, use the maps in this book to find the attractions you want to visit and their proximity to the various WDW resorts. You also can check them out at **www.disneyworld.com**. On the home page, click Tickets & Reservations; click maps on the bar near the top of the page; then pick the map you want to view.

Be sure to pick up a copy of "Disney's Shopping and Dining Guide" or "Your Handy Guide to All the Magic," both of which include a Disney Transportation map in the back. It not only shows the entire Disney road system, but also includes a handy guide that lists how to get from one place to another within Disney's World.

The best rule when using Disney transportation: Ask the driver or someone at your hotel's front desk to help you take the most direct route or the easiest one for your children. Keep asking questions along the way. Unlike missing a highway exit, missing a bus stop means your toddler may be old enough to vote before you arrive at your destination.

BY CAR

To rent or not to rent—that's the question. If you're going to stay happily immersed in everything Disney, or if you're going to stick to International Drive or Universal, you might do just as well without your own wheels. *But remember:* You'll become a virtual prisoner unless you rent a car at least a few days during your stay. In Disney's case, the least expensive properties, the All-Star resorts, are among the farthest from the Disney parks. Waits between buses can be considerable—if not unendurable, especially with kids.

During peak hours in the busy seasons, or even on an average day at park closing, you may have trouble getting a seat on the bus, something to keep in mind. Also, if you're hauling a stroller, consider the frustration factor of loading and unloading it, along with all the other kiddie paraphernalia, on and off buses, ferries, and trams. (Renting strollers in the parks will alleviate this problem.)

A car may drastically cut the commute time between the parks and hotels not directly on the monorail routes, so decide how much your time is worth and what the car will cost, and make sure to factor in the $9-per-day theme-park parking charge (but not if you're a Disney resort guest; parking is free if you stay at a Disney hotel).

In general, if you're going to spend all of your time at Disney, and you're laid-back enough to go with the flow of traffic within the transportation network, there's no sense in renting a car that will sit in the parking lot. This is especially true if you're staying at one of the Disney resorts on the monorail system. But if you're staying a week or more, you'll probably want a car for at least a day or two to venture beyond the traditional tourist areas. You can discover downtown Orlando, visit museums, tour the Space Coast, or head to the Gulf Coast. Trust me: You and your kids will need a good dose of reality after spending a few days in the Mickey madness.

If you are going to be spending the majority of your vacation outside the House of Mouse, a car is an absolute necessity (unless you plan on staying solely within the bounds of Universal Orlando for your entire trip). While there are plenty of transportation options, such as shuttles, trolleys, and taxis, using them every time you venture outside your hotel can't be done without losing your sanity (and lots of cash); don't even think of doing it!

RENTING A CAR

All the major car-rental companies are represented in Orlando and maintain desks at or near the airport (see appendix B, "Useful Toll-Free Numbers & Websites," for contact information). When you're planning your trip, poring over all those brochures, or searching through cyberspace, keep your eye out for discounts on car rentals. If you're using a travel agent, ask whether he or she has a recommendation or whether a discount is included in any packages. It also can't hurt to simply ask for the best rate available; you might just get it. Be advised that city and state rental taxes and surcharges (often not included in a quoted rate) can add almost 25% to your rental bill, so make sure to ask if taxes are included in any rate quotes that you get.

Note: Under Florida law, children under the age of 4 must ride in a car seat; children over 4 but under 6 must either ride in a car seat or wear a safety belt when riding in a vehicle. Most rental agencies in Orlando also rent car seats; just remember to ask for one when you reserve your car. They generally cost between $7 and $12 per day per seat. If you're vacationing for more than a few days or have more than one child requiring a seat, you may want to consider bringing along your own.

Be sure to ask for a seat that's the correct size for your child; an infant shouldn't be put in a seat that's too large or a toddler in a seat that's too small. Most major car-rental websites provide excellent information on choosing the proper seat restraints for your kids; **Avis**'s (**www.avis.com**) and **Hertz**'s (**www.hertz.com**) are two of the best.

All children over age 4 and under age 16 must wear seat belts—even in the back seat. It's recommended that kids sit in the back seat, especially if the car you're driving has airbags. Infants and toddlers should *never* be placed in a car seat in the front of your vehicle.

GETTING A GOOD DEAL

Car-rental rates vary even more than airline fares. The price you pay will depend on the size of the car, where and when you pick it up and drop it off, the length of the rental period, where and how far you drive it, whether you purchase insurance, and a host of other factors. A few key questions could save you hundreds of dollars:

- Are weekend rates lower than weekday rates? Ask whether the rate is the same for pickup Friday morning, for instance, as it is for Thursday night.
- Is a weekly rate cheaper than the daily rate? Even if you need the car for only 4 days, it may be cheaper to keep it for 5 or even 7.
- Does the agency assess a dropoff charge if you don't return the car to the same location where you picked it up? Is it cheaper to pick up the car at the airport compared with a downtown location?
- Are special promotional rates available? If you see an advertised price in your local newspaper, be sure to ask for that specific rate; otherwise, you may be charged the standard cost. Terms change constantly, and reservations agents are notorious for not mentioning available discounts unless you ask.
- Are discounts available for members of AARP, AAA, frequent-flier programs, or trade unions? If you belong to any of these organizations, you may be entitled to discounts of up to 30%.
- How much tax will be added to the rental bill? Local tax? State use tax?
- What is the cost of adding an additional driver's name to the contract?
- How many free miles are included in the price? Free mileage is often negotiable, depending on the length of your rental.

Tips **Fun While Driving**

Alamo Rent A Car has a **"Fun For Kids"** page on its website (**www.alamo.com**) that features printable quizzes, word games, and more to keep your kids happy while on a car trip. Several of the items on the page are Disney-related, making it even more appropriate for an Orlando-related car trip.

• How much does the rental company charge to refill your gas tank if you return with the tank less than full? Though most rental companies claim that these prices are "competitive," fuel is almost always cheaper in town. Try to allow enough time to refuel the car yourself before returning it.

Some companies offer refueling packages, in which you pay for an entire tank of gas upfront. The price is usually fairly competitive with local gas prices, but you don't get credit for any gas remaining in the tank. If a stop at a gas station on the way to the airport will make you miss your plane, by all means take advantage of the fuel-purchase option; otherwise, skip it.

Many packages are available that include airfare, accommodations, and a rental car with unlimited mileage. Compare these prices with the cost of booking airline tickets and renting a car separately to see whether these offers are good deals. See "Package Deals for Families," in chapter 2, for details on packages and where to find them.

Internet resources can make comparison-shopping easier. See "Planning Your Trip Online" in chapter 2 for tips on the best sites.

CAR-RENTAL INSURANCE

Before you drive off in a rental car, be sure that you're insured. Hasty assumptions about your personal auto insurance or a rental agency's additional coverage could end up costing you tens of thousands of dollars—even if you are involved in an accident that clearly was the fault of another driver.

If you already hold a **private auto insurance** policy, you are most likely covered in the United States for loss of or damage to a rental car and liability in case of injury to any other party involved in an accident. Be sure to find out whether you are covered in the area you are visiting, whether your policy extends to all people who will be driving the rental car, how much liability is covered in case an outside party is injured in an accident, and whether the type of vehicle you are renting is included under your contract. (Rental trucks, sport-utility vehicles, and luxury vehicles such as the Jaguar may not be covered.) There is also another area: "loss," as in "loss of income," as in the loss of the income that rental car would have made for the rental-car company. Many insurers don't cover this.

Most **major credit cards** provide some degree of coverage as well—provided that they were used to pay for the rental. Terms vary widely, however, so be sure to call your credit card company directly before you rent.

If you are **uninsured,** your credit card may provide primary coverage as long as you decline the rental agency's insurance. This means that the credit card will cover damage or theft of a rental car for the full cost of the vehicle. If you already have insurance, your credit card may provide secondary coverage—which basically covers your deductible. *Credit cards will not cover liability* or the cost of injury to an outside party and/or damage to an outside party's vehicle. If you do not hold an insurance policy, you may seriously want to consider purchasing additional liability insurance from your rental company. Be sure to check the terms, however: Some rental agencies cover liability only if the renter is not at fault; even then, the rental company's obligation varies from state to state. Bear in mind that each credit card company has its own peculiarities; call your own credit card company for details before relying on a card for coverage.

The basic insurance coverage offered by most car-rental companies, known as the **Loss/Damage Waiver (LDW)** or **Collision Damage Waiver (CDW),** can cost as much as $20 per day. The former should cover everything, including loss. It usually covers the full value of the vehicle with no deductible if an outside party causes an accident or other damage to the rental car. In all states but California, you probably will be covered in case of theft as well. Liability coverage varies according to the company policy and state law, but the minimum is usually at least $15,000. If you are at fault in an accident, however, you will be covered for the full replacement value of the car but not for liability. Most rental companies will require a police report in order to process any claims you file, but your private insurer will not be notified of the accident. Check your own policies and credit cards before you shell out money on this extra insurance, because you may already be covered.

BY BUS

Stops for the **Lynx** bus system (© 407/841-2279; www.golynx.com) are marked with a "paw" print. It will get you to Disney, Universal, and I-Drive ($1.25 adults, 50¢ kids 8–18), but it's slow and generally not tourist-friendly. I can't recommend using it, especially if you've got toddlers and younger children.

Mears Transportation (© 407/423-5566; www.mearstransportation.com) runs buses to attractions, including Kennedy Space Center, Universal Orlando, SeaWorld, and Busch Gardens in Tampa, among others. Its service is the largest in the area, and with good reason. Rates will vary based on where you are going and where you are coming from, of course, so call ahead for the particulars. Many of the area hotels use Mears for their shuttle service to the parks and attractions.

BY TAXI

Taxis line up in front of major hotels and a few smaller properties. The front desk will be happy to hail one for you. You can also call **Yellow Cab** (© 407/699-9999) and **Ace Metro** (© 407/855-0564). Rates average $2.50 for the first mile (but can run as high as $3.25 or more) and average $1.75 per mile thereafter, though sometimes you can get a flat rate. In general, cabs are economical only if you have four or five people aboard. You could actually rent your own car (depending on the model) for the price of just a few taxi rides.

Tips Look Both Ways

We don't recommend foot travel anywhere in Orlando, but occasionally, you'll have to walk across a parking lot or street. *Be careful.* In 2002, Orlando was named the most dangerous large city in the country for pedestrians by the Mean Streets study. The subsequent years haven't raised its safety level all that much. Wide roads designed to move traffic quickly and a shortage of sidewalks, streetlights, and crosswalks are to blame. So stay close to your kids, and keep a wary eye on traffic.

Note: Under Florida law, children under the age of 4 must ride in car seats in all vehicles, including taxis. For a taxi ride, you'll need to bring your own seat, making this mode of travel inconvenient for families whose kids require a seat.

FAST FACTS: Walt Disney World & Orlando

American Express There's an American Express Travel Service Office at 7618 Sand Lake Road (© **407/264-0104**).

Babysitters Several Orlando hotels, including all of Disney's resorts, offer babysitting services, usually from an outside service such as **Kids Night Out** (© **800/696-8105** or 407/828-0920; www.kidsniteout.com) or **All About Kids** (© **800/728-6506** or 407/812-9300; www.all-about-kids.com). In-room rates usually run somewhere between $10 and $15 per hour for the first child and $1 to $2 per additional child, per hour. Several Orlando resorts have good child-care facilities with counselor-supervised activity programs right on the premises with rates that run per child per hour or, in some cases, on a set schedule. The Disney resorts' programs—offered at Disney's Animal Kingdom Lodge, Beach Club, Boardwalk, Contemporary, Grand Floridian, Polynesian, and Wilderness Lodge resorts— offer supervised activities, entertainment, and meals. They're open to kids 4 to 12 (must be toilet-trained), run from 4:30 or 5pm to midnight, and cost $10 per child per hour, meal included. Reservations are suggested (© **407/939-3463**).

Business Hours Most theme parks open at 9am and stay open at least until 6 or 7pm (sometimes as late as 9pm, 10pm, or even midnight during summer and holidays). Business-office hours are generally Monday through Friday from 9am to 5pm.

Camera Repair **Colonial Photo,** 634 N. Mills Ave. in downtown Orlando (© **407/ 841-1485**), repairs most 35mm and some digital brands.

Doctors & Dentists There are basic first-aid centers in all the theme parks. There's also a 24-hour, toll-free number for the **Poison Control Center** (© **800/282-3171**).

Doctors on Call Service (© **407/399-3627**) makes house and room calls in most of the Orlando area (including the Disney resorts). **Centra Care** has several walk-in clinics listed in the Yellow Pages, including ones on Turkey Lake Road, near Universal (© **407/351-6682**); at Lake Buena Vista, near Disney (© **407/934-2273**); and on U.S. 192 (W. Irlo Bronson Hwy.) in the Formosa Gardens shopping center (© **407/397-7032**).

To find a dentist, contact **Dental Referral Service** (© **800/336-8478**; www. dentalreferral.com). Folks there can tell you the nearest dentist who meets your needs. Phones are manned weekdays from 10am to 7pm. Check the Yellow Pages for local 24-hour emergency services.

Emergencies Dial © **911** to contact the police or fire department or to call an ambulance. For less urgent requests, call © **800/647-9284**, a number sponsored by the **Florida Tourism Industry Marketing Corporation,** the state tourism-promotion board. With operators speaking over 100 languages, this source can provide directions and help with lost credit cards, medical emergencies, accidents, money transfers, airline confirmation, and much more.

Hospitals **Sand Lake Hospital,** 9400 Turkey Lake Rd. (© **407/351-8550**), is about 2 miles south of Sand Lake Road. From the WDW area, take I-4 east to the Sand Lake Road exit, and make a left on Turkey Lake Road. The hospital is 2 miles up on your right. To avoid the highway, take Palm Parkway (off Apopka–Vineland near Hotel Plaza Blvd.); it turns into Turkey Lake Road. The hospital is 2 miles up on your left. **Celebration Health** (© **407/303-4000**), located in the near-Disney town of Celebration, is at 400 Celebration Place. From I-4, take the U.S. 192 exit. At the first traffic light, turn right onto Celebration Avenue. At the first stop sign, take another right. *Note:* Be sure to check with your health care provider or insurance carrier regarding regulations for medical care outside your home area.

Internet Access You will find a few local cybercafes listed at **www.cybercafes.com** or **www.netcafeguide.com**. Most hotels and resorts provide some form of Internet access, whether via WebTV, a dataport, Wi-Fi, or a business center; charges vary.

Libraries Orange County has 14 libraries (www.ocls.lib.fl.us), including the downtown **Orlando Public Library,** 101 E. Central Blvd. (© **407/835-7323**), and **South Creek Library,** 1702 Deerfield Blvd. (© **407/858-4779**).

Lost Children Every theme park has a designated spot for adults to be reunited with lost children (or lost spouses). Ask where it is when you enter (or consult the free park-guide maps), and instruct your children to ask park personnel (not a stranger) to take them there if they get separated from you. Point out what park personnel look like. *Young children under 7 should have name tags* (concealed inside their clothing) that include parents' names and contact numbers both in Orlando and back home.

Maps AAA is an excellent source of free maps if you are a member (or someone you know is). The Orlando Convention and Visitors Bureau is another. You can pick up a copy of its official visitor map in most hotel lobbies. You can also pick up decent maps for $5 or less at most Orlando convenience and discount stores.

Newspapers & Magazines The *Orlando Sentinel* is the major local newspaper. The Friday edition of the *Sentinel* includes extensive entertainment and dining listings, as does the *Sentinel's* website, **www.orlandosentinel.com**. *Orlando Weekly* is a free alternative paper with entertainment and art listings focused on events outside tourist areas.

Pharmacies There's a **Walgreens** 24-hour pharmacy at 7650 W. Sand Lake Road (© **407/345-9497**). You can find several additional locations (some open 24 hours) near Disney, Universal Orlando, and in Kissimmee by logging on to **www.walgreens.com**. Numerous other pharmacies in and around the Orlando area, including those inside local grocery stores, are listed inside the Yellow Pages.

Post Office The post office most convenient to both Disney and Universal is at 10450 Turkey Lake Rd. (© **800/275-8777**). It's open Monday through Friday from 9am to 5pm, Saturday from 9am to noon. A smaller location, closer to Disney, is at 12133 Apopka–Vineland (S.R. 535) in Lake Buena Vista, just up the road from Hotel Plaza Boulevard (© **800/275-8777**). If all you need to do is buy stamps and mail letters, you can do that at most hotels.

Radio   Local stations include 101.1 FM (rock), 94.5 FM (R&B), 89.9 FM (jazz), 90.7 FM (classical), 92.3 FM (country), 580 AM (news), and 990 AM (Radio Disney).

Safety   Just because Minnie, Mickey, Donald, and Goofy all live here doesn't mean that a few more seedy characters aren't lurking about as well. Even in the most magical place on Earth, you shouldn't let your guard down; Orlando has a crime rate that's comparable with that of other large U.S. cities. Stay alert, and remain aware of your surroundings. It's best to keep your valuables in a safe. Most hotels today are equipped with in-room safes or offer the use of a safety deposit box at the front desk, just for that purpose. Keep a close eye on your valuables when you're in public places: restaurants, theaters, and even airport terminals. Renting a locker is always preferable to leaving your valuables in the trunk of your car, even in the theme-park lots. Be cautious, even when in the parks, and avoid carrying large amounts of cash in a backpack or fanny pack, which could be easily accessed while you're standing in line for a ride or show. And don't leave valuables unattended under a stroller; that's pretty much asking for them to be stolen.

If you're renting a car, carefully read the safety instructions that the rental company provides. Never stop for any reason in a suspicious, poorly lighted, or unpopulated area, and remember that children should never ride in the front seat of a car equipped with airbags.

One safety issue that often comes up when families with young kids visit Orlando is that of lost kids, not only at the parks, at but hotels too (and it happens a lot more than most people think). If you and your family have a safety plan in place ahead of time, you'll save lots of heartache and worry. For more on this topic, see p. 29.

Taxes   A 6.5% to 7% sales tax (depends on the county you happen to be in) is charged on all goods, with the exception of most edible grocery-store items and medicines. Hotels add another 2% to 5% in resort taxes to your bill, so the total tax on accommodations can run you up to 12%.

Telephone   Because of its growth spurt, Orlando has had to go to 10-digit dialing. If you're making a local call in Orlando's 407 area-code region, even across the street, *you must dial the 407 area code, followed by the number you wish to call,* for a total of 10 digits.

Weather   Look for the Weather Channel on your hotel TV. The *Orlando Sentinel* also includes a daily forecast; sometimes, it's even posted in hotel elevators or in the lobby. You can also get weather information from the National Weather Service, 8am to 4pm, by calling ℂ **321/255-0212**. (It answer sas National Weather Service in Melbourne, Florida, but after that, you get an option to punch in 412 on a touch-tone phone, which plugs you into the Orlando forecast.) Also check the Weather Channel online at **www.weatherchannel.com**.

Family-Friendly Accommodations

Unquestionably, families and kids are the real VIPs in Central Florida, which has more than 114,000 rooms, including scores of places located in or near the hottest tourist spots: Walt Disney World, Universal Orlando, SeaWorld, and all of International Drive. Many of these places let kids 17 and under stay free with paying adults—and some even offer free meals to preteens or roll out the red carpet in other ways!

Beautifully landscaped grounds are the rule at properties in WDW, neighboring Lake Buena Vista, Universal Orlando, and on the southern portions of I-Drive. But heavier traffic and, at times, higher prices come with those trimmings. No matter what your budget or crowd tolerance, there's something for everyone. If you're looking for an inexpensive or moderately priced motel, for instance, check out the options in Kissimmee and, to a lesser degree, on the northern end of International Drive.

Once you've decided on a date for your Orlando vacation, book your accommodations as soon as possible, especially if you want to stay at Disney or Universal. Advance reservations are a necessity if you're hunting moderate or preferred rooms in these areas. In addition to the individual listings in this chapter, there are several places to find discounts. **HotelKingdom.com** (*©* **877/766-6787** or 407/294-9600; www.hotelkingdom. com) is a good source of room or vacation rental bargains. Another good place to look is the **Orlando/Orange County Convention & Visitors Bureau** (*©* **800/ 643-9492;** www.orlandoinfo.com). You can also use the Kissimmee–St. Cloud website (**www.floridakiss.com**) or call *©* **800/333-5477.**

1 Choosing Your Orlando Hotel

There seemed to be no end to Orlando's hotel boom a few years ago. About 4,000 new rooms were added every year through 2000. Disney alone has 31 resorts, timeshares, and "official" hotels, two of them added within the last 2 years, with more than 31,000 rooms, including 784 campsites at Fort Wilderness. That's roughly 25% of the area's roster.

Orlando's tourist-based economy is showing signs of yet another growth spurt. Two major properties—the Ritz-Carlton and neighboring JW Marriott (known collectively as the Orlando Grande Lakes)—opened in mid-2003, and others, including the Omni Orlando Resort, and The Reunion Resort & Club of Orlando, followed soon after. Plans for the next few years look to be headed in the same direction as a handful of large-scale luxury resorts are scheduled to open, with other smaller-scale properties just on the horizon.

In this section, I'll give you the tools to choose the ideal hotel for your family vacation in Orlando. I discuss options for saving money on room rates, outline the amenities at Orlando hotels that most appeal to families, give details on discount hotel packages, and—most important of all when looking for a hotel in Orlando—the pros and cons of staying at a Walt Disney World resort.

SAVING MONEY ON HOTEL RATES

All of the rates cited in the following pages are what they call "rack rates." That means they're typical prices listed in the hotel brochures or that hotel reservation agents give over the telephone. *Don't pay them!* You can almost always negotiate a better price by purchasing package deals; by assuring the agents they can do better; or by mentioning that you belong to one of several organizations that receive a discount such as AARP, AAA, or a labor union. The Orlando Magicard can save you plenty of cash as well (see p. 12 for more on this cost-saving option). Even the type of credit card you use could get you a **5% to 10% discount** at some of the larger chains. Any discount you get will help ease the impact of local resort taxes, which aren't included in the quoted rates. *These taxes will add 11% to 12% to your bill, depending on where you're staying.*

The **average, undiscounted hotel rate** for the Orlando area is currently about $85 per night double, and that rate in good times climbs about 5% a year. The lowest rates at WDW are at the Pop Century and three All-Star resorts, which, depending on the season, can run from $79 to $139. They're pricier than comparable rooms in the outside world, but though they are small and basic, they are still Disney-owned and offer the same on-property advantages as Disney's more expensive resorts.

WDW's 2005 value seasons or lowest rates were generally available from January 1 to February 16, August 28 to October 4 (except Labor Day weekend), and November 27 to December 19. Regular-season rates are available from April 17 to August 27 and October 4 to November 26. Peak rates apply from February 17 to April 16, preholiday rates from November 27 through December 19, and holiday rates from December 20 through December 31. While the actual dates will shift a little (and will also change depending on the level of hotel you choose), the same general time periods should apply in 2006 and 2007; however, it's best to double-check when you make your reservations, as holiday dates, which pretty much regulate the "seasons," can change from year to year.

If you're not renting a car or staying at a Walt Disney World or Universal resort, be sure to ask when booking your room if the hotel or motel offers **transportation to the theme parks** and, if so, whether there's a charge. (You'll find this in my listings, but things sometimes change.) Some hotels and motels offer free service with their own shuttles. Others use Mears Transportation (see "Getting Around," in chapter 3). Rates can be $15 or more per person round-trip (some hotels make these arrangements for you; others require you to do it). On the other hand, if you have a car or pickup, expect to pay $9 a day to park it at Disney, Universal, and SeaWorld.

If you stay at a WDW resort or one of Disney's "official" hotels, transportation is complimentary within WDW. For more information on this and the other advantages (and disadvantages) of staying at Disney properties, see "The Perks & Downsides of Staying with Mickey," later in this chapter.

In or out of Walt Disney World, if you book your hotel as part of a **package** (see "Package Deals for Families," in chapter 2, for more details), you'll likely enjoy some kind of savings. Call the **Walt Disney Travel Company** at © **800/828-0228** or head online to **www.disneyworld.com** to book resort packages or hotel rooms at WDW.

Value **Staying for Less**

Although many folks participate in the airlines' frequent-flier programs, not many take advantage of the major hotel chains' frequent-stay clubs. Even if you don't stay in a hotel for more than your yearly vacation, you may be able to realize savings by joining its program.

Like the airlines' scheme, some hotels let you build points for staying at a participating property, dining in its restaurant, or using another partner service. Although programs vary, points can be traded for free nights; discounted rates; special perks; or, in some cases, frequent-flier miles. And the price to join is right—it's free. Simply joining a hotel club may make you immediately eligible for discounts; give you express check-in and checkout privileges; and provide free breakfasts, local calls, or a morning newspaper. And there's no reason you can't join more than one.

Here are a few frequent-stay programs that offer perks to travelers:

- **Six Continents Hotels Priority Club** (© **800/272-9273**; www.priorityclub. com) covers the Inter-Continental Resorts, Crowne Plaza hotels and resorts, Holiday Inns, and Staybridge Suites. Priority Club members get express check-in, access to discounted rates at select hotels, and other perks. Freebies vary according to hotel but often include breakfast, local phone calls, and/or parking.

- **Choice Hotels International Choice Privileges** program (© **888/770-6800**; www.guestprivileges.com) covers Sleep, Quality, Comfort, and Clarion properties. Participants receive perks such as express check-in, special rates, room upgrades based on availability, extended checkout times, and free local calls and newspapers.

- **Hyatt Hotel's Gold Passport** program (© **800/304-9288**; www.goldpassport. com) gives members a private reservation phone number and express check-in, complimentary newspapers, and access to the hotel's fitness center. You'll also receive special offers and discounted rates from select Hyatt properties.

- **Hilton HHonors Worldwide** program (© **800/548-8690**; www.hilton hhonors.com) covers Hilton, Conrad, DoubleTree, Embassy Suites, Hampton Inn, and Homewood Suites properties. It offers expedited check-in, a dedicated reservation line, late checkout, and a free daily newspaper.

Other frequent-stay programs include **Starwood Hotels Preferred Guest** (© **888/625-4988**; www.starwood.com), **Marriott Rewards** (© **801/468-4000**; www.marriottrewards.com), and **Loews First** (© **800/563-9712**; www.loews hotels.com).

Outside Disney, you'll probably be quoted a rate better than the rack rates contained in the following listings; even then, try to bargain further to ensure you get the best rates possible. Ask about discounts for students, government employees, seniors, military, firefighters, police, AFL–CIO, corporate clients, (again) AARP or AAA, holders of the Orlando Magicard, and even frequent traveler programs (whether you have hotel or airline membership). Special Internet-only discounts and packages may also be featured on hotel websites, especially those of the larger chains, and many hotels are teaming up with the airlines, offering discounted package deals. No matter where you end up staying, always ask again when you arrive if there are any additional discounts or promotions available. But never come to Orlando without a reservation: Taking chances on your negotiating skills is one thing; taking your chances on room availability is quite another. Orlando is a year-round destination, with a heavy convention and business trade, and international vacationers flock here during periods when domestic travelers don't. If you come without a reservation, you may find yourself extremely disappointed—or completely out of luck.

HOTEL RATES IN THIS CHAPTER

The hotels listed in this chapter are categorized by location and price. As you might expect, many of the inexpensive properties are the farthest from the action and/or have the most spartan accommodations.

Keep in mind, however, that this isn't one of the world's best bargain destinations. Unlike other Florida tourist areas, there are very few under-$60 motels that meet the standards demanded for listing in this book. That's why I've raised the price bar. The ones in our **inexpensive** category charge an average of less than $90 per night for a double room. Those offering $90 to $180 rooms are in the **moderate** category; $181 to $250 rooms are listed as **expensive;** and anything over $250 is **very expensive.** Any included extras (such as breakfast) are listed for each property. Orlando has peak and off seasons, often with complicated boundaries. Even remote events such as Bike Week in Daytona Beach or the International Sweet Potato Growers convention in Orlando can raise prices. These events especially affect moderately priced properties outside WDW.

The rack rates listed are per-night double, unless otherwise noted, and don't include hotel taxes of 11% to 12%. Also, most Orlando hotels and motels let **kids under 12 (and usually under 18) stay free** with a parent or guardian if you don't exceed maximum room occupancy. But to be safe, verify when booking your room.

RESERVATION SERVICES

Many of the hotels listed under "Places to Stay in the Kissimmee Area," later in this chapter, can be booked through the **Kissimmee–St. Cloud Convention & Visitors Bureau** (© 800/333-5477; www.floridakiss.com). The same goes for Orlando and the **Orlando/Orange County Convention & Visitors Bureau** (© 800/643-9492; www.orlandoinfo.com).

Florida Hotel Network (© 800/293-2419; www.floridahotels.com), **Central Reservation Service** (© 800/555-7555 or 407/740-6442; www.crshotels.com), and **Hotels.com** (© 800/246-8357; www.hotels.com) are three other services that can help with room reservations and other kinds of reservations in Central Florida.

You can book Walt Disney World hotels directly by calling © **800/828-0228** or 407/934-7639, or visiting **www.disneyworld.com.** Universal Orlando's properties can be booked by calling © **800/837-2273** or 407/363-8000, or surfing over to **www.universalorlando.com.**

Tips **Tight Squeeze**

An average hotel or motel room in Orlando has 325 to 400 square feet and two beds for four people. It's hardly a castle, but most travelers find that adequate for a short stay. For those requiring a bit more space, I've made a special note in the listings where rooms are substantially larger (or smaller) than the average.

HOTEL AMENITIES FOR FAMILIES

In the "Amenities" sections of the accommodations descriptions that follow, I mention **concierge levels** where available. In these hotels within a hotel, guests pay more to enjoy a luxurious private lounge (sometimes with great views), free continental or full breakfasts, hot and cold hors d'oeuvres served at cocktail hour, and/or late-night cordials and pastries. Rooms are usually on higher floors, and guests are pampered with special services (including private registration and checkout, a personal concierge, and nightly bed turndown) and amenities (upgraded toiletries, bathroom scales, terry robes, hair dryers, and/or more). The free food may make these rooms more economical for families than one might otherwise think (especially if you're staying in a hotel where breakfast isn't included in the rate). Ask for specifics when you reserve a room.

You'll also find counselor-supervised **child-care** or **activity centers** at some hotels. Very popular in Orlando, these can be marvelous, creatively run facilities that may offer movies, video games, arts and crafts, storytelling, puppet shows, indoor and outdoor activities, and more. Some provide meals and/or have beds where a child can sleep while you're out on the town. Check individual hotel listings for these facilities.

THE PERKS & DOWNSIDES OF STAYING WITH MICKEY

The decision on whether to bunk with the Mouse is one of the first you'll have to make when planning an Orlando vacation, and you'll probably get a strong pro-WDW argument from any younger kids in your family. In the sections "Places to Stay in Walt Disney World" and "'Official' Hotels in Lake Buena Vista," later in this chapter, you'll find information on the hotels, villas, timeshares, and campsites that are owned by Disney or are "official" hotels—those that are privately owned but have earned Disney's seal of approval. All 31, including the new Saratoga Springs Resort and Spa, are in WDW or nearby Lake Buena Vista.

In addition to their proximity to the theme parks, there are other advantages to staying at a Disney property or one of the "official" hotels. The following amenities are included at all Disney resorts, and **some** are offered by the "official" hotels, but make sure to ask when booking:

- The **Extra Magic Hour** (see the box "The Early Bird . . ." in this section).
- Guests and their baggage get free transportation from Orlando International Airport via Disney transportation to their Disney resort using **Magical Express** (albeit only until December 2006, a few months after Disney's "Happiest Celebration on Earth" ends).
- Unlimited **free** transportation on the Walt Disney World Transportation System's buses, monorails, ferries, or water taxis to and from the four WDW parks, from 2 hours prior to opening until 2 hours after closing. **Free** transportation also is provided to and from Downtown Disney West Side and Pleasure Island, Downtown Disney Marketplace, Typhoon Lagoon, Blizzard Beach, and the WDW resorts.

Three of them—the Polynesian, Grand Floridian, and Contemporary resorts—are on the Disney monorail system. This included service can save money you might otherwise spend on a rental car, parking (note, however, that parking is free if you're a Disney resort guest), and shuttles. It also means you're guaranteed admission to all the parks, even during peak times, when parking lots sometimes fill up.

- Reduced-price **children's menus** in many resort (and park) restaurants.
- **Character** breakfasts, lunches, and/or dinners at select restaurants.
- TVs equipped with the Disney Channel, **nightly bedtime stories** (Channel 22, 7–10pm, audio only), and WDW information stations.
- A **Lobby Concierge** (replacing the Guest Services desk) where you can buy tickets to all Disney parks and attractions and get information on everything Disney without standing in long lines at the parks.
- Playing privileges; preferred tee times; and, in some cases, free transportation to Disney golf courses (see "Hitting the Links," in chapter 8).
- WDW has some of the **best swimming pools** in Orlando and recently has built new ones or remodeled old ones as zero-entry or zero-grade pools, meaning that there's a gradual slope into the water on at least one side rather than only a step down. These include pools at the Grand Floridian, Animal Kingdom, and Polynesian resorts.
- Mears shuttle service (see "Getting There," in chapter 2) access for trips to non-Disney parks and attractions (fees vary), including the **Kennedy Space Center** (see chapter 11).
- On-premises Alamo car-rental (there are also car-rental desks at the Walt Disney World Swan and Dolphin but not at the other "official" hotels).
- Disney's **refillable-mug program** lets you buy—for around $12—a bottomless mug for soda, coffee, tea, and/or cocoa at its resorts. The offer is for the length of your stay, but it isn't transferable to the theme parks, and you can use it only at the property at which it is bought.

Tips **The Early Bird . . .**

Disney World's **Extra Magic Hours** allow resort guests lots of extra time at the theme parks. Each day, one of the four major theme parks opens an hour early or remains open up to 3 hours late—but only for WDW resort guests, making for a more relaxing and less-crowded experience. At press time, Disney was testing the waters by including the two water parks in its lineup. Not all the rides and attractions are running during these special periods, though, the best ones usually are, along with a handful of restaurants and shops. You can pick up a copy of the current week's Extra Magic Hours schedule at your WDW resort. A complete list of what rides are running, which shops are open, and which restaurants are serving is available at the parks.

Keep in mind that there is a catch: If you hold a ticket with a park-hopper option, you're good to go. If, however, you're holding a ticket without the hopper option, the ticket must be for admission to the park that's participating. Say you have a ticket to the Magic Kingdom without the hopper option. If Epcot is the park participating in the Extra Magic Hour that day, you'll find yourself checking out what's on TV that night instead of playing at the park.

- The **Disney Dining Plan** (an add-on to your Magic Your Way park tickets) allows you two meals and one snack per day per person (for the length of your stay) for one discounted price. Over 100 select eateries in the parks and at the resorts participate.
- Central billing allows guests to "charge" all (or most) or their purchases (including meals) made anywhere inside WDW to their room. In many cases, purchases made inside the theme parks can be delivered to your resort at no extra charge.

But there are also **disadvantages** to entering Mickey's boudoir:

- The complimentary **Walt Disney World Transportation System** can be *excruciatingly slow*. At times, you have to take a ferry to catch a bus to get on the monorail to reach your hotel. It can take an eternity (sometimes an hour or more) to get to where you need to go—even if it's just across the lagoon. And to add insult to injury, most resort bus stops are a considerable hike from the park entrances. So as you drag your kids and lug all their gear, your family's aching feet will have to wait a bit longer before they can really rest. Keep this in mind if there are fidgety kids or adults in your party.
- Resort rates are about **20% to 30% higher** than those at comparable hotels and motels away from the parks.
- Without a car or another means to get off the property, you'll be resigned either to paying WDW's higher prices or paying for a shuttle to get to Orlando's other offerings.
- Mickey, MICKEY, MICKEY . . . eek! Even the Mouse can get old after a few days unless you take a break. (Admittedly, your kids will have far less a problem with this issue than you likely will.) And if you don't spend a little time away from Mickey's monarchy, you'll miss out on the real Florida and the array of other great parks, restaurants, shops, and activities Orlando has to offer.

WALT DISNEY WORLD CENTRAL RESERVATIONS OFFICE & WALT DISNEY TRAVEL COMPANY

To book a room or package at Disney's resorts, campgrounds, and "official" hotels, call the **Central Reservation Office (CRO)**, P.O. Box 10000, Lake Buena Vista, FL 32830-1000 (© **407/934-7639**).

CRO can recommend rooms suited to your budget and needs, such as being near a particular park, those with supervised child care, or a pool large enough to swim laps. They can even recommend rooms on a particular resort that are closer to the pools or food courts. But the folks who answer the phones usually don't volunteer information about a better deal or a special *unless you ask*.

Be sure to inquire about Disney's numerous package plans, which can include meals, tickets, recreation, and other features. The right package can save you money and time, but having a comprehensive game plan first is helpful in computing the cost of your vacation in advance. This is especially true if you're traveling with more than one child; the cost per person will usually drop considerably with the right package deal.

CRO can give you information about various theme-park ticket options, the airlines, and car rentals. They can also make dinner-show reservations for you at the resort of your choice.

OTHER SOURCES FOR HOTEL PACKAGES

In addition to the Disney sources above, there are several travel companies that offer WDW packages, including **AAA** (© **800/732-1991;** www.aaa.com) and **American**

Tips **Special Treatment**

AAA (© 800/732-1991; www.aaa.com) members can take advantage of special lodging programs at select WDW resorts and preferred parking at the theme parks if they purchase a AAA Disney vacation package or prepurchase their park tickets at participating AAA locations (these cannot be purchased at the parks!). A members' Hospitality Desk located right inside the Magic Kingdom's Town Square provides basic member services.

Express Vacations (© 800/346-3607; travel.americanexpress.com/travel/personal). Almost all the major airlines offer vacation packages to Orlando, including **Delta Vacations** (© 800/872-7786; www.deltavacations.com), **American Airlines Vacations** (© 800/321-2121; www.aavacations.com), **Northwest Airlines** (© 800/225-2525; www.nwaworldvacations.com), and **Continental Airlines Vacations** (© 800/301-3800; www.coolvacations.com). Give each a call, ask for brochures, and compare offerings to find the best package for you. See "Package Deals for Families," in chapter 2, for more information on available packages.

On a slightly smaller scale than Disney, **Universal Orlando** and **SeaWorld** both offer several travel packages that can include resort stays (Universal includes both its official resorts and offsite resorts, while SeaWorld teams up with only offsite resorts), VIP access to the parks, discounts to other Orlando attractions, and cruises. One major perk that Universal Resort guests get that Disney simply can't provide, given the sheer number of its hotels, is UNIVERSAL EXPRESS (p. 242) access to most major rides in the Universal theme parks and priority seating at select Universal restaurants. This is a big plus for families with kids from tots to teens whose patience level hovers near zero. Airfare and car rentals are also available. You can book a package by calling © 888/322-5537 or 407/224-7000. On the Internet, visit **www.universalstudiosvacations.com**.

2 Places to Stay in Walt Disney World

The resorts in this section are Disney-owned or "official" Disney hotels with some of the same perks. All are on the Disney Transportation System, which means those of you who don't mind being entombed in Mouseville can do without a car.

If you decide Disney is your destination, come up with a short list of preferred places to stay; then call the WDW **Central Reservations Office** (© 407/934-7639) for rates. Web wanderers can get tons of information at **www.disneyworld.com**.

If you come by car, you will see big signs along all the major roads on Disney property, pointing the way to the various resorts. You'll find these hotels listed on the map "Walt Disney World & Lake Buena Vista Accommodations," on p. 78. If you couldn't resist bringing along Fido or Fluffy, resort guests can board their pets overnight ($11 per night per pet) at the kennels at the Transportation & Ticket Center on Seven Seas Drive, near Disney's Polynesian Resort, and the kennels (all near the park entrances) at MGM Studios, Epcot, and the Animal Kingdom (pets are not allowed in WDW hotels!). Kennels are also available at the Fort Wilderness Resort and Campground; however, Fluffy is welcome to bunk with you if you're staying at a designated campsite.

Prices in the following listings reflect the ranges available at each resort when this guide was published. Rates vary depending on season and room location, but the numbers should help you determine which places best fit your budget.

Kid's Night Out (𝄯 **407/827-5444** or via Disney 407/828-0920) provides **babysitting** services at all Disney resorts. The **supervised kids' clubs** listed at the Animal Kingdom, Beach Club, Grand Floridian, and Polynesian resorts are open to guests of any WDW resort. Disney advises parents to reserve spots for their kids in the clubs well in advance by calling 𝄯 **407/WDW-DINE** (reservations can be made up to 60 days in advance). Kids must be between 4 and 12 years of age and toilet trained. The programs run daily from 4 or 4:30pm until midnight. Dinner is included.

Note: **Rollaway beds** aren't available at WDW resorts; portable **cribs** are, at no charge. If you're carrying medications or other kid stuff that needs to be kept cool, **refrigerators** are complimentary at Disney's deluxe and moderate resorts, and can be rented at the value resorts for a charge of $10 per day, plus tax.

VERY EXPENSIVE

Disney's Beach Club Resort 𝄯𝄯𝄯   This property re-creates the grand turn-of-the-20th-century Victorian seaside resorts of Cape Cod and has a more casual ambience than its sister, the Yacht Club (detailed below), with which it shares restaurants, shops, and numerous recreational activities. Striped and floral wicker furnishings, seashells, and beach umbrellas adorn the hotel's casual interior. The Beach Club is close enough to Epcot to allow you to walk to the park, though most guests prefer to take the ferry (the parks are workout enough!). The shipwreck at Stormalong Bay (a huge free-form swimming pool and water park that sprawls over 3 acres) invites you to explore its decks, climb around, and slide 230 feet into the water waiting below. It includes a stretch of sandy beach, sand-bottom pools, whirlpools, and waterslides (including a toddler slide, so no one misses out). Room views range from the pool (more expensive) to the parking lot. Some rooms have balconies.

Note: Both the Beach Club and Yacht Club (see below) offer the chance to charter a reproduction of a 1930s mahogany runabout to **cruise Crescent Lake** or see Epcot's IllumiNations fireworks display (from $188 to $211 plus tax for up to 12 people for a 45-min. cruise to catch the fireworks; 𝄯 **407/824-2621**). A new cruise, specifically for kids ages 4 to 10 (potty trained, of course), is the **Albatross Treasure Cruise** ($28 per child). Sailing along Crescent Lake, kids follow clues and search for treasure while listening to the Legend of the Albatross. Lunch is included, and the kids get to split the booty. Reservations are highly recommended, as the cruise sails only on Wednesdays.

The **Sandcastle Club** features activities, entertainment, a meal, and a snack for youngsters ($10 per hour per child, ages 4–12, 4:30pm–midnight).

1800 Epcot Resorts Blvd. (off Buena Vista Dr.; P.O. Box 10000), Lake Buena Vista, FL 32830-0100. 𝄯 407/934-7639 or 407/934-8000. Fax 407/934-3850. www.disneyworld.com. 583 units. $305–$695 double; $495–$2,165 suite. Extra person $25. Children 17 and under stay free in parent's room. Rollaway beds not available, cribs free. AE, DC, DISC, MC, V. Free self-parking, $7 valet. Take I-4 east to Exit 67, Hwy. 536/Epcot Center Dr. Follow signs to WDW, then to the resort. Pets $9 a night. **Amenities:** 2 restaurants; grill; 4 lounges; 2 outdoor heated pools; kids' pool; 2 lighted tennis courts; Jacuzzi; watersports equipment; children's club; arcade; playground; WDW Transportation System; transportation for a fee to non-Disney theme parks; business center; salon; 24-hr. room service; babysitting; guest laundry; nonsmoking rooms. *In room:* A/C, TV, dataport, minibar, fridge, hair dryer, iron, safe.

Walt Disney World & Lake Buena Vista Accommodations

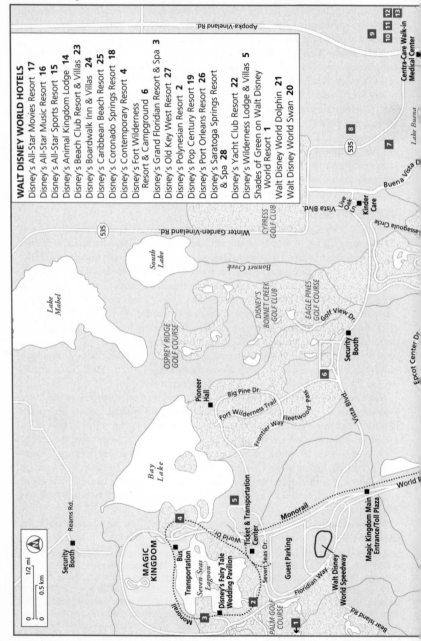

WALT DISNEY WORLD HOTELS

Disney's All-Star Movies Resort 17
Disney's All-Star Music Resort 16
Disney's All-Star Sports Resort 15
Disney's Animal Kingdom Lodge 14
Disney's Beach Club Resort & Villas 23
Disney's Boardwalk Inn & Villas 24
Disney's Caribbean Beach Resort 25
Disney's Coronado Springs Resort 18
Disney's Contemporary Resort 4
Disney's Fort Wilderness
  Resort & Campground 6
Disney's Grand Floridian Resort & Spa 3
Disney's Old Key West Resort 27
Disney's Polynesian Resort 2
Disney's Pop Century Resort 19
Disney's Port Orleans Resort 26
Disney's Saratoga Springs Resort
  & Spa 28
Disney's Yacht Club Resort 22
Disney's Wilderness Lodge & Villas 5
Shades of Green on Walt Disney
  World Resort 1
Walt Disney World Dolphin 21
Walt Disney World Swan 20

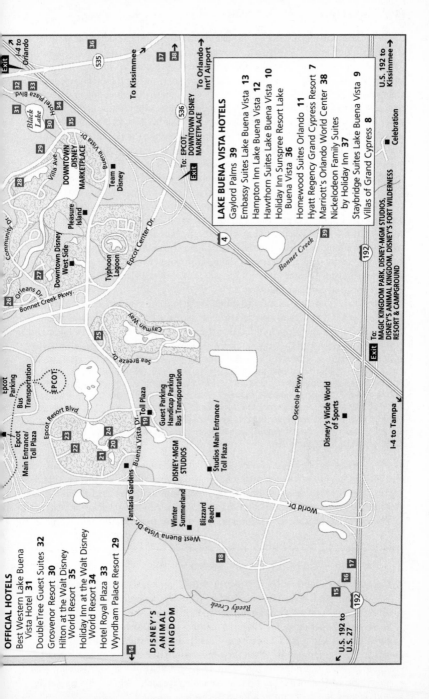

OFFICIAL HOTELS

Best Western Lake Buena Vista Hotel **31**
DoubleTree Guest Suites **32**
Grosvenor Resort **30**
Hilton at the Walt Disney World Resort **35**
Holiday Inn at the Walt Disney World Resort **34**
Hotel Royal Plaza **33**
Wyndham Palace Resort **29**

LAKE BUENA VISTA HOTELS

Gaylord Palms **39**
Embassy Suites Lake Buena Vista **13**
Hampton Inn Lake Buena Vista **12**
Hawthorn Suites Lake Buena Vista **10**
Holiday Inn Sunspree Resort Lake Buena Vista **36**
Homewood Suites Orlando **11**
Hyatt Regency Grand Cypress Resort **7**
Marriott's Orlando World Center **38**
Nickelodeon Family Suites by Holiday Inn **37**
Staybridge Suites Lake Buena Vista **9**
Villas of Grand Cypress **8**

79

Disney's Boardwalk Inn ✦✦✦ Romantics usually appreciate staying at (or at least visiting) Disney's plush 1940s-style "seaside" resort, set on 45 acres along Crescent Lake, near Epcot. It's a place to recapture a little bit of yesterday, whether that means kicking back in a rocker overlooking a village green or prowling the shops, restaurants, and clubs that line the resort's ¼-mile boardwalk. After the sun goes down, the boardwalk springs to life with street performers, food vendors, and midway games, reminiscent of the hustle and bustle of the Atlantic City Boardwalk in its heyday. (**Note:** The activity on the boardwalk reaches well into the late evening hours, as does the noise, which carries to the rooms overlooking it.) Some of the Cape Cod–style rooms have balconies, and the corner units offer a bit more space. At night, the rooms overlooking the boardwalk, mostly those in the center, enjoy a view of Epcot's fireworks display. The Inn isn't necessarily the best place for you if you have really young kids (though you'll see plenty of them here). Families with older kids and teens (who will like the posh surroundings, the Coney Island atmosphere of the Boardwalk, and the ESPN club) will do just fine. The priciest rooms overlook the boardwalk or pool; the less expensive ones overlook the parking lot but are sheltered from the boardwalk noise (good if your family is full of light sleepers). Hang on to your swimsuit if you hit the pool's **200-foot "keister coaster"** water slide, which is very popular with kids. (The pool also has spraying elephant fountains.)

Note: There is no kids' club at this hotel, so if you want to hit the Boardwalk's clubs after dark, you can hire an in-room babysitter or have the kids head to the facilities at the Yacht and Beach Club (keep in mind that the kids' club is open only until midnight).

2101 N. Epcot Resorts Blvd. (off Buena Vista Dr.; P.O. Box 10000), Lake Buena Vista, FL 32830-1000. ✆ **407/934-7639** or 407/939-5100. Fax 407/934-5150. www.disneyworld.com. 378 units. $305–$710 double; $495–$2,165 suite. Extra person $25. Children 17 and under stay free in parent's room. Rollaway beds not available, cribs free. AE, DC, DISC, MC, V. Free self-parking, valet $7. Take I-4 east to Exit 67, Hwy. 536/Epcot Center Dr. Follow signs to WDW, then to the resort. Pets $9 a night. **Amenities:** 4 restaurants; groceries; grill; 2 lounges; 3 clubs; 2 outdoor heated pools; kids' pool; 2 lighted tennis courts; croquet; health club; Jacuzzi; children's activity center; 2 arcades; playground; concierge; WDW Transportation System, transportation to non-Disney parks for a fee; business center; shopping arcade; 24-hr. room service; babysitting; guest laundry; valet; nonsmoking rooms; concierge-level rooms. In room: A/C, TV, dataport, fridge, hair dryer, iron, safe.

Disney's Boardwalk Villas ✦✦✦ Located on the same site as the Boardwalk Inn, the villas are an out-of-the-mainstream option that may make sense for those traveling in larger groups. Sold as timeshares, they're also rented to traditional tourists. Rooms range from standard-size studios to 1-, 2-, and 3-bedroom villas (the latter with 2,100 sq. ft. and beds for 12). Most have a balcony or patio and the same trimmings

---

⸢*Tips*⸣ **The Beach Club's Baby Sister**

Disney's **Beach Club Villas** (✆ **407/934-7639** or 407/934-2175; www.disney world.com) make up a resort inspired by Cape May seaside homes of the early 20th century, with clapboard exteriors and intricate white wood trim. The 280-room resort, opened in July 2002, is a member of the Disney Vacation Club that rents studios and 1- and 2-bedroom villas ($305–$449 studios, $400–$1,070 villas) to mainstream guests when their owners are not staying on the property. Amenities are shared with the Yacht Club and Beach Club resorts, with the exception of the Villa's quiet pool—which is accessible only to villa guests. It, too, is close to Epcot's International Gateway.

> ### Tips Sink Space
>
> Disney's resort rooms have notoriously cramped bathrooms (shutting the door with one person standing inside can require the skills of a contortionist). Bathing kids will be something of a challenge as well. The good news: Most rooms sport double sinks, usually set in a small dressing area outside the bathroom. (All-Star resorts have singles.) So while you may bang your shin on the shower, you won't have to wait in line to brush your teeth.

as the Boardwalk Inn, above. (They also share amenities.) Larger rooms have kitchens or kitchenettes, a good feature for those who want to prepare food or formula for kids. The service is great; the location near Epcot is convenient; and the spacious rooms are good for families traveling together.

2101 N. Epcot Resorts Blvd. (off Buena Vista Dr.; P.O. Box 10000), Lake Buena Vista, FL 32830-1000. (C) **407/934-7639** or 407/939-5100. Fax 407/934-5150. www.disneyworld.com. 520 units. Studios, Villas $305–$2,020. Extra person $25. Children 17 and under stay free in parent's room. Rollaway beds not available, cribs free. AE, DC, DISC, MC, V. Free self-parking, $7 valet. Take I-4 east to Exit 67, Hwy. 536/Epcot Center Dr. Follow signs to WDW, then to the resort. Pets $9 a night. **Amenities:** 4 restaurants; groceries; grill; 2 lounges; 3 clubs; 2 outdoor heated pools; kids' pool; 2 lighted tennis courts; croquet; health club; Jacuzzi; children's activity center; 2 arcades; playground; concierge; WDW Transportation System, transportation to non-Disney parks for a fee; business center; shopping arcade; 24-hr. room service; babysitting; guest laundry; valet; nonsmoking rooms; concierge-level rooms. *In room:* A/C, TV, dataport, kitchenette, fridge, coffeemaker, hair dryer, iron, safe, microwave.

Disney's Contemporary Resort ⭐ If location is one of your priorities, it's hard to beat this Disney resort, which is right beside the Magic Kingdom and one of only three resorts **on the monorail system** (the Grand Floridian and Polynesian are the others). The Contemporary offers great views of the Magic Kingdom and Seven Seas Lagoon from its west side and Bay Lake on its east. This 15-story concrete A-frame dates to WDW's infancy, and a complete renovation in 1999 was only the first phase of its restoration process, which has once again resumed. The result will bring the resort in line with the others in the same class and category. Rooms will be completely redecorated to reflect an upscale-Asian-Retro-yet-contemporary flair. It sounds complicated—it looks amazing! The decor will definitely appeal to adults (the flat-screen TVs are fabulous, and the new color scheme is very appealing), and with kids in tow, you'll appreciate the rounded corners, kidproof locks on the sliding doors (remember how high up you are here), and breakables placed high above a little one's reach. The pool is far less spectacular than most (it is, however, large and has a wading pool for toddlers, with a small beach area off to the left). On the plus side, the rooms can fit up to five people instead of the usual four (though space will be tight). Other kids' facilities include a playground with a good-size sandbox and a pretty decent arcade.

There's plenty for kids here, but the adult theme makes it a better choice for families with children of at least school age. Riding the monorail through—yes, it goes straight through the resort—is something kids of all ages will find very cool. If you do bunk here, avoid the Garden Wing rooms, and request the upper-floor Tower Rooms, which have nicer views and are a tad quieter than the lower-floor rooms, exposed to noisy public areas and the monorail.

4600 N. World Dr. (P.O. Box 10000), Lake Buena Vista, FL 32830-1000. (C) **407/934-7639** or 407/824-1000. Fax 407/824-3539. www.disneyworld.com. 1,008 units. $249–$720 double; $800–$1,190 suite, $405–$2,465 suites. Extra person $25. Children 17 and under stay free in parent's room. Rollaway beds not available, cribs free. AE, DC,

DISC, MC, V. Free self-parking, $7 valet. Take I-4 east to Exit 67, Hwy. 536/Epcot Center Dr. Follow signs to WDW, then to the resort. Pets $9 a night. **Amenities:** 3 restaurants (steak, New American, buffet); food court; 2 lounges; outdoor heated pool; kids' pool; 6 lighted tennis courts; fitness center; Jacuzzi; watersports equipment; kids' club; arcade; playground; concierge; WDW Transportation System, transportation to non-Disney parks for a fee; business center; salon; 24-hr. room service; babysitting; guest laundry; valet; nonsmoking rooms; concierge-level rooms. *In room:* A/C, TV, dataport, fridge, hair dryer, iron, safe.

Disney's Grand Floridian Resort & Spa   From the moment you step into the opulent, five-story, domed lobby of this Victorian-themed resort, you'll feel as if you've slipped back to an era that started in the late 19th century and lasted through the Roaring '20s. Close to the Magic Kingdom, the property is one of three on the monorail system. While a romantic choice for couples, especially honeymooners, who like luxuriating in the first-class spa and health club—the best in WDW—those with tots in tow should fear not. It's surprisingly appropriate for families (no matter what age), thanks to its numerous amenities and special options for kids.

The inviting Victorian-style rooms overlook a garden, pool, courtyard, or the Seven Seas Lagoon. The standard rooms are large enough to fit five; the dormer and Lodge Tower rooms can fit only four. Cribs, highchairs, and playpens are free of charge to guests, though you may have trouble fitting them in your room all at once. If you ask in advance, your kids will even find child-size bathrobes waiting for them in your room.

The main pool here is nice enough, but it's the new kids' pool that will grab your attention. Off to the side, in its own area near the stretch of sandy beach, lifeguards stand watch as kids splash in the waterfalls, slide down the rocky waterslide, or sink their toes in the sand. A zero entry makes it easy for younger kids to join in on the fun, though they may be more amused with the nearby dancing water. A neat little shop sells towels, swim suits, beach toys, and so much more. Kids can get their hair wrapped or make chalk drawings on the concrete. A snack bar (with a pretty good menu) is also close by.

The **Mouseketeer Clubhouse** features activities, entertainment, a meal, and a snack ($10 per hour per child, 2-hr. minimum, ages 4–12, 4:30pm–midnight). Older children might enjoy a chance to partake of a formal afternoon tea, which costs between $8.50 and $24.50 (depending on your choice of tea) per person (an a la carte menu is available as well) and is served in the Garden View Lounge from 2 to 6pm (be sure to reserve a spot well in advance by calling ✆ **407/WDW-DINE**).

If you prefer the royal treatment, the **Princess Tea Party** may be more your style. Most days (except Tuesdays and Saturdays), you and your little princess can enjoy tea for two, princess cakes, and a personal visit from Princess Aurora (aka Sleeping Beauty). Kids ages 3 to 9 receive a My Disney Doll dressed to match Aurora, along with their very own ribbon tiara, silver link bracelet, scrapbook set, and more. Most little girls come dressed in costume—as their favorite princess, of course—as this is a

---

A Piece of Yesterday, Today

The *Grand 1,* the Grand Floridian's 44-foot yacht, is available for hire for groups of 2 to 12. It cruises Seven Seas Lagoon and Bay Lake, where in the evenings, you can watch the Magic Kingdom's Wishes fireworks display in grand style. Voyages run $376 per hour and offer butler service, private dining, and a captain (✆ **407/824-2439**).

dressy affair. This extravagant experience has a price tag to match, at $200 for one child and one adult. An additional adult runs $65, while an extra child runs $135.

The hotel also offers a trio of special **Grand Adventure programs** for young children, and smaller special activities are usually offered as well. On Disney's **Pirate Cruise Adventure,** potty-trained children ages 4 to 10 depart from the Grand Floridian Marina to visit exotic "ports of call" to follow clues and collect "buried treasure." Most kids will have a jolly good time. It's offered Monday, Wednesday, and Thursday from 9:30 to 11:30am ,and the $28 price tag includes lunch. For information on the resort's two culinary-themed Adventure programs, see "Pint-Size Portionss," on p. 141.

4401 Floridian Way (P.O. Box 10000), Lake Buena Vista, FL 32830-1000. ☎ 407/934-7639 or 407/824-3000. Fax 407/824-3186. www.disneyworld.com. 867 units. $359–$890 double; $650–$2,535 suite. Extra person $25. Children 17 and under stay free in parent's room. Rollaway beds not available, cribs free. AE, DC, DISC, MC, V. Free self-parking, $7 valet. Take I-4 east to Exit 67, Hwy. 536/Epcot Center Dr. Follow signs to WDW, then to the resort. Pets $9 a night. **Amenities:** 5 restaurants; grill; 3 lounges; 2 outdoor heated pools; beach area, kids' pool; 2 lighted tennis courts; health club; spa; watersports equipment; children's center; arcade; playground; concierge; car-rental desk; WDW Transportation System, transportation to non-Disney parks for a fee; business center; shopping arcade; salon; 24-hr. room service; babysitting; guest laundry; valet; nonsmoking rooms; concierge-level rooms. *In room:* A/C, TV, dataport, minibar, fridge, hair dryer, iron, safe.

Disney's Old Key West Resort

An understated theme (at least by Disney standards) makes the Old Key West a good choice for those who prefer palms and pastels over Peter Pan and princesses all around. The sheer size of this resort, however, means that Disney transportation can be slow going at times; a rental car may be in order here. Located between Epcot and Downtown Disney West Side, this resort offers some of the quietest, homiest rooms on WDW property. Architecturally mirroring Key West at the turn of the 20th century, Old Key West is affiliated with the Disney Vacation Club—Disney's version of a timeshare—but the units are rented when not being used by owners. The 156-acre complex has tree-lined brick walkways edged by white picket fences. A tremendous sandcastle, a waterslide hidden inside, now keeps the giant pail and shovel (good for climbing on) company in the pool area. With a sandy beach, bike and boat rentals, an activity room full of games, playgrounds, pools, and numerous other recreational activities, you may have difficulties finding time for the parks. Two-bedroom villas have beds for eight; grand villas (2,202 sq. ft.) sleep 12. Villas have whirlpool tubs. All the accommodations sport balconies or patios, and all have kitchens or kitchenettes. The extra space and the kitchenettes make this a good bet for large families. There's no child care available on the premises, but you can use the kids' clubs at other Disney resorts. A variety of unique activities for both kids and adults is scheduled daily, and there are a playground, arcade, and movie rentals, too.

Warning: Old Key West has no lifeguards at any of its pools, and parents must accompany their kids to the pool at all times.

1510 N. Cove Rd. (off Community Dr.; P.O. Box 10000), Lake Buena Vista, FL 32830-1000. ☎ 407/934-7639 or 407/827-7700. Fax 407/827-7710. www.disneyworld.com. 761 units. $269–$379 studio; $350–$805 1- and 2-bedroom villas; $1,070–$1,545 grand villa. Call for extra adults. Children 17 and under stay free in parent's room. Rollaway beds not available, cribs free. AE, DC, DISC, MC, V. Free self-parking. Take I-4 east to Exit 67, Hwy. 536/Epcot Center Dr. Follow signs to WDW, then to the resort. Pets $9 a night. **Amenities:** Restaurant (American); groceries; 4 outdoor heated pools; kids' pool with sand playground; 3 tennis courts (2 lighted); Jacuzzi; sauna; watersports equipment; 2 game rooms; scheduled daily activities, WDW Transportation System, transportation to non-Disney parks for a fee; massage; babysitting; guest laundry; nonsmoking rooms. *In room:* A/C, TV, kitchen or kitchenette, fridge, coffeemaker, hair dryer, microwave.

Tips Surfing the Net in Walt Disney World

All WDW resorts will have high-speed Internet access by 2006; some will even offer Wi-Fi capability. There's a charge of $10 to use the high-speed service, and it's good for a 24-hour period (starting the minute you sign up). Depending on how often you need (or want) to use the service, you can cut costs a bit by signing up late enough in the morning that you can check your e-mail or surf the Web on two separate days while paying for only one 24-hour period.

Disney's Polynesian Resort 🎀🎀 Just south of the Magic Kingdom, the 25-acre Polynesian Resort bears some similarity to the South Pacific (torchlit walkways, the distant sound of beating drums, tropical foliage, luaus, and waterfalls), but there's no denying this is Disney World, thanks to Mickey's minions scurrying hither and yon. (And the monorail, which stops here, is a dead giveaway as well.) The resort's extensive play areas, themed swimming pools, character dining, and dinner show make it a good choice for those traveling with kids (who usually find the resort agreeably exotic). The Volcano pool, featuring a water slide, underwater jets, and nearby dancing water, is a major hit with kids, though it can get crowded. The beach is lined with canvas cabanas, hammocks, and big swings overlooking the 200-acre lagoon.

Most rooms (spread across three-story "longhouses") accommodate five; the resort will provide highchairs, playpens, and bed rails in your room upon request. If your kids are young and don't have much stamina, you might want to request a room close to the Great Ceremonial House, where the resorts' restaurants, shops, and monorail station are located. Some rooms here offer child-pleasing views of Cinderella Castle (for a price, of course), so request your desired view when making your reservation. Families with allergy sufferers or smoke-sensitive individuals should request a room in one of the resort's smoke-free buildings. At press time, the resort was undergoing extensive renovations; the lobby's been reconfigured, though it still includes all the same great shops and eateries, with some new additions tossed in. Still reflective of the islands, the guest rooms were getting a complete makeover from top to bottom to include new updated furnishings and muted earth-tone colors, giving it a far more upscale feel than before. The flat-screen TVs and covered closet spaces allow for additional space, so you can really spread out and relax.

Kids who enroll in the **Neverland Club** get activities, entertainment, movies, free video games, a meal, and a snack ($10 per hour per child, ages 4–12, 4pm–midnight). Advance reservations for the kids' club are an absolute must and can be made by calling © **407/WDW-DINE.**

Also check out the reviews of the **family-friendly Spirit of Aloha Dinner Show** (p. 120) and **'OHana** (p. 144).

600 Seven Seas Dr. (P.O. Box 10000), Lake Buena Vista, FL 32830-1000. © **407/934-7639** or 407/824-2000. Fax 407/824-3174. www.disneyworld.com. 853 units. $315–$580 double; $410–$780 concierge level; $510–$2,550 suite. Extra person $25. Children 17 and under stay free in parent's room. Rollaway beds not available, cribs free. AE, DC, DISC, MC, V. Free self-parking, $7 valet. Take I-4 east to Exit 67, Hwy. 536/Epcot Center Dr. Follow signs to WDW, then to the resort. Pets $9 a night. **Amenities:** Restaurant (Pacific Rim); cafe; 2 lounges; 2 outdoor heated pools; kids' pool; beach, watersports equipment; children's club; arcade; playground; concierge; WDW Transportation System, transportation to non-Disney parks for a fee; shopping arcade; 24-hr. room service; babysitting; guest laundry; valet; nonsmoking rooms; concierge-level rooms. *In room:* A/C, TV, fridge, hair dryer, iron, safe.

Disney's Yacht Club Resort ✿✿   This resort is a cut above its sister, the Beach Club (see above), because the rooms, views, service, and atmosphere are a step better. It's also geared more to adults and families with older children, given its far more upscale atmosphere, though young kids are catered to (this is Disney, after all). Epcot is a 10- to 15-minute walk from the front door, but you can save your energy for the parks by using the water taxi to the World Showcase's International Gateway. The theme is a turn-of-the-20th-century New England yacht club, and the atmosphere is posh, with fine leather furnishings, antique glass chandeliers, and brass accents adorning the lobby. The Yacht Club shares **Stormalong Bay,** a huge free-form, sand-bottom swimming pool and water park, with the Beach Club. It features a 230-foot water slide, cleverly hidden within a shipwreck, and a special kids' pool area, 2 to 3 feet deep, for little ones, and much more.

Rooms have beds for up to five, and most have balconies; views run from asphalt to Crescent Lake and the gardens, You would, however, have to be a contortionist to see the lake from some of the "water-view" rooms, so if this is a must, make sure that you request one with a direct view.

There's no kids' club at the hotel, though guests can park their kids at the Sandcastle Club at the Beach Club next door. *Note:* The Yacht Club offers charters of a reproduction of a 1930s mahogany runabout to **cruise Crescent Lake** or see Epcot's IllumiNations fireworks display ($188 to $211 plus tax for 45 min.; ✆ **407/824-2621**). Older kids will likely enjoy the experience. A new cruise, specifically for kids ages 4 to 10 (they must be potty trained), is the **Albatross Treasure Cruise** ($28 per child). Sailing along Crescent Lake, kids will follow clues and search for treasure while listening to the Legend of the Albatross. Lunch is included, and the kids get to split the booty. Reservations are highly recommended, as it sails only on Wednesdays.

Out with the Old . . .

Disney's **Saratoga Springs Resort and Spa** (✆ **407/827-1100** or 407/934-3400; www.disneyworld.com) is the newest of the Disney Vacation Club timeshare resorts. It opened its first phase in spring 2004 (it will eventually sport 840 rooms upon full completion in 2007) and transports guests back in time to the heyday of upstate New York's 19th-century resorts. The small resort town of Saratoga Springs is evoked through lavish gardens, Victorian architecture, bubbling springs, and a country setting. The resort's main pool brings to mind its namesake's natural springs, with "healing" waters spilling over the rocky landscaping. Kids will appreciate their own water-play area and the playground and activity center (unsupervised) that's filled with games. The spa offers an array of treatments if you're in need of some rejuvenation after a day at the parks; if you're still in the mood for a workout, there's a health club as well. Construction is ongoing, as rooms, pools, restaurants, and shops are being added as I write this. Accommodations resemble those of the other Disney vacation properties and range from studios that sleep 4 to grand villas that can sleep up to 12 people quite comfortably. Rates run from $269 to $379 for a studio to $350 to $1,545 for villas. Downtown Disney is just across the lagoon.

1700 Epcot Resorts Blvd. (off Buena Vista Dr.; P.O. Box 10000), Lake Buena Vista, FL 32830-1000. ℂ **407/934-7639** or 407/934-7000. Fax 407/924-3450. www.disneyworld.com. 621 units. $305–$525 double; $435–$695 concierge level; $540–$2,345 suite. Extra person $25. Children 17 and under stay free in parent's room. Rollaway beds not available, cribs free. AE, DC, DISC, MC, V. Free self-parking, $7 valet. Take I-4 east to Exit 67, Hwy. 536/Epcot Center Dr. Follow signs to WDW, then to the resort. Pets $9 per night. **Amenities:** 2 restaurants; grill; lounge; 2 outdoor heated pools; kids' pool; 2 lighted tennis courts; Jacuzzi; watersports equipment; croquet; arcade; playground; concierge; WDW Transportation System, transportation to non-Disney parks for a fee; business center; shopping arcade; salon; 24-hr. room service; babysitting; guest laundry; valet; nonsmoking rooms; concierge-level rooms. *In room:* A/C, TV, dataport, minibar, fridge, coffeemaker, iron, safe.

Walt Disney World Dolphin 🎭🎭   Most kids love the whimsical touch of architect

Michael Graves, who designed this Starwood resort and its sister, the Walt Disney World Swan (below). The Dolphin centers on a 27-story pyramid with two 11-story wings that are crowned by 56-foot twin dolphin sculptures that look more like the whale in *Pinocchio*. It's close to Epcot, next to the BoardWalk, and right across the street from the Fantasia Gardens minigolf courses.

On check-in, young guests get a **"Kids Passport"** that entitles them to a free ice cream cone or cup at the Dolphin Fountain or Splash Terrace restaurant after they have collected five stamps from various parts of the hotel, including restaurants, shops, and other facilities. Another nice touch for kids is the **"Straight A" Club;** if your child shows a report card filled with all "A"s, he or she gets a free ice cream.

Rooms offer views of the grounds and parts of Mouse World, all of which were completely refurbished in 2004 to include 27-inch TVs, upscale furnishings, and new decor. Corner rooms have a little more space. Unlike at the Disney-owned resorts, you can get a rollaway bed here, though space will be somewhat tight. You cannot, however, rent refrigerators, though you can get an empty minibar that really doesn't get all that cold for $12 per night (ouch!). The good news is that the hotel's $10 resort fee has been abolished.

The resort's free-form sculpted grotto pool, with waterfalls, water slide, rope bridge, and three secluded whirlpools, sprawls across 2 acres between the Dolphin and the Swan. It's a major hit with the young set. Kids enrolled in the supervised **Camp Dolphin** enjoy arts and crafts, movies, a video arcade, and dinner ($10 per hour per child, ages 4–12, 5:30pm–midnight). Be sure to reserve a space for your child well in advance by calling ℂ **407/934-4241.** The Dolphin and Swan also share a beach on Crescent Lake, the new Mandara Spa (with special programs designed specifically for teens), and a Body by Jake health club.

1500 Epcot Resorts Blvd. (off Buena Vista Dr.; P.O. Box 22653), Lake Buena Vista, FL 32830-2653. ℂ **888/828-8850** or 407/934-4000. Fax 407/934-4099. www.swandolphin.com or www.disneyworld.com. 1,509 units. $259–$409 double; $625–$3,255 suite. Extra person $25. Children 17 and under stay free in parent's room. Rollaway beds $25/night, cribs free. AE, DC, DISC, MC, V. self-parking $7, valet parking $14. Take I-4 east to Exit 67, Hwy. 536/Epcot Center Dr. Follow signs to WDW, then to the resort. Pets $9 a night. **Amenities:** 6 restaurants; grill; 2 lounges; 4 outdoor heated pools; 4 lighted tennis courts; health club; spa, watersports equipment; children's center; 2 game rooms; playground; concierge; car-rental desk; WDW Transportation System, transportation to non-Disney parks for a fee; shopping arcade; salon; 24-hr. room service; massage; babysitting; guest laundry; valet; nonsmoking rooms; concierge-level rooms. *In room:* A/C, TV, Nintendo, dataport, minibar, hair dryer, iron, safe.

Walt Disney World Swan 🎭🎭   Not to be outdone by the huge dolphins at its sis-

ter property, this high-rise Starwood resort is topped with dual 45-foot swan statues and seashell fountains. It offers a good location—close to Epcot, Fantasia Gardens, and the Boardwalk's dining and nightlife—and a chance to be in the WDW mainstream without being quite so overwhelmed by mouse decor. It shares a beach, 3-acre

---

Tips **When a WDW Property Is Not a WDW Property**

There are nine "official" Disney hotels that aren't owned by Mickey's stockholders. But there are a couple of asterisks. Walt Disney World Swan and Walt Disney World Dolphin have Uncle Walt's name, and they're on mainstream WDW resort property, but they're not Disney-owned resorts, so we consider them "officials." The good news for you: You can get discounted room rates and other special offers at the Swan and Dolphin that you won't get at a Disney-owned resort.

---

pool area, health club, a spa, a number of restaurants, and other trimmings with the Dolphin (see above). Note that the beach next to the pool offers a great view of Epcot's IllumiNations fireworks.

The hotel underwent a massive renovation in 2004 that included upgrading all its guest rooms. Rooms now sport Starwood's famous "Heavenly Beds," the perfect thing to come home to after a busy day in the parks. Guest rooms here are just a tad smaller than those at the Dolphin. The hotel offers a childproofing room kit with socket covers and a nightlight (ask for it at check-in). Alas, though the hotel has ditched its awful resort fee, it still sports the same "empty minibar" charge (don't use the minibar to store necessary medications; it's not cold enough!) as its sister property.

Kids staying at the Swan can enroll in the supervised Camp Dolphin program next door at the Dolphin and are eligible for the "Kids Passport" and "Straight A" programs as well.

1200 Epcot Resorts Blvd. (off Buena Vista Dr.; P.O. Box 22786), Lake Buena Vista, FL 32830-2786. ℂ **888/828-8850** or 407/934-3000. Fax 407/934-4499. www.swandolphin.com or www.disneyworld.com. 758 units. $259–$495 double; $865–$2,835 suite. Extra person $25. Children 17 and under stay free in parent's room. Rollaway beds $25/night, cribs free. AE, DC, DISC, MC, V. self-parking $7, valet parking $14. Take I-4 east to Exit 67, Hwy. 536/Epcot Center Dr. Follow signs to WDW, then to the resort. Pets $9 a night. **Amenities:** 4 restaurants; grill; lounge; 4 outdoor heated pools; 4 lighted tennis courts; health club; watersports equipment; children's center; 2 game rooms; playground; concierge; car-rental desk; WDW Transportation System, transportation to non-Disney parks for a fee; shopping arcade; salon; 24-hr. room service; massage; babysitting; guest laundry; valet; nonsmoking rooms; concierge-level rooms. *In room:* A/C, TV, Nintendo, dataport, minibar, hair dryer, iron, safe.

EXPENSIVE

Disney's Animal Kingdom Lodge ✦✦✦   This resort has the feel—with a little imagination—of an African game-reserve lodge, complete with thatched roofs. Not surprisingly, this is the closest you can stay to Animal Kingdom, but almost everything else on WDW property is quite a distance away. Location aside, this is a great place for families, who will appreciate the animals and activities (a lot of them quite educational) for kids.

The lodge's comfortable rooms follow a *kraal* (semicircular) design that gives patient guests a view of 130 bird species and 75 giraffes, gazelles, and other grazing animals on a 30-acre savanna. Most kids—and adults, for that matter—will find the notion of waking up to a giraffe outside their window pretty cool. (Not all rooms have savannah views—you have to pay more for that—though you can get the scenery for nothing through large picture windows in the lobby, where information displays will help your kids understand what they are seeing.) All lodge rooms have a balcony, complete with "mosquito netting" curtains, and all come with animal-identification checklists your kids can use to keep track of their sightings (you can also get these upon check-in). If you do get a room overlooking the Savannah, be sure that your children understand that dropping food and other items off the balconies to the animals is strictly *verboten*. For those staying in the concierge-level rooms, venturing beyond the main path of the savannah is allowed—provided that you sign up for an hourlong guided excursion ($45 per person).

The 9,000-square-foot pool is popular with kids and has a water slide, a wading area for young children, and a good view of the savannah. **Simba's Clubhouse,** the kids' program, offers activities, entertainment, a meal, and a snack ($10 per hour per child, ages 4–12, 4:30pm–midnight). Be sure to reserve a space for your kids well in advance (call *(C)* **407/WDW-DINE**). There are also daily **Junior Researcher** (animal familiarization) and **Junior Chef** (cookie decorating) programs, along with a long list of interesting activities that are free for children staying at the lodge (including the nightly African storytelling by the fire pit in the lobby). The resort's programs and activities are geared to children ages 4 to 10; if you're interested, ask about them at check-in. All in all, this is the best of the Disney properties when it comes to providing both an educational and entertaining environment for kids.

Warning: Because of animal-safety issues, the resort doesn't allow balloons of any sort into the rooms. You will be forced to check yours upon entry and won't get it back until departure, so to avoid upsetting little ones, do yourself a favor, and don't buy one for them at the theme parks if you're staying here.

2901 Osceola Pkwy., Bay Lake, FL 32830. *(C)* **407/934-7639** or 407/938-3000. Fax 407/939-4799. www.disneyworld. com. 1,293 units. $205–$510 double; $435–$625 concierge level; $1,030–$2,300 suite. Extra person $25. Children 17 and under stay free in parent's room. Rollaway beds not available, cribs free. AE, DC, DISC, MC, V. Free self-parking, valet parking $7. Take I-4 east to Exit 67, Hwy. 536/Epcot Center Dr. Follow signs to WDW, then to the resort. Pets $9 a night. **Amenities:** 2 restaurants (African, American); lounge; outdoor heated pool; kids' pool; health club; children's center; arcade; playground; concierge; WDW Transportation System, transportation to non-Disney parks for a fee; shopping arcade; limited room service; babysitting; guest laundry; nonsmoking rooms; concierge-level rooms. *In room:* A/C, TV, dataport, fridge, hair dryer, iron, safe.

Disney's Wilderness Lodge The geyser out back, the mammoth stone hearth in the lobby, and bunk beds for the kids are just a few reasons this resort is a family favorite.

Tips **Credit or Debit?**

If you use your debit card (instead of a credit card) as collateral against any purchases you may make during your stay, your card may be charged anywhere from $50 to $250 (or more) each and every day, whether you actually charge anything to your room or not. This can seriously deplete your checking account, leaving you with far less funds than you realize or planned on, and you won't see a credit (which can reach into the hundreds, maybe even thousands, depending on the resort) back to your account until up to 10 days after you have checked out of your resort.

Fortunately, WDW does not (at least for now) follow this practice. Instead, Disney verifies that you have sufficient funds available for room-charging privileges, basing on the amount you can "charge" on the balance of your account. No charges will be applied to your account until you check out. Be sure to ask exactly what your hotel's policy is regarding debit and credit charges the minute you check into your hotel.

The building looks like a rustic national park lodge, in part because it's patterned after the one at Yellowstone. Surrounded by 56 acres of oaks and pines, it offers a remote, woodsy setting that we find a plus but can also be a drawback: It's more difficult to access other areas via the WDW Transportation System, because the bus and water taxi are the only ways to get in and out (unless you have a car, which I would recommend if you're staying here).

The comfy rooms offer two queen beds or a queen and a set of bunk beds (which have side rails). The deluxe rooms are an especially good deal for families, as they have a seating area with a pullout couch, TV, and refrigerator that's separated from the main bedroom by French doors—perfect if parents want a little privacy after the kids are in bed. If a view is important, ask for a room with a woods view.

The geyser I mentioned "blows" periodically throughout the day and is a hit with kids. The lodge also has an immense swimming area, fed by a thundering waterfall whose water flows in from the "hot springs" in the lobby, though the water slide here is one of the shortest. The kids' program, **Cub's Den,** includes activities, entertainment, movies, video games, a meal, and a snack ($10 per hour per child, ages 4–12, 4:30pm–midnight). Reserving a place at the club for your kids is strongly suggested (call 𝒞 **407/WDW-DINE**).

The 181 units at the **Villas at Disney's Wilderness Lodge** were added in 2000. This is another Disney Vacation Club timeshare property (the Boardwalk Villas, Old Key West, and Saratoga Springs are the others) that rents vacant rooms, usually to larger groups and larger families. It offers a more upscale experience, although you get less kitchen space here than in Old Key West. The one- and two-bedroom villas have 727 and 1,080 square feet, respectively.

Note: If you have a budding engineer in your party, the lodge offers **"Wonders of the Lodge,"** a free tour touting its architecture, Wednesday through Saturday at 9am. Most kids, however, will probably find it boring. The lodge does offer a special family option that both kids and adults will enjoy: **the Flag Family program.** If you're selected, the entire family can traipse up to the Wilderness Lodge's roof in the morning (times seem to vary, so ask) and raise the American flag that flies over the resort. You'll get a picture, a certificate, and a fabulous view. If you're interested, ask at the front desk upon check-in.

901 W. Timberline Dr. (on the southwest shore of Bay Lake just east of the Magic Kingdom; P.O. Box 10000), Lake Buena Vista, FL 32830-1000. 𝒞 **407/934-7639** or 407/938-4300. Fax 407/824-3232. www.disneyworld.com. 909 units. $205–$500 lodge; $295–$1,040 villas; $360–$500 concierge; $370–$1,220 suites. Extra person $25. Children 17 and under stay free in parent's room. Rollaway beds not available, cribs free. AE, DC, DISC, MC, V. Free self-parking, $7 valet. Take I-4 east to Exit 67, Hwy. 536/Epcot Center Dr. Follow signs to WDW, then to the resort. Pets $9 a night. **Amenities:** 3 restaurants; 2 lounges; outdoor heated pool; kids' pool; 2 Jacuzzis; watersports equipment; children's center; arcade; playground; WDW Transportation System, transportation to non-Disney parks for a fee; limited room service; babysitting; guest laundry; nonsmoking rooms; concierge-level rooms. *In room:* A/C, TV, fridge, hair dryer, iron, safe.

MODERATE

Note: None of the Moderate resorts has particularly good connections to the WDW transportation network. Worse, the stops for the buses to the resorts outside the theme parks can be a long, long, long hike away from the main exits. If you opt to stay at one of these resorts, and you're lugging around young kids and the usual paraphernalia that goes along with them, I strongly suggest that you opt for a rental car.

> **Tips** **A Friendly Reminder**
>
> If you have a package delivered to your WDW resort from one of the WDW shops, it might be delivered directly to your room but also might get sent to your hotel's gift shop. If your package goes to the gift shop, a friendly reminder will be left via the telephone messaging service stating that your package has arrived and is ready to be picked up.

Disney's Caribbean Beach Resort ★★   With its moderate pricing scheme and recreational activities, the Caribbean Beach is a great choice for families who don't need a lot of frills or amenities. The resort's rooms are spread across five villages (all Disney moderate resorts have a similar general layout) of pastel buildings, each named for the islands of Aruba, Barbados, Jamaica, Martinique, and Trinidad (north and south). The lush tropical greenery adds a touch of island atmosphere. Parrot Cay, the resort's main pool area and playground, is themed as an old Spanish-style fort, complete with water cannons, water slides, and waterfalls—a popular spot with kids. Always ask for a recently refurbished room when booking.

Note: The resort's restaurants and shops are located in the central Old Port Royale complex, quite a hike from most rooms; those in the Martinique and Trinidad North areas are closest. The nearest park is Disney–MGM Studios, but it can take 45 minutes to get there if you use the Disney Transportation System.

900 Cayman Way (off Buena Vista Dr.; P.O. Box 10000), Lake Buena Vista, FL 32830-1000. ☎ **407/934-7639** or 407/934-3400. Fax 407/934-3288. www.disneyworld.com. 2,112 units. $139–$215 double. Extra person $15. Children 17 and under stay free in parent's room. Rollaway beds not available, cribs free. AE, DC, DISC, MC, V. Free self-parking. Take I-4 east to Exit 67, Hwy. 536/Epcot Center Dr. Follow signs to WDW, then to the resort. Pets $9 a night. **Amenities:** Restaurant; grill; lounge; large outdoor heated pool; 6 smaller pools in the villages; kids' pool; Jacuzzi; watersports equipment; arcade; 3 playgrounds; WDW Transportation System, transportation to non-Disney parks for a fee; limited room service; babysitting; guest laundry; nonsmoking rooms. *In room:* A/C, TV, fridge, hair dryer, iron, safe.

Disney's Coronado Springs Resort ★   Here's another clone of the Disney-moderate class. The American Southwestern theme carries through four- and five-story hacienda-style buildings with terra-cotta tile roofs and shaded courtyards, all of which surrounds a 15-acre lake. As with most WDW properties, it has an above-par pool, in this case inspired by a 46-foot Mayan pyramid with a water slide (watch out for the spitting Jaguar), and the children's pool has a spouting fountain. Keeping with the theme (which most kids adore), the playground has an archaeological dig site. The rooms are identical in size to those in the Caribbean Beach Resort; don't expect to fit more than one person into the bathroom at a time. If a member of your party has a mobility impairment, keep in mind that there are 99 disabled-access rooms at the resort. The rooms nearest the central public area, pool, and lobby tend to be noisier, but if you avoid them, you'll have a longer hike to the food court (one of the better ones in WDW) and shops. The nearest park is Animal Kingdom, but the Coronado is at the southwest corner of WDW and a good distance from much of the action.

1000 Buena Vista Dr. (near All-Star resorts and Blizzard Beach), Lake Buena Vista, FL 32830. ☎ **407/934-7639** or 407/939-1000. Fax 407/939-1003. www.disneyworld.com. 1,967 units. $139–$215 double; $280–$1,140 suite. Extra person $15. Children 17 and under stay free in parent's room. Rollaway beds not available, cribs free. AE, DC, DISC, MC, V. Free self-parking. Take I-4 east to Exit 67, Hwy. 536/Epcot Center Dr. Follow signs to WDW, then to the resort.

Pets $9 a night. **Amenities:** Restaurant; grill/food court; 2 lounges; 4 outdoor heated pools; kids' pool; health club; Jacuzzi; sauna; watersports equipment; 2 arcades; playground; WDW Transportation System, transportation to non-Disney parks for a fee; business center; salon; limited room service; massage; babysitting; guest laundry; nonsmoking rooms. *In room:* A/C, TV, dataport, fridge, hair dryer, iron, safe.

Disney's Port Orleans Resort ⭐⭐ *Value*   One of my favorite resorts for families, Port Orleans has the best location; landscaping; and, perhaps, the coziest atmosphere of the resorts in this class. This southern-style property is really a combination of two distinct resorts; the French Quarter and Riverside. The French Quarter offers magnolia trees, wrought-iron railings, cobblestone streets, and an idealistic vision of New Orleans' famous French Quarter. Riverside transports you back to Louisiana's Mississippi River towns, its rooms housed in buildings resembling grand plantation homes and the "rustic" wooden shacks of the bayou. Overall, this resort offers some romantic spots and is relatively quiet, making it popular with couples, though the pools, playgrounds, and wide array of activities make it a favorite with families as well. The recently refurbished Doubloon Lagoon pool in the French Quarter is a family favorite, with a water slide that curves out of a Sea Serpent's mouth before entering the pool. The rooms and bathrooms (equivalent to all rooms at Disney's moderate resorts) are somewhat of a tight fit for four, though the Alligator Bayou rooms have a trundle bed that allows for an extra child, and the vanity areas now have privacy curtains. Port Orleans is just east of Epcot and Disney–MGM Studios. *Note:* All 1,080 rooms in the French Quarter side reopened in March 2004 after closing for a top-to-bottom refurbishment. The 2,048 rooms in Riverside were renovated in phases throughout 2005.

2201 Orleans Dr. (off Bonnet Creek Pkwy.; P.O. Box 10000), Lake Buena Vista, FL 32830-1000. ⓒ **407/934-7639,** 407/934-5000 (French Quarter), or 407/934-6000 (Riverside). Fax 407/934-5353 (French Quarter) or 407/934-5777 (Riverside). www.disneyworld.com. 3,056 units. $139–$215 double. Extra person $15. Children 17 and under stay free in parent's room. Rollaway beds not available; cribs free. AE, DC, DISC, MC, V. Free self-parking. Take I-4 east to Exit 67, Hwy. 536/Epcot Center Dr. Follow signs to WDW, then to the individual resorts. Pets $9 a night. **Amenities:** Restaurant (American); food court; lounge; 2 outdoor heated pools; 2 kids' pools; Jacuzzi; watersports equipment; arcade; playground; WDW Transportation System, transportation to non-Disney parks for a fee; limited room service; babysitting; guest laundry; nonsmoking rooms. *In room:* A/C, TV, fridge, hair dryer, iron, safe.

Shades of Green on Walt Disney World Resort ⭐ *Value*   Shades of Green, nestled among 3 of Disney's golf courses near the Magic Kingdom, is open only to folks in the military and their spouses, military retirees and widows, 100% disabled veterans, and Medal of Honor recipients. If you qualify, don't think of staying anywhere else; it's the best bargain on WDW soil. And it's even better now, thanks to a $92 million renovation that was completed in 2004. The refit nearly doubled the room capacity of the resort and added fully ADA-compliant rooms with wide doorways and roll-in showers. In addition to the new rooms and suites (housing up to eight), existing rooms were completely overhauled. All the large rooms offer TVs with wireless

---

Tips **Value in the Eyes of the Beholder**

Disney's All-Star resorts charge a "preferred room" rate, but don't expect much for the top rate of $131. Guests who book it are paying for location: Preferred rooms are closer to the pools, food court, and/or transportation. If you've got a rental car or don't mind walking, don't bother paying extra; some of the quietest rooms at the All-Stars are the standard ones.

Tips Getting Away

If you want to enjoy the amenities and service of a Disney resort but can't do without some beach time, the Disney Vacation Club offers visitors the option of renting a room just 2 hours south of WDW at its **Vero Beach Resort** (© **407/939-7775;** www.dvcresorts.com), directly on the Atlantic Ocean, with sand, surf, and all the Disney trimmings included. Studios, standard rooms, one- and two-bedroom villas, and three-bedroom cottages are all available, ranging from about $165 to $1,105 per night. You will need to arrange for your own transportation.

---

keyboards (access to the Internet is offered for a fee), balconies or patios, and pool or golf-course views. Transportation—though slow—is available to all the Disney parks and attractions.

1950 W. Magnolia Dr. (across from the Polynesian Resort). © **888/593-2242** or 407/824-3400. Fax 407/824-3665. www.shadesofgreen.org. 587 units. $76–$116 double (based on military rank), 6- to 8-person suites $225–$250 (regardless of rank). Extra person $15. Children 17 and under stay free in parent's room. Rollaway beds not available, cribs $5/night. AE, DC, DISC, MC, V. Take I-4 east to Exit 67, Hwy. 536/Epcot Center Dr. Follow signs to WDW, then to the resort. Pets $9 a night. **Amenities:** 2 restaurants (American, Italian); 2 lounges; 2 heated outdoor pools; kids' pool; 2 lighted tennis courts; arcade; playground; activities desk; WDW Transportation System, transportation to non-Disney parks for a fee; babysitting; guest laundry; nonsmoking rooms. *In room:* A/C, TV, fridge ($5 per day), coffeemaker, hair dryer, iron, safe ($1 per day).

INEXPENSIVE

Note: All of Disney's inexpensive resorts are out of the way and offer less-than-ideal transportation connections. If you and your brood stay at one of them, I strongly recommend that you rent a car.

Disney's All-Star Movies Resort   Most kids love the larger-than-life themes at the three All-Star resorts; however, it can be Disney overload for many adults. Movies such as *Toy Story, 101 Dalmatians,* and *Fantasia* live on in a very big (and I mean BIG) way at this family-friendly resort. Gigantic larger-than-life characters such as Buzz Lightyear, Pongo, and even Mickey himself mark this resort's buildings, and the pools are themed after *The Mighty Ducks* and *Fantasia* (both usually noisy and crowded—a theme that carries throughout the resort). They, however, add the only Disney flair to what is essentially a no-frills, budget motel with basic, tiny (only 260 sq. ft.) rooms. Think old-school roadside motels, when all you expected was a clean bed and a bathroom. The soundproofing leaves something to be desired, especially with the number of children staying here. Like its two siblings (listed below), the All-Star Movies Resort is pretty isolated in WDW's southwest corner. If, like the White Rabbit, you're often "late for a very important date," renting a car is a far better choice than the Disney Transportation System.

1991 W. Buena Vista Dr., Lake Buena Vista, FL 32830-1000. © **407/934-7639** or 407/939-7000. Fax 407/939-7111. www.disneyworld.com. 1,900 units. $79–$137 double. Extra person $10. Children 17 and under stay free in parent's room. Rollaway beds not available, cribs free. AE, DC, DISC, MC, V. Free self-parking. Take I-4 east to Exit 67, Hwy. 536/Epcot Center Dr. Follow signs to WDW, then to the resort. Pets $9 a night. **Amenities:** Food court; lounge; 2 outdoor heated pools; kids' pool; arcade; playground; WDW Transportation System, transportation to non-Disney parks for a fee; limited room service; babysitting; guest laundry; nonsmoking rooms. *In room:* A/C, TV, dataport, fridge ($10 a night), safe.

Disney's All-Star Music Resort   Giant trombones and musical themes from jazz and calypso to rock and Broadway can't hide the fact that this is a clone of the All-Star Movies Resort (see above). Tiny rooms and bathrooms, where opening a door can cause injury, are the norm again. But rooms in this class do have perks: They'll save you *more than $50 a night* (in some cases, hundreds of dollars) over other Disney resorts. There is, however, a good reason for the substantial savings. The rooms, like those at the other All-Star resorts, are tiny, though a lot of folks don't come to lounge in a room. So if you're going to be inside only to sleep, the cramped quarters (maximum capacity four, but no more than two adults) may not matter so much. Note that Disney is home to a ton of cheerleading championships and other kids' events—and all the participants usually get housed at the All-Stars, making for an even noisier environment. For (relative) quiet, ask for a room on the third floor of a building. The main pools resemble a guitar and grand piano (quieter and better for older kids). The closest park is Animal Kingdom, which you can reach (not necessarily in an expedient manner) by the transportation system.

1801 W. Buena Vista Dr. (at World Dr. and Osceola Pkwy.; P.O. Box 10000), Lake Buena Vista, FL 32830-1000. ℂ 407/934-7639 or 407/939-6000. Fax 407/939-7222. www.disneyworld.com. 1,920 units. $79–$137 double. Extra person $10. Children 17 and under stay free in parent's room. Rollaway beds not available, cribs free. AE, DC, DISC, MC, V. Free self-parking. Take I-4 east to Exit 67, Hwy. 536/Epcot Center Dr. Follow signs to WDW, then the resort. Pets $9 a night. **Amenities:** Food court; lounge; 2 outdoor heated pools; kids' pool; arcade; playground; WDW Transportation System, transportation to non-Disney parks for a fee; limited room service; babysitting; guest laundry; nonsmoking rooms. *In room:* A/C, TV, dataport, fridge ($10 a night), safe.

Disney's All-Star Sports Resort   Yogi Berra said it best: "It's *déjà vu* all over again." It's a different theme, but the same routine: tight quarters like those in the All-Star Movies and Music resorts, above, but your kids, especially young ones, probably won't mind (on the contrary—sports-crazed kids love it). Rooms here are housed in buildings designed around football, baseball, basketball, tennis, and surfing motifs. For instance, the turquoise surf buildings have waves along the roofs, surfboards mounted on exterior walls, and pink fish swimming along balcony railings. Again, if your threshold for visual overload is low, you may need to visit a sanatorium once you've left this La-La Land. Surfboard Bay and the Grand Slam are the two themed pools. Note that unlike the other Disney resorts, the inexpensive ones don't provide towels at the pool, so you'll have to use the ones in your room.

One last warning: The rates and themes tempt lots of families with little kids, and the noise level can get very high, so if you're looking for a quiet family vacation, steer clear of these resorts.

1701 W. Buena Vista Dr. (at World Dr. and Osceola Pkwy.; P.O. Box 10000), Lake Buena Vista, FL 32830-1000. ℂ 407/934-7639 or 407/939-5000. Fax 407/939-7333. www.disneyworld.com. 1,920 units. $79–$137 double. Extra person $10. Children 17 and under stay free in parent's room. Rollaway beds not available, cribs free. AE, DC, DISC, MC, V. Free parking. Take I-4 east to Exit 67, Hwy. 536/Epcot Center Dr. Follow signs to WDW, then to the resort. Pets $9 a night. **Amenities:** Food court; lounge; 2 outdoor heated pools; kids' pool; arcade; playground; WDW Transportation System, transportation to non-Disney parks for a fee; limited room service; babysitting; guest laundry; nonsmoking rooms. *In room:* A/C, TV, dataport, fridge ($10 a night), safe.

Fun Fact **By the Numbers**

If you add up all the Dalmatians residing at the All-Star Movies resort—including the puppies, Pongo, and Perdita—there are actually 101 Dalmatians.

Disney's Pop Century   The newest of WDW's inexpensive—or, as Mickey calls them, value-class resorts—opened in early 2003. The massive resort began opening in stages, with some yet to open. The themes here are decade-long capsules of the 20th century, broken into two half-century blocks: the Legendary Years (1900s–40s) and the Classic Years (1950s–90s), were the first to open. The bottom line: You and the kids will get a good price and the same postage stamp–size accommodations, in this case with larger-than-life icons such as Play-Doh, a Duncan yo-yo, and eight-track tapes. Its **six swimming pools** carry shapes ranging from a crossword puzzle and soda bottle to a bowling pin and a computer. The resort is across from Disney's Wide World of Sports (p. 238).

1050 Century Dr. (P.O. Box 10000), Lake Buena Vista, FL 32830-1000. (℃ 407/934-7639 or 407/938-4000. Fax 407/938-4040. www.disneyworld.com. 5,760 units. $79–$137 double. Extra person $10. Children 17 and under stay free in parent's room. Rollaway beds not available, cribs free. AE, DC, DISC, MC, V. Free parking. Take I-4 east to Exit 67, Hwy. 536/Epcot Center Dr. Follow signs to WDW, then to the resort. Pets $9 a night. **Amenities:** Food court; lounge; 6 outdoor heated pools; kids' pool; arcade; playground; WDW Transportation System, transportation to non-Disney parks for a fee; limited room service; babysitting; guest laundry; nonsmoking rooms. *In room:* A/C, TV, dataport, fridge ($10 a night), safe.

A DISNEY CAMPGROUND

Disney's Fort Wilderness Resort & Campground   Why not take the kids camping? Pine and cypress trees, lakes, and streams surround this woodsy 780-acre resort, which offers a host of recreational opportunities for the whole family. It's close to the Magic Kingdom but quite a distance from everything else, though if you're a true outdoors type, you may want to be sheltered from some of the Mickey make-believe. There are 784 campsites for RVs, pull-behind campers, and tents (110/220-volt outlets, outdoor cooking grills, and comfort areas with showers and restrooms). Some sites are open to **pets**—at an additional cost of $5 per site, not per pet, which is cheaper than using the WDW resort kennel, where you pay $9 per pet. The 408 wilderness cabins (actually, mobile homes with an outdoor deck and grill) offer 504 square feet, enough for six people once you pull down the Murphy beds (there's also a set of bunk beds for kids), and they also have full kitchens.

Nearby Pioneer Hall is home to the popular Hoop-Dee-Doo Musical Revue, which I review on p. 310. The resort also has a nightly **campfire sing-along** where kids can roast marshmallows (you'll have to buy them or bring along your own); sing songs with Chip N' Dale; and then sit back, relax, and watch a favorite Disney flick in the outdoor theater. Pony rides at the petting farm and horse-drawn wagon and horseback rides offer a different kind of thrill than you'll find at the theme parks, especially for younger kids.

103520 N. Fort Wilderness Trail (P.O. Box 10000), Lake Buena Vista, FL 32830-1000. (℃ **407/934-7639** or 407/824-2900. Fax 407/824-3508. www.disneyworld.com. 784 campsites, 408 wilderness cabins. $39–$92 campsite double; $239–$349 wilderness cabin double. Extra person $2 campsites, $5 cabins. Children 17 and under stay free with parent. Rollaway beds not available, cribs free. AE, DC, DISC, MC, V. Free self-parking. Take I-4 east to Exit 67, Hwy. 536/Epcot Center Dr. Follow signs to WDW, then to the resort. **Amenities:** 2 restaurants (American); grill; lounge; 2 outdoor heated pools; kids' pool; 2 lighted tennis courts; watersports equipment; outdoor activities (fishing; horseback and pony rides, and hayrides; campfire programs); 2 game rooms; playground; WDW Transportation System, transportation to non-Disney parks for a fee; babysitting; guest laundry; nonsmoking cabins. *In room:* A/C, TV/VCR, kitchen, fridge, coffeemaker, outdoor grill, hair dryer (all in cabins only).

Fun Fact **Sizing Things Up**

Disney's Pop Century Resort sports a gigantic Big Wheel in its 1970s courtyard. If an actual child were to ride it, proportionally, he or she would have to weigh approximately 800 pounds.

---

3 "Official" Hotels in Lake Buena Vista

These resorts, designated "official" Disney hotels, are located on or around Hotel Plaza Boulevard, at the northeast corner of WDW. They're near Downtown Disney Marketplace, Downtown Disney West Side, and Pleasure Island. The boulevard has enough greenery to make it a nominee for Main Street, U.S.A.

Guests at these hotels enjoy some WDW privileges (see "The Perks & Downsides of Staying with Mickey," earlier in this chapter), including free bus service to the parks and the ability to purchase theme-park tickets right at the resort, but make sure when booking to ask which privileges you get, as they vary from hotel to hotel and year to year. Their locations spare you from some of the pixie dust, but the boulevard's high-speed traffic is frustrating, as it's the main thoroughfare between Downtown Disney and the free world. Also note that the Walt Disney World Dolphin and Walt Disney World Swan (listed in the previous section) should be considered the eighth and ninth "official" hotels, because they're not Disney owned. The difference is that they're on the mainstream property.

Another perk of the "official" hotels is that they generally have less-relentless Disney themes, although some do offer character breakfasts a few days each week (ask the person answering the reservation line for details and schedules). They're often much cheaper than equivalent accommodations at the Mouse's House and are usually a step above the moderate Disney-owned resorts. Almost all the resorts have kiddie pools, in-room electronic games (for an extra fee), and arcades or other activities for children.

You can make reservations for all the properties listed below through the Central Reservations Office ((C) **407/934-7639**) or through the hotel numbers included in the listings. To ensure that you get the best rates, call each hotel or its parent chain (or check their websites) to see if there are specials available.

You'll find all these hotels located on the map "Walt Disney World & Lake Buena Vista Accommodations," earlier in this chapter.

EXPENSIVE

Wyndham Palace Resort & Spa ★★ This is the most upscale and expensive of the Hotel Plaza Boulevard–area properties and is popular with families, even though it caters primarily to business travelers. For that reason, some of its best rates are offered in July and August (a bonus for families with a liberal budget). Many of the business-standard rooms have balconies or patios; kids will probably prefer the Sony PlayStation over the views. Still, ask for one above the fifth floor with a "recreation view," which face the Wyndham's pools on Recreation Island; Downtown Disney; Pleasure Island (with its brief midnight fireworks); and, in the distance, Disney–MGM Studios' Tower of Terror. If a member of the family has severe allergies, ask for one of the resort's Evergreen rooms, which offer individual air filtration systems and nonallergenic amenities. At press time, the resort offered a Disney **character breakfast** on Sundays. The Palace is known for its spacious fitness center and full-service European-style spa (massage, wraps, steam room, saunas, salon, fitness center, and more), which are open to the public. There are also three pools (one partially indoors) and a host of available recreational options.

1900 Buena Vista Dr. (just north of Hotel Plaza Blvd.; P.O. Box 22206), Lake Buena Vista, FL 32830. ℂ **800/996-3426** or 407/827-2727. Fax 407/827-6034. www.wyndham.com. 1,014 units. $149–$269 double; $209–$618 suite. Resort fee $10. Extra person $20. Children 17 and under stay free in parent's room. Rollaway beds $20/night, cribs free. AE, DC, DISC, MC, V. Free self-parking, valet parking $10. From I-4, take Exit 68, Hwy. 535/Apopka–Vineland Rd., north to Hotel Plaza Blvd. and go left. At 3rd stoplight, turn right onto Buena Vista Dr. It's the 1st hotel on the right. **Amenities:** 2 restaurants (Continental, steak); grill; 4 lounges; 3 outdoor heated pools; kids' pool; 3 lighted tennis courts; half basketball court; sand volleyball court; spa; Jacuzzi; sauna; children's center; arcade; playground; concierge; complimentary bus service to WDW parks, transportation for a fee to non-Disney parks; salon; 24-hr. room service; massage; babysitting; guest laundry; valet; nonsmoking rooms; concierge-level rooms. *In room:* A/C, TV w/PlayStation and pay movies, dataport, minibar, coffeemaker, hair dryer, iron.

MODERATE

Best Western Lake Buena Vista Hotel ⭐ (Value)   This 12-acre lakefront hotel is reasonably modern, with nicer rooms and public areas than you might find in others within the chain. Tropical-themed rooms are located in an 18-story tower, and all have balconies. Accommodations here are definitely a step above and larger than the rooms in Disney's moderate category. The views improve from the eighth floor and up, and those on the west side have a better chance of seeing something Disney. The hotel's 18th-floor lounge, Toppers, offers an excellent view of the Magic Kingdom's fireworks, but you'll have to do that one without the kids, as they aren't allowed in. The tropical pool here is decent and has a separate wading area for little ones.

You can reserve an oversize room with a sleeper sofa (about 20% larger) or a WDW fireworks-view room for $15 more a night. You can also get the same rooms with full American breakfast for up to four people for $20 more per night. (If you're a foursome, it's a reasonably good deal; if not, buy breakfast elsewhere.) *Note:* It definitely pays to surf the corporate website at **www.bestwestern.com** if you plan to stay here. It sometimes offers great deals and special rates for this hotel.

2000 Hotel Plaza Blvd. (between Buena Vista Dr. and Apopka–Vineland Rd./Hwy. 535), Lake Buena Vista, FL 32830. ℂ **800/348-3765** or 407/828-2424. Fax 407/828-8933. www.orlandoresorthotel.com. 325 units. $99–$159 standard for 4; $199–$399 suite. Resort fee $7.75. Children 17 and under stay free in parent's room. Rollaway beds $10/night, cribs free. AE, DC, DISC, MC, V. Free self-parking. From I-4, take Exit 68, Hwy. 535/Apopka–Vineland Rd., north to Hotel Plaza Blvd., and go left. It's the 1st hotel on the right. **Amenities:** Restaurant (American); grill; outdoor heated pool; kids' pool; arcade; playground; guest services desks; complimentary bus service to WDW parks, transportation for a fee to non-Disney parks; limited room service; babysitting; guest laundry; nonsmoking rooms. *In room:* A/C, TV w/pay movies, Nintendo, coffeemaker, hair dryer, iron, safe.

Tips **Yet Another Add-On**

Several of the properties in this chapter add "resort fees" to their daily room rates. That's part of an unfortunate but growing hotel trend of charging for services that used to be included in the rates, such as use of the pool; admission to the health club; or in-room coffee, phones, or safes. If it's a concern, ask if your hotel charges such a fee when booking so you don't get blindsided at check-out.

DoubleTree Guest Suites ⭐⭐ Children have their own check-in desk and theater, and they get a gift upon arrival at this hotel, the best of the "official" hotels for families traveling with little ones. (Don't forget that everyone gets a tasty **chocolate chip cookie** as a bonus!) Adults may find some of the public areas lacking in personality, though the hand-painted mural that spans the lobby and large aviary is a nice touch. All the accommodations in this seven-story hotel are two-room suites that offer 643 square feet—large by most standards—with refrigerators, microwaves, and space for up to six to catch some zzzzs. The large pool offers lush landscaping and a children's wading area. This is the easternmost of the "officials," which means that it's farthest from the other Disney action but closest to (even within walking distance of) the shops, restaurants, and activities located in the Crossroads Shopping Center or along Apopka–Vineland Road.

2305 Hotel Plaza Blvd. (just west of Apopka–Vineland Rd./Hwy. 535), Lake Buena Vista, FL 32830. ✆ **800/222-8733** or 407/934-1000. Fax 407/934-1015. www.doubletreeguestsuites.com. 229 units. $119–$249 double. Extra person $20. Rollaway beds $10/night, cribs free. Children 17 and under stay free in parent's room. AE, DC, DISC, MC, V. Free self-parking. **Amenities:** Restaurant; 2 lounges; outdoor heated pool; kids' pool; 2 lighted tennis courts; volleyball; playground; arcade; kids theater; Disney Store; concierge; car-rental desk; complimentary bus service to WDW parks, transportation for a fee to non-Disney parks; limited room service; laundry service. *In room:* A/C, TV w/pay movies, video games (fee), dataport, fridge, coffeemaker, hair dryer, iron, safe, microwave.

Grosvenor Resort *(Overrated)* This lakeside resort has a great location, within walking distance of Downtown Disney Marketplace's shops. The high-rise with low-rise wings has a British Colonial look and public areas that make for wonderful "we-stayed-here" snapshots. Unfortunately, the rooms are a hit-or-miss proposition. I've heard complaints and have seen a few examples of rooms in need of refurbishing, and the large picture in the lobby of the kids' suites with bunk beds is disappointingly deceiving, as there are only 2 of these rooms in the entire 626-room resort. Nevertheless, its frequent package deals make it popular with budget travelers, so if you choose to stay here, my best advice is to complain to the front desk if you get a dud. Ask for a Tower Room on the west side (floors 9–19) for a limited view of Lake Buena Vista. A Saturday-night mystery dinner theater ($40 adults, $11 kids 3–9) is held in the Baskerville's restaurant for an entertaining evening away from Disney. A character breakfast is also offered three mornings a week.

1850 Hotel Plaza Blvd. (just east of Buena Vista Dr.), Lake Buena Vista, FL 32830. ✆ **800/624-4109** or 407/828-4444. Fax 407/828-8192. www.grosvenorresort.com. 626 units. $86–$135 double. Resort fee $8.50. Extra person $15. Children 17 and under stay free in parent's room. Rollaway beds $18/night, cribs free. AE, DC, DISC, MC, V. Free self-parking, valet parking $8. **Amenities:** 3 restaurants; 3 lounges; 2 outdoor heated pools; 2 lighted tennis courts; fitness center; sport court; shuffleboard; volleyball; Jacuzzi; playground; concierge; car-rental desk; business center; complimentary bus service to WDW parks, transportation for a fee to non-Disney parks; babysitting; laundry service; valet. *In room:* A/C, TV w/pay movies and VCR, dataport, coffeemaker, safe.

Hilton in the Walt Disney World Resort ⭐⭐ This upscale resort welcomes many a Disney vacationer, even though business travelers constitute the bulk of its clientele. Its major claim to fame: It's the only official resort on Hotel Plaza Boulevard to offer guests Disney's Extra Magic Hour option (see p. 192 for details). The lobby boasts a nautical flair, and its public areas reflect a New England theme, sporting shingles, weathered-wood exteriors, and seafaring touches. The pleasantly decorated rooms range in size from a standard double to suites offering plenty of space in which you can relax and unwind. The newly renovated junior suites are especially spacious and can sleep up to six—great for families. Rooms on the north and west sides of floors 6 though 10 offer a view of Downtown Disney (just a short walk away) and, in the distance, the Magic Kingdom fireworks. The resort offers a variety of recreational options, including a large pool area (with two pools and plenty of space to soak up the sun) and a game room for kids.

1751 Hotel Plaza Blvd. (just east of Buena Vista Dr.), Lake Buena Vista, FL 32830. ✆ 800/782-4414 or 407/827-4000. Fax 407/827-3890. www.hilton.com. 814 units. $160–$345 double; $359–$1,500 suite. Resort fee $8.50. Extra person $20. Children 17 and under stay free in parent's room. Rollaway beds $15/night, cribs free. AE, DC, DISC, MC, V. Free self-parking, valet parking $10. **Amenities:** 4 restaurants; deli; minimarket; 3 lounges; 2 outdoor heated pools; kids' pool; fitness center; volleyball; Jacuzzi; sauna; children's center; arcade; concierge; car-rental desk; complimentary bus to WDW parks, transportation for a fee to non-Disney parks; business center; Disney Store; shopping arcade; salon; 24-hour room service; babysitting; laundry service; valet; concierge-level rooms; ATM. *In room:* A/C, TV w/pay movies, dataport, minibar, coffeemaker, hair dryer, iron, video games (fee), safe.

Holiday Inn in The Walt Disney Resort *Value*   Even after a recent $6 million facelift, this former Courtyard by Marriott is currently in the midst of extensive renovations to make it even more family friendly. The hotel is due to reopen in 2006, but be sure to contact the hotel to find out the status of the renovations.. The rooms will comfortably sleep four, and the resort offers many of the usual amenities found at a typical Holiday Inn, including a kids' pool, casual onsite dining, a "kids eat free" program, and others. For a great view of the Magic Kingdom's fireworks display, a room on the west side is best, and the higher up, the better (floors 8–14 are the best).

1805 Hotel Plaza Blvd. (between Lake Buena Vista Dr. and Apopka–Vineland Rd./Hwy. 535), Lake Buena Vista, FL 32830. ✆ 800/223-9930 or 407/828-8888. Fax 407/827-4623. www.downtowndisneyhotels.com, www.holidayinnwdw.com, or www.hiorlando.com. 323 units. $86–$129 double. Children 17 and under stay free in parent's room. AE, DC, DISC, MC, V. Free parking. **Amenities:** Restaurant; 2 lounges; "kids eat free" program; 2 heated outdoor pools; kids' pool; Jacuzzi; playground; arcade; Guest Services desk; complimentary bus service to WDW parks; transportation to non-Disney parks for a fee; car-rental desks; limited room service; laundry service; valet. *In room:* A/C, TV w/pay movies, video games (fee), coffeemaker, hair dryer, iron, safe.

Hotel Royal Plaza *⚘*   The Plaza is one of the boulevard's originals, but renovations over its 25 years (some currently under way) have kept it in relatively good shape. A favorite with budget-minded families, its hallmark is a friendly staff (some of whom have been with the hotel since the beginning) that provides good service. Poolside rooms have balconies and patios; the tower rooms have separate sitting areas, and some offer whirlpool tubs in the bathrooms. All rooms have sleeper sofas. If you want a view from up high, ask for a room facing west and WDW; the south and east sides keep a watchful eye on I-4's gridlock. **Note:** Though the pool area is attractive, located in the courtyard, hidden away from the bustling roadway nearby, there is no kiddie pool at this hotel, so families with very young children might want to look elsewhere.

1905 Hotel Plaza Blvd. (between Buena Vista Dr. and Apopka–Vineland Rd./Hwy. 535), Lake Buena Vista, FL 32830. ✆ 800/248-7890 or 407/828-2828. Fax 407/827-6338. www.royalplaza.com. 394 units. $69–$235 double; $159–$699 suite. Extra person $15. Children 17 and under stay free in parent's room. Rollaway beds not available, cribs free. AE, DC, DISC, MC, V. Free self-parking, valet parking $8. From I-4, take Exit 68, Hwy. 535/Apopka–Vineland Rd., north to Hotel Plaza Blvd., and go left. It's the 2nd hotel on the left. **Amenities:** Restaurant; lounge; outdoor heated pool; 4 lighted tennis courts; fitness center; Jacuzzi; guest services desk; complimentary bus service to WDW parks, transportation for a fee to non-Disney parks; limited room service; guest laundry; nonsmoking rooms. *In room:* A/C, TV w/pay movies, VCR, Nintendo, dataport, minibar, coffeemaker, hair dryer, iron, safe.

4 Other Lake Buena Vista–Area Hotels

The hotels in this section are within a few minutes' drive of the Disney parks (and you'll need a rental car if you stay at them). They offer great location but not Disney-related privileges given to guests in the "official" hotels, such as Disney bus service and character breakfasts. On the flip side, because you're not paying for those privileges, hotels in this category are generally a shade less expensive for comparable rooms and services.

Note: These hotels are also listed on the "Walt Disney World & Lake Buena Vista Accommodations" map in this chapter.

VERY EXPENSIVE

Gaylord Palms ✹✹✹   This Central Florida star may be a convention center, but it appeals to family vacationers, too, and it's not your run-of-the-mill resort. It could be considered a destination unto itself, offering its own entertainment, fabulous dining, shops, and recreational facilities. The 4½-acre octagonal Grand Atrium, topped by a glass dome, surrounds a miniature version of the Castillo de San Marcos, the old fort at St. Augustine. Waterfalls, lush foliage, and a rocky landscape complete the feel. Kids of all ages will likely find it worth exploring and definitely impressive—especially when they learn that humans aren't the only inhabitants of the Gaylord Palms. **"The Best of Florida LIVE"** is an ongoing exhibition that includes Gator Springs, where 15 juvenile alligators (you can actually feed them by hand) and 30 species of turtles lurk in the swamps; **Sawgrass Place** is home to four species of Florida snakes and baby alligators (known as grunts); tarpon, redfish, and snook swim about a coral reef in the **Key West's 161,000-gallon indoor ocean;** and the waterways in the eerily foggy **Everglades** are filled with bluefish, tilapia, gar, catfish, pickerel, largemouth bass, and oscars.

The resort and its rooms are divided into themes: Emerald Bay, a 362-room hotel within the hotel, has an elegant air; St. Augustine captures the essence of America's oldest city; Key West delivers the laid-back ambience of Florida's southernmost city; and the Everglades uses a misty swamp, snarling faux gator, fiber-optic fireflies, and tin-roofed shanties to muster a wild-and-woolly air. The rooms are spacious, beautifully decorated, and well appointed (the soundproofing, though, could be a bit better); each has its own balcony. The kids' pool features a huge eight-legged octopus water slide, and cabanas at the adult pool have Internet access. As is befitting a luxury resort, the service is impeccable, yet it's also extremely friendly and welcoming, not standoffish, as is the case at many other resorts of this class.

An entirely new adult recreation complex recently opened, featuring a large croquet lawn; beach volleyball court; bocce court; shuffleboard court; and The Green, a 9-hole, lighted putting green.

At 4,000-square feet, **La Petite Academy,** a branch of the well-known child-care center chain available only to resort guests ($10 per child per hour, no minimum, ages 3–14, ✆ **407/586-2505**), offers a ton of LEGO fun; a karaoke stage; an art studio; and Sega, PlayStation, and Nintendo games. The kids' **Marine Activity pool** has an octopus slide and beach play areas, and cabanas at the adult pool have Internet access. And if you need to unwind further, try the 20,000-square-foot branch of the famous **Canyon Ranch Spa.** My biggest gripe: Room-to-room and room-to-hall soundproofing should be better in this classy resort.

6000 Osceola Pkwy., Kissimmee, FL 34747. ✆ **877/677-9352** or 407/586-0000. Fax 407/239-4822. www.gaylord palms.com. 1,406 units. $239–$450 double; $625–$2,700 suites. $ Resort fee $10. Extra person $20. Kids under 18 stay free in parent's room. Rollaway beds $30/night; cribs free. AE, DC, DISC, MC, V. Self-parking $7; valet $15. **Amenities:** 5 restaurants; 4 lounges; golf (nearby); 2 outdoor heated pools; fitness center; spa; supervised children's center; concierge; tour desk; car-rental desk; free transportation to Disney parks; transportation to non-Disney parks for a fee; business center; shopping arcade; salon; room service; massage; babysitting; dry cleaning; concierge-level rooms. *In room:* A/C, TV w/pay movies and video games, dataport, coffeemaker, hair dryer, iron, safe.

Tips   Coolest Pools

My favorite hotel splash zone in Orlando is the Hyatt Regency Grand Cypress Resort's half-acre, **800,000-gallon swimming pool,** which has caves, grottoes, waterfalls, and a 45-foot water slide. The runner-up is the JW Marriott's **Lazy River,** a reasonably shallow, slow-current journey around the beautifully land-scaped Grande Lakes property. Other cool pools include the water-park–like pools (there are two) at the **Nickelodeon Family Suites by Holiday Inn,** with flumes, fountains, water guns, and more; **Stormalong Bay,** which is shared by Disney's Beach and Yacht Club resorts; the **Mayan pyramid–themed pool** at WDW's Coronado Springs resort; and the **beach pool,** with its fort and water slide, at Universal's Portofino Bay Hotel.

Hyatt Regency Grand Cypress Resort ⭐⭐⭐ *Finds*   This resort is a favorite of families seeking an upscale resort experience without Mickey Mouse extras. The lobby has lush foliage and several colorful birds, including a **macaw named Lulu** that waves to passersby and naturally attracts youthful attention. The 18-story atrium has inner and outer glass elevators (take the kids for a ride on the outers for a panoramic rush). The rooms are large and comfortable; and rollaways, cribs, bed rails, highchairs, and refrigerators are all available upon request. The rooms on the west side, from floors 7 and up, have a distant view of Cinderella Castle and the Magic Kingdom fireworks.

The Hyatt gets my vote for **Orlando's coolest pool,** a half-acre, 800,000-gallon extravaganza with caves, grottoes, 12 waterfalls, 2 waterslides, and a swinging rope bridge. A sandy beach is nearby surrounding the 21-acre lake, where canoes and paddle-boats are available for rent. Adults and kids will love it! The Hyatt shares a golf club and academy, racquet club, and equestrian center (kids' lessons are available) with its sister, the **Villas of Grand Cypress** (© **800/835-7377** or 407/239-4700; www.grandcypress. com). Younger kids (ages 5–12) can enjoy supervised play and activities (including boating, swimming, arts and crafts, video games, and horse-related activities) at **Camp Gator** (fees apply; lunch or dinner available at an additional cost).

1 N. Jacaranda (off Hwy. 535), Orlando, FL 32836. © **800/233-1234** or 407/239-1234. Fax 407/239-3800. www. hyattgrandcypress.com. 750 units. $279–$585 double; $695–$5,750 suite. Optional $13 daily resort fee (includes health club, free local calls, daily newspaper, and in-room coffee). Extra person $25. Children 18 and under stay free in parent's room. Rollaway beds and cribs free. AE, DC, DISC, MC, V. Free parking, valet $12. **Amenities:** 4 restaurants; 4 lounges; large heated outdoor pool; 45 holes of golf; 12 tennis courts (5 lighted); health club; 2 racquetball courts; spa; watersports equipment; children's center; arcade; concierge; car-rental desk; free Disney shuttle; transportation to non-Disney parks for a fee; store; salon; 24-hr. room service; in-room massage; babysitting; laundry service; valet; concierge-level rooms; equestrian center. *In room:* A/C, TV, dataport, minibar, hair dryer, iron, safe.

Marriott's Orlando World Center ⭐⭐ *Finds*   Often mistakenly overlooked by families, the World Center Marriott offers not only beautifully appointed rooms, but also an array of fun and unique recreational activities for kids of all ages. Surprisingly and somewhat unexpectedly, this resort is one of a very few that cater to both the business traveler and to families—and does it rather impressively. The lobby's centerpiece is a 28-story tower fronted by flowers and fountains. The large, comfortable, and beautifully decorated rooms sleep four, and the higher poolside floors offer views of Disney. For a large-scale resort, it is surprisingly easy to get around, as it is not spread out so much as up. The largest of its five pools has water slides and waterfalls surrounded by plenty of space to relax among the palm trees and tropical plants. There's plenty of dining right on site, ranging from counter service casual to fine dining; the **Mikado Japanese Steakhouse** (p. 156) headlines the hotel's four restaurants. The location, only 2 miles from the Disney parks, is a fabulous plus. The resort often offers deals and discounts that are especially family friendly; past deals have included a great two-room package, as well as special packages with the parks (most notably with SeaWorld and Discovery Cove).

8701 World Center Dr. (on Hwy. 536 between I-4 and Hwy. 535), Orlando, FL 32821. (℃ **800/621-0638** or 407/239-4200. Fax 407/238-8777. www.worldsbestvacation.com. 2,111 units. $159–$410 for up to 5; $750–$1,600 suite. Children 17 and under stay free in parent's room. Rollaway beds and cribs free. AE, DC, DISC, MC, V. Free self-parking, valet $16. **Amenities:** 4 restaurants; 2 lounges; 3 heated outdoor pools; heated indoor pool; kids' pool; 18-hole golf course; 8 lighted tennis courts; health club; spa; whirlpool; sauna; concierge; car-rental desk; transportation to all theme parks for a fee; business center; salon; 24-hr. room service; massage; babysitting; laundry service. *In room:* A/C, TV w/pay movies, dataport, minibar, coffeemaker, hair dryer, iron, safe.

Ritz-Carlton Orlando, Grande Lakes 🏰🏰🏰   Orlando's newest destination for deep-pocketed travelers opened in July 2003, part of a 500-acre complex that also includes a JW Marriott (see below). The posh resort's many kid-friendly options make it an attractive choice for families with plenty of extra cash. The grounds are beautiful; and the entrance and lobby area have the feel of an Italian palazzo; and kids get their own separate check-in desk and welcome kit.

All rooms have a balcony and two sinks, hand-painted Italian furniture, and plenty of room to move around in. (Kids won't mind zoning out in front of the 27-in. flat-screen TV.) The hotel will provide highchairs, cribs, rollaways, and strollers for kids on request (some for an extra fee). If you call in advance, the staff will childproof the electrical outlets in your room and remove alcoholic drinks from the minibar. Kids Suites feature a separate but adjoining room, impeccably decorated and including twin trundle beds, a closet stocked with games, a video-game system, TV, separate bathroom, pint-size table and chairs, and milk and cookies waiting upon arrival. Rooms on the west side, especially on floors 6 through 14, offer a distant view of SeaWorld and its brief nighttime fireworks, as well as the resort's pool, golf course, waterways, and woodlands. In addition to use of the resort's pools, guests can enjoy those at the JW Marriott, including the **Lazy River.** Additionally, the resort has a 40,000-square-foot, full-service spa.

The **Ritz-Kids program** has two options: an hourly one ($10 per hour per child, including snacks and beverages, no minimum, ages 4–13, 9am–10pm) and a full-day one ($55 per child, dinner included, no minimum, ages 4–13, 2–10pm). Activities include swimming, nature walks, Frisbee games, junior tennis, croquet, and more. There's a nanny service ($20 per hour for up to three kids). There's also a 75-minute **Golf Fore Kids Etiquette Class** ($25, including drinks, snack, and gift, ages 5–12, Sun and Wed) that teaches youngsters some of the sport's rules.

4012 Central Florida Pkwy. (at intersection with John Young Pkwy.), Orlando, FL 32837. (℃ **800/241-3333,** 800/576-5760, or 407/206-2400. Fax 407/206-2401. www.grandelakes.com. 584 units. $229–$399 double; $599–$5,000 suite. Extra person $30. Children 17 and under stay free in parent's room. Rollaway beds $15/night, cribs free. AE, DC, DISC, MC, V. Self-parking $8, valet $15. From I-4, take Exit 72, Hwy. 528/Bee Line Expwy. east to the John Young Pkwy., then south to Central Florida Pkwy. **Amenities:** 3 restaurants; cafe; snack bar; 2 lounges; outdoor heated pool; kids' pool; 18 holes of golf; 3 tennis courts (lighted); spa; health club; children's center; arcade; playground; concierge; free transportation to Universal and SeaWorld, transportation to Disney parks for a fee; business center; car-rental desk; salon; 24-hr. room service; babysitting; valet; nonsmoking rooms; concierge-level rooms. *In room:* A/C, TV, dataport, minibar, iron, safe.

EXPENSIVE

JW Marriott Orlando, Grande Lakes ⊛⊛   This less-expensive sister of the Ritz-Carlton Orlando (see above) is another smoke-free resort with one of the niftiest pools in Orlando, a 24,000-square-foot **Lazy River** pool that takes you on a slow, winding, tropical journey through rock formations and small waterfalls (depth 3–5 ft.). Standard rooms at the Moorish-theme resort are on par with those in Disney's moderate class and are in tiptop condition. Those on the west side, especially on floors 6 through 26, offer a distant view of SeaWorld and its brief nighttime fireworks, as well as the resort's pool, golf course, waterways, and woodlands. The hotel's playground has a sandbox where young kids like to hang out. JW junior guests are eligible for the **Ritz Kids program** and **Golf Fore Kids Etiquette Class** at the Ritz-Carlton Orlando (see above). Additionally, the two properties share pool, spa, golf, and tennis amenities.

4040 Central Florida Pkwy. (at intersection with John Young Pkwy.), Orlando, FL 32837. ℂ 800/241-3333, 800/576-5750, or 407/206-2300. Fax 407/206-2301. www.grandelakes.com. 1,000 units. $189–$369 double, $299–$4,000 suites. Extra person $25. Children 17 and under stay free in parent's room. Rollaway beds $15/night, cribs free. AE, DC, DISC, MC, V. Self-parking $8, valet $15. From I-4, take Exit 72, Hwy. 528/Bee Line Expwy. east to the John Young Pkwy., then south to Central Florida Pkwy. **Amenities:** 3 restaurants (Italian, French, American); cafe; lounge; 2 outdoor heated pools; kids' pool; 18 holes of golf; 3 tennis courts (lighted); spa; health club; children's center; arcade; playground; concierge; free transportation to Universal and SeaWorld, transportation to Disney parks for a fee; business center; car-rental desk; salon; 24-hr. room service; babysitting; nonsmoking rooms. *In room:* A/C, TV, dataport, minibar, coffeemaker, hair dryer, iron, safe.

MODERATE

Embassy Suites Lake Buena Vista ⊛   Set near the end of Palm Parkway, just off Apopka–Vineland, this fun and welcoming all-suite resort is close to all the action of Downtown Disney and the surrounding area, yet remains a quiet retreat. Each suite sleeps five and includes a separate living area (with a pullout sofa) and sleeping quarters. The roomy accommodations make it a great choice for families. Some of the other perks here include a complimentary cooked-to-order breakfast and a daily manager's reception.

⌐Tips Marriott Montage

The December 2000 christening of **Marriott Village at Little Lake Bryan,** 8623 Vineland Ave., Orlando, FL 32821 (ℂ 877/682-8552 or 407/938-9001; fax 407/938-9002; www.marriottvillage.com), brought together three of the flagship's properties in a cluster just east of Lake Buena Vista, 3 miles from WDW. No matter what your budget is, you'll likely find a room here that satisfies your needs. The resort includes a 400-room SpringHill Suites ($99–$179 double), a 388-room Fairfield Inn ($69–$119 double), and a 312-room Courtyard by Marriott ($104–$149 double). Children under 17 stay free in parent's room, and an extra person costs an additional $10.

All rooms have fridges. Each property has adult and kids' pools and activities, fitness centers, whirlpools, and guest-services desks. All offer transportation for a fee ($10–$12 per person per day) to Disney parks and non-Disney parks. There are three restaurants within walking distance. To get there, take I-4 Exit 68, Highway 535/Apopka–Vineland Road; then head south to Vineland, and go left ½ mile to the village. There's free self-parking, and valet parking costs $8.

> ### ⟨Tips⟩ Special Delivery
>
> **Gooding's Supermarkets** (✆ **407/827-1200**; www.goodings.com) offers grocery delivery service to theme park–area hotels in Lake Buena Vista, Disney, Celebration, I-Drive, and Kissimmee. There is a $50 minimum, and a $10 service charge is added to all orders. You can order groceries (but no alcohol) online up to 48 hours before your requested delivery date (delivery hours are between 9am–6pm). For details, see the website or call. This is a great service if you are staying in a hotel room with kitchen facilities, or if you have kids and want to stock your room with snacks and supplies.

8100 Lake Avenue, Orlando, Fl 32836. (✆ **800/257-8483**, or 407/239-1144. Fax 407/238-0230. www.embassysuites orlando.com. 333 units. $129–$229, Extra person (over 6-person maximum) $15. Rates include full breakfast. AE, DC, DISC, MC, V. Free self-parking, valet $7. Pets accepted. **Amenities:** Restaurant; cafe; lounge; indoor and outdoor heated pools; kids pool and play area; whirlpool and sauna; fitness center; tennis court; basketball court; business center; high-speed Internet access, laundry service; room service; free shuttle to Disney parks. *In room:* A/C, TV w/pay movies, dataport, fridge, microwave, safe, hairdryer, iron.

Hawthorn Suites Lake Buena Vista ✦ ⟨Value⟩

One of the features that is most appealing about this 5-year-old property is a floor plan that allows separation of kids and adults, which allows Mom and Dad some (relative) private time. Its 500-square-foot standard rooms have four areas: a living room with a sleeper sofa, chair, and TV; bedroom with recliner and TV; full kitchen with dining room table for four; and bathroom with vanity. Two-bedroom units are also available. I think the extras here are a big plus for families, too. The Hawthorn offers a free American breakfast buffet daily, a social hour (hors d'oeuvres, beverages, and snacks) Monday through Thursday, and a light meal on Wednesday evenings. The pool is small, but it's downright restful compared with the pools at some other hotels. The atmosphere is friendly; the service is good; and it's just 3 minutes from Hotel Plaza Boulevard. All in all, this is an excellent value choice, especially for those on a budget.

8303 Palm Pkwy. Orlando, FL 32836. (✆ **800/936-9417**, 800/527-1133, or 407/597-5000. Fax 407/597-6000. www. hawthornsuiteslbv.com. 120 units. $99–$169 for o 6 guests (8 in a 2-bedroom suite). Rates include full breakfast. Rollaway beds $10/night, cribs free. AE, DC, DISC, MC, V. Free self-parking. **Amenities:** Outdoor heated pool; exercise room; basketball court; Jacuzzi; free shuttle to Disney parks; transportation to non-Disney parks for a fee; laundry service; valet. *In room:* A/C, TV w/pay movies, dataport, kitchen, fridge, microwave, coffeemaker, hair dryer, iron.

Holiday Inn Sunspree Resort Lake Buena Vista ✦✦

Just a mile from the Disney parks, this is another hotel that caters to kids big time. They get their own check-in desk, a welcome from raccoon mascots Max and Maxine (who will tuck them in at night for a nominal fee if you make a reservation), and a fun bag with a video-game coupon and lollipop. The hotel's 231 Kid Suites have beds for up to six (bunk beds are placed in a separate sleeping area for children, which also has Nintendo video games) and themes (a jail, a fort, a space capsule, and more). All the suites have kitchenettes. Child-safety kits and outlet covers are provided upon request. If you like sleeping in, ask for a room that doesn't face the pool area (a delightful spot that's very popular with the young set).

Camp Holiday offers kids ($5 per child per hour, no minimum, ages 4–12, 11am–10pm) activities such as games, movies, arts and crafts, magic shows, and karaoke. Parents get a beeper so they can be reached easily if necessary. Free movies are also shown daily in the Castle Theater. Note also that kids under 12 eat free when accompanied by adults, though it isn't fine dining.

13351 Apopka–Vineland Rd./Hwy. 535 (between Hwy. 536 and I-4), Lake Buena Vista, FL 32821. ✆ **800/366-6299** or 407/239-4500. Fax 407/239-7713. www.kidsuites.com. 507 units. $99–$149 standard for up to 4; $119–$179 Kid Suite. Children 17 and under stay free in parent's room. Rollaway beds $10/night; cribs free. AE, DISC, MC, V. Free self-parking. Pets under 25 pounds $25. **Amenities:** Restaurant; food court; mini mart; outdoor heated pool; kids' pool; fitness center; Jacuzzi; playground; supervised children's center (fee); family activities; children's movie theater; arcade; Guest Services desk; free shuttle to Disney parks, transportation to non-Disney parks for a fee; limited room service; laundry service; valet. *In room:* A/C, TV/VCR, fridge, microwave, coffeemaker, hair dryer, iron, safe.

Homewood Suites Orlando ⊛   These moderately priced family suites are less than 2 miles from Disney, close to Downtown Disney. This hotel is a good choice if you want a little home-style comfort and the chance to perform do-it-yourself stuff in the fully equipped kitchen. The hotel has been kept up well over the years, so everything is still in good shape. The two-bedroom suites sleep up to six, offering a decent amount of room. A complimentary social hour (hors d'oeuvres, beer, and wine) that's good for Mom and Dad is held Monday through Thursday.

8200 Palm Pkwy. (off S. Apopka–Vineland Rd./Hwy. 535), Orlando, FL 32836. ✆ **800/225-5466** or 407/465-8200. Fax 407/465-0200. www.homewood-suites.com. $109–$199 double. Extra person $15. Rates include continental breakfast. Children 18 and under stay free in parent's room. Rollaway beds and cribs free. AE, DC, DISC, MC, V. Free self-parking. **Amenities:** Minigrocery; outdoor heated pool; exercise room; Jacuzzi; game room; concierge; car-rental desk; free shuttle to Disney parks, transportation to non-Disney parks for a fee; business center; babysitting; laundry service; valet; safe deposit boxes; pizza delivery. *In room:* A/C, TV/VCR w/pay movies, dataport, fully equipped/stocked kitchen, fridge, microwave, coffeemaker, hair dryer, iron, daily newspaper.

Nickelodeon Family Suites Resort by Holiday Inn ⊛⊛ *Finds* *Kids*   This all-suite property, a former Holiday Inn transformed into the first-ever Nickelodeon-branded resort, is one of the best properties in the Orlando area for families. Its two-bedroom Kid Suites feature a second bedroom for the kids with either bunk or twin beds, minikitchens, and a pullout sofa in the living area. Three-bedroom suites are also available and include more space, a second bathroom, and a full kitchen. Renovations were completed and the resort officially opened in May 2005 with an all-new lobby, an activity center full of restaurants, an arcade, shops, nightly entertainment, and redecorated rooms—all themed with Nickelodeon colors and characters. The resort's two pool areas are veritable water parks, with extensive multilevel water slides, flumes, climbing nets, and water jets. Activities are scheduled poolside, and there are also a wide variety of recreational options, including a small minigolf course, playgrounds, and sand play areas. A daily character breakfast is offered in addition to the hotel's regular breakfast buffet (at the latter, kids eat free with paying adults). There's even a spa that caters to kids!

Don't Worry; Dinners Delivered

For those of you who can't stand the thought of heading out to dinner after a long day at the parks, **Take Out Express** is a restaurant delivery service that will bring dinner to you from 4:30 to 11pm daily. Simply check out its list of participating restaurants in the area (and there are plenty of favorites to choose among) and order from their menu, and your meal will be on its way. There is a charge of $5 per restaurant (you can order from more than just one), as well as the price of your order (and don't forget to tip). Call ✆ **407/352–1170** to order or for more information.

14500 Continental Gateway (off Hwy. 536), Lake Buena Vista, FL 32821. © **877/387-5437**, 407/387-5437, or 866/GO2-NICK. Fax 407/387-1489. www.hifamilysuites.com or www.nickhotel.com. 800 units. $169–$275 suite. Children 17 and under stay free in parent's room. Rollaway beds not available, cribs free. AE, DC, DISC, MC, V. Free self-parking. **Amenities:** Restaurant; lounge; several fast-food counters; minimarket; 2 water park pools; minigolf course; fitness center; 2 Jacuzzis; 3 outdoor Ping-Pong tables; 2 shuffleboard courts; game room; complimentary recreation center for ages 4–12; tour desk; free shuttle to Disney and non-Disney parks; coin-op washers and dryers. *In room:* A/C, TV w/pay movies and VCR (some w/Nintendo), dataport, full kitchen (select suites), fridge, microwave, coffeemaker, hair dryer, iron, safe.

Staybridge Suites Lake Buena Vista ★★   This chain hotel is located just off Apopka–Vineland, close to the action of Downtown Disney and the theme parks, as well as many restaurants. An excellent choice for families, this hotel's room sizes, price, and friendly staff are three more good reasons to stay here. Featured are one- and two-bedroom suites (can sleep up to eight), all with full kitchens (some two-bedroom suites have two bathrooms). The suites have large, comfortable, separate living areas when compared with those in other all-suite hotels. A particularly unique plus to this property is the complimentary grocery shopping service offered. You can check off items on the list and drop it off at the front desk, and your items will be delivered you—even if you are not in your room. Prices run about 50¢ to $1.50 higher than those you'll find at the supermarket, but the convenience factor often makes the expense worth it for time-strapped families.

8751 Suiteside Drive, Orlando Fl. 32836. © **800/866-4549** or 407/238-0777. Fax 407/238-2640. www.ichotelsgroup. com. 150 units. $159–$299. Children 17 and under stay free in parent's room. Rates include continental breakfast. Rollaway beds not available, cribs free. AE, DC, DISC, MC, V. **Amenities:** Deli; convenience store; outdoor heated pool; children's pool; 24-hr. exercise room; Jacuzzi; 24-hr. game room; free shuttle to Disney parks; Guest Services desk; 24-hr. laundry service; nonsmoking rooms; accessible suites; complimentary grocery delivery service. *In room:* A/C, TV/VCR, kitchen, dataport, hair dryer, ironing board, iron, safe.

INEXPENSIVE

Hampton Inn Lake Buena Vista   Location rules at this modern property, which is only 1 mile from the entrance to Hotel Plaza Boulevard on the northeast corner of Disney. It's not fancy, but the price is right, and there are lots of nearby places to eat, shop, and party. It's also relatively close to Downtown Disney Marketplace. Rooms on the fourth or fifth floors have microwaves and minifridges; request one, and ask if the rate is higher than for a room on a lower floor. Some connecting rooms (useful for larger families) are available. The amoeba-shaped pool is nothing special, but it'll cool you off when you need it.

8150 Palm Pkwy., Orlando, FL 32836. © **800/370-9259** or 407/465-8150. Fax 407/465-0150. www.hamptoninnlbv.com. 147 units. $69–$149 for up to 4. 5th person $10. Rates include continental breakfast. Children 17 and under stay free in parent's room. Rollaway beds $10/night, cribs free. AE, DC, DISC, MC, V. Free self-parking. From I-4, take Exit 68, Hwy. 535/Apopka–Vineland Rd., east to Palm Pkwy., then right ¼ mile to hotel. **Amenities:** Outdoor heated pool; Jacuzzi; guest services desk; free shuttle to Disney parks; transportation to non-Disney parks for a fee; nonsmoking rooms. *In room:* A/C, TV w/pay movies, dataport, coffeemaker, hair dryer, iron.

5 Places to Stay in the Kissimmee Area

This stretch of highway (U.S. 192, also known as Irlo Bronson Memorial Highway) is within close proximity of the Disney parks. Over the past few years, a revitalization of the area has added such features as extrawide sidewalks, streetlamps, highway markers, and widened roads to make it a more friendly and appealing area to stay and play. Traffic here can nevertheless be frustrating, especially when you are trying to cross the street. Budget hotels and restaurants abound, though a few higher-priced luxury resorts are starting to appear a bit off the main drag. While Disney is close by, Universal and SeaWorld are not; they are a good 20-minute (or more) ride away. If you don't have a car, Mears Transportation (see "Getting Around," in chapter 3) is a good bet to take you there for about $15 to $20 per person, per day, round-trip.

In addition to the hotels reviewed below, the **Double Tree Resort Orlando Villas At Maingate,** 4787 West Irlo Bronson Hwy. (© **407/397-0555;** www.doubletree.com), offers spacious one-, two-, and three-bedroom town house accommodations with kitchens that are great for families and larger groups. The **Quality Suites Maingate East,** 5876 W. Irlo Bronson Hwy. (© **800/848-4148** or 407/396-8040; www.choice hotels.com), offers suites with separate bedroom and living areas, and fully stocked kitchens. *Note:* You'll find the hotels and motels described on the map "Kissimmee Area Accommodations," on p. 107.

EXPENSIVE

The Reunion Resort & Club of Orlando
This luxury resort community is still in its early phases (with a completion date set for some 10 years into the future). Currently, only the villas and some vacation homes (both available for rent to visitors) are open. The spectacular villas feature a rather unique layout. Bedrooms are located on the ground level, with the main living area and additional bedrooms on the second level (making it less likely that you'll have to drag your luggage up a flight of stairs). Some of the villas have private patios or balconies; some of the vacation homes (good for larger or extended families) have their own private pools. An extensive on-site water park opened (other pools are located throughout the property) in the summer of 2005 and includes a wave pool, water slide, lagoon, and waterfalls. Two championship golf courses are already operational. A kids' program offering a variety of supervised activities is set to begin in 2006. On the downside: The property charges an exorbitantly high "gratuity" fee.

1000 Reunion Way © 888/418-9611 or 407/662-1000. Fax 407/662-1111. www.reunionresort.com. Eventually 8,000 units. $255–$495 villas, $305–$835 homes. 9.6% gratuity fee assessed on total bill. Rollaway beds and cribs free. Free self-parking. **Amenities:** Numerous pools; water park; 3 golf courses; kids program. *In room:* A/C, TV w/pay movies, DVD/CD player, dataport, fully stocked kitchen, microwave, fridge, coffeemaker, hair dryer, iron/ironing board, safe, washer/dryer.

MODERATE

Comfort Suites Maingate East
Set back from the main drag, this fairly new and welcoming hotel is one of the nicest in the area. The lobby and accommodations—consisting of studio and one-bedroom suites—are bright and inviting. The main pool and the children's pool, with an umbrella fountain to keep everyone cool, are open around the clock. For entertainment, Old Town (a small-scale shopping, dining, and entertainment complex) is next door, and a great miniature golf course is located just in front of the property.

2775 Florida Plaza Blvd., Kissimmee, Fl 34746. © 888/782-9772 or 407/397-7848. Fax 407/396-7045. www. comfortsuitesfl.com. 198 units. $65–$150 double. Extra person $10. Rates include continental breakfast. Children 17 and under stay free in parent's room. Rollaway beds not available, cribs free. AE, DC, DISC, MC, V. Free self-parking. **Amenities:** Outdoor heated pool; kids' pool; fitness center; game room; concierge; free shuttle to Disney, Universal, and SeaWorld parks; business center; laundry service. *In room:* A/C, TV, dataport, refrigerator, microwave, coffeemaker, hair dryer, iron, safe.

Kissimmee Area Accommodations

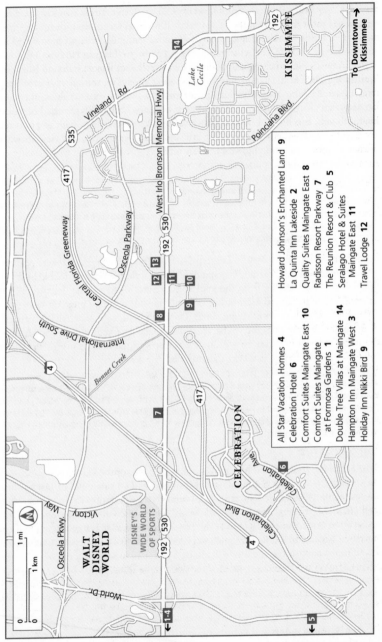

All Star Vacation Homes **4**
Celebration Hotel **6**
Comfort Suites Maingate East **10**
Comfort Suites Maingate at Formosa Gardens **1**
Double Tree Villas at Maingate **14**
Hampton Inn Maingate West **3**
Holiday Inn Nikki Bird **9**

Howard Johnson's Enchanted Land **9**
La Quinta Inn Lakeside **2**
Quality Suites Maingate East **8**
Radisson Resort Parkway **7**
The Reunion Resort & Club **5**
Seralago Hotel & Suites Maingate East **11**
Travel Lodge **12**

To Downtown → Kissimmee

Holiday Inn Nikki Bird   Spread out over 26 acres, this family-friendly resort has one of the most extensive array of recreational facilities in its class, including three pools, two toddler pools with squirting fountains, tennis courts, and more. And it's only a mile from the WDW entrance to boot. Thanks to the great landscaping, you'll never know it's located along one of the busiest stretches of highway around (the location's a big plus, as the dining and entertainment choices in this area are practically boundless). KidSuite rooms offer a separate children's sleeping area, video games, and an additional TV. Kids can play at the supervised Camp Nikki ($8 per child per hour, no minimum, ages 4–14, 11am–10pm), offering outdoor activities, such as tennis and sandcastle building, as well as indoor arts and crafts, games, and movies, all while Mom and Dad relax and enjoy some adult time.

7300 West U.S. 192, Kissimmee, Fl 34747. (C) **407/396-7300.** Fax 407/396-9196. www.holiday-inn.com. 530 units. $99–$149, extra person no charge. Children 17 and under stay free in parent's room. Rollaway beds not available, cribs free. AE, DC, DISC, MC, V. Free self-parking. **Amenities:** 2 restaurants; 1 lounge; snack/convenience store; 3 heated pools; 2 children's pools; 3 lighted tennis courts; fitness center; basketball; volleyball; horseshoes; playground; supervised children's activity center; video game room; concierge; car-rental desk; free transportation to WDW parks; laundry service; valet; safety deposit boxes. *In room:* A/C, TV w/pay movies, video games, dataport, mini fridge, microwave, coffeemaker, hair dryer, iron/ironing board, safe, CD player (in some).

Radisson Resort Parkway   Located 1½ miles from Disney, this 20-acre property was last renovated in 2001 and has standard motel-style rooms (two double beds or a king) with views ranging from the pool or courtyard to the parking lot. Aside from the reasonable prices and location, its offerings include a dining program where kids 10 and under eat free with paying adults The main pool, with waterfalls and a water slide (and a wading pool for young kids), will make sure your children won't mind spending cost-cutting time away from the parks. And the hotel is one of the few to offer free shuttle service to all the major parks.

2900 Parkway Blvd., Kissimmee, FL 34747. (C) **800/333-3333** or 407/396-7000. Fax 407/396-6792. www.radisson parkway.com. 718 units. $89–$129 for up to 5. Rollaway beds $12/night, cribs free. AE, DC, DISC, MC, V. Free self-parking. From I-4, take Exit 64A/U.S. 192 east to 1st light, Parkway Blvd., then left. **Amenities:** 2 outdoor heated pools; kids' pool; 2 lighted tennis courts; exercise room; arcade; playground; free shuttle to Disney, Universal, and SeaWorld parks; limited room service; babysitting; guest laundry; nonsmoking rooms. *In room:* A/C, TV w/movies, dataport, minibar, coffeemaker, hair dryer, iron, safe.

INEXPENSIVE

The accommodations listed here may at times lack a lot of the kid-friendly amenities, but they help stretch a family budget. Most are within a few miles of Disney, have rooms in the 300-square-foot range, and arrange transportation to the parks. Many sell attractions tickets, ***but be careful:*** Many deeply discounted ticket offers are too good to be true. Some folks land at the parks with *invalid tickets* or waste a half day or more listening to a timeshare pitch to get 30% to 40% off the regular price (single-day Disney-park tickets are $52 for adults, $42 for kids 3–9). If a discount is more than $2 to $5 per ticket, it's probably too good to be true.

Tips **Coming Soon**

Four Seasons Hotels and Resorts has purchased 400 acres in Celebration, with plans to build a 425-room hotel with an 18-hole golf course. The site will also have single-family homes.

Stick to buying tickets through the parks, or accept the modest discounts offered by such groups as AAA, AARP, and the visitor information centers listed in chapter 2.

Comfort Suites Maingate at Formosa Gardens (Value)

Just across the street from the La Quinta Inn Lakeside (see below) and up the road from WDW, this clean, comfortable place to stay has kept itself modern and in good shape. The "suites" have a small dividing wall slightly separating the living area from the sleeping quarters, but the illusion of privacy is there. Accommodations are a bit bigger than most and can squeeze in up to six. A bit of tropical landscaping gives it an inviting atmosphere and shelters guests from busy U.S. 192. At least 10 restaurants and a small shopping plaza are within walking distance, and there's a miniature-golf course right across the street.

7888 W. Irlo Bronson Memorial Hwy. (U.S. 192), Kissimmee, FL 34747. © **888/390-9888** or 407/390-9888. Fax 407/390-09811607. www.kisscomfortsuite.com. 150 units. $50–$150. Rates include continental breakfast. Children 17 and under stay free in parent's room. Rollaway beds not available, cribs free. AE, DC, DISC, MC, V. Free self-parking. **Amenities:** Bar; outdoor heated pool; kids' pool; Jacuzzi; arcade; car-rental/Guest Services desk; free shuttle to Disney, Universal, SeaWorld, and Wet 'n Wild parks; laundry service. *In room:* A/C, TV, dataport, coffeemaker, fridge, microwave, hair dryer, iron, safe.

Hampton Inn Maingate West

Built in late 1997, this inn still has a newer, nicer feel, because its upkeep is good and it doesn't have the battle scars usually found in U.S.-192 accommodations. While it's more expensive than some in its class, it's also much more modern and upbeat. The inn is located 1½ miles west of the WDW entrance road. Rates include a free continental breakfast and cookies and milk in the lobby at night.

3000 Maingate Lane, Kissimmee, FL 34747. © **800/936-9417** or 407/396-6300. Fax 407/396-8989. www.hamptoninnmaingatewest.com. 118 units. $69–$119 double. Extra person $10. Children 17 and under stay free in parent's room. Rollaway beds $10/night, cribs free. AE, DC, DISC, MC, V. Free self-parking. From I-4, take Exit 64B/U.S. 192 west 3 miles, then right on Maingate Lane (across the street from Celebration). **Amenities:** Outdoor heated pool; guest services desk; free shuttle to Disney parks, transportation to non-Disney parks for a fee; nonsmoking rooms. *In room:* A/C, TV, dataport, fridge, coffeemaker, iron, microwave.

La Quinta Inn Lakeside (★★ (Kids) (Value)

The hand-painted exteriors, lobby, and common areas of this hotel give it a unique charm not found in its hotel brethren. Just up the road from the Disney entrance, this 24-acre resort looks deceptively small when you first pull up (most of the accommodations are hidden behind the lobby area), but amenities include numerous recreational options (pools, playgrounds, and so on), a food court, a good-size convenience store, and a bountiful free breakfast. Rooms are standard in size and offerings but are nicely decorated and will comfortably sleep four. Other pluses include a child-care facility and free transport to all the major theme parks.

7769 Irlo Bronson Memorial Hwy. (U.S. 192), Kissimmee, FL 34747. © **800/531-5900** or 407/396-2222. Fax 407/396-7087. www.laquintainnlakeside.com. 651 units. $59–$139 double. Extra person $10. Rates include continental breakfast. Children 17 and under stay free in parent's room. Rollaway beds $10/night, cribs free. Discount packages available. Small pets accepted ($25 fee). AE, DC, DISC, MC, V. Free self-parking. **Amenities:** 2 restaurants; food court; 3 outdoor heated pools; 2 kids' pools; small minigolf; 2 tennis courts; exercise room; Jacuzzi; playgrounds; kids activities; Guest Services desk; free bus to Disney, Universal, and SeaWorld parks; laundry service; valet. *In room:* A/C, TV w/pay movies and PlayStation, dataport, fridge, coffee maker, hair dryer, iron, safe.

Seralago Hotel & Suites Maingate East (★★ (Kids) (Value)

Location (it's just down the road from Disney) and price are just some of the perks at this former Holiday Inn. The revamped hotel sports new colors and a bright new look but still features themed KidSuites with separate sleeping areas for your tots, as well as standard rooms and regular two-room suites. The rooms provide a reasonable amount of space for a family of five, with the two-room units sleeping up to eight. There are plenty of family recreational

> ## *Tips* Homes Away from Home
>
> Some families, especially those who like all the comforts of home or are traveling in groups of five or more, bypass motels in favor of rental condos or homes. Rates vary widely, depending on quality and location, and some may require at least a 2- or 3-night minimum. A lot of these properties are 5 to 15 miles from the theme parks and offer no transportation, so having a car is a necessity.
>
> On the plus side, most have two to six bedrooms and a convertible couch, two or more bathrooms, a full kitchen, multiple TVs and phones, and irons. Some have washers and dryers. Homes often have their own private screen-enclosed pool, while condos have a common one.
>
> On the minus side, they can be lacking in services. Most don't have daily maid service, and restaurants can be as far away as the parks. (There's another reason you'll need a car.) And unless a condo or home is in a gated community, don't expect on-site security. Some properties offer dinnerware, utensils, and salt and pepper shakers; check when you book, as amenities vary widely. Rates range from about $75 to $450 per night ($300–$3,200 per week).
>
> **All Star Vacation Homes** (© **888/249-1779** or 407-997-0733; www.allstar vacationhomes.com) is one of the area's best home and condo rental outfits, with a wide variety of properties to choose among—all of them within a 4-mile radius of Disney. Do check its website; you will be able to see the exact home you are renting, as opposed to a "typical" room. Other popular players include **Holiday Villas** (© 800/344-3959; www.holidayvillas.com), **Summer Bay Resort** (© 888/742-1100; www.summerbayresort.com), **LikiTiki Village** (© 407/239-5000), **Bahama Bay Resort** (© 888/782-9722), and **Cypress Point Orlando** (© 407/597-2700).

activities, from swimming to tennis, and the hotel's movie theater shows free family films nightly. There's a family-friendly food court, and kids 12 and under eat free (two kids per paying adult) in the hotel's cafe.

5678 Irlo Bronson Memorial Hwy. (U.S. 192), Kissimmee, FL 34746. © **800/366-5437** or 407/396-4488. Fax 407/396-8915. www.orlandofamilyfunhotel.com. 614 units. $59–$119 double. Extra person $10. Children 18 and under stay free in parent's room. Rollaway beds $10/night; cribs free. AE, DC, DISC, MC, V. Free self-parking. **Amenities:** Restaurant; food court; convenience store; lounge; 2 outdoor heated pools; toddler pool; 2 tennis courts; exercise room; basketball; volleyball; Jacuzzi; playground; arcade; Guest Services desk; free shuttle to Disney parks, transportation to non-Disney parks for a fee; limited room service; laundry service; small movie theater. *In room:* A/C, TV/VCR, video games, fridge, microwave, coffeemaker, hair dryer, iron, CD players (in some).

6 Places to Stay in the International Drive Area

The hotels and resorts listed here are 7 to 10 miles north of Walt Disney World (via I-4) and 1 to 5 miles from Universal Orlando and SeaWorld. The advantages of staying on I-Drive: It's a destination unto itself, filled with accommodations, restaurants, and small attractions; it has its own inexpensive trolley service (see "Getting Around"

International Drive Area Accommodations

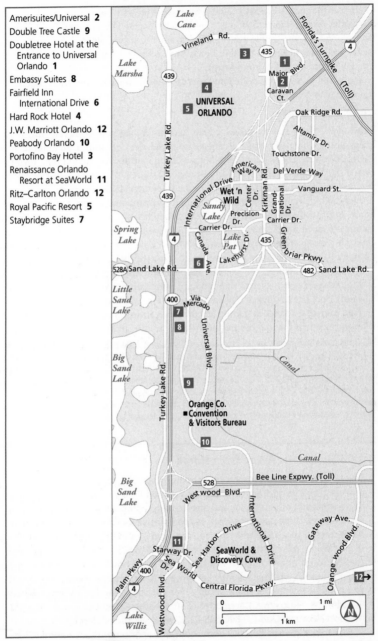

Lake Cane

Lake Marsha

Vineland Rd.

Florida's Turnpike (Toll)

435

Major Blvd.

Caravan Ct.

439

UNIVERSAL ORLANDO

Oak Ridge Rd.

Altamira Dr.

Touchstone Dr.

Del Verde Way

American Way

Vanguard St.

Grand-national Dr.

Kirkman Rd.

Turkey Lake Rd.

International Drive

Wet 'n Wild

Center Dr.

Sandy Lake

Precision Dr.

Carrier Dr.

Carrier Dr.

Greenbriar Pkwy.

439

Spring Lake

Canada Ave.

Lake Pat

Lakehurst Dr.

435

528A Sand Lake Rd.

482 Sand Lake Rd.

Little Sand Lake

400

Via Mercado

Universal Blvd.

Big Sand Lake

Canal

Orange Co. ■ Convention & Visitors Bureau

Turkey Lake Rd.

Canal

Big Sand Lake

528

Bee Line Expwy. (Toll)

Westwood Blvd.

International Drive

Gateway Ave.

Orange wood Blvd.

Starway Dr.

Sea Harbor Drive

SeaWorld & Discovery Cove

Palm Pkwy.

Sea World Dr.

400

4

Westwood Blvd.

Central Florida Pkwy.

Lake Willis

| 0 | | 1 mi |
| 0 | | 1 km |

N

in chapter 3); and it's centrally located for those who want to visit Disney, Universal, SeaWorld, *and* the downtown area. The disadvantages: The north end of I-Drive is badly congested; the shops, motels, eateries, and attractions along this stretch can be tacky; and some of the motels and hotels don't offer free transportation to the parks (the going rate is $6–$15 round-trip).

You'll find these places located on the map "International Drive Area Accommodations," in this section.

VERY EXPENSIVE

Peabody Orlando ✶✶ *Moments*   Kids and fun-loving adults flock to this hotel's main lobby, where five mallards march from the elevators into a fountain daily at 11am, accompanied by John Philip Sousa's "King Cotton March" and their own red-coated duck master (see p. 284 for more on the ducks). The show is just one of the magnets at a grand hotel that has one of the friendliest staffs in Central Florida.

That said, though it's a favorite, the Peabody is primarily a business and convention hotel, and usually sees lots of kids only during school-vacation times, when parents coming to town on business tend to bring their offspring along. This isn't the best choice for the mainstream vacationer, but if you want to stay on I-Drive and do end up here, your kids certainly won't suffer. It's classy without being stuffy, and if your budget allows the splurge, you won't be disappointed. Rooms are large and comfortable, and the west-side rooms (sixth floor and up) offer a distant view of Disney fireworks. The kids' pool has a miniwaterfall, and there are tennis courts for sports-oriented kids.

Tip: Your best chance at getting lower rates is in July and August, when the convention trade falls flat and occupancy drops to as little as 20%.

9801 International Dr. (between Bee Line Expressway and Sand Lake Rd.), Orlando, FL 32819. © 800/732-2639 or 407/352-4000. Fax 407/354-1424. www.peabodyorlando.com. 891 units. $400–$490 standard room for up to 3; $750–$1,700 suite. Extra person $15. Resort fee $8. Children 17 and under stay free in parent's room. Rollaway beds $15/night, cribs free. AE, DC, DISC, MC, V. Free self-parking, valet $10. **Amenities:** 3 restaurants; deli; 3 lounges; outdoor heated pool; kids' pool; 4 lighted tennis courts, instruction available (fee); fitness center; spa; Jacuzzi; game room; concierge; guest-services desk; shuttle to WDW and other parks for a fee; business center; shopping arcade; 24-hr. room service; valet; concierge-level rooms. *In room:* A/C, TV, dataport, minibar, hair dryer.

Smaller Homes Away from Home

Several area timeshare resorts rent rooms or apartments to tourists when the owners aren't using them. The **Disney Vacation Club** (© 407/939-7775; www.dvcresorts.com) offers studios and one- to two-bedroom apartments at its timeshare resorts. Some have small fridges and microwaves; others have full kitchens. Rates start at about $250 per night and can run up to $1,550 per night. Outside Disney World, per-night rack rates begin at $200 to $250 per night for one- and two-bedroom apartments with kitchens. As with hotel rooms, you can get major discounts off the rack rates (as low as $70 a night) for these properties if you do your homework. An especially nice choice is **Sheraton's Vistana Resort** (© 866/208-0003; www.starwoodvo.com). Another good place to look is the **Marriott Vacation Club** (© 800/845-5279; www.vacationclub.com).

One minor caveat: Because each room and apartment that's rented is individually owned, quality can vary, so be sure to specify your exact requirements when booking.

Portofino Bay Hotel   Universal Orlando's premier hotel is as grand as Disney's Grand Floridian (p. 82). It's a replica of Portofino, Italy, with a harbor and canals on which boats travel to the theme parks. The Old World ambience is carried throughout the public areas, restaurants, and rooms by a staff that tries hard to match the Peabody's friendliness.

The luxurious rooms are large (with sleeping space for up to five), and the beds have Egyptian-woven sheets. The pillows are so soft that you'll want to take them home. (Alas, they're too big for your suitcase, so ask the resort how to order one.) KidSuites have a private bedroom with a king bed and a separate room with two small beds, a beanbag chair, TV, VCRs, and CD player (your young ones will love their pint-size bathrobes). Hypoallergenic rooms are available. The drawbacks: There are stairs everywhere you turn (be prepared for some exercise), and the sheer size of the resort can make it difficult to find your way around. A $5.5 million makeover is currently under way, revamping the already-beautiful rooms and suites (all 750 of them) to be more reflective of the Mediterranean-seaside theme. The entire decor will be warmer, as the colors change to shades of green and cream with accents of jewel tones, noticeable in the new upholstery, carpeting, bedding, and curtains throughout.

The Loews hotel chain, which manages the property, is known for its child-friendly programs (including a special program for grandparents traveling with their grandchildren; call the hotel for details). **Campo Portofino** is a supervised children's activity and game center ($10 per child per hour, no minimum, ages 4–14, 5pm–midnight). **Kids Kloset** loans things such as games, books, car seats, potty seats, and other items to visiting families. The resort also supplies pagers for teens, giving them some freedom without being completely out of touch with their parents. Mom and Dad can relax while the kids are otherwise occupied at the resort's privately run **Mandara Spa** (www.mandaraspa.com), which features a state-of-the-art fitness center and full-service spa. Like many of the Disney properties, the Portofino doesn't just have swimming pools; its beach pool has a fort with a water slide (the villa pool offers several cabanas). To entertain guests in the evenings, **Musica Della Notte** (Music of the Night) has become a permanent addition to the Harbor Piazza. Guests can enjoy the music of strolling musicians performing opera, "popera," and popular music as they sit, relax, and take in the sunset. Parents will likely appreciate this more than their kids do.

One of the biggest pluses: Guests get UNIVERSAL EXPRESS access to most rides at Universal Studios Florida and Islands of Adventure, as well as seating privileges at shows and restaurants. It's a big advantage if you have fidgety children or impatient teens.

5601 Universal Blvd., Orlando Fl 32819. ✆ 800/235-6397 or 407/503-1000. Fax 407/224-7118. www.loewshotels.com/hotels/orlando. 750 units. $259–$429 double; $459–$2,200 suite and villas. Extra person $25. Children 17 and under stay free in parent's room. Rollaway beds $25/night; cribs free. AE, DC, DISC, MC, V. Self-parking $6; valet $12. Pets accepted (no fee, though deposit against damage required). **Amenities:** 4 restaurants; deli; 3 lounges; 2 outdoor heated pools (1 for concierge and suite guests only); kids' pool; bocce courts (concierge and suite guests only); fitness center; spa; watercraft rentals; playground; supervised children's center; activities; arcade; concierge; tour desk; free water-taxi transportation to Universal Orlando parks; free shuttle to SeaWorld; transportation to WDW parks for a fee; business center; shopping arcade; 24-hr. room service; babysitting; laundry service; valet; concierge-level rooms. *In room:* A/C, TV, hair dryer, iron, safe.

EXPENSIVE

Hard Rock Hotel ✰✰   You can't get any closer than this to Universal Studios at Universal Orlando. This California mission–style resort with a rock 'n' roll theme opened in 2001 with rates a level lower than its Universal sister, the Portofino (see above). The atmosphere here is bit more casual and kid friendly (though with an air of sophistication) than that of its Universal Orlando sisters. The collection of rock memorabilia found scattered throughout the public areas of the hotel is impressive. The pool area, however, takes center stage here: A tremendous oasis of palm trees and rocky landscaping surround a large free-form pool whose most unique feature is a first-rate underwater sound system. It's outfitted with 12 underwater speakers that make sure you don't miss a beat.

The rooms and amenities at the Hard Rock are a cut above those at some of Disney's comparable properties, even the Animal Kingdom Lodge (p. 87). All rooms here sleep four quite comfortably; the decor is sophisticated and modern. Though the bathrooms aren't big, there is (like at the Disney resorts) a separate dressing area that has a sink. KidSuites have a separate room with two small beds, a TV, and separate bathroom. **Camp Lil' Rock** is a supervised children's activity and game center ($10 per child per hour, no minimum, ages 4–14, 5pm–midnight). Kids' amenity bags are available on request. The hotel also offers a special package for grandparents traveling with their grandkids. Like the Portofino, the best views here are on the "bay" side, overlooking the piazza. Unfortunately, though the rooms are pretty soundproof, a few notes seep through some walls, so ask for a room that's situated away from the lobby area if you have light sleepers

There is a Hard Rock Cafe several hundred yards from the hotel, but the resort has two of its own restaurants on property. Like at the Portofino, staying here means UNIVERSAL EXPRESS access to almost every ride at Universal Studios Florida and Islands of Adventure, and seating privileges for shows and restaurants. It's a huge plus if you're here during a busy season.

5800 Universal Blvd., Orlando, FL 32819. ⓒ **800/232-7827** or 407/503-2000. Fax 407/224-7118. www.loewshotels. com/hotels/orlando. 650 units. $229–$409 double; $409–$1,770 suite. Extra person $25. Children 17 and under stay free in parent's room. Rollaway beds $25/night; cribs free. AE, DC, DISC, MC, V. Self-parking $6; valet $12. Pets accepted (no fee, though deposit against damage required). **Amenities:** 3 restaurants; grill; 2 lounges; outdoor heated pool; kids' pool; fitness center; playground; kids' club; arcade; concierge; free water-taxi transportation to Universal Studios, Islands of Adventure, and CityWalk; free shuttle to SeaWorld; transportation to WDW parks for a fee; shopping arcade; 24-hr. room service; babysitting; laundry service; valet. *In room:* A/C, TV, video games (fee), minibar, fridge (select rooms), microwave (select rooms), hair dryer, iron, safe, CD player, DVD player (fee), high-speed Internet access (fee).

Renaissance Orlando Resort at SeaWorld ⭐⭐ This stylish hotel, the classiest in the I-Drive price category, offers large rooms, and while it doesn't have much in the way of kids' amenities, it's a great location for theme-park nomads: It's across from SeaWorld and about 10 to 15 minutes from Universal Orlando and Walt Disney World. The lobby charms kids and adults alike with a 10-story atrium, koi pond (at up to 25 lb., they're huge!), free-flight aviary, and six glass elevators that overlook the atrium. Kids get a small stuffed dolphin upon check-in. East-side rooms, especially from the sixth floor up, have a nice view of SeaWorld, which is within walking distance (but watch the traffic). North- and south-side rooms have balconies overlooking the atrium. While the decor in the rooms is among the nicest I've encountered, renovations are scheduled for 2006 and will include a new color scheme and furnishings. The Mediterranean-style pool area, recently renovated, features an Olympic-size pool, two whirlpools, and a children's wading pool.

6677 Sea Harbor Dr., Orlando, FL 32821. ✆ **800/327-6677** or 407/351-5555. Fax 407/351-1991. www.renaissance hotels.com. 778 units. $149–$309 double. Extra person no charge. Children 17 and under stay free in parent's room. Rollaway beds and cribs free. AE, DC, DISC, MC, V. Free self-parking; valet parking $12. **Amenities:** 3 restaurants; grill; 3 lounges; outdoor heated pool; kids' pool; golf privileges (fee); 4 lighted tennis courts, available instruction (fee); health club; basketball; volleyball; spa; 2 Jacuzzis; sauna; playground; arcade; concierge; tour desk; car-rental desk; transportation to all the parks for a fee; business center; shopping arcade; salon; 24-hr. room service; massage; babysitting; laundry service; valet. *In room:* A/C, TV w/pay movies, dataport, minibar, fridge (select rooms), hair dryer, safe, high-speed Internet (fee), PlayStation.

Royal Pacific Resort 🅰🅰 *Value*   The third of Universal Orlando's three resorts has an open-air courtyard with an exquisite orchid garden; palm trees; waterfalls; and lagoons, including one in which a float plane with a 90-foot wingspan is docked (the scene reminds more than a few people of *Gilligan's Island*). The Royal Pacific doesn't quite succeed at creating a Polynesian paradise (you can hear the screams of riders on the Hulk Coaster from the pool area), but it's definitely the best Universal resort in the theme department.

The rooms, though smaller than those at other Universal resorts, are attractively decorated, with lovely wood accents and carvings; they are better than some at comparable Disney resorts. The **Mariner's Club** is a children's activity and game center ($10 per child per hour, no minimum, ages 4–14, 5–11pm). And the lagoon pool area—the largest in Orlando—has a beach and play area that's very popular with the young set. Kids will likely enjoy the free water-taxi ride that goes from all of Universal's resorts to its theme parks (though it's admittedly a slow ride). The addition of the Wantilan Luau Pavilion ensures that the weekly luau is held rain or shine (for more information on the luau, see p. 279). The big plus: Guests get UNIVERSAL EXPRESS access to almost every ride at Universal Studios Florida and Islands of Adventure, and seating privileges for shows and restaurants. The big minus: The self-parking lot is a very long hike from the hotel, and you have to pay $6 for that privilege.

Note: All Loews hotels are pet friendly.

6300 Hollywood Way, Orlando, FL 32819. ✆ **800/232-7827** or 407/503-3000. Fax 407/503-3202. www.loewshotels. com/hotels/orlando. 1,000 units. $179–$319 double; $279–$1,400 suite. Extra person $20. Children 17 and under stay free in parent's room. Rollaway beds $25/night, cribs free. AE, DC, DISC, MC, V. Self-parking $6, valet parking $12. From I-4, take Exit 75B, Kirkman Rd./Hwy. 435 and follow the signs to Universal. **Amenities:** 2 restaurants (Asian-Polynesian, American); 3 lounges; outdoor heated pool; kids' pool; sauna; Jacuzzi; kids' club; arcade; concierge; free water-taxi transportation to Universal Studios, Islands of Adventure, and CityWalk, free shuttle to SeaWorld, transportation for a fee to WDW parks; babysitting; valet; nonsmoking rooms. *In room:* A/C, TV, dataport, hair dryer, iron, safe.

Staybridge Suites   Like its Lake Buena Vista cousin (reviewed on p. 105), this hotel is friendly, well run, and neat as a pin. Price and spacious one- and two-bedroom suites (the latter 550 sq. ft., with beds for eight) are two of its biggest pluses. The hotel attracts both families and business travelers, and there's a supervised child-care center for kids. Courtyard rooms have balconies. The property is across the street from the Mercado shopping village and its restaurants, and just up the road from Pointe Orlando and its offerings. A free expanded continental breakfast is included in the daily rate.

8751 Suiteside Drive, Orlando Fl. 32836. ✆ **800/866-4549** or 407/238-0777. Fax 407/238-2640. www.ichotels group.com. 150 units. $159–$299. Rates include continental breakfast. Rollaway beds and cribs available at no charge. AE, DC, DISC, MC, V. **Amenities:** Deli; convenience store; outdoor heated pool; children's pool; 24-hr. exercise room; Jacuzzi; 24-hr. game room; free shuttle to Disney parks; Guest Services desk; 24-hr. laundry service; nonsmoking rooms; accessible suites; complimentary grocery delivery service. *In room:* A/C, TV/VCR, kitchen, dataport, hair dryer, ironing board, iron, safe.

MODERATE

AmeriSuites Universal   It's tough to beat the value and roominess of these kitchenette-equipped suites, especially if your goal is to be very close to the Universal theme parks without having to pay the heftier rates that come with staying on park property. The modern, spacious rooms allow your family to stretch out more than in standard hotel/motel accommodations, and the location is especially convenient if Universal Orlando is your target.

5895 Caravan Court, Orlando, FL 32819. © **800/833-1516** or 407/351-0627. Fax 407/331-3317. www.amerisuites. com. 151 units. $89–$139 for up to 4 guests. Rates include free buffet breakfast. Children 17 and under stay free in parent's room. Rollaway beds and cribs free. AE, DC, DISC, MC, V. Free self-parking. **Amenities:** Outdoor heated pool; exercise room; tour desk; free transportation to all theme parks; laundry service; valet. *In room:* A/C, TV/VCR, dataport, kitchenette, coffeemaker, hair dryer, iron, safe.

DoubleTree Castle   Built on a medieval-castle theme, this nine-story I-Drive property is entertaining from the moment you enter. Topped with spiraling turrets and two rooftop terraces, the castle is painted in pink, lavender, and gold pastels, and adorned in public areas with art, antique dolls, weaponry from around the world, and unusual timepieces. Renaissance music adds to the theme. As if that weren't enough, you get DoubleTree's famous chocolate-chip cookies upon check-in. Rooms are standard motel style, with two queen-size beds or a king-size bed. The circular pool is equipped with fountains for extra fun. The hotel sometimes shows family films on a poolside screen on weekends.

8629 International Dr., Orlando, FL 32819. © **800/952-2785** or 407/345-1511. Fax 407/248-8181. www.doubletree castle.com. 216 units. $89–$219 double; $139–$269 suites. Resort fee $2. Extra person $10. Children 17 and under stay free in parent's room. Rollaway beds $15/night, cribs free. AE, DC, DISC, MC, V. Free self-parking. Take I-4 Exit 74A, Sand Lake Rd./Hwy. 482, go east to International Dr., then south to Austrian Row. **Amenities:** Restaurant (tapas); cafe; 2 lounges; outdoor heated pool; exercise room; arcade; guest-services desk; free transportation to Disney, Universal, and SeaWorld parks; limited room service; guest laundry; valet; nonsmoking rooms. *In room:* A/C, TV w/PlayStation, dataport, fridge, coffeemaker, hair dryer, iron, safe.

DoubleTree Hotel at the Entrance to Universal Orlando   Location alone (right across the street from Universal Orlando) earns this hotel a star. Built for the convention trade, this former Radisson was just renovated and features reasonably nice rooms. Stay here and save over the Portofino Bay, Hard Rock, and Royal Pacific hotels (reviewed earlier). Rooms on the west side, floors 6 through 18, offer views of the Universal parks and CityWalk. DoubleTree's famous chocolate-chip cookies are complimentary upon check-in (though you may want to buy some to take home, because they're *that* good).

5780 Major Blvd., Orlando, FL 32819. © **800/333-3333** or 407/351-1000. Fax 407/363-0106. www.doubletree orlando.com. 742 units. $99–$209 double. Extra person $20. Children 17 and under stay free in parent's room. Rollaway beds $20/night, cribs free. AE, DC, DISC, MC, V. Free self-parking; valet parking $10. **Amenities:** 3 restaurants; grill; lounge; outdoor heated pool; kids' pool; exercise room; Jacuzzi; arcade; free transportation to Universal and SeaWorld parks, transportation for a fee to Disney/airport; salon; limited room service. *In room:* A/C, TV w/pay movies, dataport, coffeemaker, hair dryer, iron.

Embassy Suites Hotel ®   This is another hotel with a run-of-the-mill exterior hiding an impressive interior atrium highlighted by brick and wrought-iron accents, palm trees, and lush foliage. Eight floors of suites surround the atrium, some with balconies overlooking the courtyard. Suites are fairly spacious, with separate living and sleeping areas. This is one of the few hotels to offer both an indoor and an outdoor pool. Another big advantage: the proximity to I-Drive's nightlife, restaurants, and shops. There are a complimentary reception in the evenings and free transportation to Disney.

8978 International Dr., Orlando, FL 32819. ☎ **800/EMBASSY** or 407/352-1400. Fax 407/363-1120. www.embassy suites.com. 244 units. $149–$289. Extra person (over the 6-person maximum) $10.. Rates include full breakfast. Rollaway beds $15/night; cribs free. AE, DC, DISC, MC, V. Free self-parking; valet parking $8. **Amenities:** Restaurant; lounge; 2 heated pools (1 indoor, 1 outdoor); toddler pool; fitness center; game room; Guest Services desk; free transportation to Disney; 24-hour business center; room service; laundry service; valet. *In room:* A/C, TV w/pay movies, dataport, fridge, microwave, coffeemaker, hair dryer, iron.

Residence Inn Orlando International Drive 🐾

Marriott's Residence Inns were designed to offer home-away-from-home comfort for business travelers, but the concept works just as well for families. The all-suite hotel is well kept and is situated within a mile of many of International Drive's attractions, shops, and restaurants. The attractive one-bedroom suites are a roomy 500 square feet and sleep four. All have full kitchens. Some two-bedroom suites are available. An evening social hour is held Monday through Thursday. A welcome basket that includes popcorn is included in the rates. On the downside, there are neither a kids' pool nor other specifically child-friendly amenities.

7975 Canada Ave. (just off Sand Lake Rd., a block east of International Dr.), Orlando, FL 32819. ☎ **800/227-3978** or 407/345-0117. Fax 407/352-2689. www.marriott.com. 176 units. $89–$159 double; $129–$189 studio suite. Extra person $15. Children 17 and under stay free in parent's room. Rollaway beds $10/night; cribs free. Rates include buffet breakfast. AE, DC, DISC, MC, V. Free self-parking. From I-4, take Exit 74A, Sand Lake Rd./Hwy. 482, go east to Canada, then left. Pets welcome for $100 deposit (half nonrefundable), plus $10 per day. **Amenities:** Outdoor heated pool; exercise room; Jacuzzi; free bus service to Disney, transportation for a fee to the other theme parks; guest laundry; valet. *In room:* A/C, TV w/pay movies, dataport, kitchen, fridge, coffeemaker, iron, safe.

Sheraton Studio City

If you and the kids love classic Hollywood (think Bogart, Marilyn, Elvis, James Dean, and the Duke), you'll probably love the decor at this 21-story I-Drive property. Built in 1974, it got its new name and a $15.5 million makeover in 1999. Rooms have an Art Deco flavor and the personality of a high-rise motel. It's very popular with families; there are several facilities for kids; and the security is excellent (you have to show a room key to get to the guest elevators), though the service can be hit or miss.

5905 International Dr. (between Universal Blvd. and Kirkman Rd.), Orlando, FL 32819. ☎ **800/327-1366** or 407/351-2100. Fax 407/352-8028. www.sheratonstudiocity.com. 302 units. $99–$189 for up to 4; $179–$269 suites. Resort fee $3.50. Extra person $20. Children 17 and under stay free in parent's room. Rollaway beds $11/night; cribs free. AE, DC, DISC, MC, V. Free self-parking. From I-4, take Exit 75A, Kirkman Rd., south to International Dr., then right. **Amenities:** 2 restaurants; lounge; outdoor heated pool; kids' pool; exercise room; arcade; concierge; rental-car desk; free shuttle to Disney and Universal, transportation for a fee to SeaWorld; salon; limited room service; babysitting; guest laundry; nonsmoking rooms. *In room:* A/C, TV w/PlayStation, dataport, coffeemaker, hair dryer, iron, safe.

INEXPENSIVE

Fairfield Inn International Drive 🐾 *Value*

If you're looking for I-Drive's best value, it's hard to beat this one. This Fairfield combines a quiet location off the main drag; down-to-earth rates; and a clean, modern motel in one package. It's not only the best in this category, but also arguably a half step ahead of the Hampton, La Quinta, and Sierra Suites in the previous category. The rooms are very comfortable; the staff is friendly; and there are a number of restaurants within walking distance of the hotel.

8342 Jamaican Court (off International Dr. between the Bee Line Expressway and Sand Lake Rd.), Orlando, FL 32819. ☎ **800/228-2800** or 407/363-1944. Fax 407/363-1944. www.fairfieldinn.com. 135 units. $69–$84 for up to 4. Children 17 and under stay free in parents' room. Rates include continental breakfast. Rollaway beds and cribs free. AE, DC, DISC, MC, V. Free self-parking. **Amenities:** Outdoor heated pool; Guest Services desk; transportation to the parks for a fee; laundry service; valet. *In room:* A/C, TV w/pay movies, dataport, safe.

I-Drive Alternatives

If you're coming into town during peak season, and you're having trouble finding a room, the 1,052-room **Wyndham Orlando Resort,** 8001 International Dr. (© **800-WYNDHAM** or 407/351-2420; www.wyndham.com), is an impeccably landscaped property that's good for families and features numerous pools, playgrounds, and a kids' club for children ages 4–12. The 1,338-room **Caribe Royale,** 8101 World Center Dr. (© **800/823-8300** or 407/238-8000; www.cariberoyale.com), offers spacious and newly remodeled one-bedroom suites (kitchenettes) and two-bedroom villas (Jacuzzis and full kitchens). The grounds are beautifully landscaped; the pool has cascading waterfalls and a 75-foot water slide; a playground is nearby; and the service is tops.

Red Horse Inn   Built in 1972, this old-style Southwestern two-story motel is a clean bargain that's been recently refurbished. Public areas such as the reception desk boast some of the Western artwork of noted landscape artist Jack Pardue, and the Cactus Cantina Lobby Bar is decked out with real saddles (if your kids are cowboy fans, they'll love it). The location is near Universal Orlando, Wet 'n Wild, and the north I-Drive outlet malls. Guests can use the fitness center, game room, pool, and other facilities at the Red Horse's Hollywood-theme sister property, Sheraton Studio City (see above).

5825 International Dr. (between Universal Blvd. and Kirkman Rd.), Orlando, FL 32819. © **877/936-4100** or 407/351-4100. Fax 407/996-4599. www.redhorseorlando.com. 159 units. $59–$99 double. Resort fee $3.50. Extra person $10. Rates include continental breakfast. Children 17 and under stay free in parent's room. Rollaway beds $10/night, cribs free. AE, DC, DISC, MC, V. Free self-parking. From I-4, take Exit 75A, Kirkman Rd., south to International Dr., then right. Small pets welcome for $10/night. **Amenities:** Outdoor heated pool; kids' pool; concierge; free transportation to Universal and SeaWorld, transportation for a fee to Disney; babysitting; guest laundry; valet, nonsmoking rooms. *In room:* A/C, TV, dataport, safe.

Family-Friendly Dining

If you're a fast-food fan, you'll find hundreds of choices here, thanks to Orlando's 30-something years of growth as a family destination. Themed and theme-park restaurants, only a rung or two higher on the culinary scale, aren't far behind in the numbers. That's why the local cuisine isn't usually considered in the same league as that of foodie havens such as New York, San Francisco, and Las Vegas. In fairness, though, some of Orlando's 5,000-plus restaurants can go head to head with the competition. (Disbelievers should grab a chair at **Emeril's** at City-Walk or **Victoria & Albert's** at Disney's Grand Floridian Resort & Spa.)

Because most Central Florida visitors spend much of their time at Disney or Universal, I focus a lot of my energy there, but I won't leave out worthwhile restaurants beyond the parks' boundaries. In this chapter, you'll also find a sampling of what's cooking along International Drive and visit a fair share of other dining rooms that have benefited from the culinary infusion created by the attractions.

Note to parents: Keep in mind that most moderate to inexpensive restaurants have kids' menus (generally $4–$7, often including a beverage and fries), and many offer distractions, such as coloring books and mazes, to keep your little tykes busy until the food arrives. I'll make a note of those available at press time, but things change, so ask when reserving a table.

You'll also want to pay attention to the places that offer **"character meals"** (see the listings later in this chapter). Also note that the higher the meal costs, the less likely you'll be in the same dining room as a lot of little ones. So if you hanker for an evening to rekindle the romance while the kids crash in an activity center or stay with a babysitter (see chapter 4), try one of the adult restaurants I've included. (They're easy to spot—they're often the ones without kids' menus.)

For online information about area restaurants, visit **www.disneyworld.com**, **www.universalorlando.com**, **www.orlandoinfo.com**, or the websites in the listings that follow.

ADVANCED DINING RESERVATIONS AT WDW RESTAURANTS

Walt Disney World's Advanced Dining Reservation (formally known as Priority Seating) is like a reservation but less precise. It means you get the *next table available after* you arrive, but a table isn't kept empty while the eatery waits for you to arrive. Therefore, you probably will wait 15 to 30 minutes even if you arrive on time. You can make an Advanced Dining reservation 90 days (180 days if you're staying at a Disney resort) or more in advance at most full-service restaurants in the Magic Kingdom, Epcot, Disney–MGM Studios, Animal Kingdom, the Disney resorts, and Downtown Disney. Advanced Dining Reservations can also be arranged for character meals (later in this chapter) and dinner shows. To make arrangements, call © **407/939-3463.** You'll get a confirmation number for your Advanced Dining Reservation—bring it with you. Dinner shows (see chapter 10, "Entertainment for the Whole Family") can be booked up to 2 years in advance (except for Mickey's Backyard Barbecue, which accepts booking only 1 year out). Be aware, however, that these dinner shows require full payment in advance and that cancellations must be made at least 48 hours prior to the time of the show to avoid penalties.

Note: Since the Advanced Dining Reservations phone number was instituted in 1994, it has become much more difficult to obtain a table as a walk-in for the resorts' more popular restaurants. I *strongly* advise you to call as far ahead as possible, especially if you're traveling during the peak seasons. It wouldn't hurt to mark your calendar and enter the phone number into your speed dial, either. Amazingly, some restaurants can book up quite literally within only a minute or two of the phone lines opening (7am) on that 90th day out.

If you don't make your dining plans in advance, you can take your chances by making your Advanced Dining Reservations arrangements once you have arrived in the parks. In addition to the places listed below, you can always head directly to your desired restaurant to see what's available:

- **In Epcot** at Guest Relations near the entrance, near Innoventions, or right at the restaurants.
- **In the Magic Kingdom** at Guest Relations in City Hall or right at the restaurants.
- **In Disney–MGM Studios** at Guest Relations near the entrance or right at the restaurants.
- **In Animal Kingdom** at Guest Relations near the entrance. You can arrange for Advanced Dining Reservations at the Rainforest Cafe located here, but know this is a *very* popular place, so the sooner you call, the better.

Also, keep these restaurant facts in mind:

- As of July 1, 2003, *all Florida restaurants* and bars that serve food are **smoke free.**
- The Magic Kingdom (including its restaurants) serves no alcoholic beverages, but liquor is available at Animal Kingdom, Epcot, and Disney–MGM Studios restaurants and elsewhere in the WDW complex.
- All sit-down restaurants in Walt Disney World take American Express, Diners Club, Discover, MasterCard, Visa, and the Disney Visa card.
- Unless otherwise noted, restaurants in the parks **require park admission.**
- Guests at Disney resorts and official properties can make restaurant reservations through guest services or concierge desks.
- Nearly all WDW restaurants with sit-down or counter service offer children's menus with items ranging from $4 to $7, though in a few cases, they're $9 to $12. Some include beverages and fries.

Tips How Early Can You Book It?

At the time this book went to press, Advanced Dining arrangements could be made up to 180 days in advance for all character meals and for meals at the Disney resorts and theme parks, including a meal at Victoria & Albert, and up to 2 years in advance at Disney's Hoop-Dee-Doo and Spirit of Aloha dinner shows. WDW resort guests can now make Advance Dining Reservations for up to 10 days' worth of dining experiences all at once (even if it extends beyond the 180-day window)—a huge timesaver. For arrangements, call ☎ **407/939-3463.**

A NOTE ABOUT PRICES

The prices for adult meals at Orlando restaurants—except those inside the theme parks and other attractions—are no more exorbitant than you'd find anywhere else. Restaurants in this chapter are listed by location, and prices reflect the cost of an average entree per person. Restaurants in the **Inexpensive** category charge under $10 for an entree; those in the **Moderate** category charge $11 to $20. **Expensive** restaurants will set you back $21 to $30, and **Very Expensive** restaurants will top that, sometimes by a large margin.

One last note: The restaurants I list in this chapter occasionally change menus (and sometimes more than just occasionally). So items I feature here may not be on the menu when you visit. And as entrees vary, so do prices.

That said, it's time to divide and conquer.

1 Restaurants by Cuisine

AFRICAN
Boma ✿✿ (Animal Kingdom Lodge, $$$, p. 140)

Jiko—The Cooking Place ✿ (Animal Kingdom Lodge, $$$, p. 142)

AMERICAN
B-Line Diner (International Drive Area, $$, p. 154)

Cinderella's Royal Table ✿ (Magic Kingdom, $$$, p. 131)

Cosmic Ray's Starlight Café (Magic Kingdom, $, p. 132)

ESPN Club ✿ (Disney's Boardwalk, $$, p. 143)

50's Prime Time Café (Disney–MGM Studios, $$, p. 136)

Hard Rock Cafe (Universal Orlando, $$, p. 150)

Hollywood Brown Derby (Disney–MGM Studios, $$$, p. 133)

Liberty Tree Tavern ✿ (Magic Kingdom, $$, p. 132)

Panera Bread ✿ (Downtown and elsewhere, $$, p. 158)

Pecos Bills ✿ (Magic Kingdom, $, p. 132)

Planet Hollywood (Pleasure Island, $$, p. 145)

Plaza Restaurant (Magic Kingdom, $, p. 133)

Sci-Fi Dine-In Theater Restaurant (Disney–MGM Studios, $$, p. 136)

Tusker House (Animal Kingdom, $, p. 137)

BARBECUE
Bubbalou's Bodacious BBQ ✿ (Winter Park, $, p. 159)

Wild Jacks (International Drive, $$, p. 155)

BRITISH
Rose & Crown Pub & Dining Room (Epcot, $$, p. 129)

BRUNCH
Atlantis ✿ (International Drive Area, $$$$, p. 152)

CALIFORNIA
California Grill ✿✿✿ (Disney's Contemporary Resort, $$$, p. 141)

Pebbles ✿✿ (Lake Buena Vista, $$, p. 147)

Rainforest Cafe ✿ (Downtown Disney Marketplace & Animal Kingdom, $$, p. 146 and p. 137)

Wolfgang Puck Grand Café ✿ (Disney's West Side, $$, p. 147)

CANADIAN
Le Cellier Steakhouse (Epcot, $$, p. 128)

Key to Abbreviations: $$$$ = Very Expensive $$$ = Expensive $$ = Moderate $ = Inexpensive

CARIBBEAN

Bahama Breeze ✸ (International Drive, $$, p. 152)

Jimmy Buffett's Margaritaville (Universal's CityWalk, $$, p. 157)

CHARACTER MEALS

Akershus Royal Banquet Hall (Epcot, $$, p. 128)

Cape May Café (Disney's Beach Club Resort, $$, p. 161)

Chef Mickey's ✸✸ (Disney's Contemporary Resort, $$, p. 161)

Cinderella's Royal Table ✸ (Magic Kingdom, $$, p. 161)

Crystal Palace Buffet ✸ (Magic Kingdom, $$, p. 161)

Donald's Prehistoric Breakfastosaurus (Animal Kingdom, $$, p. 162)

Garden Grill ✸ (Epcot, $$, p. 162)

Liberty Tree Tavern ✸ (Magic Kingdom, $$, p. 162)

1900 Park Fare ✸ (Disney's Grand Floridian Resort & Spa, $$, p. 162)

'Ohana Character Breakfast (Disney Polynesian Resort, $$, p. 163)

Princess Storybook Character Dining (Epcot, $$, p. 163)

CHINESE

Lotus Blossom Café (Epcot, $, p. 130)

Ming Court ✸ (International Drive, $$, p. 155)

Nine Dragons (Epcot, $$, p. 129)

CUBAN

Bongo's Cuban Cafe (Disney's West Side, $$, p. 146)

Rolando's ✸ (Casselberry, $$, p. 158)

FOOD COURT

Sunshine Seasons in the Land (Epcot, $, p. 130)

FRENCH

Bistro de Paris (Epcot, $$$$, p. 124)

Chefs de France (Epcot, $$$, p. 126)

Citricos ✸ (Disney's Grand Floridian Resort & Spa, $$$$, p. 138)

GERMAN

Biergarten (Epcot, $$, p. 128)

Sommerfest (Epcot, $, p. 130)

INTERNATIONAL

Café Tu Tu Tango ✸ (International Drive, $$, p. 154)

Victoria & Albert's ✸✸✸ (Disney's Grand Floridian Resort & Spa, $$$$, p. 139)

ITALIAN

Bice ✸ (Universal's Portofino Bay Hotel, $$$$, p. 148)

L'Originale Alfredo di Roma (Epcot, $$$, p. 126)

Mama Melrose's Ristorante Italiano (Disney–MGM Studios, $$, p. 136)

Pacino's Italian Ristorante ✸ (Kissimmee, $$, p. 156)

Pastamore Ristorante ✸ (Universal's CityWalk, $$, p. 151)

Portobello Yacht Club ✸ (Pleasure Island, $$$, p. 145)

Romano's Macaroni Grill ✸ (Lake Buena Vista, $, p. 148)

Tony's Town Square Restaurant (Magic Kingdom, $$$, p. 131)

JAPANESE

Mikado Japanese Steak House ✸ (Marriott's Orlando World Center, $$$, p. 156)

Tempura Kiku (Epcot, $$$, p. 127)

Teppanyaki (Mitsukoshi) Dining Room (Epcot, $$$, p. 127)

Yakitori House (Epcot, $, p. 131)

MEXICAN

Cantina de San Angel (Epcot, $, p. 129)

San Angel Inn ✸ (Epcot, $$, p. 129)

MISSISSIPPI DELTA

House of Blues (Disney's West Side, $$, p. 146)

MOROCCAN

Marrakesh ✸ (Epcot, $$$, p. 127)

NEW ORLEANS
  Boatwright's Dining Hall (Disney's
    Port Orleans Resort, $$, p. 143)
  Emeril's 𝒜𝒜 (Universal's CityWalk,
    $$$$, p. 149)

NORWEGIAN
  Akershus Royal Banquet Hall (Epcot,
    $$, p. 128)
  Kringla Bakeri og Kafe (Epcot, $,
    p. 130)

PACIFIC RIM
  'Ohana 𝒜 (Disney's Polynesian
    Resort, $$, p. 144)
  Tchoup Chop 𝒜𝒜 (Universal's Royal
    Pacific Hotel, $$$, p. 150)

PIZZA
  Toy Story Pizza Planet
    (Disney–MGM Studios, $, p. 137)

SEAFOOD/STEAKS/CHOPS
  Artist Point 𝒜 (Disney's Wilderness
    Lodge, $$$, p. 140)
  Blackfin Seafood Grill & Bar 𝒜
    (Winter Park, $$$, p. 156)
  Cape May Café (Disney's Beach Club
    Resort, $$, p. 161)
  Charlie's Lobster House (International
    Drive, $$$$, p. 152)

Columbia Harbour House (Magic
  Kingdom, $, p. 132)
Coral Reef 𝒜 (Epcot, $$$, p. 126)
The Crab House (International Drive
  and Lake Buena Vista, $$, p. 147)
Crabby Bill's 𝒜 (Kissimmee, $$,
  p. 156)
Fishbones (International Drive area,
  $$, p. 154)
Flying Fish Café (Disney's Boardwalk,
  $$$, p. 142)
Fulton's Crab House 𝒜 (Pleasure
  Island, $$$$, p. 145)
The Palm (Universal's Hard Rock
  Hotel, $$$$, p. 149)
Todd English's Bluezoo 𝒜𝒜 (WDW
  Dolphin, $$$, p. 142)
Wild Jacks (International Drive, $$,
  p. 155)
Yachtsman Steakhouse 𝒜 (Disney's
  Yacht Club Resort, $$$$, p. 139)

SOUTHWESTERN
  Logan's Roadhouse (Kissimmee, $,
    p. 160)

TAPAS
  Café Tu Tu Tango 𝒜 (International
    Drive, $$, p. 154)
  Spoodles (Disney's Boardwalk, $$$,
    p. 142)

2 Places to Dine in Walt Disney World

From fast food on the fly to fine-dining establishments, there are literally hundreds of restaurants scattered throughout Walt Disney World, including those at the theme parks (Epcot, Magic Kingdom, Disney–MGM Studios, and Animal Kingdom), the Disney resorts, and the "official" hotels. And those totals don't include the eateries located throughout the Downtown Disney areas of Pleasure Island, West Side, and the Marketplace, some of which are listed in the Lake Buena Vista section later in this chapter. As a general rule, the food at Disney is decent enough, though only a small handful of the restaurants would truly qualify as gourmet. Portions are generally large, practically ensuring that you'll never walk away hungry, though prices match portion sizes accordingly. Be prepared to spend a rather hefty amount each day for just a few meals, a snack, and a drink (or two). Families may find sharing a good option, especially if you have very young children who tend not to eat so much when on the go. For those unwilling to share, sit-down and counter-service eateries, at least in the theme parks, do offer pint-size platters in the $4-to-$7 range.

Note: All Disney sit-down restaurants have highchairs and booster seats.

> **Tips** **Special Tastes**
>
> When it comes to eating at Disney, just because something's not on the menu doesn't mean it's not available. Looking for kosher food? Worried WDW can't entertain your vegetarian tastebuds? Disney can usually handle those diets, as well as other special dietary requirements (fat-free or sugar-free meals, or meals for those with allergies or lactose intolerance) at any of its full-service restaurants as long as guests give Disney advance notice—usually, 24 hours will do. This holds true for other dining requests, too. If you are headed to one of the resort's restaurants and know your kids may have a tough time with the menu, chicken nuggets and some other kid-friendly items can be requested in advance. It's easiest to make special requests when you make your Advance Dining Reservations (℃ **407/939-3463**) or, if you're staying at a Disney resort, by stopping by the Guest Relations desk.

IN EPCOT

The world is at your feet at Epcot, quite literally in fact. In addition to the eateries found at Future World, the World Showcase features several ethnic cuisines from around the globe, all served in some rather impressive settings. Though dining at one of the World Showcase pavilions is a traditional part of the Epcot experience, I remind you that many of the following establishments are rather overpriced when compared with an equivalent restaurant beyond the park's boundaries. Unless your budget is unlimited, you may want to consider the more casual counter-service eateries located throughout the park and save the sit-down service for somewhere else. These informal dining spots don't require Advance Dining Reservations (for details, check the Epcot guide map that you picked up upon entering the park) and often go overlooked, and unless otherwise noted, they offer **children's meals** (usually for ages 3–9). If you simply can't resist a more formal meal (and it is difficult at times), try eating lunch at the full-service restaurants when the price for a meal is much lower. Almost all the establishments listed here serve lunch and dinner daily (hours vary with park hours), and unless otherwise noted, they offer children's meals. All but one or two require theme-park admission and the $9 parking fee, too. These restaurants are located on the "Epcot Dining" map on p. 125.

Note: Because the clientele at even the fanciest Epcot World Showcase restaurant comes directly from the park, you don't have to dress up for dinner. An **Advanced Dining Reservation** (p. 119) is crucial if you want to dine at a specific table-service restaurant in Epcot; call ℃ **407/939-3463** far in advance to make one.

VERY EXPENSIVE

Bistro de Paris TRADITIONAL FRENCH   Located above Chefs de France (see below), this pricey bistro offers an intimate and elegant atmosphere overlooking the streets of Paris a-la-Epcot just below. The occasionally changing menu might include roasted veal chops with chanterelle mushrooms, rack of lamb with grilled vegetables, and seared scallops with shiitake mushrooms. It's definitely not a good choice for families, though if Mom and Dad have the night off (the kids with a sitter), by all means indulge. The restaurant has a respectable list of French wines.

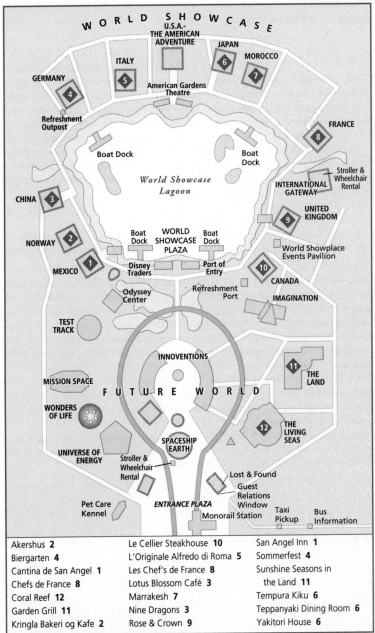

W O R L D   S H O W C A S E

U.S.A.-
THE AMERICAN
ADVENTURE

JAPAN
6

ITALY
5

MOROCCO
7

GERMANY
4

American Gardens
Theatre

Refreshment
Outpost

FRANCE
8

Boat Dock

Boat
Dock

World Showcase
Lagoon

Stroller &
Wheelchair
Rental

CHINA
3

INTERNATIONAL
GATEWAY

UNITED
KINGDOM
9

NORWAY
2

Boat
Dock

WORLD
SHOWCASE
PLAZA

Boat
Dock

World Showplace
Events Pavilion

MEXICO
1

Disney
Traders

Port of
Entry

10

CANADA

Odyssey
Center

Refreshment
Port

IMAGINATION

TEST
TRACK

INNOVENTIONS

11
THE
LAND

MISSION SPACE

F U T U R E   W O R L D

WONDERS
OF LIFE

12
THE
LIVING
SEAS

UNIVERSE OF
ENERGY

SPACESHIP
EARTH

Stroller &
Wheelchair
Rental

Lost & Found

Guest
Relations
Window

Pet Care
Kennel

ENTRANCE PLAZA

Monorail Station

Taxi
Pickup

Bus
Information

Akershus **2**	Le Cellier Steakhouse **10**	San Angel Inn **1**
Biergarten **4**	L'Originale Alfredo di Roma **5**	Sommerfest **4**
Cantina de San Angel **1**	Les Chef's de France **8**	Sunshine Seasons in
Chefs de France **8**	Lotus Blossom Café **3**	the Land **11**
Coral Reef **12**	Marrakesh **7**	Tempura Kiku **6**
Garden Grill **11**	Nine Dragons **3**	Teppanyaki Dining Room **6**
Kringla Bakeri og Kafe **2**	Rose & Crown **9**	Yakitori House **6**

France Pavilion, World Showcase. ℂ 407/939-3463. www.disneyworld.com. No kids' menu. Advance Dining Reservations strongly recommended. Main courses $24–$37 dinner. AE, DC, DISC, MC, V. Daily 5pm–1 hr. before park closes. Parking $9.

EXPENSIVE

Chefs de France TRADITIONAL FRENCH   Focusing on nouvelle cuisine, Les Chefs de France is one of the most expensive restaurants at Epcot, but not without good reason. An eye-catching, domed-glass exterior hides an Art Nouveau interior filled with candelabra and glass-and-brass partitions, that offers an intimate setting. You can credit three internationally acclaimed chefs—Paul Bocuse, Roger Verge, and Gaston LeNotre—with the menu here, which combines fresh Florida ingredients with a good dose of French imports. Light sauces (when compared with more traditional French cooking, that is) complement such tasty entrees as sautéed chicken with wild mushrooms, and Mediterranean seafood casserole. A substantial wine list complements the menu, and the desserts and pastries are among the best in the World. The service, however, can get a bit lackluster when the restaurant is busy. Older kids would fare best, though most kids will likely prefer to head elsewhere.

France Pavilion, World Showcase. ℂ 407/939-3463. www.disneyworld.com. Kids' menu w/activities, highchairs, boosters. Advance Dining Reservations. strongly recommended. Main courses $13–$18 lunch, $16–$30 dinner, kids $7. AE, DC, DISC, MC, V. Daily noon–3:30pm and 5pm–1 hr. before park closes. Parking $9.

Coral Reef ✦ SEAFOOD   We've seen both kids and adults mesmerized by the Reef's **5.6 million-gallon aquarium.** Mood is half the fun here as Disney denizens swim to "La Mer" and other classical music. Tiered seats, mainly in semicircular booths, give everyone a good view. Diners get fish-identifier sheets with labeled pictures so they can put names on the faces swimming by their tables (let the kids color or otherwise put their "signatures" on them). This is one of the most popular restaurants in all of the parks, and it's definitely a winner with kids; what could be better than a fish tank of tremendous proportions to entertain tinier tots while you eat? The menu primarily features fresh seafood and shellfish, including grilled mahimahi, Florida snapper, and salmon. A selection of landlubber fare is available as well. Wine is available by the glass.

Living Seas Pavilion, Future World. ℂ 407/939-3463. www.disneyworld.com. Kids' menu w/activities, highchairs, boosters. Advance Dining Reservations recommended. Main courses $14–$22 lunch, $16–$32 dinner, kids $5–$9. AE, DC, DISC, MC, V. Daily 11:30am–3pm and 4:30pm–park closing. Parking $9.

L'Originale Alfredo di Roma *Overrated* SOUTHERN ITALIAN   It's the most popular place in Epcot, and kids like it when the waiters occasionally burst into song. L'Originale is actually L'Replica of Alfredo De Lelio's eatery in Rome, and the menu includes his celebrated fettuccine dished out in an exhibition kitchen. On the meatier side, grilled veal chops are served with Chianti and truffle sauce, mushrooms, asparagus, and roasted

---

Fun Fact Fast Food

Disney guests eat about 10 million burgers, 8 million hot dogs, and 9½ million pounds of fries every year. That's enough fries to circle the planet three times. And it takes nearly 2 million pounds of ketchup to accompany all that fast food.

Fun Fact   Just Desserts

Playing with your food usually isn't appropriate, but WDW features plenty of places where kids can create their own decadent and delightful desserts. Kids can make Ms. Ice Cream Head at **California Grill** (p. 141), where vanilla ice cream and candy are the ingredients for making funny faces. Creating a chocolate "moose" is easy at **Le Cellier** (p. 128), in Epcot's Canadian pavilion. Real chocolate mousse is rolled in cookie crumbs, and decorated with cookie antlers and candy for its face. Troll cookies, hand-painted (iced) and decorated with candy eyes and cotton-candy hair, is the treat of choice at the **Akershus Royal Banquet Hall** (p. 128), in Norway's pavilion.

---

potatoes. Kids can choose penne with either meat sauce or a cheese sauce, or spaghetti with meatballs. The wine list is reasonably extensive. The dining-room noise level can be quite high (it's filled with families, after all), so if you want a quieter meal, ask for a seat out on the veranda—a most pleasant choice in the evenings.

Italy Pavilion World Showcase. ✆ 407/939-3463. www.disneyworld.com. Kids' menu w/activities, highchairs, boosters. Advance Dining Reservations strongly recommended. Main courses $10–$25 lunch, $17–$38 (most under $25) dinner, kids $6–$7. AE, DC, DISC, MC, V. Daily noon–park closing. Parking $9.

Marrakesh ⚜ (Finds) MOROCCAN   This dining spot exemplifies the spirit of Epcot more than any other restaurant, yet a lot of guests ignore it because they're worried the menu is too exotic. Speaking of exotic, belly dancers entertain while your eyes feast on options such as marinated beef shish kabob; braised chicken with green olives, garlic, and lemon; and roast lamb au jus. On the kids' side, the choices are grilled chicken breast, beef on a skewer, or a burger. Older kids will likely find the atmosphere to their taste. The restaurant's hand-set mosaic tiles, latticed shutters, and painted ceiling represent some 12 centuries of Arabic design. Exquisitely carved faux-ivory archways frame the dining area. There's a small selection of wine and beer for the adults in the family.

Morocco Pavilion, World Showcase. ✆ 407/939-3463. www.disneyworld.com. Kids' menu w/activities, highchairs, boosters. Advance Dining Reservations strongly recommended. Main courses $11–$22 lunch, $18–$32 dinner; $28–$30 prix fixe; kids $4–$6. AE, DC, DISC, MC, V. Daily noon–park closing. Parking $9.

Tempura Kiku JAPANESE   Only 25 guests can sit around the central counter at this smallest and most intimate of Japan's eateries, but if you get a seat, you will enjoy the tempura-battered shrimp, chicken, scallops, or beef. While the portions may be small, they are usually quite tasty. There's no kids' menu, however, making this a better bet for those with tweens and teens. For Mom and Dad, Tempura Kiku also serves sushi, sashimi, Kirin beer, plum wine, and sake, along with a handful of specialty drinks.

Japan Pavilion, World Showcase. ✆ 407/939-3463. www.disneyworld.com. No kids' menu. No Advance Dining Reservations. Main courses $9–$14 lunch, $13–$25 dinner. AE, DC, DISC, MC, V. Daily 11am–1 hr. before park closes. Parking $9.

Teppanyaki (Mitsukoshi) Dining Room JAPANESE   If you've been to any of the Japanese steakhouse chains *(teppanyakis)*, you know the drill: Diners sit around grill tables while white-hatted chefs rapidly dice, slice, stir-fry, and sometimes launch the food onto your plate with amazing skill. The theatrics should keep your kids' attention riveted. Entrees include chicken, steak, shrimp, scallops, lobster, or a combination. Kids can order grilled chicken; tempura-style shrimp; or chicken, steak, or shrimp stir-fry. As at Tempura Kiku (see above), Kirin beer, plum wine, and sake are served. The atmosphere is lively, and the noise level is generally high, so no worries with little ones here.

Japan Pavilion, World Showcase. (C) **407/939-3463.** www.disneyworld.com. Kids' menu w/activities, highchairs, boosters. Advance Dining Reservations strongly recommended. Main courses $9–$22 lunch, kids $5–$7; $16–$35 dinner, kids $5–$9. AE, DC, DISC, MC, V. Daily 11am–1 hr. before park closes. Parking $9.

MODERATE

Akershus Royal Banquet Hall NORWEGIAN   Akershus is a re-created 14th-century castle where you can sample an all-you-can eat feast of hot and cold dishes, making it a bargain for big eaters. It is also reasonably good food, though some diners will find it difficult to adapt to the Scandinavian taste. Entrees change but usually include venison stew, roast pork, gravlax, smoked mackerel, mustard herring, an array of Norwegian breads and cheeses, smashed rutabaga, and more. Cold items are served smorgasbord-style; hot items are ordered from the kitchen (and you can order as many items as your stomach can handle). The staff is friendly, and the white-stone interior, beamed ceilings, leaded-glass windows, and archways add to the authentic atmosphere. Norwegian beer and aquavit complement a list of French and California wines.

Note: The character meal options here have been expanded to include lunch and dinner. The popular Princess breakfast (p. 163) includes mostly American fare, but the lunch and dinner buffets feature a sampling of Norwegian fare along with a handful of kid-friendly favorites, including chicken, ravioli, pasta and meatballs, hot dogs, and a turkey-and-cheese roll.

Norway Pavilion, World Showcase. (C) **407/939-3463.** www.disneyworld.com. Advance Dining Reservations Required. Kids' menu w/activities, highchairs, boosters. Character breakfast adult $22, child $12; character lunch adult $24, child $13; character dinner adult $28, child $13. AE, DC, DISC, MC, V. Daily noon–park closing. Parking $9.

Biergarten GERMAN   The Biergarten, with its festive atmosphere, feels like a Bavarian village at Oktoberfest. A working waterwheel and geranium-filled flower boxes adorn the Tudor-style houses that line the dining area. An oompah band entertains with its accordions and cowbells, and guests are encouraged to dance and sing along. The all-you-can-eat buffet is filled with Bavarian fare (assorted sausages, pork schnitzel, sauerbraten, spaetzle, and sauerkraut), as well as rotisserie chicken. Though there's no child-specific menu, the buffet is extensive enough that even a picky eater should find something to his liking. Beck's and Kirschwasser—served in immense steins—are both on tap for adults.

Germany Pavilion, World Showcase. (C) **407/939-3463.** www.disneyworld.com. Advance Dining Reservations strongly recommended. Lunch buffet adult $16, child $8; dinner buffet adult $21, child $9. AE, DC, DISC, MC, V. Daily noon–3:45pm and 4pm–park closing. Parking $9.

Le Cellier Steakhouse CANADIAN   The restaurant's French Gothic facade and steeply pitched copper roofs lend it a castlelike ambience. The lantern-lit dining room resembles a wine cellar, and you'll sit in tapestry-upholstered chairs under vaulted stone arches. If you're in the mood for steak, this is the right place; offerings include the usual range of cuts, including filet, veal chop, and prime rib. Red-meat main events include the usual range of cuts, including filet, veal chop, and prime rib. Other options include seafood, pork, and pasta. The lunch menu features lighter fare, including sandwiches and salads. Kids can choose a cheeseburger, chicken nuggets, a child-size 6-ounce steak, or a hot dog. Wash down your meal with a Canadian wine, or choose among a selection of Canadian beers.

Canadian Pavilion, World Showcase. © 407/939-3463. www.disneyworld.com. Kids' menu w/activities, highchairs, boosters. Advance Dining Reservations strongly recommended. Main courses $7–$20 lunch, $16–$37 dinner, 3-course excursion $35, wine pairing $27 per person. AE, DC, DISC, MC, V. Daily noon–park closing. Parking $9.

Nine Dragons CHINESE   When it comes to decor, Nine Dragons shines, with carved rosewood furnishings and a dragon-motif ceiling. Some windows overlook the lagoon. But (is there an echo?) the food doesn't match the beautifully ornate surroundings. Main courses feature Mandarin, Shanghai, Cantonese, and Szechuan cuisines, but portions are small. The dishes include spicy beef stir-fried with squash; lightly breaded lemon chicken; and a casserole of lobster, shrimp, and scallops sautéed with ginger and scallions. If you're a group and don't mind sharing, two-person and four-person sampler plates offer a bit of everything for you to try. Kids' choices (finicky eaters, beware) are sweet-and-sour chicken or fried rice with a spring roll. You can order Chinese or California wines with your meal.

China Pavilion, World Showcase. © 407/939-3463. www.disneyworld.com. Kids' menu w/activities, highchairs, boosters. Advance Dining Reservations strongly recommended. Main courses $13–$22 lunch, $13–$39 dinner; $44 sampler for 2, $60 sampler for 4; kids' menu $5–$9. AE, DC, DISC, MC, V. Daily 11:30am–park closing. Parking $9.

Rose & Crown Pub & Dining Room BRITISH   Visitors from the United Kingdom flock to this spot, with its dark oak wainscoting, beamed Tudor ceilings, and a belly-up bar where English folk music and the occasionally saucy server entertain you as you feast your eyes and palate on a short but traditional menu. It beckons with fish and chips wrapped in newspaper (kids love 'em); bangers and mash; prime rib with Yorkshire pudding; and the best of the bunch, an English pie sampler (pork and cottage, and chicken and leek). Offerings for younger guests include macaroni and cheese, grilled chicken, and fish and chips. Wash your meal down with a pint of Irish lager, Bass Ale, or Guinness Stout.

Note: The outdoor tables (weather permitting) offer a fantastic view of IllumiNations (p. 215). These seats are first come, first served, so ask the hostess when you arrive if a patio table is available.

United Kingdom Pavilion, World Showcase. © 407/939-3463. www.disneyworld.com. Kids' menu w/activities, highchairs, boosters. Priority Seating for dining room, not for pub. Main courses $16–$19 lunch, $17–$30 dinner; kids $6–$7. AE, DC, DISC, MC, V. Daily 11am–1 hr. before park closes. Parking $9.

San Angel Inn ⭐ MEXICAN   It's always night at the San Angel, where you can feast on some of the best South of the Border cuisine in all of the theme parks. Candlelit tables set the mood, and the menu delivers reasonably authentic food; don't expect to find Americanized hard-shell tacos and nachos here. The atmosphere is more romantic than family oriented, and it's probably better for older kids rather than little ones (though you'll see them anyway). The occasional rumble of a volcano and the sounds of the distant songbirds can be heard as you wait for your dinner. *Mole poblano* (chicken brought to life with more than 20 spices, carrots, and a hint of chocolate) is one top seller. Another favorite: *filete motuleño* (grilled beef tenderloin over black beans, melted cheese, pepper strips, and fried plantains—a sweet, bananalike fruit). Chicken strips, cheeseburgers, and chicken quesadillas fill out the kids' menu.

Mexico Pavilion, World Showcase. © 407/939-3463. www.disneyworld.com. Kids' menu w/activities, highchairs, boosters. Advance Dining Reservations strongly recommended. Main courses $12–$18 lunch, $18–$24 dinner, kids $5. AE, DC, DISC, MC, V. Daily 11:30am–park closing. Parking $9.

INEXPENSIVE

Cantina de San Angel MEXICAN   Counter-service eateries are the most common places to grab a bite in the parks and are probably the best bet for families with young

---

Tips Flamed Out

If you're a smoker, don't plan on lighting up over dinner. In mid-2003, a state constitutional amendment banned smoking in Florida's restaurants, as well as at bars that earn 10% or more of their income from food.

---

kids who don't do well sitting still in the confines of a restaurant. The Cantina serves the nachos, burritos, quesadillas, and tacos not found at the San Angel Inn across the way. The wrought iron–enclosed patio overlooks the lagoon, and umbrellas shade you from the sun.

Mexico Pavilion, World Showcase. ℂ 407/939-3463. www.disneyworld.com. No Advance Dining Reservations. Meals $6–$8. AE, DC, DISC, MC, V. Daily 11:30am–1 hr. before park closes. Parking $9.

Kringla Bakeri og Kafe NORWEGIAN   The lunch-pail crowd loves this combination cafe–bakery. Grab-and-go options include a plate of smoked salmon and scrambled eggs, smoked ham and Jarlsberg cheese sandwiches, but it's the array of tempting pastries, cakes, cookies, and waffles with strawberry preserves that bring most here. Sit in the small, open-air seating area (just beyond the door, adjacent to the Stave Church), and let your kids work off excess energy at the Viking ship. Wine is sold by the glass.

Norway Pavilion, World Showcase. ℂ 407/939-3463. www.disneyworld.com. No Advance Dining Reservations. Sandwiches and salads $4–$6; pastries $3–$5. AE, DC, DISC, MC, V. Daily 11am–park closing. Parking $9.

Lotus Blossom Café CHINESE   If you're in a hurry but still in the mood for some good Chinese, this counter-service stop offers fast-food favorites such as stir-fry, egg rolls, hot-and-sour soup, sweet-and-sour chicken, and fried rice. There's a small, covered outdoor patio, though the decor is not nearly as ornate as that of its neighbor, the Nine Dragons. Chinese beer and wine are available.

China Pavilion, World Showcase. ℂ 407/939-3463. www.disneyworld.com. No Advance Dining Reservations. Meals $4–$6.50. AE, DC, DISC, MC, V. Daily 11am–park closing. Parking $9.

Sommerfest GERMAN   At the rear of the Germany pavilion, this outdoor eatery's quick-bite menu includes bratwurst and frankfurter sandwiches (one is still a hot dog) with sauerkraut. There is no specific menu for kids, making it a poor choice for really young children, although the school-age set and older kids should be fine.

Germany Pavilion, World Showcase. ℂ 407/939-3463. No Advance Dining Reservations. All items under $7. AE, DC, DISC, MC, V. Daily 11am–park closing. Parking $9.

Sunshine Seasons in the Land Value FOOD COURT   The food isn't gourmet, but of all the cafeterias and counter-service stops in Disney World, the recently renovated Sunshine Seasons (with its new earth-toned color scheme and an impressionistic decor more reflective of the Land Pavilion's theme) offers the most diversity because it has five walk-ups in one. It's especially good if you're traveling with kids who possess finicky (and varied) palates; it's often crowded with families for that very reason. There's an Asian Wok shop (stir-fry and barbecue), a wood-fired grill (Atlantic Salmon), a sandwich shop (Black Forest ham, salami, Cuban), and a soup-and-salad counter (with veggies from the Land's own gardens). There's also a small bakery. An open kitchen allows everyone to watch the behind-the-scenes action. Wine by the glass, a frosty draft, and bottled beer are also available.

Land Pavilion, Future World. ℂ 407/939-3463. www.disneyworld.com. No Advance Dining Reservations. Meals $5–$8. AE, DC, DISC, MC, V. 11am–park closing. Parking $9.

Yakitori House JAPANESE   Resembling the teahouse of the Imperial Summer Palace, this very small eatery offers a menu of *yakitori* (skewered chicken with soy sauce and sesame); teriyaki chicken and beef; and a handful of other beef, chicken, and seafood items. The food is reasonably good, though a little on the blah side, and portions are smaller than at many other Disney restaurants. There's seating both indoors and out, but no matter where you dine, you'll be overlooking tranquil Japanese gardens and a gentle waterfall.

Japan Pavilion, World Showcase. ℂ 407/939-3463. www.disneyworld.com. Advance Dining Reservations not accepted. Meals $3–$8. AE, DC, DISC, MC, V. 11am–park closing. Parking $9.

IN THE MAGIC KINGDOM

In addition to the places mentioned here, there are plenty of fast-food outlets in the park. You may find, however, that a quiet sit-down meal is an essential but all-too-brief way to get away from the forced-march madness. These restaurants are located on the "Walt Disney World & Lake Buena Vista Dining" map on p. 134–135 and "The Magic Kingdom" map on p. 178. And remember: Magic Kingdom restaurants *don't serve alcohol.* So the adult members of your party will have to go elsewhere if they like a drink with their meal.

EXPENSIVE

Cinderella's Royal Table ⭐ AMERICAN   You'll be greeted by handmaidens before making your way inside this royal restaurant—by far the most popular place to dine in Magic Kingdom. Those who enter are usually swept off their feet as they're transported back to a time when medieval kings and queens reigned (a feeling that's helped along by the Gothic interior, which includes leaded-glass windows, stone floors, and high-beamed ceilings). The servers treat you like a lord or lady (I'm not kidding; that's how they'll address you). The restaurant underwent changes to its lineup in February 2006 and now features only character meals (featuring decent but expensive food). Cinderella will host breakfast and lunch (and you'll get a free souvenir photo as part of your meal); the Fairy Godmother does hostess duty at dinner (where diners get a free lithograph).

Note: Because of its location and ambience, a meal here is sought by everyone from little girls who dream of Prince Charming to romantics seeking a more intimate meal. The problem: This is actually one of the smallest dining rooms in Disney World, making Advance Dining Reservation arrangements a must. And you'll have your work cut out for you to get one; it may very well take several calls (and a lot of flexibility on your part) to ensure a spot. And thanks to a new policy, payment (via credit card) for your meal is required in full at the time of booking (no exceptions!).

Cinderella Castle, Fantasyland. ℂ 407/939-3463. www.disneyworld.com. Advance Dining Reservations Required. Character breakfast $32 adult, $22 children 3–9; character lunch $34 adult, $23 children 3–9; character dinner $40 adults, $25 child. AE, DC, DISC, MC, V. Daily 11:30am–2:45pm and 4pm–1 hr. before park closing. Parking $9.

Tony's Town Square Restaurant ITALIAN   Inspired by the cafe in *Lady and the Tramp,* Tony's dishes up lunches and dinners of pastas and pizzas in a pleasant, if somewhat harried, dining room featuring etched glass and ornate gingerbread trim. Evening fare includes a variety of seafood, sautéed veal medallions with wild mushrooms, and breaded eggplant with tomato sauce and mozzarella cheese. With spaghetti, cheese ravioli, and cheese and pepperoni pizzas in the lineup, Tony's has one of the kid-friendliest menus in the kingdom and is a top dining spot for families with young children. Original animation cels from the movie (including the film's famous spaghetti smooch) line the walls, adding to the ambience. Additional seating is available in a sunny, plant-filled solarium.

Main Street. Ⓒ 407/939-3463. www.disneyworld.com. Kids' menu w/activities, highchairs, boosters. Advance Dining Reservations strongly recommended. Main courses $9–$12 lunch, $19–$25 dinner, kids $5–$6. AE, DC, DISC, MC, V. Daily 8:30–10:45am, noon–2:45pm, and 4pm–park closing. Parking $9.

MODERATE

Liberty Tree Tavern ✿ AMERICAN   Step into a replica of an 18th-century Colonial pub and its historic atmosphere, including oak-plank floors, pewter ware–stocked hutches, and a big brick fireplace hung with copper pots. The background music suits the period. Lunch includes sandwiches, seafood (such as cured salmon and crab cakes), salads, soups, burgers, and pot roast. The nightly character dinner (a family favorite) is a set family-style meal that includes roast turkey, carved beef, smoked pork with a mashed-potato stuffing, and macaroni and cheese—along with apple crisp and vanilla ice cream to top it off. While the fare's not all that interesting, it is appropriate to the early-American setting. The menu at lunch is similarly decent: Kids' fare includes mac and cheese, chicken strips, a cheeseburger, or hot dog.

Liberty Square. Ⓒ 407/939-3463. www.disneyworld.com. Kids' menu w/activities, highchairs, boosters. Advance Dining Reservation. Main courses $11–$15 lunch, kids $5; character dinner $22, kids $11. AE, DC, DISC, MC, V. Daily 11:30am–3pm and 4pm–park closing. Parking $9.

INEXPENSIVE

Columbia Harbour House ✿ AMERICAN/SEAFOOD   This small eatery often goes overlooked because of its size—it features only a handful of cozy little rooms, all nautically themed—but it does offer some rather decent light fare. Battered fish and shrimp—far meatier than most—sandwiches, clam chowder, and fruit are featured on the menu. Kids can choose mac and cheese or chilled chicken, though they may find the main menu to their liking.

Liberty Square. Ⓒ 407/939-3643. www.disneyworld.com. All items $5–$7, kids $4. AE, DC, DISC, MC, V. Daily 11am–park closing. Parking $9.

Cosmic Ray's Starlight Café AMERICAN   The largest of the park's fast-food spots, this cafe features an appropriately huge menu. Three separate counters, similar to a food court, serve a variety of chicken options (whole- or half-rotisserie, dark meat, white meat, fried or grilled), sandwiches, burgers, hot dogs, cheese steaks, soups, and salads. The combination of its casual atmosphere and varied menu makes Ray's a great choice for those with kids. Do note, however, that you may have to wait in more than one line here, as each station offers a different selection. Other minuses: The large dining area fills up quickly at lunch and dinner, and the noise level is generally high. *Tip:* Kosher meals are available here for direct purchase (though they're not particularly noteworthy in the taste department).

Main Street. Ⓒ 407/939-3463. www.disneyworld.com. All items $7–$14. AE, DC, DISC, MC, V. Daily 11am–park closing. Parking $9.

Pecos Bills ✿ AMERICAN   Set in an old-time saloon of sorts, this sit-and-go fast-food joint serves up burgers, hot dogs, salads, and a great Southwestern chicken wrap. Kids can choose chilled chicken or a mini-hot-dog meal. There's also a fixin's bar full of extras. Portions are large, though, like all other park dining options, and so are the prices. Its good location—just between Frontierland and Adventureland—means that those traveling clockwise through the park will probably hit the area just in time for lunch. It can get very crowded at peak meal times, though there is quite a bit of indoor and outdoor seating.

Tip: If your cravings are running more toward Mexican than American, head through the indoor seating area in the back to the seasonal **El Pirata y Perico,** a covered outdoor snack spot featuring tacos, empanadas, chips, and taco salad (all under $6). It's located in Adventureland, just across from Pirates of the Caribbean.

Frontierland. ✆ 407/939-3643. www.disneyworld.com. All items $5–$8, kids $4. AE, DC, DISC, MC, V. Daily 11 am–park closing. Parking $9.

Plaza Restaurant AMERICAN   The sundaes, banana splits, and other ice cream creations—arguably the best in WDW—at this 19th-century–inspired restaurant draw more folks than anywhere else, especially during the dog days of summer. The atmosphere and the ice cream draw tons of families. The Plaza also has tasty, if expensive, sandwiches (turkey, Reuben, cheese steak, chicken, and burgers) that come with an order of fries or potato salad. On the kids' side, choices range from a grilled cheese, PB&J, or turkey sandwich to a mini hot dog and miniburger. You can eat inside in an Art Nouveau dining room or on a veranda overlooking Cinderella Castle.

Main Street. ✆ 407/939-3463. www.disneyworld.com. Kids' menu w/activities, highchairs, boosters. Advance Dining Reservation. Meals $9–$11; ice cream $4–$6; kids $5. AE, DC, DISC, MC, V. Daily 11am–park closing. Parking $7.

AT DISNEY–MGM STUDIOS

Some of the most uniquely themed eateries in all of WDW can be found in MGM. That, however, also makes them some of the most difficult to get into, making Advance Dining Reservations a must at any of the full-service restaurants in the park. Those listed below are the best of the bunch. They're located on two maps, "Walt Disney World & Lake Buena Vista Dining" (p. 134–135) and "Disney–MGM Studios Theme Park" (p. 217).

EXPENSIVE
Hollywood Brown Derby AMERICAN   This elegant restaurant is modeled after the famed Los Angeles celebrity haunt where Louella Parsons and Hedda Hopper once held court. It features some of the finest food and the fanciest surroundings in the park—along with some of the highest prices. White linens, chandeliers, and potted palms all add to the upscale atmosphere, and over 1,500 caricatures of its most famous patrons over the years line the walls, including those of Lucille Ball, Bette Davis, and Clark Gable. Owner Bob Cobb created the original restaurant's signature Cobb salad in the 1930s. (It's so popular that this Derby serves over 31,000 of them a year.) Most kids won't be interested in that option, but hot dogs, grilled chicken, fried grouper, or mac and cheese should tempt them. Adult dinner entrees include pan-seared grouper with balsamic roasted asparagus, and mustard-crusted rack of lamb with acorn squash and sweet-and-sour cabbage. The Derby's signature dessert, grapefruit cake with cream-cheese icing, is a perfect meal capper (there are smoothies and ice cream options for younger tastes). The Derby has a full bar and a modest selection of California wines. If you're looking for a more sophisticated edge that still has kid-friendly options, this is the place (though older kids will likely fare best).

Hollywood Blvd. ✆ 407/939-3463. www.disneyworld.com. Kids' menu w/activities, highchairs, boosters. Advance Dining Reservation. Main courses $13–$19 lunch, $19–$28 dinner, kids $5–7. Fantasmic package adult $37, child $10. AE, DC, DISC, MC, V. Daily 11:30am–park closing. Parking $9.

Walt Disney World & Lake Buena Vista Dining

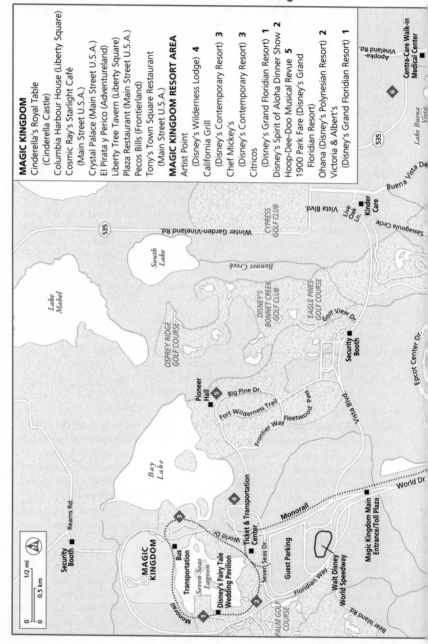

MAGIC KINGDOM

Cinderella's Royal Table
(Cinderella Castle)
Columbia Harbour House (Liberty Square)
Cosmic Ray's Starlight Café
(Main Street U.S.A.)
Crystal Palace (Main Street U.S.A.)
El Pirata y Perico (Adventureland)
Liberty Tree Tavern (Liberty Square)
Plaza Restaurant (Main Street U.S.A.)
Pecos Bills (Frontierland)
Tony's Town Square Restaurant
(Main Street U.S.A.)

MAGIC KINGDOM RESORT AREA

Artist Point
(Disney's Wilderness Lodge) **4**
California Grill
(Disney's Contemporary Resort) **3**
Chef Mickey's
(Disney's Contemporary Resort) **3**
Citricos
(Disney's Grand Floridian Resort) **1**
Disney's Spirit of Aloha Dinner Show **2**
Hoop-Dee-Doo Musical Revue **5**
1900 Park Fare (Disney's Grand
Floridian Resort)
Ohana (Disney's Polynesian Resort) **2**
Victoria & Albert's
(Disney's Grand Floridian Resort) **1**

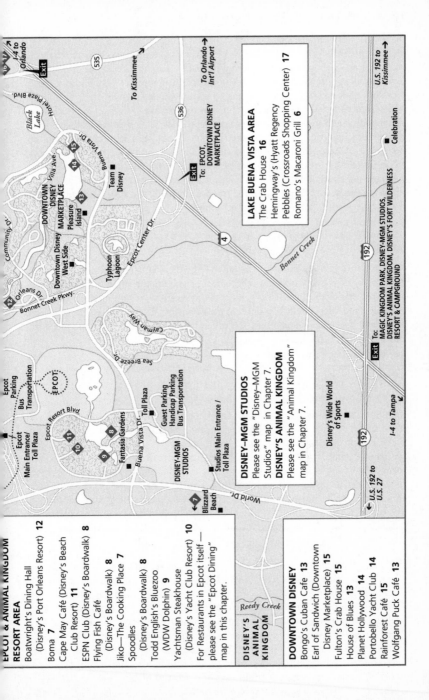

EPCOT & ANIMAL KINGDOM RESORT AREA

Boatwright's Dining Hall
(Disney's Port Orleans Resort) **12**

Boma **7**

Cape May Café (Disney's Beach
Club Resort) **11**

ESPN Club (Disney's Boardwalk) **8**

Flying Fish Café
(Disney's Boardwalk) **8**

Jiko—The Cooking Place **7**

Spoodles
(Disney's Boardwalk) **8**

Todd English's Bluezoo
(WDW Dolphin) **9**

Yachtsman Steakhouse
(Disney's Yacht Club Resort) **10**

For Restaurants in Epcot itself —
please see the "Epcot Dining"
map in this chapter.

DISNEY'S ANIMAL KINGDOM

DOWNTOWN DISNEY

Bongo's Cuban Cafe **13**

Earl of Sandwich (Downtown
Disney Marketplace) **15**

Fulton's Crab House **15**

House of Blues **13**

Planet Hollywood **14**

Portobello Yacht Club **14**

Rainforest Café **15**

Wolfgang Puck Café **13**

DISNEY-MGM STUDIOS

Please see the "Disney-MGM
Studios" map in Chapter 7.

DISNEY'S ANIMAL KINGDOM

Please see the "Animal Kingdom"
map in Chapter 7.

LAKE BUENA VISTA AREA

The Crab House **16**

Hemingway's (Hyatt Regency) **6**

Pebbles (Crossroads Shopping Center) **17**

Romano's Macaroni Grill **6**

135

MODERATE

50's Prime Time Café AMERICAN   Did you ever want to go back to when life was simpler?—well, you can here, even if it's just for a meal. The homey dining room looks just like Mom's kitchen did back in the 1950s, complete with Formica counter tops and black-and-white TVs showing clips from classics such as *My Little Margie*. The servers add to the fun, greeting diners with lines like "Hi, Sis; I'll go tell Mom you're home," and they may threaten to withhold dessert if you don't eat all your food. Kids love it. And they adore seeing their parents admonished for dinner-table infractions. The entrees—fried chicken, meatloaf, pot roast, and open-faced sandwiches, among others—aren't quite as good as Mom used to make but are decent nonetheless. The kids' cuisine (hot dogs, chicken nuggets, mac and cheese, and PB&Js) is always a hit. The desserts, including s'mores and sundaes, are worth the wait. Beer and specialty drinks (they make a mean margarita) are served.

Near the Indiana Jones Stunt Spectacular. ✆ 407/939-3463. www.disneyworld.com. Kids' menu w/activities, high-chairs, boosters. Advance Dining Reservations strongly recommended. Main courses $11–$17 lunch, $13–$20 dinner. AE, DC, DISC, MC, V. Daily 11am–park closing. Parking $9.

Mama Melrose's Ristorante Italiano ITALIAN   Set along the simulated New York street, this large warehouse-style, casual neighborhood eatery is filled with red-checkered tablecloths, wood floors, and red vinyl booths, welcoming to all that enter. The best (and safest) adult bets here are the wood-fired flatbreads (grilled pepperoni, four-cheese, portobello mushroom, and others for $12–$13). The bambino menu features pasta, pizza, and chicken Parmesan.

Near the Backlot Tour. ✆ 407/939-3463. www.disneyworld.com. Kids' menu w/activities, highchairs, boosters. Advance Dining Reservations strongly recommended. Main courses $12–$15 lunch, $12–$22 dinner, kids $5. AE, DC, DISC, MC, V. Daily 11:30am–park closing. Parking $9.

Sci-Fi Dine-In Theater Restaurant AMERICAN   This restaurant's simulated nighttime sky is filled with fiber-optic twinkling stars that look down on you as you sit in a chrome "convertible" watching a giant screen showing '50s and '60s sci-fi flicks, zany newsreels, cartoons, and B horror-movie clips, such as *Frankenstein Meets the Space Monster*. Fun-loving carhops deliver free popcorn along with your meal. The menu, almost as fun to read as the movies are to watch, features such items as Attack of the Killer Club Sandwich, the Beach Party Panic, and Red Planet. Once you're done translating, you'll choose among a selection of sandwiches, ribs, burgers, seafood,

---

Tips **The Disney Dining Plan**

Disney Resort guests can purchase the **all-new Disney Dining plan**—an add-on option to your Magic Your Way base park ticket (p. 166). The plan includes one counter-service meal, one table-service meal, and one snack per person, per night of your stay. You can actually use your meals in any order you wish until they are gone. Taxes and tips are already included, making it rather simple to use. Over 100 restaurants participate in the program, including select character dining, dinner shows, and "signature" restaurants (though these may "cost" more than one of your allotted meals, so be sure to ask). Depending on your eating habits, the program might save you a fistful of cash. Call ✆ **407/934-7639** or visit **www.disneyworld.com** for details.

pasta, steak, and salads. Kids' meals are served on souvenir glow-in-the-dark flyers. The food is average; it's the atmosphere that keeps the crowds coming. Advance Dining Reservations are highly recommended.

Note: The dining room here is fairly dark, and the clips, though pretty harmless, could scare a very young child. Take this into consideration before dining here.

Near Indiana Jones Epic Stunt Spectacular. © 407/939-3463. www.disneyworld.com. Kids' menu w/activities, high-chairs, boosters. Advance Dining Reservations strongly recommended. Main courses $12–$17 lunch, $14–$17 dinner, kids $5. AE, DC, DISC, MC, V. Daily 10:30am–park closing. Parking $9.

INEXPENSIVE

Toy Story Pizza Planet AMERICAN   The menu here is far from original but will satisfy some of the younger (and pickier) eaters in your family with pizza, salad, drinks, and desserts. It's a big favorite of kids, thanks to the array of arcade games located just next door: Avoid it if you don't want to spend the afternoon trying to pull littler ones away, or remember to bring plenty of change.

In the Muppet's Courtyard. © 407/939-3463. www.disneyworld.com. No Advance Dining Reservations. All meals $6–$9. AE, DC, DISC, MC, V. Daily 10:30am–park closing. Parking $9.

IN THE ANIMAL KINGDOM

There are few restaurants in the newest of Disney's parks, and most that exist are counter-service or grab-and-go places (though decent ones, at that). In my opinion, only two are worth listing.

MODERATE

Rainforest Cafe ✦ CALIFORNIA   Expect California fare with an island spin at this Rainforest, and its cousin, listed later in this chapter on p. 146. Menu offerings tend to be tasty and somewhat creative, with far more choices that most can contend with. That said, the cafe, like other Disney restaurants, tends to fall on the pricier side of dining. Fun dishes include Mogambo Shrimp (sautéed in olive oil and served with penne pasta), Rumble in the Jungle Turkey Wrap (with romaine, tomatoes, and bacon), and Maya's Mixed Grill (ribs, chicken breast, and shrimp). Tables situated among the dining room's vines and generally inanimate animals are usually packed; that's partially due to the lack of other full-service dining options at Animal Kingdom but also due to the actual popularity of this loud and lively establishment. Beer, wine, and other alcoholic concoctions are served.

Just outside Animal Kingdom entrance. *Admission to park not required* (though there is an entrance from inside the park, too.). © 407/938-9100. www.rainforestcafe.com. Kids' menu w/activities, highchairs, boosters. Advance Dining Reservations strongly recommended. Main courses $10–$40 (most under $25) lunch and dinner. AE, DC, DISC, MC, V. Daily 8am–11pm. Parking $9.

INEXPENSIVE

Tusker House AMERICAN   Located in the Harambe Village, this grab-and-go spot features some fast-food options that offer a bit of culinary flair. Grilled chicken salad with focaccia bread, rotisserie or fried chicken, grilled salmon, and a roasted vegetable sandwich are all on the menu here (there are chicken or mac and cheese for the kids). Beer and wine are served. The food is tasty enough, though portions are small.

In Africa, near entrance. © 407/939-3463. www.disneyworld.com. No Advanced Dining Reservations. Main courses $7–$8. AE, DC, DISC, MC, V. Daily 10:30am–4:30pm. Parking $9.

IN THE WALT DISNEY WORLD RESORTS

Most restaurants listed in this category continue the Disney trend of being above market price. On the flip side, many offer food that's a notch or two better than what you

Tips **More Kid Cuisine . . .**

Here are a few more places in the Disney resorts and parks to find food that might tickle younger tastes. Many of these are walk-up or casual eateries that don't require Advanced Dining Reservation arrangements, though you should consider making them at Narcoossee's, Grand Floridian Cafe, Big River Grille & Brewing Works, Kona Cafe, and Cap'n Jacks by calling © 407/939-3463.

- **Big River Grille & Brewing Works,** Boardwalk Resort—grilled cheese, burgers, hot dogs, PB&Js, and mac and cheese ($4.50–$5)
- **Cap'n Jacks,** Downtown Disney—grilled chicken, linguini pasta, hot dogs, and PB&J's ($5)
- **Flame Tree Barbecue,** Animal Kingdom—hot dogs and baked chicken wings ($4)
- **Grand Floridian Cafe,** Grand Floridian Resort & Spa—pizza, PB&Js, miniburgers, chicken strips, penne pasta, and mac and cheese for kids 9 and under ($5.50)
- **Kona Café,** Polynesian Resort—chicken fingers, pasta, grilled cheese, PB&Js, burgers, and hot dogs ($5.50)
- **Lottawatta Lodge,** Blizzard Beach—chicken strips, fish and chips, grilled cheese, PB&Js, burgers, and hot dogs ($4)
- **Narcoossee's,** Grand Floridian Resort & Spa—grilled fish, fish filet, petite filet, mac and cheese, chicken fingers, pasta marinara or with butter, and burgers ($6–$13)
- **Pecos Bills,** Magic Kingdom—hot dogs ($3.50)
- **Pinocchio Village Haus,** Magic Kingdom—turkey and cheese roll-up, mac and cheese ($4)
- **Pizzafari,** Animal Kingdom—cheese quesadilla and PB&Js ($4)
- **Plaza Pavilion,** Magic Kingdom—grilled chicken strips, chef salad, miniburgers, grilled cheese, turkey sandwich, and PB&J ($5–$5.50)
- **Tod English's Bluezoo,** WDW Dolphin—spaghetti, beef tenderloin, fried fish fillet, and pizza ($7–$12)
- **Toontown Farmer's Market,** Magic Kingdom—fresh fruit ($1–$1.90)
- **Typhoon Tilly's,** Typhoon Lagoon—chicken strips, fish and chips, grilled cheese, PB&Js, burgers, and hot dogs ($4)
- **Whispering Canyon Café,** Wilderness Lodge—all-you-can-eat skillet, chicken drumsticks or wraps, PB&Js, burgers, and mac and cheese ($5.50–$9)

find in the theme parks. These restaurants are located on the "Walt Disney World & Lake Buena Vista Dining" map on p. 134–135.

VERY EXPENSIVE

Citricos ✪ MODERN FRENCH   The perfect spot for a night out without the kids (even if this restaurant does welcome them), The Grand Floridian's number-two restaurant (Victoria & Albert's is number one) offers a menu featuring what the resort calls French, Alsatian, and Provençal cuisine with California and Florida touches (except when it comes to kids' cuisine, which ranges from chicken tenders to pasta and grilled tenderloin). The Old World decor includes plenty of wrought-iron railings, mosaic-tile floors, flickering amber-colored glass lights, and a spectacular show kitchen—all with an upscale artsy feel. The view of the Seven Seas Lagoon and Magic Kingdom fireworks are the bonus. Add a three-course wine pairing for $26.

4401 Floridian Way, in Disney's Grand Floridian Resort & Spa. ℭ 407/939-3463. www.disneyworld.com. Kids' menu w/activities, highchairs, boosters. Advance Dining Reservations strongly recommended. Main courses $21–$45, kids $6–$12. AE, DC, DISC, MC, V. Wed–Sun 5:30–10pm.

Victoria & Albert's 𝕱𝕱𝕱 *Finds* INTERNATIONAL   This **adult restaurant** (it's definitely not a place for the kids) is something to consider if you have a healthy budget and a desire for a romantic evening without the young 'uns. It's Disney's most elegant restaurant and truly a dining event. Dinner is next to perfect—if the portions seem small, I dare you to make it through all six courses—and the setting is exceptionally romantic. This luxurious experience begins with a personalized menu and a rose for the lady in your party. The fare changes nightly, but expect a feast fit for royalty (and costing a royal fortune). You might begin with chilled lobster roll, followed by Iranian Osetra caviar. Then pheasant consommé might precede an entree such as tamari-glazed bluefin tuna over bok choy stir-fry, or grilled prime filet with a Gorgonzola potato crouton and port wine jus. English Stilton served with a burgundy-poached pear sets up desserts such as vanilla-bean crème brûlée and Kona chocolate soufflé. The dining room is crowned by a domed, chapel-style ceiling; Victorian lamps softly light 20 exquisitely appointed tables; and your servers (always named Victoria and Albert) provide service that will have you begging to take them home. You can add a wine pairing to your meal for an extra $50 (an option I recommend).

4401 Floridian Way, in Disney's Grand Floridian Resort & Spa. ℭ 407/939-3463. www.disneyworld.com. No kids' menu. Advance Dining Reservations required. Jackets required for men. Not recommended for children. Prix fixe $95 ($105 holidays) per person, $145 with wine pairing; $125 Chef's Table, $185 with wine. AE, DC, DISC, MC, V. 2 dinner seatings daily Sept–June 5:45–6:30pm and 9–9:45pm; 1 dinner seating July–Aug 6:45–8pm. Chef's Table 6pm only. Free self- and validated valet parking.

Yachtsman Steakhouse 𝕱 SEAFOOD/STEAKS/CHOPS   Even by outside-the-park standards, the Yachtsman earns a B+ among steakhouses, and it's a good place to have a special dinner out with the kids. Its grain-fed Western beef is aged, cured, and cut here. You can see the cuts in a glass-enclosed aging room, and the exhibition kitchen provides a tantalizing glimpse of steaks, chops, and seafood being grilled over oak and hickory. Adult options range from an 8-ounce filet to a 12-ounce strip to a belly-busting 24-ounce T-bone. A filet and warm-water lobster-tail combo tops the

---

Fun Fact **Cooking for Kids**

Disney's Grand Floridian Resort & Spa offers two special cooking programs for children. **Grand Adventures in Cooking** invites up to 12 youngsters, 4 to 10 years old, to make dessert in a 2-hour decorating class ($29 per child). The **Wonderland Tea Party** gives kids the same age a 1-hour primer in cupcake decorating—with their fingers! They also feast on heart-shaped PB&Js and sip apple-juice "tea" while they play with Alice and the Mad Hatter ($29 per child). Call ℭ **407/824-3000** or 407/939-3463 for details on both programs.

Tips **For Smaller Stomachs**

If your kids aren't satisfied with the offerings on the kids' menu, try the appetizer menu. They'll have more to choose among, and the price is right. Also, always ask if half portions are available; they are generally not advertised, though some restaurants offer them upon request.

---

price chart. If you're not in the mood for beef, the Yachtsman also serves Chilean sea bass, scallops, and one daily vegetarian special. The junior menu features 6-ounce cuts of steak or prime rib, grilled chicken, chicken strips, burgers, hot dogs, and pasta. The decor includes knotty-pine beams, plank floors, and leather-and-oak chairs. The staff is very cordial. The Yachtsman has an extensive wine list, though it's not in the same league as the other two contestants in this category.

1700 Epcot Resorts Blvd., in Disney's Yacht Club Resort. ℂ 407/939-3463. www.disneyworld.com. Kids' menu w/activities, highchairs, boosters. Advance Dining Reservations recommended. Main courses $21–$80 (most over $25), kids $5–$10. AE, DC, DISC, MC, V. Daily 5:30–10pm. Free self- and valet parking.

EXPENSIVE

Artist Point ★ *Finds* SEAFOOD/STEAKS/CHOPS   Enjoy a grand view of Disney's Wilderness Lodge and rather impressive murals of the Pacific Northwest (your kids can hunt for Hidden Mickeys; see p. 220) as you dine in this two-story restaurant, whose immense windows overlook waterfalls, rocky landscaping, and the resort's erupting geyser. In keeping with the park-lodge theme, iron chandeliers hang from the ceilings, and the tables and furnishings are made of exposed wood and full of animal carvings. The menu changes seasonally and might feature the signature cedar plank-roasted wild king salmon, or grilled buffalo sirloin with sweet potato hazelnut gratin and sweet onion jam. Kids can dig into grilled chicken, baked salmon, pasta with cheese sauce, a burger, or PB&J. There's terrace seating for fair weather. Expect a reasonably extensive wine list, now exclusively featuring wines from the Pacific Northwest. *Note:* Artist Point has a much more relaxed atmosphere than some of the busier WDW resort restaurants.

Tip: If you're looking for more family-oriented dining at the Wilderness Lodge, try the **Whispering Canyon Café,** where kids can horse-race on broomsticks, and everyone gets a-hoopin' and a-hollerin' at dinner. Meals are served family style (though a la carte service is available if you so desire).

901 W. Timberline Dr., in Disney's Wilderness Lodge. ℂ 407/939-3463. www.disneyworld.com. Kids' menu w/activities, highchairs, boosters. Advanced Dining Reservations recommended. Main courses $21–$34, kids $6–$10. AE, DC, DISC, MC, V. Daily 5:30–10pm. Free self- and valet parking.

Boma ★★ *Moments* AFRICAN   One of two restaurants in the Animal Kingdom Lodge, this one is themed after an African marketplace. There's plenty of open space to roam about, a thatched roof strewn with colorful banners, and large wood tables shaped to look like tree trunks. The rear overlooks the Savannah, offering a pretty good view out the large glass windows. The show kitchen and wood-burning grill send delicious aromas wafting throughout the room and fill the dinner buffet with diverse delicacies from more than 50 African nations.

Adventurous diners can expect such treats as Moroccan seafood salad (mussels, scallops, shrimp, and couscous), curried coconut seafood stew, chicken pepper-pot soup, and much more. The watermelon-rind salad is a specialty, but don't forget to save room for the yummy desserts. Kids will appreciate the penne pasta with meatballs and tomato sauce, chicken fingers, and the large selection of fresh fruit. The restaurant is set up in sections, each with a chef who can answer your questions about the cuisine. And if there's something you particularly liked, ask for the recipe; Disney is surprisingly good about sharing its culinary secrets. And be sure to save room for the array of amazing desserts. There's also a breakfast buffet.

2901 Osceola Pkwy., at Disney's Animal Kingdom Lodge. © 407/939-3463. www.disneyworld.com. Highchairs, boosters. Advance Dining Reservations strongly recommended. Breakfast buffet $15, $8 kids 3–9; dinner buffet $25, $11 kids. AE, DC, DISC, MC, V. Daily 7–11am and 5–10pm. Free self-parking.

California Grill ☆☆☆ CALIFORNIA   Located on the Contemporary Resort's 15th floor, this stunning restaurant offers views of the Magic Kingdom and lagoon below while your eyes and mouth feast on an eclectic menu. A Wolfgang Puckish interior incorporates Art Deco elements (curved pearwood walls, vivid splashes of color, polished black granite surfaces with colorful tile accents), but the focus is an exhibition kitchen with a wood-burning oven and rotisserie where you can watch all the action as meals are prepared before your eyes. The adult menu's headliners change to take advantage of fresh market fare but may include seared yellowfin tuna, black grouper with mushroom risotto, and softshell crabs with corn salad. The Grill also has a nice sushi and sashimi menu (tuna, crab, and shrimp, among others) ranging from appetizers to large platters. Most kids will wrinkle their noses at those choices, but the Grill has options for youngsters, including cheese pizza, mac and cheese, fish and chips, grilled chicken, and a small steak. It's probably best to save this one for a night your children are with a babysitter or at a kids' club unless the kids are old enough to happily stay up for the fireworks display. The list of California wines helps complement the meal and views.

Note: It can be tough to get a table at the Grill, especially on weekends and during Disney fireworks hours, so make a reservation as early as possible. *Note:* This is one of the few WDW restaurants with a dress code; think business casual in the attire department.

⌢Tips Pint-Size Portions

If your kids are adventurous in the dining department but can't handle adult portions, several Disney restaurants allow kids to sample dishes geared to adult tastes that are served in portion sizes suited to smaller stomachs (and at smaller prices, too). Options include:

- **Artist Point** (Wilderness Lodge): Baked salmon with mashed potatoes and veggies ($9)
- **California Grill** (Contemporary): Steak with mashed potatoes and veggies ($9)
- **Citricos** (Grand Floridian): Chicken noodle soup ($2), oak-grilled filet of beef ($12)
- **Coral Reef** (Epcot): Grilled mahimahi ($9)
- **Flying Fish Café** (BoardWalk): Lettuce salad ($3), buttermilk fried fish ($8)
- **L'Originale Alfredo di Roma Ristorante** (Epcot): Fettuccine Alfredo ($7)

4600 N. World Dr., at Disney's Contemporary Resort. ℂ 407/939-3463. www.disneyworld.com. Kids' menu w/activities, highchairs, boosters. Advance Dining Reservations recommended. Main courses $20–$35, sushi and sashimi $10–$22, kids $7–$10. AE, DC, DISC, MC, V. Daily 5:30–10pm. Free self-parking.

Flying Fish Café SEAFOOD   Chefs at this Coney Island–inspired restaurant take the stage in a show kitchen that turns out adult entrees such as potato-wrapped red snapper, coriander-crusted yellowfin tuna, and oak-grilled salmon or mahimahi. It's likely none of these will tempt your offspring, but the grilled chicken or steak, fish and chips, or cheese pasta should. The atmosphere here is a bit more upscale than you'd think; kids old enough to appreciate that fact will be impressed, but this might not be the best place for kids too young to sit still. Considering the show kitchen and vibrant colors inside, this is a nice escape from the usual theme-park dining. *Note:* If you can't get a table here, ask about sitting at the counter; you get a great view of the kitchen.

2101 N. Epcot Resorts Blvd., at Disney's Boardwalk. ℂ 407/939-3463. www.disneyworld.com. Kids' menu w/activities, highchairs, boosters. Advance Dining Reservations strongly recommended. Main courses $21–$39, kids $6–$12. AE, DC, DISC, MC, V. Daily 5:30–10pm. Free self-parking.

Jiko—The Cooking Place ⚑ AFRICAN   The Animal Kingdom Lodge's signature restaurant is a nice diversion from the normal Disney restaurants and a complementary addition to the multicultural dining rooms at Epcot's World Showcase. Jiko's show kitchen, sporting two wood-burning ovens, turns out a unique menu of international cuisine with African overtones that make for interesting dining on the adult end. Dishes, depending on the season, include grilled buttermilk-curry shrimp, pan-roasted monkfish, grilled salmon with heirloom potatoes and spinach in a horseradish vinaigrette, and pomegranate-glazed quail. Kids face some usual (pizza, grilled cheese, chicken strips, PB&Js, and mac and cheese) and unusual (salmon fillets or steak) suspects. The wine list features a number of South African vintages.

2901 Osceola Pkwy., at Disney's Animal Kingdom Lodge. ℂ 407/939-3463. www.disneyworld.com. Kids' menu w/activities, highchairs, boosters. Advance Dining Reservations strongly recommended. Main courses $18–$29, kids $5.50–$8.75. AE, DC, DISC, MC, V. Daily 5:30–10pm. Free self-parking.

Spoodles TAPAS   This lively family restaurant features an open kitchen and is a good place to take the kids (the noise factor alone should indicate its popularity with the young set). The enterprising tapas menu also encourages food sharing, which increases the fun factor for adults (and is a good intro to some new cuisine for pre-teens and up). Kids face chicken fingers, cheese or pepperoni pizza, burgers, hot dogs, cheese pasta, PB&Js, and fried shrimp. Adult fare includes sautéed chile garlic shrimp, fried calamari, and a sampler platter. Entrees include Moroccan-spiced tuna and a grilled pork porterhouse with goat-cheese polenta. Spoodles has added a respectable wine list, including tableside sangria presentations.

Note: During the peak summer tourist season, thanks to its location at the Boardwalk, the wait can be long, even with Advance Dining Reservations, so this may not be the best option for famished families. Also, although Spoodles is popular, the quality here doesn't rival Café Tu Tu Tango, another tapas favorite (p. 154).

2101 N. Epcot Resorts Blvd., at Disney's Boardwalk. ℂ 407/939-3463. www.disneyworld.com. Kids' menu w/activities, highchairs, boosters. Advance Dining Reservations strongly recommended. Main courses $18–$28, tapas $6–$9, sampler $25, kids $6–$9. AE, DC, DISC, MC. V. Daily 7–11am, noon–2pm, and 5–10pm. Free self-parking.

Todd English's Bluezoo ⚑⚑ SEAFOOD   Set inside the WDW Dolphin, this is the hippest, hottest, happeningest place to dine in town. Internationally acclaimed chef Todd English has created an amazing menu of fresh seafood and coastal dishes that are served with creative flair in an artsy setting. An exhibition kitchen showcases the chefs at work, and the dining areas feature a contemporary (and very blue) decor scheme designed to evoke the ocean, with lots of hip lighting and curved walls. Appetizers include the amazing "Olive's" classico flatbread, a roasted-beet salad, and teppan-seared sea scallops. Melt-in-your-mouth entrees include lobster Bolognese, spit-roasted block of swordfish, and fresh grilled fish served with a choice of three unique sauces. Unlike those at many upscale restaurants of this caliber, the portions here are mealworthy, not miniscule. That said, the prices here are hefty and do not include side dishes (veggies, for example), which will run you an extra $5 to $7. Dress is casual (this is Disney); however, the atmosphere is definitely upscale and caters to adults. It's perfect for an evening out on the town without the kids in tow.

Tip: The front of the restaurant has a unique sectioned-off bar and lounge where live music is often featured or a DJ spins a selection of today's hottest tunes.

1500 Epcot Resort Blvd, at the WDW Dolphin. ✆ **407/934-1111.** www.disneyworld.com. Advance Dining Reservations recommended. Main courses $22–$50. AE, DISC, MC, V. Daily 3:30–11pm. Free self-parking; free valet parking (validated).

MODERATE

Boatwright's Dining Hall NEW ORLEANS   A family atmosphere (noisy), good food (by Disney standards), and reasonable prices (ditto) make Boatwright's a hit with Port Orleans Resort guests, if not outsiders. Most entrees have a Cajun/Creole spin, and portions are large. The spicy jambalaya has shrimp, chicken, and sausage. There really isn't anything French about the pot roast, but it is tasty. Boatwright's is modeled after a 19th-century boat factory, complete with the wooden hull of a Louisiana fishing boat suspended from its lofty beamed ceiling. Most kids like the wooden toolboxes on every table; each contains a salt shaker that doubles as a level, a wood-clamp sugar dispenser, a pepper-grinder-cum-ruler, a jar of unmatched utensils, shop rags (read: napkins), and a little metal pail of crayons. On the food side, they can choose pasta with cheese or sauce, grilled cheese, chicken fingers, fried shrimp, burgers, or hot dogs. (At breakfast, they can get Mickey Mouse–shaped pancakes!)

2201 Orleans Dr., in Disney's Port Orleans Resort. ✆ **407/939-3463.** www.disneyworld.com. Kids' menu w/activities, highchairs, boosters. Advance Dining Reservations recommended. Main courses $7–$11 breakfast, $14–$20 dinner, kids $5–$6. AE, DC, DISC, MC, V. Daily 7–11:30am and 5–10pm. Free self-parking.

Cape May Café *(Overrated)* SEAFOOD   This New England–style clambake offers a selection of oysters, clams, mussels, baked fish, and small peel-and-eat shrimp. Accompaniments include corn on the cob, potatoes, and other assorted veggies. Landlubbers, fear not; there is a selection of not-so-fishy fare, including pasta, barbecued pork ribs, and sirloin. The kids' bar has fried shrimp, chicken fingers, and mac and cheese. The dessert bar is popular with all ages. Though the choices are plentiful, this is still a generic resort-style buffet and nowhere near as fun as an authentic beachside clambake. The casual nautical theme carries into the restaurant from the surrounding Beach Club resort. The Cape May Café also offers a character breakfast buffet every morning (p. 161).

1800 Epcot Resorts Blvd., at Disney's Beach Club Resort. ✆ **407/939-3463.** www.disneyworld.com. Kids' menu w/activities, highchairs, boosters. Advance Dining Reservations strongly recommended. Dinner buffet $24 adults, $10 children 3–11. AE, DC, DISC, MC, V. Daily 5:30–9:30pm. Free self- and valet parking.

ESPN Club *(Finds)* AMERICAN   If you or your kids are sports enthusiasts, this is *the* place to dine in WDW. Upon entering, you will be surrounded by monitors showing

---

> **Tips Anyone Hungry?**
>
> There are plenty of places throughout Disney World to eat and eat and then eat some more, so plan on heading to these food-fests when you're plenty hungry. Disney boasts 10 **all-you-can-eat** restaurants, which is really Disney's polite way of saying feel free to eat absolutely everything in front of you.
>
> Restaurants include **'Ohana** at the Polynesian Resort, **Whispering Canyon** at the Wilderness Lodge, **Boma** at the Animal Kingdom Lodge, **Cape May Café** at the Beach Club Resort, **Crystal Palace** at the Magic Kingdom, **Liberty Tree Tavern** at the Magic Kingdom, **Garden Grill** at Epcot, **Akershus Royal Banquet Hall** (Norway) at Epcot, **Hollywood & Vine** at Disney–MGM Studios, **Chef Mickey's** at the Contemporary Resort, and **1900 Park Fare** at the Grand Floridian.

---

every possible sporting event and lots of sports-related memorabilia. The restaurant also has a small video arcade. The all-American fare includes such choices as "Boo-Yeah" chili, hot wings, and burgers. Sandwiches and salads are available as well. The service is impeccable; never have I had a waiter so quick on his feet. While the food is quite good, it's really the atmosphere—very entertaining for kids—that draws the crowds here.

2101 N. Epcot Resorts Blvd., at Disney's Boardwalk. (*C* 407/939-1177. www.disneyworld.com. Advance Dining Reservations not available. $8–$16 lunch and dinner. AE, DC, MC, V. Mon–Thurs 11:30am–1am, Fri–Sat 11:30 am–2am. Free self-parking, Valet parking $7.

'Ohana ✿ PACIFIC RIM   Its star is earned on the fun front, but the decibel level here can get a bit overwhelming, especially for those looking for a relaxing evening out. Inside, you're welcomed as a "cousin," which fits because *'Ohana* means *family* in Hawaiian. As your food is being prepared over an 18-foot fire pit, the staff keeps your eyes and ears filled with all sorts of shenanigans. The blowing of a conch shell summons a storyteller; coconut races get under way in the center aisle; and you can shed your inhibitions and shake it in the hula lessons. The edibles include a variety of skewers (think shish kabob), including turkey, shrimp, steak, and pork. You'll also find lots of trimmings and a full bar with limited wine selections (tropical alcoholic drinks are available for an added fee). *Note:* Ask for a seat in the main dining room, or you won't get a good view of the entertainment. *Note #2:* The daily character breakfast, featuring Mickey, Stitch, and plenty of friends, is one of the most popular in WDW.

1600 Seven Seas Dr., at Disney's Polynesian Resort. (*C* 407/939-3463. www.disneyworld.com. Kids' menu w/activities, highchairs, boosters. Advance Dining Reservations strongly encouraged. $25 adults, $11 children 3–11; character breakfast $18 adults, $10 kids 3–11 (p. 163). AE, DC, DISC, MC, V. Daily 7:30–11am and 5–10pm. Free self- and valet parking.

3 Places to Dine in Lake Buena Vista

In this section, we've listed restaurants located in Downtown Disney and the Lake Buena Vista area. Many of these eateries can be found on the "Walt Disney World & Lake Buena Vista Dining" map on p. 134–135. Downtown Disney is located 2½ miles from Epcot off Buena Vista Drive. It encompasses the Downtown Disney Marketplace, a very pleasant complex of shops and restaurants on a scenic lagoon; the adjoining Pleasure Island, a nighttime entertainment venue; and Downtown Disney West

Side, a slightly more upscale collection of shops, restaurants, Cirque du Soleil (p. 320), and a movie theater.

Note: Pleasure Island's restaurants don't require admission.

AT PLEASURE ISLAND
EXPENSIVE

Portobello Yacht Club ⚓ SOUTHERN ITALIAN   The pizzas here go beyond the routine to an updated *quattro formaggio* (mozzarella, Gorgonzola, Parmesan, and Fontina cheeses with sun-dried tomatoes) and *margherita* (plum tomatoes, fresh mozzarella, and basil). But it's the less-casual entrees that pack people into this place. The menu changes from time to time. You may find a nice *costoletta di vitello alla griglia* (a grilled 14-oz. veal chop with garlic whipped potatoes and asparagus) or *spaghettini alla portobello* (pasta with pieces of Alaskan king crab, scallops, shrimp, and clams in light olive oil, wine, and herbs). Steak, penne pasta with chicken, cheese pizza, spaghetti with meat sauce, chicken tenders, burgers, and hot dogs will keep most kids happy (though the service is geared more to adults, and wait times between courses can be a bit too much for little ones). Situated in a gabled Bermuda-style house filled with nautical accents throughout, the Portobello's awning-covered patio overlooks Lake Buena Vista. Its cellar is small but offers a nice selection of wine to match the meals.

1650 Buena Vista Dr., in Pleasure Island. ☎ 407/934-8888. www.levyrestaurants.com. Kids' menu w/activities, highchairs, boosters. Advanced Dining. Main courses $15–$50, pizzas $9, kids $5–$12. AE, DC, DISC, MC, V. Daily 5–11pm. Free self-parking.

MODERATE

Planet Hollywood *Overrated* AMERICAN   Some folks come for a first look, but most diners are fans who flock here for the scenery (including a planetariumlike ceiling). The compulsion is much like that of Hard Rock Cafe fans (p. 150), who go for the tunes. The Planet's servers can cop an attitude, and the food is blasé, including the kids' burgers, hot dogs, pizza, and chicken fingers. Adults will find wings, sandwiches, burgers, ribs, fajitas, pizzas, pasta, and steaks. Although it's unquestionably popular with families, and kids like the themed decor, this is not the best food in Disney World; the noise level may be too much for young children to cope with (as well as their parents); and the lines can get long during special events and in peak season.

1506 Buena Vista Dr., at Pleasure Island (look for the big globe). ☎ 407/827-7827. www.planethollywood.com. Kids' menu w/activities, highchairs, boosters. Limited Advance Dining Reservations. Main courses $9–$29 (most under $16), kids $6–$8. AE, DC, DISC, MC, V. Daily 11am–1am. Free self-parking.

AT DOWNTOWN DISNEY MARKETPLACE
VERY EXPENSIVE

Fulton's Crab House ⚓ SEAFOOD   Lobster (Maine and Australian) and crab (king and Dungeness) dominate the menu in this fun and fashionable eatery, which is housed in a replica of a (permanently moored) 19th-century Mississippi riverboat. It's one of the area's best seafood houses—and your bill will reflect that (one reason this should probably be considered only for a special family splurge, though your kids will like the atmosphere). One popular meal for two combines Alaskan king crab, snow crab, and lobster with potatoes and creamed spinach. The cioppino and Dungeness crab cakes are delicious. And there's a scattering of Florida seafood, including stone crabs (mid-Oct–mid-May). Kids can go for land (filet, grilled chicken breast, chicken tenders, burgers, hot dogs, and spaghetti) or sea (fried shrimp or fish and chips). Fulton's wine list is pretty good, too.

1670 Buena Vista Dr., aboard the riverboat docked at Downtown Disney. © 407/934-2628. www.levyrestaurants. com. Kids' menu w/activities, highchairs, boosters. Advance Dining Reservations strongly recommended. Main courses $12–$45 lunch, $16–$47 dinner, kids $5–$12. AE, DC, DISC, MC, V. Daily 11:30am–4pm and 5–11pm. Free self-parking.

MODERATE

Rainforest Cafe ✦ CALIFORNIA   Don't arrive starving at this twin to the Animal Kingdom's Rainforest Cafe (p. 137) unless you have Advance Dining Reservations. Without it, waits average 2 hours. The fare and the atmosphere at this kid-pleaser are exactly the same as those at the Animal Kingdom's version.

Downtown Disney Marketplace, near the smoking volcano. © 407/827-8500. www.rainforestcafe.com. Kids' menu w/activities, highchairs, boosters. Advance Dining Reservations strongly recommended. Main courses $10–$40 lunch and dinner (most under $25), kids $6. AE, DISC, MC, V. Sun–Thurs 11:30am–11pm; Fri–Sat 11:30am–midnight. Free self-parking.

DISNEY'S WEST SIDE
MODERATE

Bongo's Cuban Cafe *Overrated* CUBAN   Singer Gloria Estefan and her husband, Emilio, created this eatery with high expectations. This one's exterior, with a giant pineapple standing tall against the Downtown Disney skyline, is hard to miss. The interior is Art Deco with a Havana flavor, and hand-painted murals of Cuba in its heyday line the walls. A Desi Arnaz impersonator gets things going every night as the restaurant fills with loud Latin music. Alas, the food isn't great, though the prices say it ought to be. The *ropa vieja* (shredded beef) is tasty but on the dry (and sometimes cool) side, and the *arroz con pollo* (chicken with yellow rice, something of a national dish) would be a highlight if the portion matched the price. The best bet: The Cuban sandwich (thinly toasted bread with ham, pork, and cheese) is safe and sanely priced. Kid cuisine includes chicken breast or nuggets, a small steak, and burgers, but I wouldn't take children here unless they are over 10 and like Latin music. For quieter times, try the patio or upstairs lounge.

1498 Buena Vista Dr., in Disney's West Side. © 407/828-0999. www.bongoscubancafe.com. Kids' menu w/activities, highchairs, boosters. No Advance Dining Reservations. Main courses $7–$35 lunch and dinner (most under $20) dinner, kids $6–$7. AE, DC, DISC, MC, V. Daily 11am–2am. Free self-parking.

House of Blues MISSISSIPPI DELTA   Most folks come for the blues bands and Sunday Gospel Brunch (very popular with families), a foot-tapping, thigh-slapping music affair worth high marks on the entertainment side. The noise level is high, and

---

Tips A Royal Debut

In the spring of 2004, **The Earl of Sandwich** (the famous edible was allegedly invented by said earl in 1762, when he was too busy playing cards to eat a real meal—and found that putting meat between two slices of bread allowed for both) made its debut in Downtown Disney. The casual eatery offers a great selection of hot and cold sandwiches, including French roasted beef with cheddar and horseradish sauce, turkey with apple bacon and Swiss cheese, and ham with brie and dijonaise. Cobb and Chinese chicken salads are available as well. There's a small amount of indoor seating, though most diners head for the benches outside. If you're looking for a quick, light meal at a decent price (sandwiches and salads run from $4–$6), this is the place to head.

the atmosphere is informal, so you won't have to worry about any noise your kids might make. (The omelets are good, and there are enough fillers—bacon, salads, dessert, and bread—that few leave hungry.) The average food has a New Orleans flavor and includes such offerings as pan-seared voodoo shrimp, and gumbo with chicken, andouille sausage, and okra. Kids' meals include grilled cheese, chicken tenders, pizza, burgers, hot dogs, and more. The rustic backwater bayou interior has a Cajun Voodooish sort of feel and is by far the most interesting in Downtown Disney, filled (literally) with bottle caps and buttons, skeletal etchings, and hand-painted folk art.

1490 Buena Vista Dr., at Disney's West Side, beneath water tower. © **407/934-2583**. www.hob.com. Kids' menu, highchairs, boosters. No Advance Dining Reservations (except brunch). Main courses $14–$26; pizza and sandwiches $9–$11; brunch $30 adults, $15 children 3–9. AE, DISC, MC, V. Daily 11am–2am; brunch 10:30am and 1pm. Free self-parking.

Wolfgang Puck Grand Café ☞ CALIFORNIA   This restaurant's sushi bar, an artistic copper-and-terrazzo masterpiece, delivers some of the best sushi in Orlando. You can also eat gourmet pizza, with thin crusts and exotic toppings, inside or on an outdoor patio. Upstairs, the main dining room offers an upscale adult atmosphere and tables that are available only through Advanced Dining Reservations. The seasonally changing menu might feature Szechuan beef and crimini satay with a spicy vegetable stir fry and cilantro mint sauce, or pumpkin ravioli with sage, hazelnut butter, and parmesan. Desserts include a crème brûlée sampler plate. The colorful lower level can be noisy but is far more kid-friendly, offering gourmet pizza with thin crusts and exotic toppings, and burgers, chicken tenders, ravioli, and mac and cheese for youngsters. You can eat inside or on an outdoor patio. Puck's also has a grab-and-go express restaurant that sells sandwiches, pizzas, desserts, and more.

1482 Buena Vista Dr., at Disney's West Side. © **407/938-9653**. www.wolfgangpuck.com/myrestaurants. Highchairs. Reservations for dining room; Advance Dining Reservations on lower level strongly recommended. Main courses upstairs $19–$75, pizza and sushi $11–$30, kids $6–$8. AE, DC, DISC, MC, V. Daily 11am–1am. Free self-parking.

ELSEWHERE IN LAKE BUENA VISTA
MODERATE

The Crab House SEAFOOD   Even if it is a chain, this casual restaurant offers a good variety of seafood (and a handful of options for landlubbers) at satisfactory prices. The all-you-can-eat seafood and salad bar is great for those who like variety and has lots of tasty dishes. The regular menu features a variety of fish dishes; seafood; Maine lobster; and, of course, crabs—from Alaskan and king to Maryland blue. The service is friendly and relatively prompt. Fishing gear and lobster traps are spread about the casual dining room, and brown paper (good for kids to draw on) lines the tables. Outdoor patio or deck seating is available as well.

8496 Palm Parkway, Orlando, FL 32836 (just off Apopka–Vineland across and up from Hotel Plaza Blvd.) © **407/239-1888**. www.crabhouseseafood.com. Reservations accepted. Main courses $10–$24; lobster varies according to market. AE, DC, DISC, MC, V. Open daily 11:30am–11pm. Free self-parking. Take I-4 to exit 68 (535) turn right, follow past the Crossroads to Palm Parkway, and turn right. The restaurant is back a bit on the right.

Pebbles ☞☞ *Finds* CALIFORNIA   If you want to dine like a gourmet without the hefty price, this is the restaurant for you. Pebbles is a locally owned chain that has a reputation for great food and creative appetizers. Its pleasant atmosphere is styled after Key West, casual and comfortable. The portions are generous and presented with an artistic flair. The Pebbles twin filets are seared and then bathed in a golden lager, and delivered with caramelized onions and three-cheese mashed potatoes. The Mediterranean

Salmon is sprinkled with artichokes, capers, feta, polenta, and a balsamic demi-glaze. Some lighter bites include crab cakes with Key lime remoulade, and baked chèvre coconut shrimp with sweet-and-sour sauce. Choices for the younger set include PB&J, pizza, grilled cheese, pasta, and chicken fingers. *Note:* Pebbles also has a location in Winter Park, at 2516 Aloma Ave. (© **407/678-7001**).

12551 Apopka–Vineland Rd., in the Crossroads Shopping Center. © **407/827-1111**. www.pebblesworldwide.com. Kids' menu w/activities, highchairs, boosters. Reservations not accepted. Main courses $10–$28. AE, DC, DISC, MC, V. Sun–Thurs noon–11pm; Fri–Sat 11am–11pm. Free self-parking. Take the I-4 Hwy. 535/Apopka–Vineland Rd. exit north to the Crossroads Shopping Center on the right.

INEXPENSIVE

Romano's Macaroni Grill ★ *Value* NORTHERN ITALIAN Though it's part of a multistate chain, Romano's has the down-to-earth cheerfulness of a Mom-and-Pop joint. The laid-back atmosphere makes it a good place for families looking for a casual dinner at a good price. The menu offers thin-crust pizzas made in a wood-burning oven and topped with such items as barbecued chicken. The grilled chicken portobello (simmering between smoked mozzarella and spinach orzo pasta) is worth the visit. Equally good is an entree of grilled salmon with a teriyaki glaze and spinach orzo pasta. Kids' options include pizza, lasagna, spaghetti, grilled chicken, and corn dogs, and all of them come with a dessert and a drink with free refills! Mom and Dad can get premium wines by the glass.

12148 Apopka–Vineland Rd. (just north of County Rd. 535/Palm Pkwy.). © **407/239-6676**. www.macaronigrill.com. Kids' menu w/activities, highchairs, boosters. Main courses $6–$15 lunch, kids $5; $8–$17 dinner (most under $12), kids $4. AE, DC, DISC, MC, V. Sun–Thurs 11am–10pm; Fri–Sat 11am–11pm. Free self-parking. Take I-4 Exit 68, Hwy. 535/Apopka–Vineland Rd. north and continue straight when Hwy. 535 goes to the right. Romano's is about 2 blocks on the left.

4 Places to Dine in Universal Orlando

Universal Orlando stormed onto the restaurant scene with the opening of its dining and entertainment venue, CityWalk, set between Universal Studios Florida and Islands of Adventure. But Universal's sudden entry onto the food front doesn't mean quality was lost in the rush. Two of its restaurants (Emeril's and Tchoup Chop) make our all-star team, and several others offer cuisine ranging from respectable light bites to dependable dinners. And of course, this is theme-park-ville, so family-friendliness is a given at most of the restaurants.

Note: Most of the restaurants below can be found on the "CityWalk" map on p. 323. All the hotel restaurants listed can be found on the "International Drive Area Dining" map on p. 153.

VERY EXPENSIVE

Bice ★ ITALIAN Universal Orlando's newest restaurant, appropriately located in the romantic Italian setting of the Portofino Bay Hotel, replaces the Delfino Riviera. The new family-owned and -operated restaurant (part of a Milan-based international chain) still features Italian fare served in an upscale atmosphere, though the operation is now a bit more down to earth. The extensive menu includes such items as a Belgian endive salad in a light Dijon mustard dressing with gorgonzola cheese and toasted walnuts; spaghetti with Maine lobster, cherry tomatoes, and braised green onions; and veal chops in a porcini sauce. The dining room overlooks the waters along the piazza of the hotel, itself a beautiful and romantic setting; try to get a table on the patio. The

Tips **The Bubba Gump Shrimp Co.**

Universal recently added a Bubba Gump Shrimp Co. (**www.bubbagump.com**) to its CityWalk lineup of unique eateries. Though not yet open at press time, the chain is known across the country for its casual family-friendly atmosphere and diverse menu—not to mention pretty good seafood.

interior decor is a bit less impressive, though still nice enough, with its fresco ceiling and muted lighting. The service can be a bit standoffish and snooty. This is another spot best saved for an evening out *sans* the kids.

5601 Universal Studios Blvd., in the Portofino Bay Hotel. ☎ **407/503-3463** or 407/503-1415. Reservations recommended. Main courses $18–$48. AE, MC, V. Daily 5:30–10:30pm. Free 3-hr. validated self-parking, valet parking $10. From I-4, take Exit 75B, Kirkman Rd./Hwy. 435, and follow the signs to Universal.

Emeril's *★★* NEW ORLEANS   It's hard to get short-term reservations for dinner (less than 3–4 weeks in advance) at Emeril's unless your stars are aligned or you come at the opening bell and take your chances with no-shows. If you do get in, you'll find the dynamic, Creole-inspired cuisine is worth the struggle. Best bets include the andouille-crusted redfish (an extremely moist white fish with roasted pecan-vegetable relish and meunière sauce) and a quacker trilogy that includes pan-seared duck breast, confit leg, and Hudson Valley foie gras with dirty rice and crispy parsnip strips. If you want some vino with your meal, no problem; the back half of the building is a glass-walled, 12,000-bottle, aboveground wine cellar. Prices at Emeril's are high enough that the restaurant can afford tons of legroom between tables and an assortment of pricey abstract paintings on the walls.

Emeril Lagasse originally had few offerings penciled in for kids (in keeping with the adult atmosphere of his restaurants outside Florida) but quickly adjusted his menu to suit Orlando's family atmosphere, and now your children can feast on a minifilet, fried shrimp, cheese tortellini, chicken tenders, or a wood-oven pizza. He's also gone on record to say that parents introducing their kids to fine dining shouldn't make it a chore but rather emphasize the special nature of the occasion. And that's exactly what this meal should be for your kids—a special treat (though I would leave younger ones with a sitter).

Note: Lunch costs about two thirds what you'll spend on dinner, and the menu has many of the same entrees. It's also easier to get a reservation, and the dress code is more casual; jackets are recommended for gents at dinner, although that goes against the grain after a long day in the parks.

6000 Universal Studios Blvd., in CityWalk. ☎ **407/224-2424.** www.emerils.com. Kids' menu w/activities, highchairs, boosters. Reservations necessary. Main courses $18–$28 lunch, $31–$50 dinner, kids $7.50–$17. Daily 11:30am–2:30pm; Sun–Thurs 5:30–10pm; Fri–Sat 5:30–11pm. AE, DISC, MC, V. Parking $9 (free after 6pm). From I-4, take Exit 75B, Kirkman Rd./Hwy. 435, and follow the signs to Universal.

The Palm STEAKS/SEAFOOD   This upscale restaurant in the Hard Rock Hotel is the 23rd member of a chain started more than 75 years ago in New York. The food is good, though, as is the case with most Disney and Universal restaurants, somewhat overpriced for the value received. Beef and seafood rule a menu headlined by a 36-ounce New York strip steak for two ($71). Smaller appetites and budgets can feast on broiled crab cakes, veal piccata, and lamb chops. The kids' menu (steak, chicken, pasta, and burgers) is pricey, though not quite as expensive as Emeril's. The decor leans toward the upscale supper clubs of the '30s and '40s, and the walls are lined with caricatures of celebrities and other famous people. Older kids will likely be impressed with the atmosphere, but this isn't the place to bring little ones.

5800 Universal Blvd., in the Hard Rock Hotel. ℂ 407/503-7256. www.thepalm.com. Reservations recommended. Main courses $9–$38, kids $8–$18. AE, DC, DISC, MC, V. Mon–Sat 5–11pm; Sun 5–10pm. Free 3-hr. validated self-parking, valet $10. From I-4, take Exit 75B, Kirkman Rd./Hwy. 435, and follow the signs to Universal.

EXPENSIVE

Tchoup Chop ✿✿ PACIFIC RIM   Pronounced "chop chop," the Royal Pacific Hotel's headline restaurant and Emeril Lagasse's second in Orlando is named for the location of his original restaurant: Tchoupitoulous Street in New Orleans. It's a nice place for a special night out for the family and a good spot to introduce your kids to the pleasures of fine dining; they'll likely be very taken with the atmosphere. The interior blends colorful flowers, sculpted gardens, and miniwaterfalls with Batik fabrics, carved wood grilles, and glass chandeliers. The exhibition kitchen offers a look at the chefs making your meal in woks or on wood-burning grills. Tchoup Chop's January 2003 coming out introduced a Polynesian- and Asian-influenced menu with temptations such as macadamia nut–crusted Atlantic salmon with ginger soy butter sauce, braised Kobe beef short ribs with ham-hock red beans, and smoked oyster–stuffed quail with crispy spinach. The chefs solicited opinions from both parents and kids when formulating the kids' menu, so your offspring will find treats such as tempura chicken nuggets, stir-fried shrimp with noodles, chicken spring rolls, and burgers.

6300 Hollywood Way, in Universal's Royal Pacific Hotel. ℂ 407/503-2467. www.emerils.com. Kids' menu w/activities, highchairs, boosters. Reservations strongly recommended. Main courses $13–$34, kids $8–$12. AE, DISC, MC, V. Daily 11:30am–2pm; Sun–Thurs 5:30–10pm; Fri-Sat 5:30–11pm. Valet parking $5. From I-4, take Exit 75B, Kirkman Rd./Hwy. 435, and follow the signs to Universal.

MODERATE

Hard Rock Cafe *Overrated* AMERICAN   The largest Hard Rock Cafe on the planet features a 1959 pink Cadillac spinning above the bar. With its size, however, comes

---

Tips **More Kid Cuisine II . . .**

Here are a few additional places for your smaller fry to grab a bite in the Universal resorts and parks. You can find additional information on the Internet at **www.universalorlando.com**.

- **Confisco Grille,** Islands of Adventure—mac and cheese, cheese pizza, chicken tenders, burgers, and ravioli ($6–$8).
- **Finnegan's Bar & Grill,** Universal Studios Florida—grilled cheese, chicken fingers, burgers, mac and cheese, and PB&Js ($5–$8).
- **Lombard's Landing,** Universal Studios Florida—chicken fingers, fried fish, burgers, and linguine with marinara sauce ($6.75–$8).
- **Mythos,** Islands of Adventure—chicken fingers, cheese pizza, ravioli, ham- and-cheddar wrap, and burgers ($6–$8).
- **NASCAR Cafe,** CityWalk—chicken fingers, cheese pizza, spaghetti, burgers, and corn dogs ($6).

that much more noise—and the sound levels are loud. Kids love it, but adults shouldn't even think about having a conversation here. The menu is the same found at Hard Rocks around the world and includes burgers, chicken, okay steaks, and fried this-and-that. And of course, it has its very own souvenir shop, too. The food is average American fare; it's the experience that draws people in. *Note:* The adjacent Hard Rock Live! is a huge venue for concerts.

6000 Universal Studios Blvd., near Universal CityWalk. ☎ 407/351-7625. www.hardrock.com. Kids' menu w/activities, highchairs, boosters. Reservations not accepted. Main courses $9–$23, kids $7. AE, MC, V. Daily 11am–11pm. Parking $9 (free after 6pm). From I-4, take Exit 75B, Kirkman Rd./Hwy. 435, and follow the signs to Universal.

Jimmy Buffett's Margaritaville CARIBBEAN   The casual, laid-back atmosphere may take you away to paradise, but the noise level after 4pm makes it futile for Parrotheads and plain folk alike to try to talk with their table mates—although most folks come to Margaritaville to sing and get stupid, not to gab. Given that introduction, it should come as no surprise that I recommend you bring kids here for lunch only, before the hard partying starts. The back "Porch of Indecision" offers the quietest spot in the place to dine. Despite the cheeseburgers in paradise (yes, they're on the menu at $8–$9), the menu has Caribbean leanings and includes a Cuban meatloaf survival sandwich, Creole shrimp marinara, Jimmy's jammin' jambalaya, and corn-and-crab bisque. And while it's not contending for a critic's-choice award, it's fairly tasty grub. Kids' choices include a small cheeseburger in paradise, mac and cheese, chicken fingers, spaghetti and meatballs, and PB&Js. If you don't thirst for margaritas ($6–$8 a pop; ouch!), the drink menu is almost as long as the main menu and features domestic and imported beer, as well as some unique tropical concoctions.

1000 Universal Studios Plaza, in CityWalk. ☎ 407/224-2155. www.universalorlando.com. Kids' menu w/activities, highchairs, boosters. Reservations not accepted. Main courses $8–$22 (most under $15), kids $6–$8. AE, DISC, MC, V. Daily 11am–midnight. Parking $9 (free after 6pm). From I-4, take Exit 75B, Kirkman Rd./Hwy. 435, and follow the signs to Universal.

Pastamore Ristorante ✿ SOUTHERN ITALIAN   This family-style restaurant greets you with display cases brimming with mozzarella and other goodies lurking on the menu. Speaking of menus, Pastamore's may have the longest kids' menu in O-Town: chicken parmigiana, chicken fingers, grilled shrimp, filet mignon, fettuccine alfredo, fried cheese ravioli, spaghetti and tomato sauce, pizza, and burgers. I highly recommend it for families with kids of all ages. On the adult side, the antipasto primo is a meal unto itself. The mound includes bruschetta, eggplant caponata, melon con prosciutto, grilled portobello mushrooms, olives, a medley of Italian cold cuts, plum tomatoes, fresh mozzarella, and more. The menu also features such traditional offerings as veal Marsala, chicken piccata, shrimp scampi, fettuccine Alfredo, lasagna, and pizza. The food is actually pretty interesting, and the presentation isn't bad, either. There's an open kitchen allowing a view of the chefs. Pastamore has a basic beer and wine menu. You can also eat in a cafe where a lighter menu—breakfast fare and sandwiches—is served from 8am to 2am.

1000 Universal Studios Plaza, in CityWalk. ☎ 407/363-8000. www.universalorlando.com. Kids' menu w/activities, highchairs, boosters. Reservations accepted. Main courses $7–$18, kids $5–$12. AE, DISC, MC, V. Daily 5pm–midnight. Parking $9 (free after 6pm). From I-4, take Exit 75B, Kirkman Rd./Hwy. 435, and follow the signs to Universal.

5 Places to Dine in the International Drive Area

International Drive has one of the area's larger collections of fast-food joints, but the midsection and southern third also have some of this region's better restaurants. South

---

Value **Self-Service Suppers**

If you're on a tight budget, and your room has a kitchen or a spot to sit and grab a bite, consider dining in a night or two and saving a few bucks. Area grocers, many with delis that turn out ready-to-eat treats, include **Albertson's** near I-Drive (7524 Dr. Phillips Blvd.; ℭ **407/352-1552**; www.albertsons.com) and **Gooding's** in Lake Buena Vista (Crossroads Shopping Plaza, 12521 Hwy. 535/ Apopka–Vineland Ave.; ℭ **407/827-1200**; www.goodings.com). You can find more locations and options in the Orlando Yellow Pages under "Grocers."

I-Drive is 10 minutes by auto from the Walt Disney World parks. Most of the restaurants listed here are located on the "International Drive Area Dining" map on p. 153.

VERY EXPENSIVE

Atlantis ☞ SUNDAY BRUNCH   The signature restaurant at the Renaissance Orlando Resort at SeaWorld has a respectable evening menu (steaks, chops, and seafood), but the family favorite here is Sunday's champagne brunch, which is served in the resort's huge atrium. Themes change monthly, but the 100-item menu often has treats such as quail, duck, lamb chops, Cornish hen, clams, mussels, sea bass, sushi, and more. Although there isn't a kid-specific menu, with that many choices—including yummy pastries!—young diners are sure to find some things they like.

6677 Sea Harbour Dr., in the Renaissance Orlando Resort. ℭ 407/351-5555. www.renaissancehotels.com. No kids' menu; highchairs, boosters. Reservations recommended. Sunday brunch $32 adults, $16 children. AE, DC, DISC, MC, V. Sun 10:30am–2pm. Free self-parking, valet parking $9. From I-4, take Exit 71/Central Florida Pkwy. east, and follow the signs to SeaWorld.

Charlie's Lobster House SEAFOOD   This 17-year-old, good-time eatery cranks out a menu bursting with treats from the Gulf of Mexico, Pacific, and Atlantic in a setting straight out of New England. Fish and shellfish specialties include pan-roasted Maine lobster, grilled or blackened yellowfin tuna, Alaskan king-crab legs, Maryland-style crab cakes, and broiled shrimp with lump-crab stuffing. Landlubbers can choose among a handful of steaks, including filets and strips. Although Charlie's is kid-friendly, there are only a few menu options specifically for small fry (shrimp, chicken fingers, and burgers).

8845 International Dr., in the Mercado Shopping Plaza. ℭ 407/352-6929. www.charlieslobsterhouse.com. Kids' menu, highchairs, boosters. Reservations suggested. Main courses $19–$46, kids $7. AE, DC, DISC, MC, V. Daily 5–10pm. Free self-parking. From I-4, take Exit 74A, Sand Lake Rd./Hwy. 528, east to International Dr., and then south.

MODERATE

Bahama Breeze ☞ CARIBBEAN   This chain restaurant sports a creative menu that offers a variety of delicious sandwiches and chicken, fish, and pasta entrees with Caribbean twists. Try starting with the Creole baked goat cheese before moving on to the Cuban sandwich, one of the most authentic around. If that is not to your liking, try the pan-seared pork or Bahamian chicken kabobs. Kids can dine on chicken fingers, cheese pizza, mac and cheese, and grilled cheese. The atmosphere is island casual, with rich wood and wicker throughout. On a warm evening, ask to eat outside. Once famous for its long waits, the restaurant now accepts call-ahead reservations; be sure to make one. You can pass the time watching chefs working in the open kitchen if you

International Drive Area Dining

For Restaurants in Universal Orlando's CityWalk, please see the "CityWalk" map in chapter 10.

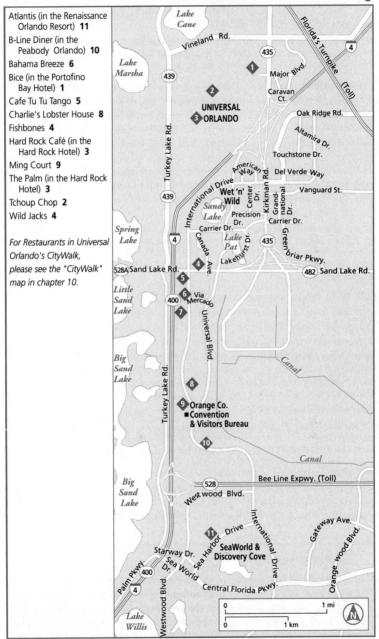

forget. *Note:* A second branch is located in Lake Buena Vista at 8735 Vineland Ave., near the I-4 intersection (© **407/938-9010**).

8849 International Drive, Orlando. © **407/248-2499.** www.bahamabreeze.com. Kids' menu w/activities, highchairs, boosters. Same-day reservations are available. Lunch and dinner $9–$25. AE, DISC, MC, V. Mon–Fri 4pm–1:30am; Sat noon–1:30am; Sun noon–1am. Free self-parking. From I-4, take exit 74A, follow I-Drive 1 mile south.

B-Line Diner AMERICAN   You and your kids can sink into upholstered booths or belly up to the counter on a stool in this rather upscale version of a '50s-style diner with a fabulous dessert case (the cakes are a major hit with all ages, as are the yummy sundaes and shakes). The round-the-clock menu features comfort foods such as a chicken pot pie that's as good as what Mom made; a ham-and-cheese sandwich on a baguette; and roast pork with grilled apples, sun-dried cherry stuffing, and brandy–honey sauce. The kids' menu offers chicken fingers, spaghetti, grilled cheese, and burgers. Portions are hearty, but so are the prices for diner fare. Though it is a diner-style restaurant, the atmosphere's not particularly kid-friendly unless your children are older or exceptionally well behaved.

9801 International Dr., in the Peabody Orlando. © **407/345-4460.** www.peabodyorlando.com. Kids' menu w/activities, highchairs, boosters. Reservations not accepted. Main courses $4–$16 at breakfast, $7–$18 at lunch, $9–$26 (most under $18) at dinner, kids $6–$10. AE, DC, DISC, MC, V. Daily 24-hr. free self- and validated valet parking. From I-4, take Exit 74A, Sand Lake Rd./Hwy. 528, east to International Dr., and then south. Hotel is on the left across from the Convention Center.

Café Tu Tu Tango *Finds* INTERNATIONAL/TAPAS   Designed like a Spanish artist's loft, this eclectic eatery offers performance or art experiences while you munch on appetizer-size minimeals. The atmosphere—there's frequently an artist bringing a canvas to life—should keep your children reasonably entertained. The portions are small, but the tastes are big. The roasted pears on pecan crisps—topped with Spanish blue cheese and a balsamic reduction—are a must. The kids' menu has grilled cheese, spaghetti, pizza (they can exercise their creativity by designing their own personal pie), chicken fingers, and corn dogs. The staff is fabulous, and your server will be happy to educate you about the menu or make suggestions. Wine is available by the glass or bottle.

8625 International Drive. © **407/248-2222.** www.cafetututango.com. Reservations accepted but not required. Tapas (small plates) $4–$11. AE, DC, DISC, MC, V. Sun–Thurs 11:30am–11pm; Fri–Sat 11:30am–midnight. Free self-parking. From I-4, take exit 74A, Sand Lake Rd./Hwy 528, east to International Drive, and then south. It is on the left.

Fishbones SEAFOOD   The fish at this nautically themed restaurant is hand-picked daily to ensure freshness and taste. You can create your own meal by mixing and matching sauces and salsas to enhance your selected fish (there are plenty of varieties to choose among). If fish isn't your dish, other offerings include rack of lamb, prime

---

Tips **Room Service**

For those of you who would rather take a break from eating out, there are Orlando restaurants that are more than willing to come to you. A local delivery service, Take Out Express, will deliver takeout from a number of area restaurants (even more than one at a time, for an extra charge) right to your hotel room. The delivery cost is about $5 to order from one restaurant, with a separate (though lower) delivery charge for each additional restaurant you order from. Call © **407/352-1170** for details or to order.

rib, and duck. Portions are large; the atmosphere is friendly; and children are catered to with a special kids' menu.

6707 Sand Lake Rd., off of International Dr. © 407/352-0135. Main courses $13–$40 (most below $25). AE, MC, V. Sun–Thurs 5–10:30pm, Fri–Sat until 11pm. Free self-parking. From I-4 take exit 74A, and go east on SR 482 (Sand Lake Rd.) ⅓ mile.

Ming Court ✹ CHINESE   Local patronage and a diverse menu make this one of Orlando's most popular Chinese eateries (which was recently named 1 of the top 100 Chinese restaurants in the country by a major restaurant trade publication). Start with the duck lettuce cup before going on to the lightly battered, deep-fried chicken breast; it's got plenty of zip from a delicate lemon–tangerine sauce. If you're in the mood for beef, there's a grilled filet mignon that's seasoned Szechuan style (the topping has toasted onions, garlic, and chili). The mildly innovative menu is extensive, featuring the freshest ingredients (there's not a freezer on site). Portions are sufficient; there's a moderate wine list; and the service is quite good.

The candlelit interior is decorated in soft earth tones and creates a romantic atmosphere. Glass-walled terrace rooms overlook lotus ponds filled with colorful koi and a plant-filled area under a lofty skylight ceiling. A musician plays classical Chinese music on a *zheng* (a long zither) at dinner. The children's menu features a boxed meal featuring their choice of Oriental-style shrimp, pork, beef, or chicken (and french fries!) and comes with a story for kids to read along with their dinner. *Tip:* The restaurant's website is extensive and features lots of information on, and photos of, individual dishes.

9188 International Dr., between Sand Lake Rd. and Bee Line Expressway. © 407/351-9988. www.ming-court.com. Reservations recommended. Main courses $7–$13 lunch, $13–$36 dinner; dim sum mostly $3–$5. AE, DC, DISC, MC, V. Daily 11am–2:30pm and 4:30–10:30pm. Free self-parking. From I-4, take Exit 74A, Sand Lake Rd./Hwy. 528, east to International Dr., and then south. It's on the right.

Wild Jacks BARBECUE/STEAKS   Your family should come hankering red meat or not come at all to this chuckwagon-style eatery. Jacks serves Texas-size (and sometimes Texas-tough) hunks of cow grilled on an open pit and served with jalapeño smashed potatoes and corn on the cob. It's a family-friendly spot that's a good place to bring the kids; the interior, filled with mounted buffalo heads, long-stuffed jack-a-lopes, and more twitch-and-twang country/Western music than a city slicker can endure in a lifetime, should prove diverting for the young set. The ribs are generally moist and tender, but at crowded times, when the kitchen gets backed up, they may be dry and chewy. The menu also has chicken, salmon, and pork, but it's not a good idea to experiment in a beef house, even a marginal one. Kids have a range of choices, from pint-size steaks, ribs, and burgers to pasta and chicken tenders. Wash the meal down with an icy longneck (there is a wine list, but it's very basic).

7364 International Dr. (between Sand Lake Rd. and Carrier Dr.). © 407/352-4407. Kids' menu w/activities, highchairs, boosters. Reservations accepted. AE, DC, DISC, MC, V. Main courses $11–$21, kids $6.50. Daily 4–10pm. Free self-parking. From I-4, take Exit 74A, Sand Lake Rd./Hwy. 528, east to International Dr., and then go south. It's on the right.

6 Places to Dine Elsewhere in Orlando

There's life in other areas, as locals and enterprising visitors discover, though many of them aren't as child-friendly as those near the theme parks and may not have a kids' menu. We list the family-friendly establishments off the beaten track below, as well as a few options that are best reserved for nights out on your own or for special forays with older kids and teens.

Note: The restaurants in this part of the chapter are located on the "Dining Elsewhere in Orlando" map on p. 157.

EXPENSIVE

Blackfin Seafood Grill & Bar ☞ SEAFOOD   One of Orlando's better marine cuisineries (along with Crabby Bill's, which is listed a little later in this chapter), Blackfin is a classy and casual eatery for those flexible enough to get to the region's north end. Menu headliners include oak-grilled pompano or orange swordfish in lemon butter, delicately blackened wahoo with pan-seared sesame mayonnaise, and red snapper with a Parmesan crust. Landlubbers find an oak-grilled veal chop with a shiraz demi-glacé and herb-roasted chicken breasts delivered with wild rice. On the kiddie side, the limited options include corn dogs, chicken nuggets, spaghetti, and rock shrimp.

460 N. Orlando Ave., Winter Park. ⓒ 407/691-4653. Kids' menu, highchairs, boosters. Reservations recommended. Main courses $25–$40 (most under $30), kids $3–$6. AE, DC, DISC, MC, V. Sun–Wed 5–10pm; Thurs–Sat 5–11pm. Free self-parking. From I-4 Exit 88, go east on Lee Rd.; turn south on US 17-92/N. Orlando Ave. It's located on the east side.

Mikado Japanese Steak House ☞ JAPANESE   This restaurant offers a tastier meal and a more intimate atmosphere than the other Japanese steakhouses in the area. The sushi menu is one of the area's best, as is its *teppanyaki.* Here, the chefs slice, dice, and send the occasional piece of chicken, seafood, and beef from their grill to your plate, and the chef's addition of a few extra special spices make it the best *teppanyaki* around. Your children will likely find the atmosphere exotic and cool, but be aware that the kids' menu is very limited, though pint-size portions of the teppanyaki entrees are available and likely much better than the grilled cheese, pizza, and burgers. Shoji screens lend intimacy to a dining area where windows overlook rock gardens, reflecting pools, and a palm-fringed pond. Sake, from the restaurant lounge, may be in order for Mom and Dad.

8701 World Center Dr. (off Hwy. 536), in Marriott's Orlando World Center. ⓒ 407/239-4200. Reservations recommended. Main courses $16–$35. AE, DC, DISC, MC, V. Daily 6–10pm. Free self- and validated valet parking. Take I-4 Exit 67/Hwy. 536 east to the Marriott World Center.

MODERATE

Crabby Bill's ☞ SEAFOOD   This fun, friendly member of a small central Florida chain was launched by "Crabby Bill" Loder in 1975 and continues to deliver quality seafood to diners who dig in from family-style tables. In season, the grouper is fresh and fabulous. (I recommend trying it broiled, which keeps it juicy, but you also can order it blackened or fried, including in a sandwich.) If the oysters on the half shell are farm-raised in Texas (ask), they're small but very sweet. The house specialties—no surprise here—include stone-crab claws (Oct–May) as well as king, snow, and blue crabs. The menu also has a variety of fried, grilled, broiled, or blackened fish. Kids will find burgers, chicken fingers, fried shrimp or fish, mac and cheese, and spaghetti and meatballs (all dishes are served with Oreos—sure to please your kids' palate).

5030 E. Irlo Bronson Memorial Hwy./U.S. 192, Kissimmee (between Poinciana Blvd. and Vineland Rd.). ⓒ 321/677-0303. www.crabbybills.com. Reservations not necessary. Main courses $9–$25 (most under $14), sandwiches $4.50–$7, kids $3–$4. AE, DC, DISC, MC, V. Daily 11:30am–10pm.

Pacino's Italian Ristorante ☞ NORTHERN ITALIAN   The house specialty at this family-friendly spot, veal osso buco, is a delicious collision of veal shank, mushrooms, Barolo wine, herbs, and mushrooms. At 32 ounces, the porterhouse steak is a belly-buster; and the house's *frutti di mare* has shrimp, calamari, clams, and scallops sautéed with white wine and herbs, and heaped onto a mound of linguine. Pasta-loving kids get

Dining Elsewhere in Orlando

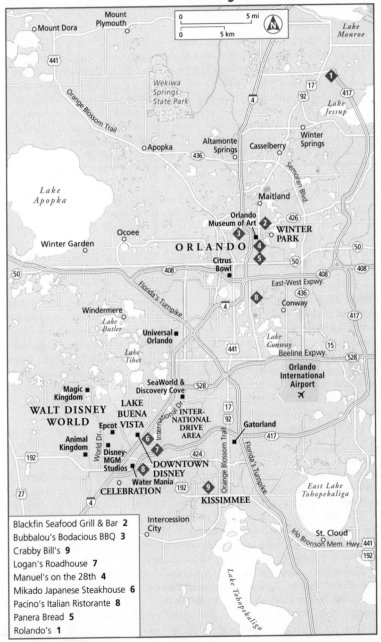

Blackfin Seafood Grill & Bar **2**
Bubbalou's Bodacious BBQ **3**
Crabby Bill's **9**
Logan's Roadhouse **7**
Manuel's on the 28th **4**
Mikado Japanese Steakhouse **6**
Pacino's Italian Ristorante **8**
Panera Bread **5**
Rolando's **1**

Value Bargain Buffets

I won't list them all, but if you spend time on International Drive or U.S. 192/Irlo Bronson Memorial Highway between Kissimmee and Disney, you'll see billboards peddling all-you-can-eat breakfast buffets for $4 to $6. All these spots welcome kids and are a good way to fill your family's tanks early and skip (or at least go easy on) lunch, especially if your day is in the theme parks, where lunches are overpriced. Breakfast buffets are served by **Golden Corral,** 8033 International Dr. (© 407/352-6606); **Ponderosa Steak House,** 6362 International Dr. (© 407/352-9343) and 7598 U.S. 192 W. (© 407/396-7721); and **Sizzler Restaurant,** 9142 International Dr. (© 407/351-5369) and 7602 U.S. 192 W. (© 407/397-0997).

---

their choice of spaghetti, lasagna, and pizza, while those craving something from the animal food group can dig into chicken tenders. The ceiling's fiber optics help create an illusion of dining under the stars; there's a patio if you want the real thing. Some servers can be a little aloof, but the price and taste make up for it.

5795 W. Irlo Bronson Memorial Hwy./U.S. 192, Kissimmee. © 407/396-8022. www.pacinos.com. Kids' menu w/activities, highchairs, boosters. Reservations accepted. Main courses $13–$27 (most under $20), pizza $9–$11, kids $4–$5. AE, MC, V. Daily 4–10pm. Free self-parking. From I-4, take Exit 64A/U.S. 192 exit east 1 mile.

Panera Bread *Finds* AMERICAN   This trendy cafe–bakery is a great place for a light meal, and its quick growth in the area (there are several locations) attests to its popularity among locals and visitors alike. The cafe menu offers a variety of delicious soups (broccoli cheddar, black bean, vegetable sirloin, and others) and salads (Asian sesame chicken, Caesar, and more). But the real main events are sandwiches, such as turkey with chipotle mayonnaise, roast beef with creamy horseradish sauce, portobello and mozzarella panini, and a dozen others. While there isn't a kid-specific menu, most young appetites would be happy to dive into the bakery menu (caramel pecan or very chocolate brownies, bear claws, and cherry Danish) or a PB&J on French bread from the cafe menu.

296 E. Michigan St., Orlando. © 407/481-9880. www.panerabread.com. Reservations not accepted. Main courses $7–$14, baked goods $1–$5. AE, DISC, MC, V. Mon–Sat 6:30am–9:30pm; Sun 7am–8:30pm. Free self-parking. From I-4, take Exit 80B, U.S. 17/92, go north to Michigan, and then right 1½ miles.

Rolando's *Finds* CUBAN   If you like neighborhood-style Cuban cuisine, you won't be disappointed here. This mom-and-pop restaurant serves large portions of traditional Cuban fare, such as *arroz con pollo* (chicken with yellow rice); *ropa vieja* (shredded beef); and, if you call a few hours or a day in advance, *paella* (fish and shellfish served on a bed of rice). I also recommend Rolando's roast chicken, which is brushed with crushed garlic, white-wine vinegar, cumin, and oregano, and then briefly deep-fried. Entrees are served with yucca (a chewy root) or plantains (a cooked bananalike fruit). Kids' options include mac and cheese, a ham-and-cheese sandwich, and chicken fingers. The plain dining room has Formica tables, old photographs of Cuba, and potted philodendrons suspended from the ceiling. Soft lighting adds a smidgen of ambience, and there's a very limited beer-and-wine list.

870 E. Hwy. 436/Semoran Blvd., Casselberry. © 407/767-9677. Kids' menu, highchairs, boosters. Reservations accepted. Main courses $4–$6 lunch, $8–$18 dinner, kids $4–$5. AE, DC, DISC, MC, V. Mon–Fri 11am–9:30pm; Sat noon–10pm; Sun noon–8:30pm. Free self-parking. From I-4, take Exit 82A, Hwy. 408/East–West Expwy., head east, and make a left on Hwy. 436.

INEXPENSIVE

Bubbalou's Bodacious BBQ ☆ *Value* BARBECUE   You can smell the hickory smoke emerging from this family-friendly restaurant for blocks, the tangy scent cutting through the humid Florida air. This is, hands down, some of the best barbecue you'll find anywhere. And if nothing else, you have to love the name. There are other things on the menu. If you can eat the night or day away, go for "The Big-Big Pig" platter (beef, sliced pork, and turkey with fixin's). There also are several barbecue baskets, combos, dinners, and sandwiches, as well as side orders ranging from fried pickles and okra to collard greens and black-eyed peas. The uninitiated should stay away from the "Killer" sauce, which produces a tongue buzz that's likely to last for hours; you might even taste-test the mild before moving up to the hot. The beans are the perfect side dish (if you don't mind producing methane hours later). Your kids have a

---

Not Just Fries Anymore

Some of you may not be able to go your entire vacation without a trip to McDonald's for a Big Mac. If you just can't pass up a trip to Mickie D's for a fast-food fix, the good news is that Orlando has a handful of uniquely themed McDonald's unlike any you'll find in your neighborhood. All of them sport eclectic menus, which, in addition to the usual fare, add (among other items) pizzas, portobello eggplant, turkey wraps, panini, and crème brûlée cheesecake.

The 24-hour McDonald's **European Café**, 7344 Sand Lake Road, Orlando, (© 407/264-0776), boasts two levels with plenty of glass to allow sunlight to pour in. You won't mistake it for a European cafe (it's still a McDonald's, so don't get too carried away), but cool features include a pool table and arcade games on the second level, and fabulous views of the sand lakes.

The **Ancient Ruins** branch, located at 5401 Altamira Dr. (© 407/345-9477), is themed (wonder of wonders) on the ancient ruins of Greece, complete with broken columns, stone walls, and frieze-style moldings.

Moving on to Africa, the **Club Safari** location, 2944 S. Kirkman Rd. (© 407/296-6265), boasts an African Safari theme complete with rich wooden fixtures, African masks and artwork, crystal chandeliers, and animal prints galore. Animatronic toucan and Tiki figures sing jungle jingles, and you can't help but take note of the 13-foot bronze giraffe and two bronze tigers keeping watch.

Chrome shines everywhere you turn at the **Motorcycle McDonald's,** 5400 S. Kirkman Rd. (© 407/352-1526). Tail pipes, shocks, and various other bike parts adorn the restaurant's walls.

Finally, the **world's largest McDonald's** can also be found in Orlando, right on 6875 Sand Lake Rd. (© 407/351-2185). The location boasts a huge tubular maze with 25,000 feet of twists, turns, sliding, crawling, and jumping space for kids to play in. Another unique feature: You can book hotels, transportation, buy attraction tickets, and get daily park information, all while enjoying your fries and a Coke (or in this case, maybe a gourmet coffee).

choice of barbecued chicken or chicken strips, grilled cheese, burgers, or corn dogs. And there's takeout (including special family packs) available if you want to head back with something to snack on in your hotel room.

1471 Lee Rd., Winter Park (about 5 min. from downtown Orlando). © **407/628-1212.** www.bubbalous.com. Kids' menu, highchairs, boosters. Reservations not accepted. Main courses $4–$13, kids $3.50–$4. AE, MC, V. Mon–Thurs 10am–9pm; Fri–Sat 10am–10pm. Free self-parking. Take I-4 Exit 88, Lee Rd./Hwy. 423, and follow your nose; Bubbalou's is on the left, next to a dry cleaner's.

Logan's Roadhouse *Kids* SOUTHWESTERN   Set along the busy thoroughfare of U.S. 192 in Kissimmee, this laid-back eatery serves up a varied menu of Southwestern favorites and barbecue. Kick back and relax a spell, and go ahead and throw those peanut shells on the floor (your mom won't yell at you here). Standouts include the San Antonio chicken wraps; the mesquite-grilled salmon, chicken, and pork; and the barbecued chicken and ribs. You can also get, however, a host of sandwiches, salads, seafood, steaks, burgers, and rib-sticking sides. The casual roadhouse decor, friendly service, and varied menu full of kid-friendly favorites (including chicken, burgers, hot dogs, mac and cheese, and steak tips) make this one a great choice for families.

4510 Irlo Bronson Memorial Highway (U.S. 192 at the intersection of International Drive South), Kissimmee. © **407/ 390-0500.** www.logansroadhouse.com. Main courses $6–$17, kids $5–$7. AE, DISC, MC, V. Sun–Thurs 11am– 10:30pm, Fri–Sat 11am–11:30pm. Free self-parking. Take exit 64 towards Celebration, and follow U.S. 192 (the restaurant is on your left).

7 Only in Orlando: Dining with Disney Characters

Dining with your favorite costumed characters is a treat for many Disney fans, but it's a truly special occasion for those under 10. Some of the most beloved movie characters seemingly come to life, shaking hands, hugging, signing autographs, and posing for family photos (most never speak, with the exception of the princesses and a very small handful of others—just so you know). These are huge events—it's not uncommon for Chef Mickey's, listed below, to have **1,600 or more guests on a weekend morning**—so make reservations as far in advance as possible (when you book your room, if not earlier), and don't expect more than just a few moments of one-on-one, but what time there is, is sure to bring a smile to little ones' faces.

The prices for character meals are much the same, no matter where you're dining. Breakfast (most serve it) runs $17 to $32 for adults and $9 to $10 for children 3 to 11; those that serve dinner charge $22 to $39 for adults and $10 to $13 for kids. The prices vary a bit, though, from location to location.

To make reservations for WDW character meals, call © **407/939-3463.** American Express, Diners Club, Discover, MasterCard, Visa, and the Disney Visa Card are accepted at all character meals.

You'll find all the restaurants mentioned in this section on the map, "Walt Disney World & Lake Buena Vista Dining," earlier in this chapter. For Internet information, go to **www.disneyworld.com**.

Note: Although the character appearances below were accurate when this book went to press, lineups and booking requirements change frequently (as do menus and prices). I strongly recommend against promising children they will meet a specific character at a meal. And you should never mention dining with the characters unless your Advance Dining Reservation arrangements are confirmed first; character meals book up quickly, and trying to arrange Advance Dining Reservation too late in the game (or, worse, attempting to walk in) will mostly likely result in disappointment. If you have your heart set on meeting a certain character, call to confirm his or her appearance when making your Advance Dining Reservation arrangement.

Cape May Café   The Cape May Café, a delightful New England–themed dining room, serves lavish buffet breakfasts (eggs, pancakes, bacon, pastries) hosted by **Admiral Goofy** and his crew: **Chip 'n' Dale** and **Pluto** (characters may vary). Its location at the Beach Club Resort makes it a great way to start the day when you're on your way to nearby Epcot.

1800 Epcot Resorts Blvd., at Disney's Beach Club Resort. $18 adults, $10 children. Daily 7:30–11am.

Chef Mickey's 😊😊   The whimsical Chef Mickey's offers buffet breakfasts (eggs, bacon, sausage, pancakes, fruit) and dinners (entrees change daily; salad bar, soups, vegetables, ice cream with toppings). Aside from the characters, kids will enjoy watching the monorail go by overhead as it passes through the Contemporary Resort. **Mickey, Minnie, and various pals** make their way to every table while meeting and mingling with guests. While this is one of the largest restaurants offering character dining, if you plan on dining here during spring break and around the holidays, it's best to make Advance Dining Reservation arrangements well ahead of time.

4600 N. World Dr., at Disney's Contemporary Resort. Breakfast $18 adults, $10 children; dinner $27 adults, $12 children. Daily 7–11:30am and 5–9:30pm.

Cinderella's Royal Table 😊   Cinderella Castle—the most recognized icon in all of the WDW resort, not to mention the center of the Magic Kingdom—serves character breakfast buffets daily (a variety of breakfast favorites, including scrambled eggs, bacon, Danish) and, as of February 2006, serves character lunches and dinners as well. Hosts vary (the Fairy Godmother was hosting dinners as this book went to press), but **Cinderella** always puts in an appearance. This is one of the most popular character meals in the park and the hardest to get into, so **reserve far, far in advance** (reservations are taken 180 days in advance, and you must pay for your meal in full with a credit card at time of booking). To have the best shot at getting in, be flexible about your seating arrangements and dining times, and call Disney exactly at 7am EST on your first date of reservations eligibility (if you aren't sure what date that is, call Disney, and they'll help you figure it out). If you get through on your first try (lucky you!), tell the reservations clerk you want Cinderella's Table for whatever date you've picked. Don't even think about requesting a specific time; take whatever you can get (most reservations will be gone by 7:15am).

In Cinderella Castle, at the Magic Kingdom. Breakfast $32 adult, $22 children 3–9; lunch $34 adult, $23 children 3–9; dinner $40 adults, $25 children 3–9. Daily 8am–10:20am, noon–3pm; 4pm–park closing. Theme-park admission required.

Crystal Palace Buffet 😊   The prettiest of the Magic Kingdom's restaurants, the Crystal Palace features a glass exterior that glimmers in sunlight. **Winnie the Pooh and pals** hold court here throughout the day. The restaurant serves breakfast (eggs, French toast, pancakes, bacon, and more), lunch, and dinner. The latter features a long list of hot and cold entrees that usually include some type of poultry, beef, seafood, an array of veggies, salads, and kid-friendly favorites. The dessert buffet includes a make-your-own-sundae bar.

At Crystal Palace, in the Magic Kingdom. Breakfast $18 adults, $10 children; lunch $20 adults, $11 children; dinner $23 adults, $12 children. Daily 8–10:30am, 11:30am–2:45pm, 4pm–park closing. Theme-park admission required.

Other Casts of Characters

Not wanting to feel left out, Universal Orlando and SeaWorld have instituted their own character dining experiences. Like Disney's meals, these are very popular experiences, so be sure to reserve your spot as far in advance as possible.

At Islands of Adventure, the **Confisco Grill** is home to a character breakfast buffet where Spider-Man, Captain America, the Cat in the Hat, and Thing 1 and Thing 2 all join in on the fun. It runs Thursday through Sunday from park opening until 10:30am. The cost is $16 adults and $10 kids 3 to 9. Call ✆ **407/224-4012** for more information or to make reservations.

At SeaWorld, you can chow down on a buffet lunch right alongside the killer whales at the daily **Dine with Shamu,** at the Shamu Stadium. The cost is $32 adults and $18 children ages 3 to 9; park admission is required but not included in the cost. The **Shamu and Crew** character breakfast buffet, held at the Seafire Inn in the Waterfront district, is offered only seasonally, during the park's Halloween and Christmas celebrations. The action takes place 8:45 to 10:15am. The cost is $15 adults and $10 children ages 3 to 9; park admission is required but not included in the cost. For both character experiences, call ✆ **800/327-2420,** or check out **www.seaworld.com** for more information or to make a reservation.

Donald's Prehistoric Breakfastosaurus   **Donald, Goofy,** and **Pluto** host a buffet breakfast (eggs, bacon, French toast) in Dinoland U.S.A.'s Restaurantosaurus.

In Dinoland U.S.A., at Disney's Animal Kingdom. $17 adults, $9 children. Daily park opening–10am. Theme-park admission required.

Garden Grill ☞   There's a "Momma's-in-the-kitchen" theme at this revolving restaurant, where hearty, family-style meals are hosted by **Mickey** and **Chip 'n' Dale.** (Mickey sure gets around, eh?) Lunch and dinner (chicken, fish, steak, vegetables, potatoes) are served.

In the Land Pavilion at Epcot. Lunch $20 adults, $10 children; dinner $22 adults, $10 children. Daily noon–3pm, 5–8pm. Theme-park admission required.

Liberty Tree Tavern ☞   This Colonial-style 18th-century pub offers character dinners hosted by **Minnie, Goofy, Pluto,** and **Chip 'n' Dale.** The family-style meals include salad, roast turkey, ham, flank steak, cornbread, and apple crisp with vanilla ice cream.

In Liberty Square, in the Magic Kingdom. $22 adults, $10 children. Daily 4pm–park closing. Theme-park admission required.

1900 Park Fare ☞   The elegant Grand Floridian offers breakfast (eggs, French toast, bacon, pancakes) and dinner buffets (steak, pork, fish) at the exposition-themed 1900 Park Fare. Big Bertha—a French band organ that plays pipes, drums, bells, cymbals, castanets, and xylophone—provides music. **Mary Poppins, Alice in Wonderland, and friends** appear at breakfast; **Cinderella and friends** show up for Cinderella's Gala Feast at dinner.

4401 Floridian Way, at Disney's Grand Floridian Resort & Spa. Breakfast $17 adults, $10 children; dinner $26 adults, $11 children. Daily 7:30–11am and 5–9pm.

'Ohana Character Breakfast

Traditional breakfasts (eggs, pancakes, bacon) are prepared in an 18-foot fire pit and served family style. **Mickey, Stitch, and friends** appear, and children are given the chance to parade around with Polynesian musical instruments.

1600 Seven Seas Dr., in 'Ohana at Disney's Polynesian Resort. $17 adults, $9 children. Daily 7:30–11am.

Princess Storybook Character Dining

Snow White, Mary Poppins, Princess Aurora, Pocahontas, or **Belle** might show up at the morning character meal buffet (scrambled eggs, French toast, sausage, bacon, potatoes). Disney also offers character dining here during lunch and dinner. Both meals feature family-style service and offer some Norwegian specialties in addition to traditional American fare.

At Akershus Castle in Epcot's Norway Pavilion. Breakfast $22 adults, $12 children; lunch adults $24, children $13; dinner adults $28, children $13. Daily 7:30am–park closing. Theme-park admission required.

6

What Kids Like to See & Do in Walt Disney World

The Walt Disney World stable has grown to include an array of themed resorts, hundreds of restaurants and shops, nightclub venues, smaller attractions, and four major theme parks: the Magic Kingdom, Epcot, Disney–MGM Studios, and Animal Kingdom. And with the economy showing signs of recovery, park attendance is once again on the rise. WDW attracted nearly 42 million paying customers in 2004, according to estimates by *Amusement Business* magazine. All four Disney parks make the country's top five in attendance (the remaining park on the list is Disneyland in California). But that should hardly surprise you; they offer a fanciful, self-sufficient vacation where wonderment, human progress, and old-fashioned family fun are the key themes. The Disney Imagineers show off their creative capabilities through spectacular parades and fireworks displays, 3-D and CircleVision films, nerve-racking thrill rides, and adventurous journeys through time and space. Though they're expensive, you'll seldom hear people complain about failing to get their money's worth; an evening out at home, including the cost of a babysitter, can add up to almost as much without nearly the same return.

One reason people keep coming back for more is that rides and shows are periodically updated. And if something doesn't quite work, Disney usually fixes it. As part of this process, the company interviews some of its park-goers to decide how well, or poorly, things are working.

There have been changes and additions as Walt Disney World has matured, and new rides and attractions periodically enter the mix, including Epcot's **Soarin'**, where guests fly over the landscapes of California while surrounded by a gigantic projection screen, and Disney–MGM Studios' **Lights, Motors, Action! Extreme Stunt Show,** featuring a behind-the-scenes look at stunts and special effects.

But before I dive into the action, giving you details of these and other exciting experiences, let me take care of some basic business.

1 Essentials

GETTING INFORMATION IN ADVANCE

Before leaving home, call or write to Walt Disney World Co., Box 10000, Lake Buena Vista, FL 32830-1000 (© **407/934-7639**), for a vacation DVD and planning CD. You can view this online as well. Both are valuable planning aids. When you call, also ask about special events that will be going on during your visit. While I list big-time events under "When to Go," in chapter 2, many other events may be of interest to you.

Once you've arrived in town, Guest Services and the concierge desks in hotels (especially Disney properties and "official" hotels) have up-to-the-minute information about

Walt Disney World Parks & Attractions

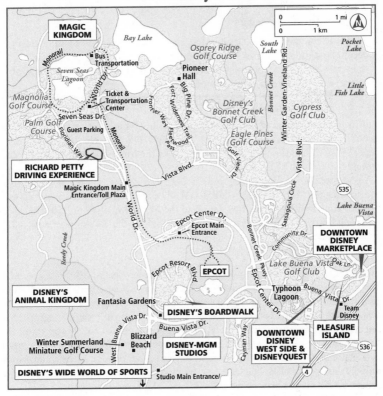

happenings in the parks. Stop by to ask questions and get literature, including maps and a schedule of park hours and events. If you have questions your hotel's personnel can't answer, call Disney at © **407/824-4321.**

There are also information areas at City Hall in the Magic Kingdom and Guest Relations at Epcot, Disney–MGM Studios, and Animal Kingdom.

If you're hooked into the Internet or have a local library with Internet access, try **www.disneyworld.com**, which features entertaining and regularly updated information on the parks.

You can also consult the Orlando/Orange County Convention & Visitors Bureau site (**www.orlandoinfo.com**). Another good site, **www.floridakiss.com**, is sponsored by the Kissimmee–St. Cloud Convention & Visitors Bureau. It, too, has an attractions link.

GETTING TO WDW BY CAR

The interstate exits to all Disney parks and resorts are well marked. Once you're off I-4, there are signs directing you to individual destinations. If you miss your exit, *don't panic.* Simply get off at the next one, and turn around. It may take a little more time, but it's safer than cutting across five lanes of traffic to make the off ramp—or, worse, to risk a fender bender. Drive with extra caution in the attractions area. Disney drivers are divided into two categories: cast members in a hurry to make their shift and

---

Tips **Tighter Security**

Guards at the gates at all Disney parks check a variety of carry-ins, including backpacks and large purses. They also have been known to check guests' IDs, so be sure to bring a government-issued photo identification card. All this, of course, means it takes a little longer to get to the action.

---

tourists in a hurry to get to the fun (and trying to drive while looking at a map). Both can often pull some rather stupid moves. The new WDW Western Beltway, currently under construction, should help alleviate some of the congestion both along I-4 and throughout areas of WDW.

Upon entering WDW grounds, you can tune your radio to **1030 AM** when you're approaching the Magic Kingdom or **850 AM** when approaching Epcot for park information. Tune to **1200 AM** when departing the Magic Kingdom or **910 AM** when departing Epcot. TVs in all Disney resorts and "official" hotels also have park information channels.

PARKING

All WDW lots are tightly controlled; the Disney folks have parking down to a science. You park where they tell you to park—or here comes security. I can't stress enough to *WRITE DOWN your parking place (lot, row, and space number) on something (that you won't lose) so you can find your vehicle later.* At the end of the day, you'd be surprised at just how many white minivans there are dotting the massive lot. If you think the catchy names will help jar your memory, think again. After a day at the parks, you'll have more characters swimming around in your head than you can count—each sounding all too familiar. The last thing you and your kids will want to do is play a game of "Let's guess where we left the car."

Visitors will likely need to ride the free trams in the massive Magic Kingdom lots (unless you've booked your vacation through AAA and can park up close in the AAA lot), but some folks decide to skip them and walk to the gates at Epcot, Disney–MGM Studios, and Animal Kingdom. *Some won't have a choice. Disney has cut tram service to parking areas closest to the entrances to its parks.* Guests who can't make the hike can have a driver drop them at special unloading areas outside the entrances. Special lots are available for travelers with disabilities (call © **407/824-4321** for details) right near the entrances as well. If your kids are young, and the tram is available, I recommend you use it; your children are in for enough walking once they're in the parks, and it's best to preserve their energy for the fun stuff. If you do end up walking from your car, be careful! These lots aren't designed for pedestrians. Tourists make for some of the worst, least attentive drivers around—especially when they're in a hurry to get to the park too.

At press time, parking had just been raised to $9 at the four major WDW parks ($10 for RVs). Disney resort guests do not have to pay for parking.

TICKETS & PASSES

In January 2005, Disney revamped its entire ticketing structure (now called **Magic Your Way**), giving visitors who stay here for a few days far better deals than those who come for just a day. Whereas before you had a limited number of ticket options (a 1-day, one-park ticket or a multiday, multipark pass), the new system allows guests to customize their tickets by first purchasing a base ticket for a set fee and then allowing them to purchase add-ons, including a park-hopper option; a no-expiration option; and the option to include admission to some of Disney's smaller venues, such as Pleasure Island, the water parks, and DisneyQuest (the latter is known as the Magic Plus Pack option).

You can purchase your base tickets for durations running from a single day to several days, with the latter being the most cost effective; the longer you stay, the less you'll pay per day. If you crunch the numbers, tickets good for at least 4 days will cost almost $10 less per day than a single-day ticket would; buy a 6-day ticket, and your per-day price drops by almost 50%. Do note, however, that under the new system, tickets now expire 14 days from the first day of use unless you add on a no-expiration feature (you don't, however, have to use the tickets on consecutive days within that 14-day period).

The following don't include *the 6 to 6.5% sales tax* (Disney actually falls in two different counties) unless noted. *Note:* Price hikes are frequent occurrences, so call (© 407/824-4321) or visit WDW's website (**www.disneyworld.com**) for the most up-to-the-minute pricing.

Note: All tickets include unlimited use of the WDW transportation system. Bear in mind that Disney considers children 10 and older adults for pricing purposes, and children under 3 aren't charged admission.

One-day/one-park tickets, for admission to the Magic Kingdom, Epcot, Animal Kingdom, or Disney–MGM Studios, are $63 for adults and $52 for children ages 3 to 9. Ouch! **Four-day base tickets** (one park per day) are $195 adults and $160 children ages 3 to 9. A **7-day base ticket** (one park per day) costs $204 for adults (about $29 a day) and $165 for kids ages 3 to 9 (about $24 a day).

Adding on a **Park Hopper** option to your ticket allows you unlimited admission to the Magic Kingdom, Epcot, Animal Kingdom, and Disney–MGM Studios for the duration of your base ticket. Pricing for the Park Hopper is the same for adults and children and costs $40 above the price of your base ticket (no matter how many days that ticket is valid for). So if you purchase a single-day base ticket, adding the Park Hopper will cost an additional $40 (for a total of $103 for an adult—not very cost effective), but if you purchase a 7-day base ticket, the Park Hopper add-on will still cost you only $40 (for a total of $244—a very good deal).

If you add a **Magic Plus Pack** option to your base ticket, you'll get several admissions to some of WDW's smaller attractions: Blizzard Beach, Typhoon Lagoon, DisneyQuest, Pleasure Island, and Disney's Wide World of Sports Complex. The number of visits allowed depends on the number of days your base ticket is good for (three visits for base tickets covering 1–3 days, four visits for 4- and 5-day tickets, five visits for 6-day tickets, and six visits for any base ticket over 7 days). This option adds $50 to the cost of your base ticket, and, like the Park Hopper, the longer you stay at Disney, the more cost effective the option becomes. If you plan on visiting only one smaller attraction while at WDW, paying the separate admission fee is cheaper and smarter than opting for the Magic Plus Pack.

The **Premium Ticket** is a base ticket that comes with the Magic Plus Pack and Park Hopper options. The only way you'll save money by buying this ticket is if you do so in advance.

A **1-day ticket to Typhoon Lagoon, Blizzard Beach,** or **DisneyQuest** is $34 for adults and $28 for children.

A **1-day ticket to Pleasure Island** is $10 for a single-club pass and $21 for a multiclub pass. Because this is primarily an 18-and-over entertainment complex, there's no bargain price for children.

If you're planning an extended stay or going to visit Walt Disney World more than once during the year, **annual passes** ($415–$539 adults, $365–$475 children) are another great option. Florida residents can get a break on park prices by choosing 10% off a 1-day ticket, a free hopper option, or a 3-day park pass for the price of a 2-day pass. Residents get a discount on annual passes as well.

OPERATING HOURS

All of Disney's theme parks are open 365 days a year. Hours of operation vary throughout the year and can be influenced by special events, so it's a good idea to call to check opening/closing times. The **Magic Kingdom** and **Disney–MGM Studios** are generally open from 9am to 6 or 7pm, with hours often extended to 9pm and sometimes as late as midnight during major holidays and summer. **Animal Kingdom** usually is open from 8 or 9am to 5 or 6pm but sometimes closes as late as 7pm.

Epcot's Future World is generally open from 9 or 10am to 6 or 7pm and occasionally later. **Epcot's World Showcase** usually opens at 11am or noon and closes at 9pm. Once again, there are extended holiday and summer hours.

Typhoon Lagoon and **Blizzard Beach** are open from 10am to 5pm most of the year (with extended hours during summer and some holidays). Note that during the summer and holiday periods, the water parks can fill up early and close to new visitors, so if you plan on visiting one of them at a busy time of year, do it early or pretty late in the day. Both parks are closed on a rotating basis during the winter for maintenance.

2 Making Your Visit More Enjoyable

HOW I'VE MADE THIS CHAPTER USEFUL TO PARENTS

Before every listing in the major parks, you'll note the **Recommended Ages** entry, which tells which ages will most appreciate that ride or show. Though most families want to do everything, this guideline is helpful in planning your daily itinerary. In the ride ratings, I also indicate whether a ride will be more enjoyable for kids than for adults, or vice versa. Many, even a couple in the Magic Kingdom, are too intense for young kids, and one bad experience can spook them for a good long time (even beyond your vacation). You'll also find any *height and health restrictions* noted in the listings.

I've also given you a few other yardsticks that will help evaluate the rides for your kids: **Ryan** (age 12), **Austin** (age 10), **Nicolas** (age 8), **Hailey** (age 6), and **Davis** (age 4) have all happily added their two cents to the mix. This bunch have made more than just a few trips to the theme parks right alongside me, and they've provided plenty of pint-size insight and information, and a pound's worth of opinions along the way.

BEST TIME OF YEAR TO VISIT

Because of the large number of international visitors, there's really no off season at Disney, but during the winter months, usually mid-January through March, crowds are smaller (except weekends), and though the weather can be unpredictable in January, the rest of the time, it's generally mild. The crowds also thin from mid-September until the week before Thanksgiving and in May, before Memorial Day weekend (though weekends can get crowded with locals). *Summer is among the worst times.* The masses throng to the parks. It's also humid and hot, *Hot,* **HOT.** If you can skip a summer visit, you won't have to worry about the possibility of a hurricane (admittedly rare—up until the last few years, anyway) or an electrical storm (an almost-daily occurrence here). *Tip:* Summer may be bad, but periods around major holidays are the absolute worst due to immense crowds. The 2 weeks on either side of Easter, and mid-December through the first weekend in January, are practically intolerable. Admittedly, the festive atmosphere and holiday decor make Disney World that much more fun for the family, but if the thought of standing in absurdly long lines and dealing with massive crowds doesn't make you merry, don't even think of coming here to celebrate the season.

BEST DAYS TO VISIT

The busiest days at all parks are generally Saturday and Sunday. Seven-day guests usually arrive and depart on one of these days, so fewer of them turn the turnstiles, but weekends are when locals and Florida commuters invade. Beyond that, Monday, Thursday, and Saturday are pretty frantic in the Magic Kingdom; Tuesday and Friday are hectic at Epcot; Sunday and Wednesday are crazy at Disney–MGM Studios; and Monday, Tuesday, and Wednesday are a zoo at Animal Kingdom. Crowds tend to thin later in the day, so if you're going to visit during the busy season and have the luxury of the Park Hopper option, you'll bump into fewer guests the later you visit. This also applies to the water parks.

The big attractions at Animal Kingdom are, clearly, the animals, and the best time to see them is at the opening bell or late in the day, when things are cooler. You'll also get a decent midday glimpse of some of them during the cooler months.

PLAN YOUR VISIT

How you plan your time at Walt Disney World will depend on a number of factors. These include the ages of any children in your party; what, if anything, you've seen on previous visits; your interests; and whether you're traveling at peak time or off season. Preplanning is always essential. So is choosing age-appropriate activities.

Nothing can spoil a day in the parks more than a child devastated because he or she can't do something that was promised. Before you get to the park, review this book

---

Tips New Kid on the Block

Disney has introduced a new kind of tour guide. **Pal Mickey** is a 10½-inch-tall plush toy with quite a personality. Turn him on, and he'll happily help you tour the parks, letting you know when the parades are about to start, announcing show times, and telling you where to find all your favorite characters. He shares stories, sings songs, plays games, and spouts off plenty of Disney trivia, too. Designed for 5- to 10-year-olds (who find him a ton of fun), Pal Mickey's wireless technology allows him to pick up sound clips from signals located throughout the parks, but he'll also interact with you at the resorts, and back home, he'll voice prerecorded facts and jokes. He's available for purchase ($65, not including sales tax). He'll keep kids entertained in those long theme-park lines, and his timesaving tips, including ride height restrictions, can be quite helpful. Pal Mickey operates on three AA batteries. A Spanish version is available as well.

Tips   **Parental Touring Tip**

Many of the attractions at Walt Disney World offer a **Parent Switch program,** designed for parents traveling with small children. While one parent rides an attraction, the other stays with the kids not quite ready to handle the experience; then the adults switch places without having to stand in line again. Notify a cast member if you wish to participate when you get in line. Most other Orlando theme parks offer this option, too.

and the suggested ages for children, including *height restrictions.* The WDW staff won't bend the rules despite the pitiful wails of your little ones. *Note:* Many rides that have minimum heights also have enough turbulence to make them unsuitable for folks with neck, back, or heart problems; those prone to motion sickness; and pregnant women.

Unless you're staying for more than a week, you can't experience all the rides, shows, or attractions included in this chapter. A ride may last only 5 minutes, but you may have to wait an hour or so, even if you use FASTPASS (detailed shortly). You'll wear yourself and your kids to a frazzle trying to hit everything. It's better to follow a relaxed itinerary, including leisurely meals and some recreational activities, than to make a demanding job out of trying to see and do it all.

CREATE AN ITINERARY FOR EACH DAY

Watch the previously mentioned *Walt Disney World Vacation* DVD, peruse the planning CD, read the detailed descriptions in this book, and then plan your trip to include those shows and attractions that pique your family's interest and excitement.

At the same time, consider your loyalties. My younger kids could spend all day in Tomorrowland, spinning around like space rangers with Woody and Buzz Lightyear, but touring Toontown is of far less interest to them. Put the rides featuring your favorite characters, or your kids' favorites, at the top of your list. It's a good idea to make a daily itinerary, putting your choices in some kind of sensible geographical sequence so you're not zigzagging all over the place. Consult the maps in this book, and familiarize yourself in advance with the layout of each park. Also recognize that rides or exhibits nearest an entrance may be busiest when the gates open. That's because a lot of people visit the first thing they see, even if the more popular attractions are deeper into the park.

I repeat this advice: Schedule sit-down shows, recreational activities (a boat ride or a refreshing swim late in the afternoon), and at least some unhurried meals if time permits. This will save you and your kids from exhaustion and aggravation. Breaks in the day will give your family the much-needed opportunity to recharge their batteries and rest weary feet. And *be flexible!* My suggested itineraries that follow allow you to see a great deal of the parks as efficiently as possible. If you have the luxury of a multiday pass, you can divide and conquer at a slower pace, and even repeat some favorites.

Tips FASTPASS

If lines aren't your thing—well . . . you had better turn back now. Lines are a part of the deal at Disney (and the other parks, too, for that matter). On the other hand, if you're savvy, you can usually avoid the worst of them if you take advantage of Disney's FASTPASS system. The free system allows you to wait on a far shorter line at some of the park's most popular attractions. Seems easy enough, right? Well, it is. There is, however, a small price to be paid for skipping the big lines. Here's the drill:

Hang onto your ticket stub when you enter, and head to the hottest ride on your list. If it's a FASTPASS attraction (noted in the guide map you get when you enter), you'll see a sign marking the FASTPASS kiosk just near the entrance. Feed your ticket into the ticket-taker. *Note:* Every member of your group must get an individual FASTPASS. Retrieve both your ticket and your FASTPASS slip. Printed on the slip are two times. You can return any time during that 1-hour window and enter the ride (there's a much shorter and faster line for FASTPASS holders). Be sure to keep your slip handy, as you'll need it to get in the right line.

Note II: Early in the day, your 1-hour window may begin as soon as 40 minutes after you feed the FASTPASS machine, but later in the day, it may be hours later. Initially, Disney allowed you to do this on only one ride at a time. Now your FASTPASS ticket has a time printed when you can get a second FASTPASS, usually about 2 hours after you got the first one, though it can sometimes be as soon as 45 minutes later, even if you haven't used the first pass yet.

Note III: Don't think you can fool Disney by feeding your ticket stub in multiple times, figuring you can hit the jackpot for multiple rides or help others in your group who lost their tickets. These "smart" stubs will reject your attempts by spitting out a coupon that says "Not A Valid FASTPASS."

Note IV: FASTPASS slips can run out. So if you have your heart set on a ride, and it's the middle of the peak season, be sure to head to your chosen attraction's FASTPASS machine as soon as you can. Tickets for top rides often run out by the early afternoon, sometimes even earlier.

SUGGESTED ITINERARIES

My suggested itineraries will allow you to cover most of the ground in each park in as efficient a manner as possible. Do note, though, that using FASTPASS may require you to double back to a land you've already covered.

There are a ton of ways to see the parks, and I feel, time and budget permitting, it's often better to do it in limited doses—those where you spend 2 or more days in a park at a casual pace. I'm offering suggested itineraries as options for those on a tighter schedule. The following itineraries are organized to get the most out of the least amount of time. I break things into one game plan for families with younger kids and another for those with older kids and teenagers. With few exceptions (I note them later), Disney World doesn't have enough true stomach-turning thrill rides to warrant a special itinerary for take-no-prisoners teens and adults. Frankly, the only Orlando park in that class is Universal's Islands of Adventure, which I tackle in chapter 7, "What Kids Like to See & Do Beyond Disney."

A Day in the Magic Kingdom with Younger Kids

Consider making Advanced Dining reservations for dinner at **Cinderella's Royal Table** (© 407/939-3463), located inside Cinderella Castle.

If you have very young kids (preschool to around age 7 is the perfect age), go right to the **Walt Disney World Railroad** station on Main Street, and take the next train. Get off at **Mickey's Toontown Fair** to meet Mickey, Minnie, and the gang. Ride the **Barnstormer at Goofy's Wiseacre Farm**, a mini–roller coaster, and explore **Mickey's** and **Minnie's Country Houses**.

If your kids are 8 or older, start the day at **Tomorrowland**, and brave **Buzz Lightyear's Space Ranger Spin** and **Space Mountain**. (Little ones like the **Tomorrowland Indy Speedway**, but there's not much else for them here.)

Most kids under 10 will find something that's fun in Fantasyland, including **Dumbo the Flying Elephant**, **Peter Pan's Flight**, **Mickey's PhilharMagic**, **It's a Small World**, **The Many Adventures of Winnie the Pooh**, and **Cinderella's Golden Carousel**.

Afterward, lunch at Cosmic Ray's Starlight Café or the Columbia Harbour House in **Liberty Square**.

Next, head west to **Liberty Square**. Most kids over 10 will appreciate the Animatronic history lesson in the **Hall of Presidents** show. Before leaving, visit the **Haunted Mansion**; then move to **Frontierland**. **Splash Mountain** and **Big Thunder Mountain Railroad** are best suited for those 8 and older; **Country Bear Jamboree** is fun for the younger set; while **Tom Sawyer Island** allows kids over 7 a great place to run around and parents a well deserved sit-down (unless they're keeping watch over their younger adventurers).

Go to **Adventureland** next. Ride **The Magic Carpets of Aladdin**, **Pirates of the Caribbean**, and **Jungle Cruise**; then let the kids burn some energy in the **Swiss Family Treehouse**. Younger kids (ages 4–8) will appreciate the **Enchanted Tiki Room**.

Consult the guide map available as you enter the park, and if the **Wishes** fireworks display and **SpectroMagic** are scheduled, be sure to watch them.

A Day in the Magic Kingdom with Older Kids & Teenagers

As I mentioned earlier, consider making an Advanced Dining reservation at **Cinderella's Royal Table** (© 407/939-3463) if you want a sit-down dinner.

From Main Street, cut through the center of the park to Frontierland, and challenge **Splash Mountain**; then ride **Big Thunder Mountain Railroad**.

Next, go to Liberty Square, and visit the **Haunted Mansion** and **Hall of Presidents**.

After lunch at Liberty Tree Tavern, cut diagonally through the park, past Cinderella Castle, and into Tomorrowland to ride **Space Mountain** and **Buzz Lightyear's Space Ranger Spin**.

If time permits, head to Adventureland for the **Jungle Cruise** and **Pirates of the Caribbean**; then, if it's scheduled, end the day with the **Wishes** fireworks display.

A Day in Epcot with Younger Kids

Remember to get an Advanced Dining reservation if you want to eat in the park (call © 407/939-3463 before you arrive). For dinner, I suggest the **Mitsukoshi Teppanyaki Dining Room** in the World Showcase's Japan exhibit or the **Coral Reef** restaurant in the Living Seas. The **Sunshine Seasons** in The Land is a good choice for lunch because of its diversity. See other options in chapter 5, "Family-Friendly Dining."

While the least desirable of the parks for young kids, Epcot has added a number of activities and attractions to keep them entertained.

Future World, near the front of the park, is the best place to start. Begin your day at Imagination! and its two great shows: **Journey into Imagination with Figment** and *Honey, I Shrunk the Audience.*

Next, visit **Innoventions.** On its East Side, all but the smallest kids will appreciate today's and tomorrow's high-tech gadgets at the **House of Innoventions.** Building a robot to take home at **Fantastic Plastic Works** will appeal to younger kids. Over on the West Side, kids and adults find it hard to leave **Video Games of Tomorrow,** while younger kids can learn about fire safety in a fun and unique way at **Where's the Fire?**

After heading to the **Living Seas** to **Turtle Talk with Crush** and do some deep-sea exploration (and if your kids are over the 40" minimum), make your way to **The Land** for a ride high above California's impressive landscape on **Soarin'.** Break for a late lunch; then you're off to the **World Showcase.** The meticulously detailed pavilions of 11 nations surround a big lagoon that you can cross by boat if your feet need a break. Tinier tykes may get bored, but those 5 and up can create cultural crafts to take home at the **Kidcot fun stops** along the way.

Norway delivers a history lesson and boat ride to the time of the Vikings aboard the *Maelstrom;* **China** and **Canada** feature fabulous 360-degree movies (China also has the engaging **Dragon Legend Acrobats**); and **Germany's Biergarten** is filled with oompah music (little kids usually love the model train set up right nearby). Also, take in the show and concerts at **U.S.A.—The American Adventure** before ending your day with **IllumiNations.**

A Day in Epcot with Older Kids & Teenagers

If you want to eat in the park, make an Advanced Dining reservation before you arrive, if possible (call *©* **407/ 939-3463**). For dinner, I suggest the **San Angel Inn** in the World Showcase's Mexico exhibit or the **Coral Reef** restaurant in the Living Seas. The **Sunshine Seasons Food Fair** in The Land is a good family choice for lunch because of its diversity. See other options in chapter 5, "Family-Friendly Dining."

Future World, near the front of the park, is the best place to start. Skip **Spaceship Earth,** at least for now. If you must, save the ride through history till the end of the day—when your feet will appreciate the rest. Go straight to **Body Wars,** which is in the **Wonders of Life** pavilion to the left of Spaceship Earth. Next is **Mission: Space,** where you can train as the astronauts do. Follow up with next-door-neighbor **Test Track.** Then cut to the west to **Imagination** for *Honey, I Shrunk the Audience.*

After a late lunch, visit **The Land** to ride **Soarin';** then head to **Innoventions.** On its East Side, check out the high-tech gadgets at the **House of Innoventions;** then head to the West Side, for **Video Games of Tomorrow.**

Next, head to the **World Showcase** for a cultural trip around 11 of the world's nations.

Norway delivers a history lesson and boat ride to the time of the Vikings aboard the *Maelstrom;* **China** and **Canada** feature fabulous 360-degree movies (China also has the engaging **Dragon Legend Acrobats**); **Japan's Matsuriza** drummers shouldn't be missed; and the **United Kingdom** offers scheduled interactive comedy with the **World Showcase Players.** Also, take in the show and concerts at **U.S.A.—The American Adventure** before ending your day by watching **IllumiNations.**

A Day at Disney–MGM Studios with Younger Kids

The layout and size of this park make it easier to backtrack from one area to another.

If you want to eat dinner in the park, make Advanced Dining reservations (© **407/939-3463**) ahead of time. The **Hollywood Brown Derby** is a decent sit-down option but one that's pricey for families (see chapter 5, "Family-Friendly Dining," for more information on dining options). For lunch, try **Toluca Legs Turkey Co.,** where the smoked turkey legs are one of the best grab-and-go meals in any park (you can also get hot dogs). **Voyage of the Little Mermaid** is a must for the young (in years or yearnings); the same goes for **Jim Henson's Muppet*Vision 3-D,** a truly fun show for all ages.

Sounds Dangerous Starring Drew Carey is a good chance to rest weary feet, though most of the show takes place in total darkness—not a place for little ones. The explosions and noise in the **Indiana Jones Epic Stunt Spectacular** and the new **Lights, Motors, Action! Extreme Stunt Show** may be too much for tinier tots, but most kids ages 5 and older will love the action.

Visit the *Honey, I Shrunk the Kids Movie Set;* then check your show schedule for favorites such as **Playhouse Disney—Live on Stage!** (great for little kids) and *Beauty and the Beast.* At night, *don't miss* **Fantasmic!** if your kids are 5 and older.

A Day at Disney–MGM Studios with Older Kids & Teenagers

Remember to make Advanced Dining reservations (© **407/939-3463**) ahead of time if you want to eat in the park. The **Hollywood Brown Derby** is a decent sit-down option but one that's pricey for families (see chapter 5, "Family-Friendly Dining," for more restaurant options). For lunch, consider **Toluca Legs Turkey Co.,** where the smoked turkey legs are one of the best grab-and-go meals in any park (you can also get hot dogs).

Head directly to the **Twilight Zone Tower of Terror.** It's a high-voltage ride that's not for the young or faint of heart, but adrenaline-crazed kids and teens will keep coming back for more. The same goes for the **Rock 'n' Roller Coaster,** with its incredible takeoff speed, three inversions, and rock 'n' roll music that will blow you (or at least your eardrums) away. Then make your way over to the impressive and high-energy **Lights, Motors, Action! Extreme Stunt Show**.

The park is small, so backtracking isn't as much of a concern here. Consider bypassing attractions that have long lines, saving them for later, or use FASTPASS where you can. **Star Tours** and the **Indiana Jones Epic Stunt Spectacular** have the longest lines after the thrill rides mentioned above.

Jim Henson's Muppet*Vision 3-D is a truly fun show for all ages. Afterward, watch (and maybe win at) **Who Wants to Be a Millionaire—Play It!;** then go on the ton-of-fun **Backlot Tour.** At night, *don't miss* **Fantasmic!**

A Day at Animal Kingdom for Kids of All Ages

I'm not breaking this park into separate itineraries for older and younger age groups because there are few things here that can't be done by most kids, no matter how old they are. Instead, I'll suggest age appeal for those attractions that warrant it.

Be here when the gates open, usually around 8 or 9am. (Call Disney information at ✆ **407/824-4321** to check the time.) This will give you the best chance of seeing animals, because they're most active in the morning air (the next-best time is late in the afternoon, although some can be seen throughout the day if you come here during cooler months). If you want to eat at the **Rainforest Cafe,** make Advanced Dining reservations by calling ✆ **407/939-3463.**

Flame Tree Barbecue, Pizzafari, and **Tusker House Restaurant** are fair lunch stops.

The size of the park (500 acres) means a lot of travel once you pass through the gates. Don't linger in the **Oasis** area or around the **Tree of Life;** instead, head directly to the back of the park to be first in line for **Kilimanjaro Safaris.** This will allow your family to see animals before it gets hot and the lines become monstrous. Work your way back through Africa, visiting **Pangani Forest Exploration Trail** and its lowland gorillas (this may be too long and lifeless for younger kids). Then head to the **Tree of Life** on Discovery Island for **It's Tough to Be a Bug!** Older kids, teens, and adults should ride **Dinosaur** and **Primeval Whirl** in Dinoland U.S.A., a good choice if you get there before lines form or if you use FASTPASS. Younger kids deserve some time at the **Boneyard** and on **TriceraTop Spin** in Dinoland, as well as a trip to **Camp Minnie-Mickey,** on the other side of the park, to meet their favorite characters. Make sure to see the park's (and WDW's) best show, **Festival of the Lion King,** while you're there.

Trek through the jungles on the **Maharajah Jungle Trek** in Asia. Older kids and teens will love tackling **Kali River Rapids,** a great way to cool off at the end of the day (and yes, they will get soaked), or meeting a yeti on Disney's newest thriller, **Expedition Everest** (opening in summer 2006).

SERVICES & FACILITIES IN THE PARKS

ATMs Money machines are available near the entrances to all parks and usually at least one other place inside (see the handout guide map as you enter the park). They honor cards from banks using the Cirrus, Honor, and PLUS systems.

Baby Care All parks have a Baby Care Center that's equipped with private rooms designated for breast-feeding, changing, and feeding, and that sell baby-care basics. All women's restrooms, and some men's, are equipped with changing tables.

Cameras & Film Film, batteries, Kodak disposable cameras, and some digital supplies are sold at various locations in all parks (at much higher prices than those in the free world).

Car Assistance If you need a battery jump or other assistance, raise the hood of your vehicle, and wait for security to arrive.

First Aid All parks have stations marked on the handout guide maps.

Lost Children Every park has a designated spot for lost children to be reunited with their families. In the Magic Kingdom, it's City Hall or the Baby Care Center; in Epcot, the Earth Center or the Baby Care Center; in Disney–MGM Studios, Guest Relations; and in Animal Kingdom, Discovery Island. *Children under 7 should wear name tags inside their clothing;* older children and adults should have a prearranged

---

Tips **Smoking Alert**

WDW parks do not sell cigarettes, and Disney prohibits smoking in shops, attractions, restaurants, and ride lines. Smokers are allowed to light up only in designated outdoor areas.

---

meeting place in case your group gets separated. If that happens, tell the first park employee you see; many employees wear the same type of clothing, and all have special name tags. For more on lost children, see "Traveling Safely with Your Child," in chapter 2.

Package Pickup   Nearly all WDW stores can arrange for packages to be sent to the front of the park. Allow at least 3 hours for delivery. If you're staying at a Disney resort, you can also have all packages purchased by 7pm sent to your hotel room (they will be delivered by noon the next day).

Parking   At press time, Disney charged $9 for car, light-truck, and van parking, and $10 for RVs.

Pets   Don't leave yours in a parked car, even with a window cracked open. Cars are death traps in Florida's sun. Only service animals are permitted in the parks, but there are five kennels at WDW (© **407/824-6568;** $6 per day, $9 overnight for resort guests, $11 overnight for those staying elsewhere). The ones at the Transportation and Ticket Center in the Magic Kingdom and near the entrance to Fort Wilderness board animals overnight. Day accommodations are offered at kennels just outside the Entrance Plaza at Epcot (the only location offering walking services) and at the entrances to Disney–MGM Studios and Animal Kingdom. *Proof of vaccination is required.*

Shops   In addition to the ones listed in the following pages, most of Disney's rides have small gift shops featuring souvenirs based on that ride's theme.

Stroller Rental   Strollers are available near all the park entrances. The cost for a single is $10 per day, or $8 per day for a length-of-stay rental. A double costs $18 per day, or $16 per day for a length-of-stay rental. *Tip:* Because strollers often have to be parked outside attractions, it's easy to get confused about whose stroller is whose. Attach a brightly colored piece of cloth or some other identifier so that someone doesn't accidentally walk off with your stroller. If it does go astray (and many will), just bring your receipt to the stroller rental location, and you can get a replacement.

Tip Boards   Each park has a tip board that tells visitors the approximate waiting time at all the major rides and attractions. In Magic Kingdom it's at the end of Main Street on the left as you face the castle; in Epcot, the digital board is in Innoventions Plaza; at MGM, it's at the intersection of Hollywood and Sunset boulevards; and inside Animal Kingdom, you'll find it just over the bridge to Discovery Island.

Wheelchair Rental   A wheelchair is $10 per day, or $8 per day for a length-of-stay rental. Electric wheelchairs rent for $35, including a $5 deposit.

3 The Magic Kingdom

America's most popular theme park, the 107-acre Magic Kingdom is filled with over 40 attractions (with new experiences being added almost yearly), unique shops, and themed restaurants. Its centerpiece and most recognizable symbol, Cinderella Castle, forms the hub from which its **seven themed lands** reach out.

ARRIVING   From the immense parking lot, you have to walk to the tram that will take you to the ticket and transportation center, and then wait for a ferry or monorail to take you to the entrance, where before entering, you'll have to pass through security for a bag check. All told, the time it takes to get from your car to Main Street U.S.A. is somewhere around **35 to 45 minutes,** sometimes longer. And that total doesn't include the time spent in lines if you have to stop at Guest Relations, purchase your tickets, or rent a stroller. You'll face the same agony (complicated by escaping crowds) on the way out, so relax. This is one of the most crowded parks, so plan to arrive an hour before the opening bell or an hour or two after.

Each of the parking lot's sections is named for Disney characters (Goofy, Pluto, Minnie, and so on), and aisles are numbered. I can't stress enough just how important it is *to write down where you left your vehicle;* you would be amazed at how many cars look just like yours!

The most important thing you can do upon arriving at the park is to pick up a copy (or two) of the Magic Kingdom **guide map** (if you can't find one at the turnstiles, stop at City Hall or the nearest shop). It provides an array of detailed information about available guest services, restaurants, and attractions. The *Times Guide* (separate from the guide map) will be your key to the daily schedules for show times, parades, fireworks, character meet-and-greets, and park hours.

If you have questions, all park employees are very knowledgeable, and City Hall, on your left as you enter, is an information center—and, like Mickey's Toontown Fair, a great place to meet costumed characters. Character greeting places are also featured on the map, so make note of them if you have little ones along.

HOURS   The park is open from at least 9am to 6 or 7pm, sometimes later—as late as midnight during major holidays and summer.

TICKET PRICES   Tickets are $63 for adults and $52 for children 3 to 9. Kids under 3 get in free. See "Tickets & Passes," on p. 166, for information on multiday passes and other add-on options.

SERVICES & FACILITIES IN THE MAGIC KINGDOM

Most of the following are noted on the handout guide maps in the park:

ATMs   Machines inside the park honor cards from banks using the Cirrus, Honor, and PLUS systems. They're near the main entrance, in Frontierland, and in Tomorrowland.

Baby Care   Located next to the Crystal Palace at the end of Main Street, the Baby Care Center is furnished with a nursing room with rocking chairs and toddler-size toilets. Disposable diapers, formula, baby food, and pacifiers are sold at a premium (read: bring your own, or pay the price). There are changing tables here, as well as in all women's restrooms and some men's.

Cameras & Film   Film, Kodak disposable cameras, and limited digital supplies are available throughout the park.

The Magic Kingdom

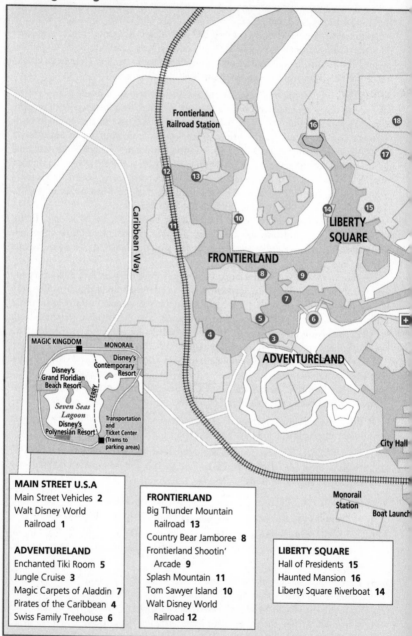

Frontierland
Railroad Station

LIBERTY
SQUARE

FRONTIERLAND

Caribbean Way

ADVENTURELAND

MAGIC KINGDOM　　**MONORAIL**

Disney's
Contemporary
Resort

Disney's
Grand Floridian
Beach Resort

Seven Seas
Lagoon

FERRY

Disney's
Polynesian Resort

Transportation
and
Ticket Center
(Trams to
parking areas)

City Hall

Monorail
Station

Boat Launch

MAIN STREET U.S.A

Main Street Vehicles **2**
Walt Disney World
   Railroad **1**

ADVENTURELAND

Enchanted Tiki Room **5**
Jungle Cruise **3**
Magic Carpets of Aladdin **7**
Pirates of the Caribbean **4**
Swiss Family Treehouse **6**

FRONTIERLAND

Big Thunder Mountain
   Railroad **13**
Country Bear Jamboree **8**
Frontierland Shootin'
   Arcade **9**
Splash Mountain **11**
Tom Sawyer Island **10**
Walt Disney World
   Railroad **12**

LIBERTY SQUARE

Hall of Presidents **15**
Haunted Mansion **16**
Liberty Square Riverboat **14**

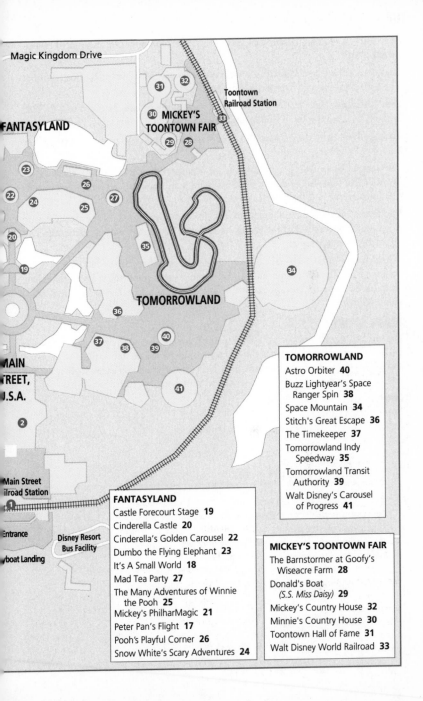

Magic Kingdom Drive

Toontown Railroad Station

31 · 32

30 **MICKEY'S TOONTOWN FAIR**

FANTASYLAND

29 · 28

23

26

22 · 24 · 25

27

20

19

35

34

TOMORROWLAND

36

37 · 38

40

39

MAIN STREET, U.S.A.

41

2

Main Street Railroad Station

1

Entrance

Disney Resort Bus Facility

yboat Landing

TOMORROWLAND
Astro Orbiter **40**
Buzz Lightyear's Space
 Ranger Spin **38**
Space Mountain **34**
Stitch's Great Escape **36**
The Timekeeper **37**
Tomorrowland Indy
 Speedway **35**
Tomorrowland Transit
 Authority **39**
Walt Disney's Carousel
 of Progress **41**

FANTASYLAND
Castle Forecourt Stage **19**
Cinderella Castle **20**
Cinderella's Golden Carousel **22**
Dumbo the Flying Elephant **23**
It's A Small World **18**
Mad Tea Party **27**
The Many Adventures of Winnie
 the Pooh **25**
Mickey's PhilharMagic **21**
Peter Pan's Flight **17**
Pooh's Playful Corner **26**
Snow White's Scary Adventures **24**

MICKEY'S TOONTOWN FAIR
The Barnstormer at Goofy's
 Wiseacre Farm **28**
Donald's Boat
 (S.S. Miss Daisy) **29**
Mickey's Country House **32**
Minnie's Country House **30**
Toontown Hall of Fame **31**
Walt Disney World Railroad **33**

First Aid It's located beside the Crystal Palace next to Baby Care and staffed by registered nurses.

Lockers Lockers are located in the arcade below the Main Street Railroad Station. The cost is $5, plus a $2 refundable deposit.

Lost Children Lost children in the Magic Kingdom are usually taken to City Hall or the Baby Care Center. *Children under 7 should wear name tags* inside their clothing.

Package Pickup Any package can be sent to package pickup near City Hall. Allow 3 hours for delivery.

Pet Care Day boarding is available at the Transportation and Ticket Center for $6 (© 407/824-6568). The center also boards animals overnight ($9 for Disney or official hotel guests, $11 for others). Proof of vaccination is required.

Strollers They can be rented at the Stroller Shop near the entrance to the Magic Kingdom. The cost is $10 for a single and $18 for a double, with a discounted rate for a length-of-stay rental.

Wheelchair Rental For wheelchairs, go to the gift shop to the left of the ticket booths at the Transportation and Ticket Center, or to the Stroller and Wheelchair Shop inside the main entrance to your right. The cost is $10; for electric ones, $35, plus a $5 deposit.

MAIN STREET, U.S.A.

Designed to model a turn-of-the-20th-century American street (although it ends in a 13th-c. European castle), this is the gateway to the Kingdom and is filled with shops and on-the-run eateries. Don't dawdle on Main Street when you enter; leave it for the end of the day, when you're heading back to your hotel.

Main Street Vehicles
Frommer's Rating: C
Recommended Ages: Mainly nostalgic adults

Frommer's Rates the Rides

Because there's so much to do, I'm shifting from the star-rating system used for rooms and restaurants to one that has a little more range. You'll notice that most of the grades below are *As, Bs,* and *Cs.* That's because Disney designers have done a reasonably good job on the attractions front. But occasionally, my ratings show *Ds* for Duds.

Here's what **Frommer's Ratings** mean:

A+	=	Your trip wouldn't be complete without it.
A	=	Put it at the top of your "to-do" list.
B+	=	Make a real effort to see or do it.
B	=	It's fun but not a "must see."
C+	=	A nice diversion; see it if you have time.
C	=	Go if there's no wait and you can walk right in.
D	=	Don't waste your time.

Tips A Cut Above

The Harmony Barber Shop on Main Street (near the firehouse), its entrance marked by signature candy-striped poles, is a real working barber shop. It's open daily from 9am to 5pm and gives hundreds of haircuts each week. If your child gets his or her first cut here, Disney throws in several extras—bubbles, stickers, and a special set of mouse ears—to mark the occasion. Kids 12 and under can get a cut for about $14; cuts for adults cost around $17. To jazz up the experience, kids and adults can add some color to their coif (thanks to a special colored hair gel) for just $5.

Ride a horse-drawn trolley, jitney, vintage fire engine, or horseless carriage *only* if you don't mind waiting around. Otherwise, there are far, far better things to see and do throughout the realm.

Walt Disney World Railroad

Frommer's Rating: B

Recommended Ages: All ages

You can board an authentic 1928 steam-powered train for a 15-minute trip clockwise around the perimeter of the park. This is a good way to save wear and tear on your feet *if* you're headed to one of its three stations: the park entrance, Frontierland, and Mickey's Toontown Fair, in that order.

   Davis's Rating: "Let's go again . . . can we?" (Of course, he could've just as easily ridden the monorail all day, too.)

ADVENTURELAND

Cross the bridge marked by Tikis and torches as the rhythm of beating drums sound in the distance. As you make your way through lush jungle foliage, trees hung with Spanish moss, dense vines, and stands of palm and bamboo, you are transported to an exotic locale where swashbuckling adventures await you and your kids.

The Enchanted Tiki Room

Frommer's Rating: B for kids

Recommended Ages: 2–10 and older adults

The large, hexagonal Tiki Room serves up a Polynesian atmosphere, with its thatched roof, bamboo beams, tapa-bark murals, and torches. Inside, guests are entertained by the likes of Iago (from *Aladdin*) and Zazu (from *The Lion King*), as well as an ensemble of boisterous tropical birds (over 200 of them, in fact), along with chanting totem poles and singing flowers that whistle, warble, and tweet. Overall, it's good family fun, but be aware that it's rather loud, and a brief simulated tropical storm, with crackling thunder and flashes of lightning, combined with the multitude of audio and visual effects, may be a bit too overwhelming for very young children.

Jungle Cruise

Frommer's Rating: C+ (B for the foot-weary)

Recommended Ages: 4–adult

It's a nostalgic ride for many an adult but a yawner for many older kids and teens. You'll sail through the African veldt in the Congo, an Amazon rainforest, and along the Nile in Egypt as your boat captain offers somewhat corny but humorous commentary on your travels. You'll encounter dozens of exotic Animatronic animals, ranging from playful elephants to lions, tigers, and alligators as you sail through dense tropical and subtropical foliage (most of it is real). You'll pass a Cambodian temple guarded by snakes, a rhino chasing terrified African beaters as they clamor up a totem pole for safety, and a jungle camp taken over by apes. While you're waiting to board, read the prop menu. It includes fricassee of giant stag beetle and barbecued three-toed skink. Most boat captains keep up an amusing-if-corny banter. It's a nice break from the park madness if the line isn't long or you use FASTPASS.

Magic Carpets of Aladdin
Frommer's Rating: A for tykes and parents
Recommended Ages: 2–8
Younger kids will appreciate this ride's gentle ups and downs as they fly through the sky on the colorful magic carpets. The view of Agrabah from above is impressive, but be prepared as you make your way around the genie's giant bottle: The spitting camels have pretty good aim, making it likely that you'll get squirted with water (similar to One Fish, Two Fish, Red Fish, Blue Fish at Universal Orlando's Islands of Adventure; see p. 263). If there's a downside here, it's that you may find yourself wishing for smaller lines (though they're not nearly as unbearable as some you'll encounter in Fantasyland).

Pirates of the Caribbean
Frommer's Rating: B+
Recommended Ages: 6–adult
The release of the Oscar-nominated film, and soon-to-be-released sequel, has revitalized the popularity of this oldie but goodie (alas, no Johnny Depp here, though your kids will have fun spotting the scenes appropriated by the movie). After making your way through dark and dank dungeons, guests board a boat and set sail for a small Caribbean town, its shores teeming with pillaging Animatronic pirates who carouse, chase wenches, and wreak general havoc. There are plenty of gunfire and cannonballs flying through the air as the marauders battle one another, with you, of course, caught up in the middle. The effects are great, as is the yo-ho-ho music of "A Pirate's Life for Me" that plays in the background (you won't be able to stop yourself from humming along). The bonus here is an immense covered queue area that will protect you and your stroller-bound children from both sun and rain (this ride offers the only covered stroller parking in the park). *Tip:* Nod hello to the parrot (Peglegged Pete) above the entrance plaza, and he may offer you his own greeting.

Nicolas's Rating: "The pirates in the movie were better, but the ride is pretty cool. I liked the waterfall part the best." The shop at the end of the ride is a favorite shopping spot for all my pirates, big and little alike.

Tips **One for You . . . One for Me**

Disney's trying out something new: a map made just for preschoolers and their parents. It highlights all the kid-friendly hot spots, ranging from stroller rental locations to the baby-care center to all restrooms. It also lists which rides are most appropriate and must-sees for the younger set. The map is usually obtainable at the parks' Guest Services desks and at stroller rental locations.

Swiss Family Treehouse
Frommer's Rating: C
Recommended Ages: 4–12

This attraction, based on the 1960 Disney movie version of *Swiss Family Robinson,* includes a few more comforts from home than did the original. After climbing its many, many steps, you'll finally reach the treehouse, its rooms filled with mahogany furnishings, decorative accents, and running water. If your kids are nervous about heights, this one's not a good choice; visitors will find themselves walking along a rope-suspended bridge high above the ground, not to mention the climbing that's required to make it up and down all the stairs that lead around this 50-foot banyan tree. The "tree," designed by Disney Imagineers, has 330,000 polyethylene leaves sprouting from a 90-foot span of branches; although it isn't real, it's draped with actual Spanish moss. It's a good place for kids to work off some excess energy, though things can get crowded up there. *Note:* People with limited mobility, beware; this attraction requires a lot of climbing.

FRONTIERLAND

From Adventureland, step into the wild and woolly past of the American frontier, where Disney cast members are clad in denim and calico; sidewalks are wooden; rough-and-tumble architecture runs to log cabins and rustic saloons; and the landscape is Southwestern scrubby with mesquite, cactus, yucca, and prickly pear.

Big Thunder Mountain Railroad
Frommer's Rating: A
Recommended Ages: 8–adult

This roller coaster earns high marks for what it is: a ride designed for those not quite up to the lunch-losing thrills of Rock 'n' Roller Coaster at Disney–MGM Studios (p. 222) or Dueling Dragons and Incredible Hulk Coaster at Islands of Adventure, listed in chapter 7. Think of Big Thunder as *Roller Coasters 101.* (Survive, and graduate to the next level.) It sports fun hairpin turns and dark descents rather than sudden, steep drops and near collisions. Your runaway train covers 2,780 feet of track and careens through the ribs of a dinosaur, under a thundering waterfall, past spewing geysers, and over a bottomless volcanic pool. Animatronic characters (such as a long johns–clad fellow in a bathtub) and critters (goats, chickens, donkeys) enhance the scenic backdrop, along with several hundred thousand dollars' worth of authentic antique mining equipment. *Note:* You must be at least 40 inches tall to ride. Also, Disney discourages expectant mothers; people prone to motion sickness; and those with heart, neck, or back problems from riding. It also may be too intense for some kids under 8.

  Austin's Rating: *"It's even better at night!!"* (He rode it both during the day and at night, and loved it every time.) **Ryan's Rating:** "It's no kid's ride, that's for sure." (It may not be the Hulk, but it's got plenty of zip just the same. It even thrills a few adults, too!)

Country Bear Jamboree *(Finds*
Frommer's Rating: B+
Recommended Ages: 3–adult, but the younger, the better

This is a foot-stomping hoot, though older kids and teens may hate it. Like many of the shows and rides in the Magic Kingdom, it doesn't have a companion in the other parks because it opened when the park did (in 1971!) and dates to a time when entertainment was simpler but still fun. But it still has the power to bridge the generations

> **Tips** **A (Baker's) Dozen Suggestions for Fewer Headaches**
>
> 1. **Be a leader, not a follower:** Try going against the grain, and head left toward Adventureland to begin your day (most visitors sprint for Tomorrowland). If you have the time and aren't a slave to the compressed itinerary of a 1-day visit, make your way to one (maybe two) major attractions early on; then save the others for early on your second day, when crowds are lightest. Pick up a FASTPASS when and wherever you can. And try to make mealtimes a bit earlier or later than usual—11am or 2pm for lunch and 4 or 7pm for dinner. Even a few minutes can make all the difference in the restaurant lines.
> 2. **Note your car's location:** That big red Hummer in the next space may not be there when you get out. Write your lot and row number on something with ink that won't run if it gets wet.
> 3. **Avoid the rush:** I-4 can get horribly crowded at times, so be ready for bumper-to-bumper traffic from 7 to 9am, from 4 to 7pm, and often in between. Check your map for secondary roads and alternative routes, and try to leave the parks a half hour before closing, when crowds disburse in droves.
> 4. **Be realistic:** You aren't going to be able to do everything in every park (believe me, I've tried). As a group, list three or four "must-do" things each day. If you can, consider splitting up, with each adult taking one or more kids—one heading for the thrill rides; the other for the tamer, tot-friendly attractions. If time allows, you can always backtrack later, and this way, no one really misses out on the fun.
> 5. **Timing is everything:** I often laugh when I see people racing to make a tram and then gunning for the turnstiles. Relax—the park isn't going anywhere. And rushing just to wait in line seems rather silly, doesn't it? Once inside the park, mix it up a bit; stagger the attraction lines with indoor shows or even breaks on a shady bench.
> 6. **Call ahead:** If a sit-down dinner in a special restaurant is important to you, make sure to make Advanced Dining Reservations (© **407/939-3463**) before your visit.
> 7. **Set a spending limit:** Kids should know they have a set amount to spend on take-home trinkets (if they do, they generally spend more

(and the A/C is a blessing on hot summer days). The 15-minute show stars a troupe of fiddlin', strummin', and harmonica-playin' bears (audio-Animatronic, of course) belting out lively tunes and woeful love songs. The chubby Trixie, decked out in a satiny skirt, laments lost love as she sings "Tears Will Be the Chaser for Your Wine." Teddi Barra descends from the ceiling in a swing to perform "Heart, We Did All That We Could." In the finale, the cast joins in a rousing singalong.

Frontierland Shootin' Arcade

Frommer's Rating: C

wisely). You should, too. Sticking to your budget will be beneficial in the end, but building in a small contingency "fun" fund for emergencies is still a good idea.

8. **Take a break:** If you're staying at a WDW property, spend the midafternoon napping (don't laugh; you may need a nap) or unwinding in the pool. Return to the parks for a few more attractions and the closing shows. (Get your hand stamped when you leave, and you'll be readmitted without charge.)

9. **Dress comfortably:** This may seem like common sense, but judging by the limping, blistered crowds trudging the parks, most people don't understand the immeasurable amount of walking they'll be doing. Wear comfortable, broken-in walking shoes or sneakers (you know, the ones that won't give you blisters just because you put them on), and skip the sandals and mules that can fall off or cause you to trip.

10. **Don't skimp on the sunscreen:** The Florida sun can be relentless, even in the shade, under the clouds, or in the cooler months. A bad first-day burn can ruin your trip, not to mention your skin. Dress appropriately; wear lightweight, light-colored clothing, and bring along hats (especially for toddlers and infants, even if they'll be in a stroller). If you must show off your skin, slather it in sunscreen (with at least a 30 SPF rating). This is especially important for children. Make sure that you and your kids drink plenty of water in summer to prevent dehydration. Bringing a pair of sunglasses is a smart move, too.

11. **Travel light:** Don't carry large amounts of cash. The Pirates of the Caribbean aren't the only thieves in WDW. There are ATMs in the parks and most resorts if you run short.

12. **Get a little goofy:** Relax, put on those mouse ears, eat that extra piece of fudge, and sing along at the shows. Don't worry about what the staff thinks; they've seen it all (and they're dressed pretty goofily, too).

13. **Take measure of your kids:** This guide, park maps, and information boards outside the more adventurous rides list minimum heights. If you know the restrictions early, you can avoid disappointment in the parks. Trust us—WDW won't budge because of sad faces or temper tantrums when your safety is involved.

Recommended Ages: 8–adult

Combining state-of-the-art electronics with a traditional shooting-gallery format, this arcade presents an array of targets (slow-moving ore cars, buzzards, and gravediggers) in an 1850s boomtown scenario. Fog creeps across the graveyard, and the setting changes as a calm, starlit night turns stormy with flashes of lightning and claps of thunder. Coyotes howl; bridges creak; and skeletal arms reach out from the grave. If you hit a tombstone, it might spin around and mysteriously change its epitaph. To keep things authentic, newfangled electronic firing mechanisms loaded with infrared bullets are concealed in vintage buffalo rifles. Fifty cents buys you 25 shots. It's good for a few minutes of fun for kids over 5.

Splash Mountain
Frommer's Rating: A+
Recommended Ages: 8–adult
If you need a quick cooling off, this is the place to go—because you and your kids will get wet! Some kids may find it a little intimidating upon inspection, but most have a blast while riding it. Based on Disney's 1946 film *Song of the South,* Splash Mountain takes you flume-style down a flooded mountain, past 26 colorful scenes that include backwoods swamps, bayous, spooky caves, and waterfalls. Riders are caught in the bumbling schemes of Brer Fox and Brer Bear as they chase the ever-wily Brer Rabbit, who, against the advice of Mr. Bluebird, leaves his briar-patch home in search of for-tune and the "laughing place." The music from the film forms a delightful audio back-drop. Your hollow-log vehicle twists, turns, and splashes, sometimes plummeting in darkness as the ride leads to a 52-foot, 45-degree, 40-mph splashdown in a briar-filled pond. *Note:* You must be at least 40 inches tall to ride. Also, expectant mothers; peo-ple prone to motion sickness; and those with heart, neck, or back problems shouldn't climb aboard.

   Austin's Rating: "Ahhhhhhhhhhhh!!! . . . let's go again!" (Sloshing albeit quickly back to the end of the line for yet another go.)

Tom Sawyer Island
Frommer's Rating: C for most, B+ for kids who need to burn any extra energy
Recommended Ages: 4–12
   Huck Finn's raft will take you on a 2-minute journey across the River of America to the densely forested Tom Sawyer Island, where kids can explore the narrow passages of Injun Joe's cave (complete with such scary sound effects as whistling wind), a walk-through windmill, a serpentine abandoned mine, and Fort Longhorn. The island's two bridges—one a suspension bridge, the other made of barrels floating on top of the water—create quite a challenge for anyone trying to cross. Maintaining your balance is difficult at best if (or should I say when) the other guests are jumping up and down—but that's half the fun. Narrow, winding dirt paths lined with oaks, pines, and sycamores create an authentic backwoods atmosphere. It's easy to get briefly lost and stumble upon some unexpected adventure, but for younger children, the woods and caves can pose a real problem; toddlers who can't easily find their way back to you or who may get scared by darkness and eerie noises should be watched very carefully. Aunt Polly's Dockside Inn, which serves up sandwiches and such, and has outdoor tables on a porch overlooking the river, is the perfect spot for a relaxing lunch after all that running around; as a bonus, it's generally not as crowded as eateries on the main-land. Check the schedule, though; it's open only seasonally.

LIBERTY SQUARE

Pass through Frontierland into this small area, and you'll suddenly find yourself in the middle of Colonial America, standing in front of the Liberty Tree, an immense live oak decorated with 13 lanterns symbolizing the first 13 colonies. The entire area has an 18th-century, early American feel, complete with Federal and Georgian architec-ture, quaint shops, and flowerbeds bordering manicured lawns. You may even encounter a fife-and-drum corps marching along the cobblestone streets.

Fun Fact **It's a Dirty Job . . .**

The Disney parks are usually fairly clean, but there's one notable spot in the Magic Kingdom that takes pride in its dreary image. To maintain the Haunted Mansion's worn appearance, employees spread hundreds (maybe thousands) of bags of a special dust all over the home's interior and also string up plenty of real-looking cobwebs. It takes a lot of effort to keep the place looking bedraggled, which may explain why your haunted hosts are only a handful of Disney cast members without smiles plastered on their faces.

Hall of Presidents
Frommer's Rating: B+ for school age and adults
Recommended Ages: 8–adult

American presidents from George Washington to George W. Bush are represented by extremely lifelike audio-Animatronic figures (arguably, the best in WDW). If you look closely, you'll see them fidget and whisper during the performance. The show begins with a film projected on a 180-degree, 70mm screen. It talks about the importance of the Constitution; then the curtain rises on America's leaders, and as each comes into the spotlight, he nods or waves with presidential dignity. Then Lincoln rises and speaks, occasionally referring to his notes. In a tribute to Disney thoroughness, painstaking research was done in creating the figures and scenery, with each president's costume reflecting period fashion, fabrics, and tailoring techniques.

Haunted Mansion
Frommer's Rating: A
Recommended Ages: 6–adult

What better way to show off Disney's eye for detailed special effects than through this ride, where "Grim Grinning Ghosts" come out to socialize—or so the ride's theme song goes. The queue here is one of the most amusing in the park, as it winds through a graveyard filled with tombstones whose epitaphs are sure to make you chuckle. Upon entering, you're greeted by a ghostly host, who encloses you in a windowless portrait gallery (are those eyes following you?) where the floor seems to descend (actually, it's the ceiling that's rising), and the room goes dark (the only truly scary moment). Darkness, spooky music, eerie howling, and mysterious screams and rappings enhance its ambience. Your vehicle . . . err , Doom Buggy takes you past a ghostly banquet and ball, a graveyard band, a suit of armor that comes alive, cobwebdraped chandeliers, a ghostly talking head in a crystal ball, and more. Keep your eyes on the mirror you pass at the end of your ride, as you'll find another passenger in your buggy. . . . Boo! The experience is more amusing than terrifying; most children 6 and older will be fine, but those younger (and even some of the older ones) may not be so amused.

Hailey's Rating: "I was a little scared, but Mom kept reminding me it was all pretend." As fun as it can be for some, the special effects can spook even those you'd least expect.

Liberty Square Riverboat *Overrated*
Frommer's Rating: C
Recommended Ages: All ages

An impressive looking steam-powered stern-wheeler aptly named the *Liberty Belle* departs for cruises along the Rivers of America, allowing thrill-ride-weary passengers and tired-out toddlers the chance to rest and relax. As you pass along the shores of Frontierland, the Indian camp, wildlife, and wilderness cabin will make it seem as though you're traveling through the wild and woolly West. Older kids will definitely be bored.

FANTASYLAND

The most fanciful land in the park, Fantasyland features attractions that bring classic Disney characters to life. It is by far the most popular land in the park for young children, who can sail over Merry Ole London and Never Land, ride in a honey pot through the Hundred-Acre Wood, and fly with Dumbo. If your kids are under 8, you'll find yourself spending a lot of your time here.

Cinderella Castle *Moments*

Frommer's Rating: A (for visuals)
Recommended Ages: All ages

There's actually not a lot to do here, but it's the Magic Kingdom's most widely recognized symbol, and I guarantee that you won't be able to pass it by without a look. It's not as though you could miss it anyway. The fairytale castle looms over Main Street U.S.A., its 189-foot-high Gothic spires taking center stage from the minute you enter the park.

One of the most popular restaurants in the park, **Cinderella's Royal Table** (p. 131), is set inside the castle—along with a shop or two. Mosaic murals depict the Cinderella story, and Disney family coats of arms are displayed over a fireplace. An actress portraying Cinderella, dressed for the ball, often makes appearances in the lobby. The Castle Forecourt Stage features live shows daily, so be sure to check the daily *Times Guide*'s schedule for **Cinderella's Surprise Celebration** and **Cinderellabration.**

Cinderella's Golden Carousel *Moments*

Frommer's Rating: B+, A for carousel fans
Recommended Ages: All ages

One of the most beautiful attractions at Disney, the Golden Carousel is as enchanting to look at as it is to ride. Built by the Philadelphia Toboggan Co. in 1917, the carousel toured many an amusement park in the Midwest long before Walt Disney bought it and brought it to Orlando 5 years before the Magic Kingdom opened. Disney artisans meticulously refurbished it, adding 18 hand-painted scenes from *Cinderella* on a wooden canopy above the horses. Its organ plays Disney classics such as "When You Wish upon a Star." Adults and children alike adore riding the ornate horses round and round; there are even a few benches for the littlest tykes in the family. The ride is longer than you might expect, but the lines can get lengthy as well, so check back a bit later if your timing is off the first time around.

Dumbo the Flying Elephant

Frommer's Rating: B+ for young kids and parents
Recommended Ages: 2–6

This is a favorite of the preschool set, a fact that will quickly become apparent when you see the line wrapping around, and around, and around. Much like Magic Carpets of Aladdin (p. 182), the miniature Dumbos fly around in a circle, gently rising and dipping as you control them from inside the elephant. If you can stand the brutal lines—much of which can be out in the blazing sun—this ride is almost sure to make your little one's day.

It's a Small World
Frommer's Rating: B+ for youngsters and first-timers
Recommended Ages: 2–8

Recently refurbished to spruce up some of its older displays, It's a Small World is one of those rides that you just have to do because it's been there since the beginning; it's a classic (built for the 1964 World's Fair before being transplanted to Disney), and in this day and age, it's nice to see that some things don't change (or at least not too much). Besides, it's a big favorite of younger kids. And as much as some adults pooh-pooh it, I'd take bets they come out smiling and singing right along with their kids. If you don't know the song, you will by the end of the ride (and probably ever after), as the hard part is trying to get it *out* of your head. As you sail along, you'll pass through the countries of the world, each filled with appropriately costumed audio-Animatronic dolls greeting you by singing "It's a Small World" in tiny Munchkin voices. The cast of thousands includes Chinese acrobats; Russian kazatski dancers; Indian snake charmers; French cancan girls; and . . . well, you get the picture. To truly experience everything Disney, this one's a must.

Ryan's Rating: "No way! I'm not going on that." (On the other hand, Nicolas, Hailey, and Davis all loved it, mesmerized by the scenery and the song.)

Mad Tea Party
Frommer's Rating: C+
Recommended Ages: 4–adult

Traditional amusement-park ride it may be, but it's still a family favorite—maybe because it is so simple. The mad-tea-party scene in *Alice in Wonderland* was the inspiration for this one, and riders sit in giant pastel teacups set on saucers that careen around a circular platform while the cup, saucer, and platform all spin round and round. Occasionally, the woozy Dormouse pops out of a big central teapot to see just what's going on. Tame as it may appear, this can be a pretty active, even nauseating ride, depending on how much you spin your teacup's wheel. Adolescents seem to consider it a badge of honor if they can turn the unsuspecting adults in their cup green; you have been warned!

Hailey's and **Nicolas's Rating** (in chorus): "Faster, faster . . . let's make Mom turn green!" (They must have read my review. Ugh!)

The Many Adventures of Winnie the Pooh
Frommer's Rating: B
Recommended Ages: 2–8 and their parents

This fun ride features the cute and cuddly little fellow, along with Eeyore, Piglet, and Tigger. You board a golden honey pot and ride through a storybook version of the Hundred-Acre Wood, keeping an eye out for Heffulumps, Woozles, Blustery Days,

---

Tips Playtime for Pooh

Pooh's Playful Spot, located just across from The Many Adventures of Winnie the Pooh (handy, don't you think?) in Fantasyland, is a toddler-friendly play area complete with a treehouse; honey pots; slides; water fountains; crawl-through logs; and, fortunately, benches for parents in need of a rest while they watch their little ones run about.

(*Tips* **Not So Fast**

If you're tackling rides with preshows, such as Mickey's PhilharMagic, don't try to be the first one inside. Hang back in the crowd a little, and you may land in the center of the theater, where the seats are better. Folks who rush in are shooed to the theater's far side.

---

and the Floody Place. Kids, especially those 3 to 5, love it, but prepare yourself for *very, very* long lines if you don't use FASTPASS.

Mickey's PhilharMagic

Frommer's Rating: A+

Recommended Ages: All ages

This late-2003 arrival is by far the most amazing 3-D movie production I've ever laid eyes on and a must-see for all ages. Popular Disney characters—including Ariel, Simba, and Aladdin—are brought to 3-D life on a 150-foot screen (the largest wrap-around screen on the planet) as they try to help (or, in some cases, hinder) the attempts of Donald Duck to retrieve Mickey's magical sorcerer's hat before the Mouse discovers it's missing. It's the first time the classic Disney characters have ever been rendered in 3-D. Even if you're not a big fan of shows, this is one you should see. Like (but far better than) the whimsical **Jim Henson's Muppet*Vision 3-D** (p. 220) at Disney–MGM Studios, the show combines music, animated film, puppetry, and special effects that tickle several of your senses. The kids will love the animation and effects, and parents will enjoy the nostalgia factor.

Peter Pan's Flight

Frommer's Rating: A for kids and parents

Recommended Ages: 3–8

Another of Disney's simple pleasures, this is a classic ride that's fun for the whole family. You'll fly through the sky in your very own ship (much like Captain Hook's), gliding over familiar scenes from the adventures of Peter Pan. Your adventure begins in the Darlings' nursery and includes a flight over an elaborate nighttime cityscape of Merry Ole' London before you move on to Never Land. There, you encounter mermaids, Indians, Tick Tock the Croc, the Lost Boys, Princess Tiger Lilly, Tinker Bell, Hook, and Smee, all while listening to the theme, "You Can Fly, You Can Fly, You Can Fly." It's *very* tame fun for the young and young at heart.

   Davis's Rating: "Look, look—it's Tinkerbell, and Peter, and the crocodile, and . . ." Well, you get the idea. This one is always a hit with my younger set; the older ones, however, run the other way, especially when they see the never-ending lines for Never Land.

Snow White's Scary Adventures

Frommer's Rating: C

Recommended Ages: 4–8

While Disney has changed the ride a bit since it debuted, attempting to make it less scary for the small children for whom it was intended, it still features the wicked witch rather predominantly (though Snow White appears far more often than before). Many of the scenes are pleasant, including such happier moments from the movie as the scenes at the wishing well and Snow White riding away with the prince to live happily ever after. The audio-Animatronic dwarfs and bright colors are also far from menacing. Even so, this ride still has plenty of scary moments if your child is under 5 (and those any older likely won't even want to ride), so if the lines are long, think about passing this one up.

MICKEY'S TOONTOWN FAIR

Wondering where to find Mickey? Instead of walking about the park, as he did many years ago, the Mouse now holds court in Toontown. The candy-striped **Judge's** and **Toontown Hall of Fame** tents inside this zone are where kids get a chance to meet many of their favorite Disney characters, including Mickey, Minnie, Donald, Goofy, and Pluto. The entire area (small as it may be) is filled with a whimsical collection of cartoonish attractions geared mostly to those under 6 (making it one of the more crowded spots in the park).

The Barnstormer at Goofy's Wiseacre Farm (Finds

Frommer's Rating: A for kids and parents
Recommended Ages: 4 and up
This mini–roller coaster is the twin of Woody Woodpecker's Nuthouse Coaster (which it likely inspired) at Universal Studios Florida (p. 255). It's designed to look and feel like a cropduster that flies slightly off course and right through the Goofmeister's barn. The ride has very little in the dip-and-drop department but a little zip on the spin-and-spiral front. *Note:* The 60-second ride has a 35-inch height minimum, and expectant mothers are warned not to ride it.

Nicolas's Rating: "Wow, that was cool!" It even gets squeals from some adults.

Donald's Boat (SS *Miss Daisy*)

Frommer's Rating: B+ for kids
Recommended Ages: 2–10
The good ship *Miss Daisy* offers plenty of interactive fun for kids who enjoy getting wet. Watch out as you make your way around the surrounding "waters," as the leaks squirting from the boat are practically unavoidable—but that's half the fun (you can tell by the little squeals of joy from those who've been doused). *Tip:* The nearby Toon Park (a 40-inch height *maximum*) is a small covered playground with slides and a small playhouse for dryer adventures. There are also a handful of covered benches for weary parents in need of a momentary break.

(Tips It Ain't Fair, But . . .

Disney rides sometimes break down or need routine maintenance that can take them out of commission for a few hours, a day, a week, or sometimes months. Test Track at Epcot, for example, occasionally experiences technical difficulties. And It's a Small World recently closed for a few months in 2004 for renovations.

Many, but not all, of the ride rehabs are listed on the Disney website (www.disneyworld.com). Deb's Unofficial Walt Disney World Information Guide site (www.allearsnet.com) lists most ride rehabs as well. The moral of the story: Err on the side of caution, and don't make promises to kids about specific rides just in case something happens. Note that refurbishments and technical difficulties are unfortunate but part of the deal; neither Disney nor Universal will discount or refund any tickets when rehabs occur.

> (*Value* **Extra Magic—Extra Time**
>
> The free **Extra Magic Hour** program allows Disney resort guests (as well as those staying at the WDW Swan, the WDW Dolphin, and the Hilton at the Walt Disney World Resort) some extra playtime in the parks. Under the program, a select number of attractions, shops, and restaurants at one of the four major Disney parks open an hour early on scheduled mornings, and those at another park remain open up to 3 hours after official closing on scheduled evenings. And because only resort guests can participate in the Extra Magic Hour, crowds are almost nonexistent, and lines are much shorter—not to mention that the temperatures are usually a lot more agreeable early in the morning and later in the evening.
>
> To enter a park for the morning Extra Magic Hour, you must present your Disney-resort room key and park ticket. For the evening Extra Magic Hour, your room key, park ticket, and a special wristband (for every member in your group) are required. You can obtain the wristband at the park scheduled to remain open that evening, but no earlier than 1 hour prior to park closing.
>
> *Warning:* If you hold a ticket with a Park Hopper add-on (see p. 167 for information on Disney ticketing options), you can attend any Extra Magic Hour at any park. But if you hold a base ticket with no park-hopping privileges, you can attend the Extra Magic Hour only at the park where you're spending your day. So if you have only a base ticket, and you go to the morning Magic Hour at Epcot and spend the day there, you cannot head over to Magic Kingdom's evening Magic Hour on the same day. Call © **407/824-4321** or visit **www.disneyworld.com** for details.

Mickey's & Minnie's Country Houses

Frommer's Rating: B for younger kids
Recommended Ages: 2–8

These separate cottages offer a lot of visual fun and a small bit of interactive play for youngsters, but they're usually crowded; the lines flow like molasses. Mickey's place is more for looking than touching, though it does feature a small garden and garage playground. Minnie's lets kids play in her kitchen, where popcorn goes wild in a microwave, a cake bakes and then deflates in the oven, and the utensils strike up a symphony of their own.

TOMORROWLAND

This land represents the future as envisioned in the '20s and '30s—a galactic, science fiction–inspired community inhabited by humans, aliens, and robots.

Astro Orbiter

Frommer's Rating: B
Recommended Ages: 4–10

While touted as a tame ride much like the ones you might have ridden when you were a child and the carnivals came to town, it does offer a bit of unexpected uneasiness.

Its "rockets" are on arms attached to "the center of the galaxy" and move up and down while orbiting the planets, but they also tilt to the side—and when you're on top of the two-story tower, looking down from your perch can make you rather anxious. Because of the ride's limited capacity, the line tends to move at a snail's pace, so unless it's short, skip this one.

Buzz Lightyear's Space Ranger Spin
Frommer's Rating: A+ for kids and parents
Recommended Ages: 3 and up

Recruits stand ready as Buzz Lightyear briefs you on your mission. The evil emperor Zurg is once again up to no good, and Buzz needs your to help save the universe. As you cruise through "space," you'll pass through scenes filled with brightly colored aliens, most of whom are marked with a big "Z," so you know where to shoot. Kids love using the dashboard-mounted laser cannons as they spin through the sky (filled with gigantic toys instead of stars). If they're good shots, they can set off sight-and-sound gags with a direct hit from their lasers (my 4-year-old, however, aims just about everywhere but at the target and still has loads of fun). A display in the car keeps score. This ride uses the same technology as Universal Studios Florida's Men in Black Alien Attack (p. 253), but it's aimed at a younger audience; therefore, it's far tamer.

   Davis's and **Nicolas's Rating:** "To infinity and beyond . . . again! Come on, Mom, again!!!" (It's one of the best rides in the park and fun for the entire family.)

Space Mountain
Frommer's Rating: B+
Recommended Ages: 10–adult

This cosmic roller coaster usually has *long* lines (but it has FASTPASS), and most guests find only marginal entertainment value in the preride space-age music and exhibits (meteorites, shooting stars, and space debris whizzing overhead). Once aboard your rocket, you'll climb and dive through the inky, starlit blackness of outer space. The hairpin turns and plunges make it seem as if you're going at breakneck speed, but your car doesn't go any faster than 28 mph. The front seat of the train offers the best bang, but Space Mountain is one of the first generation of modern, dark-side coasters and, therefore, somewhat outdated. If you like dark or semidark thrill rides, you'll be much happier with Rock 'n' Roller Coaster at Disney–MGM Studios. *Note:* Riders must be at least 44 inches tall. Also, expectant moms; people prone to motion sickness; and those with heart, neck, or back problems shouldn't climb aboard.

   Ryan's Rating: "That was soooooooo cool!" (In other words, it's a good coming-of-age test for thrill-ride junkies of the near future and those not willing to ride the real biggies.)

Stitch's Great Escape *(Overrated*
Frommer's Rating: C-
Recommended Ages: 5–10

⌐Tips Best Protein Snack in the Parks

For our money, you can't beat the smoked-turkey drumsticks sold for just over $5 in WDW parks, including at The Lunching Pad in Tomorrowland. Apparently, a lot of folks agree; Disney sells about 1.6 million of them a year.

In 2003, the scarier **ExtraTERRORestrial Alien Encounter** was closed permanently to make way for this newer, (allegedly) more family-friendly attraction. Unfortunately, Disney missed the mark a bit on this one. Even though it features the mischievous experiment 626, otherwise known as Stitch—a favorite of many younger kids—the ride isn't really that child-friendly (at least not for the young set). It's not particularly exciting, either. Upon entering the attraction, guests are briefed on their responsibilities as newly recruited alien prison guards. Suddenly, an alarm sounds; a new prisoner is arriving, and the pandemonium begins. Stitch, after appearing by teleportation, is confined in the middle of the room, but only momentarily; the ride isn't called Stitch's Great Escape for nothing. Guests are seated around the center stage, overhead restraints on their shoulders (which are slightly uncomfortable unless you are sitting straight up when they are lowered) allowing them to "feel" special sensory effects. It's the attraction's long periods of darkness and silence that make this one inappropriate for younger children—a fact made apparent by some of the screams you'll hear from the audience. *Note:* There's a 40-inch height requirement.

The Timekeeper
Frommer's Rating: C+
Recommended Ages: 8–adult
This Jules Verne/H. G. Wells–inspired multimedia show combines CircleVision and IMAX footage with audio-Animatronics. It's hosted by a robot/mad scientist (Robin Williams) and his assistant, 9-EYE, a flying, camera-headed 'droid that moonlights as a time-machine test pilot. In this escapade, the audience hears Mozart as a young prodigy playing for French royalty, visits medieval battlefields in Scotland, watches da Vinci work, and floats in a hot-air balloon over Moscow's Red Square. Voices include Jeremy Irons and Rhea Perlman. Older kids will like the robot, but younger ones will get bored and restless. *Note:* You have to stand during the entire show, which is open only seasonally.

Tomorrowland Indy Speedway
Frommer's Rating: B+ for kids, D for tweens, teens, and childless adults
Recommended Ages: 4–10
Younger kids love this ride, especially if they get the chance to drive one of the gas-powered, mini–sports cars—though they may need the help of a parent's foot to push down on the gas pedal—for a 4-minute spin around the track. Tweens and teens, however, hate it: Speeds reach a mere 7 mph, which for most is *incredibly* slow, and the steering is atrocious (even I can't control the cars without bumping the rail that it follows). The slow speed seems to work well for young kids (who also think the bumping around is fun). The long lines move even slower than the ride does, so be prepared to wait this one out. There's a 52-inch height minimum to take a lap without an older rider along with you. *Note:* It carries Disney's warning that expectant mothers and people with heart, neck, or back problems shouldn't climb aboard, likely because of the potential for getting bumped as you try to board or disembark.

Tomorrowland Transit Authority
Frommer's Rating: C, B+ for tired adults or toddlers
Recommended Ages: All ages
After making your way up a moving walkway, you'll spot the futuristic train cars that will take you on a tour of Tomorrowland from high above the ground. The engineless train runs on a track and is powered by electromagnets, creating no pollution and little noise, and using little power. Narrated by a computer guide named Horack I, TTA

Moments **Where to Find Characters**

Mickey's Toontown Fair was designed as a place where kids can meet and mingle with their favorite characters all day at the Judge's Tent and Toontown Hall of Fame Tent. Mickey and others are stars in residence. In **Fantasyland,** look for Ariel's Grotto and Fantasyland Character Festival for daily greetings. **Main Street** (Town Square), **Adventureland** (at Pirates of the Caribbean and near Magic Carpets of Aladdin), and **Liberty Square** (at the Diamond Horseshoe) are other hot spots. I've occasionally caught a few near the Galaxy Palace Theater in **Tomorrowland** as well. If your child has an autograph book for characters to sign, have it out and ready with a pen for Goofy to plop down his signature. And have your camera ready and waiting if you want to capture a picture of your kids with Pluto. And bring lots of patience; you won't be the only parent waiting for the Kodak moment.

---

offers an overhead view of Tomorrowland, including a brief interior look at Space Mountain. Lines are often nonexistent, as most riders are parents awaiting the return of their children from Space Mountain or those with tired toddlers in need of a brief respite from the activity below.

Walt Disney's Carousel of Progress *(Overrated*
Frommer's Rating: C
Recommended Ages: 5–10
Open only seasonally, when the crowds are at their peak, the Carousel of Progress offers more of a respite from the hustle and bustle of the crowds than it does an interesting experience. It debuted at the 1964 World's Fair before Disney decided to include it in his collection. The ride emigrated from Disneyland to Disney World in 1975 and was refurbished to its original state just over 10 years ago. The entire show rotates through scenes illustrating the state of technology from the 1900s to the 1940s. Most adults find it rather boring, but kids willing to sit still for a few minutes may actually learn a thing or two.

PARADES, FIREWORKS & MORE

You can pick up a guide map when you enter the park. It should include an **entertainment schedule** that lists all kinds of special goings-on for the day. These include concerts, encounters with characters, holiday events, and the major happenings listed next.

Share a Dream Come True Parade
Frommer's Rating: B
Recommended Ages: All ages
This is the Magic Kingdom's newest parade. Floats topped by gigantic themed snow globes with Disney characters inside them make their way through the park and up Main Street daily.

SpectroMagic *(Moments*
Frommer's Rating: A
Recommended Ages: All ages
This 20-minute after-dark production combines fiber optics, holographic images, clouds of liquid nitrogen, old-fashioned twinkling lights, and a soundtrack featuring

classic Disney tunes. Mickey, dressed in an amber-and-purple grand magician's cape, makes an appearance in a confetti of light. You'll also see the SpectroMen atop the title float, as well as Chernabog, *Fantasia's* monstrous demon, who unfolds his 38-foot wingspan. It takes the electrical equivalent of seven lightning bolts (enough to power a fleet of 2,000 over-the-road trucks) to bring the show to life.

SpectroMagic is held only on a limited number of nights. See your entertainment schedule for availability. When it is held, there are usually two showings: one earlier in the evening and the next one near closing time. If you have little kids, go to the early showing. If you have older kids and teens, the later showing is usually less crowded (and you face shorter ride lines while the first production is going on). No matter which showing you attend, this one is worth having the kids stay up for; it's a memorable experience for the entire family.

Wishes (Moments

Frommer's Rating: A+

Recommended Ages: All ages

This breathtaking 12-minute fireworks display replaced the old **Fantasy in the Sky** fireworks in October 2003. The show, narrated by Jiminy Cricket and with background music from several Disney classics, is the story of a wish coming true, and it borrows one element from the old one: Tinker Bell still flies overhead. The fireworks go off nightly during summer and holidays and on selected nights (usually Mon and Wed–Sat) the rest of the year. See your entertainment schedule for details. Numerous good views of the action are available, so long as you're standing on the front side of the castle; get too far off to the side or behind the display, and it loses much of its impressive and meticulously choreographed visual effect. Disney hotels close to the park (Grand Floridian, Polynesian, Contemporary, and Wilderness Lodge) also offer excellent views.

4 Epcot

Epcot is an acronym for *Experimental Prototype Community of Tomorrow,* and it was Walt Disney's dream for a planned city. Alas, after his death, it became a theme park—Central Florida's second major theme park, which opened in 1982. Its aims are described in a dedication plaque: "May Epcot entertain, inform, and inspire. And, above all . . . instill a new sense of belief and pride in man's ability to shape a world that offers hope to people everywhere."

Ever growing and changing, Epcot occupies 300 vibrantly landscaped acres. If you can spare it, take a little time to stop and smell the roses on your way to and through the two major sections: Future World and World Showcase.

Epcot is so big that hiking the World Showcase end to end (1⅓ miles from the Canada pavilion on one side to Mexico on the other) can be exhausting (that goes double for your kids). That's why some folks are certain that Epcot stands for "Every Person Comes out Tired." Depending on how long you intend to linger at each country in World Showcase, this part of the park can be experienced in 1 day. One way to conserve energy is to take the launches across the lagoon from the edge of Future World to Germany or Morocco. But most visitors simply make a leisurely loop, working clockwise or counterclockwise from one side of the Showcase to the other.

Unlike Magic Kingdom, much of Epcot's parking lot is close to the gate. Parking sections are named for themes (Harvest, Energy, and so forth), and the aisles are numbered.

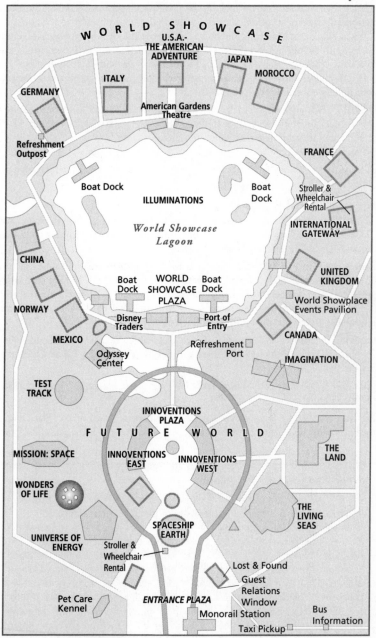

While some guests are happy to walk to the gate from nearer areas, trams are available, but these days mainly to and from the outer areas.

If you plan to eat lunch or dinner here and haven't already made Advanced Dining Reservations (© **407/939-3463**), you can make them at Guest Services or at the restaurants, many of which are described in chapter 5, "Family-Friendly Dining."

Before you get under way, check the map's schedule and incorporate any shows you want to see into your itinerary.

HOURS   Future World is usually open from 9 or 10am to 6 or 7pm but sometimes later during major holidays and the summer. World Showcase doesn't open until 11am or noon, and it usually closes at 9pm but sometimes later.

TICKET PRICES   Ticket are $63 for adults, $52 for children 3 to 9, and free for children under 3. See "Tickets & Passes," earlier in this chapter, for information on multiday passes and add-on options.

SERVICES & FACILITIES IN EPCOT

ATMs   The machines here accept cards issued by banks using the Cirrus, Honor, and PLUS systems, and are located at the front of the park, in Italy, and near the bridge between World Showcase and Future World.

Baby Care   Epcot's Baby Care Center is by the first-aid station near the Odyssey Center in Future World. It's furnished with a nursing room with rocking chairs; disposable diapers, formula, baby food, and pacifiers are for sale. There are also changing tables in all women's restrooms, as well as in some of the men's restrooms. Disposable diapers are also available at Guest Relations.

Cameras & Film   Film, batteries, Kodak disposable cameras, and limited digital supplies are available throughout the park, including at the Kodak Camera Center at the Entrance Plaza.

First Aid   The First Aid Center, staffed by registered nurses, is located near the Odyssey Center in Future World.

Lockers   Lockers are to the west of Spaceship Earth, outside the Entrance Plaza, and in the Bus Information Center by the bus parking lot. The cost is $5 a day, plus a $2 deposit.

Tips Fun for Kids at Epcot

Epcot is the least kid-friendly of the Disney parks (especially for the preschool and toddler set), but there are still plenty of things for your kids to do.

Be sure to pick up a guide map and entertainment schedule as you enter the park. Folks with children can and should grab a copy of the *Epcot Kids' Guide,* which uses a yellow K in a red square to note **Kidcot Funstops** inside the World Showcase. These play and learning stations are for the younger set (geared to ages 4–8) and allow them to stop at various World Showcase countries, create cultural crafts, get autographs, have their Kidcot passports stamped (these are available for purchase in most Epcot stores and make a great souvenir), and chat with cast members native to those countries. Your kids will get the chance to learn about different countries and make a souvenir to bring home. For more information, stop in at Guest Services when you get into the park. The stations open at 1pm daily.

Lost Children Lost children in Epcot are usually taken to Earth Center or the Baby Care Center, where lost-children logbooks are kept. *Children under 7 should wear name tags* inside their clothing.

Package Pickup Any package you purchase can be sent to the Gift Stop near Spaceship Earth. Allow 3 hours for delivery. There's also a package-pickup location at the World Traveler at the International Gateway entrance in the World Showcase.

Parking It's $9 for cars, pickups, and vans, and $10 for RVs.

Pet Care Day accommodations are offered at kennels just outside the Entrance Plaza at Epcot for $6 (© **407/824-6568**). Proof of vaccination is required. Walking service (available only at the Epcot kennel) costs $2.50 per walk. Four other kennels are located in the WDW complex.

Strollers These can be rented from special stands on the east side of the Entrance Plaza and at World Showcase's International Gateway. The cost is $10 for a single and $18 for a double, with a discount available for length-of-stay rentals.

Wheelchair Rental Rent wheelchairs inside the Entrance Plaza to your left, to the right of ticket booths at the Gift Shop, and at World Showcase's International Gateway. The cost for regular chairs is $10. Electric wheelchairs cost $35 a day, plus a $5 refundable deposit.

FUTURE WORLD

Future World is on the front end of Epcot, the first area mainstream guests see after entering the park. Its icon is a huge geosphere known as Spaceship Earth—aka that giant silver golf ball. The focus here is on discovery, scientific achievements, and tomorrow's technologies in areas running from energy to undersea exploration. This zone offers two thrill rides that will get the adrenaline pumping in your teens and several attractions that will appeal to the small fry in your party.

Imagination
Frommer's Rating: B+
Recommended Ages: 6–adult

In this pavilion, even the fountains are magical. "Water snakes" arc in the air, offering kids a chance to dare them to "bite." (Little kids love them, and it's a good place for them to work off a little energy and you to get a great photo.) Figment, the pavilion's much-loved mascot (see below), makes an occasional appearance.

The 3-D **Honey, I Shrunk the Audience** show is one of the big attractions here, deserving an **A rating** by itself. Based on the Disney hit *Honey, I Shrunk the Kids* film, you're terrorized by mice and, once you're shrunk, by a large cat; then you're given a good shaking by a gigantic 5-year-old. Vibrating seats and creepy tactile effects enhance dramatic 3-D action. Finally, everyone returns to proper size—except the family dog, which creates the final surprise.

Figment, the crazy-but-lovable purple dragon, stars in the **Journey into Your Imagination** ride. Things begin with an open house at the Imagination Institute, with Dr. Nigel Channing taking you on a tour of labs that demonstrate how the five senses capture and control one's imagination, except that you never get to touch and taste once Figment arrives to prove that it's far, far better to set your imagination free. He invites you to his upside-down house, where a new perspective enhances your imagination. "One Little Spark," an upbeat ditty that debuted when the attraction opened in 1983, has been brought back and incorporated into the ride.

Moments **Top-10 Orlando Family Attractions**

For Very Young Kids:

1. **Caro-Seuss-El** Cowfish, elephant birds, and other wacky critters inhabit this Islands of Adventure merry-go-round (p. 262).
2. **A Day in the Park with Barney** The purple dinosaur drives some adults batty, but little Universal Studios guests love him (p. 251).
3. **Jim Henson's Muppet*Vision 3-D** Don't miss Kermit, Miss Piggy, and the rest of the crew at Disney–MGM Studios (p. 220).
4. **Voyage of the Little Mermaid** Puppets, film, and special effects make for a lively show, also at Disney–MGM Studios (p. 224).
5. **If I Ran the Zoo** Let the little ones play with Seussian creatures at this 19-station, interactive playland at Islands of Adventure (p. 262).
6. **Ketchakiddie Creek** Disney's Typhoon Lagoon has lots of wet fun for the younger set (and older guests, too; p. 235).
7. **Magic Carpets of Aladdin** Watch out for spitting camels on this wheel-and-spoke kids' ride at Disney's Magic Kingdom (p. 182).
8. **Cinderella's Golden Carousel** Built in 1917, this grand old Magic Kingdom carousel delights plenty of adults, too (p. 188).
9. **Mickey's & Minnie's Country Houses** The utensils and furniture create some surprises inside these houses at Mickey's Toontown Fair in the Magic Kingdom (p. 192).
10. **One Fish, Two Fish, Red Fish, Blue Fish** Your little ones can fly their funky fish up and down as they spin above ground level at Islands of Adventure's Seuss Landing (p. 263).

For Kids 6–12 & Older:

1. **Big Thunder Mountain Railroad** Hold onto your skivvies, as this runaway train at Disney's Magic Kingdom provides its share of thrills and chills (p. 183).
2. **Popeye & Bluto's Bilge-Rat Barges** Arguably, this Islands of Adventure entry is the best faux-whitewater ride in Florida (p. 265).
3. **Indiana Jones Epic Stunt Spectacular/Lights, Motors, Action! Extreme Stunt Show** Both offer edge-of-your-seat excitement at Disney–MGM Studios (p. 219).
4. **Dudley Do-Right's Ripsaw Falls** Expect to get wet on this Islands of Adventure log ride that reaches 50 mph (p. 265).
5. **The Barnstormer at Goofy's Wiseacre Farm** The Magic Kingdom's mini–roller coaster is the fairest of this genre (p. 191).
6. **Woody Woodpecker's Nuthouse Coaster** But Islands' minicoaster is just half a click behind Goofy's in the fun factor (p. 255).
7. **Jimmy Neutron's Nicktoon Blast** Help Jimmy battle Yokians ,and meet SpongeBob and other 'toons at one of Universal Studios Florida's newest attractions (p. 253).

8. **Splash Mountain**   The Magic Kingdom's wettest ride will launch you at 40 mph down a 52-foot, 45-degree slope (p. 186). **Jurassic Park River Adventure**   Made from the same mold as Splash Mountain, this Islands of Adventures wild ride adds hissing dinosaurs to the special effects (p. 266).

9. **Soarin'**   You'll fly high over California's spectacular landscape by hang-glider at Epcot (p. 204).

10. **Kali River Rapids**   Animal Kingdom's raft ride isn't quite up to Popeye & Bluto's at Islands, but it's still a ton of wet fun (p. 233).

For Thrill-Seeking Teens & Parents:

1. **Incredible Hulk Coaster**   In Florida, it doesn't get any scarier than this Islands of Adventure rocket ride, which offers seven rollovers and two deep drops (p. 264).

2. **Rock 'n' Roller Coaster**   You won't find a faster giddyup-and-go than this 0-to-60-mph, Aerosmith-supported stretch limo at Disney–MGM Studios (p. 222).

3. **Dueling Dragons**   Test your courage on one of two coasters that hit speeds of 60 mph and come within 12 inches of each other at Islands of Adventure (p. 267).

4. **Summit Plummet**   Hang onto your swimsuit as you fall 120 feet at 60 mph—sans vehicle!—at this Blizzard Beach water slide (p. 237).

5. **The Twilight Zone Tower of Terror**   If you want to see what it's like to fall in an elevator, yo-yo style, tackle this Disney–MGM test of your nerve (p. 223).

6. **The Amazing Adventures of Spider-Man**   Bar none, this Islands of Adventure entry is the best 3-D simulator and action ride east of the Mississippi River (p. 263).

7. **Mission: Space**   Get ready to launch (maybe your lunch) if you climb aboard Epcot's new motion simulator, which NASA astronauts helped design and test (p. 205).

8. **Kraken**   Speaking of launching, SeaWorld's signature thrill ride is a floorless, open-sided roller coaster that hits 65 mph while making seven loops (p. 276).

9. **Revenge of the Mummy**   Inside darkened Egyptian tombs with a thousand-year-old mummy screeching "Death is only the beginning!" will make you glad you live in more modern times (p. 254).

10. **Test Track**   Run your six-passenger convertible through a host of tests at this GM-sponsored attraction, which features a 65-mph speed burst on an elevated straightaway (p. 206).

Moments **Behind the Scenes: Special Tours in Walt Disney World**

In addition to the greenhouse tour in Epcot's The Land pavilion (p. 204), the Disney parks offer a number of walking tours and learning programs, some of which are suitable for kids. The tours are subject to change. The tours listed below represent the most popular choices available at press time. Times, days, and prices also change. It's best to call ahead to Disney's tour line, © **407/939-8687,** to make reservations or get additional information.

- Epcot's **Seas Aqua Tour** lends you a wetsuit and then takes you on a 2½-hour journey that includes a 30-minute swim in the 5.7 million-gallon Living Seas Aquarium, home to some 65 marine species. The tour includes a souvenir T-shirt and group photo. The cost is $100; park admission is not required; and it's open to guests 8 and older (those under 18 must be accompanied by an adult). It's offered daily at 12:30pm.

- The **Family Magic Tour** explores the nooks and crannies of the Magic Kingdom in the form of a 2-hour scavenger hunt. You meet and greet characters at the end. Children and adults are $25 per person. You must also buy admission tickets to the park and book in advance. If you have young kids and want to do a special tour, this is the one to take. It begins daily at 11:30am outside City Hall. It's sometimes held at 9:30am, too.

- The **Magic Behind Our Steam Trains** tour (ages 10 and up) is a fun one for locomotive buffs. A pair of inveterate conductors give you insight other guests don't get into the history and present operations of the little engines that could. Tours run Monday, Tuesday, Thursday, and Saturday at 7:30am; the cost is $40 per person, plus park admission.

Several tours are offered only to those age 16 and older. Most of these are aimed at adults (photos are not permitted on these backstage tours, and photo ID is a must). A few that might appeal to teens are:

- The 3½-hour **Hidden Treasures of World Showcase** explores the architectural and entertainment offerings of Epcot's 11 "nations." The $59 tours (plus admission) are at 9:45am on Tuesday and Thursday. If you're interested

Once you disembark from the ride, head for the **"What If"** labs, where your kids can burn lots of energy while exercising their imaginations at a number of interactive stations that allow them to conduct music, and experiment with video.

Innoventions East and West

Frommer's Rating: B+ for hungry minds and game junkies

Recommended Ages: 8–adult

Innoventions East, behind Spaceship Earth and to the left as you enter the park, features the **House of Innoventions.** It's a preview of tomorrow's smart house, but many of its products are already on the market (at astronomical prices). Its refrigerator has an Internet-savvy computer that can make your grocery list and place the order. A smart picture frame can store and send photos to other smart frames. And its toilet in your teen's getting both an educational and entertaining tour, this is a good choice.

- The 4½-hour **Keys to the Kingdom** tour provides an orientation to the Magic Kingdom and a glimpse into the high-tech systems behind the magic. It's $58 (park admission required) and is held daily at 8:30, 9:30, and 10am. It's got some interesting insights into the park, and you will get treated to a ride or two, so if your teen is wild about Disney, it's not a bad bet.

- At the top of the price chain ($199 per person) is **Backstage Magic,** a 7-hour, self-propelled bus tour through areas of Epcot, the Magic Kingdom, and Disney–MGM Studios that aren't seen by mainstream guests. The 10am weekday tour is limited to 20 people age 16 or older, and you might have trouble getting a date unless you book early. Some will find this one isn't worth the price, but if you or your teen have a brain that must know how things work or simply want to know more than your family or friends, you might find it's worth the cost. You'll see WDW mechanics and engineers repairing and building Animatronic beings from attractions such as "It's a Small World." You'll peek over the shoulders of cast members who watch closed-circuit TVs to make sure other visitors are surviving the harrowing rides. And at the Magic Kingdom, you'll venture into the tunnels used for work areas, as well as corridors for the cast to get from one area to the others without fighting tourist crowds. It's not unusual for tour-takers to see Snow White enjoying a Snickers bar, find Cinderella having her locks touched up at an underground salon, or view woodworkers as they restore the hard-maple muscles of the carousel horses. Park admission *isn't* required, and lunch is included.

- **Backstage Safari** at Animal Kingdom ($65 per person plus park admission) offers a 3-hour look at the park's veterinary hospital as well as lessons in conservation, animal nutrition, and medicine (Mon, Wed, Thurs, and Fri). If your teen dreams of veterinary school, this is a good bet; otherwise, it may be a bit boring for her. *Note:* You won't see many animals.

has a seat warmer, automatic lid opener and closer, and a sprayer and blow dryer that eliminate the need for toilet paper if you're worldly. The **Internet Zone** profiles tomorrow's online games for kids, including laser tag with Disney characters. **Opportunity City** is the latest addition and features an online game, Hot Shot Business. Across the plaza at **Innoventions West,** crowds flock to **Video Games of Tomorrow,** which has nearly three dozen game stations. **Where's the Fire?,** geared to smaller kids, teaches the basics of fire safety and demonstrates how firefighters fight fires with the help of a pump truck.

Note: A new Underwriters Laboratories exhibit at Innoventions East, the **Test the Limits Lab,** has six kiosks that let kids and fun-loving adults try out a variety of products. In one, you can pull a rope attached to a hammer that crashes into a TV screen to see if it's shatter resistant. In another, you can push a button that releases a magnet that falls onto a firefighter's helmet.

The Land

Frommer's Rating: B+ for environmentalists and gardeners, C for others
Recommended Ages: 8–adult

The largest of Future World's pavilions highlights food and nature.

Living with The Land is a 13-minute boat ride through three ecological environments (a rainforest, an African desert, and the windswept American plains), each populated by appropriate audio-Animatronic denizens. New farming methods and experiments ranging from hydroponics to plants growing in simulated Martian soil are showcased in real gardens. If you'd like a more serious overview, take the 45-minute **Behind the Seeds** guided walking tour of the growing areas, offered daily. Sign up at the Green Thumb Emporium shop near the entrance to Food Rocks. The cost is $8 for adults and $6 for children 3 to 9. *Note:* It's really geared to children.

Circle of Life combines spectacular live-action footage with animation in a 15-minute motion picture based on *The Lion King*. In this cautionary environmental tale, Timon and Pumbaa are building a monument to the good life called Hakuna Matata Lakeside Village, but their project, as Simba points out, is damaging the savanna for other animals. The message: Everything is connected in the great circle of life.

On the new **Soarin'**, a copy of a popular attraction at Disney's California Adventure theme park, guests are seated in a giant projection-screen dome and then allowed to fly through the sky, 40 feet into the air, over the landscapes of California. This amazing adventure is enhanced by sensory effects as guests are treated to the sights, sounds . . . and smells (think orange blossoms and pine trees) of a dozen locations in California, including the Golden Gate Bridge, the redwood forests, Napa Valley, Yosemite, and more. You really will feel almost as though you're flying through the sky. *Note:* The ride carries a 40-inch height minimum. For the best experience, try to get seated in the first row; if you're not sanguine about heights, the third row is the charm.

The Living Seas

Frommer's Rating: B
Recommended Ages: 8–adult

This pavilion contains a 5.7 million-gallon saltwater aquarium including coral reefs inhabited by some 4,000 sharks, barracudas, parrotfish, rays, dolphins, and other critters. While waiting in line, visitors pass exhibits tracing the history of undersea exploration,

---

Moments Kids in the Kitchen

During the Epcot Food and Wine Festival in the fall, future cooks can take advantage of a free **Junior Chefs program** at The Land, which lets kids ages 3 to 10 assist real-life chefs in baking Nestle Toll House cookies. Your children will get their own chef's hats and a couple of cookies to take home (though most can't resist eating them right away). It usually runs about every hour or so (check when you get to the pavilion). There's no need to reserve a spot for your child. Just show up for the Junior Chef storefront in the Sunshine Seasons Food Fair on the first floor about 10 minutes before the program is set to begin. Your kids will have a great time, and you'll get lots of opportunities to take pictures.

including a diving barrel used by Alexander the Great in 332 B.C. and Sir Edmund Halley's first diving bell (1697).

A 2½-minute multimedia preshow about today's ocean technology is followed by a 7-minute film demonstrating the formation of the earth and seas as a means to support life.

After the films, you enter "hydrolators" for a hokey "descent" to the simulated ocean floor. Upon arrival, you can journey through rooms and more rooms for close-up views through acrylic windows of the denizens, including manatees and other marine life. Be sure to check out the adorable **Turtle Talk with Crush,** which debuted in late 2004. Crush (from *Finding Nemo*) chitchats with passersby from behind his undersea movie screen, engaging them in conversation and telling a joke or two. This is a first-of-its-kind attraction, using digital projection and voice-activated animation to create a real-time experience. Your kids will get a huge kick out of it; you will, too. Young kids will also have fun in **Bruce's Shark World,** an interactive, toddler-friendly play area.

Note: The **Epcot DiveQuest** program enables certified divers (ages 10–14 must have an adult accompany them) to participate in a 3-hour adventure that includes a 40-minute dive in the Living Seas aquarium. The program costs $140. Call © **407/ 939-8687** for more information. Keep in mind, however, that you get far more for your money at Discovery Cove (p. 280) if you want to swim with the dolphins.

Mission: Space
Frommer's Rating: A+
Recommended Ages: 10–adult

This $100 million attraction seats up to four riders at a time in a simulated flight to the Red Planet. You'll assume the role of commander, pilot, navigator, or engineer, depending on where you sit, and must complete related jobs vital to the mission (don't worry if you miss your cue; you won't crash). The ride uses a combination of visuals, sound, and centrifugal force to create the illusion of a launch and trip to Mars. Even veteran roller-coaster riders who tried the simulator said the sensation mimics a liftoff, as riders are pressed into their seats and the roar and vibration trick the brain during the launch portion of the 4-minute adventure. NASA helped design and tweak this attraction. *Note:* Riders must be at least 44 inches tall. If you're claustrophobic, have a low tolerance for loud noises, or have stuffy sinuses, you should avoid the ride. If spinning causes you to get dizzy or motion-sick, this isn't the ride for you, either, though you can reduce the effects by focusing straight ahead. Speaking from experience, taller guests may have difficulty seeing the screen the way it was meant to be viewed—and shorter guests may have trouble reaching some of the gear.

Austin's and **Nicolas's Rating:** "That was the coolest ride here—even better than Test Track (see below). Can we go again?" Not until I stop spinning!

Spaceship Earth *(Overrated)*
Frommer's Rating: C
Recommended Ages: All ages

This massive, silvery geosphere symbolizes Epcot. That makes it a must-do for many, though it's something of a yawner—another slow-track journey back in time to trace the progress of communications. Long lines can be avoided by saving it until late in the day, when you might be able to just walk in. The 15-minute show/ride takes visitors to the distant past, where an audio-Animatronic Cro-Magnon shaman recounts the story of a hunt while others record it on cave walls. You advance thousands of years to ancient Egypt, where hieroglyphics adorn temple walls and writing is recorded on

> (*Tips* **Visual & Audio Assistance**
>
> Complimentary guided-tour audiocassette tapes and players are available at Guest Relations to assist visually impaired guests, and personal translator units are available to amplify the audio at some Epcot attractions (inquire at Earth Station). For more information on services available to those with disabilities at Disney World, see p. 36.

papyrus scrolls. You'll progress through the Phoenician and Greek alphabets, the Gutenberg printing press, and the Renaissance, trying not to notice that several of these guys look an awful lot like Barbie's dream date, Ken. Technologies develop at a rapid pace, through the telegraph, telephone, radio, movies, and TV. It's but a short step to the age of electronic communications. You're catapulted into outer space to see Spaceship Earth from a new perspective, returning for a finale that places the audience amid interactive global networks.

Ryan's, Nicolas's, and **Austin's Rating:** "*Zzzzzzzzz.*" The scenery is impressive, but overall, it's too tame even for me—*eeeeek!*

Test Track

Frommer's Rating: A+

Recommended Ages: 8–adult

Test Track is a $60 million marvel that combines GM engineering and Disney Imagineering. Most of you will have a blast. The line can be more than an hour long in peak periods, so consider the FASTPASS option (but remember to get one early, before they run out). The last part of the line snakes through displays about corrosion, crash tests, and other things from the GM proving grounds (you can linger long enough to see them even with FASTPASS). The 5-minute ride follows what looks to be an actual highway. It includes braking tests, a hill climb, and tight S-curves in a 6-passenger convertible. The left front seat offers the most thrills as the vehicle moves through the curves. There's also a 12-second burst of speed that reaches 65 mph on the straightaway (no traffic!).

Note: Riders must be at least 40 inches tall. Also, expectant mothers; people prone to motion sickness; and those with heart, neck, or back problems shouldn't test the track.

Note II: This is the only attraction in Epcot that has a single-rider line, which allows singles to fill in vacant spots in select cars. If you're part of a party that doesn't mind splitting up and riding in singles, you can shave off some serious waiting time by taking advantage of this option. FASTPASS offers the same time savings without the break up, but Test Track is often in such demand that the last FASTPASS for the *day* is often gone by 11am, so if you don't catch it early enough, the single-rider line is the only option you'll have.

Note III: Test Track often experiences technical difficulties. and to add insult to injury, it's one of the few rides in Epcot that closes due to inclement weather. If you know a storm's brewing in the afternoon, be sure to head here early in the day.

Nicolas's and **Austin's Rating:** "It's really fast. Let's go again; it's better than when Mom drives!" (Indeed, that last burst provides quite a rush.)

Universe of Energy

Frommer's Rating: B+

Recommended Ages: 6–adult

Sponsored by Exxon, this pavilion has a roof full of solar panels and a goal of better-ing your understanding of America's energy problems and potential solutions. Its headline ride, **Ellen's Energy Adventure,** features comedian Ellen DeGeneres being tutored (by Bill Nye the Science Guy) to be a *Jeopardy!* contestant. On a massive screen in Theater I, an animated motion picture depicts the Earth's molten begin-nings, its cooling process, and the formation of fossil fuels. You move back in time 275 million years into an eerie, storm-wracked landscape of the Mesozoic Era, a time of violent geological activity. Here, giant audio-Animatronic dragonflies, earthquakes, and streams of molten lava threaten you before you enter a steam-filled tunnel deep in the bowels of a volcano. When you emerge, you're in Theater II and the present. In this new setting, which looks like a NASA Mission Control room, a 70mm film pro-jected on a massive 210-foot wraparound screen depicts the challenges of the world's increasing energy demands and the emerging technologies that will help meet them. Your moving seats now return to Theater I, where swirling special effects herald a film about how energy affects our lives. It ends on an upbeat note, with a vision of an energy-abundant future and Ellen as a new *Jeopardy!* champion.

Note: Most kids enjoy the ride, though younger children may find the dinosaur scenes and parts of the movies rather frightening and too intense to be tolerable.

Wonders of Life

Frommer's Rating: B

Recommended Ages: 10–adult

Housed in a vast geodesic dome fronted by a 75-foot replica of a DNA strand, this pavilion offers some of Future World's most engaging shows and attractions for older kids. *Note:* This pavilion operates seasonally, so call ahead to find out if it will be open when you're at the park.

The *Making of Me,* starring Martin Short, is a captivating 15-minute motion pic-ture combining live action with animation and spectacular *in utero* photography to create a sweet introduction to the facts of life. Don't miss it, although the presentation may prompt some questions from young children; therefore, I recommend it for ages 10 and up. Short travels back in time to witness his parents as children, their meeting at a college dance, their wedding, and their decision to have a baby. Along with him, we view his development inside his mother's womb and witness his birth.

During the very popular **Body Wars** ride, you're reduced to the size of a cell for a medical rescue mission inside the immune system of a human body. Your objective: Save a miniaturized immunologist who has been accidentally swept into the blood-stream. This motion-simulator ride takes you on a wild journey through gale-force winds in the lungs and pounding heart chambers. Engineers designed this ride from the last row of a car, so that's where to sit to get the most bang for your buck. Although you know they're part of the Disney show, it's a little eerie passing through derma topic purification stations to undergo miniaturization. It's not as good as the similarly built **Star Tours** at Disney–MGM studios (p. 223), but it definitely has its moments and is popular with teens. This one isn't a smart choice for those prone to motion sick-ness or who generally prefer to be stirred rather than shaken. *Note:* Riders must be at least 40 inches tall. Also, steer clear if you're an expectant mother or have heart, neck, or back problems.

Moments **Water-Fountain Conversations**

Many an ordinary item at Disney World has hidden entertainment value for you and your kids. Take a drink at the water fountain in Innoventions Plaza (the one right next to Mouse Gear), and it may beg you not to drink it dry. No, you haven't gotten too much sun; the fountain actually talks (much to the delight of kids and the surprise of unsuspecting adults). A few more talking fountains are scattered around Epcot. The fountains aren't the only items at WDW that will chat you up. I've kibitzed with a walking-and-talking garbage can (named PUSH) in Magic Kingdom and a personable palm tree (who goes by Wes Palm) at Animal Kingdom. Ask a Disney employee to direct you if you and your kids want to meet one of these conversational contraptions.

Dancing fountains can be found throughout the park as well. Kids love chasing the shooting droplets and spouting streams of water; getting wet is just a bonus. Some of the fountains are lit, making them fun well into the evening hours. In addition to the large fountain display outside Imagination, smaller spots can be found to the left of Innoventions and on the way to Mission: Space, as well as near the bridge leading to the World Showcase.

Little kids also love the sparkling, twinkling lights embedded in the walkway between Innoventions and Mission: Space. And be sure to catch the Innoventions Fountains show, where the waters dance to the beat of recorded music, and are accented by lights and changing colors.

In the hilarious, multimedia **Cranium Command,** Buzzy, an audio-Animatronic brain-pilot-in-training, is charged with the seemingly impossible task of controlling the brain of an average 12-year-old boy. Charles Grodin, Jon Lovitz, Bob Goldthwait, George Wendt, and Kevin Nealon and Dana Carvey (as Hans and Franz) play the boy's body parts. It's another must-see attraction (recommended for ages 8 and up; it's not frightening, but younger kids may have trouble grasping some of the content) and has a loyal following among Disney veterans. The audience is seemingly seated inside Bobby's head as Buzzy guides him through a day of typical preadolescent traumas such as running for the school bus, meeting a girl, fighting bullies, and a run-in with the school principal.

The pavilion also has **Fitness Fairgrounds,** large areas filled with fitness-related shows, exhibits, and participatory activities, including a film called *Goofy About Health.* It's a good place for young children to expend some energy while learning valuable concepts about nutrition and physical fitness.

WORLD SHOWCASE

This community of 11 miniaturized nations surrounds the 40-acre World Showcase Lagoon on the park's southern side. All the showcase's countries have authentically indigenous architecture, landscaping, background music, restaurants, and shops. The nations' cultural facets are explored in art exhibits, song and dance performances, and innovative rides, films, and attractions. And all the employees in each pavilion are natives of the country represented.

All pavilions offer some kind of live entertainment throughout the day. Times and performances change, but they're listed in the guide map. World Showcase opens between 11am and noon daily, so there's time for a Future World excursion if you arrive earlier.

Note: With the exception of those with an appreciation of world geography and cultures, most young kids will find little of interest here other than a few tame rides and some activities as Kidcot Funstop stations (p. 198). There are, however, **regular appearances by characters** at Showcase Plaza (consult the daily schedule for times).

Canada

Frommer's Rating: A
Recommended Ages: 8–adult

Our neighbors to the north are represented by architecture ranging from a mansard-roofed replica of Ottawa's 19th-century French-style Château Laurier (here called Hôtel du Canada) to a British-influenced stone building modeled after a famous landmark near Niagara Falls.

An Indian village complete with a rough-hewn log trading post and 30-foot replicas of Ojibwa totem poles signifies the culture of the Northwest. The Canadian wilderness is reflected by a rocky mountain; a waterfall cascading into a whitewater stream; and a miniforest of evergreens, stately cedars, maples, and birch trees. Don't miss the stunning floral displays of azaleas, roses, zinnias, chrysanthemums, petunias, and patches of wildflowers inspired by the Butchart Gardens in Victoria, British Columbia.

The pavilion's highlight attraction is *O Canada!*—a dazzling 18-minute, 360-degree CircleVision film that shows Canada's scenic splendor, from a dogsled race to the thundering flight of thousands of snow geese departing an autumn stopover near the St. Lawrence River. If you're looking for foot-tapping live entertainment, **Off Kilter** raises the roof with New Age Celtic music as well as some get-down country music. Days and times vary.

Northwest Mercantile carries sandstone and soapstone carvings; fringed leather vests; duck decoys; moccasins; an array of stuffed animals; Native American dolls; Native American spirit stones; rabbit-skin caps; heavy knitted sweaters; and, of course, maple syrup.

China

Frommer's Rating: A
Recommended Ages: 10–adult

Bounded by a serpentine wall that snakes around its perimeter, the China pavilion is entered via a triple-arched ceremonial gate inspired by the Temple of Heaven in Beijing, a summer retreat for Chinese emperors. Passing through the gate, you'll see a half-size replica of this ornately embellished red-and-gold circular temple, built in 1420 during the Ming dynasty. Gardens simulate those in Suzhou, with miniature waterfalls; fragrant lotus ponds; and groves of bamboo, corkscrew willows, and weeping mulberry trees.

Reflections of China 🎭🎭 is a 20-minute movie that explores the culture and landscapes in and around seven Chinese cities. Shot over a 2-month period in 2002, it visits Beijing, Shanghai, and the Great Wall (begun 24 c. ago!), among other places. **Land of Many Faces** is an exhibit that introduces China's ethnic peoples, and entertainment is provided daily by the amazing and child-pleasing **Dragon Legend Acrobats** 🎭🎭.

The **Yong Feng Shangdian Shopping Gallery** features silk robes, lacquer and inlaid mother-of-pearl furniture, jade figures, cloisonné vases, brocade pajamas, silk rugs and embroideries, wind chimes, and Chinese clothing. Artisans occasionally demonstrate calligraphy.

Austin's Rating: "Whoa! It looks like the real deal!" (He's been fortunate enough to have traveled to Beijing and Shanghai.)

France
Frommer's Rating: B
Recommended Ages: 8–adult

This pavilion focuses on La Belle Epoque, a period from 1870 to 1910 in which French art, literature, and architecture flourished. It's entered via a replica of the beautiful cast-iron Pont des Arts footbridge over the Seine. It leads to a park with bleached sycamores, Bradford pear trees, flowering crape myrtle, and sculptured parterre flower gardens inspired by Seurat's painting *A Sunday Afternoon on the Island of La Grande Jatte.* A one-tenth–scale replica of the Eiffel Tower constructed from Gustave Eiffel's original blueprints looms overhead.

The highlight is *Impressions de France,* which is definitely more for the older set than for young kids. Shown in a palatial sit-down theater a la Fontainebleau, this 18-minute film is a scenic journey through diverse French landscapes projected on a vast 200-degree wraparound screen and enhanced by the music of French composers. The antics of **Serveur Amusant,** a comedic waiter, and the visual comedy of **Le Mime Roland** delight both children and adults, as do the yummy pastries at Boulangerie Patisserie.

The covered arcade has shops selling French prints and original art, cookbooks, wines (there's a tasting counter), French food, Babar books, perfumes, and original letters of famous Frenchmen ranging from Jean Cocteau to Napoleon. Another marketplace/tourism center revives the defunct Les Halles, where Parisians used to sip onion soup in the wee hours.

Germany
Frommer's Rating: B
Recommended Ages: 8–adult

Enclosed by castle walls and towers, this festive pavilion is centered on a cobblestone *platz* (square), with pots of colorful flowers girding a fountain statue of St. George and the Dragon. An adjacent clock tower is embellished with whimsical glockenspiel figures that herald each hour with quaint melodies. The pavilion's **Biergarten** (p. 128) was inspired by medieval Rothenberg and features a year-round Oktoberfest and its music. And 16th-century facades replicate a merchant's hall in the Black Forest and the town hall in Römerberg Square.

The shops here carry Hummel figurines; crystal; glassware; cookware; Anton Schneider cuckoos; cowbells; Alpine hats; German wines (there's a tasting counter, if Mom or Dad wants to give one a try); and specialty foods, toys (German Disneyana, teddy bears, dolls, and puppets), and books. An artisan demonstrates molding and painting Hummel figures; another paints detailed scenes on eggs. Background music runs from oompah bands to Mozart symphonies.

Tip: Model-train enthusiasts and kids enjoy the exquisitely detailed miniature version of a small Bavarian town, complete with working train station. Even the littlest members of your party will be fascinated as they watch the trains dart in and out of tunnels and stations.

Italy

Frommer's Rating: B

Recommended Ages: 10–adult

One of the prettiest World Showcase pavilions, Italy lures visitors over an arched stone footbridge to a replica of Venice's intricately ornamented pink-and-white Doge's Palace. Other architectural highlights include the 83-foot Campanile (bell tower) of St. Mark's Square, Venetian bridges, and a piazza enclosing a version of Bernini's Neptune Fountain. A garden wall suggests a backdrop of provincial countryside, and citrus, cypress, pine, and olive trees frame a formal garden. Gondolas are moored on the lagoon.

Shops carry cameo and filigree jewelry, Armani figurines, kitchenware, Italian wines and foods, Murano and other Venetian glass, alabaster figurines, and inlaid wooden music boxes.

In the street-entertainment department, the seemingly lifeless forms of **Imaginum, A Statue Act,** fascinate visitors young and old daily, and the **Character Masquerade,** featuring traditional Carnevale masks and costumes, will generate enthusiasm as well.

Japan

Frommer's Rating: A

Recommended Ages: 8–adult

> ### (Finds) Great Things to Buy at Epcot
>
> Sure, *you* want to be educated about the cultures of the world, but for most of us, the two big attractions at the World Showcase for families are eating and shopping. Dining options are explained in chapter 5, "Family-Friendly Dining." This list gives you an idea of additional items available for purchase.
>
> If you'd like to check out the amazing scope of Disney merchandise at home, everything from furniture to bath toys, you can order a catalog by calling ℭ **800/237-5751** or surfing the Web to **www.disneystore.com**.
>
> - The toys and piñatas draw folks to the Mexico pavilion, and the silver jewelry is beautiful. Choose among a range of merchandise that goes from a simple flowered hair clip to a kidney-shaped stone-and-silver bracelet.
> - There are lots of great sweaters available in the shops of Norway, and it's really tough to resist the Scandinavian trolls. They're ugly, but you have to love them. Your kids will love the LEGO that's for sale.
> - Discover Disney trading pins and Coca-Cola memorabilia in the shops of U.S.A.—The American Adventure.
> - Your funky teenager might like the Taquia knit cap, a colorful fezlike chapeau, that's available in Morocco. There are also a variety of celestial-patterned pottery available in vases and platters, and, for the little princesses, a Jasmine character costume.
> - Toy soldiers, British games, candy, and music tapes are popular in the United Kingdom. Tennis fans may be interested in the Wimbledon shirts, shorts, and skirts. There are also a nice assortment of rose-patterned tea accessories, Shetland sweaters, tartans, pub accessories, and loads of other stuff from the United Kingdom.

A flaming red *torii* (gate of honor) on the banks of the lagoon and the graceful blue-roofed Goju No To pagoda, inspired by a shrine built at Nara in A.D. 700, welcome you to this pavilion, which focuses on Japan's ancient culture. In a traditional Japanese garden, cedars, yews, bamboo, "cloud-pruned" evergreens, willows, and flowering shrubs frame a contemplative setting of pebbled footpaths, rustic bridges, waterfalls, exquisite rock landscaping, and a pond of golden koi. It's a haven of tranquility in a park that's anything but.

The **Yakitori House** is based on the renowned 16th-century Katsura Imperial Villa in Kyoto, designed as a royal summer residence and considered by many to be the crowning achievement of Japanese architecture. Exhibits ranging from 18th-century Bunraki puppets to samurai armor take place in the moated **White Heron Castle,** a replica of the Shirasagi-Jo, a 17th-century fortress overlooking the city of Himeji. There's also a gallery that puts on temporary exhibits (at press time, it featured a very kid-friendly display of **Japanese Tin Toys**).

The drums of **Matsuriza**—one of the best performances in the World Showcase—entertain guests daily (the show is loud, but kids love it). The **Mitsukoshi Department Store** (Japan's answer to Macy's) is housed in a replica of the Shishinden (Hall of Ceremonies) of the Gosho Imperial Palace, built in Kyoto in A.D. 794, and is popular with kids of all ages. It sells lacquerware, kimonos, kites, fans, dolls in traditional costumes (children love them), Pokémon and Hello Kitty items (ditto), origami books, samurai swords, Japanese Disneyana, bonsai trees, Japanese foods, Netsuke carvings, pottery, and modern electronics.

Mexico

Frommer's Rating: A

Recommended Ages: 8–adult

You'll hear the music of marimbas and mariachi bands as you approach Mexico, fronted by a Mayan pyramid modeled on the Aztec temple of Quetzalcoatl (God of Life) and surrounded by dense Yucatán jungle landscaping. Upon entering the pavilion, you'll be in a museum of pre-Columbian art and artifacts.

Down a ramp, a small lagoon is the setting for **El Rio del Tiempo** (River of Time), where visitors board boats for an 8-minute cruise (reasonably entertaining for the young set) through Mexico's past and present. Passengers get a close-up look at the Mayan pyramid. **Mariachi Cobre,** a 12-piece band, plays Tuesday to Saturday.

Shops in and around the **Plaza de Los Amigos** (a "moonlit" Mexican *mercado* with a tiered fountain and street lamps) display an array of leather goods, baskets, sombreros, piñatas, pottery, embroidered dresses and blouses, maracas, jewelry, serapes, colorful papier-mâché birds, and blown-glass objects (an artisan occasionally gives demonstrations). The Mexican Tourist Office also provides travel information.

Morocco

Frommer's Rating: A

Recommended Ages: 10–adult

This exotic pavilion has architecture embellished with geometrically patterned tile work, minarets, hand-painted wood ceilings, and brass lighting fixtures. (The king of Morocco took a personal interest in the project and sent royal artisans to help in its construction, and the result is one of the most authentic atmospheres at the World Showcase.) It's headlined by a replica of the Koutoubia Minaret, the prayer tower of a 12th-century mosque in Marrakech. The Medina (old city), entered via a replica of an arched gateway in Fez, leads to **Fez House** (a traditional Moroccan home) and the

Tips **Stay Tuned**

Disney hasn't added a new "nation" to World Showcase since Norway became the 11th country in 1988. But the latest buzz has Spain possibly becoming the 12th, with a pavilion that would blend the city of Toledo with some architectural highlights of Madrid and Barcelona.

narrow, winding streets of the souk, a bustling marketplace where all manner of authentic handcrafted merchandise is on display. Here, you can browse or purchase pottery, brassware, hand-knotted Berber or colorful Rabat carpets, ornate silver and camel-bone boxes, straw baskets, and prayer rugs. There are weaving demonstrations in the souk periodically during the day. The Medina's rectangular courtyard centers on a replica of the ornately tiled Najjarine Fountain in Fez, the setting for musical entertainment.

Treasures of Morocco is a three-times-per-day, 35-minute guided tour (1–5pm) that highlights this country's culture, architecture, and history (older kids will find it enjoyable and educational, but this is not for the young set). The pavilion's **Gallery of Arts and History** contains an ever-changing exhibit of Moroccan art, and the Center of Tourism offers a continuous three-screen slide show. Morocco's landscaping includes a formal garden, citrus and olive trees, date palms, and banana plants. On the entertainment side, **Mo'Rockin'** plays Arabian rock music on traditional instruments on Tuesday through Saturday.

Norway
Frommer's Rating: B+
Recommended Ages: 10–adult

This pavilion is centered on a picturesque cobblestone courtyard. A *stavekirke* (stave church), styled after the 13th-century Gol Church of Hallingdal, has changing exhibits. A replica of Oslo's 14th-century **Akershus Castle,** next to a cascading woodland waterfall, is the setting for the featured restaurant (p. 128). Other buildings simulate the red-roofed cottages of Bergen and the timber-sided farm buildings of the Nordic woodlands.

Maelstrom, a boat ride in a dragon-headed Viking vessel, traverses Norway's fjords and mythical forests to the music of Peer Gynt. Along the way, you'll see images of polar bears prowling the shore; then trolls cast a spell on the boat. The watercraft crashes through a narrow gorge and spins into the North Sea, where a storm is in progress. (This is a relatively calm ride that's fine for all but the littlest kids, though it's not recommended for expectant mothers or folks with heart, neck, or back problems.) The storm abates, and passengers disembark safely to a 10th-century Viking village to view the 5-minute 70mm film *Norway,* which documents 1,000 years of history. **Spelmanns Gledje** entertains with Norwegian folk music.

Shops sell hand-knit wool hats and sweaters, troll dolls, toys (there's a LEGO table, where kids can play), wood carvings, Scandinavian foods, and jewelry.

United Kingdom
Frommer's Rating: B
Recommended Ages: 8–adult

The U.K. pavilion takes you to Merry Olde England through **Britannia Square,** a London-style park with a copper-roof gazebo bandstand, a stereotypical red phone booth, and a statue of the Bard. Four centuries of architecture are represented along quaint cobblestone streets; there's a traditional British pub; and a formal garden with low box hedges in geometric patterns, flagstone paths, and a stone fountain replicates the landscaping of 16th- and 17th-century palaces. Of special interest for the kids is a small, traditional hedge maze that features topiaries shaped like Disney characters at the back of the pavilion. *Note:* Characters, especially from British stories such as *Winnie the Pooh* and *Alice in Wonderland,* tend to show up here quite often.

The **British Invasion,** a group that impersonates the Beatles daily except Sunday; pub pianist **Pam Brody** (Tues, Thurs, Fri, and Sun); and the comedic acting troupe the **World Showcase Players** (daily), provide entertainment. High Street and Tudor Lane shops display a broad sampling of British merchandise, including toy soldiers; Paddington bears; personalized coats of arms; Scottish clothing (cashmere and Shetland sweaters, golfwear, tams, and tartans); English china; Waterford crystal; and pub items such as tankards, dartboards, and the like. A tea shop occupies a replica of Anne Hathaway's thatched-roof 16th-century cottage in Stratford-on-Avon. Other emporia represent the Georgian, Victorian, Queen Anne, and Tudor periods. Background music ranges from "Greensleeves" to the Beatles.

U.S.A.—The American Adventure
Frommer's Rating: A
Recommended Ages: 8–adult
Housed in a vast Georgian-style structure, **The American Adventure** is a 29-minute dramatization of U.S. history, utilizing a 72-foot rear-projection screen; rousing music; and a large cast of lifelike audio-Animatronic figures, including narrators Mark Twain and Ben Franklin. The adventure begins with the voyage of the *Mayflower* and encompasses major historic events. You'll view Jefferson writing the Declaration of Independence, Matthew Brady photographing a family about to be divided by the Civil War, the stock-market crash of 1929, Pearl Harbor, and the *Eagle* heading toward the moon. Teddy Roosevelt discusses the need for national parks. Susan B. Anthony speaks out on women's rights; Frederick Douglass, on slavery; and Chief Joseph, on the plight of Native Americans. It's one of Disney's best historical productions and offers great entertainment for the entire family. Entertainment includes the **Spirit of America Fife & Drum Corps;** the **Voices of Liberty,** an a cappella group that sings patriotic songs; and **AMERICAN VYBE,** which features the sounds of swing, jazz, and gospel.

Formal gardens shaded by live oaks, sycamores, elms, and holly complement the 18th-century architecture. **Heritage Manor Gifts** sells autographed presidential photographs, needlepoint samplers, quilts, pottery, candles, Davy Crockett hats, American

---

Tips Cruise Control

There are two cruise-style options for watching Epcot's IllumiNations fireworks display (below) from World Showcase Lagoon. You can charter the 1930s vintage speedboat *Breathless* ($180, up to seven people) or catch the show aboard a less romantic but less expensive pontoon boat ($140, up to 10 people). Both rides last 45 to 50 minutes, and you must rent the entire boat for your family or find your own boatmates. For information or to reserve a boat, call © 407/939-7529.

history books, historically costumed dolls, classic political campaign buttons, and vintage newspapers with banner headlines such as "Nixon Resigns!"

A NIGHTTIME SPECTACLE

IllumiNations *Moments*

Frommer's Rating: A+

Recommended Ages: 3–adult

Little has changed since Epcot's millennium version of IllumiNations ended on January 1, 2001. This 13-minute grand nightcap continues to be a blend of fireworks, lasers, and fountains in a display that's signature Disney. The show is worth the crowds that flock to the parking lot when it's over (just be sure to keep a firm grip on young kids). *Tip:* Stake your claim to your favorite viewing area a half hour before show time (listed in your entertainment schedule). The ones near Showcase Plaza have a head start for the exits. Another good place for viewing the show is the terrace at the Rose & Crown Pub in the United Kingdom (p. 213).

   Ryan's Rating: "That was cool—better than the Magic Kingdom's fireworks." Thanks to its added dimensions—lasers and fountains—my kids found it more interesting than the Wishes fireworks display (p. 196).

5 Disney–MGM Studios

You'll probably see the Tower of Terror and the Earrfel Tower, the water tank with mouse ears, before you enter this park, which Disney bills as "the Hollywood that never was and always will be." Once inside, you'll find pulse-quickening rides such as **Rock 'n' Roller Coaster,** movie- and TV-themed shows such as **Jim Henson's Muppet*Vision 3-D,** and a spectacular laser-light show called **Fantasmic!** The main streets include Hollywood and Sunset boulevards, where movie sets remember the golden age of Hollywood. New York Street is lined with miniature renditions of Gotham's landmarks (the Empire State, Flatiron, and Chrysler buildings), and there are mock-ups of San Francisco, Chinatown, and other places. You'll find some of the best street performing in the Disney parks here. More important, it's a working movie and TV studio where shows are occasionally in production.

   Arrive early. Unlike Epcot, MGM's 154 acres of attractions are easier to see in 1 day. The parking lot reaches to the gate, but trams serve most areas. Pay attention to your parking location; this lot isn't as well marked as the Magic Kingdom's. Again, write your lot and row number on something you can find at day's end.

   If you don't get a *Disney–MGM Studios Guide Map* and entertainment schedule as you enter the park, you can pick one up at Guest Relations or most shops. Straight off, check show times, and work out an entertainment schedule based on highlight attractions and geographical proximity. My favorite MGM restaurants are described in chapter 5, "Family-Friendly Dining."

   There's a Tip Board listing the day's shows, ride closings, and other information at the corner of Hollywood and Sunset boulevards.

HOURS   The park is usually open from 9am to at least 6 or 7pm, with extended hours sometimes as late as midnight during holidays and summer.

TICKET PRICES   A 1-day park ticket is $63 for adults and $52 for children 3 to 9. Kids under 3 get in free.

SERVICES & FACILITIES IN DISNEY–MGM STUDIOS

ATMs   ATMs accepting cards from banks using the Cirrus, Honor, and PLUS systems are to the right of the entrance and near Toy Story Pizza Planet.

Baby Care   MGM has a small Baby Care Center to the left of the entrance, where you'll find facilities for nursing and changing. Disposable diapers, formula, baby food, and pacifiers are for sale. Changing tables are also in all women's restrooms and some men's restrooms.

Cameras & Film   Film, Kodak disposable cameras, and limited digital supplies are available throughout the park.

First Aid   The First Aid Center, staffed by registered nurses, is in the Entrance Plaza adjoining Guest Relations and the Baby Care Center.

Lockers   Lockers are located alongside Oscar's Classic Car Souvenirs, to the right of the Entrance Plaza after you pass through the turnstiles. The cost is $5, plus a $2 deposit.

Lost Children   Lost children at Disney–MGM Studios are taken to Guest Relations, where lost-children logbooks are kept. *Children under 7 should wear name tags* inside their clothing.

Package Pickup   Any purchase can be sent to Oscar's Super Service in the Entrance Plaza. Allow 3 hours for delivery.

Parking   It's $9 a day for cars, light trucks, and vans, and $10 for RVs.

Pet Care   Day accommodations for $6 are offered at kennels to the left and just outside the entrance (© **407/824-6568**). There are also four other kennels in the WDW complex. Proof of vaccination is required.

Strollers   Strollers can be rented at Oscar's Super Service, inside the main entrance, for $10 for a single and $18 for a double. Discounts are available for length-of-stay rentals.

Wheelchair Rental   Wheelchairs are rented at Oscar's Super Service, inside the main entrance. The cost for regular chairs is $10 a day. Electric wheelchairs rent for $35, plus a $5 refundable deposit.

MAJOR ATTRACTIONS & SHOWS

American Film Institute Showcase
Frommer's Rating: C
Recommended Ages: 10–adult
This shop and exhibit area is the final stop on the Backlot Tour (see below) and looks at the efforts of the editors, cinematographers, producers, and directors whose names roll by in the blur of credits. It also showcases the work of the American Film Institute's Lifetime Achievement Award winners, including Bette Davis, Jack Nicholson, and Elizabeth Taylor. A special exhibit here, **"Villains: Movie Characters You Love to Hate,"** features the costumes and props of several notable bad guys, including Darth Vader.

Beauty and the Beast—Live on Stage
Frommer's Rating: B+
Recommended Ages: All ages
A 1,500-seat covered amphitheater is the home of this 30-minute, live, Broadway-style production of *Beauty and the Beast* that's adapted from the movie. Musical highlights

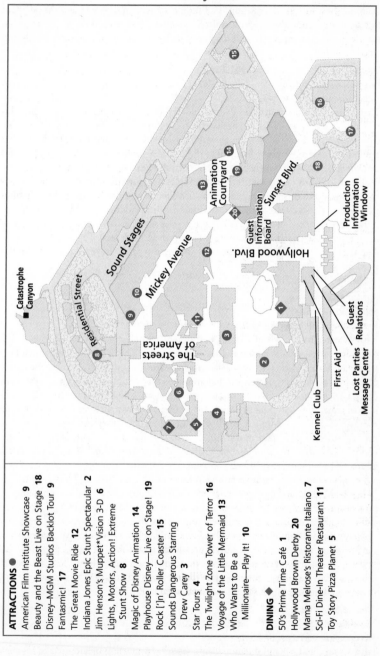

Disney–MGM Studios Theme Park

ATTRACTIONS ●

American Film Institute Showcase **9**
Beauty and the Beast Live on Stage **18**
Disney–MGM Studios Backlot Tour **9**
Fantasmic! **17**
The Great Movie Ride **12**
Indiana Jones Epic Stunt Spectacular **2**
Jim Henson's Muppet*Vision 3-D **6**
Lights, Motors, Action! Extreme Stunt Show **8**
Magic of Disney Animation **14**
Playhouse Disney—Live on Stage! **19**
Rock ['In' Roller Coaster **15**
Sounds Dangerous Starring Drew Carey **3**
Star Tours **4**
The Twilight Zone Tower of Terror **16**
Voyage of the Little Mermaid **13**
Who Wants to Be a Millionaire—Play It! **10**

DINING ◆

50's Prime Time Café **1**
Hollywood Brown Derby **20**
Mama Melrose's Ristorante Italiano **7**
Sci-Fi Dine-In Theater Restaurant **11**
Toy Story Pizza Planet **5**

217

from the show include the rousing "Be Our Guest" opening number and the poignant title song featured in the romantic waltz-scene finale. The sets and costumes are lavish, and the production numbers are pretty spectacular. It's a treat for the whole family and a great place to rest your feet. There are usually four or five shows a day.

Disney–MGM Studios Backlot Tour
Frommer's Rating: B+
Recommended Ages: 6–adult
This 35-minute tram tour takes you behind the scenes for a close-up look at the vehicles, props, costumes, sets, and special effects used in movies and TV shows. On many days, you'll see costume makers at work in the wardrobe department (Disney has around 2 million garments here). But the real fun begins when the tram heads for **Catastrophe Canyon,** where an earthquake in the heart of oil country causes canyon walls to rumble. A raging oil fire, massive explosions, torrents of rain, and flash floods threaten you and other riders before you're taken behind the scenes to see how filmmakers use special effects to make such disasters (little kids may get a little intimidated if they aren't warned in advance). The preshow is almost as interesting. While waiting in line, you can watch entertaining videos hosted by several TV and movie stars. The Backlot Tour is a solid ride that's of the same type as Universal Studios Florida's Earthquake—The Big One (p. 252).
   Hailey's Rating: "How'd they do that? That was cool."

Fantasmic! *(Moments*
Frommer's Rating: A+
Recommended Ages: All ages
Disney mixes heroes, villains, stunt performers, choreography, laser lights, and fireworks into a spectacular end-of-the-day extravaganza. This is a 25-minute visual feast where the Magic Mickey comes to life in a show featuring shooting comets, great balls of fire (our apologies to Jerry Lee), and animated fountains that really charge the audience. The cast includes 50 performers, a giant dragon, a king cobra, and 1 million gallons of water, just about all of which are orchestrated by a sorcerer mouse that looks more than remotely familiar. You'll probably recognize other characters, as well as musical scores from Disney movie classics such as *Fantasia, Pinocchio, Snow White and the Seven Dwarfs, The Little Mermaid,* and *The Lion King.* You'll also shudder at the animated villainy of Jafar, Cruella ee Ville, and Maleficent in the battle of good versus evil, part of which is projected onto huge water-mist screens. The amphitheater holds 9,000 souls, and during holidays and summers, it's often standing room only, so arrive early. (There is sometimes an additional show earlier in the evening.) *Note:* The show's loud pyrotechnics may frighten younger children.
   Nicholas's Rating: He was wide-eyed and smiling but silent. This isn't a good show for anyone with sensitive ears, including adults. If someone in your family has that problem, bring earplugs or cotton balls to deaden the sound effects. Be aware as well that the show can be frightening for younger kids, thanks to the occasional eerie music, lighting, after-dark setting, and scary characters.

The Great Movie Ride
Frommer's Rating: C for most, B+ for adults who love classics
Recommended Ages: 8–adult
Film footage and 50 audio-Animatronic replicas of movie stars are used to re-create some of the most famous scenes in filmdom on this 22-minute ride through movie

Tips Dinner & a Show

At press time, Disney was offering preferred seating at the end-of-the-day spectacular, **Fantasmic!**, along with a fixed-price dinner at one of Disney–MGM's sit-down restaurants. All you need to do is make Advanced Dining Reservation arrangements (© **407/939-3463**) and request the Fantasmic! package for the Hollywood Brown Derby ($37 adults, $10 kids 3–11), Mama Melrose's Ristorante Italiano ($29 adults, $10 kids), or Hollywood & Vine ($22 adults, $10 kids). You'll get your line pass at the restaurant and instructions on getting to the special entrance to the preferred-seating area of the show.

Note: The prices above are for a fixed-price meal and do not include sales tax, tip, or alcoholic beverages; if you order off the menu, you'll pay more. The prices also don't include a reserved seat at Fantasmic!, only a pass that will get you into the preferred-seating area (you must arrive at least 30 min. in advance—a much shorter wait than usual and a boon if you have restless kids).

history. You'll relive magic moments from the 1930s through the present, starring Gene Kelly; Jimmy Cagney; John Wayne; Julie Andrews; Marlon Brando; and arguably the best Tarzan, Johnny Weissmuller, giving his trademark yell while swinging across the jungle. The action is enhanced by special effects, and outlaws hijack your tram en route. So pay attention when the conductor warns, "Fasten your seat belts. It's going to be a bumpy night." The ride appeals mostly to adults and film buffs (younger kids and teens may not recognize some of the classic movies depicted), but it's a great place to rest your feet with tired toddlers while your older kids are off riding the Tower of Terror. The setting is a full-scale reproduction of Hollywood's famous Mann's Chinese Theatre, complete with handprints of the stars out front. *Tip:* Some of the movie scenes, especially the ones from *Alien,* can frighten young kids.

Honey, I Shrunk the Kids Movie Set
Frommer's Rating: B+
Recommended Ages: 3–10
Let the kids catch up to you in the exhaustion category as they ride talking ants, slide through a film canister, get slimed by a giant dog's sinuses, crawl through LEGO-ville, and get chilled by a sneaky hose. It's a fabulous larger-than-life playground that young kids will love.

Indiana Jones Epic Stunt Spectacular
Frommer's Rating: A+
Recommended Ages: 6–adult
Visitors get a peek into the world of movie stunts in this dramatic 30-minute show, which re-creates major scenes from the Indiana Jones series. The show opens on an elaborate Mayan temple backdrop. Indy crashes onto the set via a rope, and as he searches with a torch for the golden idol, he runs into booby traps. Then a boulder straight out of *Raiders of the Lost Ark* chases him! The set is dismantled to reveal a colorful Cairo marketplace where a swordfight ensues, and the action includes virtuoso bullwhip maneuvers, gunfire, and a truck bursting into flames. An explosive finale takes place in a desert scenario. Music and a narrative enhance the action. Throughout the production, guests get to see how elaborate stunts are pulled off. Arrive early

(Finds) Find the Hidden Mickeys

Hidden Mickeys (HM, for short) started as an inside joke among early Disney Imagineers and soon became a park tradition. Today, dozens of subtle Mickey images—usually silhouettes of his world-famous ears, profile, or full figure—are hidden (more or less) in attractions and resorts throughout the Walt Disney empire. No one knows how many, because sometimes, they exist only in the eye of the beholder. See how many Hidden Mickeys you can locate during your visit (keeping track of them is a cool game for kids and will keep them entertained throughout their visit). And be sharp-eyed about it. Those bubbles on your souvenir mug might be forming one. Here are a few to get you started:

In the Magic Kingdom:

- In the Haunted Mansion banquet scene, check out the arrangement of the plate and adjoining saucers on the table.
- In the Africa scene of It's a Small World, note the purple flowers on a vine on the elephant's left side.
- While riding Splash Mountain, look for Mickey lying on his back in the pink clouds to the right of the *Zip-A-Dee Lady* paddle-wheeler.

At Epcot:

- In Imagination, check out the little girl's dress in the lobby film of *Honey, I Shrunk the Audience,* one of five HMs in this pavilion.
- In The Land pavilion, don't miss the small stones in front of the Native American man on a horse and the baseball cap of the man driving a harvester in the *Circle of Life* film.
- As you cruise through the Mexico pavilion on El Rio del Tiempo, notice the arrangement of three clay pots in the marketplace scene.
- In Maelstrom in the Norway pavilion, a Viking wears Mickey ears in the wall mural facing the loading dock.

and sit near the stage if you want a shot at being picked as an audience participant. Alas, it's *a job for adults only.*

Austin's Rating: "The airplane scene is so great with all the explosions!" This show definitely keeps you on the edge of your seat at times.

Jim Henson's Muppet*Vision 3-D

Frommer's Rating: A+

Recommended Ages: All ages

This must-see film stars Kermit and Miss Piggy in a delightful marriage of Jim Henson's puppets and Disney audio-Animatronics, special-effects wizardry, 70mm film, and cutting-edge 3-D technology. The action includes flying Muppets, cream pies, and cannonballs, plus high winds, fiber-optic fireworks, bubble showers, and even an actual spray of water. Kermit is the host; Miss Piggy sings "Dream a Little Dream of Me"; Statler and Waldorf critique the action (which includes numerous mishaps and disasters); and Nicki Napoleon and his Emperor Penguins (a full Muppet orchestra)

- There are four HMs inside Spaceship Earth, one of them in the Renaissance scene, on the page of a book behind the sleeping monk. Try to find the other three.

At Disney–MGM Studios:
- On the Great Movie Ride, there's an HM on the window above the bank in the gangster scene.
- At Jim Henson's Muppet*Vision 3-D, take a good look at the top of the sign listing five reasons for turning in your 3-D glasses, and note the balloons in the film's final scene.
- In the Twilight Zone Tower of Terror, note the bell for the elevator behind Rod Serling in the film. There are at least five other HMs in this attraction.
- Outside Rock 'n' Roller Coaster, look for two in the rotunda's tile floor.
- By the way, the park's least Hidden Mickey is what's called the Earrfel Tower, Disney–MGM Studios' tall water tower, which is fitted with a huge pair of Mouseket-EARS.

In Animal Kingdom:
- Look at the Boneyard in Dinoland U.S.A., where a fan and two hard hats form an HM.
- There are 25 Hidden Mickeys at Rafiki's Planet Watch, where Mickey lurks in the murals, tree trunks, and paintings of animals.

In the Resort Areas:
- HMs are on the weather vane atop the Grand Floridian Resort & Spa's convention center and in the interactive fountains at the entrance to Downtown Disney Marketplace, and one forms a giant sand trap next to the green at the Magnolia Golf Course's 6th hole.

You can learn more at **www.hiddenmickeys.org**.

provide music from the pit. In the preshow area, guests view an entertaining video on overhead monitors. Note the Muppet fountain out front and the Muppet version of a Rousseau painting inside. The 25-minute show (including the 12-min. video preshow) runs continuously. *Tip:* Sweetums, the giant but friendly Muppet monster, usually interacts with a few kids sitting in the front rows during the show.

Hailey's Rating: "I thought I could reach out and touch stuff." That's how realistic the in-your-face, 3-D action is!

Lights, Motors, Action! Extreme Stunt Show

Frommer's Rating: A

Recommended Ages: 6–adult

MGM's newest addition debuted in mid-2005—and it's a biggie. Taking its cue from the original show at Disneyland Paris, this stunt show features high-flying, high-speed movie stunts full of pyrotechnic effects and more. Like the **Indiana Jones Epic Stunt Spectacular** (p. 219), the storyline has the audience following the filming of an

In the Words of Walt Disney

A family picture is one the kids can take their parents to see and not be embarrassed.

action-packed movie (in this case, a spy thriller set in a Mediterranean village). Over 40 vehicles are used in the show, including cars, motorcycles, and watercraft—each modified to perform the rather spectacular stunts. It's entertaining and certainly offers its share of thrills, but it's not as engaging as the Indiana Jones production unless you're a family of car buffs. The show is part of the redevelopment of the MGM back-lot area that's also seen the addition of new cityscapes of San Francisco and Chicago, among others. Check the entertainment schedule for show times.

Magic of Disney Animation

Frommer's Rating: B

Recommended Ages: 8–adult

Once hosted by Walter Cronkite and Robin Williams, the new version of **Magic of Disney Animation** features Mushu the dragon from Disney's *Mulan* as he co-hosts a theater presentation in which some of Disney's animation secrets are revealed. The Q & A session that follows allows guests to ask questions about the animation process before attempting their own Disney character drawings under the supervision of a working animator. Joining in on the fun for a meet-and-greet opportunity are the stars of *The Incredibles,* including Elastigirl, Frozone, and Mr. Incredible.

Playhouse Disney—Live on Stage!

Frommer's Rating: B

Recommended Ages: 2–5

Younger audiences love this 20-minute show, in which they meet characters from Bear in the Big Blue House, The Book of Pooh, and other stories. The show encourages preschoolers to dance, sing, and play along with the cast. If your kids are the right age, don't miss it. The action happens several times a day. Check your show schedule.

Rock 'n' Roller Coaster *(Moments*

Frommer's Rating: A+

Recommended Ages: 10–adult

Some say this is one of Disney's attempts to go head to head with Universal Orlando's Islands of Adventure. True or not, this inverted roller coaster is one of the best thrill rides at WDW. Kids looking for an adrenaline rush will demand to ride it. It's a fast-and-furious indoor ride in semidarkness. You sit in a 24-passenger "stretch limo" out-fitted with 120 speakers that blare Aerosmith at 32,000 watts! Flashing lights deliver a variety of messages and warnings, including "Prepare to merge as you've never merged before." Then, faster than you can scream "I want to live!" (2.8 sec., actually), you shoot from 0 to 60 mph and into the first gut-tightening inversion at 5Gs. It's a real launch (sometimes of lunch), followed by a wild ride through a make-believe California freeway system. One of three inversions cuts through an O in the Hollywood sign. The ride lasts 3 minutes, 12 seconds—the running time of Aerosmith's hit "Sweet Emotion." *Note:* Riders must be at least 48 inches tall, and expectant moms; people prone to motion sickness; and those with heart, neck, or back problems shouldn't try this ride.

Nicolas's Rating: "Wow!" That was the last thing he said as he headed back to the end of the line.

Sounds Dangerous Starring Drew Carey

Frommer's Rating: C+

Recommended Ages: All ages

Drew Carey provides laughs while dual audio technology provides some hair-raising effects during this 12-minute show at ABC Sound Studios. You'll feel like you're right in the middle of the action of a TV pilot featuring undercover police work and plenty of mishaps. Even when the picture disappears, and the theater is plunged into darkness, you continue on Detective Charlie Foster's chase via headphones that show off "3-D" sound effects. Most of this attraction takes place in total darkness, which will likely disturb young kids.

Tip: After the show is over, check out **Sound Works,** which offers interactive activities that allows you and your kids to experiment with different sound effects.

Star Tours

Frommer's Rating: B+

Recommended Ages: 8–adult

Cutting-edge when it opened, this galactic journey, based on the original *Star Wars* trilogy (George Lucas collaborated on the ride), is now a couple of rungs below the latest technology but is still fun. The preshow, which should eventually be updated with characters from *Episode III: Revenge of the Sith,* now has R2-D2 and C-3PO running an intergalactic travel agency (it offers some of the best detailing of any preshow at Disney World). Once inside, you board a 40-seat spacecraft for a journey that greets you with sudden drops, crashes, and oncoming laser blasts as it careens out of control. This is another of those virtual-simulator rides where you go nowhere but feel like you do. If you or your kids have sensitive stomachs, try to ride up front, where you won't get tossed around as much. *Note:* Riders must be at least 40 inches tall. Also, expectant mothers; people with neck, back, and heart problems; and those prone to motion sickness shouldn't ride.

The Twilight Zone Tower of Terror *(Moments*

Frommer's Rating: A+

Recommended Ages: 10–adult

This is a truly stomach-lifting (and dropping) ride, and Disney continues to fine-tune it to make it even better: A January 2003 upgrade added random drop sequences with individual features, meaning that you might get a different fright from ride to ride. The legend says that during a violent storm on Halloween night 1939, lightning struck the Hollywood Tower Hotel, causing an entire wing and an elevator full of people to disappear. And you're about to meet them as you become the star in a special episode of . . . *The Twilight Zone.* En route to this formerly grand hotel, guests walk past overgrown landscaping and faded signs that once pointed the way to stables and

---

Tips **Tune Time**

Weekdays from noon to 4pm, you can watch B. B. Good broadcast his Radio Disney show live from a studio next to Sounds Dangerous Starring Drew Carey. You can tune into the show and others on Radio Disney at 990 on your AM dial.

> ⌒ *Tips* **Call Ahead**
>
> Disney–MGM is home to some of Disney World's most unique restaurants (see chapter 5, "Family-Friendly Dining," for more details). If you plan to dine in any of them, be sure to make Advanced Dining Reservations (preferably before you arrive, but if not, the minute you arrive at your hotel or in the park). Waiting until lunch or dinnertime will almost ensure that you'll miss out, especially at the Sci-Fi Dinner Theater and The Prime Time Cafe.

tennis courts; the vines over the entrance trellis are dead; and the hotel is a crumbling ruin (it's some of Disney's best theme work). Eerie corridors lead to a dimly lit library, where you can hear a storm raging outside. After various spooky adventures, the ride ends in a dramatic climax: a 13-story free fall in stages. Some believe this rivals Rock 'n' Roller Coaster in the thrill department (one of the Imagineers who helped design the tower admitted that he's too scared to ride his own creation). At 199 feet, it's the tallest ride in the World, and it's a grade above Doctor Doom's Fearfall at Islands of Adventure. *Note:* You must be at least 40 inches tall to ride. Expectant moms; people prone to motion sickness; and those with heart, neck, or back problems shouldn't try to tackle it. If you're scared of heights or darkness, this one isn't for you either. **And one final amusing tidbit:** If you decide to back out before taking the plunge, there is an escape route from the hotel—via an elevator.

Voyage of the Little Mermaid
Frommer's Rating: B+
Recommended Ages: 4–adult
Hazy lighting creates an underwater effect in a reef-walled theater and helps set the mood for this charming musical based on the Disney feature film, which charms even older kids and adults. The show combines live performers with more than 100 puppets, movie clips, and innovative special effects. Sebastian sings the movie's Academy Award–winning song, "Under the Sea"; the ethereal Ariel shares her dream of becoming human in a live performance of "Part of Your World"; and the evil Ursula, 12 feet tall and 10 feet wide, belts out "Poor Unfortunate Soul." It has a happy ending, as most of the young audience knows it will; they've seen the movie. This 17-minute show is a great place to rest your feet on a hot day, and you get misted inside the theater to further cool you off.

Who Wants to Be a Millionaire?—Play It!
Frommer's Rating: B+
Recommended Ages: 8–adult
Contestants can't win $1 million, but they can win points used to buy prizes ranging from collectible pins to a leather jacket or a 3-night cruise on one of Disney's cruise ships. Based on Disney–owned ABC TV's game show, the theme-park version features lifelines (such as asking the audience or calling a stranger on two phones set up in the park). Contestants get a shot at up to 15 multiple-choice questions in the climb to the top. Games run continuously in the 600-seat studio. Audience members play along on keypads. And unlike on the TV show, the entire audience competes to get in the hot seat; the fastest to answer qualifying questions become contestants.

PARADES, PLAYGROUNDS & MORE

Disney Stars and Motor Cars is a motorcade filled with a procession of Disney characters in their chariots. The parade is popular enough that if you decide to skip it, you'll find shorter lines at the park's primo rides (check the parade schedule in your park map).

6 Animal Kingdom

Disney's fourth major park opened in 1998 and combines exotic animals, the elaborate landscapes of Asia and Africa, and the prehistoric lands of the dinosaur. Animals, architecture, and lush surroundings take center stage here, with a handful of rides thrown in for good measure.

Although it's 500 acres, the park can easily be toured in a single day, usually less. A conservation venue as much as an attraction, you won't find animals displayed throughout the park as in other venues such as **Busch Gardens** (p. 327). Animal habitats at Animal Kingdom are re-created in a natural manner, which unfortunately means that at times, you'll have to search a bit to find them. Most of the animals can be found around the Kilimanjaro Safari and the Pangani Forest Expedition Trail. The animal theme does, however, carry throughout the park in its rides, shows, and architecture. Plus one of the best shows in all of Disney—the **Festival of the Lion King**—is here, so be sure to put it on your to-do list.

Animal Kingdom is divided into the **Oasis,** a shopping area near the entrance that has limited animal viewing; **Discovery Island,** home of the Tree of Life, which is the park's icon; **Camp Minnie-Mickey,** which is mainly a character meet-and-greet area; **Africa,** the main animal-viewing area, which is dedicated to the wildlife in Africa today; **Asia,** which has a river raft ride, animal exhibits (including Bengal tigers and giant fruit bats), and a bird show; and **Dinoland U.S.A.,** which has rides, games, and the Boneyard play area.

Tip: At press time, Asia was being readied for the Animal Kingdom's long-awaited thrill ride "**Expedition Everest.**" Debuting mid-2006, this high-speed, coasterlike train ride moves forward and backward through glaciers, waterfalls, and canyons of the Himalayas before climaxing with an encounter with a yeti.

The park covers more than 500 acres, and your feet (and most definitely your kids') will tell you that you've covered the territory at the end of the day. Most of the rides are accessible to guests with disabilities, but the hilly terrain, large crowds, narrow passages, and long hikes can make for a strenuous day if there's a wheelchair-bound person in your party or you're schlepping lots of baby stuff. Anyone with neck or back

---

Moments You Want Characters?

Characters and hot spots change, but as of this writing, the best bets at Disney–MGM Studios are (see the handout *Times Guide* for exact schedules and lineups):

Toy Story Friends At Al's Toy Barn.

Mickey & Friends Mickey Avenue between Backlot Tour and Who Wants to Be a Millionaire?—Play It!

Monsters, Inc. On Commissary Lane.

Power Rangers On the Streets of America.

problems, as well as pregnant women, may not be able to enjoy rides like **Kali River Rapids** and **Dinosaur.**

The 145-foot-tall **Tree of Life** is in the center of the park. It's an intricately carved free-form representation of animals, handcrafted by a team of artists over the period of a year. It's not nearly as tall or imposing as Spaceship Earth at Epcot or Cinderella Castle in the Magic Kingdom. The tree is impressive, though, with 8,000 limbs; 103,000 leaves; and 325 mammals, reptiles, bugs, birds, dinosaurs, and Mickeys carved in its trunk, limbs, and roots. (One cool game to play with your young kids is to see how many animals they can find represented in the trunk.) For more on the tree, see "Discovery Island Trails," below.

ARRIVING From the parking lot, walk or (where available) ride one of the trams to the entrance. If you do walk, watch out for the trams and autos, because the lot isn't designed for pedestrians. Also, make certain to note where you parked (section and row). Lot signs aren't as prominent as in the Magic Kingdom, and the rows look alike when you come back out; I've gotten a bit confused on more than one occasion. Upon entering the park, consult the handout guide map for special events or entertainment. If you have questions, ask park staffers.

HOURS Animal Kingdom is open at least from 8 or 9am to 5pm, but it sometimes stays open an hour or so later.

TICKET PRICES The ticket prices are $63 for adults and $52 for children 3 to 9. See "Tickets & Passes," earlier in this chapter, for information on multiday options.

SERVICES & FACILITIES IN ANIMAL KINGDOM

ATMs Animal Kingdom has an ATM near Garden Gate Gifts to the right of the entrance. It accepts cards from banks using the Cirrus, Honor, and PLUS systems.

Baby Care The Baby Care Center is located near Creature Comforts gift shop on the west side of the Tree of Life, but as in the other Disney parks, you'll find changing tables in both restrooms, and you can buy disposable diapers at Guest Relations.

Cameras & Film You can drop film off for same-day developing at the Kodak Kiosk in Africa and Garden Gate Gifts near the park entrances. Cameras and film are available in Disney Outfitters in Safari Village; at the Kodak Kiosk in Africa, near the entrance to the Kilimanjaro Safari; and in Garden Gate Gifts.

First Aid The First Aid Center, which is staffed by registered nurses, is located near the Creature Comforts gift shop on the west side of the Tree of Life.

Lockers Lockers ($5, plus a $2 deposit) are located in Garden Gate Gifts to your right as you enter the park. They're also located to the left, near the Rainforest Cafe.

Lost Children A center for lost children is near Creature Comforts at the Baby Care Center on the west side of the Tree of Life. At the risk of rehashing, *make your younger kids wear name tags* inside their clothing.

Package Pickup Packages can be sent to the front of the park at Garden Gate Gifts. Allow 3 hours for delivery.

Parking The cost is $9 a day for cars, light trucks, and vans, and $10 for RVs.

Pet Care Pet facilities are located outside the park entrance ($6 per day; © 407/ 824-6568). There are four other kennels located in the WDW complex. Proof of vaccination is required.

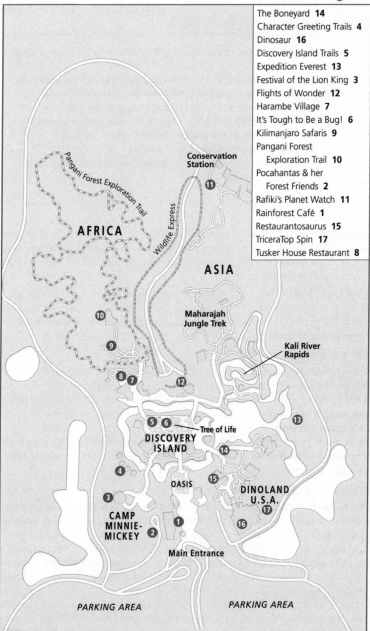

Animal Kingdom

The Boneyard **14**
Character Greeting Trails **4**
Dinosaur **16**
Discovery Island Trails **5**
Expedition Everest **13**
Festival of the Lion King **3**
Flights of Wonder **12**
Harambe Village **7**
It's Tough to Be a Bug! **6**
Kilimanjaro Safaris **9**
Pangani Forest
  Exploration Trail **10**
Pocahantas & her
  Forest Friends **2**
Rafiki's Planet Watch **11**
Rainforest Café **1**
Restaurantosaurus **15**
TriceraTop Spin **17**
Tusker House Restaurant **8**

Pangani Forest Exploration Trail

Conservation Station

11

Wildlife Express

AFRICA

ASIA

Maharajah
Jungle Trek

Kali River
Rapids

10

9

8 7

12

13

5 6 — Tree of Life

DISCOVERY
ISLAND

14

4

15

OASIS

DINOLAND
U.S.A.

3

17

CAMP
MINNIE-
MICKEY

2

16

1

Main Entrance

PARKING AREA

PARKING AREA

Tips Animal Kingdom Tip Sheet

1. Arrive at the park's opening, or stay until near closing for the best view of the animals.
2. **Kilimanjaro Safaris** is one of the most popular rides and the best place to see a lot of animals in one sitting. But in summer, the animals can be scarce except near park opening and closing times. If you can hoof it there first thing, do it. If not, try late in the day. The same applies to viewing the gorillas on the **Pangani Forest Exploration Trail.**
3. The **Festival of the Lion King** show is a must.
4. Looking for Disney characters? Go to the Character Greeting Trails in **Camp Minnie-Mickey.**

Strollers   Stroller rentals are available at Garden Gate Gifts to the right as you enter the park ($10 for a single, $18 for a double; discounts available for length-of-stay rentals). There are also satellite locations deeper into the park; ask a Disney employee to steer you in the right direction.

Wheelchair Rental   You can rent wheelchairs at Garden Gate Gifts, to the right as you enter the park. Rentals are $10 for a standard wheelchair and $35 for an electric wheelchair, plus a $5 refundable deposit. Ask Disney employees for other rental locations scattered throughout the park.

THE OASIS

This painstakingly designed landscape of streams, grottoes, and miniwaterfalls sets the tone for the rest of the park. This is a good place to see wallabies, tiny deer, giant anteaters, sloths, iguanas, tree kangaroos, otters, and macaws (*if,* I remind you *ad nauseum,* you get here early or stay late). But thick cover provides a jungle tone and sometimes makes seeing the animals difficult. There are no rides in this area, and aside from the animals, it's mainly a pass-through zone. Those guests traveling with eager children will probably have more time to enjoy these exhibits on the way out—if everyone isn't too pooped.

DISCOVERY ISLAND

Like Cinderella Castle in the Magic Kingdom and Spaceship Earth in Epcot, the 14-story **Tree of Life** located here has been designed to be the park's central landmark. The manmade tree and its carved animals are the work of Disney artists. Teams of them worked for a full year creating the various sculptures, and it's worth a stroll on the walks around its roots, but most folks are smart to save it for the end of the day. (Much of it can be seen while you're in line for **It's Tough to Be a Bug!** or on **the Discovery Island Trails.**) The intricate design makes it seem as though a different animal appears from every angle. One of the creators says he expects it to become one of the most-photographed works of art in the world. (He's probably a Disney shareholder.) There's a wading pond directly in front of the tree that often features flamingos.

Discovery Island Trails
Frommer's Rating: B
Recommended Ages: All ages

The old, pre-FASTPASS queue for It's Tough to Be a Bug! provides a leisurely path through the root system of the Tree of Life and a chance to see real, not-so-rare critters, such as axis deer, red kangaroos, otters, flamingos, lemurs, Galapagos tortoises, ducks, storks, and cockatoos. Again, the best viewing times are early or late in the day.

It's Tough to Be a Bug!

Frommer's Rating: A, C for young ones scared silly from sensory effects
Recommended Ages: 5–adult

This show's cuteness quotient is enough to earn it a B+. But it goes a rung higher thanks to the preshow: To get to the theater, you have to wind around the Tree of Life's 50-foot base, giving you a front-row look at this manmade marvel. After you've passed that, grab your 3-D glasses, and settle into a sometimes-creepy-crawly seat. Based on the film *A Bug's Life,* the special effects in this multimedia show are pretty impressive. It's *not a good one for very young kids* (it's dark and loud, and I've seen 4-year-olds reduced to hysteria by the effects) or bug haters of any age, but for others, it's a fun, sometimes poignant look at life from a smaller perspective. Flick, Hopper, and the rest of the cast—ants, beetles, and spiders—literally deliver some in-your-face action. And the show's finale always leaves the crowd buzzing.

DINOLAND U.S.A.

Enter by passing under Olden Gate Bridge, a 40-foot brachiosaurus reassembled from excavated fossils. Speaking of which, until late summer 1999, this land had three paleontologists working on the very real skeleton of Sue, a monstrously big *Tyrannosaurus rex* unearthed 9 years earlier in the Black Hills of South Dakota. They patched and assembled the bones here because Disney helped pay for the work. Alas, Sue's permanent home is at Chicago's Field Museum, but Dinoland U.S.A. has a replica cast from her 67 million-year-old bones. It's marked as **Dino-Sue** on park guide maps.

The Boneyard

Frommer's Rating: B
Recommended Ages: All ages

Kids love the chance to slip, slither, slide, and slink through this giant playground and dig site, where they can discover the real-looking remains of triceratops, T rex, and other vanished giants. They can even play music on a "xylobone." Contained within a latticework of metal bars and netting, this area is popular but not as inviting as the *Honey, I Shrunk the Kids* play area in Disney–MGM Studios (p. 219).

DINOSAUR

Frommer's Rating: B
Recommended Ages: 8–adult

Tips Dehydration Alert!

Animal Kingdom can get very hot, especially during summer. Bring bottled water (unless you want to pay 2½ times the free-world price), and get refills at fountains inside the park. Remember to bring sunscreen and wide-brimmed hats *for the whole family,* and plan to ride Kali River Rapids during the hottest part of the day (bring a change of clothes as well, because you will get soaked).

Fun Fact It Costs to Recycle

The animals here deposit more than 1,600 tons of dung a year. Disney pays a company to haul it away and then buys some of it back as compost for landscaping.

This ride hurls you through the darkness in CTX Rover "time machines" back to the time when dinosaurs ruled the Earth. The expedition takes you past an array of snarling and particularly ferocious-looking dinosaurs, one of which decides you would make a great munchie. What started out as a journey back through time becomes a race to escape the jaws of an irritated and rather ugly Carnotaurus. Young children may find the large lizards and the darkness a bit frightening, and the ride a bit jarring. But until Expedition Everest opens in 2006, this motion simulator/track ride combo is as close as Animal Kingdom gets to a thrill ride. *Note:* You must be 40 inches or taller to climb aboard. Also, expectant mothers; people with neck, back, and heart problems; and those prone to motion sickness shouldn't ride.

Ryan's Rating: "That was pretty cool. I liked all the bumps, but we look goofy in that photo." If you have the presence of mind to smile when you hear the T rex roar, your souvenir photo (it's snapped on the sly) will look a lot better. The cost of one: Ouch! ($17 for an 8×10).

Primeval Whirl

Frommer's Rating: B+

Recommended Ages: 8–adult

Disney introduced this spinning, freestyle twin roller coaster in 2002 in an effort to broaden the park's appeal to young kids (odd, as this ride has a pretty tall height minimum). You control the action through its wacky maze of curves, peaks, and dippity-do-dahs, encountering faux asteroids and hokey cutouts of dinosaurs. This is a cross between those old carnival coasters of the '50s and '60s, and a more daring version of the Barnstormer at Goofy's Wiseacre Farm (p. 191). *Note:* The ride carries a 48-inch height minimum. Expectant moms, as well as those with neck, back, or heart problems and folks prone to motion sickness, should stay planted on firm ground.

TriceraTop Spin

Frommer's Rating: B+ for tykes and parents

Recommended Ages: 2–7

Cut from the same cloth as the Magic Carpets of Aladdin (p. 182), this is another minithrill for youngsters (and another ride with long lines). In this case, cars that look like cartoon dinosaurs are attached to arms that circle a hub while moving up and down and all around. This ride, Primeval Whirl, and an arcade-game area make up a Dinoland U.S.A. miniland called Chester & Hester's Dino-Rama. It's a great spot to take little ones.

CAMP MINNIE-MICKEY

Disney characters are the main attraction in this land, designed in the same vein as an Adirondack resort. Aside from those characters, however, this zone for the younger set *isn't as kid-friendly as* rivals Mickey's Toontown Fair in the Magic Kingdom (reviewed earlier in this chapter) or Woody Woodpecker's KidZone in Universal Studios Florida (see "Universal Studios Florida," in chapter 7).

Character Greeting Trails *(Moments*
Frommer's Rating: A for younger kids, D for waiting parents
Recommended Ages: 2–8

Some say this is a must-do for people traveling with children; I say run the other way—quickly. If, however, your kids are hooked on getting every character autograph possible, this is the place to go. A variety of Disney characters, from Winnie the Pooh and Pocahontas to Timon and Baloo, have separate trails where you can meet and mingle, snap photos, and get those autographs. Mickey, Minnie, Goofy, and Pluto even make periodic appearances. Be aware, however, that the lines for these meet-and-greet opportunities are at times excruciatingly long, so unless your kids are really gung-ho on collecting the characters' signatures, don't even think of coming here.

Festival of the Lion King *(Finds*
Frommer's Rating: A+
Recommended Ages: All ages

Almost everyone in the audience comes alive when the music starts in this rousing 28-minute show in the Lion King Theater. It's one of the top three theme-park shows in Central Florida, and it thrills young and old alike. The production celebrates nature's diversity with a talented, colorfully attired cast of singers, dancers, and life-size critters leading the way to an inspiring singalong that gets the entire audience caught up in the fun. Based loosely on the animated film, this stage show blends the pageantry of a parade with a tribal celebration. The action takes place both on stage and around the audience. Even though the pavilion has 1,000 seats, it's best to arrive at least 20 minutes early.

Pocahontas and Her Forest Friends
Frommer's Rating: C
Recommended Ages: All ages

The wait can be nightmarish, and the 15-minute show isn't close to the caliber of Festival of the Lion King. In this one, Pocahontas, Grandmother Willow, and some forest creatures (a raccoon, turkey, porcupine, snake, and some rats) hammer home the importance of treating nature with respect. If you must, go early. The theater has only 350 seats, but it allows standing-room crowds.

AFRICA

Enter through the town of Harambe, a run-down representation of an African coastal village poised on the edge of the 21st century. Costumed employees will greet you as you enter the buildings. The whitewashed structures, built of coral stone and thatched with reed by African craftspeople, surround a central marketplace rich with local wares and colors.

Kilimanjaro Safaris
Frommer's Rating: A+ early or late, B+ other times

Tips Pin Mania

Pin buying, collecting, and trading can reach frenzied proportions among Disney fans, including many cast members. All the theme parks have special locations set aside for the fun, which are marked on the handout guide maps. You can learn more about the madness (and the rules of pin-trading etiquette) on the Internet at **www.dizpins.com** and **www.officialdisneypintrading.com**.

Fun Fact Did You Know?

Tobacco products aren't the only things unavailable in the theme parks. You can't buy chewing or bubble gum, either. It seems that too many guests stuck it under tables, benches, and chairs—or tossed it on sidewalks, where it often hitched a ride on the soles of the unsuspecting.

Recommended Ages: All ages

Animal Kingdom doesn't have many rides, but the animals you'll see on this one make it a winner as long as your timing is right; they're scarce at midday during most times of year (cooler months the exception), so I recommend that you ride as close to park opening or closing as possible. If you don't make it in time for one of the first or last journeys, the lines can be horrific, so a FASTPASS may be in order.

A large, rugged truck takes you through the African landscape (though just a few years ago, it was a cow pasture). The animals usually seen along the way include giraffe, black rhinos, hippos, antelopes, Nile crocodiles, zebras, wildebeests, cheetahs, and a pair of lions that may offer half-hearted roars toward some gazelles that are safely out of reach. Early on, a shifting bridge gives riders a brief thrill; later, there's a bit of drama (a la Disney) as you help catch some poachers. While everyone has a good view, photographers may get a few more shots when sitting on the left side of their row.

Hailey's Rating: "Where'd they all go?" An afternoon safari ride on a summer day has its disadvantages, but my kids are far from early risers.

Pangani Forest Exploration Trail (Finds

Frommer's Rating: B+, A if you're lucky enough to see the gorillas

Recommended Ages: All ages

The hippos put on quite a display (and draw a riotous crowd reaction) when they do what comes naturally and use their tails to scatter it over everything above and below the surface. There are other animals here, including ever-active mole rats, but the **lowland gorillas** are the main event. The trail has two gorilla-viewing areas: One sports a family, including a 500-pound silverback, his ladies, and his children; the other has bachelors. Guests who are unaware of the treasures that lie herein often skip or rush through it, missing a chance to see some magnificent creatures. That said, they're not always cooperative, especially in hot weather, when they spend most of the day in shady areas out of view. There's also a new **Endangered Animal Rehabilitation Center** with Colobus and Mona monkeys. Most children are usually delighted if they catch a glimpse of the playful meerkats, which young kids will recognize as the models for Timon in *The Lion King. Note:* The walk and frequent dearth of animal sightings can make this the wrong choice for families with restless little ones.

Rafiki's Planet Watch (Overrated

Frommer's Rating: C

Recommended Ages: All ages

Board an open-sided train (the Wildlife Express) near Pangani Forest Exploration Trail for a trip to the back edge of the park, which has three attractions. **Conservation Station** offers a behind-the-scenes look at how Disney cares for animals (and the entrance mural is loaded with Hidden Mickeys). You'll pass nurseries and veterinarian stations. But these facilities need to be staffed to be interesting, and that's not always the case.

Habitat Habit! is a trail with small animals such as cotton-top tamarins. The **Affection Section's** petting zoo has rare goats and potbellied pigs.

ASIA

Disney's Imagineers have outdone themselves in creating the kingdom of **Anandapur.** The intricately painted artwork at the front is appealing, and it also seems to make the lines move a tad faster.

Flights of Wonder
Frommer's Rating: B
Recommended Ages: All ages

This live-animal action show has undergone several transformations since the park opened. It's a low-key break from the madness and has a few laughs, including Groucho the African yellow-nape, which entertains the audience with op-*parrot*-ic a cappella solos, and the just-above-your-head soaring of a Harris hawk and a Eurasian eagle owl. Young kids will especially enjoy it.

Kali River Rapids
Frommer's Rating: B+
Recommended Ages: 6–adult

Its churning water mimics real rapids, and optical illusions have you wondering whether you're about to go over the falls. The ride begins with a peaceful tour of lush foliage, but soon you're dipping and dripping as your tiny craft is tossed and turned. You *will* get wet. (Bring a plastic garbage bag for your valuables or store them in a locker before riding. The rafts' center storage areas alone likely won't keep them dry.) The lines can be long, but keep your head up and enjoy the marvelous art overhead and on beautiful murals. *Note:* There's a 38-inch height minimum. Expectant moms; people with neck, back, and heart problems; and those prone to motion sickness shouldn't ride it.

Ryan's and **Nicolas's Rating:** "Wow, the water is *c-c-c-cold!* But the ride is a blast." The experience was made better, postride, when he and his brothers manned the water cannons near the exit and fired at other raft riders (yet another reason you'll emerge soaked after this one).

Maharajah Jungle Trek
Frommer's Rating: B
Recommended Ages: 6–adults

Tips Moving Mountains

If there's a knock against Animal Kingdom, it's that it doesn't pack a lot of punch in the adrenaline department due to its lack of thrill rides. But naysayers will be quieted in mid-2006 by the debut of **Expedition Everest,** Animal Kingdom's first true thrill ride. You'll begin on a seemingly casual trek to the snowcapped peak of Mount Everest, passing through an Asian mountain range and dense bamboo forests, and moving past glacier fields and pounding waterfalls. But your journey will quickly get off track and become a high-speed train ride that sends you careening along rough and rugged terrain, moving backward and forward, along icy mountain ledges and through darkened caves—only to end up confronting the Abominable Snowman. My adrenaline is running already.

Disney keeps its promise to provide up-close views of animals with this exhibit. If you don't show up in the midday heat, you may see Bengal tigers through a wall of thick glass, while nothing but air separates you from dozens of giant fruit bats hanging in what appears to be a courtyard. Some have wingspans of 6 feet. (If you or your kids have a phobia, you can bypass this, though the bats are harmless.) There are lots of spots for your kids to get good views of the animals. Guides are on hand to answer questions, and you can also check a brochure that lists the animals you may spot; it's available on your right as you enter. You'll be asked to recycle it as you exit.

PARADES

Mickey's Jammin' Jungle Parade at Animal Kingdom is an interactive street party featuring whimsical, colorful animals and characters on expedition. The music and overall atmosphere are lively, and the one-of-a-kind visuals are some of the best in all the parks.

7 Disney Water Parks

Walt Disney World has two renowned water parks in which guests can cool off: **Typhoon Lagoon** and **Blizzard Beach.** The parks have attracted more than 50 million people since they opened, and both offer a slate of cool rides and good swimming areas, including great spots to take young kids. *Note:* All the attractions mentioned in this section can be found on the "Walt Disney World Parks & Attractions" map on p. 165.

TYPHOON LAGOON

Ahoy swimmers, floaters, run-aground boaters!

A furious storm once roared 'cross the sea

Catching ships in its path, helpless to flee . . .

Instead of a certain and watery doom

The winds swept them here to TYPHOON LAGOON.

Such is the Disney legend relating to **Typhoon Lagoon** ✸✸✸, which you'll see posted on consecutive signs as you enter the park. Located off Buena Vista Drive between the Downtown Disney Marketplace and Disney–MGM Studios, this is the ultimate in water-theme parks. Its fantasy setting is a palm-fringed island village of ramshackle, tin-roofed structures, strewn with cargo, surfboards, and other marine wreckage left by the "great typhoon." A storm-stranded fishing boat (the *Miss Tilly*) dangles precariously atop 95-foot Mount Mayday, the steep setting for several attractions. Every half hour, the boat's smokestack erupts, shooting a 50-foot geyser of water into the air.

ESSENTIALS

HOURS   The park is open from at least 10am to 5pm, with extended hours during some holiday periods and summer (© **407/560-4141;** www.disneyworld.com).

⌐Tips Closed for the Winter

Both Disney water parks are refurbished on a rotating basis for a month or more each winter. So if a water park is on your itinerary, ask in advance about closings.

ENTRANCE FEES   A 1-day ticket (before 6.5% tax) to Typhoon Lagoon is $34 for adults and $28 for kids 3 to 9.

HELPFUL HINTS   In summer, arrive no later than 9am to avoid long lines. The park is often filled to capacity by 10am and then is closed to later arrivals. Beach towels ($2) and lockers ($5 and $8) can be rented, and beachwear can be purchased at **Singapore Sal's.** Light fare is available at two eateries: **Leaning Palms** and **Typhoon Tillie's.** A beach bar called **Let's Go Slurpin'** sells beer and soft drinks. There are picnic tables (consider bringing picnic fare; you can keep it in your locker until lunch). Guests aren't permitted to bring their own flotation devices, and glass bottles are prohibited.

ATTRACTIONS IN THE PARK
Castaway Creek
Hop onto a raft or an inner tube, and meander along this 2,100-foot lazy river that circles most of the park. It tumbles through a misty rainforest, by caves and secluded grottoes, and on into the sunshine, all the while passing along some of Disney's meticulously maintained tropical foliage. Tubes are included in the admission price.

Crush 'n' Gusher
The newest thrill to splash onto the scene is a first-of-its-kind water coaster, featuring three separate experiences to choose among. The **Banana Blaster, Coconut Crusher,** and **Pineapple Plunger** each offer steep drops, twists, and turns of varying degrees as you're sent careening through an old, rusted-out fruit factory. Intense jets of water actually propel riders back uphill at one point.

Ketchakiddie Creek
Many of the park's other attractions require guests to be older children, teens, or adults, but this section is a *kiddie area exclusively for 2- to 5-year-olds.* An innovative water playground, it has bubbling fountains to frolic in, mini–water slides, a pint-size "whitewater" tubing run, spouting whales and squirting seals, rubbery crocodiles to climb on, grottoes to explore, and waterfalls to loll under. It's also small enough for you to take good home videos or photographs.

Shark Reef
Guests are given free equipment (and instruction) for a 15-minute swim through this very small snorkeling area, which includes a simulated coral reef populated by about 4,000 parrotfish; angelfish; yellowtail damselfish; and other cuties, including small rays and sharks. If you don't want to get in, you can observe the fish via portholes in a walk-through viewing area.

Typhoon Lagoon Surf Pool *(Moments*
This large (2.75-million gal.) and lovely lagoon is the size of two football fields and is surrounded by a white sandy beach. It's the park's main swimming area. The chlorinated water has a turquoise hue much like the Caribbean. **Large waves** (about 6 ft.) roll through the deeper areas every 90 seconds. A foghorn sounds to warn you when one is coming. Young children can wade in the lagoon's more peaceful tidal pools—**Blustery Bay** or **Whitecap Cove**—but don't let little ones near the main pool without direct supervision, as a wave can easily knock a child over. The lagoon also is home to a **special weekly surfing program** (p. 292).

   Ryan's Rating: "I'm not getting out!" (Well, he did, but not without a fuss. If your kids love the water, you may have the same problem.)

> (*Tips*) **Water Park Dos & Don'ts**
>
> 1. Go in the afternoons, about 2pm, even in summer, if you can stand the heat that long and want to avoid crowds. The early birds usually are gone by then.
> 2. Go early in the week, when most of the weeklong guests are filling the lines at the theme parks.
> 3. Kids can get lost just as easily at a water park as at the other parks, and the consequences can be tragic. All Disney parks have lifeguards, usually wearing bright red suits, but to be safe, make yourself the first line of safety for the kids in your crew (children 10 and under must be accompanied by an adult to get into the parks).
> 4. Women should wear a securely attached one-piece bathing suit unless they want to put on a show for the rest of the crowd. And all bathers should remember **the "wedgie" rule** on the more extreme rides, such as Summit Plummet (at Blizzard Beach, below). *What's the wedgie rule?* It's a principle of physics that says you may start out wearing baggies and end up in a thong.
> 5. Use waterproof sunscreen with an SPF of at least 30, and drink plenty of fluids. Despite all that water, it's easy to get dehydrated in summer.

Water Slides

Humunga Kowabunga consists of three 214-foot Mount Mayday slides that propel you down the mountain on a serpentine route through waterfalls and bat caves and past nautical wreckage before depositing you in a bubbling catch pool; each offers slightly different views and 30-mph thrills. There's seating for non-Kowabunga folks whose braver kids have commissioned them to "Watch me." *Note:* You must be 48 inches or taller to ride this. **Storm Slides** offer a tamer course through the park's man-made caves.

Whitewater Rides

Mount Mayday is the setting for three whitewater rafting adventures: **Keelhaul Falls, Mayday Falls,** and **Gangplank Falls**, all offering steep drops coursing through caves and passing lush scenery. Keelhaul Falls has the most winding route, Mayday Falls has the steepest drops and fastest water, and the slightly tamer Gangplank Falls uses large tubes so that the whole family can pile on.

BLIZZARD BEACH

Blizzard Beach 🎭🎭🎭, arguably the most popular water park in North America, is the younger of Disney's water parks, a 66-acre "ski resort" in the midst of a tropical lagoon centering on the 90-foot, uh-oh, Mount Gushmore. There's a legend for this one as well. Apparently, a freak snowstorm dumped tons of snow on Walt Disney World, leading to the creation of Florida's first—and, so far, only—mountain ski resort (complete with Ice Gator, the park's mascot). Naturally, when temperatures returned to their normal broiling range, the snow bunnies prepared to close up shop, when they realized—this is Disney; happy endings are a must—that what remained of their snow resort could be turned into a water park featuring the fastest and tallest waterlogged "ski" runs in the country. The base of Mount Gushmore has a sand beach with several other attractions, including a wave pool and a smaller version of the mount for younger children. The park is located off World Drive, just north of the All-Star Movie, Music, and Sports resorts.

ESSENTIALS

HOURS It's open from at least 10am to 5pm, with extended hours during holiday periods and summer (© **407/560-3400;** www.disneyworld.com).

ENTRANCE FEES A 1-day ticket to Blizzard Beach is $34 (before the 6.5% tax) for adults and $28 for children 3 to 9.

HELPFUL HINTS Arrive at or before opening to avoid long lines and to be sure you get in. Beach towels ($2) and lockers ($5 and $8) are available, and you can buy the beachwear you forgot to bring at the **Beach Haus.** You can grab something to eat at **Avalunch** and **Lottawatta Lodge** (burgers, hot dogs, nachos, pizza, and sandwiches).

MAJOR ATTRACTIONS IN THE PARK

Cross Country Creek

Inner-tubers can float lazily along this park-circling, 2,900-foot creek, but beware of the mysterious cave, where you'll get splashed with melting ice. It's a good ride for the entire family.

Melt-Away Bay

Waterfalls of melting "snow" feed this 1-acre bobbing wave pool, which features relatively calm waves.

Runoff Rapids

Another tube job, this one lets you careen down any of three twisting-turning runs, one of which sends you through darkness.

Ski-Patrol Training Camp

Designed for preteens, it features a rope swing, a T-bar drop over water, slides like the wet and slippery **Mogul Mania** from the Mount, and a challenging ice-floe walk along slippery floating icebergs. It's a good spot for kids not up to the more adrenaline-pumping slides in the park.

Slush Gusher

This super-speedy slide travels along a snow-banked gully. *Note:* It has a 48-inch height minimum.

Snow Stormers

These three flumes descend from the top of Mount Gushmore and follow a switch-back course through ski-type slalom gates.

Summit Plummet *(Moments*

Read *every* speed, motion, vertical-dip, wedgie, and hold-onto-your-breastplate warning in this guide. Then test your bravado in a bullring, a space shuttle, or dozens of other death-defying hobbies as a warmup. This puppy starts pretty slow, with a lift ride to the 120-foot summit. Then . . . well . . . kiss any kids or religious medal you may be carrying, because if you board, you *will enter* Disney World's fastest body slide, a test of your courage and swimsuit that virtually goes straight down and has you moving *sans* vehicle at 60 mph by the catch pool (aka stop zone). *Note:* It has a 48-inch height minimum. Also, expectant mothers and people with neck, back, and heart problems shouldn't ride.

Ryan's Rating: "Uh. No way!" (I don't blame him. Even the hardiest rider may find this one hard to handle; a veteran thrill-seeker I know described the experience as "15 seconds of paralyzing fear.")

Teamboat Springs

One of Disney World's longest whitewater raft rides, your six-passenger raft twists down a 1,200-foot series of rushing waterfalls.

Tike's Peak

This kid-size version of Mount Gushmore offers short water slides, rideable animals, a snow castle, a squirting ice pond, and a fountain play area for young guests. If you have kids under 48 inches in height, this is the place to take them.

Toboggan Racers

Here's an eight-lane slide that sends you racing head first over exhilarating dips into a snowy slope.

8 Other WDW Attractions

Note: All the attractions mentioned in this section can be found on the "Walt Disney World Parks & Attractions" map on p. 165.

FANTASIA GARDENS & WINTER SUMMERLAND

Fantasia Gardens Miniature Golf ⭐⭐, located off Buena Vista Drive across from Disney–MGM Studios, offers two 18-hole miniature courses drawing inspiration from the Walt Disney classic cartoon of the same name. You'll find hippos, ostriches, and alligators on the **Fantasia Gardens** course, where the Sorcerer's Apprentice presides over the final hole. It's a good bet for beginners and kids. Seasoned minigolfers probably will prefer **Fantasia Fairways,** which is a scaled-down golf course complete with sand traps, water hazards, tricky putting greens, and holes ranging from 40 to 75 feet.

Santa Claus and his elves provide the theme for **Winter Summerland** ⭐⭐ (Disney reports that Santa built it as a vacation resort for his off-duty elves), which has two 18-hole miniature golf courses across from Blizzard Beach on Buena Vista Drive. The **Winter** course takes you from an ice castle to a snowman to the North Pole (it's reportedly the easier of the two courses and the best one for young kids and beginners). The **Summer** course is pure Florida, from sandcastles to surfboards to a visit with Santa on the "Winternet."

Tickets at both venues are $10 for adults and $8 for children 3 to 9. Both are open from 10am to 10 or 11pm daily. For information about Fantasia Gardens, call ⓒ **407/ 560-4582.** For information about Winter Summerland, call ⓒ **407/560-3000.** You can find both on the Internet at **www.disneyworld.com**.

DISNEY'S WIDE WORLD OF SPORTS

The 200-acre Disney's Wide World of Sports complex has a 7,500-seat professional baseball stadium, 10 other baseball and softball fields, six basketball courts, 12 lighted tennis courts, a track-and-field complex, a golf driving range, and six sand volleyball courts. It's a haven for sports fans and wannabe athletes.

Note: The **Hess Sports Field North** opened in the spring of 2005, the first expansion of the Wide World of Sports venue since its opening in 1997. The addition features 20 acres of playing fields, with space for four football/soccer fields and four baseball–softball diamonds.

Finds DisneyQuest

The reaction that visitors have upon experiencing this popular attraction is often the same. No matter whether it's kids just reaching the video-game age, teens who are firmly hooked, or adults who never outgrew _Pong_, they leave saying, "Awesome!"

This five-level virtual-video arcade has everything from nearly old-fashioned pinball to virtual games and rides. Want appetizers?

Aladdin's Magic Carpet Ride puts you astride a motorcycle-type seat and flies through the 3-D Cave of Wonders. **Invasion! An ExtraTERRORestrial Alien Encounter** has the same kind of intensity. Your mission is to save colonists from intergalactic bad guys. One player flies the virtual module, while others fire weapons.

Pirates of the Caribbean: Battle for Buccaneer Gold puts you and three mates in 3-D helmets so that you can battle pirate ships virtual-reality style. One plays captain, steering your ship, while the others assume positions behind cannons to blast the blackhearts into oblivion. Each time you do, you're rewarded with some doubloons, but beware of the sea monsters that can gobble you and your treasure. In the final moments, you come face to face with a ghost ship, which can send you to Davy Jones's Locker.

Songmaker has short lines, perhaps for a reason: It involves karaoke. Step into a phone booth–size recording studio to make your own CD, and buy it for $10.

Try the **Mighty Ducks Pinball Slam** if you're a pinball fan. It's an interactive, life-size game in which you ride platforms and use body English to score points.

If you have an inventive mind, stop in at **CyberSpace Mountain** ✭✭, where Bill Nye the Science-Turned-Roller-Coaster-Guy helps you create the ultimate loop-and-dipster, which you can then ride in a simulator. It's a major hit with the coaster-crazy crowd.

Finally, if you need some quiet time, sign up at **Animation Academy** for a minicourse in Disney cartooning. There are also snack and food areas for those who need something more tangible than virtual refreshment.

DisneyQuest (_©_ **407/828-4600**; www.disneyquest.com) is located in Downtown Disney West Side, on Buena Vista Drive. The admission ($34 for adults and $28 for kids 3–9; prices don't include 6% sales tax) allows you unlimited play from 11:30am to 11pm (until midnight Fri–Sat). Unfortunately, heavy crowds tend to gather here after 1pm, which can cut into your fun and patience.

The complex is located on Victory Way, just north of U.S. 192 (west of I-4; _©_ **407/ 939-1500**; www.disneyworldsports.com). It's open daily from 10am to 5pm; the cost is $10 adults and $7.50 kids 3 to 9. Organized programs and events include:

- The **Multi-Sports Experience,** which challenges guests with a variety of activities, covering many sports: football, baseball, basketball, hockey, soccer, and volleyball. It's open on select days.

- The **Atlanta Braves** play 16 spring-training games during a 1-month season that begins in early March. Tickets cost $13 to $21. For tickets, call Ticketmaster (© **407/939-4263**). In addition to the Braves, the facility hosts the **Tampa Bay Buccaneers'** spring training camp.
- The **NFL, NBA, NCAA, PGA,** and **Harlem Globetrotters** also host events, sometimes annually and sometimes more frequently, at the complex. Admission varies by event.

Disney's Wide World of Sports is located on Victory Way, just north of U.S. 192 (west of I-4; © **407/939-1500;** www.disneyworld.com).

What Kids Like to See & Do Beyond Disney

Younger members of your party may not draw battle lines in so many words, but older kids may boldly declare they like one ride, show, or theme park better than another.

Veteran vacationers call it the Great Theme-Park War—the ongoing, "anything-you-can-do-we-can-do-better," knock-down-drag-out battle between the Magic Mickey and top-ranked challenger Universal Orlando, which each year since 1999 has chipped away at what was once Walt Disney World's virtual monopoly. Still, make no mistake: Disney is king, leading in theme parks (4–2) and smaller attractions (9–1). It has a 2-to-1 edge in nightclub venues and a huge lead in restaurants, and, when it comes to hotel rooms, its lead is insurmountable.

Nevertheless, Universal is making a stand. It had a substantial growth spurt in 1999, bolstering its original theme park, **Universal Studios Florida (USF),** with a second one, **Islands of Adventure,** that's the top park in town for teens and offers the city's largest collection of thrill rides. Universal also added a nightclub and restaurant complex, **CityWalk,** and three luxury resorts: **Portofino Bay,** the **Hard Rock Hotel,** and the **Royal Pacific Resort.**

USF opened two new kid-friendly rides in 2003—**Jimmy Neutron's Nicktoon Blast** and **Shrek 4-D**—and it replaced Kongfrontation (much to my disappointment) in 2004 with **Revenge**

of the Mummy, an indoor roller coaster with more than just thrills in store. There's also the **Fear Factor Live** stunt show—featuring reality TV a la Universal Studios—which began running in 2005. Furthermore, Universal Orlando has more than 2,000 adjoining acres on which to expand, and while the company's lips are sealed, speculations are that plans include at least two more hotels, a golf course, and possibly 300 acres of additional rides and attractions in upcoming years.

A few miles south, **SeaWorld** and its sister park, **Discovery Cove,** also grab a share of the Orlando action (especially with the kid set). With what seems like an explosive expansion, SeaWorld has added new shows (in 2003, *Odyssea* arrived; *Mystify* joined up in 2004; and the all-new *Blue Horizons* debuted in 2005); as well as the **Waterfront,** a 5-acre shopping, dining, and entertainment area. And SeaWorld plans to open a brand-new water park right across the street in 2007.

Aside from greater variety, these players mean more multiday packages and special deals for you. To compete with Disney, SeaWorld and Universal Orlando teamed up on multiday pass options a few years back. They offer a **FlexTicket** that also includes admission to **Wet 'n Wild** (a Universal-owned water park) and **Busch Gardens** in Tampa. (Unfortunately for you, Universal, SeaWorld, and Busch Gardens also rival Disney with single-day tickets that, without tax, cost $63 for adults and $52 for children 3–9.)

While the wars rage on in the traditional tourist areas, it has finally dawned on the rest of Orlando that Central Florida is one of the world's favorite vacation destinations.

Since the early 1990s, downtown Orlando has gotten a makeover that woos hundreds of thousands to its attractions, nightclubs, and restaurants. Recent expansions at the **Orlando Museum of Art** and the **Orlando Science Center** show that the city is trying to grab its share of the tourist pie. This expansion means visitors can enjoy the spoils: more variety, greater opportunities, and a world beyond the theme parks.

THE FLEXTICKET The most economical way to see the various "other-than-Disney" parks is with these passes, which counter Disney's Magic Your Way Park Hopper tickets. With the **FlexTicket,** you pay one price to visit any of the participating parks as many times as you want during a 14-day period. At press time, a four-park pass to Universal Studios Florida, Islands of Adventure, Wet 'n Wild, and SeaWorld was $190 for adults and $156 for children 3 to 9. A five-park pass, which adds Busch Gardens in Tampa, was $235 for adults and $200 for kids. The **FlexTicket** can be ordered through **Universal** (© **800/711-0080** or 407/363-8000; www.universalorlando.com),

SeaWorld (© **800/327-2424** or 407/351-3600; www.seaworld.com), or **Wet 'n Wild** (© **800/992-9453** or 407/351-9453; www.wetnwild.com).

Note: There's a round-trip shuttle available to Busch Gardens (p. 327) that's free for FlexTicket buyers (it's $10 for other guests; © **800/221-1339**).

UNIVERSAL EXPRESS This is Universal's answer to Disney's FASTPASS. UNIVERSAL EXPRESS has two tiers. Guests of the Portofino Bay, Hard Rock, and Royal Pacific hotels (see chapter 4, "Family-Friendly Accommodations") need only to show their room keys to get at or near the front of the line for most rides. Single-day and multiday ticket buyers who don't stay at a Universal resort can obtain one express pass at a time. Waits are usually 15 minutes or less. Guests can return for more when their reservations are used or expire (and, like at Disney, can get a second ticket 2 hr. after the first is issued). Guests can also purchase the **Universal Express Plus Pass,** which allows them to use the express lines at rides all day long. Pass prices vary, depending on the time of year, and have ranged from $15 to $39 per pass in the past. While the system is available throughout the day, passes (even the Plus passes) are not unlimited and can run out during busier times. Call © **407/363-8000** or go to **www.universalorlando. com** for more information.

1 Universal Studios Florida

Even with fast-paced grownup rides based on blockbusters such as *The Mummy, Twister, Terminator, Men in Black,* and *Back to the Future,* Universal Studios Florida is a ton of fun for kids. As a plus, it's a working motion-picture and TV production studio, so occasionally, you may catch some live filming being done. Even if there isn't a film or show in production, you can see reel history displayed in the form of some 40 actual sets exhibited along Hollywood Boulevard and Rodeo Drive. And there are plenty of action shows and rides, including **Revenge of the Mummy, Twister . . . Ride It Out, Earthquake—The Big One, Back to the Future . . . The Ride, Jaws, Terminator 2: 3-D Battle Across Time,** and **Fear Factor Live!**

After a period of quiet on the expansion front, 2003 saw Universal add two new attractions—**Jimmy Neutron's Nicktoon Blast,** and **Shrek 4-D**—and 2004 saw the

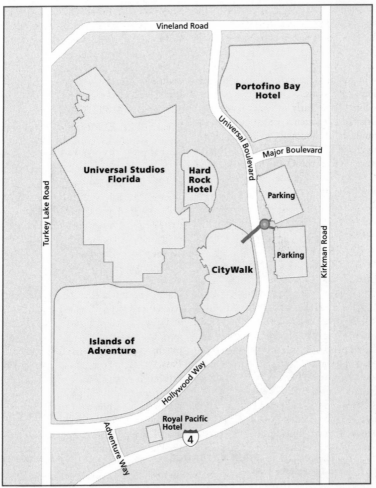

debut of **Revenge of the Mummy,** a ride based on the hit film *The Mummy.* Universal also replaced some stale shows and characters with fresh ones (see "Universal Has New Characters & Shows," on p. 249). As a result, the park is better than it's ever been as a place to bring the kids.

ESSENTIALS

GETTING TO UNIVERSAL BY CAR   Universal Orlando is a half mile north of I-4 Exit 75B, Kirkman Road/Highway 435. There may be construction in the area, so follow the signs directing you to the parks.

PARKING   If you park in the multilevel garages, remember the theme and row in your area to help you find your car later. Or do it the old-fashioned way: Write it down.

Universal Studios Florida

NEW YORK

5th Ave.

7th Ave.

PRODUCTION CENTRAL

Amblin Ave.

8th Ave.

57th St.

Park Ave.

Delancey St.

42nd St.

Canal St.

South St.

South St.

BATTERY PARK

Hollywood Blvd.

HOLLYWOOD

Nickelodeon Way

THE FRONT LOT

Plaza of the Stars

Rodeo Drive

CELEBRITY CIRCLE

MAIN ENTRANCE

BUS/TAXI PICKUP

← Exit to Turkey Lake Road

CityWalk See CityWalk Map in Chapter 10

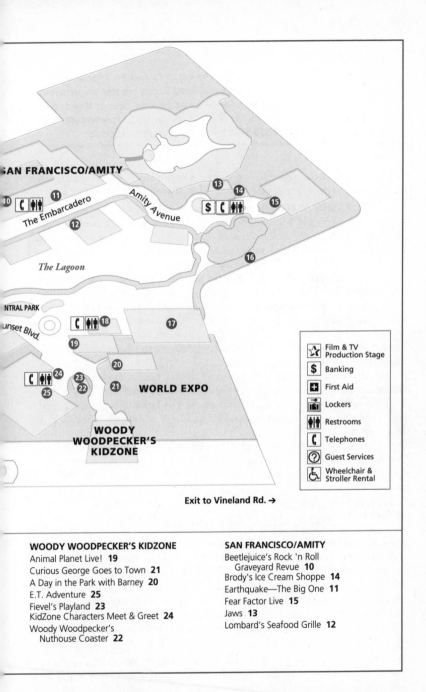

SAN FRANCISCO/AMITY

The Embarcadero

Amity Avenue

The Lagoon

NTRAL PARK

unset Blvd.

WORLD EXPO

WOODY WOODPECKER'S KIDZONE

☆	Film & TV Production Stage
$	Banking
➕	First Aid
🔒	Lockers
🚻	Restrooms
☎	Telephones
?	Guest Services
♿	Wheelchair & Stroller Rental

Exit to Vineland Rd. →

⟨*Tips* ⟩ Shorter Days

Like Disney, Universal juggles park hours to adjust for varying attendance due to seasonal shifts and holidays. The hours listed in this chapter are generally accurate, but sometimes, the parks close earlier, or some rides or shows open later. To avoid disappointment, check the park's website at **www.universal orlando.com** or call ⓒ **407/363-8000** for up-to-the-minute schedules.

Parking costs $9 for cars, light trucks, and vans. Valet parking is $16. Universal's garages are connected to its parks and have moving sidewalks, but it's still a long walk.

TICKETS, PASSES & TOURS   At press time, a **1-day ticket** costs $63 (plus 6% sales tax) for adults and $52 for children 3 to 9. A **2-day, 2-park pass** is $108 for adults and children, and includes one of three options: **1.** You get one free child's ticket with the purchase of an adult ticket, as well as 2 free days in the parks (for a total of 4 consecutive days); **2.** You can double the number of days on your tickets (for a total of 4 consecutive days); or **3.** You can get a no-expiration option that lets you visit the parks on nonconsecutive days (or lets you save your second day for another visit to the city). Universal also sells a **2-park Annual Power Pass** that's good for an entire year except for about 30 or so blackout dates, mainly during summer and around the December holidays. It costs $120, regardless of age. **The Preferred Annual Pass** has no blackout dates, includes free parking and discounts on dining and merchandise, and costs $180 per person.

All multiday passes let you move between Universal Studios Florida and Islands of Adventure. *Multiday passes also give you free access to the CityWalk clubs at night.* See the beginning of this chapter for information on the **FlexTicket,** which provides multiple-day admission to Universal Studios Florida, Islands of Adventure, SeaWorld, and Wet 'n Wild.

Because both Universal parks are within walking distance of each other, you won't lose much time jockeying back and forth, which is not the case at Disney. Nevertheless, it's a long walk for tykes and people with limited mobility, so consider a stroller or wheelchair.

There are also 5-hour **VIP tours** at either Universal Studios Florida or Islands of Adventure, which include a guided tour and line-cutting privileges at a number of high-profile attractions, for $100 per person. A 6-hour, two-park VIP tour covers both parks and costs $125 per person. Tours also include morning coffee, bottled water, a soda, discounts on dining and merchandise, a music CD, and free valet parking. Prices for both tours do not include 6.5% tax and *do not cover admission to the parks!* For more information on the VIP tour, call ⓒ **407/363-8295** or send an e-mail to **viptours@universalorlando.com**. Tours start at 10am and noon daily. If you plan on visiting during peak season, money isn't an issue, and you aren't staying at one of the Universal resorts, this is a good way to experience the best of the park without having to spend most of your day in lines.

HOURS   The park is open 365 days a year, usually at least from 9am to 6pm, though it's open later in summer and around holidays. The best bet is to call before you go so that you're not caught by surprise.

MAKING YOUR VISIT MORE ENJOYABLE
PLANNING YOUR VISIT

You can get information before you leave home by calling **Universal Orlando Guest Services** at ℂ **800/711-0080,** 407/224-4233, or 407/363-8000. Ask about travel packages as well as theme-park information. You can also write to Guest Services, 1000 Universal Studios Plaza, Orlando, FL 32819-7601.

ONLINE   Find information about Universal Orlando at **www.universalorlando.com**. Orlando's daily newspaper, the *Orlando Sentinel,* also produces Orlando Sentinel Online at **www.orlandosentinel.com**. Additionally, there's a lot of information about the parks, hotels, restaurants, and more at the Orlando/Orange County Convention and Visitors Bureau site: **www.orlandoinfo.com**.

INFORMATION FOR VISITORS WITH SPECIAL NEEDS

Guests with disabilities should go to **Guest Services,** located just inside the main entrance, for a *Rider's Guide for Rider Safety & Guests with Disabilities,* a Telecommunications Device for the Deaf (TDD), or other special assistance. You can rent a standard wheelchair for $8 or an electric one for $40 (both require a credit card imprint, a driver's license, or $50 as a deposit). You can reserve them 24 hours or more in advance by calling ℂ **407/224-6350.** You can arrange for sign-language interpreting services at no charge by calling ℂ **888/519-4899** (toll-free TDD), 407/224-4414 (local TDD), or 407/224-5929 (voice). Make arrangements for an appointment with an interpreter 1 to 2 weeks in advance. Information is also available at **www.universal orlando.com**.

Tip: The *Rider's Guide* is also a great tool for parents, as it describes in great detail the various rides' special effects, warnings, height requirements, and general guest services information at both Universal parks.

PETS   You can board your small animals at the shelter located inside the parking garages for $10 a day (no overnight stays), but you must provide food and return to walk them periodically. Ask the attendant when you pay for parking to direct you to the kennel. Note that all Universal resorts allow small pets to stay with you in your room.

HOW WE'VE MADE THIS CHAPTER USEFUL TO PARENTS

As in chapter 6, "What Kids Like to See & Do in Walt Disney World," before every listing in the major parks, you'll note the **Recommended Ages** entry that tells which ages will most appreciate that ride or show. This guideline is helpful in planning your daily itinerary. In our ride ratings, I've indicated whether a ride will be more enjoyable for kids than for adults. Fewer of Universal Orlando's rides and shows appeal to very young kids than at some of the Disney parks, and one bad experience can spook your small fry for a long time. You'll also find any **height and health restrictions** noted in the ride and show listings that follow.

For the Universal and SeaWorld parks, I'm also going to rely on my kids—**Ryan** (age 12), **Austin** (age 10), **Nicolas** (age 8), **Hailey** (age 6), and **Davis** (age 4)—for ratings. My five kids have happily shared their opinions, good and bad, after tackling the parks with me on more than just a few occasions. On select rides, I'll give you their views and reviews.

BEST TIME OF YEAR TO VISIT

As at Walt Disney World, there's really no off season for Universal, but the week after Labor Day until mid-December (excluding Thanksgiving week) and January to mid-May (excluding spring break) are known for smaller crowds, cooler weather, and less-humid air. The summer months, when the masses throng to the parks, are the worst time for crowds and hot, sticky, humid days. During cooler months, you also won't have to worry about daily thunderstorms.

If you're planning a trip from mid-February to mid-April, keep in mind that a raucous Mardi Gras celebration goes on in the evenings (schedules have varied over the years, including only weekends at first and then daily celebrations during the last 2 weeks, so check with Universal for the most up-to-date schedule). It's a very grownup event, with lots of alcohol flowing and a separate ticket price. It's definitely not suitable for younger children. The park is still open for all during the day but generally closes earlier than usual. (The same is true in Oct at Universal's Islands of Adventure, which hosts the very grownup, not to mention frightening, Halloween Horror Nights.)

Some of the park's best rides are action-based thrill rides, which means your options are limited if you're pregnant; are prone to motion sickness; or have heart, neck, or back problems. The same applies to smaller children. Review the rides and restrictions on the following pages or when you enter the park so that you don't stand in line for something you're unable to experience. (There are stationary areas available at some moving rides. Check your park guide for information, as well as the boards in front of each ride; then ask the attendants for help as you enter.) A child-swap program (allowing parents to switch off on rides without having to stand in line twice) is available at the rides as well.

THE BEST DAYS TO VISIT

Go near the end of the week, on a Thursday or Friday. The pace is somewhat fast Monday through Wednesday, with the heaviest crowds on weekends and during summers and holidays.

CREATE AN ITINERARY

Pick three or four things that you must see or do, and plan your day along a rough geographical guide. Universal Studios Florida is relatively small, so walking from one end of the park to the other isn't as daunting as it is in some of the Disney parks, but the sometimes-long lines still dictate that you remain flexible.

CHOOSE AGE-APPROPRIATE RIDES/SHOWS

Here, as in Walt Disney World, height and age restrictions aren't bent to accommodate a screaming child. Even where restrictions don't exist, some shows have loud music and pyrotechnics that can frighten kids. And in a few cases, Universal employs a PG-13 rating, which suggests that a ride or show may not be suitable for preteens. Check the attraction descriptions that follow to make sure your child won't be unduly disappointed or frightened.

Moments Universal Has a Few 'Toons, Too

While the options pale in comparison to with, Universal has character meet-and-greets on a rotating basis. At **Universal Studios Florida,** you may run into Woody Woodpecker, SpongeBob SquarePants, Scooby-Doo, Jimmy Neutron, and others. At **Islands of Adventure,** the cast may include Spider-Man, Popeye and Olive Oyl, Beetle Bailey, the Cat in the Hat, Betty Boop, or Boris and Natasha.

Universal Has New Characters & Shows

Universal Studios Florida has replaced some of its old (read: stale, if you've been there a few times) street characters and shows in favor of new ones. The occasionally changing lineup includes **Lucy and Ricky Ricardo; Doc Emmit Brown; Fiona, Shrek, and Donkey; SpongeBob SquarePants;** the *Men in Black* agents; and the *Madagascar* menagerie. *Note:* Characters rotate or appear seasonally.

SUGGESTED ITINERARIES

A Suggested Itinerary for Families with Young Children

Waste no time: Hoof it to Woody Woodpecker's KidZone, where you and your heirs can spend most of the day. If they're 36 inches or taller, don't miss multiple rides on **Woody Woodpecker's Nuthouse Coaster.** Try to make an early pit stop at **Fievel's Playland** (especially its water slide, which is slow-moving and has longer lines after 10:30am). Then take a leisurely pace to see **E.T. Adventure, A Day in the Park with Barney,** and **Animal Planet Live!**

Take a lunch break, and don't leave before visiting the wet-and-wild **Curious George Goes to Town.** Round out the day with a stop at **Shrek 4-D.**

A Suggested Itinerary for Older Children, Teens & Adults

A single day is usually sufficient to see the park if you arrive early and keep a fairly brisk pace. Skip the city sidewalks of the main gate and **Terminator 2: 3-D Battle Across Time** until later. Go to the right, and tackle **Men in Black Alien Attack** and **Back to the Future . . . The Ride** and the **Fear Factor Live!** stunt show. Then make a counterclockwise loop, visiting **Jaws, Earthquake—The Big One, Revenge of the Mummy,** and **Twister . . . Ride It Out.** Break for lunch somewhere in that bunch; tackle the 'toons in the new **Jimmy Neutron's Nicktoon Blast** and the **Shrek 4-D** adventure; then catch the fun in **Terminator 2: 3-D Battle Across Time.**

A second day lets you revisit some of your favorites or see those you missed. With the pressure to hit all the major rides lessened, you can get to the **Universal Horror Makeup Show** and **Beetlejuice's Rock 'n Roll Graveyard Revue,** and then head back to the rides you liked most for a second go-round.

SERVICES & FACILITIES IN UNIVERSAL STUDIOS FLORIDA

ATMs Machines accepting cards from banks using the Cirrus, Honor, and PLUS systems are to the right of the main entrance (outside and inside the park) and in San Francisco/Amity, near Lombard's Landing restaurant.

Baby Care Changing tables are in men's and women's restrooms; there are nursing facilities at Family Services, just inside the main entrance and to the right. Diapers, food, formula, and infant supplies aren't sold at the parks.

Cameras & Film Film, disposable cameras, and limited digital supplies are available at the On Location shop in the Front Lot, just inside the main entrance. One-hour photo developing is available, though I don't recommend paying park prices.

Car Assistance   Battery jumps are provided. If you need assistance with your car, raise the hood and press the blue button at one of the guest-assistance stations located throughout the garage to call for security.

First Aid   The First Aid Center is located between New York and San Francisco, next to Louie's Italian Restaurant on Canal Street. There's also one just inside the main entrance next to Vacation Services.

Lockers   Lockers are across from Guest Services, near the main entrance, and cost $8 and $10 a day. Lockers are also available at select rides.

Lost Children   If you lose a child, go to Guest Services near the main entrance, or contact any park employee for assistance. *Children under 7 should wear name tags* inside their clothing.

Pet Care   A kennel is available ($10 a day) near the newest parking lot. Ask the parking attendant for directions upon entering the toll plaza. Overnight boarding is not permitted. Remember to bring food and proof of vaccination. You will be responsible for walking your pet.

Stroller Rental   Strollers can be rented in Amity and at Guest Services, just inside the entrance to the right. The cost is $10 for a single and $16 for a double.

Wheelchair Rental   Regular wheelchairs can be rented for $12 in Amity and at Guest Services, just inside the main gate. Electric wheelchairs are $40. Both require a signed agreement and a $50 deposit.

MAJOR ATTRACTIONS AT UNIVERSAL STUDIOS FLORIDA

Rides and attractions at this park have cutting-edge technology such as OMNIMAX 70mm film projected on seven-story screens to create terrific special effects. While waiting in line, you'll be entertained by excellent preshows—better than those at the Disney parks. Universal, as a whole, takes itself less seriously than the Mouse That Roared, and the atmosphere is peppered by subtle reminders that in the competitive theme-park industry, it's not a small world after all.

Animal Planet Live!
Frommer's Rating: B+ for kids and parents
Recommended Ages: All ages
Get a behind-the-scenes look at the Animal Planet television network through a multimedia show that combines video with live actors. The stars can include primates, a fox, a raccoon, and a dog. Members of the audience occasionally get to participate in the fun. If your kids love animals, it's a must.

Back to the Future . . . The Ride
Frommer's Rating: A+
Recommended Ages: 8–adult

Value **Money Saver**

You can save 10% off your purchase at many Universal Orlando gift shops or eateries by showing your AAA (American Automobile Association) card. This discount isn't available at food and merchandise carts or on tobacco, candy, film, collectibles, and sundry items.

Frommer's Rates the Rides

As I do for the Disney parks in chapter 6, "What Kids Like to See & Do in Walt Disney World," I'm using a grading system to score the Universal Orlando and SeaWorld rides in this chapter. (I'll return to the star-rating system toward the end of the chapter, when I explore some of Orlando's smaller attractions.) Most of the grades below are As, Bs, and Cs. That's because the major parks' designers have done a pretty good job on the attractions. But you'll also find a few Ds for Duds. Here's what the Frommer's ratings mean:

A+ = Your trip wouldn't be complete without it.
A = Put it at the top of your "to-do" list.
B+ = Make a real effort to see or do it.
B = It's fun but not a "must see."
C+ = A nice diversion; see it if you have time.
C = Go if it appeals to you but not if there's a wait.
D = Don't waste your time.

Blast through the space–time continuum in 1 of 24 flight simulators built to look like the movie's famous DeLorean. Along the way, you'll dive into blazing volcanic tunnels, collide with Ice Age glaciers, thunder through caves and canyons, and briefly get swallowed by a dinosaur in an eye-crossing multisensory adventure. You twist and turn; you dip and dive—all the while feeling as though you're really flying. Sit in one of the car's back seats to avoid ruining the illusion (in the front seat, you can lean forward and see your neighbors careening hydraulically in the next bay). It's pretty bumpy and might not be a good idea if you're prone to dizziness or motion sickness. *Note:* Heed the health warnings displayed at the ride, which has a 40-inch height minimum. Also, Universal recommends that expectant mothers skip this ride.

Nicolas's Rating: "AHHHHHHHH!" (My thoughts exactly! It's a pretty rough but really fun, wild ride.)

Beetlejuice's Rock 'n Roll Graveyard Revue
Frommer's Rating: C+ for classic rock fans, C for others
Recommended Ages: 10–adult
This rock musical stars Dracula, Wolfman, the Phantom of the Opera, Frankenstein and his bride, and Beetlejuice. The fun includes pyrotechnic special effects, some adult jokes, and MTV-style choreography. It's loud and lively enough to scare some small children and frazzle some older adults. *Note:* It carries Universal's PG-13 rating, meaning that it may not be suitable for preteens.

A Day in the Park with Barney
Frommer's Rating: A+ for tiny tots and their parents, D for everyone else
Recommended Ages: 2–6
Set in a parklike theater-in-the-round, this 25-minute musical stars the Purple One, Baby Bop, and BJ. It uses song, dance, special effects, and interactive play to entertain the kids. This could be the highlight of the day for preschoolers (parents can console

themselves with their kids' happiness). The playground adjacent to the theater is really unique ,with chimes to ring, treehouses to explore, and lots more to intrigue wee ones.

Davis's Rating: His big, goofy smile said it all: He adored the entire experience as he sang and danced right along with Barney and his pals. But my over-8 set couldn't stand having to hang around any longer than was required of them. The theater is air-conditioned, but even in the hottest months, that's not enough to entice me to spend another minute around Barney; he smile on my son's face, however, was.

Earthquake—The Big One
Frommer's Rating: A
Recommended Ages: 6–adult
After a short preshow, you climb on a BART train in San Francisco for a peaceful sub-way ride, but just as you pull into the Embarcadero Station, there's an earthquake—a big one, 8.3 on the Richter scale! As you sit helplessly trapped, slabs of concrete col-lapse around you; a propane truck bursts into flames; a runaway train hurtles your way; and the station floods (65,000 gal. of water cascade down the steps). **Note:** Uni-versal says expectant moms should skip this one.

Ryan's, Austin's, and Nicolas's Rating: "That was way cool." (Surprisingly, the noise, flames, and other special effects didn't bother the youngest of the three.)

E.T. Adventure
Frommer's Rating: B for preteens and their families
Recommended Ages: All ages
You'll soar with E.T. on a mission to save his ailing planet, through the forest and into space aboard an intergalactic bicycle. You'll also meet some characters created by Steven Spielberg for the ride, including Botanicus, Tickli Moot Moot, Horn Flowers, and Tympani Tremblies. This family favorite (young kids especially adore it) is defi-nitely a charmer. If there is a knock, it's that there are two waiting areas: inside and outside. And wait you will. **Note:** No lap riders here, so you'll have to take advantage of the child swap if you have very small children.

Jaws
Frommer's Rating: B+
Recommended Ages: 6–adult
As your boat heads into the 7-acre, 5 million-gallon lagoon, a dorsal fin appears on the surface. Then what goes with the fin—a 3-ton, 32-foot, mechanical great white shark—tries to sink its urethane teeth into your hide (or at least your boat's). A 30-foot wall of flame that surrounds the vessel truly causes you to feel the heat in this $45 million attraction. We won't tell you exactly how it ends, but in spite of a captain who

---

Tips Quiet on the Set

The latest addition to USF's spectacular shows is **Fear Factor Live.** Having debuted in the spring of 2005, it's the first reality show (based on NBC's block-buster hit *Fear Factor*) to become a theme-park attraction. Audience members perform stunts that test their courage; strength; and, at times, their stomachs—similar to the stuff on the hit TV show but live in Orlando. You can catch the show in the venue set between Jaws and Men in Black, where the park's Wild Wild West Stunt Show once reigned supreme.

Fun Fact **Goodbye Kong, Hello Mummy**

Kongfrontation was part of Universal Studios Florida when it opened in 1990, but the ride closed in September 2002, replaced in the spring of 2004 with **Revenge of the Mummy**. (I guess they didn't know they'd be releasing Oscar-winner Peter Jackson's new Kong movie).

---

can't hit the broad side of a dock with his grenade launcher, some lucky Orlando restaurant will be serving blackened shark tonight. (*Tip:* The effects of this ride are far more spectacular after dark.) *Note:* While it lacks a height requirement, the shark may be too intense for kids younger than 6, and Universal recommends that expectant mothers avoid it.

Warning: Universal has put Jaws on a limited operational schedule—it's open only during peak seasons and select times—so if it's on your to-do list, check ahead of time to see if it will be running when you're visiting.

Jimmy Neutron's Nicktoon Blast

Frommer's Rating: A
Recommended Ages: 6–adult

Buckle up for one of the park's newer rides. In this one, you climb aboard Jimmy's Rocket Pod, which hurtles you through hyperspace thanks to a motion simulator, sophisticated computer graphics, state-of-the-art ride technology, animation, and programmable motion-based seats. Your task: Defeat the evil Yokians, egg-shaped aliens that have stolen Jimmy's latest invention, the Mark IV rocket, and are threatening to take over Universal Orlando and the rest of the world. The attraction also features Jimmy's robot dog, Goddard; his nemesis, Cindy Vortex; and popular characters from several other cartoons, including SpongeBob SquarePants, Rugrats, Wild Thornberrys, and Fairly Odd Parents. *Note:* You must be 40 inches or taller to join Jimmy's Air Force.

Hailey's Rating: "Wow, it's the best ride here!" (Arguably, for kids it is, though the fact that she's a huge Nickelodeon fan may have something to do with it too.)

Men in Black Alien Attack

Frommer's Rating: A+
Recommended Ages: 6–adult

Armageddon may be upon us unless you and your mates fly to the rescue and destroy the alien menace. Once aboard your six-passenger cruiser, you'll buzz the streets of New York, using your "zapper" to splatter up to 120 bug-eyed targets. You have to contend with return fire and distractions such as light, noise, and clouds of liquid nitrogen (aka fog), any of which can spin you out of control. Your laser tag–style gun fires infrared bullets. Earn a bonus by hitting Frank the Pug (to the right, just past the alien shipwreck). The 4-minute ride relies on 360-degree spins rather than speed for its thrill factor. At the conclusion, you're swallowed by a giant roach (it's 30 ft. tall, with 8-ft. fangs and 20-ft. claws) that explodes, dousing you with bug guts as you blast your way to safety and into the pest-control hall of fame—maybe. When you exit, Will Smith rates you anywhere from galaxy defender to bug bait. (There are 38 possible scores; those assigned to less than full cars suffer the scoring consequences.) *Note:* Guests must be at least 42 inches tall to climb aboard this $70 million ride. *Note II:* Men in Black often has a *much* shorter line for single riders. Even if you're not alone but have older kids and are willing to be split up, get in this line, and hop right on a vehicle that has less than six passengers.

Ryan's, Austin's, and **Nicolas's Rating:** "Very cool! Gross, but very cool." (Of course, we immediately had to head back to the end of the line to ride again . . . and again.)

Revenge of the Mummy
Frommer's Ratings: A+
Recommended Ages: 10 and up

Ten years in the making, the $40 million Revenge of the Mummy made its debut in 2004. The indoor roller coaster uses a sophisticated propulsion system to hurtle riders through the shadowy, darkened tombs of ancient Egypt (all spectacularly re-created) while trying to escape the curse of the mummy. The sound system (enhanced by 200 speakers and surround-sound technology in the coaster cars) will spook you, too. Highly advanced robotics are used to bring to life some pretty scary-looking skeletal warriors, one of whom jumps aboard your car; even Imhotep himself makes an appearance. Overhead flames, fireballs, and creepy creatures combine with surprising twists, turns, stops, and starts to make for a thrill like no other in the park. And just when you think it's over . . . well, I have to leave some surprises for you. *Note:* Guests must be 48 inches tall to ride, and the normal back, neck, motion-sickness, and pregnancy warnings apply. I would also add phobia warnings for darkness, bugs, pyrotechnic effects, and special effects that jump out at you.

Austin's Rating: "What a cool coaster! First you go forward, then backward, and it's so smooth—scary, too!" (Riding the movies takes on a whole new meaning here!)

Shrek 4-D
Frommer's Rating: B+
Recommended Ages: All ages

Universal Studios' second new ride is a 20-minute show that can be seen, heard, felt, and smelled thanks to film; motion simulators; OgreVision glasses; and other special effects, such as water spritzers. The attraction picks up where the movie left off—allowing you to join Shrek and Princess Fiona on their honeymoon (at least, the G-rated portions of it). After one of the most amusing preshows in the park (featuring a ghostly Lord Farquaad, the Three Little Pigs, Pinocchio, and the Magic Mirror), you're settled in specially designed seats in the main auditorium and then transported to the fairy-tale realm of Duloc. The screen comes alive as you help Shrek and Donkey rescue Fiona from her kidnappers: Lord Farquaad and his knights. Along the way, spiders will try to crawl on you, and you'll ride a dragon that spritzes you when she clears her sinuses. The theater's seats are pneumatic air-propulsion nodules that are capable of turning and tilting (though not dramatically). Again, if your kids don't like touchy-feely special effects, they may get upset at certain points while experiencing this attraction.

Terminator 2: 3-D Battle Across Time
Frommer's Rating: A
Recommended Ages: 10–adult

This is billed as "the quintessential sight and sound experience for the 21st century!" The same director who made the movie, Jim Cameron, supervised this $60 million production. After a slow start, it builds into an impressive experience featuring the *Ahnud* (on film), along with other original cast members. It combines 70mm 3-D film (utilizing three 23-ft.-×-50-ft. screens) with thrilling technical effects and live stage action that includes a custom-built Harley-Davidson "Fat Boy." *Note:* The crisp 3-D effects are among the best in any Orlando park, but Universal has given this show a PG-13 rating, meaning that the violence and loud noise may be too intense for pre-teens. That may be a little too cautious, but some kids under 10 may be frightened. The rest may proclaim that they want to go back.

Ryan's Rating: "The action, the motorcycle—what a cool show."

Twister . . . Ride It Out
Frommer's Rating: A
Recommended Ages: 8–adult

Visitors from the twister-prone Midwest may find this re-creation a little too close to the real thing. An ominous funnel cloud, five stories tall, is created by swirling 2 million cubic feet of air per minute (that's enough to fill four full-size blimps), and the sound of a freight train fills the theater at rock-concert level as cars, trucks, and a cow fly about while the audience stands just 20 feet away. It's the windy version of *Earthquake* and packs quite a wallop. Crowds have been known to applaud when it's over.

Note: This show, too, comes with a PG-13 rating. Its loudness and intensity certainly can be too much for children under 8. Also, readers who have visited Universal Studios Hollywood in California will find Twister similar in theme to that park's Backdraft attraction, although (sacrilege!) the one in California offers a better overall experience.

Woody Woodpecker's Nuthouse Coaster
Frommer's Rating: A+ for kids and parents, B+ for others
Recommended Ages: 5–adult

This is the top attraction in Woody Woodpecker's KidZone, an 8-acre concession Universal Studios made several years ago after being criticized for having too little for young visitors. This ride is a kiddie coaster that will thrill some moms and dads, too. While only 30 feet at its peak, it offers quick, spiraling turns while you sit in a miniature steam train. The ride lasts only 55 seconds, and waits can be 30 minutes or more, but few kids will want to miss it. It's very much like The Barnstormer at Goofy's Wiseacre Farm in the Magic Kingdom (p. 191).

Hailey's and **Nicolas's Rating:** "We're going again . . . !" (They finally quit after four trips. I have to say I enjoyed sitting down while I waited for them to run out of steam.)

Note: Its height minimum is 36 inches.

ADDITIONAL ATTRACTIONS

The somewhat corny **Universal Horror Makeup Show** gives behind-the-scene looks at what goes into (and oozes out of) some of Hollywood's most frightening monsters. It has a PG-13 rating and may frighten young kids. **Lucy, A Tribute** is a remembrance of America's queen of comedy that will bore most kids after a few minutes, and the **Blues Brothers** launch their foot-stomping revue several times a day on Delancy Street (most kids will find it entertaining).

Back at Woody Woodpecker's KidZone, **Fievel's Playland** is a wet, Western-themed playground with a house to climb and a water slide for small fry (the ride lines can get long, but most little kids love it). **Curious George Goes to Town** is filled with whimsical watery fun, from fountains to ball-shooting cannons. Bring a change of clothes; you and your kids will get wet.

SHOPPING AT UNIVERSAL STUDIOS FLORIDA

Every major attraction has a theme store attached, many of them selling some rather unique merchandise. Although the prices are high when you consider you're just buying a souvenir, the **Hard Rock Cafe** shop in adjacent CityWalk is extremely popular and has a small but diverse selection of Hard Rock everything (including memorabilia with astronomical sticker prices). For just about everything else a la Universal, the **Universal Studios Store** carries a rather decent selection of toys, T-shirts, and souvenirs.

More than two dozen other shops in the park sell collectibles. Be warned, though, that unlike Walt Disney World, where Mickey is everywhere, Universal's shops are specific to individual attractions. If you see something you like, buy it; you probably won't find it in another store. If you did forget to pick something up, there's a shop-by-phone service. Call © **407/224-5800,** and describe the item and where you think you saw it; the likelihood is that they'll be able to help you out. There is a Universal store at Orlando International Airport, but it mainly carries the usual souvenirs.

Note: Universal has a service similar to Disney's in which you can have your purchases delivered to the Universal Studios Store at the front of the park. Allow 3 hours.

GREAT BUYS AT UNIVERSAL STUDIOS FLORIDA

Here's a sampling of the more unusual gifts available at some of the Universal stores. Of course, in addition to these options, you can find the standard tourist fare, with a staggering array of mugs, key chains, T-shirts, and the like. We've tried to include things you wouldn't find (or consider buying) anywhere else:

- **Back to the Future—The Store** Real fans of the movie series will find lots of intriguing stuff here, but one of the most interesting items is a miniature version of a DeLorean.
- **E.T.'s Toy Closet and Photo Spot** This is the place for plush stuffed animals, including a replica of the alien namesake.

Universal Cuisine

The best restaurants in the theme park are just outside the main gates at CityWalk, Universal's restaurant and nightclub venue. But there are more than a dozen places to eat inside the park. Here are my favorites:

Best Sit-Down Meal: Lombard's Seafood Grille combines a waterfront location with a varied menu of seafood, steak, pasta, chicken, and burgers, plus a kids' menu ($11–$35). It's located across from Earthquake—The Big One.

Best Counter Service: Universal Studio's Classic Monster Cafe is one of the newest park eateries. It serves salads, pizza, pasta, and rotisserie chicken ($6–$15). It's off 7th Avenue near Shrek 4-D.

Best Place for Hungry Families: Similar to a mall food court, the **International Food and Film Festival** offers a variety of food in one location. With options ranging from stir-fry to fajitas, it's a place where a family can split up and still eat under one roof. There are kids' meals for under $4 at most locations. The food is far from gourmet but a cut above regular fast food. Main courses run from $6 to $12. It's located near the back of Animal Planet Live! and the entrance to Back to the Future . . . The Ride.

Best Snack: The floats ($3–$6) at **Brody's Ice Cream Shop** are just the thing to refresh you on a hot summer afternoon. Brody's is located near Jaws.

- **MIB Gear**   If you find yourself in need of a ray gun or alien blaster, this is the place to buy everything out of this world.
- **Quint's Surf Shack**   This is the place to go for a different kind of T-shirt. Tropical colors, with subtle Universal logos, are the thing here.
- **Universal Studios Store**   This store, near the entrance, sells just about everything when it comes to Universal apparel, and there are plenty of toys as well.

2 Islands of Adventure

Universal's second theme park opened in 1999 with a colorful and cleverly themed collection of fast and sometimes-furious rides. At 110 acres, it's the same size as its big brother, Universal Studios Florida, but it seems larger, and it's definitely *the* Orlando destination for thrill-ride junkies. Roller coasters roar above pedestrian walkways, and water rides slice through the park. The trade-off: There are few shows. If you have teens in tow, this is unquestionably the top park in town for them. If you have little children, the options aren't as extensive, but Islands does offer plenty of places to play for young kids.

Expect total immersion in the park's various "islands." From the wobbly angles and Day-Glo colors in **Seuss Landing** to the lush foliage of **Jurassic Park,** Universal has done a good job of differentiating various sections of this $1 billion park (unlike Universal Studios Florida, where the cityscapes tend to blend together, making it hard to tell whether you're in San Francisco or New York). It's also done an outstanding job of differentiating Islands from Disney or any other Orlando park. The closest competitor in Florida is Busch Gardens in Tampa, but this attraction clearly has the edge on the ride front—at least when it comes to diversity.

The adventure is spread across six islands: the **Port of Entry,** a pass-through zone that has a collection of shops and restaurants, and five themed areas: **Seuss Landing, The Lost Continent, Jurassic Park, Toon Lagoon,** and **Marvel Super Hero Island.** The park offers a concentration of thrill rides and coasters, plus generous play areas for kids.

ESSENTIALS

GETTING TO ISLANDS OF ADVENTURE BY CAR   Universal Orlando is a half mile north of I-4 Exit 75B, Kirkman Road/Highway 435. There may be construction in the area, so follow the signs directing you to the park.

PARKING   If you park in the multilevel garage, make a note of the row and theme in your area to help you find your car later. Parking costs $9 for cars, light trucks, and vans. Valet parking is available for $16.

TICKETS, PASSES & TOURS   A **1-day ticket** costs $63 (plus 6.5% sales tax) for adults and $52 for children 3 to 9. A **2-day two-park pass** is $108 for adults and $100 for children 3 to 9. All multiday passes let you move between Universal Studios Florida and Islands of Adventure. *Multiday passes also give you free access to the City-Walk clubs at night.* Because the parks are within walking distance of each other, you won't lose much time jockeying back and forth, unlike the situation at Disney. Nevertheless, it's a long walk for tykes and people with limited mobility, so consider a stroller or wheelchair.

For more information on multiday pass options and VIP tours, see "Tickets, Passes & Tours," in the Universal Studios Florida section earlier in this chapter.

Tips Some Practical Advice for Island Adventurers

1. **The Shorter They Are . . .** *Nine of the 14 major rides at Islands of Adventure have height restrictions.* Dueling Dragons and the Incredible Hulk Coaster, for instance, deny access to anyone under 54 inches. For those who want to ride but come with little kids, there's a baby or child swap at all the major attractions, allowing one parent to ride while the other watches the tykes. But sitting in a waiting room isn't much fun for the little ones. So take your child's height into consideration before coming to the park or at least some of the islands.

2. **Cruising the Islands**   If you hauled your stroller with you on your vacation, bring it with you to the park. It's a very long walk from your car, through the massive parking garage and the nighttime entertainment district, CityWalk, before you get to the fun. Carrying a young child and the accompanying paraphernalia, even with a series of moving sidewalks, can make the long trek seem even longer—especially at the end of the day.

3. **The Faint of Heart**   Even adults riding without children need to heed all the ride restrictions. Expectant mothers; guests prone to motion sickness; and those with heart, neck, or back trouble will be discouraged—with good reason—from riding most primo attractions. There's still plenty to see and do, but without the roller coasters, Islands of Adventure isn't so special.

4. **Beat the Heat**   Several rides require that you wait outside; though most queues are covered to protect you from the sizzling Florida sun, the heat is a different matter. Bring some bottled water (freeze it the night before) with you for the long waits (a 99¢ free-world bottle costs $2.50 or more if you buy it here), or take a sip or two from the fountains smartly placed in the queues. Make sure your kids wear hats and sunscreen, and get enough to drink as well. Also, beer, wine, and liquor are more available at the Universal parks than at the Disney ones, but booze, roller coasters, and hot weather can make for a messy mix.

5. **Cash in on Your Card**   You can save 10% on your purchases at any gift shop or on a meal at Islands of Adventure by showing your AAA (American Automobile Association) card. This discount isn't available at food or merchandise carts. And tobacco, candy, film, collectibles, and sundry items aren't included.

HOURS   The park is open 365 days a year, generally from 9am to 6pm, though often later, especially in summer and around holidays, when it's sometimes open until 9pm or later. Also, during Halloween Horror Nights, the park closes around 5pm, reopens at 7pm (with a new admission), and remains open until at least midnight. The best bet is to call before you go so that you're not caught by surprise.

Islands of Adventure

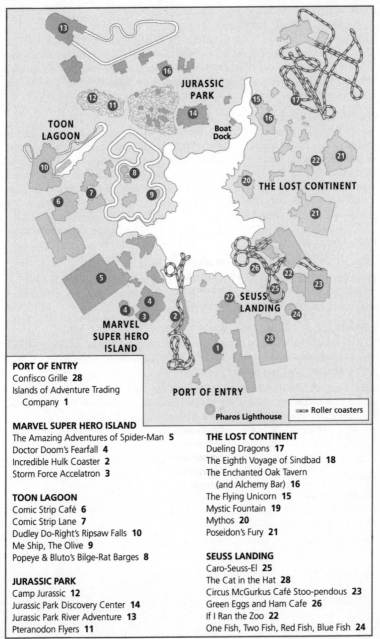

JURASSIC PARK

TOON LAGOON

Boat Dock

THE LOST CONTINENT

MARVEL SUPER HERO ISLAND

SEUSS LANDING

PORT OF ENTRY

Pharos Lighthouse

⊨⊨⊨ Roller coasters

PORT OF ENTRY
Confisco Grille **28**
Islands of Adventure Trading
   Company **1**

MARVEL SUPER HERO ISLAND
The Amazing Adventures of Spider-Man **5**
Doctor Doom's Fearfall **4**
Incredible Hulk Coaster **2**
Storm Force Accelatron **3**

TOON LAGOON
Comic Strip Café **6**
Comic Strip Lane **7**
Dudley Do-Right's Ripsaw Falls **10**
Me Ship, The Olive **9**
Popeye & Bluto's Bilge-Rat Barges **8**

JURASSIC PARK
Camp Jurassic **12**
Jurassic Park Discovery Center **14**
Jurassic Park River Adventure **13**
Pteranodon Flyers **11**

THE LOST CONTINENT
Dueling Dragons **17**
The Eighth Voyage of Sindbad **18**
The Enchanted Oak Tavern
   (and Alchemy Bar) **16**
The Flying Unicorn **15**
Mystic Fountain **19**
Mythos **20**
Poseidon's Fury **21**

SEUSS LANDING
Caro-Seuss-El **25**
The Cat in the Hat **28**
Circus McGurkus Café Stoo-pendous **23**
Green Eggs and Ham Cafe **26**
If I Ran the Zoo **22**
One Fish, Two Fish, Red Fish, Blue Fish **24**

259

MAKING YOUR VISIT MORE ENJOYABLE
PLANNING YOUR VISIT
You can get information before you leave by calling 📞 **800/711-0080,** 407/224-4233, or 407/363-8000. Ask for information about travel packages, as well as theme-park information. You can also write to Guest Services, 1000 Universal Studios Plaza, Orlando, FL 32819-7601. For online information, see "Planning Your Visit" for Universal Studios Florida, earlier in this chapter.

INFORMATION FOR VISITORS WITH SPECIAL NEEDS
Guests with disabilities should go to **Guest Services,** located just inside the main entrance, for a *Rider's Guide for Rider Safety & Guests with Disabilities,* a Telecommunications Device for the Deaf (TDD), or other special assistance. You can rent a standard wheelchair for $12 or an electric one for $40 (both require a $50 deposit and a signed rental contract). You can reserve them 24 hours or more in advance by calling 📞 **407/224-6350.** You can arrange for sign-language interpreting services at no charge by calling 📞 **888/519-4899** (toll-free TDD), 407/224-4414 (local TDD), or 407/224-5929 (voice). Make arrangements for an appointment with an interpreter 1 to 2 weeks in advance. Check **www.universalorlando.com** for more information.

THE BEST DAYS TO VISIT
Like Universal Studios Florida, it's best to visit Islands near the end of the week, on a Thursday or Friday. The pace is somewhat fast Monday to Wednesday, with the heaviest crowds on weekends and during summer and holidays.

SERVICES & FACILITIES AT ISLANDS OF ADVENTURE
ATMs   Machines accepting cards from banks using the Cirrus, Honor, and PLUS systems are located outside and to the right of the main entrance, and in the Lost Continent, near the bridge to Jurassic Park.

Baby Care   There are baby-swap stations at all the major attractions. This allows one parent to wait while the other rides. Nursing facilities are located in the Guest Services building in the Port of Entry. Look for the FAMILY SERVICES sign. There are no infant supplies sold anywhere in the park, so come prepared with diapers, food, and other necessities.

Cameras & Film   Film, disposable cameras, and digital supplies are available at De Foto's Expedition Photography, to the right just inside the main entrance.

Car Assistance   Battery jumps are provided. If you need assistance with your car, raise the hood, and press the blue button at one of the guest-assistance stations located throughout the garage to call for security.

First Aid   There's one just inside and to the right of the main entrance, and another in the Lost Continent, across from Oasis Coolers.

Lockers   Lockers are across from Guest Services near the main entrance and cost $8 or $10 a day. There are also lockers near the Incredible Hulk Coaster in Marvel Super Hero Island, the Jurassic Park River Adventure in Jurassic Park, and Dueling Dragons in the Lost Continent. The lockers at Dueling Dragons and the Incredible Hulk Coaster are free for the first 45 minutes. Thereafter, or at the Jurassic Park River Adventure, they're $2 per hour, to a maximum of $14 per day. You're not supposed to—and shouldn't—take things on these rides, so put them in a locker, or give them to a nonrider for safekeeping.

Lost Children   If you lose a child, go to Guest Services, near the main entrance, or go to the first park employee you see. *Children under 7 should wear name tags inside their clothing.*

Pets   You can board your small animals at the shelter in the parking garages for $10 a day (no overnight stays). You need to bring food, stopping back occasionally to walk them. Ask the attendant where you pay for parking to direct you to the kennel.

Ride Restrictions   Many of the park's attractions have minimum height requirements (see the listings that follow). Universal also recommends that expectant mothers steer clear of some rides (also noted in the listings).

Stroller Rental   Look to the left as you enter through the turnstiles. The cost is $10 for a single and $16 for a double.

Wheelchair Rental   Regular wheelchairs can be rented for $12 in the center concourse of the parking garage or to your left as you enter the turnstiles of the main entrance. Electric wheelchairs are $40. Both require a signed rental agreement and a $50 deposit.

SUGGESTED ITINERARIES

For Families with Young Kids

If you have kids under 10, enter and go to the right to **Seuss Landing,** an island where everything is geared to the young and young at heart. You'll easily spend the morning or longer exploring real-life interpretations of the wacky, colorful world of Dr. Seuss. (The wild colors make for some good photographs.) Be sure to ride **The Cat in the Hat; One Fish, Two Fish, Red Fish, Blue Fish;** and **Caro-Seuss-El.** After all that waiting in line, let the little ones burn some energy playing in **If I Ran the Zoo.**

Grab lunch at the **Green Eggs and Ham Cafe** (yes, they really are green). Next, head to the **Lost Continent** to ride the **Flying Unicorn** (36-in. height minimum) and talk to the **Mystic Fountain;** then let them play in **Camp Jurassic** or watch a "hatching" at the **Discovery Center** in **Jurassic Park.** They can have some more interactive fun in **Toon Lagoon** aboard **Me Ship, The Olive,** and meet characters on the **Toon Trolley** and Comic Strip Lane. Those 40 inches or taller can end the day in **Marvel Super Hero Island** by riding the **Amazing Adventures of Spider-Man.**

For Families with Older Kids & Teens

Head left from Port of Entry to **Marvel Super Hero Island,** and ride the **Incredible Hulk Coaster, The Amazing Adventures of Spider-Man,** and **Doctor Doom's Fearfall.** (If you arrive early, the line will be short for your first choice, but you'll have to wait or use UNIVERSAL EXPRESS for the others.) There should be time to squeeze in **Dudley Do-Right's Ripsaw Falls** in **Toon Lagoon** before you break for lunch at **Comic Strip Café** or **Blondie's: Home of the Dagwood.**

Now that you're fully refueled, ride **Popeye & Bluto's Bilge-Rat Barges;** then move to **Jurassic Park,** where you can ride **Jurassic Park River Adventure** and visit the **Discovery Center.** End your day in the **Lost Continent,** where you can catch the show in **Poseidon's Fury** and then test your courage aboard **Dueling Dragons.**

Tips **Finding Your Way**

Other-than-English park maps are available at Guest Services in the Port of Entry in French, German, Japanese, Portuguese, and Spanish.

PORT OF ENTRY

This "greeting card" to the park is lined with interesting shops and an array of eateries. If you plan to save shopping for the end of the day, return to **Islands of Adventure Trading Company,** which offers a variety of merchandise linked to attractions throughout the park—from Jurassic T-shirts to stuffed Cat in the Hat dolls.

SEUSS LANDING

This 10-acre island, inspired by the works of the late Theodore Seuss Geisel, is awash in Day-Glo colors, whimsical architecture, and curved trees (the latter were downed and bent by Hurricane Andrew before the park acquired them). Needless to say, the main attractions here are aimed at the younger set, though anyone who loved the good Doctor as a child will enjoy some nostalgic fun on these rides. And those who aren't familiar with his work will enjoy the visuals; Seussian art is like Dalí for kids.

Caro-Seuss-El

Frommer's Rating: A+ for young kids, parents, and carousel lovers

Recommended Ages: All ages

Forget tradition. This not-so-average carousel gives you a chance to ride seven whimsical characters of Dr. Seuss (a total of 54 mounts), including cowfish, elephant birds, and mulligatawnies. They move up and down as well as in and out. Their eyes blink and heads bob as you twirl through the riot of color surrounding the ride. *Note:* A special ride platform lets guests in wheelchairs experience the up-and-down motion of the ride, making this a great stop for visitors with disabilities.

The Cat in the Hat

Frommer's Rating: A for preteens, C+ for teens and adults

Recommended Ages: All ages

Any Seuss fan will recognize the giant candy-striped hat looming over the entrance to this ride and probably the chaotic journey. Comparable with but spunkier than It's a Small World at Magic Kingdom (p. 189), The Cat in the Hat is among the signature children's experiences at Islands of Adventure. Love or hate the idea, *do it,* and earn your stripes. Your couch travels through 18 scenes retelling *The Cat in the Hat*'s tale of a day gone very much awry. You, meanwhile, spin about and meet Thing 1 and Thing 2, in addition to other characters. The highlight is a revolving 24-foot tunnel that alters your perceptions and leaves your head with a feeling oddly reminiscent of a hangover.

Note: Pop-up characters may be scary for riders under 5, and expectant moms are discouraged from riding The Cat.

If I Ran the Zoo

Frommer's Rating: A for the very young

Recommended Ages: 2–7

This 19-station interactive play land features flying water snakes and a chance to tickle the toes of a Seussian animal. Kids also can spin wheels, explore caves, fire water cannons, climb, slide, and otherwise burn off some excited energy. It's perfect for the preschool set.

One Fish, Two Fish, Red Fish, Blue Fish

Frommer's Rating: B+ for kids and parents

Recommended Ages: 2–7

This kiddie charmer is similar to the Dumbo ride (p. 188) at Magic Kingdom (including the ridiculously long line), although this one has a few added features. Your controls allow you to move your funky fish up or down 15 feet as you spin around on an arm attached to a hub. All the while, a song belts out rhyming flight instructions. Watch out for "squirt posts," which spray unsuspecting riders who don't follow the rhyme. Actually, even the most careful driver is likely to get wet.

MARVEL SUPER HERO ISLAND

Thrill junkies love the twisting, turning, stomach-churning rides on this island filled with building-tall murals of Marvel Super Heroes. Fans can **Meet the Marvel Super Heroes** in front of The Amazing Adventures of Spider-Man (for times, check your guide map, handed out when you enter, or grab a copy at Guest Services). And the munch crowd can dig into sandwiches and burgers at **Captain America Diner** (in the $6–$10 range) and **Cafe 4** for pizza, pasta, and sandwiches ($4–$12).

The Amazing Adventures of Spider-Man *(Finds*

Frommer's Rating: A+

Recommended Ages: 8–adult

The original Web master stars in this exceptional show/ride (arguably the best in town), which features 3-D action and special effects. The story line: You're on a tour of the *Daily Bugle* when—yikes!—something goes horribly wrong. Peter Parker suddenly encounters evil villains and becomes Spider-Man. This high-tech ride isn't stationary, like the Back to the Future ride at Universal Studios Florida (p. 250). Cars twist and spin, plunge and soar through a comic-book universe. Passengers wearing 3-D glasses squeal as computer-generated objects fly at their 12-person cars. There's a simulated 400-foot drop that feels an awful lot like the real thing. *Note:* Expectant mothers and those with heart, neck, or back problems shouldn't ride. There's a 40-inch height minimum.

Ryan's Rating: "I think I left my stomach back there." (He isn't the only one. This ride is unsuitable for young children and squeamish adults—though closing your eyes momentarily can help. If you are neither, it's an absolute must.)

Tip: Waits can be 45 minutes even on an off day (and sometimes a whole lot longer), so use UNIVERSAL EXPRESS if necessary. The ride also offers a single-rider line that can drastically reduce waiting times. So if it's an option on the day you're here, and you've got older kids or teens who won't mind splitting up, take advantage of it.

Doctor Doom's Fearfall

Frommer's Rating: C+

Recommended Ages: 8–adult

Look! Up in the sky! It's a bird, it's a plane . . . uh, it's you falling 150 feet, if you're courageous enough to climb aboard this towering metal skeleton. The screams that can be heard at the ride's entrance add to the anticipation of a big plunge followed by smaller ones. The plot? You're touring a lab when—are you sensing a recurring theme here?—something goes wrong as Doctor Doom tries to cure you of fear. You're fired to the top, with feet dangling, and dropped in intervals, feet first, leaving your stomach at several levels. The experience isn't nearly up to the Tower of Terror's at Disney–MGM Studios (most of the velocity moves in the "up" direction, not the down one), but it's still frightful (and you do get a neat view of the entire park). The waiting times can also be scary, but the teens who flock here don't seem to mind too much. *Note:* Expectant mothers and those with heart, neck, or back problems shouldn't ride. If you or your kids are scared of heights, don't even think about getting on this one. Minimum height is 52 inches.

Incredible Hulk Coaster (Finds
Frommer's Rating: A+
Recommended Ages: 10–adult

Bruce Banner is working in his lab when—yes, again—something goes wrong. But this rocking rocket of a ride makes everything oh, so right, except maybe your heart-beat and stomach. From a dark tunnel, you burst into the sunlight while accelerating from 0 to 40 mph in 2 seconds. While that's only two thirds the speed of Disney–MGM's Rock 'n' Roller Coaster, this is in broad daylight; there's a lot more motion still to come; and you can *see* the asphalt! From there, you spin upside down 128 feet from the ground, feel weightless, and careen through the center of the park over the heads of other visitors. Coaster-lovers will be pleased to know that this ride, which lasts 2 minutes and 15 seconds, includes seven inversions and two deep drops. The ride, however, is extremely smooth, making it one of the better coaster experiences for all types of riders. Sunglasses, change, and an occasional set of car keys lie in a mesh net beneath the ride—proof of its motion and the fact that most folks don't heed the warnings to stash their stuff in the nearby lockers. As a nice touch, the 32-passenger metal coaster glows green at night (riders who ignore all the warnings occasionally turn green as well).

Austin's Rating: "That was sooooooo smoooooooth, and you shot off like a rocket." (Adrenaline-seeking teens not only love this ride, but also often wait in an even longer line to get a front-row seat for all the action.)

Note: Expectant mothers and those with heart, neck, or back problems shouldn't ride it. Riders must be at least 54 inches tall.

Storm Force Accelatron
Frommer's Rating: C+
Recommended Ages: 4–adult

Despite the exotic name, this ride is little more than a spinoff of the Magic Kingdom's Mad Tea Party—spinning teacups that, in this case, have a 22nd-century design. While aboard, you and the X-Men's super heroine, Storm, try to defeat the evil Magneto by converting human energy into electrical forces. To do that, you need to spin faster and faster. In addition to some upset stomachs (your kids will be happy to give

---

Tips Out of Sight . . .

If your kids are at the age where they are just starting to test the more intense thrill rides, they may overreach once or twice. To be on the safe side, tell your kids that if they find a ride a little too intense, they should hang on and *close their eyes.* A lot of the thrills at many of the parks are visually driven, and the intensity will come down a notch or two if you can't see what's coming. The only exception to this is **Mission: Space** at Epcot (p. 205), where shutting your eyes may actually cause even more disorientation.

you one), the spiraling creates a thunderstorm of sound and light that gives Storm all the power she needs to blast Magneto into the ever-after (or until the next riders arrive). This ride is sometimes closed during off-peak periods. *Note:* Expectant moms are advised not to ride this ride.

TOON LAGOON

More than 150 life-size sculpted cartoon images—characters range from Betty Boop and Flash Gordon to Bullwinkle and Cathy—let you know you've entered an island dedicated to your favorites from the Sunday funnies. Many of the selected characters will probably be more familiar to parents than to children, but Popeye is present, and the cool rides mean your kids will be happy anyway.

Dudley Do-Right's Ripsaw Falls

Frommer's Rating: A
Recommended Ages: 7–adult

The setting and effects at WDW's Splash Mountain are better, but the adrenaline rush here is higher. The staid red hat of the heroic Dudley can be deceiving: The ride that lies under it has a lot more speed and drop than onlookers suspect. Six-passenger logs take you around a 400,000-gallon lagoon before launching you into a 75-foot drop at 50 mph. At one point, you're 15 feet below the surface. Though the water is contained on either side, you *will* get wet. Younger kids may be a bit intimidated by the whole experience, but most children who make the height requirements like it.

Austin's Rating: "I'm soaked . . . but what a rush! Just when you think you're done, it makes another dip and dive." (It may not, however, be as much of a rush for the taller members of your family: One of the ride's biggest knocks is that its passenger logs are pretty cramped, especially if you have long legs.)

Note: Once again, expectant mothers and folks with heart, neck, or back problems should do something else. Riders must be at least 44 inches tall.

Me Ship, *The Olive*

Frommer's Rating: B+
Recommended Ages: 4–adult

This three-story boat is a family-friendly play land with dozens of interactive activities from bow to stern. Kids can toot whistles, clang bells, or play the organ. Sweet Pea's Playpen is a favorite of younger guests. Kids 6 and up will love Cargo Crane (adults will like it, too), where they can drench riders on Popeye & Bluto's Bilge-Rat Barges (see below). *Note:* If you or your kids are shutterbugs, the second and third deck of the good ship offer *great views and photo ops* of the Incredible Hulk Coaster and some of the rest of Islands of Adventure.

Popeye & Bluto's Bilge-Rat Barges

Frommer's Rating: A
Recommended Ages: 6–adult

This is the same kind of ride with the same kind of raft as Kali River Rapids at Animal Kingdom (p. 233), but it's a bit faster and bouncier. You'll be squirted by mechanical devices as well as the water cannons fired by guests at Me Ship, *The Olive* (see above). The 12-passenger rafts bump, churn, and dip (14 ft. at one point) along a whitewater course lined with Bluto, Sea Hag, and other villains. You will get soaked—and then drenched for good measure. Kids find this a whole lot less intimidating than some of the other rides at Islands. *Note:* Yes, once again, expectant mothers and people with heart, neck, or back problems shouldn't ride this one. Riders must be at least 42 inches tall.

Tips **Up, Up & Away**

Strength and fitness folks can get a little extra workout at the small **rock-climbing venue** ($5 per person) outside the Thunder Falls Terrace restaurant in Jurassic Park. If you or the kids are looking for a more economical and less strenuous option, try walking the elevated trails and climbing the net ladders beneath the Pteranodon Flyers attraction, also in Jurassic Park (see below).

Austin's Rating: "The water is *c-c-cold*" (a blessing on hot summer days but less so in Jan.).

JURASSIC PARK

All the basics and some of the high-tech wizardry from Steven Spielberg's wildly successful films are incorporated into this lushly landscaped tropical locale that includes a replica of the visitor center from the movie. There's something here for every child in your party, from teens to toddlers. Expect long lines at the River Adventure and pleasant surprises at the Discovery Center.

Camp Jurassic
Frommer's Rating: A+ for young children
Recommended Ages: 2–7
This play area, similar in theme to the Boneyard in WDW's Animal Kingdom, has everything from lava pits with dinosaur bones to a rainforest and amber mines. Watch out for the spitters that lurk in dark caves. The multilevel play area has plenty of places for kids to crawl, explore, and spend energy. Young kids need close supervision, though. It's easy to get turned around inside the caverns.

Jurassic Park Discovery Center
Frommer's Rating: B+
Recommended Ages: All ages
Here's an amusing, educational pit stop that has life-size dinosaur replicas and some interactive games, including a sequencer that pretends to combine your DNA with a dinosaur's. The "Beasaur" exhibit allows you to see and hear as the huge reptiles did. You can play the game show You Bet Jurassic (grin) and scan the walls for fossils. The highlight is watching a velociraptor "hatch" in the lab. Because there are a limited number of interactive stations, this can consume a lot of time on busy days.

Jurassic Park River Adventure
Frommer's Rating: A
Recommended Ages: 7–adult
After a leisurely raft tour along the river, some raptors escape and could hop aboard your boat at any moment. The ride lets you literally come face to face with "breathing" inhabitants of Jurassic Park. At one point, a *Tyrannosaurus rex* decides you look like a tasty morsel, and at another point, spitters launch venomous lungers your way. The only way out: an 85-foot plunge in your log-style life raft that will leave you dripping. If your stomach can take only one flume ride, this one's a lot more comfortable than Dudley Do-Right (see earlier), and the atmosphere is better. ***Note:*** Expectant mothers and those with heart, neck, or back problems shouldn't ride. Guests must be at least 42 inches tall.

Austin's and **Nicolas's Rating:** "The drop was definitely scary . . . in a fun sort of way, but definitely scary." (It's steep and quick enough to lift your fanny out of the seat. Fact is, when Spielberg rode it, he made them stop the ride and let him out before the plunge.)

Pteranodon Flyers
Frommer's Rating: C+
Recommended Ages: All ages (sort of—see restrictions below)
The 10-foot metal frames and simple seats are flimsy, but this quick spin around Jurassic Park offers a great bird's-eye view. The landing is bumpy, and you'll swing side to side throughout, which makes some riders queasy. Unlike the traditional gondolas in sky rides, on this one, your feet hang free from the two-seat skeletal flyer, and there's little but a restraining belt between you and the ground. *Note:* That said, this is a child's ride. Single passengers must be between 36 and 56 inches tall; adults can climb aboard *only* when accompanying someone that size. And because this ride launches only two passengers every 30 to 40 seconds, it can consume an hour of your day, even in the off season. So although it is nice, and your little ones will love it, pass it up if you're pressed for time.

Nicolas's Rating: "That was cool. It was like flying, but the wait was horrible." The swaying adds a little thrill to the equation, but we waited over an hour for this one, and it wasn't even a particularly crowded day.

THE LOST CONTINENT
Although it's mixed its millennia—ancient Greece with a medieval forest—Universal has done a good job of creating a foreboding mood in this section of the park, whose entrance is marked by menacing stone griffins. This is another section that offers at least one attraction that every child in your party will find to their liking.

Dueling Dragons *(Moments*
Frommer's Rating: A+
Recommended Ages: 10–adult
Maniacal minds created this thrill ride, sending two roller coasters right at each other at high speeds (when both are running, which isn't always the case). True coaster crazies will love the intertwined set of leg-dangling racers that climb to 125 feet, invert five times, and three times come within 12 inches of each other as the two dragons battle and you prove your bravery by tagging along. A couple of thrill junkies (after riding this one for the third time in a day) revealed that this is where they head in Orlando when they want the ultimate adrenaline rush (though it's not as smooth a ride as the Hulk Coaster). Teens flock here in droves. For the best ride, try to get one of the two outside seats in each of the eight rows. If you want to get into the front seat, there's a special (yes, longer!) line near the loading dock so that daredevils can claim the first car. *Note:* Expectant mothers and those with heart, neck, or back problems shouldn't ride. (Why aren't you surprised?) Riders must be at least 54 inches tall.

Fun Fact Coaster Tidbit
One Dueling Dragon coaster seems to have an obvious advantage over the other. The Fire Dragon can reach speeds up to 60 mph, while the Ice Dragon has a top end of only 55 mph.

Eighth Voyage of Sindbad (Overrated)
Frommer's Rating: C+
Recommended Ages: 6–adult
The mythical sailor is the star of a stunt demonstration that takes place in a 1,700-seat theater decorated with blue stalagmites and eerie, gloomy shipwrecks. The show has water explosions and dozens of pyrotechnic effects, including a 10-foot circle of flames. But it doesn't come close to the quality of the Indiana Jones stunt show at Disney–MGM Studios. Young kids will probably like it, though a few of the characters may scare younger kids; you can take solace in the fact that you get to rest your feet. **Note:** This show is closed from time to time, including during the run of Halloween Horror Nights (p. 22).

Flying Unicorn
Frommer's Rating: A+ for kids and parents, B+ for others
Recommended Ages: 5–adult
The Flying Unicorn is a small roller coaster that travels through a mythical forest on the Lost Continent, next to Dueling Dragons. It's very much like Woody Woodpecker's Nuthouse Coaster at Universal Studios Florida (p. 255) and The Barnstormer at Goofy's Wiseacre Farm in the Magic Kingdom (p. 191). That means a fast corkscrew run that is sure to earn squeals, but probably not at the risk of someone's losing his lunch. It's the perfect introductory coaster for the young set. **Note:** Here's another one that expectant moms are warned not to ride. The Unicorn has a 36-inch height minimum.

Mystic Fountain
Frommer's Rating: B+ for kids
Recommended Ages: 3–8
Located just outside Sindbad's theater, this interactive "smart" fountain delights younger guests (and usually provides a cool photo op or two for parents). It can see and hear, leading to a lot of kibitzing with those who stand before it. If you want to stay dry, don't get too close when it starts "spouting" its wet wisdom. On the other hand, if you need a quick cool-off—go for it.

Poseidon's Fury
Frommer's Rating: B+
Recommended Ages: 6–adult
Clearly, this is the park's best show—though with a lack of competition, that's something of a backhanded compliment. The story line revolves around a battle between Poseidon, god of the sea, and the evil Darkenon. Speaking of revolving, you'll pass through a small room that has a 42-foot vortex where 17,500 gallons of water swirl around you, barrel roll–style. (If you wear glasses, note that they will fog up completely when you pass through the vortex; take them off if you can.) In the battle royale, the protagonists hurl 25-foot fireballs at each other. It's more interesting than frightening, but it's not worth the long lines that often plague it, so if you're on a tight schedule, use UNIVERSAL EXPRESS or skip it. **Note:** The fireballs, explosive sounds, and rushing water may be a little too intense for children under 6.

SHOPPING AT ISLANDS OF ADVENTURE
There are more than 20 shops within the park, offering a variety of theme merchandise. You may want to check out **Cats, Hats & Things** for special Seussian souvenirs, books, and T-shirts. **Jurassic Outfitters** and **Dinostore** feature a variety of stuffed and

plastic dinosaurs, plus safari-themed clothing. Superhero fans should check out **The Marvel Alterniverse Store** and the **Spider-Man Shop. Toon Extra** has the largest selection of souvenirs in Toon Lagoon. **Islands of Adventure Trading Company** is a good stop on the way out if you're still searching for something that will help you or the folks back home remember your visit.

Note: Universal has a service similar to Disney's in which you can have your purchases delivered to the front of the park. Allow 3 hours. Universal also has a shop-by-phone service. Call © **407/224-5800,** and describe the item and where you think you saw it; the likelihood is that they'll be able to help you out and have it shipped to you.

DINING AT ISLANDS OF ADVENTURE

There are a number of stands where you can get a quick bite to eat, as well as a handful of full-service restaurants. The park's creators have taken some extra care to tie in restaurant offerings with the theme. The **Green Eggs and Ham Cafe** may be one of the few places on earth where you'd be willing to eat tinted huevos. (It sells an egg-and-ham sandwich for about $7.) There are dozens of sit-down restaurants, eateries, and snack carts. To save money, look for the kiddie menus, offering a children's meal and a small beverage for $6. Also consider combo meals, which usually offer a slight price break. **Thunder Falls Terrace** in Jurassic Park, for instance, offers a rib-and-chicken combo as well as other options in the $8-to-$13 range.

Here are some of our other favorites at Islands:

- **Best Sit-Down Restaurant**   At **Mythos** on the Lost Continent, choose among selections such as cedar-planked salmon, lobster and corn bisque, a wrap of the day, and wood-fired pizzas. The atmospheric, cavelike setting is pleasant. This is a grownup dining affair, best suited to adults and children over age 10. Entrees cost $10 to $23, and Mythos is usually open from 11:30am to 3:30pm daily.
- **Best Atmosphere for Adults & Teens**   The **Enchanted Oak Tavern (and Alchemy Bar),** also in the Lost Continent, also has a cavelike interior, which looks like a mammoth tree from the outside and is brightened by an azure skylight with a celestial theme. The tables and chairs are thick planks, and the servers are clad in "wench wear." Try the chicken/rib combo with waffle fries for about $13. Mom and Dad can sample 1 of the 45 types of beer on the menu.
- **Best Atmosphere for Kids**   The fun never stops under the big top at **Circus McGurkus Cafe Stoo-pendous** in Seuss Landing, where animated trapeze artists swing from the ceiling. Kids' meals, including a souvenir cup, are $6 to $7. The adult menu features fried chicken, lasagna, spaghetti, and pizza ($7–$12). Try the fried chicken platter or the lasagna.
- **Best Diversity**   **Comic Strip Café,** located in Toon Lagoon, is a four-in-one, counter service–style eatery offering burgers, Chinese food, Mexican food, and pizza and pasta ($6–$9).

Also, several restaurants (see chapter 5, "Family-Friendly Dining") are just a short walk from the park in Universal's entertainment complex, CityWalk.

⎛Fun Fact⎞ Food for Thought

The green eggs at the Green Eggs and Ham Cafe get their color from a variety of spices, not food dye.

> ⌒ *Tips* **Great Things to Buy at Islands of Adventure**
>
> Here's a sampling of some of the more unusual wares available at Islands of Adventure. It represents a cross-section of tastes:
>
> **Jurassic Outfitters**   There are plenty of T-shirts with slogans like "I Survived [the whatever ride]."
>
> **Spider-Man Shop**   This shop specializes in its namesake's paraphernalia, including red Spidey caps covered with black webs and denim jackets with logos.
>
> **Toon Extra**   Where else can you buy a miniature stuffed Mr. Peanut beanbag, an Olive Oyl-and-Popeye frame, or a stuffed Beetle Bailey? Life doesn't get any better for some of us.
>
> **Treasures of Poseidon**   Located in the Lost Continent, it carries an array of blue glassware, including tumblers, stuffed animals, and toys.

3 SeaWorld

Cleverly disguised as a theme park—or, as SeaWorld likes to call itself, an adventure park—this popular 200-acre marine park lets guests explore the mysteries of the deep and learn about the oceans and their inhabitants, all while having tons of fun. SeaWorld combines wildlife-conservation awareness (otherwise known as edutainment), actual marine-life care, and plain old fun all in one fell swoop. While that's what Disney is attempting with its latest park, Animal Kingdom, the message here is subtle and a more inherent part of the experience.

SeaWorld's beautifully landscaped grounds center on a 17-acre lagoon and include flamingo and pelican ponds and a lush tropical rainforest. Shamu, a killer whale, is the star of the park, along with his expanding family, which includes baby whales. The pace is much more laid-back than at either Universal or Disney, and it's a good way to break up a long week trudging through the other parks. Close encounters at feeding pools are among the real attractions (so be sure to budget a few extra dollars to buy fishy handouts for the sea lions and dolphins, who've turned begging into an art form).

SeaWorld manages a few thrills and chills. **Journey to Atlantis** is a high-tech water ride similar to Splash Mountain at Disney's Magic Kingdom and Jurassic Park River Adventure at Universal Orlando's Islands of Adventure. And **Kraken** is a floorless roller coaster that sports seven inversions, much like coasters such as Montu and Kumba at SeaWorld's sister, Busch Gardens in Tampa (p. 327). But this park doesn't try to compete with the wonders of WDW or Universal. Instead, it lets you discover the crushed-velvet texture of a stingray or the song of the seals. And your children will enjoy that every bit as much as the techno wonders elsewhere.

ESSENTIALS
GETTING TO SEAWORLD BY CAR   The marine park is south of Orlando and Universal, north of Disney. From I-4, take Exit 72, Beeline Expressway/Highway 528, and follow the signs.

SeaWorld

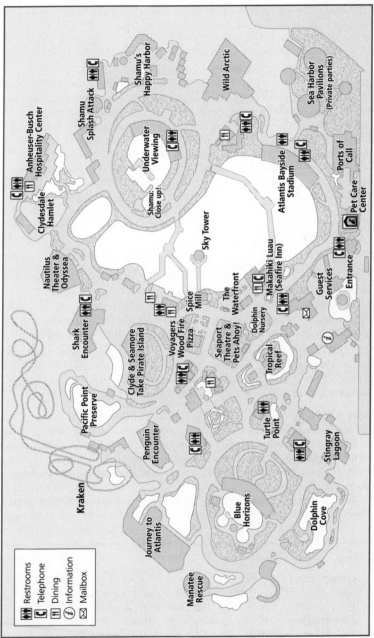

Restrooms
Telephone
Dining
Information
Mailbox

Kraken

Journey to Atlantis

Manatee Rescue

Blue Horizons

Penguin Encounter

Pacific Point Preserve

Shark Encounter

Clyde & Seamore Take Pirate Island

Voyagers Wood Fire Pizza

Nautilus Theatre & Odyssea

Turtle Point

Stingray Lagoon

Dolphin Cove

Seaport Theatre & Pets Ahoy!

Dolphin Nursery

Tropical Reef

Spice Mill

The Waterfront

Makahiki Luau (Seafire Inn)

Guest Services

Entrance

Sky Tower

Clydesdale Hamlet

Anheuser-Busch Hospitality Center

Shamu Splash Attack

Shamu: Close up!

Underwater Viewing

Shamu's Happy Harbor

Wild Arctic

Atlantis Bayside Stadium

Sea Harbor Pavilions (Private parties)

Ports of Call

Pet Care Center

PARKING   Parking costs $8 for cars, light trucks, and vans. The lots aren't huge, and most folks can walk to the entrance. Trams also run. Note the location of your car. SeaWorld characters such as Wally Walrus mark sections, but at the end of a long day, it's easy to forget where you parked.

TICKET PRICES   At press time, a **1-day ticket** cost $62 for ages 10 and over, and $50 for children 3 to 9, plus 6.5% sales tax. (The price typically goes up $2 per year.) The park's new online ticketing allows you to go to its website, **www.seaworld.com**; buy your ticket over the Internet; print it at home; and take the printout right to the turnstiles. *Note:* SeaWorld sometimes offers promotions that net you a second day free.

See p. 242 for information on the **FlexTicket,** multiday admission tickets for Sea-World, Universal Orlando, Wet 'n Wild, and Busch Gardens.

SeaWorld's **Adventure Express Tour** ($89 adults and $79 kids, *plus park admission*) is a 6-hour guided excursion that includes front-of-the-line access to Journey to Atlantis, Kraken, and Wild Arctic; reserved seating at two animal shows; lunch; and a chance to touch or feed penguins, dolphins, stingrays, and sea lions (𝐶 **800/406-2244** or 407/363-2380). It's the only way to dodge park lines, though these aren't as long as Disney's or Universal's.

HOURS   The park is usually open from 9am to 6pm and sometimes later, 365 days a year. Call 𝐶 **800/327-2424** or 407/351-3600 for more information.

MAKING YOUR VISIT MORE ENJOYABLE
PLANNING YOUR VISIT
Get information before you leave by writing to **SeaWorld Guest Services** at 7007 SeaWorld Dr., Orlando, FL 32801, or call 𝐶 **800/327-2424** or 407/351-3600.

ONLINE   SeaWorld information is available at **www.seaworld.com**. The *Orlando Sentinel* newspaper produces *Orlando Sentinel Online* at **www.orlandosentinel.com**. You can also get a ton of information from the Orlando/Orange County Convention & Visitors Bureau website, **www.orlandoinfo.com**.

INFORMATION FOR VISITORS WITH SPECIAL NEEDS
The park publishes an accessibility guide for guests with disabilities, although most of its attractions are easily accessible to those in wheelchairs (it's available online at **www.seaworld.com** in the "Park Information" section). SeaWorld also provides a Braille guide for the visually impaired. For the hearing-impaired, there's a very brief synopsis of shows. Sign-language interpreting services are available at no charge but must be reserved by calling 𝐶 **407/363-2414** at least a week in advance of your visit. Assisted-listening devices are available at select attractions for a $20 refundable

---

Tips **Shuttle Service**

SeaWorld and Busch Gardens in Tampa, both owned by Anheuser-Busch, have a shuttle service that offers $10 round-trip tickets to get you from Orlando to Tampa and back. The 1½- to 2-hour one-way shuttle runs daily and has five pickup locations in Orlando, including at Universal and on I-Drive (𝐶 **800/221-1339**). The schedule allows about 7 hours at Busch Gardens. The service is free if you have a FlexTicket.

> ⌒Tips **New Dining Programs**
>
> SeaWorld is diving deeper into the restaurant game with **Dine with Shamu** (© 800/327-2424 or 407/351-3600 for information and reservations; www.seaworld.com), a reservations-only seafood buffet served poolside with Shamu as a special guest. While eating, guests can mingle and question Sea-World trainers. The menu also includes chicken, beef, and salads. The cost is $34 for adults and $18 for kids 3 to 9, in addition to park admission. Reserving a spot 2 to 3 weeks in advance is usually more than enough unless you're coming in one of the crunch periods (summer, holidays), when you should reserve as soon as your travel plans are firm.
>
> **Sharks Underwater Grill** is an underwater venue with floor-to-ceiling windows where diners can dig into Florida and Caribbean treats while watching denizens swim by in the Shark Encounter exhibit. Menu prices are $16 to $26 for adults, and $6 to $12 for kids 3 to 9 (pasta, hot dogs, chicken breast, steak, and popcorn shrimp), and theme-park admission is required. You can make a reservation for a meal here by calling © 800/327-2420; for more information, head online to **www.seaworld.com**.
>
> Other eating options once you're inside the park include the **Seafire Inn** (stir-fry, burgers, coconut shrimp, chicken, and salads) and **Voyagers** (wood-fired pizza, grilled salmon, smoked chicken, and focaccia club sandwiches).

deposit. For a complete rundown of all of your options, head to Guest Services when you enter the park; you can also call © **407/351-3600** for more information.

BEST TIME OF YEAR TO VISIT
Because this is a mostly outdoor, water-related park, you may want to keep in mind that even Florida gets a tad nippy during January and February. SeaWorld has smaller crowds from January through April and from just after Labor Day until just before Thanksgiving.

BEST DAYS TO VISIT
Weekends, Thursday, and Friday are busy days at this park. Monday through Wednesday are usually better days to visit, because tourists coming for a week go to the Disney and Universal parks early in their stays, saving SeaWorld for the end, if at all.

FAMILY-FUN ACTIVITIES
Because it has few thrill rides, SeaWorld has few restrictions, but you may want to check out the special tour programs offered through the education department. SeaWorld lives up to its reputation for making education fun, and these wonderful experiences will entertain both you and your kids. They are well worth the extra expense. There are four 1-hour options: **Polar Expedition Tour** (touch a penguin), **Predators** (touch a shark), **Saving a Species** (see manatees and sea turtles), and a **Behind the Scenes Tour.** All cost $16 for adults and $12 for children 3 to 9, *plus park admission.* Call © **407/363-2380** for information or © **800/406-2244** for reservations.

BUDGET YOUR TIME

SeaWorld has a leisurely pace because its biggest attractions are up-close encounters with the animals. Don't be in a rush. This park can easily be enjoyed in a day. Its layout and the many outdoor exhibits give it an open feel. Because of the large capacity and walk-through nature of many of the attractions, crowds generally aren't a concern except at Journey to Atlantis and Kraken. Wild Arctic also draws a sizable crowd, and you'll need to arrive at Shamu Stadium in plenty of time for the show. But the lines here don't reach Disney's proportions even at peak times, so relax. Isn't that what a vacation is supposed to be about?

SERVICES & FACILITIES AT SEAWORLD

ATMs An ATM is located at the front of the park. It accepts Cirrus-, Honor-, and PLUS-affiliated cards.

Baby Care Changing tables are in or near most women's restrooms and in the men's restroom at the front entrance near Shamu's Emporium. You can buy diapers in machines located near changing areas and at Shamu's Emporium. There's a special area for nursing mothers near the women's restroom at Friends of the Wild gift shop, near the center of the park.

Cameras & Film Film, disposable cameras, and limited digital supplies are available at stores throughout the park.

First Aid First Aid Centers staffed with registered nurses are behind Stingray Lagoon and near Shamu's Happy Harbor.

Lockers Lockers are located next to Shamu's Emporium, just inside the park entrance. The cost is $8 a day, plus a $2 deposit.

Lost Children Lost children are taken to the Information Center. A parkwide paging system helps reunite guests. *Children under 7 should wear name tags.*

Pet Care A kennel is available between the parking lot and the main gate. The cost is $6 a day (no overnight stays).

Strollers Dolphin-shaped strollers can be rented at the Information Center near the entrance. The cost is $10 for a single and $17 for a double.

Wheelchair Rental Regular wheelchairs are available at the Information Center for $8; electric chairs are $35.

MAJOR ATTRACTIONS

Blue Horizons
Frommer's Rating: A
Recommended Ages: All ages

This isn't your run-of-the mill aquatic animal act. Inside the park's partially covered, open-air stadium, Atlantic bottlenose dolphins, false killer whales, exotic and colorful birds, divers, and elaborately costumed aerialists perform in this new Broadway-style show. A young girl's image of the sea and sky sets the story line as acts are performed both high above and below the water. The spectacular stage is filled with clouds, bubbles, and waves, making for an impressive and colorful backdrop. The animals and actors alike impress with spectacular and graceful stunts as they perform to an original musical score (recorded by the Seattle Symphony Orchestra).

Clyde & Seamore Take Pirate Island
Frommer's Rating: A
Recommended Ages: All ages

A lovable sea lion and otter, with a supporting cast of walruses and harbor seals, appear in this fish-breath comedy with a swashbuckling conservation theme. It's corny, but don't hold it against the animal stars. With all those high-tech rides at the other parks, you need a break, and this one delivers some laughs. Watch out if you enter late; the mime entertaining the audience may make you part of the preshow.

Clydesdale Hitching Barn
Frommer's Rating: C+ (A for horse lovers)
Recommended Ages: All ages

Here is where you will find all the famous Clydesdale horses. Guests can walk through; see the grand beasts; and, in some instances, watch them being hitched up for the occasional parade through the park.

Journey to Atlantis
Frommer's Rating: A
Recommended Ages: 8–adult

Taking a cue from Disney's Imagineers, SeaWorld has created a story line to go with this $30 million water ride. It has to do with a Greek fisherman and ancient Sirens in a battle between good and evil. But what really matters is the drop: a wild plunge from an altitude of 60 feet, in addition to lugelike curves and a shorter drop. Journey to Atlantis breaks from SeaWorld's edutainment formula and offers good old-fashioned fun. There's no hidden lesson—just a splashy thrill when you least expect it. And yes, you will get wet. *Note:* Riders must be at least 42 inches tall. Expectant moms, as well as folks with heart, neck, or back problems, should find some other way to pass the time.

Austin's Rating: "I like that better than Splash Mountain." (I agree that this ride has a slight edge over that Magic Kingdom ride, but the Jurassic Park River Adventure, p. 266, wins the battle of Orlando's water coasters, though it's also the scariest.)

Kat 'N' Kaboodle
Frommer's Rating: C+
Recommended Ages: All

This street show, located at the new Waterfront area, features 16 exotic breeds of furry felines, including Bengals, Persians, Sphynxes, and Siamese. They entertain the crowds with acrobatics and amazing feats, as well as interact with the audience.

Tips What's Old is New Again

Look for yet another new show to make an appearance late in 2006. While Shamu still reigns supreme, **Believe** is the first change in SeaWorld's signature whale show in over 8 years. Freshening things up a bit, the production will be set to a special musical score to create a more fanciful flair. An all-new set and screens will complete the look. At the same time, three new thrillers (though for the younger set) are scheduled to debut: a Shamu-themed roller coaster; a jellyfish-shaped samba-tower ride; and a whirling, twirling beach-bucket ride.

Key West at SeaWorld

Frommer's Rating: A+ for kids, B+ for adults
Recommended Ages: All ages

This Caribbean-style village has island food, entertainers, and street vendors. But the big attractions are the hands-on encounters with harmless Southern diamond and cownose rays; Sea Turtle Point, the home of threatened and endangered species; and Dolphin Cove, where you can feed smelt to the namesakes. *Warning:* If you have a soft heart (and little kids are major softies for these animal encounters), it's easy to spend $20 feeding the critters.

Davis's and **Hailey's Rating:** "They're so soft and tickly!" (Indeed, those brave enough to feed the toothless rays likely will find one of their funny bones brushed—and their arms and shirts quite wet.)

Kraken

Frommer's Rating: A+
Recommended Ages: 10–adult

SeaWorld's deepest venture onto the field of thrill-ride battle starts slow, like many coasters, but it ends with pure speed. Kraken is named for a massive, mythological, underwater beast kept caged by Poseidon. This 21st-century version offers floorless and open-sided 32-passenger trains (the better for you to see what awaits you) that plant you on a pedestal high above the track. When the monster breaks loose, you climb 151 feet, fall 144 feet, hit speeds of 65 mph, go underground three times (spraying bystanders with water), and make seven loops during a 4,177-foot course. It may be the longest 3 minutes, 39 seconds of your life. For adventurous teens, this is *the* top attraction in the park, and the lines can get very long. *Note:* Kraken carries a 54-inch height minimum. Expectant moms, as well as folks with heart, neck, or back problems, should skip this one.

Manatee Rescue

Frommer's Rating: B+
Recommended Ages: All ages

Today, the West Indian manatee is an endangered species. There are as few as 3,200 remaining in Florida's wild. Underwater viewing stations, innovative cinema techniques, and interactive displays combine here for a tribute to these gentle marine mammals. While this isn't as good as seeing them in the great outdoors, it's as close as most folks get, and it's a much roomier habitat than the tight quarters their kin have at the Living Seas in Epcot.

Odyssea

Frommer's Rating: B+
Recommended Ages: All ages

This 30-minute, Cirque du Soleil–style stage show opened at SeaWorld's Nautilus Theater in July 2003. The show combines circus acrobatics, comedy, colorful costumes, music, and special effects to create a mythical underwater atmosphere. The special effects are good, and the aerial stunts are even better. You and your kids will be entranced.

Penguin Encounter *(Overrated)*

Frommer's Rating: C; B for young kids
Recommended Ages: All ages

A Seasonal Production

In addition to its regular productions, SeaWorld stages a few shows only sea-sonally, including *Mistify*, a nighttime spectacular combining fireworks and fountains on the lagoon. During summer months, guests are treated to the spe-cial-effects extravaganza nightly. If you're dining at the Spice Mill restaurant in the Waterfront, you can even enjoy dinner with the show.

Here, you are transported by moving sidewalk through Arctic and Antarctic displays. You'll get a glimpse of penguins as they preen, socialize, and swim at bullet speed in their 22°F (–5°C) habitat. You'll also see puffins and murres in a similar, separate area. While it gives you a nice view of the penguins (and they are always a hit with the kids), the surroundings in the viewing area leave a bit to be desired, especially among so many other elaborate and well-done exhibits.

Pets Ahoy!
Frommer's Rating: B
Recommended Ages: All ages
Eighteen cats, 12 dogs, 3 potbellied pigs, and a horse are joined by birds and rats to perform comic relief in a 25-minute show held several times a day. Almost all the stars were rescued from animal shelters. It's a charmer that appeals to young and old.

Rico & Roza's Musical Feast
Frommer's Rating: C
Recommended Ages: All
This amusing 25-minute show takes place several times a day at the Waterfront's Seafire Inn. The review celebrates family, food, and fun as proprietors Rico and Roza entertain guests with many a merry musical tune, a dash of comedy, a tall tale or two, and a little interaction with the audience. Though you can see the show without eat-ing at the inn, I think it makes for a very entertaining dining experience, especially with younger children, who at times require a diversion to make it through a meal.

Shamu Adventure *(Moments*
Frommer's Rating: A+
Recommended Ages: All ages
Everyone comes to SeaWorld to see the big guy. The featured event is a well-choreo-graphed show planned and carried out by very good trainers and very smart Orcas. The whales (reaching 25 ft. and 10,000 lb.) really dive into their work. The fun builds until the video monitor flashes an urgent Weather Watch and one of the trainers utters the fateful warning: "Uh-oh!" Hurricane Shamu is ready to make landfall. At this point, a lot of folks remember the warnings posted throughout the grandstand: *If you want to stay dry, don't sit in the first 14 rows.* Those who didn't pay attention get one last chance to flee. Then the Orcas race around the edge of the pool, creating huge waves of *icy* water and profoundly soaking anything in range. Veteran animal handler Jack Hanna also makes a video appearance on the huge overhead monitors, compli-ments of ShamuVision. A nighttime version of this show, **Shamu Rocks America,** offers more of a party atmosphere and less of an educational experience. The whales perform to the beat of the somewhat loud rock 'n' roll music, and special effects are more predominant. All of it adds up to a very entertaining show for all ages. *Note:* Arrive 30 minutes early for a good seat. The stadium is large, but it fills quickly.

Ryan's, Austin's, and **Nicolas's Ratings** (in unison): "That's *f-f-freezing!*" (I warned them, but they insisted on sitting in the splash zone. Bring extra clothes and shoes!)

Shamu's Happy Harbor
Frommer's Rating: A for kids
Recommended Ages: 3–12

This 3-acre play area has a four-story net tower with a 35-foot crow's-nest lookout, water cannons, remote-controlled vehicles, nine slides, a submarine, tunnels, and a water maze. It's *one of the most extensive play areas* at any park and a great place for kids to unwind. Bring extra clothes for the kids (and maybe for yourself, too), because it's not designed to keep you dry. Smaller kids will require close supervision, however, as they can easily get lost in all the action—and unlike at many other play areas in other parks, there are several escape routes here.

Shark Encounter
Frommer's Rating: B
Recommended Ages: 3–adult

Remember Terrors of the Deep? Well, it's been renamed Shark Encounter, which also was the exhibit's original name. Pools out front have small sharks and rays (feeding

---

Moments **More Active Fun**

SeaWorld offers three other hands-on programs. The 9-hour **Marine Mammal Keeper Experience** allows you to work alongside the marine-mammal experts, learning how to feed and care for the aquatic inhabitants at the park. You'll also enjoy up-close encounters with dolphins, sea lions, beluga whales, and walruses ($399 per person; minimum 13 years old and 52 in. tall). The program includes 7 days of consecutive park admission, lunch, a career book, and a T-shirt.

Sharks Deep Dive gives snorkelers and divers a chance to have limited, hands-off contact with the 58 sharks, including a nearly 9-foot sand tiger, in the Shark Encounter area. Two at a time, guests don wetsuits for a 30-minute encounter inside a cage that rides a 125-foot track. Part of the cage is above water, but participants can dive up to 8 feet underwater for a close-up look at the denizens. The cost is $150 for certified divers and $125 for snorkelers (minimum age 10). The price includes a souvenir booklet, T-shirt, and snorkel gear but *does not include the required park admission fee.*

The new 2-hour **Beluga Interaction Program** gives you an up-close, hands-on encounter (about 30 min.) with these mammoth whales ($179, minimum age 13, and you must know how to swim). The price includes a book on whales and a souvenir photo but *does not include the mandatory park admission fee.*

The programs are not open to expectant mothers. Call ℂ **407/370-1382** or visit **www.seaworld.com** for more information. *Note:* If you're willing to splurge on only one program, we'd opt for Discovery Cove (see below) over this one because it's much more hands-on.

Tips On the Waterfront

SeaWorld's 5-acre Waterfront area, which debuted in late spring 2003, added a seaport-themed village to the park's landscape. On High Street, look for a blend of shops; **Kat 'N' Kaboodle** (p. 275); and the Seafire Inn restaurant, where lunch includes a musical revue called **Rico & Roza's Musical Feast** (p. 277). At Harbor Square, the funny Seaport Symphony orchestra has chefs making music with pots and pans. The park also is adding street performers, including a crusty old captain who tells fish tales and makes music with bottles and brandy glasses. Also at the Waterfront is an array of eateries, including the Spice Mill, Voyagers Wood Fire Pizza, and the Seafire Inn.

---

isn't allowed here). The interior aquariums have big eels, beautiful but poisonous lionfish, hauntingly still barracudas, and bug-eyed pufferfish. This isn't a tour for the claustrophobic, because you have to walk through an acrylic tube beneath hundreds of millions of gallons of water. Also, small fry may find the swimming sharks a little too much to handle. *Note:* Part of this exhibit has given way to a new restaurant, **Sharks Underwater Grill** (p. 273).

Wild Arctic
Frommer's Rating: B+
Recommended Ages: All ages for exhibit; 6–adult for ride
Enveloping guests in the beauty, exhilaration, and danger of a polar expedition, Wild Arctic combines a high-definition adventure film with flight-simulator technology to display breathtaking Arctic panoramas. After a hazardous flight over the frozen north, you emerge into an exhibit where you can see a playful polar bear or two, beautiful beluga whales, and walruses performing aquatic ballets (on different levels, you can see them both above and below the surface). Small kids and those prone to motion sickness may find the ride bumpy. There's a separate line if you want to skip the flight and just see the critters.

ADDITIONAL ATTRACTIONS
The park's other attractions include **Pacific Point Preserve,** a 2½-acre natural setting that duplicates the rocky home of California sea lions and harbor seals. Tropical fish and sea creatures at the **Tidepool** offer a hands-on experience for all ages. The **Tropical Reef** surrounds guests with aquariums filled with a variety of sea creatures to look at. Here, you can touch the sea urchins, starfish, and anemones. **Tropical Rain Forest,** a bamboo-and-banyan-tree habitat, is the home of cockatoos and other birds. And **Turtle Point** showcases sea turtles swimming in the lagoon or lounging on the beach and sand dunes. The **Anheuser-Busch Hospitality Center** lets you indulge in free samples of Anheuser-Busch beers and then stroll through the stables to watch the famous Budweiser Clydesdale horses being groomed. **The Extreme Zone** tests your climbing and jumping skills with a rock wall and trampoline jump (both for an additional fee). Even shopping is an experience at SeaWorld; at **Oysters Secret,** guests can watch as pearl divers dive in search of just the right oyster, which will be pried open for the pearl inside. Guests can have the pearls made into jewelry.

The **Makahiki Luau** is a full-scale dinner show featuring South Seas–style food (mahimahi in piña colada sauce, Hawaiian chicken, and sweet-and-sour pork) while you're entertained by music and dance of the Pacific Islands. It's hardly haute cuisine or Broadway but is very much on par with Disney's Spirit of Aloha Dinner Show (p. 310). It's held daily at 6:30pm. Park admission is not required. The cost is $43 for adults and $28 for children 3 to 9. Reservations are required and can be made by calling © 800/327-2420 or online at **www.seaworldorlando.com**.

SHOPPING AT SEAWORLD

SeaWorld doesn't have nearly as many shops as Walt Disney World and Universal Orlando, but with the opening of the Waterfront, it has added some rather unique boutiques, including **Allura's Treasures,** featuring fanciful dolls, mermaids, and fairies, jewelry, and more. **Tropical Traders** is filled with handcrafted gifts made by artisans from exotic ports all over the world. There are, of course, also lots of cuddly toys for sale around the park. Where else can you get a stuffed manatee but at **Manatee Cove**? The **Friends of the Wild** gift shop (it's near Penguin Encounter) has one of the largest and most varied selections in the park. The shop attached to **Wild Arctic** is good for plush toys as well. **Shamu's Emporium,** near the entrance, is one of the largest stores in the park, featuring an array of souvenirs ranging from T-shirts to toys.

And because of the Anheuser-Busch connection, the gift shop outside the entrance to the park offers a staggering array of Budweiser-related items.

DISCOVERY COVE: A DOLPHIN ENCOUNTER

Anheuser-Busch spent $100 million building SeaWorld's sister park, which debuted in 2000. The price is $279 per person (plus the 6.5% sales tax) for ages 6 and up if you want to swim with the dolphins. It's $179 if you just want to enjoy the fishes and other sea life without having the dolphin experience. In order to make the experience a bit more tolerable in the cost department, admission includes a 7-day consecutive pass to either SeaWorld or Busch Gardens Tampa Bay. You can upgrade this feature to a 14-day combination pass for both parks for an additional $30.

If you've never gone for a dip with a dolphin, words hardly do it justice. It's exhilarating and exciting—exactly the kind of thing that can make for a most memorable vacation.

The actual dolphin encounter deserves an **A+ rating.** It's open only to those ages 6 and older (younger guests or those who don't want to participate in the dolphin swim can take part in the other activities).

The park has a cast of more than 2 dozen dolphins, and each of them works 2 to 4 hours a day. Many of them are mature critters that have spent their lives in captivity, around people. They love having their bellies, flukes, and backs rubbed. They also have an impressive bag of tricks. Given the proper hand signals, they can make sounds much like a human passing gas, chatter in dolphin talk, and do seemingly effortless 1½ gainers in 12 feet of water. They take willing guests for rides in the piggyback or missionary position. They also wave "hello" and "goodbye" with their flippers, and take great pleasure in roaring by guests at top speed, creating waves that drench them.

The dolphin experience lasts 90 minutes, about 35 to 40 minutes of which is spent in the lagoon with one of them. Trainers use the rest of the time to teach visitors about these remarkable mammals.

The rest of the day isn't nearly as exciting, but it is wonderfully relaxing. Discovery Cove doesn't deliver thrill rides, water slides, or acrobatic animal shows; that's what SeaWorld, Disney, and Universal are for. This is where you come to get away from all that.

Here's what you get for your money, with or without the dolphin encounter:

- A limit of *no more than 1,000 other guests a day.* (The average daily attendance at Disney's Magic Kingdom is 41,000.) This ensures that your experience will be more relaxing and private, which is really part of what you are paying for in the first place anyway.

- Lunch, a towel, locker, sunscreen, snorkeling gear (including a flotation vest), a souvenir photo, and free parking are also part of the deal.

- Other 9am-to-5:30pm activities include a chance to swim near (but on the other side of the Plexiglas from) **barracudas and black-tip sharks.** There are no barriers between you and the gentle rays and brightly colored tropical fish in a new 12,000-square-foot lagoon, where some of the rays are 4 feet in diameter. The 3,300-foot Tropical River is a great place to swim or float in a mild current; it goes through a cave, two waterfalls, and a large aviary where you can also take a stroll, becoming a human perch for some of the 30 exotic bird species. There are also beach areas for catching a tan.

- As mentioned above, 7 days of **unlimited admission** to SeaWorld and/or Busch Gardens Tampa Bay (park admission normally costs $62 a day for adults and $50 for children 3–9).

One other option is Discovery Cove's **Trainer For a Day ticket,** which for $449 ($479 with a 14-day park pass) allows guests 6 and older to also have a dolphin-training encounter; participate in guided snorkeling tours; feed fish; and interact with other critters, including rays. A paying adult must accompany guests ages 6 to 12.

You can drive to Discovery Cove by following the above directions to SeaWorld and then following the signs. Unlike other parks, Discovery Cove doesn't have a parking charge. For up-to-the-minute information, call ✆ **877/434-7268** or go to **www. discoverycove.com**.

If you plan on trying this adventure, I recommend making a reservation far, far in advance. With the limited number of guests admitted and the number of people who want a chance to swim with the fishes, this park gets booked very quickly. *Note:* There is an ever-so-small chance of getting in as a walk-up customer. The park reserves a small number of tickets daily for folks whose earlier dolphin sessions were canceled due to bad weather. The best chance for last-minute guests comes during any extended period of good weather.

4 Other Area Attractions

There are—surprise!—a number of cool things in Orlando for families that don't revolve around Mickey, the Hulk, or Shamu. Now that I've covered the monster parks, we're going to explore some of Central Florida's best smaller attractions.

IN KISSIMMEE

Kissimmee's tourist strip is on Walt Disney World's southern border and extends about 2 miles west and 8 to 10 miles east. Irlo Bronson Memorial Highway/U.S. 192, the highway linking the town to WDW and points west, is under perpetual construction, and the development clutter can make it hard to see some smaller destinations. Check with your hotel's front desk or the attractions for updates that might make finding them a little easier.

Note: The following prices don't include the 6.5% to 7% sales tax unless otherwise noted.

Gatorland ⭐ *Finds* **All ages** Founded in 1949 with only a handful of alligators living in huts and pens, Gatorland now houses thousands of alligators (including a rare blue one) and crocodiles on its 70-acre spread. Breeding pens, nurseries, and rearing ponds are situated throughout the park, which also displays snakes, toads, insects, turtles, and a Galápagos tortoise. Its 2,000-foot boardwalk winds through a cypress swamp and breeding marsh. There are four shows. **Gator Wrestlin'** uses the old "put-them-to-sleep" trick, but it's more of an environmental-awareness program. The **Gator Jumparoo** is a crowd-pleaser in which the big reptiles lunge 4 or 5 feet out of the water to snatch a hunk of meat from a trainer's hand. **Up Close Encounters** is a new show that features a variety of wildlife, including some venomous snakes. And **Jungle Crocs of the World** showcases some of the world's toothiest carnivores. Younger kids will enjoy the new **train ride** through the park; **Lilly's Pad,** a wet-and-dry play area; and **Allie's Barnyard,** a small petting zoo. While you're here, try the smoked gator ribs or nuggets in the open-air restaurant, or grab a gator-skin souvenir in the gift shop. Allow 4 to 5 hours. *Tip:* Additional parking, a whole new facade, and additional landscaping are being added as the park undergoes an extensive million-dollar renovation—its largest in over 10 years.

This one's a huge hit with all five of my kids (and me too!).

Note: Gatorland's new **Trainer for a Day** program lets up to five guests get up-close and personal with the gators for a day (or 2 hours, in this case). The $100, 2-hour experience puts you side by side with trainers and includes a chance to wrangle some alligators (minimum age 12). Advance reservations are required, and admission to the park is included.

Tip: Printable discount coupons and special Internet ticket prices are available at the park's website. Be sure to check it out before you leave home.

14501 S. Orange Blossom Trail (U.S. 441; between Osceola Pkwy. and Hunter's Creek Blvd.). © 800/393-5297 or 407/855-5496. www.gatorland.com. Admission $20 adults, $9.95 children 3–12. Daily 9am–5 or 6pm usually, but closing times vary by season. Free parking. From I-4, take Exit 65/Osceola Pkwy. east to U.S. 17/92/441, and go left/north. Gatorland is 1½ miles on the right.

Green Meadows Petting Farm **All ages** Families can take a break from the razzle-dazzle and get a taste of country at this 300-critter farm that features pigs, chickens, ducks, geese, donkeys, and more. The 2-hour guided tour includes a chance to milk a cow, and the farm also has pony rides, train rides, and hayrides. The emphasis is on teaching children and their tagalongs about life on a farm. Allow about 3 to 4 hours. *Tip:* Check out the farm's website for discount admission coupons.

1368 S. Poinciana (5 miles south of U.S. 192). © 407/846-0770. www.greenmeadowsfarm.com. Admission $19 adults; free for children 2 and under. Daily 9:30am–4pm. From I-4, take Exit 64A/U.S. 192 east about 5 miles; then go south on Poinciana.

Tips Out With the Old . . .

In 2005, **Water Mania,** the Kissimmee water park that drew families to its doors by the thousands, was sold. At press time, there was no word as to what, if any, future the park may have. Meanwhile, insiders are wondering whether the park will reopen under its new ownership or whether it has closed its doors forever.

Orlando Area Attractions

DINNER SHOWS◆

Arabian Nights **13**

Dolly Parton's Dixie
  Stampede **12**

Fiasco's Circus & Magic
  Dinner Show **6**

Medieval Times **16**

Pirates Dinner
  Adventure **5**

Sleuths Mystery
  Dinner Show **7**

Mount Plymouth

Lake Monroe

0   5 mi

0   5 km

Wekiwa Springs State Park

Lake Jessup

○Apopka

Altamonte Springs

Casselberry

Winter Springs

Lake Apopka

441

Maitland **2**

WINTER PARK **3**

Winter Garden ○

Ocoee ○

ORLANDO

Citrus Bowl■

East-West Expwy

Windermere

Lake Butler

Conway

Universal Orlando **7** **4** **8** **5** **6** **9** **10** **11**

Lake Tibet

Lake Conway

Beeline Expwy.

Orlando International Airport ✈

Magic Kingdom■

WALT DISNEY WORLD

LAKE BUENA VISTA

International Drive

INTER-NATIONAL DRIVE AREA **12**

Gatorland **15**

Epcot■

Animal Kingdom■

Disney-MGM Studios■

DOWNTOWN DISNEY

CELEBRATION **13**

Intercession City ○

KISSIMMEE **16** **17**

East Lake Tohopekaliga

St. Cloud **18**

14

ATTRACTIONS●

Audubon of Florida-National Center
  for Birds of Prey **2**

Central Florida Zoo **1**

Fantasy of Flight **17**

Forever Florida **18**

Gatorland **15**

Green Meadows Petting Farm **14**

Orlando Science Center **3**

Peabody Ducks **11**

Skull Kingdom **4**

Titanic—Ship of Dreams **9**

Wet 'n Wild **8**

Wonder Works **10**

Have Some Extra Time?

Wonder Works is just the spot to spend a couple of hours (less than 2) if you're in need of a less-intense evening or rainy-afternoon activity. This upside-down building's exterior catches the eye, and it's just as interesting on the inside, with an array of unique hands-on exhibits that include the bed of nails, the bridge of fire, the WonderCoaster, and more. There's plenty to do for kids ages 4 to 12, who (among other options) can stomp on giant piano keys to make music or create sheets of bubbles with bubble machines. Call ℂ **407/351-8800** or surf the Internet to **www.wonderworksonline.com** for more information.

INTERNATIONAL DRIVE AREA

These attractions are a 10- to 15-minute drive from the Disney area and 5 to 10 minutes from Universal Orlando. Most appeal to special interests, but one is free (the Peabody Ducks' show), and another, Wet 'n Wild, is in the same class as Disney's water parks.

Peabody Ducks 🐦 *Moments* **All ages** One of the best shows in town is short but sweet and, more important, *free.* And your children, especially young kids, will love it. The Peabody Orlando's five mallards march into the lobby each morning, accompanied by John Philip Sousa's "King Cotton March" and their own red-coated duck master. They get to spend the day splashing in a marble fountain. Then, in the afternoon, they march back to the elevator and up to their fourth-floor "penthouse." Donald Duck never had it this good. And there are multiple crews, so every couple of months, they get to rotate back to the farm for some extra R&R. Allow 1 hour.

9801 International Dr. (between the Bee Line Expwy. and Sand Lake Rd.). ℂ **800/732-2639** or 407/352-4000. Free admission. Daily at 11am and 5pm. Free self-parking, valet parking $8. From I-4, take Exit 74A, Sand Lake Rd./Hwy. 528, east to International Dr., and then south. Hotel is on the left across from the Convention Center.

Skull Kingdom **Age 10 and up** As you wander the stone halls inside the Skull Castle, you'll be taunted and terrified by a cast of ghoulish characters second in Central Florida only to the crew at Universal Orlando's Halloween Horror Nights, but this show runs year-round. The night show (after 5pm) on weekends is far more intense than the day show. It's not for children under 10. Allow about 30 minutes to walk through the castle. The **Chamber of Magic** dinner show (all-you-can-eat pizza and drinks) can be combined with the haunted tour.

5933 American Way (just off the intersection of International Dr. and Universal Blvd., 3 blocks east of Universal Orlando). ℂ **407/354-1564**. www.skullkingdom.com. Admission day show $9 per person, night show $14 per person; magic dinner show $20 adult, $16 kids under 7; magic show, dinner, and the haunted tour $28 adults, $24 kids under 7. Free parking. Mon–Fri 10am–5pm; Sat–Sun 6pm–midnight. From I-4, take Exit 75A/Hwy. 435 south to American Way, and look for the giant skull castle.

Wet 'n Wild 🐦🐦 **All ages** Who knew people came in so many shapes and sizes? Stacked or stubby, terribly tan or not, all kinds come here, so there's no reason to be bashful about squeezing into a bathing suit and going out in public. The 25-acre Wet 'n Wild is America's third-most-popular water park (behind Blizzard Beach and Typhoon Lagoon, respectively). **Disco H2O,** the park's newest addition, debuted in 2005; it's an enclosed flume ride where a four-passenger raft sends you flying through the sights and sounds of the '70s, complete with mirrored lights and disco tunes blasting in the background. Other options include **The Flyer,** a six-story, four-passenger toboggan run through 450 feet of banked curves; the **Surge,** which is one of the longest (580 ft. of curves) and fastest multipassenger tube rides in the Southeast; and **Black Hole,** a two-person, spaceship-style raft that makes a 500-foot twisting, turning voyage through darkness (all three rides require that children 36–48 in. be accompanied by an adult). You can also ride **Raging Rapids,** a simulated whitewater run with a waterfall plunge; **Blue Niagara,** a 300-foot, six-story loop-and-dipster that also has a plunge (48-in. height minimum); **Knee Ski,** a cable-operated, half-mile kneeboarding course that's open in warm-weather months only (56-in. height minimum); **Der Stuka,** a six-story, free-fall speed slide; and **Mach 5,** which has a trio of twisting, turning flumes. The park also has a large kids' area with miniversions of the big rides. If you enjoy the water, plan on spending a full day here.

Note: In addition to the admission prices below, Wet 'n Wild is part of the multiday **FlexTicket package** that includes admission to Universal Orlando (which owns this attraction), SeaWorld, and Busch Gardens in Tampa (see the beginning of this chapter for more information).

6200 International Dr. (at Universal Blvd.). © 800/992-9453 or 407/351-1800. www.wetnwild.com. Admission $34 adults, $28 children 3–9. Hours vary seasonally, but the park usually is open at least 10am–5pm daily weather permitting (it's one of the few water parks open year-round). You can rent tubes ($4), towels ($2), and lockers ($5); all require a $2 deposit. Parking is $6 for cars, light trucks, and vans. From I-4, take Exit 75A/Hwy. 435 South, and follow the signs.

ELSEWHERE IN CENTRAL FLORIDA

The listings that follow are out of the mainstream tourist areas, meaning that you won't have to battle heavy crowds. The Central Florida Zoo and Orlando Science Center are close enough to incorporate a visit to Winter Park if you choose to make a day of it.

Central Florida Zoo *Finds*   **All ages**   This community zoo has come a long way since it was born in 1923, when a circus came to town, leaving a monkey and a goat behind. The monkey rode the goat in the earliest show. Today, the animal collection includes beautiful clouded leopards, cheetahs, and black-footed cats, all of which are endangered. You'll also meet a ham of a hippo named Geraldine, as well as black howler monkeys, siamangs, American crocodiles, a banded Egyptian cobra, a Gila monster, hyacinth macaws, barred owls, bald eagles, and dozens of other species. The zoo has half-price admission for everyone Thursdays from 9 to 10am and all day Tuesdays for seniors 60 and over. Allow 2 to 3 hours. *Tip:* One-year memberships that include additional perks and free admission to this and 100 other participating zoos and aquariums across the country are available. A family membership is $50, which, depending on your family's size, may be more economical than purchasing individual tickets.

(Tips   Back in Action

After closing its doors in 2003, **Cypress Gardens Adventure Park** (© 863/324-2111; www.cypressgardens.com) has reopened and now features 38 thrill rides, an all-new water ski show, and the beautiful botanical gardens that started it all. A soon-to-be-opened water park will feature plenty of wild raft rides, a children's play area, and other aquatic fun. Call or visit the website for up-to-date details.

3755 NW U.S. 17/92, Sanford. ✆ 407/323-4450. www.centralfloridazoo.org. Admission $8.95 adults, $6.95 seniors, $4.95 children 3–12. Daily 9am–5pm. Free parking. Take I-4 Exit 104 right onto Orange Ave., turn left at the traffic light on Lake Monroe Rd., and then right on U.S. 17/92. The zoo is on the right.

Forever Florida   All ages   The 4,700-acre Crescent J Ranch is a nature preserve that offers a chance to see native wildlife, Florida flora, and a working cattle ranch by guided tour. Options include touring by horseback; bike; covered wagon; and Cracker coach, a funky buggy that puts riders on a perch 10 feet above ground level. Allow a half day or longer to get here, take the tour, and see the grounds, which also include a pony-riding ring (there are ponies set aside for young kids to ride), hiking trails, and a petting zoo. Especially cool for kids is the **Fossil Dig,** a sandpit that has real fossils (dinosaur bones and so on) for them to unearth.

4755 N. Kenansville Rd., St. Cloud (southeast of Kissimmee). ✆ 866/854-3837. www.foreverflorida.com. Tours and rides from $20 adult, $15 kids on up to $89 per person, higher for overnights. Sun–Thurs 9am–5pm; Fri–Sat 9am–8pm; first tours at 10am. Free parking. Take I-4 Exit 64A/U.S. 192 east about 15 miles to U.S. 441; then go south 7½ miles to Forever Florida on the left.

Orlando Science Center ★★ *Finds*   **All ages**   The four-story center, the largest of its kind in the Southeast, provides 10 exhibit halls that allow visitors to explore everything from Florida swamps to the arid plains of Mars to the human body. There's also a **Weird Science** hall (hosted by Dr. Dare and his creation, Frankenboy), featuring a number of interactive sound, graphics, animation, and video kiosks. One of the big attractions is the **Dr. Phillips CineDome,** a 310-seat theater that presents large-format films, planetarium shows, and laser-light extravaganzas. In **KidsTown,** little folks wander in exhibits representing a miniature version of the big world around them. In one section, there's a pint-size community that includes a construction site, park, and wellness center. **Science City,** located nearby, includes physics lessons and a power plant, and **123 Math Avenue** uses puzzles and other things to make learning math fun. Children of all ages will find at least one or two (and often more) memorable experiences waiting for them. Allow 3 to 4 hours, more if your family has inquiring minds.

777 E. Princeton St. (between Orange and Mills aves., in Loch Haven Park). ✆ 888/672-4386 or 407/514-2000. www.osc.org. Admission (includes exhibits, CineDome film, and planetarium show) $15 adults, $14 seniors 55 and older, $9.95 children 3–11. Tues–Thurs 9am–5pm; Fri–Sat 9am–9pm; Sun noon–5pm. Parking available in a garage across the street for $3.50. Take I-4 Exit 85/Princeton St. east, and cross Orange Ave.

5 Attractions Outside Orlando

Just outside Orlando, you'll find a couple more places to visit. **Fantasy of Flight** offers a look at the yesterday, today, and tomorrow of aviation, as well as a simulator. It's a good way for aviation buffs to spend a morning or an afternoon. And a short drive from beautiful Winter Park, about 30 minutes from the theme-park hubbub, the **Audubon of Florida—National Center for Birds of Prey** offers your kids the chance to get up close and personal with eagles, hawks, and other magnificent raptors.

Audubon of Florida—National Center for Birds of Prey ★ *Finds*   **Age 8 and up**   In addition to being a rehabilitation center—one of the biggest and most successful in the Southeast—this is a great place to get to know winged wonders that roost here and earn their keep by entertaining the relatively few visitors who come. It's a wonderful chance for your kids to get an up-close look at these magnificent birds in a relaxed setting. You can get a close look at hams such as Elvis, the blue suede shoe–wearing American kestrel; Daisy, the polka-dancing barn owl; and Trouble, a bald eagle born with a misaligned beak. Allow 2 hours.

1101 Audubon Way, Maitland. © **407/644-0190**. www.adoptabird.org or www.audubonofflorida.org/conservation/cbop.htm. Recommended donation $5 adults, $4 children 3–12. Tues–Sun 10am–4pm. From Orlando, go north on I-4 Exit 88, Lee Rd./Hwy. 423, turn right/east, and at the first light (Wymore Rd.) go left and then right/east at the next light (Kennedy Blvd.). Continue a half-mile to East Ave., turn left, and go to the stop sign at Audubon Way. Turn left, and the center is on the right.

Fantasy of Flight   **Age 8 and up**   Wannabe flyboys and -girls can have all sorts of fantasies in this attraction, which takes guests to the days when earthlings, in this case pilots, went sky diving . . . because they had no other choice. The fun includes flying a fighter simulator outfitted with the sights, sounds, and (hang onto your lunch) motion of a World War II combat plane. Immersion experiences give you the feeling of flying through stratosphere clouds. Exhibits include a Douglas B-23 Dragon, an Fi-103 Flying Bomb, an F4U-4 Corsair, and a replica of the *Spirit of St. Louis*. You also can tour an airplane restoration shop. Allow 2 to 3 hours.

1400 Broadway Blvd., Polk City. © **863/984-3500**. www.fantasyofflight.com. Admission $25 adults, $23 seniors 60 and over, $14 children 5–12. Daily 9am–5pm. Free parking. Take I-4 south of Orlando to Exit 44/Hwy. 559, and turn north to the attraction.

8

Orlando for Active Families

The majority of Orlando's visitors often overlook the fact that there are plenty of fun and exciting things to do beyond the boundaries of the theme parks. Activities range from relaxing to adventurous and even outrageous, with many far more laid-back in pace and price than the theme parks.

Championship golf courses, lakes for boating and fishing, hot air ballooning, and even hang gliding and surfing are all available in and around Orlando. If you and your kids are looking for a little four-legged fun, you can giddy-up on horseback or stretch out and sing along on an old-fashioned hayride. Central Florida's rather lengthy menu of indoor and outdoor recreation venues ensure that everyone in the family, no matter what their age or interests, will find something fun (and often unique) to do.

Those of you staying with the Mouse will certainly find plenty to do without having to stray too far; however, even the Mickster can't top some of Central Florida's true treasures. Orlando's many parks, preserves, and waterways offer those willing to venture beyond theme-park boundaries a chance to explore Florida's more natural side. To get to most of these, you'll need a car (or you'll face a costly taxi or limo ride), because they're out of the mainstream tourist areas. *Note:* Two additional treasures worth noting, the Canaveral National Seashore and Merritt Island National Wildlife Refuge, are within a reasonable driving distance of Walt Disney World, so be sure to check out chapter 11, "Side Trips from Orlando," for all the details.

1 Sports

Walt Disney World and the surrounding areas have plenty of recreational options for those who believe the theme parks aren't the be-all and end-all of Orlando's existence. Most of those that are listed below are open to everyone, no matter where you're staying. The prices listed don't include tax unless otherwise noted. For further information about WDW recreational facilities, call © **407/939-7529,** or on the Internet, go to **www.disneyworld.com,** and click the recreation link.

AIRBOATING   You can glide across the surface of local waters at **Boggy Creek Airboat Rides** in Kissimmee (© **407/344-9550;** www.bcairboats.com), where you'll pay $19 per adult and $15 per child for half-hour tours. Other choices include **Airboat Rides "Old Fashioned"** (© **407/568-4307;** www.airboatrides.com), which charges $37 per adult and $20 per child for 90 minutes; and **A-Awesome Airboat Rides** (© **407/568-7601,** www.airboatride.com), which charges $40 per adult and $25 per child for a 90-minute ride along the St. Johns River, in Christmas, east of Orlando. Both of the latter require reservations.

BALLOONING   There are several places in the area to experience an early-morning hot air balloon flight, including **Orange Blossom Balloons** in Lake Buena Vista (𝄐 407/239-7677; www.orangeblossomballoons.com) and **Blue Water Balloons** (𝄐 800/586-1884 or 407/894-5040, www.bluewaterballoons.com). Sunrise flights are available daily, and all flights, which last approximately 1 hour, are followed by a champagne toast (sorry, kids) at the conclusion of the flight and a breakfast buffet or picnic afterward. Children who make the age grade will probably be delighted with the view and the unique sensation, unless they (or you) don't see eye to eye with heights. Blue Water offers hotel pickup at no extra charge. Rates for both run approximately $175 per adult and $95 per child ages 10 to 15.

BICYCLING   Bike rentals (single and multispeed adult bikes, tandems, baby seats, and children's bikes—including those with training wheels) are available from the **Bike Barn** (𝄐 407/824-2742) at Fort Wilderness Resort and Campground at Walt Disney World. Rates for each bike are $8 per hour, $22 per day (surrey bikes run $18–$22 per half hour), regardless of age. Fort Wilderness offers a lot of good bike trails. Many of the other Disney resorts also offer bicycle rentals at similar rates. Either call your hotel in advance or inquire upon check-in.

BOATING   With the many manmade lakes and lagoons dotting the WDW landscape, it's no surprise that Disney owns a navy of pleasure boats. **Capt. Jack's** at Downtown Disney rents Water Sprites and canopy boats ($24–$27 per half-hour, including tax), pontoons ($42 per half hour, tax included), and sailboats ($20–$30 per hour, tax included). For information, call 𝄐 **407/828-2204.** The **Bike Barn** at Fort Wilderness (𝄐 **407/824-2742**) rents canoes and paddleboats ($7 per half hour). At both sites, kids must be at least 12 to rent a boat, and those under 18 cannot rent without a signed parental waiver.

FISHING   There are several fishing excursions offered on Disney waterways, including Bay Lake and Seven Seas Lagoon. The lakes are stocked, so you may catch something, but true anglers probably won't find it much of a challenge. The excursions can be arranged 2 to 90 days in advance by calling 𝄐 **407/939-2277.** A license isn't required. The fee is $200 to $395 for up to five people for 2 hours ($90 for each additional hour), including refreshments, gear, guide, bait, and tax. Children above the toddler stage are permitted on these tours when accompanied by an adult; however, an hourlong excursion just for kids ages 6 to 12 is available for $30.

A less-expensive alternative: Rent fishing poles at the **Bike Barn** (𝄐 **407/824-2742**) to fish in the Fort Wilderness canals. Pole rentals cost $6 per hour, $10 per day (not including tax). Bait is $3.50 to $3.65. A license isn't necessary.

Outside the realm, **A Pro Bass Guide Service** (𝄐 **800/771-9676** or 407/877-9676; www.probassguideservice.com) offers guided bass-fishing trips along some of Central Florida's most picturesque rivers and lakes. Hotel pickup is available; the cost is $260 for 2 people per half day, $360 for a full day. A license is $17.

HANG GLIDING   Flying from 2,000 feet in the air, you'll get the chance to glide through the sky—with a little help from your instructors. If you're a thrill-ride junkie, this is the real deal. The **Wallaby Ranch** (𝄐 **863/424-0070,** www.wallaby.com) is located in Davenport, just south of Kissimmee.

HAYRIDES   The hay wagon departs **Pioneer Hall** at Disney's Fort Wilderness nightly at 7 and 9:30 for 45-minute old-fashioned hayrides with singing, jokes, and games. Most kids will find it enjoyable, though some teens may think it corny. The

Tips   Hitting the Links

Walt Disney World operates five 18-hole, par-72 golf courses and one 9-hole, par-36 walking course, so if you want to work on your putting and need some time away from the kids (who will most likely prefer an outing on one of Disney's mini-golf courses—see p. 238), you'll have plenty of options. All are open to the public and offer pro shops, equipment rentals, and instruction. The rates are $99 to $159 per 18-hole round for resort guests ($10 more if you're not staying at a WDW property). Twilight specials are available for $60 to $80 per person. For tee times and information, call © 407/939-4653 up to 7 days in advance (up to 30 days for Disney resort and "official" property guests). Call © 407/934-7639 for information about golf packages.

Beyond Mickey's shadow, try **Celebration Golf Club** (© 888/275-2918 or 407/566-4653; www.celebrationgolf.com), which has an 18-hole regulation course (greens fees $65–$129) that kids under 17 are eligible to play and a 3-hole junior course for 5- to 9-year-olds. Note that there is a dress code at the club, so be sure to ask ahead so that your kids are decked out in suitable attire. **Champions Gate** (© 888/554-9301 or 407/787-4653; www.champions gategolf.com) offers 36 holes designed by Greg Norman, where greens fees will set you back $55 to $170, and the David Leadbetter Golf Academy (© 407/787-3330; www.davidleadbetter.com). **Orange County National** (© 407/656-2626; www.orangecountynationalgolf.com) has 36 Phil Ritson–designed holes; greens fees run $50 to $150.

Golf magazine recognized the 45 holes designed by Jack Nicklaus at the **Villas of Grand Cypress** ✹✹✹ resort (p. 291) as among the best in the

cost is $8 for adults, $4 for children ages 3 to 9, and free for kids 2 and under. An adult must accompany children under 12. No reservations. Call © **407/824-2832** for more information.

HIKING   The **Nature Conservancy's Disney Wilderness Preserve** (© **407/682-3664;** www.nature.org/florida) is a 12,000-acre, little-discovered getaway from the theme-park madness. It has 7 miles of trails at the headwaters of the Everglades ecosystem, just south of Orlando. Self-guided trails range from a half-mile interpretive trail, good for younger kids, to a 4.5-mile hiking trail for adults and teens. Picnic facilities are available along the trails. Admission costs $3 adults, and $2 for kids ages 6 to 17 and Nature Conservancy members. It's open Monday through Friday in summer from 9am to 5pm; it's open daily from 9am to 5pm the rest of the year. The preserve also features Sunday-afternoon **buggy rides** ($12 adults, $6 kids).

HOOPS & MORE   Disney's **Multi-Sports Experience** at Disney's Wide World of Sports (p. 239) lets you and the kids try your hands at basketball, football, and soccer. Admission is $10 for adults and $7.50 for children 3 to 9. It's open on select days (© **407/939-1500**).

nation. Tee times begin at 8am daily. Special rates are available for children under 17, and the resort even runs a 5-day summer golf program for kids interested in the game. For information, call © **407/239-1909.** The course is generally restricted to guests or guests of guests (rates run approximately $120–$180 per round), but there's limited play available to those not staying at the resort. Fees run approximately $180 to $250.

With more than 150 courses located throughout the Orlando area, it's simply impossible to list them all. There are, however, several additional courses and academies worth noting: **Hawk's Landing Golf Club and Academy** (© 407-238-8660) at the World Center Marriott; the **Legacy, Independence,** and soon-to-open **Tradition** golf courses, as well as the **National Golf School,** all located at **Reunion Resort & Club of Orlando** (© 888/418-9610, or 407/662-1000); and the **Ritz Carlton Golf Club** and **Grande Pines Golf Club,** both located at the **Grande Lakes Orlando** (© 407/393-4814), where the only golf-caddy concierge program around is available to make your game all it can be. The program offers advice, helpful hints, caddy services, food and beverage service, and much more.

Also consider **Golfpac** (© **800/486-0948** or 407/260-2288; www.golfpac orlando.com), an organization that packages golf vacations with accommodations and other features, and prearranges tee times at more than 40 Orlando-area courses. The earlier you call (months, if possible), the better your options. **Advanced Tee Times USA** (© **800/374-8633;** www.teetimes usa.com) and **Golforlando** (© **800/981-8656;** www.golforlando.com) are two other reservation services that offer packages and course information.

HORSEBACK RIDING   Disney's Fort Wilderness Resort and Campground Disney's Fort Wilderness Resort and Campground offers 45-minute guided trail rides several times a day. The cost is $32 per person. Children must be at least 9 years old. Maximum rider weight is 250 pounds. If you or your children have never ridden before, the tame horses and gentle terrain make this ride a good introductory experience. For information and reservations up to 30 days in advance, call © **407/824-2832.**

The **Villas of Grand Cypress** opens its equestrian center to outsiders, and has programs and options for riders of all ages and all skill levels. You can go on a 45-minute walk-trot trail ride (offered four times daily) for $45, though your children must be at least 10 years of age to participate. A 30-minute private lesson is $55; an hour's lesson is $100. A private junior lesson (15 min.) is available for riders age 2 to 9 for $25. A host of other package options is offered. For more information, call © **800/835-7377** or 407/239-1938 or go online to **grandcypress.com.**

Another choice outside the world of Walt Disney is the **Horse World Riding Stables,** 3705 Poinciana Blvd. (© **407/847-4343;** www.horseworldstables.com), in Kissimmee. The stables offer nature-trail rides and individual riding lessons. Rates for a 1-hour ride start at $39 for ages 6 and up; the cost is $17 for kids 5 and under who ride with an adult. Reserve in advance.

HORSE-DRAWN-CARRIAGE RIDES Disney offers evening carriage rides at two of its resort locations: **Fort Wilderness Resort and Campground** and the **Port Orleans Resort.** The 30-minute rides cost $30 for up to four people. Most kids will enjoy the ride and the sightseeing opportunity. For information, call © **407/824-2832.**

JOGGING Many of the Disney resorts have scenic jogging trails. For instance, the **Yacht** and **Beach Club** resorts share a 2-mile trail; the **Caribbean Beach Resort's** 1.4-mile promenade circles a lake; **Port Orleans** has a 1.7-mile riverfront trail; and **Fort Wilderness's** tree-shaded 2.3-mile jogging path has exercise stations about every quarter mile. Pick up a jogging-trail map at any Disney property's Guest Services desk.

PARASAILING The **Sammy Duvall Watersports Centre** (© **407/939-0754;** www.sammyduvall.com) at Disney's Contemporary Resort will take you up to 600 feet above Seven Seas Lagoon and Bay Lake on a flight that lasts 8 to 12 minutes. The cost runs approximately $90 for one rider and $140 for two riders. Kids over 2 are eligible if they fly in tandem with someone else (minimum weight 115 lb.), though you'll have to judge whether your child is up to such an experience. While older kids and teens would probably fare well, younger children likely wouldn't. Everyone who goes up has to sign a waiver, and parents have to sign off on their kids' participation. You can reserve a spot up to 90 days in advance.

SCUBA DIVING AND SNORKELING Believe it or not, even inland, you can scuba and snorkel in the Florida waterways. **Fun 2 Dive Scuba and Snorkeling Tours** (© **407/322-9696;** www.fun2dive.com) and **Orlando Dive and Snorkel Tours** (© **407/466-1668;** www.floridamanateetours.com) both offer the chance to swim and snorkel with manatees (and other wildlife), as well as other eco-tour opportunities. Prices at Fun 2 Dive (which also offers scuba lessons and deep-sea fishing excursions) run approximately $85 per person (with a maximum of 6 people) to swim and snorkel; at Orlando Dive and Snorkel, the fun starts at $28 per person, plus $10 for rental gear.

SKATING On the occasional rainy afternoon (or even on a good day) **Vans Skatepark** (© **407/351-3881;** www.vans.com) offers skateboarders (beginners or advanced) the chance to ride the day away on the ramps, bowls, street courses, and more. Safety equipment is required (and available for rent if you don't have your own), and those under 18 are required to have a parent or guardian sign a waiver (in front of a Vans employee or a notary). Rates run approximately $12 per session for non-members and $5 for members (requiring a 1-year commitment) on weekdays; $15 and $7, respectively, on weekends and holidays. Sessions are 2 hours long and run at scheduled times. Equipment is available for rent, from boards to helmets and pads (cost runs about $2 to $5). Private lessons, camps, and birthday parties are also offered. The park is located in the Festival Bay Mall at the far north end of International Drive.

SURFING It's true. The creative minds at Disney have added a way for you to learn how to catch a wave and "hang ten" at the Typhoon Lagoon water park (p. 234). Tuesdays and Fridays, instructors from **Carroll's Cocoa Beach Surfing School** show up for an early-bird session in the namesake lagoon, which has a wave machine capable of 8-footers. The 2½-hour sessions are held before the park opens to the general public and are limited to 14 people. Minimum age is 8. The $135-per-person cost (including tax) doesn't include park admission, which you'll have to pay if you want to hang around after the lesson (*©* **407/939-7529**). You'll also need alternative transportation to get here if you're staying in Walt's World, because the Disney transportation system doesn't service Typhoon Lagoon until official park-opening time.

SWIMMING   Almost all of Orlando's resorts have their own pools, some of which are rather unique or rather extensive (and discussed in more detail in chapter 4, "Family-Friendly Accommodations"), but if you're not satisfied with the one at your hotel, the **YMCA Aquatic Center,** 8422 International Dr. (*©* **407/363-1911**), has a full fitness center, racquetball courts, an indoor Olympic-size pool, and a heated 25-meter pool for kids. All pools have lifeguards. Admission is $10 per person and $25 for families.

TENNIS   There are 26 lighted tennis courts scattered throughout the Disney properties and the Wide World of Sports Complex. Most are free and open to resort guests on a first-come, first-served basis. Call *©* **407/939-7529** for more information. The **Racquet Club at the Contemporary Resort,** with six clay courts, all lit for evening play, will cost you $8 per hour to play, and reservations are required. Private lessons are available for $40 to $50, depending on the lesson's duration. The courts at the Grand Floridian are for Grand Floridian guests only

The **Grand Cypress Racquet Club** (*©* **407/239-1944;** www.grandcypress.com) features 12 courts, 5 of which are lit for night play. Racquetball courts, a clubhouse, and pro shop are available as well. Clinics are offered daily, with private lessons ($70 per hour, $40 per half\ hour) and semiprivate ($85 per hour) lessons available as well.

WATER-SKIING & WAKEBOARDING   Water-skiing trips (including boats, drivers, equipment, and instruction) can be arranged Tuesday through Saturday at **Walt Disney World** by calling the **Sammy Duvall Watersports Centre** at Disney's Contemporary Resort (*©* **407/939-0754;** www.sammyduvall.com). Make reservations up to 14 days in advance. The cost for skiing is $140 per hour for up to five people. You also can arrange for wakeboarding for up to four people; rates run $80 for a half hour and $140 for an hour. There's no minimum age, although I wouldn't recommend this for children under 8 and definitely not for those at all uncomfortable in the water.

Outside Disney, you can get some time behind a boat or at the end of an overhead cable at the **Orlando Watersports Complex,** which has lights for nighttime thrill-seekers. Teens will likely think the nighttime option cool, but kids under 8 and those not completely comfortable in the water aren't the best candidates for this activity. The complex is located close to Orlando International Airport at 8615 Florida Rock Road. Prices for skiing (including lessons) begin at about $21 an hour for a cable and $35 a half hour behind a boat. The complex offers a number of specials and discounts aimed at kids and families; call or check the website to see what's being offered during the time of your visit. For information, call *©* **407/251-3100** or go to **www.orlandowater sports.com**. Another good option is **Buena Vista Water Sports** (*©* **407/239-6939;** www.bvwatersports.com), located closer to all the action at Lake Bryan in Lake Buena Vista. And finally, there are **Sea-Doo rentals,** and water-ski and wakeboard lessons and rides. Passes are available from 1 hour ($21) to all day ($40) to all week ($186). Cable lessons (lasting 1 hour) run $65, and those under the age of 10 who pass the lesson receive a 2-hour cable pass free of charge.

In 2005, the indoor **Ron Jon Surf Park** (*©* **321/799-8880;** www.ronjons.com) opened at the Festival Bay shopping center on International Drive. It features wave pools for intermediate- and pro-level surfers and bodyboarders, as well as wave pools for novice wave riders. Lessons and clinics are available.

Moments **The Multisports Experience**

In 2002, Disney replaced its NFL Experience at the Wide World of Sports complex with an expanded multisports venue that lets you test your skills not only at football, but also at baseball, basketball, hockey, soccer, and volleyball. Admission is $11 for adults and $7.75 for kids 3 to 9. It's open on select days. For information and event schedules, call © **407/939-1500** or head online to **www.disneyworldsports.com**.

---

2 Spectator Sports

Orlando is not a sporting town of the same caliber as, say, a New York or Chicago, but it still is home to one major franchise and a number of other sporting teams. If you and your kids are sports nuts, you won't have to forgo your fix while in town.

BASEBALL

The **Atlanta Braves** call Disney's Wide World of Sports (p. 240) 7,500-seat baseball stadium—dubbed Cracker Jack Stadium in 2002—their spring-training home. They play 18 games during a 1-month season that begins in March. The smaller setting makes for a far more intimate experience for kids than a regular-stadium game would, and the atmosphere is usually a lot more relaxed. Tickets are $13 to $21. For information, call © **407/828-3267.** You can get tickets through **Ticketmaster** (© **407/839-3900**).

BASKETBALL

The 17,500-seat TD Waterhouse Centre—known in a previous life as the Orlando Arena—is the home court of the NBA's **Orlando Magic** (© **407/896-2442**; www.nba. com/magic), which plays 41 of its regular-season games here from October to April. To get there, take I-4 east to Exit 83B, Hwy. 50/U.S. 17/92 (Amelia St.), turn left at the traffic light at the bottom of the off ramp, and follow the signs. Single-game tickets ($25–$175) can be hard to find. The team schedules special theme nights and promotions throughout the season, many of them family-related; and its mascot, Stuff (that really is his name) the Dragon, is a hit with kids. For up-to-the-minute parking information, tune your car radio to 1620 AM.

3 Playing on the Green: Orlando's Parks & Playgrounds

After several days of barnstorming through the theme parks and other tourist attractions, a day in the area's nature parks can be a refreshing break. Need I also mention that it will help you recover from sticker shock—digging deeply into your wallet day after day?

CITY PARKS

Lake Eola Park   All ages   More than a million people visit this 20-acre park each year. The 0.9-mile sidewalk that circles the downtown lake offers a good course for hikers and joggers. Visitors can feed the live birds that inhabit the park, catch a tan on the lawn, or burn some calories cruising the lake in swan-shaped paddleboats. There are a playground for kids and toddlers, and several concessions, picnic areas, and restrooms. This park is also the home of several annual events, including the Fourth of July fireworks blast.

195 N. Rosalind Ave. ℂ **407/246-2827.** Free admission. Open 8am–10pm. Take I-4 to Anderson St. in downtown Orlando, go east past City Hall, cross Orange and Magnolia aves., and then turn left at Rosalind and into the park.

Turkey Lake Park   All ages   This 36-acre city park was originally a citrus grove and has one of the most natural settings of all Orlando's parks. The park—last renovated in December 2002—has a swimming pool, large picnic pavilions, a lake stocked with fish, a large children's playground and two smaller ones, nature and jogging trails, an 18-hole disc-golf course, a farm-animal petting zoo, and a boardwalk running through a scrub-pine habitat. It also has an ecology center.

3401 S. Hiawassee Rd. ℂ **407/299-5581.** Open 8am–5pm, sometimes later. $4 per vehicle. Take I-4 to Kirkman Rd., go north to Conroy; west/left to Hiawassee; and then north to the park, which is just past the Florida Turnpike.

STATE PARKS & PRESERVES

Wekiwa Springs State Park   All ages   The namesake springs and river provide a fertile habitat for white-tailed deer, gray foxes, bobcats, raccoons, and (careful here) black bears. The waters here also offer some of the best paddling venues in Central Florida. Canoe rentals are $14 for 2 hours and $2 per hour thereafter. There are bicycle and hiking trails, and the park also has picnic, grilling, volleyball, and camping areas.

1800 Wekiva Springs Rd., Sanford. ℂ **407/884-2008.** www.floridaparks.com/stprks/centralstateparks.htm. Open 8am to sundown. $4 per vehicle. Take I-4 to Exit 94; then take SR 434 West to Wekiwa Springs Rd. or SR 436 to Wekiwa Springs Rd. near Apopka.

4 Kids' Camps & Classes

It's hard to imagine, but this mecca of theme parks also has some of the coolest kids' camps around. **SeaWorld** features a few that may even pass for a few points of extra credit. Keep in mind, however, these are summer camps, and as your kids are likely between teachers, it's best to check with your school's guidance counselor where your child or children attend class to find out whether extra credit for attending camp is agreeable.

SeaWorld (see chapter 7, "What Kids Like to See & Do Beyond Disney") offers six resident camps during the summer:

- **Ocean Explorers.** Designed for grades 5 and 6, this program allows kids to interact with dolphins, snorkel in a shark cage, check out the rehabilitation facilities, play at the park, and sleep next to the beluga whales and the dolphins. Duration: 6 days. Price: $895 per child.
- **Ultimate Florida Adventure.** Appropriate for grades 7 through 9, this 10-day camp takes campers on an expedition to snorkel in the Florida Keys, airboat through the Everglades, canoe along Florida's waterways, and see the sights in St. Augustine. Then it's back to SeaWorld and Discovery Cove for lessons about preservation and rehabilitation programs, and encounters with dolphins and stingrays, with plenty of playtime in the parks and more. Duration: 10 days. Price: $1,975 per child.
- **Career Camp** includes three separate camps designed by grade: Career Camp for grades 7 through 9, Advanced Career Camp for grades 10 through 12, and Coastal Career Camp for grades 10 through 12. The programs include lessons on what it takes to train and work with the park's animals, and to maintain and enrich the animal exhibits. Kids train with animal experts, and learn about animal rescue and rehabilitation. The Coastal program includes snorkeling in the Florida

National Marine Sanctuary (in the Florida Keys), touring Key West, airboating through the Everglades, canoeing along the waterways, and more. All the career camps include plenty of fun at the theme park, including a day with the dolphins, sharks, stingrays, and other critters at Discovery Cove (p. 280), as well as at Sea-World. Duration: 6 days. Price: $1,195 per child for the career camps; the Coastal camp runs 10 days at a cost of $1,995 per child.

The cost of the camps includes meals, lodging, equipment, and more. For more information, call © **800/327-2424** or check out **www.seaworld.org**. Due to the camps' popularity, SeaWorld recommends making reservations between the preceding December and February.

Day camps (both half day and full day) are available for younger kids (preschool through 8th grade) that include behind-the-scenes tours, enrichment sessions on training and animal care, rescue and rehabilitation, and plenty of time at the parks to play. Weeklong camps run throughout the summer, with 1-day camps running at select times throughout the year (generally around a holiday). Prices for summer weeklong preschool camps run approximately $189, for both your child and the participating (required) adult. Daylong seasonal camps cost $45. Prices for the summer camps run approximately $219 for half-day camps and $299 for full-day camps. Special 1-day holiday camps cost $45 per child. All camps include up-close animal encounters, activities, crafts, a T-shirt and water bottle, lunch, and a snack. (The exception: Single-day seasonal camps do not include lunch.)

You'll find a variety of additional kids' camps throughout the Central Florida area, including at **Craig Carrol's Surfing School,** over in Cocoa Beach (offered by the same folks who hang ten at Disney's Typhoon Lagoon; p. 234); skate camps offered at **Vans Skate Park** (p. 292); and plenty of great (though often far less unique) camps at the area's better resorts, including select WDW resorts (see p. 295 for more details on these offerings).

9

Shopping for the Whole Family

Except for mouse ears and other tourist trinkets, Orlando has few products to call its own. Generally speaking, the merchandise and the malls won't be all that different from those you have at home. Still, many of you need some kind of shopping fix, and goofy souvenirs often are among your priorities—especially for the kids. After all, what else says "theme park" better than a pair of Mickey Mouse ears? (Except perhaps a blinking Buzz Lightyear, a Cinderella glass slipper, a Spider-Man outfit . . . you get the idea.)

But before putting your credit cards in high gear, consider these words to the wise: If you're going to ring registers in the theme parks, you're going to pay top dollar. Alas, most official Disney and Universal merchandise is available only in company stores. But when it comes to other goods, plan a day away from tourist central, and be as savvy here as you are at home. You can find a lot of what you want, and at the best possible prices, by knowing what is *and isn't* a bargain.

1 The Shopping Scene

SHOPPING HOURS & SALES TAXES

Generally speaking, neighborhood stores in Orlando open daily at around 9 or 10am and don't close before 5pm at the very earliest. An exception would be some of the stores in Downtown Orlando, which are usually closed on Sundays. Malls and major shopping centers tend to open around 10am, often not closing before 9 or 10pm, except on Sundays, when they usually close around 5 or 6pm. Stores in all Orlando theme parks generally stay open from the official park-opening time until just after the official park-closing time (giving you that last-minute opportunity to buy your child that stuffed Mickey or Cat in the Hat that she never knew she couldn't live without).

At all the Disney resorts, you'll usually find at least one shop that's open by 8am and keeps going until 10 or 11pm. Stores in the Downtown Disney Marketplace are usually open daily from 9:30am until around 11 or 11:30pm; those in Downtown Disney West Side usually stay open from around 10:30am until 11pm (midnight on Friday and Saturday). The shops at Pleasure Island don't open until 7pm, but they also don't close until 1am.

The shops at Universal Orlando's CityWalk open at 11am and don't close until 2am.

Sales tax in Osceola County, which includes Kissimmee, the U.S. 192 corridor, and *all of Disney's All-Star resorts,* is 7%. In Orange County, which includes the International Drive area, SeaWorld, Universal Orlando, most (but not all) of Disney World, and most of the lesser attractions, it's 6.5%. The tax is charged on every purchase except most edible grocery items and medicines.

(Tips) Setting Limits

The theme parks are filled one end to the other with shops of every sort, and unless they've been properly prepared, your kids could catch a serious case of the "Buy me" flu. (You might also, but that's a whole different ballgame.) And nothing will sour a vacation faster than your kids whining at the sight of every storefront (again, there are plenty of them) that they want Mickey this and Mickey that.

Depending on your child's age, you'll need to set buying limits and make sure that your children know them in advance. Souvenirs aren't cheap in Disney or Universal, and if you give your kids a set spending limit and stick to it, they may even learn a lesson or two about value shopping and getting their money's worth (my own spend far more wisely—and much less quickly—with only their own money in hand). Personally, I set a total vacation allowance and then remind the kids along the way of how many parks and attractions they will need to allot for in their budget. If your kids seem overanxious to spend early on, you may need to jog their memory. Or you might find that setting a fixed allowance per park works better for your family; it all depends on your kids. Older kids (and even some younger ones) might be persuaded to set aside portions of their allowance for use as souvenir money, with a few subtle reminders tossed in well ahead of time, of course. Special chores that pay more than the going rate can help out as well.

Another suggestion: Set specific shopping times so your kids won't be continually bugging you every time you pass a souvenir shop (keeping in mind that almost every ride will dump you into stores filled with shelves of souvenirs). If Susie and Timmy know ahead of time that they'll be getting their toy at the end of the day, they won't worry about passing up that store at the end of the ride. (It will also save you the trouble of carrying around a giant stuffed animal the whole day if you're not staying on park property, where you can have it delivered to your resort.) There are times an exception may be necessary, however, as some of the shops inside WDW, and many stores at Universal and SeaWorld, carry ride- or area-specific merchandise that may not be found elsewhere in the park. So if you promised a Spider-Man shirt to your budding web-slinger or a Cat in the Hat doll to your young Seuss fan, you'll need to pay up after you ride, or you'll be heading back to a store before you leave for the day.

GREAT SHOPPING AREAS

CELEBRATION   Though not the best place to head if you're the shop-'til-you-drop type, this is a rather pleasant spot to stroll leisurely along quaint streets filled with upscale shops, coffeehouses, and restaurants. Celebration, after all, is a Disney-designed community, making it practically the perfect little town. It's a throwback to mid-20th-century mainstream America, when Main Street shopping was in style. Market Street and the area just surrounding it are home to a dozen or so shops, a couple of art galleries, a handful of restaurants, and a three-screen theater. The storefronts,

Orlando Shopping

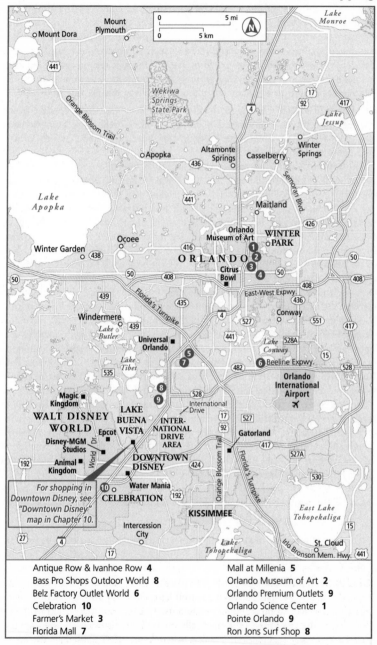

Antique Row & Ivanhoe Row **4**	Mall at Millenia **5**
Bass Pro Shops Outdoor World **8**	Orlando Museum of Art **2**
Belz Factory Outlet World **6**	Orlando Premium Outlets **9**
Celebration **10**	Orlando Science Center **1**
Farmer's Market **3**	Pointe Orlando **9**
Florida Mall **7**	Ron Jons Surf Shop **8**

especially the galleries and gift shops, offer interesting and unique merchandise, though you'll find that there's a price to pay for perfection. The real attraction here is the relaxing, picture-perfect atmosphere. The high prices, however, may make for more window-shopping than actual spending. If, by chance, Celebration reminds you of the movie *The Truman Show*, you're not alone. The movie was filmed in Seaside, a Florida Panhandle community that inspired the builders of this burg. This would be a far better place to head for an afternoon out without the kids in tow (© 407/566-2200).

DOWNTOWN DISNEY   With three distinct areas—West Side, Pleasure Island, and the Marketplace—Downtown Disney (© 407/939-2648; www.downtowndisney. com) is chock full of some of the most unique shops in Orlando, as well as many restaurants and entertainment venues.

The best shops in the Marketplace include the 50,000-square-foot **World of Disney** (p. 308), the largest store in Downtown Disney. There are rooms and more rooms filled with everything Disney, from toys and trading pins to clothes and collectibles—and everything (and I mean everything) in between. I always stop in at the **LEGO Imagination Center** (p. 307) when I'm in town. The shop, currently undergoing renovations, is filled with LEGO blocks designed for everyone from toddlers to tweens, Bionicles, T-shirts, and trinkets. **Once Upon a Toy** (p. 307) is one of the best stores in the Marketplace and the best toy store I've ever been in. It's stocked from floor to ceiling with games and toys, many of them classics—you know, the ones you played with while growing up. Its 16,000 square feet of space is divided into three separate sections: the first is filled with board games; the second is loaded with stuffed animals, building sets, and Playskool toys; the third features action figures, vehicles, and videos. **Team Mickey's Athletic Club** is filled with character clothing with a sporty spin. Other smaller but similarly interesting shops include **Summer Sands,** featuring the hottest in beachwear from top names such as Quicksilver and Calvin Klein; **Pooh Corner,** which offers everything Pooh that you can think of; and **The Art of Disney,** where you can buy limited-edition animation cels and other Disney collectibles.

Notable stores at West Side include **Magic Masters,** where you can load up on magic tricks for your budding Harry Houdini; **Magnetron,** which sells a huge variety of magnets (though, strangely enough, no Disney ones); and **Celebrity Eyeworks Studio,** where your teens can pick up a copy of those cool shades their favorite star was sporting in his or her last film. *Note:* For details on the music-related **Guitar Gallery** and **Virgin Megastore,** see "Music," later in this chapter.

⎛Tips Getting your Fill

The neatest new way to buy toys at several Downtown Disney stores (especially Once Upon a Toy) is in bulk . . . sort of. Toys such as Lincoln Logs and Mr. Potato Head, as well as a few others, can be purchased by the piece. Here's how it works: You pick out a box (there are two sizes to choose between), and fill it with as many (or few) pieces as you can fit inside. The only stipulation: You have to be able to close the lid properly. No matter how many pieces you've stuffed inside, the price of the box remains the same. If you've got good space-saving skills, buying your toys this way may net you a very good deal. (Here's a hint to get you started: Mr. Potato Head has a hole in his back, so fill it up, and you'll fit more pieces in your box.)

Tips **Ship It**

Because Orlando is geared to travelers, many retailers offer to ship packages home for a few dollars more (Disney definitely does). So if you're pondering an extra-large or rather fragile purchase, or even just one you'd rather not have to carry, ask. If a retailer doesn't offer such a service, check with your hotel. Many a concierge or business-center staffer can arrange a pickup by United Parcel Service, the U.S. Postal Service, or other carrier. Anything's better than dragging that 6-foot stuffed Goofy through the friendly skies.

INTERNATIONAL DRIVE AREA (*Note:* Locally, this road is always referred to as **I-Drive.**) Extending 8 or so miles northeast of Disney between Highway 535 and the Florida Turnpike, this busy thoroughfare is one of the most popular tourist districts in the area, in part because it is filled with so many restaurants, shops, hotels, and attractions. From indoor surfing and glow-in-the-dark golf to dozens of themed restaurants and shopping spots, this is *the* tourist strip in central Florida. Its main shopping draw is the **Orlando Premium Outlets,** just off south I-Drive (see below). Another I-Drive shopping spot, **Pointe Orlando** (© 407/248-2838; www.pointe orlandofl.com), features a collection of restaurants, clubs, and specialty shops. A major renovation, currently in the works, will add even more retailers to this outdoor complex, as well as brand-new landscaping and lighting in order to create a more inviting atmosphere. **The Mercado** (© 407/345-9337; www.themercado.com) is a Mediterranean-style marketplace on I-Drive that's filled with specialty shops, restaurants, and attractions; often, live entertainment is featured here in the evenings.

KISSIMMEE Skirting the south side of Walt Disney World, Kissimmee centers on U.S. 192/Irlo Bronson Memorial Highway, as archetypal of modern American cities as Disney's Main Street is of America's yesteryear. U.S. 192 is lined end to end with budget motels, smaller attractions, and almost every fast-food restaurant known to humankind (though a handful of good eateries can be found here as well). Kissimmee does not offer the fabulous array of shopping options found elsewhere in Orlando. The shopping here is notable for the quantity, not necessarily the quality, but it's a good place to pick up some knickknacks, a cheap souvenir, or white-elephant gifts.

WINTER PARK Just north of downtown Orlando, Winter Park (© 407/644-8281; www.winterpark.org) is the place many of central Florida's old-money families call home. It began as a haven for Yankees trying to escape the cold. Today, its centerpiece is Park Avenue, which has quite a collection of upscale shops—Ann Taylor, Bari's, Williams-Sonoma, and Restoration Hardware, among others—along its cobblestone route, with many an upscale restaurant and occasional art galleries as well. Its quaint atmosphere and boutique-style shops make for a great place to spend a relaxing afternoon, just not with the kids along (though there are plenty of shops where you can buy something to take back to them). To get here, take I-4 Exit 87, Fairbanks Avenue/Highway 426, east past U.S. 17/92 to Park Avenue, and turn left.

SHOPPING AT DISNEY'S THEME PARKS

You'll find dozens of places to buy everything from trinkets to treasures at the WDW parks, many of which have shops bearing themes and merchandise from specific rides and lands. Most of the stores carry merchandise that will appeal to both kids and adults, so everyone can shop together without getting bored. And if you're staying at a Disney resort, the stores will ship your purchases straight to your room, so you won't have to carry everything around with you. (If you're not staying on Disney property, you can have shops send your merchandise to the package pickup stations at each park, where you can get them before you leave, but you'll have to allot at least 3 hr. for them to get there.)

Here are some favorites from each of the parks.

MAGIC KINGDOM The **Emporium** on Main Street has a huge collection of everything Disney, from clothing to collectibles. You won't have to stop there, however; the entire row of shops, each filled with clothing, toys, memorabilia, and more, is interconnected. The **Toontown Hall of Fame Tent,** in Mickey's Toontown Fair, has an avalanche of things (including a large selection of sweets) kids under 7 will beg you to buy.

EPCOT *Careful:* With all the cultural products (edible and otherwise), a stroll around the World Showcase can break your bank unless you keep your wits about you. The headliners include China's **Yong Feng Shangdian Shopping Gallery,** which features silk robes, lacquer and inlaid mother-of-pearl furniture, jade figures, cloisonné vases, brocade pajamas, silk rugs and embroideries, wind chimes, and Chinese clothing. Artisans occasionally demonstrate calligraphy. **Mitsukoshi Department Store** (Japan's answer to Macy's) sells lacquerware, kimonos, kites, fans, dolls in traditional costumes, origami books, samurai swords, Japanese Disneyana, bonsai trees, Japanese foods, Netsuke carvings, pottery, modern electronics, and Pokémon cards (your kids will be thrilled). Shops in and around the **Plaza de Los Amigos** display an array of leather goods, baskets, sombreros, piñatas, pottery, embroidered dresses, maracas, serapes, colorful papier-mâché birds, and blown-glass objects (an artisan occasionally gives demonstrations). And Canada's **Northwest Mercantile** carries sandstone and soapstone carvings, fringed leather vests, duck decoys, moccasins, an array of stuffed animals, Native American dolls, Native American spirit stones, rabbit-skin caps, heavy knitted sweaters, and maple syrup. If you have little ones in tow, don't miss a stop at **MouseGear** in Future World's Innoventions East; it's loaded with toys and stuffed animals for the young set, and some of the best Epcot and Disney merchandise in all WDW.

DISNEY–MGM STUDIOS The best shopping at this park is aimed more at older kids and teens than very young kids. **Animation Courtyard Shops** carry collectible cels, with costumes from Disney classic films, plush, and pins, for the younger set. **Sid Cahuenga's One-of-a-Kind** sells autographed photos of the stars, original movie posters, and star-touched items such as canceled checks signed by Judy Garland and

---

Tips **Where Was That?**

If you arrived home (or even to your hotel room) only to realize that you forgot to buy that special souvenir, you're in luck. If you were at any of the Disney theme parks at the time you saw the item, call ✆ **407/363-6200;** if you were anywhere at Universal Orlando, call ✆ **407/224-5800.** Tell the customer-service rep the park you were in and describe the item; you'll likely be able to order it by phone and have it sent to your home.

others. Parents will be suitably impressed. **Celebrity 5 & 10,** modeled after a 1940s Woolworth's, has stocked its shelves with housewares a la Mickey. If you're with little ones, your best bet is the **Stage One Company Store,** which carries Muppet-themed souvenirs; **Legends of Hollywood**, which carries Pooh-and-friends clothing; and **L.A. Cinema Storage,** with its Mr. Potato Head station.

ANIMAL KINGDOM   **Creature Comforts** on Discovery Island focuses on kids' things, including themed toys and clothing. **Mombasa Marketplace** in Africa has a nice selection of safari clothing and African-themed gifts. And if you or your kids are into yesterday, don't miss a look through **Chester & Hester's Dinosaur Treasures.** The store is themed after the Dinosaur ride (p. 229) and has plush dinosaurs, T-shirts, and ball-style caps. The **Island Merchantile** (off to the side of the TriceraTop Spin) has tons of really unique little trinkets I didn't spot anywhere else in WDW, much of it for under $5 (though there are plenty of higher-priced items as well).

Though not inside the Big Four theme parks, the shops at Blizzard Beach and Typhoon Lagoon sell loads of bathing suits, towels, beach toys, and more. Kids into skateboarding will appreciate the selection of branded merchandise at both water parks as well.

SHOPPING AT UNIVERSAL'S THEME PARKS

At **Universal Studios Florida,** I'm stuck on **Back to the Future—The Store** and its miniature version of a DeLorean (kids 6 and up will like browsing here); the **Men in Black Gear Shop,** filled floor to ceiling with alien blasters of every kind; and the **Universal Studios Store,** near the park entrance, which appeals to all ages and sells just about everything when it comes to Universal apparel.

Next door at **Islands of Adventure,** there are more than 20 shops within the park, offering a variety of themed merchandise. You may want to check out **Cats, Hats & Things** and **Dr. Seuss' All the Books You Can Read** for special Seussian storybooks and souvenirs, especially with little kids in tow. **Jurassic Outfitters** and **Dinostore** feature enough plush and plastic dinosaurs to populate a geologic period, as well as safari-style clothing and souvenir T-shirts. Superhero fans should check out the **Spider-Man Shop,** and if your kids are into comic books, the **Comic Shop** offers a great selection of titles (Marvel comics only, of course). **Islands of Adventure Trading Company** is a good stop on the way out if you're still searching for something to help your kids remember their visit. The store carries a wide variety of theme merchandise geared to visitors of all ages.

FACTORY OUTLETS

Sure, you probably have one of these in (or at least near) your own hometown, and you won't get appreciatively better savings here. But if you're seeking school clothes, summer clothes, or just something to wear while you're in town, the two outlet malls below are some of the best in Orlando (and among the few places on the planet where you can get official theme-park merchandise at discounted prices).

Belz Factory Outlet World   This is the largest of the Orlando factory-outlet centers. It has 170 stores in 2 enclosed malls and 4 shopping annexes. It offers a wide range of merchandise, and in a few cases, the savings can be 75% off retail prices, but as is the case with most outlets, *most buys here are no better than what you'll find in discount houses in or near your town.* There are more than a dozen shoe stores (Bass, Nike, Rockport, and so on); nearly as many housewares shops (Fitz & Floyd, Oneida, and

---

Tips **Homegrown Souvenirs**

Oranges, grapefruit, and other citrus products rank high on the list of local products. **Orange Blossom Indian River Citrus,** 5151 S. Orange Blossom Trail, Orlando (© 800/624-8835 or 407/855-2837; www.orange-blossom.com), is one of the top sellers during the late-fall-to-late-spring season. If your kids are fruit-lovers, it's a great place to get a tasty souvenir. Alligator-skin leather goods are a specialty in the gift shop at **Gatorland Zoo,** 14501 S. Orange Blossom, Orlando (© 407/855-5496; www.gatorland.com).

---

more); a Universal Studios Outlet; and 60-some clothing shops for men, women, and children (Gap, Levi's, Van Heusen, OshKosh B'Gosh, Izod, Guess Jeans, and others). You can also shop for books, records, electronics, sporting goods, health and beauty aids, jewelry, toys, gifts, accessories, lingerie, and hosiery. 5401 W. Oak Ridge Rd. © 407/ 352-9611. www.belz.com. From I-4, take Exit 74B, and turn north on I-Drive, continuing to the mall. Near Universal Orlando.

Orlando Premium Outlets *Kids* *Finds*   Opened in June 2000, this 440,000-square-foot outlet center offers shoppers the atmosphere of a beautiful outdoor shopping mall filled with landscaping and natural lighting. It's inviting instead of outlet-ish. It's billed as Orlando's only upscale outlet and is by far the best choice for a great shopping experience in Orlando. It has 110 tenants, including Disney and Universal outlets, Coach, Donna Karan, Kenneth Cole, Nike, Polo/Ralph Lauren, Timberland, and Tommy Hilfiger. Others include DKNY, Fendi, Hugo Boss, Nautica, Salvatore Ferragamo, and Versace. Some of the best buys are at Banana Republic, and the selection at all the stores is fabulous. Set just between S.R. 535 and I-Drive, it's easily accessible from either location. 8200 Vineland Ave. © 407/238-7787. www.PremiumOutlets.com. From I-4, take Exit 68, Apopka-Vineland Rd./Hwy. 535 right/south to the first light; then go left at the first light to the outlet. Near SeaWorld.

THE MALLS

Florida Mall   The exciting news at this popular shopping spot is the arrival of Nordstrom to combat the opening of Mall at Millenia (see below). Other anchors include Burdines, Dillard's, JCPenney, Sears, and Saks, to go along with an Adam's Mark Hotel and more than 250 specialty stores, restaurants (Buca di Beppo, Le Jardin, and Ruby Tuesday), a food court, and entertainment venues. No fewer than 10 stores offer children's clothing, and there are three toy stores as well. Strollers can be rented at several locations inside the mall. If you have young children, this is definitely your best bet for a mall excursion. 8001 S. Orange Blossom Trail. © 407/851-6255. www.shop simon.com. Take I-4 Exit 74A, Sand Lake Rd./Hwy. 482, and look for it on the corner of Orange Blossom and Sand Lake.

Mall at Millenia   This 1.3 million-square-foot upscale center made quite a splash on the mall scene when it debuted in October 2002, with anchors that include Bloomingdale's, Macy's, and Neiman Marcus. In addition to the heavyweight anchors, Millenia offers 200 specialty stores that include Cartier, Chanel, Crabtree & Evelyn, Giorgio's of Palm Beach, Gucci, Louis Vuitton, Swarovski, and Tiffany & Co. Your label-conscious teens will find the rarified air here to their liking, though you, like me, may find it a bit too nose-in-the-air snooty. The mall is 5 miles from downtown Orlando and offers shuttle service to some hotels. 4200 Conroy Rd. (at I-4 near Universal Orlando). *C* **407/363-3555.** www.mallatmillenia.com. Take I-4 Exit 74A, Sand Lake Rd./Hwy. 482 east to the John Young Pkwy./Hwy. 423, and go north to Conroy and then west to the mall.

2 Shopping A to Z

Most visitors to Orlando will spend their time—and money—shopping in the theme parks. That's what the city is renowned for, after all. But if you aren't happy confining your credit card purchases to Disney, Universal, and SeaWorld, there are a few other shopping opportunities for family spending in the Orlando area.

ANTIQUES

If you can think of nothing better than a relaxing afternoon of bargain-hunting or scouring thrift and antiques shops, check out **Antique Row** and **Ivanhoe Row** on North Orange Avenue (stretching from Colonial Dr./Hwy. 50 to Lake Ivanhoe), in downtown Orlando. This collection is a long way from the manufactured fun of Disney. The shops are an interesting assortment of the old, the new, and the unusual. **Flo's Attic,** 1800 N. Orange Ave. (*C* **407/895-1800**), and **A. J. Lillun,** 1913 N. Orange Ave. (*C* **407/895-6111**), sell traditional antiques. Kids who like perusing cool old stuff will enjoy the experience, but if your children aren't into that sort of experience, they'll likely be bored stiff.

To get there, take I-4 Exit 85/Princeton Street, and turn right on Orange Avenue. Parking is limited, so stop wherever you find a space along the street.

BOOKS

All the major bookstore chains have stores in the Orlando area, though there are one or two local shops as well. This is a city that caters to kids, so almost all bookstores have well-stocked children's sections.

Barnes & Noble   This branch of the nationwide chain offers a wide selection of books for all ages. It's open daily from 9am to 11pm. 7900 Sand Lake Rd. *C* **407/345-0900.**

B. Dalton   This store has a large selection of children's books, as well as bestsellers and magazines. It's open 10am to 10pm Monday through Saturday, 11am to 9pm on Sunday. 9101 International Dr. *C* **407/363-0500.**

Borders   A cafe is a welcome addition to this store's collection of books, appealing to all ages. It's open 9am to 10pm Monday through Thursday, until 11pm Friday, and 9am to 9pm Sunday. 1051 W. Sand Lake Rd. *C* **407/826-8912.**

Brandywine Books   This local bookstore specializes in rare, out-of-print, and used hardbacks. It's open 10:30am to 5pm Monday through Saturday. 114 S. Park Ave., Winter Park. *C* **407/644-1711.**

Long's Christian Book & Music Store   Families looking for Christian-oriented reading material should head for this local shop. It sells cassettes, CDs, videos, church supplies, and cards, in addition to a large selection of books and Bibles. Long's is open 9am to 9pm Monday through Saturday. 1610 Edgewater Dr. *C* **407/422-6934.**

Waldenbooks   This member of the popular chain features a large selection of children's books in its Walden Kids section, as well as bestsellers and other books appealing to all ages. It's open 10:30am to 9pm Monday through Saturday, noon to 6pm Sunday. 8001 S. Orange Blossom Trail, in the Florida Mall. *C* **407/859-8787.**

COMICS

Coliseum of Comics   This regional chain has five locations spread across Central Florida, including this Orlando store. It is a large purveyor of new and used comics (X-Men, Spider-Man, Superman, and more), as well as toys, games, videos, and collectible game cards. If your kids are comics-crazed, it's a sure bet they'll love this store. There's also a branch in Kissimmee at 1180 E. Vine St. (© **407/870-5322**). The stores usually are open from 10am to 6pm Monday through Thursday, closing at 11pm on Friday and at 9pm on Saturday, Sundays from noon to 6pm. 4722 S. Orange Blossom Trail. © **407/240-7882**. www.coliseumofcomics.com.

FARMERS' MARKETS

You can shop for fresh produce, plants, baked goods, and crafts every Saturday from 8am to 2:30pm at the downtown Orlando **farmers' market.** It's located at the intersection of North Magnolia and East Central. Get more information at **www.downtown orlando.com**.

HAIRCUTS

The **Harmony Barber Shop** on Main Street in Disney's Magic Kingdom is a real scissor shop (with an atmospheric old-fashioned decor) where you can get your hair cut from 9am to 5pm daily. The barbers are incredibly friendly, give a good cut, and are an absolute marvel with kids. Adult haircuts are $17; kids' are $14. If it's your child's first haircut, Disney barbers will throw in a certificate, pixie dust, bubbles, and a set of special mouse ears. The shop is near the beginning of Main Street, set back in by the firehouse. If you're lucky, Disney's barbershop quartet, the Dapper Dans, will serenade you and your kids as you get your locks shorn. There are also beauty shops located at Disney's Contemporary, Coronado Springs, Yacht and Beach Club Resorts, as well as at the Grand Floridian.

MUSEUM STORES

Orlando Museum of Art   The museum not only has some exciting exhibits for kids and their caretakers, but also a wonderful shop featuring jewelry, books, videos, posters, and Dale Chihuly glass art. You can access the store without having to pay admission to the museum. It's open 10am to 4pm Tuesday through Friday, noon to 4pm Saturday through Sunday. 2416 N. Mills Ave., in Loch Haven Park. © **407/896-4231**. www.omart.org.

MUSIC

Guitar Gallery in Downtown Disney West Side (© **407/827-0118**) is a retail shop with more than 150 custom, collector, rare, and unique guitars. (One ivory-and-rosewood number sports a $25,000 price tag!) There are hand-decorated guitars, including a "Wonderland" Washburn created by Sammy Hagar and his son, and an Ibanez model with a hand-carved Egyptian scene on its wooden face. Guitars are suspended from hand-brushed aluminum walls and encased in rotating display cases. There are a few things here that won't cost you a second mortgage. It's more of a collector's shop, but if you have a budding musician, or your kids have a guitar-playing hero, they'll probably enjoy a quick stop here. The store is open daily 10:30am to 11pm, sometimes later.

The 49,000-square-foot **Virgin Megastore,** also in Downtown Disney West Side (© **407/828-0222**), stocks more than 150,000 titles on CDs and cassettes; has 2,000 CD-ROM and video-game titles; and also sells books, magazines, and graphic novels. If you have preteens and teens with you, they'll be in music heaven. The store also has

CD listening stations, video stations, game demo stations, a cafe with indoor and outdoor seating, and an outdoor stage for concerts. It's open 11am to midnight Sunday through Thursday, until 1am Friday through Saturday.

SCIENCE STORES

Orlando Science Center   The center's (p. 286) store has a fun selection of mindbending puzzles, interactive science games, theme clothing, and jewelry that will appeal to kids of all ages. You can access the shop without having to pay admission to the museum. It's open 9am to 5pm Tuesday through Thursday, 9am to 9pm Friday and Saturday, and noon to 5pm Sunday. 777 E. Princeton St., between Orange and Mills aves., in Loch Haven Park. (C) 407/514-2230. www.osc.org.

SPORTS STUFF

Bass Pro Shops Outdoor World   This is the retail version of fishing and hunting (including archery) heaven. Located in Belz's Festival Bay shopping center, this store also features areas for watersports equipment, camping gear, and outdoor apparel, as well as a golf pro shop and an aquarium. If your family interests trend toward the outdoors, this is a worthy shopping stop. The store is open daily, usually 9am to 6pm, except Christmas. 5156 International Dr. (C) 407/563-5200. www.basspro.com.

Ron Jon Surf Shop   Also located in Belz's Festival Bay, this is a mini version of the wild and wacky Ron Jon's in Cocoa Beach. That means if you're looking for legitimate surfboards and gear, swimwear, T-shirts, or Ron Jon bumper stickers, this is the place to find it. It's open 9am to 10pm Monday through Saturday and 10am to 7pm on Sunday. 5156 International Dr. (C) 407/481-2555. www.ronjons.com.

SWEETS

Downtown Disney has two favorite spots for sweet satisfaction in Orlando.

Candy Cauldron ((C) 407/828-1470), on Disney's West Side, will satisfy your and your kids' sweet tooth with 200 temptations, such as fudge, caramel apples, cotton candy, chocolate candies and fruit, and truffles. This candy-coated heaven is open 10:30am to 11pm daily.

At the Marketplace, **Ghirardelli Soda Fountain and Chocolate Shop** ((C) 407/934-8855), a branch of the famous San Francisco institution, sells truffles, doublechocolate mocha bars, and more. But Ghirardelli's is famous for its ice cream concoctions, and if you've promised your kids fountain drinks, this is the place to come. Ghirardelli's has a tantalizing selection of cones, floats, shakes, malts, and ice cream sodas. The hot fudge sundae here is a classic. Hours are 9:30am to 11pm daily.

TOYS

Need a way to keep the kids distracted while you shop for toys in peace? In the Downtown Disney Marketplace, the **LEGO Imagination Center** ((C) 407/828-0065) has a nifty outdoor play area in front where kids can build monster robots, race cars, and other creations There are LEGO pirate ships, cowboy towns, and high-rise dollhouses, as well as the traditional LEGO buckets of building blocks. It's open 9:30am to 11pm daily.

Also in the Disney Marketplace, **Once Upon a Toy** ((C) 407/934-7775) is a 16,000-square-foot store created by Disney and the Hasbro toy company. It's a toylover's nirvana. You can buy a Mr. Potato Head with Disney parts (or build your own on one of five touch screens), a Clue board game based on WDW's *Haunted Mansion* attraction, a Disney theme-park version of Monopoly, and a Play-Doh play set based on Disney's It's a Small World attraction. There also are Disney character dolls and miniature versions of Disney's monorail system. Other toys include Lincoln Logs (adults will marvel at the miniature replica of Disney's Wilderness Lodge displayed by the logs), Tinker Toys, and *Star Wars* memorabilia. The store is open 9:30am to 11pm daily. *Tip:* This is a great place for taking snapshots of the kids, as the store is loaded with backdrops, including a child-size version of the Walt Disney World Railroad and a Peter Pan–themed castle.

Kids, especially those 12 and under, and parents can browse for hours in the mammoth **World of Disney** (© **407/828-1451**), a Downtown Disney Marketplace store with a dozen themed rooms, featuring toys, dolls, and other trinkets a la Disney. You'll also find Disney art, clocks, and clothing in sizes ranging from infant to adult. Just keep an eye on the kids; the store is so big (about half a million sq. ft.), it's easy for the little shoppers (and big ones, too) to wander off.

10

Entertainment for the Whole Family

Most visitors, after a week of pounding the theme-park pavement, are desperately in need of yet another week off just to recover from the experience. This, however, may not include the kids, who are allowed the luxury of sleeping at times when the adults are otherwise occupied driving back to the hotel, scurrying about organizing for the next day's activities, packing for the trip home, or simply keeping watch over their kids. A lot of vacationers, especially first-timers, burn the candle at both ends, completely wearing themselves out. The result: They'll likely need a vacation from their vacation. (Your kids will probably bemoan the fact that the vacation is over.)

Some of you know the feeling. You're simply not willing to miss a beat even after a long day at the parks, or have older kids and teens whose interest won't be flagging at the end of the day. You want after-hours adventure, and in the last decade, Orlando's tourism czars have built a bundle of entertainment to satisfy your family's cravings.

The success of Central Florida's dinner shows, video arcades, cultural-arts programs, and adult nightclub districts—including Universal's **CityWalk, Downtown Disney West Side,** and **Pleasure Island**—shows that many visitors have the pizzazz to pick up the pace even after a day of toting their toddlers and teens around Mickeyville and Universal.

Check the "Calendar" section of Friday's *Orlando Sentinel* for up-to-the-minute details on local clubs, visiting performers, concerts, movies, and events. It has hundreds of listings, many of which are online at **www.orlandosentinal.com**. The *Orlando Weekly* is a free magazine found in red boxes throughout central Florida. It highlights the more offbeat and often more of-the-minute performances. You can see it online at **www.orlandoweekly.com**. Another good source on the Internet is **www.orlandoinfo.com**, operated by the Orlando/Orange County Convention & Visitors Bureau.

Note: In addition to the places I list in this chapter, there are several great nighttime options for families, including end-of-evening productions in the theme parks (see chapters 6 and 7 for more information), sporting events at Disney's Wide World of Sports (see p. 238), and after-dark minigolf at Disney's miniature courses (p. 238).

1 Dinner Shows

IN WALT DISNEY WORLD

The Magic Mickey offers tons of nighttime entertainment aimed at the whole family, including laser-light shows, fireworks, and IllumiNations (p. 215). There also are three dinner shows worthy of special note: the Hoop-Dee-Doo Musical Revue, the Spirit of Aloha Dinner Show, and a third production that's an occasional player.

Tips **If You're Lucky . . .**

Mickey's Backyard BBQ (📞 407/939-3463; www.disneyworld.com) is a seasonal offering at Pioneer Hall at Fort Wilderness Resort & Campground, where Tom Sawyer and Huck Finn allow you onto their home turf to have a thigh-slapping time and a feast in a covered outdoor pavilion. Expect Mickey and his pals to join you for a meal that includes barbecued pork ribs, baked chicken, hot dogs, corn on the cob, baked beans, macaroni and cheese, watermelon, beer, wine, lemonade, iced tea, and dessert. (There's no specific menu for kids, but there are plenty of options on the regular menu that will satisfy them.) The storytelling, games, and character appearances make this a huge thrill for most young kids. The 3-hour meals start at 6:30pm and cost $39 for adults, $25 for kids 3 to 9, including tax and tip. It happens only on Tuesdays and Thursdays . . . sometimes. So **call.**

Note: While they offer entertainment, don't expect haute cuisine. The food, though good, takes a back seat to the show. Also note that all three dinner experiences require that you *pay in full with a credit card at the time of booking.* If you cancel your dinner plans at least 48 hours in advance, you will get a full refund.

Disney's Spirit of Aloha Dinner Show *(Moments* **All ages** While not quite as much in demand as the Hoop-Dee-Doo, the Polynesian Resort's delightful 2-hour show is like a big neighborhood party. Disney's Spirit of Aloha Dinner Show features Tahitian, Samoan, Hawaiian, and Polynesian singers, drummers, and dancers who entertain you while you feast on a menu that includes tropical appetizers, lanai-roasted chicken, Polynesian wild rice, South Seas vegetables, dessert, wine, beer, and other beverages. It all takes place 5 nights a week in an open-air theater (dress for nighttime weather, and bring the sweaters) with candlelit tables, red-flame lanterns, and tapa-bark paintings on the walls. Reservations should be made 60 to 90 days in advance (but can be made up to 2 years in advance), especially during peak periods such as summer and holidays. Show times are 5:15 and 8pm Tuesday through Saturday. 1600 Seven Seas Dr. (at Disney's Polynesian Resort). 📞 407/939-3463. www.disneyworld.com. Reservations required. Adults $50, kids 3–11 $25, including tax. Free parking.

Hoop-Dee-Doo Musical Revue *ᐖᐖᐖ (Moments* **All ages** This is Disney's most popular show, so make reservations *early.* The reward: You feast on a down-home, all-you-can-eat barbecue: fried chicken; smoked ribs; salad; corn on the cob; baked beans; bread; strawberry shortcake; and your choice of coffee, tea, beer, wine, sangria, or soda. (There's no kids' menu, but your kids shouldn't have much of a problem finding something to their liking.) While you stuff yourself silly in Pioneer Hall, performers in 1890s garb lead you in a foot-stomping, hand-clapping, high-energy show that includes a lot of corny jokes you haven't heard since second grade. Kids of all ages love it (and some may be selected to participate in the proceedings). *Note:* Be prepared to join in on the fun, or else the singers and dancers, along with the rest of the crowd, may humiliate you until you do. It's easy to get caught up in this lively and entertaining family show.

Reservations should be made 60 to 90 days in advance or earlier (you can make them up to 2 years in advance), especially during peak periods such as summer, spring break, and holidays. Show times are 5, 7:15, and 9:30 nightly, and shows last roughly 2 hours. 3520 N. Fort Wilderness Trail (at Fort Wilderness Resort and Campground). 𝄢 **407/939-3463**. www.disneyworld.com. Reservations required. Adults $50, kids 3–9 $25, including tax and tip. Free parking.

ELSEWHERE IN ORLANDO

Outside Mickey's monarchy, Orlando has an active dinner-theater scene, but keep in mind that the city is a family destination—and the dinner shows are very reflective of that. You won't find sophisticated offerings like those in major cultural centers such as New York, London, or Paris. Most of the local dinner shows focus on pleasing the kids, so if you're looking for fun, you'll find it, but if you want critically acclaimed entertainment, look elsewhere. You also won't find four-star food, but dinners are certainly palatable enough, with some a bit better than others. Attending a show is considered by many to be a quintessential Orlando experience, and if you arrive with the right attitude, you'll most likely have an enjoyable evening. Your children certainly will.

Note: Discount coupons to the dinner shows below can often be found inside the tourist magazines that are distributed in gas stations and tourist information centers; you'll also find them in many non-Disney hotel lobbies and sometimes on the listed websites. Trust me—you'll appreciate having them when you add up your bill.

Arabian Nights   Age 5 and up   If you're a horse fancier, this is *the* attraction to see in Central Florida, and your kids will be impressed by the equestrian acrobatics even if you aren't hoof-happy. Arabian Nights is one of the classier dinner-show experiences. It stars many of the most popular breeds, from chiseled Arabians to hard-driving Andalusians to beefcake Belgians. They giddy-up through performances that include Wild West trick riding, chariot races, slapstick comedy, and bareback bravado. Though locals rate it No. 1 among Orlando dinner shows, do note that my kids preferred the action of some of Orlando's other offerings. On most nights, the performance here opens with a ground trainer working one-on-one with a black stallion. The dinner served during the 2-hour show includes salad; a choice of prime rib, grilled chicken, chicken tenders, chop steak, or lasagna; vegetables; garlic mashed potatoes; rolls; dessert; wine, beer, and unlimited soda pop. Special diets can be accommodated with advance notice. Show times vary, but there is at least one show nightly. *Tip:* Book your tickets online, and you'll save about $10 to $15 per person off the regular admission price. 6225 W. Irlo Bronson Memorial Hwy. (U.S. 192), Kissimmee. 𝄢 **800/553-6116** or 407/239-9223. www.arabian-nights.com. Reservations recommended. $40–$50 adults, $20–$31 children 3–11. Free parking.

⌒Tips   Supper at SeaWorld . . .

While it may not appeal to some children (the 8-and-older squad should be okay), **SeaWorld's Makahiki Luau,** 7007 SeaWorld Dr. (𝄢 **800/327-2424** or 407/ 363-2559; www.seaworld.com), is another option during your Orlando visit. The show is a celebration of Hawaiian music and dance, and the menu offers mahimahi in piña colada sauce, Hawaiian chicken, sweet-and-sour pork, fried rice, vegetables, fruit, banana lava cake, and beverages. There isn't a kids' menu per se, but you can order a hot dog or chicken tenders for those whose tastes refuse to accept menu fare. The price is $43 for adults and $28 for children 3 to 9. Park admission is not required. A holiday version runs during the Christmas season.

A Universal Luau

Universal Orlando's Royal Pacific Resort offers its own luau on Saturday nights (year-round) and Friday nights (late May–September). The Wantilan Luau features entertainment from various Polynesian islands, including drum performances, dancing, and music. The menu features a variety of island cuisines (including the ubiquitous roast pig); a special kids' menu; and unlimited wine, beer, mai tais, and nonalcoholic drinks. The price (including tax and tip) is $50 for adults and $29 for kids age 12 and under. You're guaranteed a luau rain or shine, but in bad weather, the action moves indoors, and the atmosphere is not as good. Call ⓒ **407-503-DINE** for more information.

Dolly Parton's Dixie Stampede Dinner & Show   Age 4 and up   Here's a hootin'-n-hollerin' good time. This $28 million venture is similar to the ones the actress and country singer has in other southern locations, although the venue is slightly larger. While horses have less of a role than at Arabian Nights (see above), the Quarter Horses, Appaloosas, Belgians, and others that perform here help put on a fun "God Bless the U.S.A." show that opens with a herd of bison charging around the arena. Any weaknesses in the early themes and songs are forgotten when the fun and games begin, including a rivalry that pits half the audience (the North) against the other half (the South) in a who-can-cheer-and-stomp-the-loudest battle. The blue-versus-gray competition continues in a number of offbeat events, including a chicken chase using four kids from the audience, pig races, a game of toilet-seat horseshoes, and more. Some may blink at the Civil War theme, but your kids will have a great time. The vittles (plan to eat with your fingers; they don't give you utensils) include a small rotisserie chicken (whole); a slice of smoked pork tenderloin; a potato wedge; corn on the cob' creamy vegetable soup; dessert; and unlimited coffee, tea, or Pepsi—and reversing the original rule to keep up with the competition, beer and wine are now served. Vegetarians have a choice of lasagna and a fruit bowl (in addition to the other fixin's). There's no specific menu for kids, and be advised that *children ages 3 and under are free only if they sit on a parent's lap*. Show times vary, but there is at least one show nightly, and during the Christmas season, you can enjoy a special holiday version of the show. As Dolly said at the June 18 opening, "It's fun for families, and I'm gettin' rich on it." 8251 Vineland Ave. (across from Orlando Premium Outlets), Orlando. ⓒ 866/443-4943 or 407/238-4455. www.dixiestampede. com. Reservations recommended. $47 adults, $20 children 4–11. Free parking. From I-4, take Exit 68, Apopka–Vineland Rd./Hwy. 535 right/south to the first light, and then go left at the first light to the outlet.

Fiasco's Circus & Magic Dinner Show   Age 6 and up   Guests at Orlando's newest dinner show laugh their way through dinner as circus-style performers entertain with magic tricks and acts that are really more comedic in nature than magical; the entire evening is filled with Monty Pythonesque mishaps and mayhem. The menu, representing dishes from all over the world, is the largest around, offering over 100 items (a nice departure from the fixed meals offered at other dinner theaters), including lots of options for kids. When purchasing your tickets, you can choose between the interactive or the "safe" zone seating, so be sure to specify your preference, or you may find yourself part of the show. 7430 Universal Blvd. ⓒ 866-GO-FIASCO or 407/226-7220. www.fiascosdinnershow.com. Reservations recommended. $45 adults, $25 kids 3–9 (on Thursday, one child enters free per paying adult). Free parking.

Medieval Times   Age 5 and up   Orlando has one of the eight Medieval Times shows in the North America, and this is the show my kids rate No. 1 in town. Inside, guests gorge themselves on barbecued spare ribs, herb-roasted chicken, soup, appetizer, potatoes, dessert, and beverages (including beer). But because this is the 11th century, you eat with your fingers from metal plates while knights mounted on Andalusian horses run around the arena, jousting and clanging to please the fair ladies. Arrive 90 minutes early for good seats and to see the Medieval Village, a re-created Middle Ages settlement. A new storyline, "Knights of the Realm," introduced in 2004, adds to the action a touch of romance between one of the knights and the princess. Show times vary, but there is at least one performance nightly. While I recommend it for kids over 5, mine have all been to the show at varying ages from 9 months right on up. They have always appreciated the chance to scream and yell as loud as they can while stomping their feet during dinner, as this is not so well received at home. The biggest concern when bringing very young kids is definitely the noise level. 4510 W. Irlo Bronson Memorial Hwy. (U.S. 192), Kissimmee. ✆ **800/229-8300** or 407/396-1518. www.medievaltimes.com. Reservations recommended. $49 adults, $33 children 3–11. Free parking.

Moments Prime Rib & a Side of Murder

Ever dream about being Sherlock Holmes? **Sleuths Mystery Dinner Show** ⭐⭐, 8267 International Drive (✆ **800/393-1985** or 407/363-1985; www.sleuths.com), is an interactive dinner show staged in an intimate theater setting where guests play detective and try to solve a whodunit murder mystery.

A roster of suspects and impending victims (OK, they're really actors) interact with guests throughout the experience, which includes a preshow where you're introduced to the characters and served appetizers and a salad. When the actual performance begins, the actors both entrance and, at times, reduce you to hysterical laughter. Then it's time for dinner, which includes a choice of a Cornish game hen, prime rib (for $3 more), or lasagna. While eating, you discuss clues with the other detectives at your table (the round tables seat eight). Each table is given the opportunity to interrogate the suspects (which can get quite hilarious, depending on the amount of alcohol—adults get unlimited wine and beer—people have consumed before they get to ask their questions). The suspects duly questioned, a mystery dessert is served; then the murderer is revealed. It makes for a very entertaining yet relaxing evening out.

Eleven different productions (each is about 2–2½ hr. long) are offered throughout the year, so you can keep coming back for more. There are two mystery shows designed specifically for kids (I'd recommend that they be at least 8 years old), but other performances probably are best for teens at least 16 years of age. Admission costs $47 adults and $24 kids 3 to 11. For kids' performances, the cost is $28 adults and $16 kids 3 to 11. Reservations are recommended.

To get here, from I-4 East take exit 75A; at the light, turn right onto Universal Blvd.; and then turn right into Gooding's Plaza. Parking is free.

Pirates Dinner Adventure **Age 5 and up** The special-effects show at this theater includes a full-size ship in a 300,000-gallon lagoon, circus-style aerial acts, a lot of music, and a little drama. It's a big hit with pirate-happy kids. Dinner includes an appetizer buffet with the preshow, followed by roast chicken and beef, rice, vegetables, dessert, and coffee. The kids' menu has chicken fingers. After the show, you're invited to the Buccaneer Bash dance party, where you can mingle with cast members. Show times vary, but there is at least one show nightly. This is the only dinner show I've come across that has highchairs for young kids. *Note:* While many of the dinner shows have violent scenes, this one in particular features a great deal of fistfighting throughout the show. 6400 Carrier Dr. ✆ **800/866-2469** or 407/248-0590. www.orlandopirates.com. Reservations recommended. $45 adults, $28 children 3–11. Free parking. Take I-4 Exit 74A, Sand Lake Rd./Hwy. 482, north to Carrier; turn right.

2 Arcades & Fun Centers

DisneyQuest **Age 7 and up** This five-level arcade usually inspires awe in children just reaching the video-game stage, firmly hooked teens, and nostalgic adults who never outgrew Pac-Man.

While you will find a few things for the younger set—such as video and pinball games—this high-tech arcade is geared more to older children, teens, and adults. Options include **Aladdin's Magic Carpet,** a virtual-reality adventure that puts you astride a motorcyclelike seat for a journey into the 3-D Cave of Wonders; **Invasion! An ExtraTERRORestrial Alien Encounter,** in which you and three others in your space module try to save colonists from intergalactic bad guys; **Pirates of the Caribbean: Battle for Buccaneer Gold,** another 3-D VR adventure that has you and your shipmates fighting blackhearts; the **Mighty Ducks Pinball Slam,** a life-size pinball game in which body English and reflexes help you score; and **CyberSpace Mountain,** in which you build, and then ride, your own simulated roller coaster. For more on this attraction, see "DisneyQuest" on p. 239.

Warning: Heavy crowds after 1pm can significantly cut into your game time. Downtown Disney West Side. ✆ **407/828-4600.** www.disneyquest.com. $34 adults, $28 kids 3–9. Open daily 11:30am–11pm, sometimes to midnight.

Fun Spot **Age 4 and up** This throwback amusement park on the north end of International Drive, near Universal Orlando, has something for just about everyone in the family. There are bumper cars, bumper boats, a carousel, kiddie rides, spinning teacups, a Ferris wheel, several go-kart tracks, and a lift-and-drop ride that's a tame version of Universal's Doctor Doom's Fearfall (p. 263). General admission is free; you can pay as you play or ride. Tokens for the primo games (such as simulators, video games, and pinball) cost 25¢ each; 120 for $25; 400 for $75; or, if you're bringing an entourage, 1,000 for $175. Most games take 2 to 4 tokens. There's also a $5.25 play-all-day arcade (older pinball, PlayStation2, X-Box, Pac-Man, and sports games). Rides run from $3 per $6 per for the go-karts to an array of multiride armbands ($9.95 kids 2–6, $20 ages 5–7, $30 age 10 and up—this one includes the go karts). 5551 Del Verde Way. ✆ **407/363-3867.** www.fun-spot.com. Mon–Fri 2–11pm (10am–midnight in summer); Sat–Sun 10am–midnight.

3 Movies

There are several theaters scattered through tourist and high-traffic areas in Central Florida, many of them conveniently located to those staying near the theme-park

---

Tips Ghostly Experience

Orlando Ghost Tours (© 407/423-5600; www.hauntedorlando.com) puts a different spin on the city's nightlife with 2-hour walking tours that explore downtown's spookier side. The tours include narratives (some funnier than others) on Florida history and folklore, followed by a chance to use "ghost-finding" equipment in a haunted building. If your kids are over 6, aren't easily spooked, and are into the supernatural and ghost stories, it's good fun. The cost is $25 adults, $20 college students, and $15 for kids 6 to 12. Tours run Wednesday through Saturday at 8pm.

---

areas. Most theaters offer discounted ticket pricing for children under 12 and discounted matinees (though, really, who's going to sit in a movie theater instead of the theme parks?); some also offer discounts to students (bring ID). I definitely recommend that you head for those theaters that offer stadium seating (the ones I recommend below have it), so that even the shortest members of your party will get to see the picture.

AMC Theatres has a 24-screen complex at Pleasure Island in Downtown Disney (© 407/298-4488) that seats 6,000—the largest in the southeast. It's got stadium seating and digital sound systems in most of its theaters. **Universal Cineplex** at City-Walk (© 407/354-5998; www.citywalk.com) has 20 screens, stadium seating, and a state-of-the-art projection system.

Muvico Pointe 21 houses 21 screens (surprise!) in the Pointe Orlando shopping center on International Drive (© 407/926-6843; www.pointeorlandofl.com), including an IMAX screen that's nearly six-and-a-half stories high. All the theaters have stadium seating and top-of-the-line sound systems.

You can find other theaters, movies, and times in the *Orlando Sentinel* newspaper or at its website, **www.orlandosentinel.com/entertainment/movies**.

4 Theater

Orlando Youth Theatre **Age 4 and up** Here's a nifty way for families to keep the "kid" theme going outside the parks. This theater by the young includes 6- to 18-year-olds presenting shows such as *James and the Giant Peach* and *Alice in Wonderland,* as well as drama and improv in fall and spring, and during summer camps. 128 W. Church St. © 407/254-4930. www.orlandoyouththeatre.com. Tickets $8.

5 Concert Venues

Florida Citrus Bowl With 70,000 seats, the bowl is the largest venue in the area for rock concerts, which in the past have featured such heavyweights as Elton John and the Rolling Stones. It's also home of the Capital One Florida Citrus Bowl (see chapter 2). 1610 W. Church St. (at Tampa St.). © 407/849-2001 for event information, 407/849-2020 to get box-office information, 877/803-7073 or 407/839-3900 to charge tickets via Ticketmaster. www.orlandocentroplex.com. Parking $5–$6.

TD Waterhouse Centre Formerly the Orlando Arena, this 17,500-seat venue has a résumé that includes the NBA's Orlando Magic (see "Spectator Sports," in chapter 8), as well as big-name concert performers such as Garth Brooks, Elton John, and Bruce Springsteen. It also features family-oriented entertainment, including the Ringling Bros. Barnum & Bailey Circus in January, and a slate of cultural offerings such as Broadway-style shows, ballets, plays, and symphony performances. 600 W. Amelia St. (between I-4 and Parramore Ave.). ℭ **407/849-2001** for event information, 407/849-2020 to get box-office information, 877/803-7073 or 407/839-3900 for tickets through Ticketmaster. www.orlandocentroplex. com. Parking $5–$6.

6 Dance

Orlando Ballet   **Age 7 and up**   Formerly called the Southern Ballet Theatre, this troupe stages the holiday favorite *The Nutcracker* annually (on select days, a child gets in free with a paying adult to this ballet), as well as a comedic version of the cherished classic, called the *Nutty Nutcracker.* Performances are usually held in the Bob Carr Performing Arts Centre during the 2 weeks preceding Christmas and feature the Orlando Philharmonic Orchestra. One cool program run during the holidays offers a "character" breakfast that lets families dine with characters from *The Nutcracker.* Call for details if you'll be visiting in December. 401 W. Livingston St. ℭ **407/426-1739** for information, 877/803-7073 or 407/839-3900 to get tickets via Ticketmaster. www.orlandoballet.org. Tickets $10–$60. Parking $5–$6.

7 Night Out for Mom & Dad

If you're so inclined, take advantage of the various babysitting services I tell you about in chapter 4, and step out for at least 1 night of fun *sans* the kids.

The places described here can be located on the map "Downtown Disney" on p. 319. For information about nighttime activities throughout Downtown Disney, call ℭ **407/939-2648.**

PLEASURE ISLAND

This 6-acre complex of nightclubs, restaurants, and shops, not to mention a multi-screen movie theater, will not disappoint those in search of an exciting night on the town. Guests can walk the grounds and enjoy the sights, sounds, and surroundings free of charge, but if you want to enter the clubs, admission is required. A single admission price—$21 plus tax—allows you to club-hop and celebrate New Year's Eve into the wee hours every night of the week. If you prefer to head to a single club (though it may be difficult to stick to just one), admission is $11 (though the Comedy Club and the Adventurers Club don't offer single-club admission prices, so it's all or nothing if you want to hang at either of them—and you do). If you have a Premium or Magic Plus Pack admission ticket (see p. 166 for more on Disney's ticket options), you can use one of your Plus options for a 1-night admission to all clubs on Pleasure Island. Pay special attention to **Mannequins** (listed a little later). This club is the cream of Pleasure Island's crop and fills quickly, so late arrivals may be left at the door.

Pleasure Island is designed to look like an abandoned waterfront industrial district with clubs in its lofts and warehouses. But the streets are decorated with brightly colored lights and balloons. Dozens of searchlights play overhead, and rock music emanates from the bushes. You'll be given a map and show schedule when you enter the park. Take a look at it, and plan your evening around the shows that interest you. The mood is always festive, especially at midnight, which is celebrated with a high-energy street party, live entertainment, a barrage of fireworks, and showers of confetti.

In addition to the clubs, there are shops and eateries (with outdoor umbrella tables) on the island. **Planet Hollywood** (p. 145) is adjacent. (You don't need an admission ticket to eat at any of the Pleasure Island restaurants.)

For more information on Pleasure Island's clubs and events, call ℂ **407/939-2648** or surf over to **www.disneyworld.com**. Clubs are open daily from 7pm to 2am; shops open at 7pm, and some are open until 1am. There's free self-parking, but as the night wears on, spots can become very hard to find.

Although this is Disney, it's essentially a bar district where liquor is served. *Kids under 18 must be accompanied by a parent or legal guardian* if they want to come here. If you do choose to bring older children (and they should be at least 10 or older), use the same rules you use at home. Your preteens and teens might think it cool to be allowed to hang out in most of the clubs, even if it is with Mom and Dad, but this is still an adult environment, and you're better off leaving them to alternatives better suited to their age group. If you do let them tag along, bring 'em early (the later it is, the more adult the area becomes), and stick to the Comedy Warehouse, Rock 'n' Roll Beach Club, 8Trax, and Motion (all described below).

Tips On the Boardwalk

Disney's Boardwalk has a few options for folks searching for off-the-field nightlife. Street performers sing, dance, and do a little juggling and magic most evenings on the outdoor promenade.

Atlantic Dance (ℂ **407/939-2444** for limited recorded information) features Top-40 and '80s dance hits Tuesday through Thursday, and live bands on Friday and Saturday nights. It's open to everyone 21 and over. Hours are 9pm to 2am, and admission is free.

The rustic saloon-style **Jellyrolls** (ℂ **407/939-5100**) offers dueling pianos and a boisterous crowd. Strictly for the over-21 set, it's popular with visiting business travelers and is usually packed to the rafters on weekends. There's an $8 cover after 7pm.

If you're looking to hoist a pint, the **Big River Brewery and Grill** (ℂ **407/560-0253**) serves microbrewed beer, as well as steaks, ribs, chicken, fish, sandwiches, and salads. Prices range from $7 to $27, and there's no cover. It's open Monday through Thursday from 11:30am to 1am, Friday through Sunday from 11:30am to 2am. It's near Atlantic Dance.

If you're a sports nut, look no farther than **ESPN Sports** (ℂ **407/939-3463**; www.disneyworld.com), where 100 monitors—there are even a few in the bathrooms—broadcast sporting events from around the world. Need I say more? There's a full-service bar, but there are also a restaurant and a small arcade, so if you're stuck for the night with the kids, you all will have something to do.

Disney's Boardwalk can be a cheap night out if you enjoy strolling and people-watching (and if you stay out of the restaurants and clubs). The whole area has something of a midway atmosphere reminiscent of Atlantic City's heyday.

(Tips **The Luck of the Irish**

The Great Irish Pubs of Florida, Inc. (the company that created the Nine Fine Irishmen pub in Las Vegas's New York–New York Hotel & Casino), brought the luck of the Irish to Downtown Disney just as this book was going to press. **Raglan Road** opened in late 2005 on the former site of the Pleasure Island Jazz Company. The pub immerses guests in a wholly Irish environment that includes custom-made furnishings direct from the Emerald Isles. Entertainment includes Irish storytelling, dance, and music. Guests can dine on a menu of traditional Irish fare created by well-known Irish chef Kevin Dundon. Pleasure Island admission is not required to get into this pub. For more information, check out **www.disneyworld.com**.

Here's the club lineup:

Adventurers Club　The most unique of Pleasure Island's clubs occupies a multi-story building that, according to legend, was designed to house the library and archae-ological-trophy collection of island founder and compulsive explorer Merriweather Adam Pleasure, a figment of Disney's imagination. It's also the global headquarters of the Adventurers Club, which Pleasure headed until he vanished at sea in 1941. The plush club is chock full of artifacts: early aviation photos; hunting trophies; shrunken heads; Buddhas; goddesses; and a mounted "yakoose," a half yak, half moose that occasionally speaks, whether you've been drinking or not. In the eerie Mask Room, more strange sounds are heard, and the 100 or so masks move their eyes and make odd pronouncements. Also on hand are Pleasure's zany band of globetrotting friends and servants, played by skilled actors who interact with guests while staying in char-acter. Comedy, cabaret, and other shows run in various rooms within the club. It's easy to see why it's the most popular place on the island; it's a hoot.

BET Soundstage　This club grooves—loudly—to the sounds of reggae, the smooth moves of traditional R&B, and the rhyme of hip-hop. If you like the BET Cable Network, you'll love it. You can boogie on an expansive dance floor or kick back on an outdoor ter-race. The club also serves Caribbean-style finger food and periodically has concerts for a separate charge (© **407/934-7666**). You must be 21 to enter (and they will check!).

Comedy Warehouse　Housed in the island's former power plant, the Comedy Warehouse has tiered seating. A troupe of comics—the Who, What, and Warehouse Players—performs 45-minute improvisational comedy shows based on audience sug-gestions. This is Disney, so the shows are neither as risqué as those at other improv clubs nor candidates for anyone's top 10, but if you like your comedy relatively clean, you're in luck. There are several shows nightly, and drinks are served. Arrive early.

8Trax　Disco and bell bottoms rule in this 1970s-style club, where some 50 TV monitors air diverse shows and videos over the dance floor. A DJ plays everything from "YMCA" to "The Hustle" while the disco ball spins. All you need to bring are your polyester and patent leather. If you grew up during the Reagan years, you can relive your musical past on Thursday nights, when the tunes fast-forward to the '80s.

Mannequins Dance Palace　Housed in a vast dance hall with a small-town movie-house facade, Mannequins is supposed to be a converted mannequin warehouse

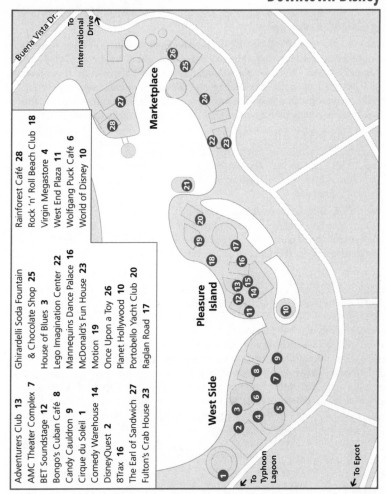

To International Drive

Buena Vista Dr.

Marketplace

Pleasure Island

West Side

To Typhoon Lagoon

To Epcot

Adventurers Club **13**	Ghirardelli Soda Fountain
AMC Theater Complex **7**	& Chocolate Shop **25**
BET Soundstage **12**	House of Blues **3**
Bongo's Cuban Café **8**	Lego Imagination Center **22**
Candy Cauldron **9**	Mannequins Dance Palace **16**
Cirque du Soleil **1**	McDonald's Fun House **23**
Comedy Warehouse **14**	Motion **19**
DisneyQuest **2**	Once Upon a Toy **26**
8Trax **16**	Planet Hollywood **10**
The Earl of Sandwich **27**	Portobello Yacht Club **20**
Fulton's Crab House **23**	Raglan Road **17**

Rainforest Café **28**	
Rock 'n' Roll Beach Club **18**	
Virgin Megastore **4**	
West End Plaza **11**	
Wolfgang Puck Café **6**	
World of Disney **10**	

(remember, you're still in Disney World). This high-energy club has a big rotating dance floor, and it's a local favorite—so much so that it's one of the toughest clubs in Orlando to get into, so arrive early, especially on weekends. Those who get in will find three levels of bars and hangout spaces that are festooned with elaborately costumed mannequins and moving scenery suspended from the overhead rigging. A DJ plays contemporary tunes filtered through speakers powerful enough to wake Sleeping Beauty, and there are high-tech lighting effects. You must be 21 to get in, and they're very serious about it. Have your ID ready, even if you learned to dance to the Beatles.

Motion Pleasure Island's newest dance club is a hyperactive joint that features Top-40 tunes and alternative rock, and appeals to younger or young-at-heart partyers. The club uses moody blue lighting, but the outer-space idea eluded me; it just looks like a cool, high-tech dance club. The club usually doesn't open until 9pm and doesn't heat up until later in the evening.

Rock 'n' Roll Beach Club   Once the laboratory in which Pleasure developed a unique flying machine, this three-story structure today houses an always-crowded dance club where live bands play classic rock from the '60s through the '90s. There are bars on all three floors, including one that serves international brews. The first level contains the dance floor. The second and third levels offer air hockey, pool tables, basketball machines, pinball, video games, darts, and a pizza-and-beer stand.

DISNEY'S WEST SIDE

This area adjoins Pleasure Island and offers additional shops, restaurants, and a 24-screen AMC Theater (see "Movies," earlier in this chapter). Older kids and teens will find DisneyQuest (p. 314) an alluring, if crowded, enticement. The two most popular adult entries are:

Bongo's Cuban Café *(Overrated*   Created by Cuban-American singer Gloria Estefan and her husband, Emilio, the cafe is Downtown Disney's version of old Havana. There are leopard-spotted chairs and mosaic bar stools shaped like bongo drums (and a Desi Arnaz impersonator every night). There's no dance floor to speak of, though you could

---

Finds   **Not Your Ordinary Circus**

Lions and tigers and bears?

Oh, no. But neither you nor your kids will feel cheated.

This Disney partnership with the famed no-animals circus is located in Downtown Disney West Side. **Cirque du Soleil,** which translates to "circus of the sun" and flutters off the tongue as *"SAIRK doo so-LAY,"* is nonstop energy. At times, it seems all 64 performers are on stage simultaneously, especially during the intricately choreographed trampoline routine. Trapeze artists, high-wire walkers, an airborne gymnast, a posing strongman, mimes, and two zany clowns cement a show called *La Nouba* (it means "Live it up") into a five-star performance. You may not be able to explain it to your kids in advance, but most of them (especially those 8 and up) will come away impressed and amazed. And so will you.

This production is more than equal to Cirque du Soleil's other famous shows in Las Vegas. That said, though *La Nouba* is a ton of fun, it's also one of the priciest shows in town. If you're on a tight or even modest budget, it may be gut-check time: Can you blow your entertainment allowance for a day or 2 on 90 minutes of fun? There are three ticket categories: $95 for adults and $76 for kids 3 to 9 (plus tax) for center-of-the-theater seats; $75 and $56, respectively, for seats to the right and left of the stage; and $61 and $49 for the very upper levels to the left and right, and the far left and right of the stage. Shows are at 6 and 9pm, 5 nights a week, but times and nights rotate (the show was dark Sun and Mon at press time), and sometimes there's a matinee, so call ahead (© **407/939-7600**) or check the show's website (**www.cirquedusoleil.com**) for information and tickets.

cha-cha on the patio, an upstairs number that overlooks the rest of West Side. It's a great place to sit back and bask in the Latin rhythms. While the mood is good, the food is a little lacking. Open daily 11am to 2am. © **407/828-0999**. www.bongoscubancafe. com. No reservations or cover charge. Free self-parking.

House of Blues   Several well-known artists have performed here, including Jethro Tull, Cyndi Lauper, Quiet Riot, Duran Duran, and others. The barnlike building, with three tiers, may be a little difficult for those with disabilities to maneuver, but there really isn't a bad seat in the house. The atmosphere is dark and boozy, perfect for the bluesy sounds that raise the rafters. The dance floor is big enough to boogie without doing the Bump with a stranger. You can dine in the adjoining restaurant (p. 146) on baby back ribs, Louisiana crawfish, jambalaya, New Orleans–style shrimp, and Cajun meatloaf. You have to see it to believe, with its voodooish atmosphere and extremely ornate decor. There's also a Sunday gospel brunch (see p. 147 for more about the menu). © **407/934-2583**. www.hob.com. Cover charges vary by event/artist. Free self-parking.

CITYWALK

Located between the Islands of Adventure and Universal Studios Florida theme parks, this nightclub, restaurant, and shopping district competes nose to nose with Disney's Pleasure Island. It's open daily from 11am, but the hours of many clubs and restaurants vary, so call in advance if you're interested in a specific venue. Most clubs stay open until 2am and will not allow anyone under 21 to enter after a certain time (see listings below for details).

At 30 acres, CityWalk (© **407/363-8000** or 407/224-9255; www.citywalk.com or www.universalorlando.com) is five times larger than Pleasure Island. Alcohol is prominently featured here, and the nights can get pretty wild, so an adult should accompany all teens, young children, and party-hearty peers. Better yet—don't bring the kids at all unless you're heading to the movies or one of the theme restaurants for dinner.

Unlike at Pleasure Island, you can walk the district for free at night, or visit individual clubs and pay an individual cover charge. CityWalk also offers two **party passes.** A pass to all clubs costs $9.95 plus tax. For $13 plus tax, you get a club pass and a movie at Universal Cineplex (© **407/354-3374**). Universal also offers free club access to those who buy multiday theme-park tickets (see chapter 7). If all you want on your night out is dinner and a movie, CityWalk's **Meal & Movie Deal** nets you dinner (an entree and a soft drink from a limited menu) at one of the district's restaurants and a movie ticket for $20, including tax and gratuity. Kids get no special price or meals; CityWalk is aimed at the moms and dads taking the night off. To get your tickets, ask at the CityWalk Guest Services Ticket Window or call © **407/224-CITY.**

Daytime parking in the Universal Orlando garages costs $9, but parking is free after 6pm. To get to CityWalk, take I-4 Exit 74B (westbound) or 75A (eastbound), and follow the signs to the parks.

Bob Marley—A Tribute to Freedom   This hybrid bar–restaurant has a party atmosphere that will make the food more appealing as the night wears on. The clapboard building is said to be a replica of Marley's home in Kingston. Jamaican vittles— such as meat patties; jerk snapper; and the brew of champions, Red Stripe beer—are served under patio umbrellas amid portraits of the original Rastamon. If you try an Extreme Measure, have a designated driver. Local and national reggae bands perform on a microdot stage. Open daily 4pm to 2am. © **407/224-2262**. www.bobmarley.com. Cover charge $7 after 8pm, more for special acts. Must be 21 or over after 10pm.

⟨Tips Chilling Out

You can grab a margarita to go and "chill" in the brightly colored wooden chairs (think of Adirondacks) outside Jimmy Buffet's Margaritaville. It's a perfect spot to watch the crowds scurrying to and from the theme parks.

CityJazz   The cover charge at this club includes the **Downbeat Jazz Hall of Fame** (with memorabilia from Louis Armstrong, Ella Fitzgerald, and other greats). The two-story, 10,500-square-foot building houses more than 500 pieces of memorabilia representing Dixieland, swing, bebop, and modern jazz. It also has a state-of-the-art sound system and stage. Graphic murals and oversize black-and-white photographs set the mood. Acts of national renown perform frequently. It's a real treat for true jazz fans, who can sip cocktails while browsing. Open Sunday through Thursday 8pm to 1am, and Friday and Saturday 7pm to 2am. ✆ **407/224-2189.** Cover charge $7 (more for special events). Must be 18 to get in.

Decades Cafe   This theme joint serves steak, ribs, and barbecue in a setting filled with music and movie memorabilia from the past 40 years. On Friday and Saturday nights, there's a DJ. Open weekdays from 4pm until closing; weekends from 11:30am. ✆ **407/224-3663.** Cover charge $5 on weekends.

the groove   This often-crowded multilevel club features a huge dance floor, a number of bars, and a handful of lounges for just hanging out. Three unique themed lounges are outfitted in blue, green, and red; each features its own decor, style of music, bar, and specialty drink to fit its ambience. There are a high-tech sound system (read: *LOUD*) and a spacious dance floor in a room gleaming with chrome. Most nights, a DJ plays tunes featuring the latest in hip-hop, jazz fusion, techno, and alternative rock. Bands occasionally play the house, too. Try the upper-level patio for a brief reprieve. Open daily from 9pm to 2am. ✆ **407/363-8000.** Cover charge $7. Must be 21 to get in.

Hard Rock Cafe/Hard Rock Live   The first concert hall to bear the Hard Rock name is next door to the largest Hard Rock Cafe in the world (p. 150). This building, fashioned to look like an ancient coliseum, has a 2,500-seat concert venue. Call ahead to find out what acts will be featured during your visit. Tickets for big-name performers sell fast. A lot of bands only your teens will probably know play the venue, but oldies such as Crosby Stills & Nash, Bob Dylan, and the Moody Blues have performed here. Concerts generally begin about 8pm. The sound system is loud, and the sightlines are pretty decent. The Cafe is open daily 11am to midnight. ✆ **407/351-5483.** www.hardrock.com. Tickets $6–$150, depending on concert.

Jimmy Buffett's Margaritaville   Flip-flops and flowered shirts are the proper apparel here. Music from the maestro is piped throughout the building, with live music performed on a small stage inside later in the evening. A Jimmy soundalike strums on the spacious back porch. True Parrotheads know the lyrics at least as well as the singers. Barwise, there are three options. The Volcano erupts margarita mix; the Land Shark has fins hanging from the ceiling; and the 12 Volt, is . . . well, a little electrifying—we'll leave it at that. If you opt for dinner among the palm trees, go for the true Key West experience. Early in the day, that means a cheeseburger (in paradise); later, it's conch fritters, one of many kinds of fish (pompano, sea bass, dolphin), and

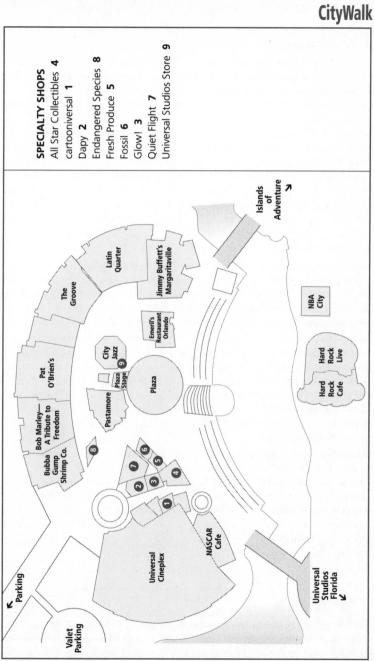

SPECIALTY SHOPS

All Star Collectibles **4**
cartooniversal **1**
Dapy **2**
Endangered Species **8**
Fresh Produce **5**
Fossil **6**
Glow! **3**
Quiet Flight **7**
Universal Studios Store **9**

Key lime pie. Open daily 11am to 2am. (See p. 151 for more on the food here.) *C* **407/224-2155.** Cover $5 after 10pm.

Latin Quarter This two-level restaurant–nightclub offers you a chance to absorb the salsa-and-samba culture of 21 Latin nations. It's filled with the music of the merengue, the mambo, and the tango, along with a bit of Latin rock thrown in for good measure; be prepared to move your hips. The surprisingly intimate atmosphere features mountainous architecture and waterfalls surrounding the dance floor; you'll feel like you're dancing in a Mayan temple The sound system is loud enough to blow you into the next county, but before that happens, you can leave on your own to see a Latin American art gallery. Open Monday through Friday 5pm to 2am, and Saturday and Sunday noon to 2am. *C* **407/224-3663.** Cover $5–$10.

NASCAR Café This one-of-a-kind, NASCAR-licensed eatery is a must for gearheads, though its basic vittles (so-so steaks, chicken, pork chops, shrimp, and sandwiches, most under $8) won't win culinary awards. The kids' menu has spaghetti, pizza, corn dogs, and more ($6). Race-related souvenirs and video games fill the first floor. Open daily 11am to 11pm or later. *C* **407/224-7223.**

NBA City If you're a fan of the NBA, this one's a must. Hoops and memorabilia hang from the walls, and TV monitors play seemingly every game on the airwaves. The mixed menu ($5–$20) ranges from steaks and chicken to fish, pasta, and sandwiches. The kids' menu ($6 including soda) has burgers, hot dogs, grilled cheese, chicken nuggets, and more. Fans young and old will like it, but if you're looking for better-than-average food, look elsewhere. Daily 11am to midnight or later. *C* **407/363-5919.**

Pat O'Brien's Just like the French Quarter, which is home to the original Patty O's, drinking, drinking, and more drinking are the highlights here. Creole treats and sandwiches (most $8–$10) take up only a page or two of the menu; the rest is filled with wild alcoholic libations. Enjoy the piano bar or the flame-throwing fountain while you suck down the drink of the Big Easy: the Hurricane. Although you can order a soft drink, Pat O'Brien's primarily promotes the hard stuff, and no one under 21 is permitted after 9pm (a kids' menu is available until then, but this is *not* the place to take them!). If your plans for the evening fall anything short of full intoxication (unless you're the designated driver for the aforementioned planners), this may not be the place for you. There's a limited menu of sandwiches and treats like jambalaya and shrimp Creole ($8–$10). Open daily from 4pm to 2am. *C* **407/363-8000.** www.pat obriens.com. Cover charge $5 after 9pm. You must be 21 to enter after 9pm.

NIGHTLIFE ELSEWHERE IN ORLANDO

Pleasure Island, Downtown Disney, and CityWalk are the biggest nighttime draws for most tourists and some locals. However, the dozens of clubs and bars on International

---

Tips **Free Ride**

A free public transportation system called **Lymmo** (*C* **407/841-2279;** www.go lynx.com) runs in a designated lane through the downtown area. But because Lymmo stops running at 10pm (midnight on Fri and Sat), it may stop moving before you do. So stash enough cash for a taxi if you're going to party late into the night.

Other Places to Party

In addition to the other clubs listed in this section, downtown hot spots include **Chillers, the Big Belly Brewery,** and **Lattitudes,** 33 W. Church St. (© 407/939-4270)—three separate clubs located in a single trilevel building that are all geared to the young-adult crowd with an atmosphere that's very casual. Another nighttime complex lined with clubs and bars is **Wall Street Plaza (www.wallstplaza.net),** a "meet market" on Wall Street that's home to **The Globe** (© 407/849-9904), a European patio cafe; **Slingapours** (© 407/849-9904), a dance club with an indoor and outdoor patio for relaxing; **Waitiki** (© 407/849-0471), a retro Tiki lounge and restaurant; the **Monkey Bar** (© 407/849-0471), a hip martini lounge and cocktail bar; **One-Eyed Jacks** (© 407/648-2050) and the **Loaded Hog** (© 407/649-1918), both party bars; the **Tuk Tuk Room** (© 407/849-9904), a cocktail-and-sushi lounge; and the **Wall Street Cantina** (© 407/420-1515), a bar that serves mean margaritas.

Drive, along Orange Avenue, and in the rest of downtown Orlando attract most home-grown night owls, business travelers who want to stay as far as possible from the Mickey madness, and a small number of enterprising tourists who venture north at night. If Mom and Dad are truly looking to avoid kids on their evening out, heading to one of the spots below is their best bet.

Cricketers Arms Pub   Regardless of whether you're British or just a sympathizer, this pub is a fun place to party. As the name implies, cricket (and soccer) matches are featured on the telly. Nightly entertainment ranges from karaoke to live bands (usually blues or soft rock). The revelry offers a good excuse to try a pint or two of any of the 17 beers and ales on tap, such as Boddingtons, Fullers ESB, and Old Speckled Hen. There's also a fun menu that offers English standards such as cottage pie and fish and chips, among others ($3.50–$14). Open daily from noon to 2am. 8445 International Dr. © 407/354-0686. www.cricketersarmspub.com. Free parking.

11

Side Trips from Orlando

Although many visitors to Orlando never venture outside the city, an excursion away from Orlando's theme parks can allow you and your kids time to recharge your batteries while enjoying some of Central Florida's other unique and sometimes more natural offerings.

Many families who vacation in Orlando (especially those using the FlexTicket pass; see p. 242) eventually drive or shuttle it an hour and a half west on I-4 to another major theme park, **Busch Gardens,** as well as some of Tampa's big-league spectator sports and smaller attractions, including the **Museum of Science and Industry.** Others—especially those with space-crazed kids—head an hour east on Highway 528 to the Space Coast, where "having a blast" takes on new meaning. Rockets really do blast off from the **John F. Kennedy Space Center** at Cape Canaveral, which is also the home of **Canaveral National Seashore** and, nearby, some of Florida's finest surfing spots. The coastal areas offer a combination of entertainment and education (be it astronomy or the natural sciences) that the whole family will enjoy.

1 Tampa

84 miles W of Orlando

Busch Gardens theme park, with its wild animals and even wilder rides, is Tampa Bay's biggest draw for families. While you're in town, you can also visit the much less frantic exhibits at the Lowry Park Zoo; educate your kids (and yourself) at the Florida Aquarium; and, in warmer months, take a refreshing plunge at the Adventure Island water park. You can do Tampa as a day trip out of Orlando, or you can spend a day or two exploring the city with your kids (I've provided accommodations and dining choices below for those of you who choose to go that route); your choice will depend on your family's interests, your remaining stamina (after hitting all of Orlando's offerings), and how much vacation time you have. Most people with only a week's vacation won't do more than travel to Busch Gardens before heading back to Mickeyville. If you've got more time, a day or two in Tampa is a fun and slightly less frenetic place than Orlando to wind down your vacation.

GETTING THERE

BY CAR   From Orlando, take Interstate 4 west (it's really southwest), which can take you to the downtown area, or Interstate 275 North, which goes to Busch Gardens and other northside attractions.

BY SHUTTLE   **Busch Gardens** and **SeaWorld Orlando,** both owned by Anheuser-Busch, offer daily shuttle service between those parks for $10. The 1½- to 2-hour run (each way) has seven pickup locations in Orlando, including SeaWorld, International

Drive, and Universal Orlando (© **800/221-1339**). The schedule allows about 5 to 7 hours at Busch Gardens, and the service is free if you buy a FlexTicket (p. 242).

VISITOR INFORMATION   Contact the **Tampa Bay Convention & Visitors Bureau,** 400 N. Tampa St., Tampa, FL 33602-4706 (© **800/448-2672,** 800/368-2672, or 813/223-2752; www.visittampabay.com), for advance information. Once you're downtown, head to the bureau's **visitor information center** at 400 N. Tampa St. (Channelside), Suite 2800 (© **813/223-1111**). It's open Monday through Saturday from 9:30am to 5:30pm.

EXPLORING THE PARKS & MORE

Adventure Island   If the summer heat gets to you before one of Tampa's famous thunderstorms brings late-afternoon relief, your family can take a waterlogged break at this 25-acre outdoor water park near Busch Gardens Tampa Bay (see below). You can also frolic here during the cooler days of spring and fall, when the water is heated. Adults and teens enjoy Key West Rapids, Tampa Typhoon, Gulf Scream, Wahoo Run, and other exciting water rides (there are height requirements on many of these thrill rides, usually starting at 48 in.). Young children can have a ton of fun in the miniature wave pool, water jets, bubbling springs, and aqua gym at Fabian's Funport. Lifeguards are there to supervise all the attractions and activities. There are also places to picnic and sunbathe, a games arcade, a volleyball complex, and an outdoor cafe. If you forget to bring your own, a surf shop sells bathing suits, towels, and suntan lotion.

10001 Malcolm McKinley Dr. (between Busch Blvd. and Bougainvillea Ave.). © 813/987-5600. www.4adventure.com. Admission $33 adults, $31 children 3–9, plus tax; free for children 2 and under. 2-day combination tickets with Busch Gardens Tampa Bay (1 day each) $68 adults, $58 children 3–9, free for children under 3. Website sometimes offers discounts. Parking $5. Mid-Mar–Labor Day daily 10am–5pm; Sept–Oct Fri–Sun 10am–5pm (extended hours in summer and on holidays). Closed Nov–mid-Mar. Take exit 50 off I-275, and go east on Busch Blvd. for 2 miles. Turn left onto McKinley Dr. (N. 40th St.); entry is on right.

Busch Gardens Tampa Bay ✹✹✹   If you have time for a day trip, this venerable theme park is a don't-miss attraction for children and adults, who can see, in person, all those wild beasts you've watched on *Animal Planet*—and you'll get better views of them here than at Disney's Animal Kingdom in Orlando (see "Animal Kingdom," in chapter 6). Busch Gardens has several thousand animals living in naturalistic environments that help carry out the park's overall African theme, including an 80-acre plain that's strongly reminiscent of the real Serengeti of Tanzania and Kenya, upon which zebras, giraffes, and other animals graze. Unlike the animals on the real Serengeti, however, the grazing animals have nothing to fear from lions, hyenas, crocodiles, and other predators, which are confined to enclosures—as are hippos and elephants. *Tip:* Before you leave home, spend some time with your kids on the park's website (**www. buschgardens.com**), which offers some wonderful educational information about the animals and environments in the park.

Timbuktu, near the center of the park, is a great place for smaller kids to enjoy miniature train and motorcycle rides, as well as the whimsical **Carousel Caravan. Dumphrey's Special Day,** a show at the Dragon's Tale Theater, and the entire **Land of Dragons,** with its treehouse, slides, and miniature rides, make this pint-size play area another high point for younger guests.

The entire family can enjoy the **Skyride cable cars** that glide high above the park; the Clydesdale barn, where these large horses are groomed several times daily; **Ubanga-Banga Bumper Cars;** and the arcade area, though the games here can significantly

Tampa

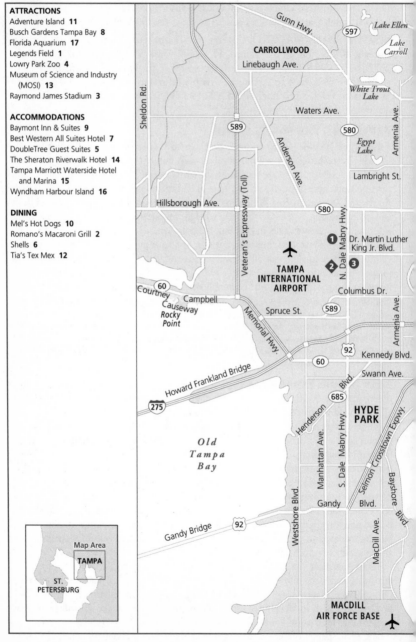

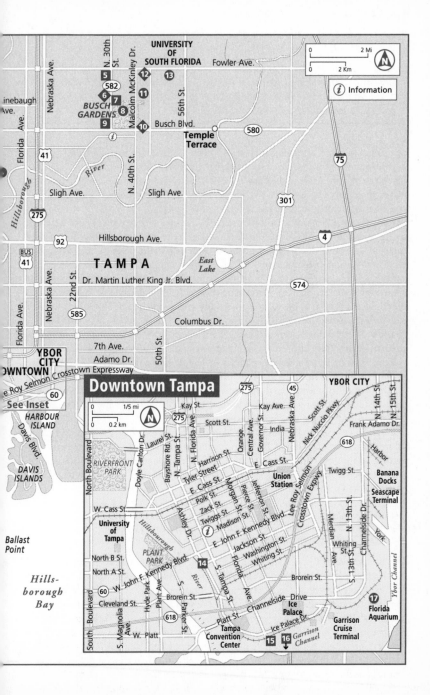

UNIVERSITY
OF
SOUTH FLORIDA

Fowler Ave.

N. 30th St.

5 582

Nebraska Ave.

12 **13**

Malcolm McKinley Dr.

56th St.

inebaugh
Ave.

6 **7** **11**

BUSCH
GARDENS **8**

9

10 Busch Blvd.

580

Florida Ave.

41

i

N. 40th St.

**Temple
Terrace**

River

Hillsborough

275

Sligh Ave.

Sligh Ave.

301

92

Hillsborough Ave.

BUS
41

TAMPA

*East
Lake*

4

Nebraska Ave.

22nd St.

Dr. Martin Luther King Jr. Blvd.

574

Florida Ave.

585

50th St.

Columbus Dr.

**YBOR
CITY**

7th Ave.

OWNTOWN

Adamo Dr.

Roy Selmon Crosstown Expressway

See Inset

60

*HARBOUR
ISLAND*

Davis Blvd.

*DAVIS
ISLANDS*

*Ballast
Point*

*Hills-
borough
Bay*

Downtown Tampa

275

45

YBOR CITY

N. 14th St
N. 15th St

0   1/5 mi

Kay St.

Kay Ave.

Scott St.

India

Central Ave.

Governor

Scott St.

Nebraska Ave.

Nick Nuccio Pkwy.

Frank Adamo Dr.

0   0.2 km

275

N. Florida Ave.

Bayshore Rd.

N. Tampa St.

Harrison St.

Orange

E. Cass St.

Lee Roy Selmon

618

Harbor

North Boulevard

*RIVERFRONT
PARK*

Doyle Carlton Dr.

Laurel St.

Tyler Street

E. Cass St.

Polk St.

Twigg St.

**Banana
Docks**

**Seascape
Terminal**

Ashley Dr.

Zack St.

Morgan St.

Pierce St.

Jefferson St.

**Union
Station**

Crosstown Expwy

N. 13th St.

Meridan
Ave.

Channelside Dr.

York

**University
of
Tampa**

W. Cass St.

Hillsborough

Twiggs St.

Madison St.

i

E. John F. Kennedy Blvd.

Jackson St.

Washington St.

Florida

Whiting St.

Whiting
St.

N. 13th St.

S. 13th St.

Ybor Channel

*PLANT
PARK*

North B St.

North A St.

River

14

Brorein St.

60

W. John F. Kennedy Blvd.

Hyde Park Ave.

Plant Ave.

S. Tampa Ave.

Cleveland St.

Brorein St.

618

South Boulevard

S. Magnolia
Ave.

Parker St.

Platt St.

W. Platt

Channelside Drive

**Ice
Palace**

**Florida
Aquarium**

17

Ice Palace Dr.

**Garrison
Cruise
Terminal**

**Tampa
Convention
Center**

15 **16** *Garrison
Channel*

(*Tips* **Flexing Your Muscle**

Busch Gardens is part of the Orlando-Tampa **FlexTicket,** which also includes Universal Studios Florida, Islands of Adventure, SeaWorld, and Wet 'n Wild. The ticket, which allows unlimited admission to the five parks over a 14-day period, costs $225 for adults and $190 for children 3 to 9.

---

dent your budget. A baby-animal nursery, petting zoo, and elephant and hippo exhibits are other family favorites. Ditto for **Curiosity Caverns,** where bats, reptiles, and small mammals that are active in the dark are kept in cages. Note that the latter is housed in one of those faux tunnels made of concrete and stucco, and the area is kept dark, so it could be frightening for some kids under 5.

Older thrill-ride fans find an enterprising mix of six roller coasters. The newest and by far the scariest is **SheiKra,** America's first and only dive coaster (and one of only three in the world), along with the **Montu, Kumba, Gwazi, Python,** and **Scorpion,** all with minimum height requirements of 42 to 54 inches. The park also has a pair of water rides: **Tanganyika Tidal Wave** (48-in. minimum height) and the **Stanley Falls Flume** (an aqua version of a roller coaster that's tame enough for most kids 7 or 8 and older). Near the back of the park, **Rhino Rally** puts you in a Land Rover for a bouncy ride through habitat that includes white rhinos, gazelles, Watusis, and wildebeests. A "flash flood" turns the Rovers into rafts that float down a short manmade river. While not particularly scary, the frantic feeling of a narrow escape combined with the rough ride may not be suitable for those under 6. The **R. L. Stine's Haunted Lighthouse 4-D** offers fun and surprises for adults and older kids.

The park also offers exotic architecture, craft demonstrations, an alligator-and-turtle exhibit, a hospitality house with free beer for adults, and the **Ka Tonga** and **Moroccan Roll** song-and-dance shows.

Note: You can get to Busch Gardens from Orlando via shuttle buses, which pick up at area hotels between 8 and 10:15am for the 1½- to 2-hour ride, with return trips starting at 5pm and continuing until the park closes. Round-trip fares are $10 per person. (It's free if you have a FlexTicket.) Call © **800/221-1339** for schedules, pickup locations, and reservations.

3000 E. Busch Blvd. (at McKinley Dr./N. 40th St.). © **888/800-5447** or 813/987-5283. www.buschgardens.com. Admission $58 adults, $48 children 3–9, plus tax; free for children 2 and under. Website offers discounts. Daily 10am–6pm (extended hours to 7 and 8pm in summer and on holidays). Parking $7. Take I-275 north of downtown to Busch Blvd. (exit 50), and go east 2 miles. From I-75, take Fowler Ave. (exit 54), and follow the signs west.

Florida Aquarium 🦊🦊 See more than 5,000 aquatic animals and plants that call Florida home at this entertaining and informative attraction, which appeals to all ages. The exhibits follow a drop of water from the pristine springs of the **Florida Wetlands Gallery;** through a mangrove forest in the **Bays and Beaches Gallery;** and out onto the **Coral Reefs,** where an impressive 43-foot-wide, 14-foot-tall panoramic window lets you look out on schools of fish and lots of sharks and stingrays. The **No Bone Zone** is an exhibit on invertebrate sea life that features a child-pleasing touch tank where kids can stroke sea stars and crabs, among others. Also worth visiting is the **"Explore a Shore"** aquatic discovery zone, where kids can explore the two-story pirate ship, scale the coral-reef rock, crawl through the wave tunnel, or slide down the water slide (with water cannons, jet sprays, and more). Lockers and a changing area are nearby (you will get wet). You can also go out on the bay to look for birds and sea life on 90-minute Dolphin Quest cruises in the *Bay Spirit*, a 64-foot, diesel-powered catamaran.

Note: If your children are 8 and older, a cool "Behind the Scenes" eco-tour program gives you an inside look at how the aquarium feeds and houses its marine residents and also offers up-close encounters with some of the animals. Older kids (and those certified to dive) can dive with the sharks for $150. Kids 6 and up can swim with the fishes (if the kids are under 9 years old, you'll be swimming too) for $75.

701 Channelside Dr. © 813/273-4000. www.flaquarium.net. Admission $18 adults, $15 seniors, $13 children 3–11, free for children under 3. Dolphin Quest $19 adults, $18 seniors, $14 children 2–13, free for children under 2. Combination aquarium admission and eco-tour $31 adults, $28 seniors, $21 children 3–11, free for children under 3. Eco-tours only $20 adults, $19 seniors, $15 children 8–11. Premium Pass including admission, eco-tour, and behind-the-scenes tour $36 adult, $33 seniors, $26 children 3–11. Website sometimes offers discounts. Parking $5. Daily 9:30am–5pm. Closed Thanksgiving, Christmas. Take I-4 West to exit 1E (22nd and 21st sts.), and head down 21st St. to Hwy. 60, make a right off Hwy. 60 onto Channelside Dr.

Lowry Park Zoo ✿   The opportunity to view 3,000-pound manatees, Komodo dragons, Persian leopards, and rare red pandas makes this a worthwhile excursion. With lots of greenery, bubbling brooks, and cascading waterfalls, this 24-acre zoo displays animals in settings similar to their natural habitats. Other major exhibits include a Florida wildlife display, an Asian Domain, Primate World, an Aquatic Center, a free-flight aviary with a birds-of-prey show, a hands-on Discovery Center, and an endangered-species carousel ride that's a real hit for children as well as carousel-lovers of all ages. **Wallaroo Station** has kids' rides, a small water park, a kangaroo walkabout, and

---

Moments   **Special Tours at Busch Gardens**

Busch Gardens offers a number of special options that are geared to families and kids.

Although you and your kids will get close to Busch Garden's predators, hippos, and elephants in their glass-walled enclosures, the only way to mingle with the grazers is on a tour. The best is a VIP **Animal Adventure Tour,** on which you'll roam the plains in the company of a zoologist. These 2-hour excursions cost a pricey $120 per person (in addition to the park's entry fee) and usually leave about 1:30pm daily. The park provides bottled water on the tours but advises all participants to wear hats and lots of sunscreen. You can reserve spots on the tours (which fill up fast) by calling © **813/984-4043** or surfing the Web to **www.buschgardens.com**. *Children under 5 are not permitted.*

Another (though less attractive) alternative is the 30-minute, zoologist-led **Serengeti Safari Special Tour,** in which you and 19 other people ride out among the grazers on the back of a flatbed truck. Five of these tours are offered daily, and they are worth the extra $34 per person, regardless of age. Reserve a space by calling © **813/984-4043** or heading online to **www.buschgardens.com**. You can by pick up your tickets for the tours at the Adventure Tour Center, located in the Morroccan Village at the main entrance. *Children under 5 are not allowed on the tour.*

a petting zoo. In 2004, a **Safari-Africa** exhibit opened, featuring elephants, meerkats, and reticulated giraffe. The **Rhino Reserve** is where you'll find a white rhino, and the **Treetop Skyfari** offers guests a bird's-eye view of the animal habitats below. Kids will have fun feeding the giraffes, and camel rides are available as well. Lowry Park has one of Florida's three manatee hospitals and rehabilitation centers. It's also a sanctuary for Florida panthers and red wolves. The zoo also occasionally offers fun and educational classes and programs where kids can get an up-close encounter with some animals. Cost depends on the individual program. Call the zoo or consult its website (an excellent and entertaining resource for kids) for more information.

Tip: If you're a member of your local zoo, you may be eligible for discounted or free admission to the Lowry Zoo. Call ahead and ask.

1101 W. Sligh Ave. ℂ 813/935-8552 or 813/932-0245 for recorded information. www.lowryparkzoo.com. Admission $15 adults, $14 seniors, $11 children 3–11, free for children 2 and under. Parking free. Daily 9:30am–5pm. Closed Thanksgiving, Christmas. Take I-275 to Sligh Ave. (exit 48), and follow the signs.

Museum of Science and Industry (MOSI) 🎔🎔 A great place to take the kids on a rainy day, MOSI is the largest science center in the Southeast and has more than 450 interactive exhibits. You can step into the **Gulf Hurricane** and experience 74-mile-per-hour winds, defy the laws of gravity in the unique *Challenger* space experience, and explore the human body in **The Amazing You.** If your heart is up to it, you can ride a bicycle across a 98-foot-long cable suspended 30 feet above the lobby (don't worry; you'll be harnessed to the bike). Your kids will likely find the dinosaurs in the lobby awe inspiring. The new **Kids In Charge,** a 45,000-square-foot space dedicated entirely to kids and the largest children's science center in the country, is filled with four unique interactive exhibits that will stimulate curiosity and encourage learning. You can also watch stunning movies in Florida's first IMAX dome theater (free with admission) or take a 5-minute ride in a flight simulator. Outside, trails wind through a 47-acre nature preserve with a butterfly garden. The museum also has a planetarium.

4801 E. Fowler Ave. (at N. 50th St.). ℂ 813/987-6100. www.mosi.org. Admission $16 adults, $14 seniors, $12 kids. With the Kids in Charge museum $20 adults, $19 seniors, $18 children 2–12, free for children under 2. Admission includes IMAX movies. Daily 9am–5pm Monday through Friday, 9am–7pm Saturday and Sunday. From downtown, take I-275 north to the Fowler Ave. E. exit (exit 51). Take this 2 miles east to museum, on right.

SPECTATOR SPORTS

National Football League fans can catch the **Tampa Bay Buccaneers** at the modern, 66,000-seat Raymond James Stadium, 4201 N. Dale Mabry Hwy., at Dr. Martin Luther King, Jr. Boulevard (ℂ 813/879-2827; www.buccaneers.com), August through December. Single-game tickets (starting at $30) are *very* hard to come by.

The National Hockey League's **Tampa Bay Lightning** play in the St. Pete Times Forum, beginning in October (ℂ 813/301-6500; www.tampabaylightning.com). You can usually get single-game tickets ($8–$155) on game day.

New York Yankees fans can watch the Bronx Bombers during baseball spring training from mid-February to the end of March at Legends Field (ℂ 813/879-2244 or 813/875-7753; www.legendsfieldtampa.com), opposite Raymond James Stadium. This scaled-down replica of Yankee Stadium is the largest spring-training facility in Florida, with a 10,000-seat capacity. Tickets are $10 to $16. The club's minor-league team, the **Tampa Yankees** (same phone and website), plays at Legends Field April through August.

Value **Discount Packages**

Many Tampa hotels combine tickets to major attractions such as Busch Gardens in their packages, so always ask about special deals.

WHERE TO STAY

If you're going to Busch Gardens, Adventure Island, Lowry Park Zoo, or MOSI, the motels I list in the "Near Busch Gardens" section are much more convenient than those downtown, about 7 to 12 miles to the south (and about a 20- to 30-minute drive in traffic). Most of these are also geared to families, so you're more likely to find kid-friendly amenities in them. The downtown Tampa hotels are geared to business travelers, but staying there will put you near the Florida Aquarium and reasonably close to the sports venues listed above. For the latter, you can also check with your favorite chain, many of which have places in the Westshore area, a few miles west of downtown.

Room rates at most hotels in Tampa vary little from season to season. This is especially true downtown, where the hotels do a brisk convention business all year. Hillsborough County adds 12% tax to your hotel-room bill.

NEAR BUSCH GARDENS

In addition to the hotels listed below, a good option in the area is **DoubleTree Guest Suites,** 11310 N. 30th St. (© **877/655-5697** or 813/971-7690; www.doubletree tampa.com), which offers all the comforts of home (including a kitchenette), spacious accommodations, and those famous tasty DoubleTree cookies.

Baymont Inn & Suites *Value*   Banana trees (though fake) and a parrot cage welcome guests to the terra cotta–floored lobby of this comfortable and convenient member of the small, cost-conscious chain. Rooms are spacious, and have ceiling fans and desks. The two-room suites feature a king-size bed in the bedroom and a pullout couch in the sitting room; all suites have refrigerators and microwave ovens. It's designed for business travelers, but small families should do just fine, and the free breakfast will help fuel you and the kids. Outside, a courtyard with an unheated swimming pool has plenty of space for sunning. There's no restaurant on the premises, but plenty of restaurants are within walking distance.

9202 N. 30th St. (at Busch Blvd.), Tampa, FL 33612. © **866/999-1111** or 813/930-6900. Fax 813/930-0563. www.baymontinns.com. 143 units (9 suites). Winter $65–$100 double; off-season $60–$80 double. Children under 18 stay free in parent's room. Rollaway beds (just 2) and cribs are available at no charge. Rates include breakfast and local phone calls. AE, DC, DISC, MC, V. **Amenities:** Outdoor pool; games room; coin-op washers and dryers. *In room:* A/C, TV w/Nintendo, dataport, coffeemaker, hair dryer, iron.

Best Western All Suites Hotel *Rfr* *Value*   This three-story, all-suite hotel is the most beachlike vacation venue you'll find close to the park, and it's an attractive spot for families. Whimsical signs lead you around a lush tropical courtyard with a heated freshwater pool (popular with kids and adults alike); hot tub' and a lively, sports-oriented tiki bar. The bar can get noisy before closing at 9pm, and ground-level units are musty, so ask for an upstairs suite away from the action if you have little ones with early bedtimes. Suite living rooms are well equipped with fridges and microwaves, and separate bedrooms have narrow screened patios or balconies. Great for kids, the 11 "family suites" have bunk beds in addition to a queen-size bed for parents and also sport VCRs. The hotel restaurant has a good kids' menu.

Behind Busch Gardens, 3001 University Center Dr. (faces N. 30th St. between Busch Blvd. and Fowler Ave.), Tampa, FL 33612. ℭ 800/786-7446 or 813/971-8930. Fax 813/971-8935. www.thatparrotplace.com. 150 units. Winter $99–$119 suite for 2; off-season $99–$119 suite for 2. Children under 17 stay free in parent's room. No rollaway beds, cribs available at no charge. Rates include hot and cold breakfast buffet. AE, DC, DISC, MC, V. **Amenities:** Restaurant (breakfast and dinner only); bar; heated outdoor pool; access to nearby health club; Jacuzzi; games room; limited room service; laundry service; coin-op washers and dryers. *In room:* A/C, TV, dataport, fridge, coffeemaker, hair dryer, iron, microwave.

DOWNTOWN TAMPA

If the two hotels I list below are sold out, another good option is **The Sheraton Riverwalk Hotel,** 200 N. Ashley St. (ℭ 800/325-3535 or 813/223-2222, www.starwood hotels.com). Set on the east bank of the Hillsborough River, this former Radisson hotel recently underwent an $8.5 million renovation before reopening in November 2005 as a Sheraton. Half the comfortable rooms face west and have views from their balconies of the Arabesque minarets atop the University of Tampa campus across the river—quite a scene at sunset (your kids should be suitably impressed). There isn't much here that's especially aimed at the kid set, but they should find no fault with the pool that overlooks the riverfront.

Tampa Marriott Waterside Hotel and Marina 𝕉𝕉   This luxurious 22-story hotel occupies downtown's most strategic location—beside the river and between the Tampa Convention Center and the St. Pete Times Forum—and was built for the business set, though it's not a bad choice for families. Opening onto a riverfront promenade, the towering, three-story lobby (look out for those palm trees) should suitably impress. The third floor has a fully equipped spa, modern exercise facility, and outdoor heated pool where kids and parents can relax. About half the guest quarters have balconies overlooking the bay or city (choice views are high up on the south side). The regular rooms are spacious enough and can easily fit a family of four (you can ask for a refrigerator), though they're dwarfed by the 720-square-foot suites.

700 S. Florida Ave. (at St. Pete Times Forum Dr.), Tampa, FL 33602. ℭ 800/228-9290 or 813/221-4900. Fax 813/ 221-0923. www.marriott.com, www.tampawaterside.com. 717 units. $129–$254 double; $450–$1800 suite. AE, DC, DISC, MC, V. Weekend rates available. Valet parking $14; no self-parking. **Amenities:** 3 restaurants; 3 bars; heated outdoor pool; health club; spa; Jacuzzi; concierge; activities desk; car-rental desk; business center; salon; limited room service; massage; babysitting; laundry service; coin-op washers and dryers; boat dock, concierge-level rooms. *In room:* A/C, TV, fax, dataport (with high-speed Internet), fridge, coffeemaker, hair dryer, iron, video games (fee).

Tips **On the Go with Babies in Tow**

If you're headed to Tampa for an overnight and don't want to have to schlep all the baby gear along—or if you decide last minute to stay and have left all yours in Orlando, **Baby's Away** (ℭ 800/252-0254 or 813/933-0035; www.babys away.com) will come to the rescue. It rents strollers, cribs (though most hotels have them), beach equipment, and plenty more. If you're in need of other necessities, the University Mall (ℭ 813/971-3456; www.universitymalltampa. com) is just a minute or two away from the Busch Gardens area hotels listed above, and there's a Walgreens nearby as well.

Wyndham Harbour Island 🏮🏮🏮   Close enough to downtown but still worlds away on its own 177-acre island, this tropical-flaired Wyndham insists that you're here on vacation and not stuck in some insipid downtown convention hotel. Rooms overlook the harbor and are hypercomfortable, with pillowtop mattresses and large bathrooms with Golden Door products. Fridges and microwaves are available for an extra fee. Luna di Mare is the hotel's exquisite Italian restaurant, overlooking the water and offering an extensive wine list, seafood, and chops—perfect for an evening out without the kids along. Guest privileges at the Harbour Island Athletic Club include full workout facilities, tennis courts, racquetball courts, and a full-service spa. Stroll the boardwalk to fully appreciate your surroundings.

725 S. Harbour Island Blvd., Tampa, FL 33602. © 877/999-3223 or 813/229-5000. Fax 813/229-5322. www.wyndham. com/hotels/TPAHI/main.wnt. 299 units. $199–$289 double, $495–$895 suite. AE, DC, DISC, MC, V. Weekend rates available. Valet parking $12; no self-parking. **Amenities:** 2 restaurants; 3 bars; heated outdoor pool; access to nearby health club; access to spa; Jacuzzi; concierge; activities desk; car-rental desk; business center; salon; limited room service; massage; babysitting; laundry service. *In room:* A/C, TV, fax, high-speed Internet (fee), coffeemaker, hair dryer, iron, video games (fee), fridge (fee), microwave (fee), VCR (fee).

WHERE TO DINE

As with the hotels, I have organized the restaurants that follow by geographic area: In & Near Busch Gardens, and West of Downtown. You can find a number of fast-food and chain eateries on Kennedy Boulevard, west of Dale Mabry.

IN & NEAR BUSCH GARDENS

You'll find several national chains and family restaurants east of I-275 on Busch Boulevard and Fowler Avenue.

Mel's Hot Dogs 🏮🏮 *Value* AMERICAN   Catering to everyone from businesspeople on a lunch break to hungry families craving inexpensive all-beef hot dogs, Mel Lohn's red-and-white cottage offers everything from "bagel-dogs" to bacon/cheddar Reuben-style hot dogs. All choices are served on a poppyseed bun and can be ordered with french fries and a choice of coleslaw or baked beans. The decor highlights all things hot dog, and the pictures, articles, and memorabilia that line the walls highlight the restaurant's history; there's also an eye-catching red wienermobile usually parked out front. Your kids will love it—and so will you. But just in case hot-dog mania hasn't won you over, there are a few alternative choices (chicken, beef, and veggie burgers, and terrific onion rings). Children's meals include hot dogs, corn dogs, hamburgers, or chicken nuggets, all of which come with fries, dessert, and a toy. Be sure to say hello to Mel; he usually greets everyone who enters his doors with a smile and a story.

4136 E. Busch Blvd., at 42nd St. © 813/985-8000. Kids' menu, highchairs, booster seats. Reservations not accepted. Most items $4–$12, kids $4–$4.50. No credit cards. Sun–Thurs 11am–8pm; Fri–Sat 11am–9pm.

Shells 🏮 *Value* SEAFOOD   You'll see Shells restaurants in many parts of Florida, and with good reason, for this casual chain consistently provides excellent value for families. Each branch has virtually identical menus, prices, and hours. Particularly good for adults are the spicy Jack Daniel's buffalo shrimp and scallop appetizers. Main courses range from the usual fried-seafood platters to pastas and charcoal-grilled shrimp, fish, steaks, and chicken. Kids can dig into fried chicken, shrimp, fish, or macaroni and cheese while they color on their placemats.

11010 N. 30th St. © 813/977-8456. www.shellsseafood.com. Kids' menu, highchairs, booster seats, placemats with crayons. Reservations not accepted. Main courses $9–$20, kids $3–$5. AE, DISC, MC, V. Sun–Thurs 4–10pm; Fri–Sat 4–11pm.

Tia's Tex Mex *(Value* SOUTHWEST　Create your own combination platter from a list that includes tamales, chicken flautas, chalupas, tacos, and enchiladas (all the taco shells here are made with vegetable oil). Or dig into one of the menu standards, such as mesquite-grilled shrimp with chipotle glaze, or sizzling steak or chicken fajita skillets. The younger set's menu offers corn dogs, chicken fingers, tacos, and grilled-cheese sandwiches. And your kids will also be kept busy by crayons and word games on their placemats.

2815 Fowler Ave. (between I-275 and Bruce B. Downs Blvd.). ✆ 813/972-7737. www.tiastexmex.com. Kids' menu, highchairs, booster seats, placemats with crayons and word-scramble game. Reservations recommended. Main courses $7–$15, kids $4–$5. AE, DC, DISC, MC, V. Daily 11am–10pm, except Thanksgiving and Christmas.

WEST OF DOWNTOWN

In addition to the restaurant listed below, you'll find the usual chain restaurants in town, including T.G.I. Friday's, Carrabba's, and Chili's, along North Dale Mabry, near Raymond James Stadium.

Romano's Macaroni Grill *☆ (Value* ITALIAN　Romano's is a small chain with a nice family atmosphere (you can definitely hear the buzz of conversation), and unlike most of Tampa's better restaurants, it's not oriented toward the business crowd. The staff will put jug wine on your table and deliver entrees such as veal piccata, chicken Marsala, shrimp scampi, and a meaty lasagna, which are reasonably priced and pretty tasty. Kids can feast on a grilled macaroni-and-cheese sandwich, a corn dog, pizza, or chicken fingers, among others, all of which come with refillable soft drinks and dessert. This place also offers stuff to keep the young ones busy while Mom and Dad eat their meals.

14904 N. Dale Mabry Hwy. ✆ 813/264-6676. www.macaronigrill.com. Kids' menu, highchairs, booster seats, placemats with crayons and word games. Reservations accepted. Main courses lunch $6–$15, kids $4; dinner $8–$19, kids $4. AE, MC, V. Daily 11am–10pm.

2 Cocoa Beach, Cape Canaveral & Kennedy Space Center

46 miles SE of Orlando

Today, this once-sleepy region, known to many as the imaginary home of *I Dream of Jeannie*, now welcomes crowds attracted primarily by Kennedy Space Center, which is not only the launching pad for the U.S. space program, but also a tourist attraction that thrills hundreds of thousands of visitors each year. A visit to the space center is usually an awe-inspiring experience for even the most jaded kids (and has launched many dreams about becoming an astronaut). If your kids' interests tend more toward natural life on earth, the area is also home to 72 miles of sandy beaches (the closest beach to Orlando's attractions); some of the best surfing anywhere around; and wildlife, at the zoo (the Brevard Zoo, which offers exhibits on par with Tampa's Lowry Park Zoo, listed earlier in this chapter), or in its more natural state—in the wild.

GETTING THERE

BY CAR　From Orlando, take Highway 528 (a toll road), exit on Highway 407, and go to Highway 405/NASA Parkway; then follow the signs east to the space center.

BY SHUTTLE　**Mears Transportation** (✆ 407/423-5566; www.mearstransportation. com) runs Kennedy Space Center shuttles Monday, Wednesday, and Friday from Lake Buena Vista and U.S. 192 (near Disney) and International Drive (near Universal).

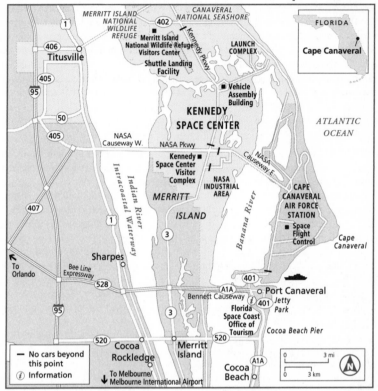

The cost is $21 per person round-trip (ages 3 and under free), and the trip allows for 7 hours at the center.

VISITOR INFORMATION For information about the area, contact the **Florida Space Coast Office of Tourism/Brevard County Tourist Development Council,** 8810 Astronaut Blvd., Suite 102, Cape Canaveral, FL 32920 (© **800/872-1969** or 321/868-1126; www.space-coast.com). The office is in the Sheldon Cove building, on Florida A1A a block north of Central Boulevard, and is open Monday through Friday, 8am to 5pm.

The office also operates an information booth at the Kennedy Space Center Visitor Complex (see below).

EXPLORING THE ATTRACTIONS

Brevard Zoo Howard and Max, a pair of white rhinos, are the newest additions at this delightful small-town zoo. The rhinos occupy a brand-new Expedition Africa exhibit that also features ostriches and giraffes (you and your kids can hand-feed the latter, whose 18-in. tongues usually startle when they snake out to grab a snack!). Other residents include dingoes, red kangaroos, wallabies, cottontop tamarins, crocodiles, howler monkeys, bald eagles, red wolves, and river otters. There's a hands-on petting zoo featuring a miniature horse, miniature donkey, fallow deer, and goats. The zoo also offers a 10-minute train tour of the grounds ($3 for ages 2 and up), educational kayak trips ($5; kids must be at least 5), a tropical garden inhabited by flying fox bats and muntjac deer, a free-flight aviary, and alligator feedings usually 3 days a week (check the schedule or website below for days and times; they change, as do the gators' appetites over the year).

8225 N. Wickham Rd., Melbourne (just east of I-95 Exit 73/Wickham Rd.). (C) 321/254-9453. www.brevardzoo.org. Admission $9 adults, $8 seniors, $6 children 2–12, free for kids under 2. Daily 10am–5pm. No admissions after 4:15pm. Closed Thanksgiving and Christmas.

John F. Kennedy Space Center ✹✹✹   Whether you and your kids are space buffs or not, you'll appreciate the sheer grandeur of the facilities and technological achievements displayed at NASA's primary space-launch facility, which is rich in history. This is where Alan Shepard, America's first man in space, and Neil Armstrong, the first human on the moon, started their memorable journeys.

Because all roads other than FL 405 and FL 3 are closed to the public in the space center, you must begin your visit at the **Kennedy Space Center Visitor Complex.** A bit like a themed amusement park, this privately run complex has had an ambitious $130 million renovation and expansion, and operators continue to tweak its offerings, so check the complex's website or call in advance to see whether tours and exhibits have changed. Also check beforehand to see what's happening on the day you intend to be here, and arrive early to plan your visit. You'll need at least 2 hours to see the highlights on the bus tour through the center, up to 5 hours if you linger at the stops along the way (or if you've got small kids and end up making lots of stops), and a full day to see and do everything here.

The visitor complex has real NASA rockets and the actual Mercury Mission Control Room from the 1960s. Exhibits look at early space exploration and where it's going in the new millennium. There are a rocket garden, where kids of all ages can explore spacecraft, including a shuttle; a daily "Encounter" with a real astronaut; several dining venues; and a shop selling a variety of space memorabilia and souvenirs. Two space-related IMAX movies (one in 3-D) shown on five-and-a-half-story-high screens are informative and entertaining.

While you could spend your entire day at the visitor complex, you must take a **KSC Tour** to see the actual space center, where rockets and shuttles are prepared and launched. Plan to take the bus tour early in your visit, and be sure to hit the restrooms before boarding the bus; there's only restroom out on the tour. The buses depart every 10 minutes or so, and you can reboard as you wish. They stop at the **LC-39 Observation Gantry,** with a dramatic 360-degree view over launch pads where space shuttles blast off; the **International Space Station Center,** where scientists and engineers prepare additions to the space station now in orbit; and the impressive **Apollo/Saturn V Center,** which includes artifacts, photos, interactive exhibits, and the 363-foot **Saturn V,** the most powerful rocket ever launched by the United States.

Kids will appreciate the **Mad Mission to Mars,** where they can explore the cosmos via a combination of live action, 3-D animation, and theatrical effects.

Don't miss the **Astronaut Memorial,** a moving black-granite monument that has the names of the U.S. astronauts who have died on missions or while in training (including the names of those who perished in the 2003 *Columbia* tragedy). The 60-ton structure rotates on a track that follows the movement of the sun (on clear days, of course), causing the names to stand out above a brilliant reflection of the sky.

Tips **Out to Launch**

If you'd like to see a shuttle launch at the **Kennedy Space Center,** first call
© 321/867-5000 or check NASA's official website (www.ksc.nasa.gov) for a
schedule of upcoming takeoffs. You can buy launch tickets at the Kennedy Space
Center Visitor Complex (© 321/449-4444) or online at www.ksctickets.com. *A*
word of caution: Shuttle launches are frequently delayed due to weather,
equipment malfunctions, or other factors, so you might have to make multiple
visits to see one. If you don't have that flexibility, the launch window may be
delayed beyond your going-home date.

If you can't get into the space center, other good viewing spots are on the
causeways leading to the islands and on U.S. 1 as it skirts the waterfront in
Titusville. The **Holiday Inn Riverside–Kennedy Space Center,** on Washington
Avenue (U.S. 1) in Titusville (© 800/465-4329 or 321/269-2121; www.holidayinn
ksc.com), also has a clear view of the launch pads across the Indian River. I've
watched from the beach at the Holiday Inn Oceanfront, and hearing and feeling the distant rumbles of the shuttle at takeoff is an incredible experience.
Note, however, that area motels raise their rates and often book up during
launch periods.

The **U.S. Astronaut Hall of Fame** (located on FL 405 just west of the center) features displays, exhibits, and tributes to the heroes of the Mercury, Gemini, and Apollo
space programs. There's also a collection of spacecraft, including a Mercury 7 capsule,
a Gemini training capsule, and an Apollo 14 command module. And in "Simulator
Station," guests can experience the pressure of four times the force of gravity, ride a
rover across Mars, and land the space shuttle. Kids around age 7 and up will think the
experience out of this world, and adults will be suitably impressed as well.

Note: Pay an extra $20 per adult and $13 per child 3 to 11 over the cost of regular
admission, and you and your kids can **have lunch with a real-life astronaut.** It's usually a thrilling treat for kids old enough to appreciate it. The schedule of astronauts
changes frequently, and you'll need to book in advance (call the space center to check
availability and book your lunch, or do it online at the center's website). Lunch is
included in the price, though there's no kids' menu.

Future space explorers, ages 14 and up (though those under 18 must be accompanied by a parent), can see and feel what space flight is really like at the **ATX** or Astronaut Training Experience. It's an out-of-this-world experience that includes a full day
of hands-on training, mission simulations, and exploration (as well as a T-shirt and
VIP tour of the Kennedy Space Center). At $225 per astronaut, space flight can, how-
ever, get rather expensive. Call © 321/449-4400 to reserve a space.

A $160 million, 10-year development plan was announced by the center as this book
went to press. The Shuttle Launch Experience, scheduled to open in 2007, will be the
first of many new additions to the complex. Custom-designed motion platforms, special
simulator seating, multiple video screens, and audio and visual effects will combine to
re-create the feeling of blasting off into space (think Mission: Space at Epcot; p. 205).

NASA Pkwy. (FL 405), 6 miles east of Titusville, ½ mile west of FL 3. © 321/449-4444 for general information, or
321/449-4444 for guided bus tours and launch reservations. www.kennedyspacecenter.com. Maximum Access Admission $37 adult, $30 children 3–11. Standard Admission passes $30 adult, $20 children 3–11. Guided tours $22 adult,

$16 children. All tours and movies free for children under 3. Daily 9am–5:30pm. Shuttle-bus tours daily 9:45am–2:15pm. Closed Christmas and some launch days.

BEACHES & WILDLIFE REFUGES

To the north of the Kennedy Space Center, **Canaveral National Seashore** 🏕🏕 is a protected 13-mile barrier island backed by cabbage palms, sea grapes, palmettos, marshes, and Mosquito Lagoon. This is a great area for watching herons, egrets, ibises, willets, terns, and other birds. You might also glimpse dolphins and manatees in the lagoon. It's a nice quiet spot for a family picnic. The beaches near parking lots 1 and 2 have lifeguards, in case you want to take a swim. Note that the park runs special Junior Ranger programs for children ages 6 to 12; ask at the visitor center or check the park's website.

The main **visitor center** is at 7611 S. Atlantic Ave., New Smyrna Beach, FL 32169 (*©* **321/867-4077** or 321/867-0677 for recorded information; www.nps.gov/cana), on Apollo Beach, at the north end of the island. The southern-access gate to the island is 8 miles east of Titusville on FL 402, just east of FL 3.

Its neighbor to the south and west is the 140,000-acre **Merritt Island National Wildlife Refuge** 🏕🏕, home to hundreds of species of shorebirds, waterfowl, reptiles, alligators, and mammals, many of them endangered. Stop and pick up a map and other information at the visitor center, on Highway 402 about 4 miles east of Titusville. The center has a quarter-mile-long boardwalk along the edge of the marsh and has displays showing the animals you may see here. You can see them from the 7-mile-long Black Point Wildlife Drive or one of the nature trails through the hammocks and marshes. The visitor center is open Monday through Friday from 8am to 4:30pm, Saturday from 9am to 5pm (closed Sun Apr–Oct). Admission is free. For more information and a schedule of interpretive programs, contact the refuge at P.O. Box 6504, Titusville, FL 32782 (*©* **321/861-0667;** www.nbbd.com/godo/minwr).

Note: Those parts of the national seashore near the Kennedy Space Center and all of the refuge close 4 days before a shuttle launch and usually reopen the day after a launch.

OUTDOOR ACTIVITIES

FISHING   If you and your kids like to fish, head to Port Canaveral for catches such as snapper and grouper. **Jetty Park** (*©* 321/783-7111), at the south entry to the port, has a fishing pier equipped with a bait shop (see "Beaches & Wildlife Refuges," above). The south bank of the port is lined with charter boats, and you can go deep-sea fishing on the *Miss Cape Canaveral* (*©* 321/783-5274 or 321/648-2211 in Orlando; www.misscape.com), one of the party boats based here. All-day voyages (including all gear, bait, breakfast, lunch, and unlimited soft drinks) depart daily at 8am and cost $50 to $65 for adults, $45 to $60 for seniors, $40 to $55 for students 11 to 17, and $30 to $45 for kids 6 to 10. Be sure to bring hats, sunscreen, and shoes with good traction for you and the kids.

SURFING   Rip through some occasionally awesome waves (by Florida's standards, not California's or Hawaii's) at the **Cocoa Beach Pier** area or down south at **Sebastian Inlet.** Get outfitted at Ron Jon Surf Shop, and learn how to hang five or ten with the store's **Cocoa Beach Surfing School** 🏕, 150 E. Columbia Lane (*©* **321/868-1980;** www.cocoabeachsurfingschool.com). It offers equipment and lessons for beginners or pros at area beaches (kids must be at least 8 and able to swim in order to participate). Private lessons run approximately $50 for 1 hour, $85 for 2, and $120 for 3;

semiprivate (two kids only) and group lessons are offered at slightly discounted prices. Be sure to bring along a towel, flip-flops, sunscreen, and a lot of nerve. The school also offers 5-day surfing camps that cover water safety and surfing instruction for kids age 8 to 16 from May to August. The cost is $250 per child and does not include lunch or snacks.

WHERE TO STAY

The hotels listed below are all in Cocoa Beach, the closest resort area to Kennedy Space Center, about a 30-minute drive to the north. If they're booked up, you can also try the new **Four Points Sheraton Cocoa Beach Surf Company,** 4001 N. Atlantic Ave. (© **800/368-7764;** www.starwoodhotels.com), which opened in December 2005. Though small, its 75 well-appointed and spacious rooms and suites are located just a block from the beach.

Note: You'll pay a 4% hotel tax on top of the Florida 6% sales tax here.

DoubleTree Hotel Cocoa Beach Oceanfront 𝘍 This six-story hotel is a good choice for families and was extensively renovated in late 2004 after suffering some damage from Hurricane Frances. Your kids should be suitably thrilled with the chain's signature chocolate-chip cookies upon check-in. All rooms have balconies with ocean views and easy chairs, and 10 suites have living rooms with sleeper sofas and separate bedrooms. A charming dining room facing the beach serves decent Mediterranean fare (there's a kids' menu, and highchairs are available) and opens to a bilevel brick patio with water cascading between two heated swimming pools. The beach is a short walk away.

2080 N. Atlantic Ave., Cocoa Beach, FL 32931. © 800/552-3224 or 321/783-9222. Fax 321/799-3234. www.cocoa beachdoubletree.com. 148 units. $119–$194 double; $185–$275 suite. Children under 18 stay free in parent's or grandparent's room. Rollaway beds $15, cribs available at no charge. AE, DC, DISC, MC, V. **Amenities:** Restaurant; bar; 2 heated outdoor pools; exercise room; games room; limited room service; laundry service; coin-op washers and dryers; concierge-level rooms. *In room:* A/C, TV, dataport, coffeemaker, hair dryer, iron.

Holiday Inn Cocoa Beach Oceanfront Resort 𝘍𝘍 Set on 30 beachside acres, this sprawling family-oriented complex, last renovated in 2004 (after that year's flurry of hurricanes had taken their toll), offers a wide variety of spacious hotel rooms, efficiencies, and two-level lofts, and is the best bet in town for families with young kids. A few of the suites are themed KidSuites with bunk beds, VCRs, and PlayStations for the kids; other suites feature sitting rooms with pullout couches. All suites come with refrigerators and microwaves. Most accommodations are in 1960s-style motel buildings flanking a long central courtyard where you'll find tropical foliage surrounding the tennis courts, a small playground area, the pool, and plenty more. The pirate-themed kids' pool is popular with little ones, and adults can relax in the tropical-themed Olympic-size pool or the hot tub. Only those rooms directly facing the beach or pool have patios or balconies; the rest are entered from exterior corridors. There's direct access to the beach.

1300 N. Atlantic Ave. (FL A1A, at Holiday Lane), Cocoa Beach, FL 32931. © 800/206-2747 or 321/783-2271. www. hicentralflorida.com/hicocoabeach. Fax 321/783-8878. 500 units. $69–$220 double. Resort fee $4.95. Children under 18 stay free in parent's room. Rollaway beds $11, cribs available at no charge. AE, DC, DISC, MC, V. **Amenities:** 2 restaurants; 2 bars; heated outdoor pool; kiddie pool; 2 tennis courts; exercise room; Jacuzzi; watersports equipment rentals; games room; concierge; limited room service; laundry service; coin-op washers and dryers. *In room:* A/C, TV, dataport, coffeemaker, hair dryer, iron.

WHERE TO DINE

On the **Cocoa Beach Pier,** at the beach end of Meade Avenue, you'll get a fine view down the coast to accompany the seafood offerings at **Atlantic Ocean Grill** (© 321/ 783-7549) and the fairly good pub fare at adjacent **Marlins Good Times Bar & Grill** (same phone). Another good casual option is **Grills Restaurant and Tiki Bar,** 505 Glen Cheek Dr. (© **321/868-2226;** www.visitgrills.com), an open-air waterfront eatery that's friendly enough to bring the kids along. Your children will likely get a kick out of watching the fishing boats come in with the catch of the day, and when there's live entertainment out on the deck, the occasional squeak or squeal easily goes unnoticed. Main courses on the immense menu (chicken, beef, pasta, seafood galore, and more) run $3 to $16.

Note: All the restaurants we list below provide kids crayons or other activities to keep them busy during mealtimes.

Bernard's Surf *ℛ* SEAFOOD/STEAKS   Photos on the walls testify that many astronauts—and Russian cosmonauts, too—come to these adjoining establishments to celebrate their landings. It all started as Bernard's Surf, which has been serving standard steak-and-seafood fare in a nautically dressed setting since 1948. Bernard's offers house specials such as stone-crab claws; Florida lobster tails stuffed with crab; chargrilled red snapper; and a belly-busting platter of shrimp, scallops, grouper, crab cakes, lobster, and oysters. Little mates can choose fried flounder, shrimp, chicken fingers, and clams, burgers, or pasta marinara. All kids' meals include fries and ice cream.

2 S. Atlantic Ave. (at Minuteman Causeway Rd.), Cocoa Beach. © 321/783-2401. Reservations recommended. Kids' menu, highchairs, booster seats, placemats with crayons. Main courses $14–$55, kids $5. AE, DC, DISC, MC, V. Mon–Thurs 4–10pm; Fri–Sat 4–11pm. Closed Christmas.

Fischer's Seafood Bar & Grill *ℛ (Value)* SEAFOOD/STEAKS   The fresh seafood also finds its way into this adjoining bar and grill, a friendly, *Cheers*-like lounge popular with the locals. Fischer's menu features fried combo platters, shrimp and crab-claw meat sautéed in herb butter, and mussels with wine sauce over pasta, to mention a few worthy selections. Fischer's also provides sandwiches, burgers, and other pub fare, and it has the same 25¢ happy-hour oysters and spicy wings as a branch of

---

Chowing Down in Nearby Titusville

Dixie Crossroads, 1475 Garden Street (© **321/268-5000;** www.dixiecrossroads. com), in nearby Titusville, is a must-stop restaurant for families. Well worth the 20-minute drive from the Cape, this unpretentious, family-owned eatery earns high marks for its southern hospitality and superior service—oh, and the food's pretty good, too. Rock shrimp is the specialty, but the seafood of any sort is worth trying. Landlubbers can dine on chicken, steaks, and ribs. Kids can choose items from their own menu or share a plate for $2.95 (a deal unheard of anywhere else). Prices are easy on the pocketbook, with a good portion of the menu costing under $12 (all-you-can-eat entrees run up to $34). Hand-painted murals adorn the walls; fish ponds (where kids can feed the fish for a quarter), a butterfly garden, walking trails, and fountains make it an experience, not just a meal. The booths are large (fitting 6 easily), but be prepared for a wait, because this very popular spot can get quite crowded.

Rusty's Seafood & Oyster Bar (see below), which also has a branch in this complex. Fischer's kiddie menu has most of the same options as Bernard's (though cheaper), plus a grilled-cheese sandwich.

2 S. Atlantic Ave. (at Minuteman Causeway Rd.), Cocoa Beach. (✆ **321/783-2401**. Reservations not accepted. Kids' menu, highchairs, booster seats, placemats with crayons. Main courses $9–$16, sandwiches and salads $4–$9, kids $3. AE, DC, DISC, MC, V. Mon–Thurs 11am–10pm; Fri–Sat 11am–11pm. Closed Christmas.

Rusty's Seafood & Oyster Bar *Value* SEAFOOD   This lively sports bar ,beside Port Canaveral's manmade harbor, offers inexpensive chow ranging from very spicy seafood gumbo to a pot of seafood that will give most families their fill of steamed oysters, clams, shrimp, crab legs, potatoes, and corn on the cob. Raw or steamed fresh oysters and clams from the raw bar are first rate and a very good value, as is a lunch buffet on weekdays. Seating is available indoors or out, but the inside tables have the best view of fishing boats and cruise liners going in and out of the port (which should keep nautically minded children entertained). The kids' menu offers chicken nuggets, fried shrimp, burgers, grilled-cheese sandwiches, and spaghetti.

Note: Daily happy hours, from 3 to 6pm, see beer drafted at 60¢ a mug, and tons of raw or steamed oysters and spicy buffalo wings go for 25¢ each. As a result, lots of couples and adults will congregate here. It's a busy and sometimes-noisy joint, especially on weekend afternoons, but the clientele tends to be somewhat older and better behaved than at some other pubs along the banks of Port Canaveral. So it's unlikely that you'll encounter a problem by bringing your kids here (and any noise they make will likely get lost in the din).

There's another **Rusty's** in the Bernard's Surf/Fischer's Seafood Bar & Grill restaurant complex in Cocoa Beach (see above). It has the same menu.

628 Glen Cheek Dr. (south side of the harbor), Port Canaveral. (✆ **321/783-2033**. Kids' menu, highchairs, booster seats, placemats with crayons. Main courses $7–$25, sandwiches and salads $4–$7, lunch buffet $6 adults, $3 kids. AE, DC, DISC, MC, V. Sun–Thurs 11am–11:30pm; Fri–Sat 11am–12:30am (lunch buffet Mon–Fri 11am–2pm).

Appendix A:
For International Visitors

Whether it's your first visit or your tenth, a trip to the United States may require advance planning. This chapter will provide you essential information, helpful tips, and advice for the most common problems that international visitors may encounter while vacationing in Orlando.

1 Preparing for Your Trip

ENTRY REQUIREMENTS

Check at any U.S. embassy or consulate for current information and requirements. You can also obtain a visa application and other information online at the **U.S. State Department's** website, at **www.travel.state.gov**.

VISAS The U.S. State Department has a **Visa Waiver Program** allowing citizens of certain countries to enter the United States without a visa for stays of up to 90 days. At press time, these included Andorra, Australia, Austria, Belgium, Brunei, Denmark, Finland, France, Germany, Iceland, Ireland, Italy, Japan, Liechtenstein, Luxembourg, Monaco, the Netherlands, New Zealand, Norway, Portugal, San Marino, Singapore, Slovenia, Spain, Sweden, Switzerland, and the United Kingdom. Citizens of these countries need only a valid machine-readable passport and a round-trip air or cruise ticket in their possession upon arrival. For those holding passports that are not machine readable, a visa will be required. *Note:* All passports issued after October 2005 require a digital photograph and, if issued after October of 2006, require an integrated chip. If you first enter the United States, you may also visit Mexico, Canada, Bermuda, and/or the Caribbean islands, and return to the United States without a visa. Further information is available from any U.S.

embassy or consulate. Canadian citizens may enter the United States without visas; they need only proof of residence.

Citizens of all other countries must have (1) a valid, machine-readable passport that expires at least 6 months later than the scheduled end of their visit to the United States, and (2) a tourist visa, which may be obtained without charge from any U.S. consulate.

To obtain a visa, the traveler must submit a completed application form, with a 1½-inch-square photo, and demonstrate binding ties to a residence abroad. Usually, you can obtain a visa at once or within 24 hours, but it may take longer during the summer rush from June through August. If you cannot go in person, ask the nearest U.S. embassy or consulate about applying by mail. Your travel agent or airline office may also be able to provide you visa applications and instructions. The U.S. consulate or embassy that issues your visa will determine whether you will be issued a multiple- or single-entry visa and any restrictions regarding the length of your stay.

British subjects can obtain up-to-date visa information by calling the **U.S. Embassy Visa Information Line** ((C) **0891/ 200-290**) or by visiting the "Visas to the U.S." section of the American Embassy London's website, at **www.usembassy. org.uk**.

Irish citizens can obtain up-to-date visa information through the **Embassy of the U.S. Dublin,** 42 Elgin Rd., Dublin 4, Ireland (© **353/1-668-8777**), or by checking the "Consular Services" section of the website, at **http://dublin.usembassy. gov**.

Australian citizens can obtain up-to-date visa information from the **U.S. Embassy Canberra,** Moonah Place, Yarralumla, ACT 2600 (© **02/6214-5600**), or by checking the U.S. Diplomatic Mission's website, at **http://usembassy-australia.state.gov/consular**.

Citizens of **New Zealand** can obtain up-to-date visa information by contacting the **U.S. Embassy New Zealand,** 29 Fitzherbert Terrace, Thorndon, Wellington (© **644/472-2068**), or get the information directly from the "For New Zealanders" section of the website, at **http://usembassy.org.nz**.

MEDICAL REQUIREMENTS Unless you're arriving from an area known to be suffering from an epidemic (particularly cholera or yellow fever), inoculations or vaccinations are not required for entry into the United States. If you have a medical condition that requires **syringe-administered medications,** carry a valid signed prescription from your physician; the Federal Aviation Administration (FAA) no longer allows airline passengers to pack syringes in their carry-on baggage without documented proof of medical need. If you have a disease that requires treatment with **narcotics,** you should also carry documented proof with you; smuggling narcotics aboard a plane is a serious offense that carries severe penalties in the United States.

For **HIV-positive visitors,** requirements for entering the United States are somewhat vague and change frequently. According to the latest publication of *HIV and Immigrants: A Manual for AIDS Service Providers,* the Immigration and Naturalization Service (INS) doesn't require a medical exam for entry into the United States, but INS officials may stop individuals because they look sick or because they are carrying AIDS/HIV medicine. For up-to-the-minute information, contact **AIDSinfo** (© **800/448-0440** or 301/519-6616 outside the U.S.; www.aidsinfo.nih.gov) or the **Gay Men's Health Crisis** (© **212/367-1000;** www. gmhc.org).

DRIVER'S LICENSES Foreign driver's licenses are mostly recognized in the

---

Visitor Information Abroad

There are several **Orlando Tourism Offices** outside the United States. You can get information from the following sources:

- **Argentina** © **0800-999-1749,** www.orlandoinfo.com/argentina
- **Belgium** © **32-2/705-7897,** www.orlandoinfo.com
- **Brazil** © **0800/556652,** www.orlandoinfo.com/brasil
- **Canada** © **1-800-646-2079,** www.orlandokissimmee.com/canada
- **Germany** © **0800-100-7325,** www.orlandoinfo.com/de
- **Japan** © **3-3501-7245,** www.orlandoinfo.com/japan
- **Latin America** © **407/363-5872,** www.orlandoinfo.com/latinoamerica
- **Mexico** © **01-800/800-4636,** www.orlandoinfo.com/mexico
- **Spain** © **407/363-5872,** www.orlandoinfo.com/espana
- **United Kingdom** © **0800-018-6760,** www.orlandoinfo.com/uk

United States, although you may want to get an international driver's license if your home license is not written in English.

PASSPORT INFORMATION

Safeguard your passport in an inconspicuous, inaccessible place, like a money belt. Make a copy of the critical pages, including the passport number, and store it in a safe place separate from the passport itself. If you lose your passport, visit the nearest consulate of your native country as soon as possible for a replacement. Passport applications are downloadable from the websites listed below.

Note: The International Civil Aviation Organization has recommended a policy requiring that *every* individual who travels by air have a passport. In response, many countries are now requiring that children, even infants, must be issued their own passport to travel internationally, whereas before, those under 16 or so may have been allowed to travel on a parent's or guardian's passport.

You can pick up a passport application at any of 28 regional passport offices or most travel agencies. Canadian children who travel must have their own passport. However, if you hold a valid Canadian passport issued before December 11, 2001, that bears the name of your child, the passport remains valid for you and your child until it expires. Passports cost C$87 for those 16 years and older (valid 5 years), C$37 for children 3 to 15 (valid 5 years), and C$22 for children under 3 (valid 3 years). Applications, which must be accompanied by two identical passport-size photographs and proof of Canadian citizenship, are available at travel agencies throughout Canada or from the central **Passport Office,** Department of Foreign Affairs and International Trade, Ottawa, ON K1A 0G3 (© **800/567-6868;** www.dfait-maeci.gc.ca/passport). Processing takes 5 to 10 days if you apply in person or about 3 weeks by mail.

FOR RESIDENTS OF THE UNITED KINGDOM

To pick up an application for a standard 10-year passport (5-year passport for children under 16), visit the nearest passport office, major post office, or travel agency. You can also contact the **United Kingdom Passport Service** at © **0870/571-0410** or visit its website, at www.passport. gov.uk. Passports are £42 for adults and £25 for children under 16, with another £30 fee if you apply in person at a passport office. Processing takes about 2 weeks (1 week if you apply at the passport office).

FOR RESIDENTS OF IRELAND

You can apply for a 10-year passport (€57) at the **Passport Office,** Setanta Centre, Molesworth Street, Dublin 2 (© **01/671-1633;** www.irlgov.ie/iveagh). Those under age 18 and over 65 must apply for a €12 3-year passport. You can also apply at 1A South Mall, Cork (© **021/272 525**), or over the counter at most main post offices.

FOR RESIDENTS OF AUSTRALIA

You can get an application from your local post office or any branch of Passports Australia, but you must schedule an interview at the passport office to present your application materials. Call the **Australian Passport Information Service** at © **131-232,** or visit the government website, at www.passports.gov.au. Passports for adults are A$150, and passports for those under 18 are A$75.

FOR RESIDENTS OF NEW ZEALAND

You can pick up a passport application at any New Zealand Passports Office or download an application from its website. Contact the **Passports Office** at © **0800/225-050** in New Zealand or 04/474-8100 or log on to www.passports. govt.nz. Passports for adults are NZ$71, and passports for children under 16 are NZ$36.

Size Conversion Chart

Women's Clothing

American	4	6	8	10	12	14	16	
French	34	36	38	40	42	44	46	
British	6	8	10	12	14	16	18	

Women's Shoes

American	5	6	7	8	9	10		
French	36	37	38	39	40	41		
British	4	5	6	7	8	9		

Men's Suits

American	34	36	38	40	42	44	46	48
French	44	46	48	50	52	54	56	58
British	34	36	38	40	42	44	46	48

Men's Shirts

American	$14\frac{1}{2}$	15	$15\frac{1}{2}$	16	$16\frac{1}{2}$	17	$17\frac{1}{2}$
French	37	38	39	41	42	43	44
British	$14\frac{1}{2}$	15	$15\frac{1}{2}$	16	$16\frac{1}{2}$	17	$17\frac{1}{2}$

Men's Shoes

American	7	8	9	10	11	12	13
French	$39\frac{1}{2}$	41	42	43	$44\frac{1}{2}$	46	47
British	6	7	8	9	10	11	12

CUSTOMS
WHAT YOU CAN BRING IN

Every visitor more than 21 years of age may bring in, free of duty, the following: (1) 1 liter of wine or hard liquor; (2) 200 cigarettes, 100 cigars (but not from Cuba), or 3 pounds of smoking tobacco; and (3) $100 worth of gifts. These exemptions are offered to travelers who spend at least 72 hours in the United States and who have not claimed them within the preceding 6 months. It is altogether forbidden to bring into the country foodstuffs (particularly fruit, cooked meats, and canned goods) and plants (vegetables, seeds, tropical plants, and the like). Foreign tourists may carry in or out up to $10,000 in U.S. or foreign currency with no formalities; larger sums must be declared to U.S. Customs on entering or leaving, which includes filing Form CM 4790. For details regarding U.S. Customs and Border Protection, consult your nearest U.S. embassy or consulate, or **U.S. Customs** (✆ **202/927-1770;** www.customs. ustreas.gov).

WHAT YOU CAN TAKE HOME

U.K. citizens returning from a non-EU country have a customs allowance of 200 cigarettes, *or* 100 cigarillos, *or* 50 cigars, *or* 250g of smoking tobacco; 2 liters of still table wine; 1 liter of spirits or strong liqueurs (over 22% volume), *or* 2 liters of fortified wine, sparkling wine, or other liqueurs; 60cc (ml) perfume; 250cc (ml) of toilet water; and £145 worth of all other goods, including gifts and souvenirs. People under 17 cannot have the tobacco or alcohol allowance. For more information, consult **HM Customs & Excise** at ✆ **0845/010-9000** (from outside the U.K., 020/8929-0152) or **customs. hmrc.gov.uk**.

For a clear summary of **Canadian** rules, request the booklet *I Declare* from the **Canada Customs and Revenue Agency** (© **800/461-9999** in Canada, or 204/983-3500; www.cbsa-asfc.gc.ca/E/ pub/cp/rc4044/). Canada allows its citizens a C$750 exemption, and you're allowed to bring back duty-free 200 cigarettes, 50 cigars or cigarillos, 200 tobacco sticks, and 200g manufactured tobacco; and 53 imperial ounces of wine, *or* 40 imperial ounces of liquor, *or* 8.5 liters of beer or ale. Canadian citizens under 18 or 19, depending on their province, cannot have the tobacco or alcohol allowance. In addition, you're allowed to mail gifts to Canada valued at less than C$60 a day, if they're unsolicited and don't contain alcohol or tobacco (write on the package "Unsolicited gift, under $60 value"). All valuables should be declared on the Y-38 form before departure from Canada, including serial numbers of valuables you already own, such as expensive foreign cameras. *Note:* The C$750 exemption can be used only once a year and only after an absence of 7 days.

The duty-free allowance in **Australia** is A$900 or, for those under 18, A$450. Citizens age 18 and over can bring in 250 cigarettes *or* 250 grams of loose tobacco and 2.25 liters of alcohol. If you're returning with valuables you already own, such as foreign-made cameras, you should file Form B263. A helpful brochure, available from Australian consulates and Customs offices, is *Know Before You Go*. For details, consult the **Australian Customs Service** at © **1300/363-263** or **www.customs. gov.au**.

The duty-free allowance for **New Zealand** is NZ$700. Citizens over 17 can bring in 200 cigarettes, *or* 50 cigars, *or* 250 grams of tobacco (or a mixture of all three if their combined weight doesn't exceed 250g), plus 4.5 liters of wine or beer and 1.125 liters of liquor. New Zealand currency does not carry import or export restrictions. Fill out a certificate of export, listing the valuables you are taking out of the country; that way, you can bring them back without paying duty. Most questions are answered in a free pamphlet, available at New Zealand consulates and Customs offices: *New Zealand Customs Guide for Travellers, Notice no. 4.* For more information, contact **New Zealand Customs,** The Customhouse, 17–21 Whitmore St., Box 2218, Wellington (© **0800/428-786** or 04/473-6099; www. customs.govt.nz).

HEALTH INSURANCE

Although it's not required of travelers, health insurance is highly recommended. Unlike many European countries, the United States usually does not offer free or low-cost medical care to its citizens or visitors. Doctors and hospitals are expensive, and in most cases, they will require advance payment or proof of coverage before they render their services. Policies can cover everything from the loss or theft of your baggage and trip cancellation to the guarantee of bail in case you're arrested. Good policies will also cover the costs of an accident, repatriation, or death. Packages such as **Europ Assistance's "Worldwide Healthcare Plan"** are sold by European automobile clubs and travel agencies at attractive rates. **Worldwide Assistance Services, Inc.** (© **800/777-8710;** www. worldwideassistance.com), is the agent for Europ Assistance in the United States.

Though lack of health insurance may prevent you from being admitted to a hospital in nonemergencies, don't worry about being left on a street corner to die: The American way is to fix you now and bill the living daylights out of you later.

If you get sick or are injured, there are basic first-aid centers in all Orlando theme parks. **Doctors on Call Service** (© **407/399-3627**) is a group that makes house and room calls in most of the Orlando area, including the Disney resorts. **Centra Care** has several walk-in clinics listed in the Yellow Pages, including ones on Turkey Lake Road, near Universal (© **407/351-6682**); at Lake Buena Vista, near Disney (© **407/934-2273**); and on U.S. 192 (W. Irlo Bronson Memorial Highway) in the Formosa Gardens Shopping Center (© **407/397-7032**). Prescriptions can be filled at pharmacies such as **Walgreens** and **Eckerd Drugs,** which have some stores open 24 hours a day; all are listed in the Yellow Pages. Many discount stores, such as **Kmart** and **Target,** and grocers such as **Publix and Goodings** also have pharmacies.

INSURANCE FOR BRITISH TRAVELERS   Most big travel agents offer their own insurance and will probably try to sell you their package when you book a holiday. Think before you sign. **Britain's Consumers' Association** recommends that you insist on seeing the policy and reading the fine print before buying travel insurance. **The Association of British Insurers** (© **020/7600-3333;** www.abi.org.uk) gives advice by phone and publishes *Holiday Insurance,* a free guide to policy provisions and prices. You might also shop around for better deals: Try **Columbus Direct** (© **0870/033-9988;** www.columbus direct.net).

INSURANCE FOR CANADIAN TRAVELERS   Canadians should check with their provincial health plan offices or call **Health Canada** (© **866/225-0709;** www.hc-sc.gc.ca) to find out the extent of their coverage and what documentation and receipts they must take home in case they are treated in the United States.

MONEY

CURRENCY   The U.S. monetary system is very simple: The most common **bills** are the $1 (colloquially, a "buck"), $5, $10, and $20 denominations. There are also $2 bills (seldom encountered), $50 bills, and $100 bills (the last two are usually not welcome as payment for small purchases). All the paper money was recently redesigned, making the famous faces adorning them disproportionately large. The old-style bills are still legal tender.

There are seven denominations of coins: 1¢ (1 cent, or a penny); 5¢ (5 cents, or a nickel); 10¢ (10 cents, or a dime); 25¢ (25 cents, or a quarter); 50¢ (50 cents, or a half dollar); the gold "Sacagawea" coin worth $1; and, prized by collectors, the rare, older silver dollar.

Note: The "foreign-exchange bureaus" so common in Europe are rare even at airports in the United States and nonexistent outside major cities. It's best not to change foreign money (or traveler's checks denominated in a currency other than U.S. dollars) at a small-town bank or even a branch in a big city. In fact, leave any currency other than U.S. dollars at home; it may prove a greater nuisance to you than it's worth.

You can exchange foreign currency at **Guest Relations** windows at all four Disney parks, at **City Hall** in the Magic Kingdom, and **Earth Station** at Epcot. Currency can also be exchanged at Walt Disney World resorts and at the **SunBank** across from Downtown Disney Marketplace. There are also currency exchanges at Guest Services at Universal Orlando and SeaWorld.

Travel Tip

Keep a copy of all your travel papers separate from your wallet or purse, and leave a copy with someone at home in case of an emergency.

> ## (Tips) Walt Disney World Services for International Visitors
>
> Disney welcomes millions of international guests every year and offers a phone service that provides information in many languages ((📞 **407/824-2222**). Here are other services in Disney theme parks and resorts:
>
> - **Ears to the World** are personal translator units that translate over 25 of Disney's shows and attractions into French, German, Portuguese, Japanese, and Spanish. They're available at Guest Relations just inside the Magic Kingdom, Epcot, Disney–MGM Studios, and Animal Kingdom.
> - Detailed guidebooks and maps to the four major parks are available in Spanish, French, German, Portuguese, and Japanese at the five International Information Centers (marked by an "i" on handout guide maps) in the theme parks and Downtown Disney.
> - Menus in Spanish, French, German, Portuguese, and Japanese are available at all theme-park restaurants that offer table or counter service.
> - Theme-park cast members who speak a foreign language sport a gold badge with the flag of that country on their name tag.
> - Resort phones are equipped with software that expedites international calls by allowing guests to dial directly to international destinations. All public telephones provide instructions in French, German, Portuguese, and Japanese. International calling cards can be found in vending machines just inside the main entrances of the four major theme parks.
> - There's also online help at **www.disneyworld.com**. Once you're on the website, go to the bottom of the screen, and click International Sites.
> - Currency exchange of up to $100 is available at Guest Relations in each of the four major theme parks and all the WDW resorts. Note, however, that you won't get the best rate if you do so; it's better to withdraw cash from an ATM.

TRAVELER'S CHECKS Though traveler's checks are widely accepted, make sure that they're denominated in U.S. dollars, as foreign-currency checks are often difficult to exchange. The three traveler's checks that are most widely recognized—and least likely to be denied—are **Visa, American Express,** and **Thomas Cook.** Be sure to record the numbers of the checks, and keep that information in a separate place in case they get lost or stolen. Most businesses are pretty good about taking traveler's checks, but you're better off cashing them in at a bank (in small amounts, of course) and paying in cash. Remember: You'll need identification, such as a driver's license or passport, to change a traveler's check.

CREDIT CARDS & ATMS Credit cards are the most widely used form of payment in the United States: **Visa** (Barclaycard in Britain), **MasterCard** (Euro-Card in Europe, Access in Britain, Chargex in Canada), **American Express, Diners Club, Discover,** and **Carte Blanche.** There are, however, a handful of stores and restaurants that do not take credit cards, so be sure to ask in advance. Most businesses display a sticker near their entrance to let you know which cards they accept. (**Note:** Businesses may require a minimum purchase, usually around $10, to use a credit card.)

It is strongly recommended that you bring at least one major credit card. You must have a credit or charge card to rent a car. Hotels and airlines usually require a credit card imprint as a deposit against expenses, and in an emergency, a credit card can be priceless.

You'll find **automated teller machines (ATMs)** just about everywhere in Orlando, including the theme parks. Some ATMs will allow you to draw U.S. currency against your bank and credit cards. Check with your bank before leaving home, and remember that you will need your personal identification number (PIN) to do so. Most accept Visa, Master-Card, and American Express, as well as ATM cards from other U.S. banks. Expect to be charged up to $4 per transaction, however, if you're not using your own bank's ATM.

One way around these fees is to ask for "cash back" at grocery stores that accept ATM cards and don't charge usage fees. Of course, you'll have to purchase something first. The same is true at most U.S. post offices.

ATM cards with major credit card backing, known as debit cards, are now a commonly acceptable form of payment in most stores and restaurants. Debit cards draw money directly from your checking account. Some stores enable you to receive cash back on your debit-card purchases as well.

SAFETY

Walt Disney World and Orlando are safe in general, and the theme parks are even safer, but crime free, they're not. You can take some general precautions to minimize your chances of being the victim of a crime.

GENERAL SUGGESTIONS Although Florida's tourist zones are generally safe,

U.S. urban areas tend to be less safe than those in Europe or Japan. You should always stay alert. This is particularly true of large American cities. If you're in doubt about which neighborhoods are safe, don't hesitate to make inquiries with the hotel front desk staff or the local tourist office.

Avoid deserted areas, especially at night, and don't go into public parks after dark unless there's a concert or similar occasion that will attract a crowd.

Avoid carrying valuables with you on the street, and keep expensive cameras or electronic equipment bagged or covered when not in use. If you're using a map, try to consult it inconspicuously—better yet, study it before leaving your room. Hold your pocketbook—better yet, sling the strap across your chest—and put your billfold in an inside pocket. In theaters, restaurants, and other public places, keep possessions in sight.

Always lock your room door; don't assume that once you're inside the hotel, you are automatically safe and no longer need to be aware of your surroundings. Hotels are open to the public, and in a large hotel, security may not be able to screen everyone who enters.

DRIVING SAFETY Driving safety is important, too, and carjacking is not unprecedented. Question your rental agency about personal safety, and ask for a traveler-safety brochure when you pick up your car. Obtain written directions—or a map with the route clearly marked—from the agency showing how to get to your destination. (Many agencies now offer the option of renting a cellphone for the duration of your car rental; check with the rental agent when you pick up the car. Otherwise, contact **InTouch USA** at ✆ **800/872-7626** or www.intouchusa. com for short-term cellphone rental.) And if possible, arrive and depart during daylight hours.

If you drive off a highway and end up in a dodgy-looking neighborhood, leave the area as quickly as possible. If you have an accident, even on the highway, stay in your car with the doors locked until you assess the situation or until the police arrive. If you're bumped from behind on the street or are involved in a minor accident with no injuries, and the situation appears to be suspicious, motion to the other driver to follow you. Never get out of your car in such situations. Go directly to the nearest police precinct, well-lit service station, or 24-hour store.

Park in well-lit and well-traveled areas whenever possible. Always keep your car doors locked, whether the vehicle is attended or unattended. Never leave any packages or valuables in sight. If someone attempts to rob you or steal your car, don't try to resist the thief/carjacker. Report the incident to the police department immediately by calling ✆ **911.**

2 Getting to the U.S.

Twenty or so cities scattered throughout Europe, Central America, Mexico, and Canada offer direct air service to **Orlando International Airport (www. state.fl.us/goaa).**

Major airlines offering service to and from Orlando out of international destinations include **Air Canada** (✆ **888/247-2262;** www.aircanada.ca), **AeroMexico** (✆ **800/237-6639;** www.aeromexico. com), **American** (✆ **800/433-7300;** www.americanair.com), **British Airways** (✆ **800/247-9297;** www.british-airways. com), **Continental** (✆ **800/525-0280;** www.continental.com), **Delta** (✆ **800/221-1212;** www.delta.com), **Iberia** (✆ **800/772-4642** in the U.S.; www. iberia.com), **Icelandair** (✆ **800/223-5500** in the U.S. or 020/7874-1000 in the U.K.; www.icelandair.com), **Northwest** (✆ **800/225-2525;** www.nwa.com), **United Airlines** (✆ **800/241-6522;** www.ual.com), **US Airways** (✆ **800/428-4322;** www.usairways.com), and **Virgin Atlantic** (✆ **800/862-8621;** www.virgin-atlantic.com).

AIRLINE DISCOUNTS The smart traveler can find numerous ways to reduce the price of a plane ticket simply by taking time to shop around. For example, overseas visitors can take advantage of the APEX (Advance Purchase Excursion) reductions offered by all major U.S. and European carriers. For more money-saving airline advice, see "Getting There," in chapter 2. For the best rates, compare fares, and be flexible with the dates and times of travel.

IMMIGRATION & CUSTOMS CLEARANCE Visitors arriving by air, no matter what the port of entry, should cultivate patience and resignation before setting foot on U.S. soil. Getting through immigration control can take as long as 2

⸝Tips **Prepare to Be Fingerprinted**

As of January 2004, many international visitors traveling on visas to the United States will be photographed and fingerprinted at Customs in a new program created by the Department of Homeland Security called **US-VISIT.** Non-U.S. citizens arriving at airports and on cruise ships must undergo an instant background check as part of the government's efforts to deter terrorism by verifying the identity of incoming and outgoing visitors. For more information, go to the Homeland Security website, at **www.dhs.gov/dhspublic.**

hours on some days, especially on summer weekends, so be sure to carry this guidebook or something else to read. This is especially true in the aftermath of the September 11, 2001, terrorist attacks, when U.S. airports have considerably beefed up security clearances. According to Orlando International Airport's website, the average time between deplaning and leaving the airport for an international visitor is 46 minutes.

People traveling by air from Canada, Bermuda, and certain countries in the Caribbean can sometimes clear Customs and Immigration at the point of departure, which is much quicker.

3 Getting Around the U.S.

BY PLANE Some large airlines offer transatlantic or transpacific passengers special discount tickets under the name **Visit USA,** which allows mostly one-way travel from one U.S. destination to another at very low prices. Unavailable in the United States, these discount tickets must be purchased abroad in conjunction with your international fare. This system is the easiest, fastest, and cheapest way to see the country. Obtain information well in advance from your travel agent or the airline, because the conditions attached to these discount tickets can be changed without notice.

BY TRAIN International visitors (excluding Canada) can buy a **USA Railpass,** good for 15 or 30 days of unlimited travel on Amtrak (© **800/USA-RAIL;** www.amtrak.com). Prices in 2005 for a 15-day pass were $295 off peak, $440 peak; a 30-day pass costs $385 off peak, $550 peak. The pass is available through many foreign travel agents. If you plan on spending time only on the East Coast of the United States, prices in 2005 for a 15-day East pass were $210 off peak, $325 peak; a 30-day pass costs $270 off peak, $405 peak. With a foreign passport, you can also buy passes at some Amtrak offices in the United States, including locations in San Francisco, Los Angeles, Chicago, New York, Miami, Boston, and Washington, D.C. Reservations are generally required and should be made as early as possible.

BY CAR You're going to need a car to get around Orlando unless you're committed to staying at Disney, riding shuttles, or paying a premium for cabs. Relying on public transportation is futile except in the downtown area.

To rent a car, you need a major credit card and a driver's license (sometimes, a hefty cash deposit can be used instead of a credit card). You must also be at least 25 years old. Some companies rent to younger people but add a daily surcharge, which can run as high as $20 per day. There are two gas (petrol) options when renting a car: returning it with a full tank or bringing it back empty and paying the rental company's rate upfront. Refueling on your own is the more cost-effective option, but if you have an early flight home, you may not want to waste the time to refuel on the way to the airport. All the major car-rental companies are represented in Florida (see appendix B, "Useful Toll-Free Numbers & Websites," for the contact information for these companies).

If you plan to rent a car in the United States, you probably won't need the services of an additional automobile organization. If you're planning to buy or borrow a car, automobile-association membership is recommended. **AAA, the American Automobile Association** (© **800/222-4357;** travel.aaa.com), is the country's largest auto club and supplies its members maps; insurance; and, most important, emergency road service. The cost of joining runs from $63 for singles to $87 for two members, but if you're a member of a foreign auto club with reciprocal arrangements, you can enjoy free AAA service in America. See "Automobile Organizations," in "Fast Facts" later in this chapter, for more information.

BY BUS   Bus travel is often the most economical form of public transit for short hops between U.S. cities, but it can also be slow and uncomfortable—certainly not an option for everyone (particularly when Amtrak, which is far more luxurious, offers similar rates). **Greyhound/Trailways** (*©* 800/231-2222; www.greyhound. com), the sole nationwide bus line, offers an **International Ameripass** that must be purchased before coming to the United States or by phone through the Greyhound International Office at the Port Authority Bus Terminal in New York City (*©* 212/971-0492). The pass can be obtained from foreign travel agents or through Greyhound's website (order at least 21 days before your departure to the U.S.) and costs less than the domestic version. Passes cost as follows in 2005: 4 days ($179), 7 days ($239), 10 days ($289), 15 days ($349), 21 days ($419), 30 days ($479), 45 days ($529), and 60 days ($639). You can get more info on the pass at the website or by calling *©* 402/330-8552. In addition, special rates are available for seniors, students, and children.

FAST FACTS: For the International Traveler

Automobile Organizations Auto clubs will supply maps, suggested routes, guidebooks, accident and bail-bond insurance, and emergency road service. The **American Automobile Association (AAA)** is the major auto club in the United States. If you belong to an auto club in your home country, inquire about AAA reciprocity before you leave. You may be able to join AAA even if you're not a member of a reciprocal club; to inquire, call AAA (*©* 800/222-4357). AAA is actually an organization of regional auto clubs; so look under "AAA Automobile Club" in the White Pages of the telephone directory. AAA has a nationwide emergency-road-service telephone number (*©* 800/AAA-HELP).

Business Hours Offices are usually open weekdays from 9am to 5pm. Banks are open weekdays from 9am to 4m or later and sometimes Saturday mornings. Stores typically open between 9 and 10am and close between 5 and 6pm from Monday through Saturday. Stores in shopping complexes and malls tend to stay open late, until about 9pm on weekdays and weekends, and many malls and larger department stores are open on Sundays.

Currency & Currency Exchange See "Entry Requirements" and "Money" in "Preparing for Your Trip," earlier in this chapter.

Drinking Laws The legal age for purchase and consumption of alcoholic beverages is 21; proof of age is required and often requested at bars, nightclubs, and restaurants, so it's always a good idea to bring ID when you go out. Beer and wine often can be purchased in supermarkets.

Do not carry open containers of alcohol in your car or any public area that isn't zoned for alcohol consumption. The police can fine you on the spot. And nothing will ruin your trip faster than getting a citation for DUI ("driving under the influence"), so don't even think about driving while intoxicated.

Electricity Like Canada, the United States uses 110 to 120 volts AC (60 cycles), compared with 220 to 240 volts AC (50 cycles) in most of Europe, Australia, and New Zealand. If your small appliances use 220 to 240 volts, you'll need a 110-volt transformer and a plug adapter with two flat parallel pins to operate them here. Downward converters that change 220 to 240 volts to 110 to 120 volts are difficult to find in the United States, so bring one with you.

Embassies & Consulates All embassies are located in the nation's capital, Washington, D.C. Some consulates are located in major U.S. cities, and most nations have a mission to the United Nations in New York City. If your country isn't listed below, call for directory information in Washington, D.C. (© **202/555-1212**), or log on to **www.embassy.org/embassies**.

The embassy of **Australia** is at 1601 Massachusetts Ave. NW, Washington, DC 20036 (© **202/797-3000**; www.austemb.org). There are consulates in New York, Honolulu, Houston, Los Angeles, and San Francisco.

The embassy of **Canada** is at 501 Pennsylvania Ave. NW, Washington, DC 20001 (© **202/682-1740**; www.canadianembassy.org). Other Canadian consulates are in Buffalo (New York), Detroit, Los Angeles, New York, and Seattle.

The embassy of **Ireland** is at 2234 Massachusetts Ave. NW, Washington, DC 20008 (© **202/462-3939**; www.irelandemb.org). Irish consulates are located in Boston, Chicago, New York, San Francisco, and other cities. See the website for a complete listing.

The embassy of **Japan** is at 2520 Massachusetts Ave. NW, Washington, DC 20008 (© **202/238-6700**; www.embjapan.org). Japanese consulates are located in many cities, including Atlanta, Boston, Detroit, New York, San Francisco, and Seattle.

The embassy of **New Zealand** is at 37 Observatory Circle NW, Washington, DC 20008 (© **202/328-4800**; www.nzemb.org). New Zealand consulates are located in Los Angeles, Salt Lake City, San Francisco, and Seattle.

The embassy of the **United Kingdom** is at 3100 Massachusetts Ave. NW, Washington, DC 20008 (© **202/588-7800**; www.britainusa.com). Other British consulates are available in Atlanta, Boston, Chicago, Cleveland, Houston, Los Angeles, New York, San Francisco, and Seattle.

Emergencies Call © **911** to report a fire, call the police, or get an ambulance anywhere in the United States. This is a toll-free call. (No coins are required at public telephones.)

The Florida Tourism Industry Marketing Corporation, the state tourism-promotions board, sponsors a help line (© **800/647-9284**). With operators **speaking over 100 languages,** it can provide general directions, and can help with lost travel papers and credit cards, minor medical emergencies, accidents, money transfer, airline confirmation, and much more.

Gasoline (Petrol) Petrol is known as gasoline (or simply gas) in the United States, and petrol stations are known as both gas stations and service stations. At press time, the cost of gasoline in the United States is abnormally high ($2.50 a gallon in Orlando) and fluctuating drastically. Taxes are already included in the printed price. One U.S. gallon equals 3.8 liters or .85 imperial gallon.

Holidays Banks; government offices; post offices; and many stores, restaurants, and museums are closed on the following legal national holidays: January 1 (New Year's Day), the third Monday in January (Martin Luther King, Jr., Day), the third Monday in February (Presidents' Day, Washington's Birthday), the last Monday in May (Memorial Day), July 4 (Independence Day), the first Monday in September (Labor Day), the second Monday in October (Columbus Day), November 11 (Veterans' Day/Armistice Day), the fourth Thursday in November (Thanksgiving Day), and December 25 (Christmas). Also, the Tuesday following the first Monday in November is Election Day and is a federal-government holiday in presidential-election years (held every 4 years, and next in 2008).

Legal Aid As an international tourist, you'll probably never become involved with the American legal system. If you are stopped for a minor infraction, such as speeding or some other traffic violation, never attempt to pay the fine directly to a police officer; you may be arrested on the much more serious charge of attempted bribery. Pay fines to the clerk of the court (© **407/836-6000** in Orlando or © **407/343-3530** in Kissimmee). If you're accused of a more serious offense, it's wise to say and do nothing before consulting a lawyer. Under U.S. law, an arrested person is allowed one telephone call to a party of his or her choice. Call your embassy or consulate.

Mail If you want to receive mail on your vacation, and you aren't sure of your address, your mail can be sent to you, in your name, c/o General Delivery at the main post office of the city or region where you expect to be. The post office nearest Disney and Universal is at 10450 Turkey Lake Rd., in Orlando (© **800/275-8777**). The ZIP code is 32819. You must pick up your mail in person and produce proof of identity (driver's license, passport, and so on).

Often found at intersections, mailboxes are blue with a red-and-white stripe and carry the inscription U.S. MAIL. Make sure you see this inscription; overnight-delivery companies also often have dropoff boxes along the road. Don't forget to add the five-digit postal code, or ZIP code, after the two-letter abbreviation of the state to which the mail is addressed (FL for Florida, NY for New York, and so on).

At press time, domestic postage rates were 24¢ for a postcard and 39¢ for a letter. For international mail, a first-class letter of up to ½ ounce costs 84¢ (63¢ to Canada and Mexico); a first-class postcard costs 75¢ (55¢ to Canada and Mexico); and a preprinted postal aerogramme costs 75¢. For more information, see **pe.usps.gov**.

Measurements See the chart on the inside front cover of this book for details on converting metric measurements to U.S. equivalents.

Smoking Heavy smokers have it rough in Florida: Smoking is banned in public buildings, sports arenas, elevators, theaters, banks, lobbies, restaurants, offices, stores, bed-and-breakfasts, many small hotels, and bars. Inside the theme parks, you can smoke only in designated outdoor areas.

Taxes The United States doesn't have a VAT (value-added tax) or other tax assessed on most things at a national level. In Florida, however, purchases are taxed at a rate of 6.5% to 7%, depending on the county. Hotel taxes in and around Orlando can push the totals up to 11% or even 12%.

Telephone, Telegraph, Telex & Fax The telephone system in the United States is run by private corporations, so rates, especially for long-distance service and operator-assisted calls, can vary widely. Generally, hotel surcharges on long-distance and local calls are astronomical, so you're usually better off using a **public pay telephone,** which you'll find clearly marked in most public buildings and private establishments, as well as on the street. They can also be found at most convenience grocery stores and gas stations. Many convenience groceries and pharmacies sell **prepaid calling cards** in $5 or $10 increments or by the number of minutes you choose; these can be the least expensive way to call home. Many public phones at airports now accept American Express, Master-Card, and Visa credit cards. **Local calls** made from public pay phones in most locales cost either 35¢ or 50¢. Pay phones do not accept pennies, and few will take anything larger than a quarter.

You may want to lease a cellphone for the duration of your trip.

Most long-distance and international calls can be dialed directly from any phone. **For calls within the United States and to Canada,** dial 1, followed by the area code and the seven-digit number. **For other international calls,** dial 011, followed by the country code, city code, and the telephone number of the person you are calling.

Calls to area codes **800, 888, 877,** and **866** are toll free. However, calls to numbers in area codes **700** and **900** (chat lines, bulletin boards, "dating" services, and so on) can be very expensive—usually a charge of 95¢ to $3 or more per minute, and they sometimes have minimum charges that can run as high as $15 or more.

For **reversed-charge or collect calls,** and for person-to-person calls, dial 0 (zero, not the letter O), followed by the area code and number you want; an operator will come on the line, and you should specify that you are calling collect, person to person, or both. If your operator-assisted call is international, ask for the overseas operator.

For **local directory assistance** ("information"), dial 411; for long-distance information, dial 1, followed by the appropriate area code and 555-1212.

Most telegraph and telex services in the United States are provided by **Western Union.** You can dictate a telegram over the phone by calling ℂ **800/325-6000,** or use the number to check on the nearest location to wire money or have it sent to you.

Most hotels have **fax machines** available for guest use (be sure to ask about the charge to use it). A less expensive way to send and receive faxes may be at stores such as **The UPS Store** (formerly Mail Boxes Etc.), a national chain of retail packing-service shops. (Look in the Yellow Pages directory under "Packing Services.")

The United States has two kinds of telephone directories. The **White Pages** list private households and business subscribers in alphabetical order. The inside front cover lists emergency numbers for police, fire, ambulance, poison-control center, crime victims' hotline, and so on. The first few pages will tell you how to make long-distance and international calls, complete with country codes and area codes. Government numbers are usually printed on blue paper within the White Pages. Printed on yellow paper, the so-called **Yellow Pages** list all local services, businesses, industries, and houses of worship according to activity, with an index at the front or back. (Drugstores/pharmacies and restaurants are also listed by geographic location.) The Yellow Pages also include city plans or detailed area maps, postal ZIP codes, and public-transportation routes.

Time The United States is divided into six time zones. From east to west, they are Eastern Standard Time (EST), Central Standard Time (CST), Mountain Standard Time (MST), Pacific Standard Time (PST), Alaska Standard Time (AST), and Hawaii Standard Time (HST). **Orlando,** like most of Florida, is on **Eastern Standard Time.** When it's noon in Orlando, it's 7am in Honolulu, 8am in Anchorage, 9am in Vancouver and Los Angeles, 11am in Winnipeg and New Orleans, and 5pm in London.

Daylight saving time takes effect at 2am the first Sunday in April until 2am the last Sunday in October, except in Arizona, Hawaii, the U.S. Virgin Islands, and Puerto Rico. Daylight saving moves the clock 1 hour ahead of standard time. (A new law will extend daylight saving time in 2007; clocks will change the second Sunday in March and the first Sunday in November.)

Tipping Tips are a very important part of certain workers' salaries, so it's necessary to leave appropriate gratuities. In hotels, tip **bellhops** at least $1 per bag ($2–$3 if you have a lot of luggage), and tip the **chamber staff** $1 to $2 per day (more if you've left a disaster area for him or her to clean up). Tip the **doorman** or **concierge** only if he or she has provided you some specific service (for example, calling a cab for you or obtaining difficult-to-get theater tickets). Tip the **valet-parking attendant** $1 every time you get your car.

In restaurants, bars, and nightclubs, tip **service staff** 15% to 20% of the check; tip **bartenders** 10% to 15%; tip **checkroom attendants** $1 per garment; and tip **valet-parking attendants** $1 per vehicle.

As for other service personnel, tip **cab drivers** 15% of the fare; tip **skycaps** at airports at least $1 per bag ($2–$3 if you have a lot of luggage); and tip **hairdressers** and **barbers** 15% to 20%.

Toilets You won't find public toilets or restrooms on the streets in most U.S. cities, but they can be found in hotel lobbies, bars, restaurants, museums, department stores, railway and bus stations, and service stations. Large hotels and fast-food restaurants are probably the best bet for good, clean facilities. If possible, avoid the toilets at parks and beaches, which tend to be dirty; some may be unsafe. Restaurants and bars in resorts or heavily visited areas may reserve their restrooms for patrons. Some establishments display a notice indicating this. You can ignore this sign or, better yet, avoid arguments by paying for a cup of coffee or a soft drink, which will qualify you as a patron.

Appendix B:
Useful Toll-Free Numbers
& Websites

AIRLINES
Aer Lingus
☎ 800/474-7424 in the U.S.
☎ 01/886-8888 in Ireland
www.aerlingus.com

Aero Mexico
☎ 800/237-6639
www.aeromexico.com

Air Canada
☎ 888/247-2262
www.aircanada.ca

Air New Zealand
☎ 800/262-1234 or 800/262-2468 in the U.S.
☎ 800/663-5494 in Canada
☎ 0800/737-767 in New Zealand
www.airnewzealand.com

Air Tran Airlines
☎ 800/247-8726
www.airtran.com

Alaska Airlines
☎ 800/426-0333
www.alaskaair.com

American Airlines
☎ 800/433-7300
www.aa.com

American Trans Air
☎ 800/225-2995
www.ata.com

America West Airlines
☎ 800/235-9292
www.americawest.com

British Airways
☎ 800/247-9297

☎ 0345/222-111 or 0845/77-333-77 in the U.K.
www.british-airways.com

Continental Airlines
☎ 800/525-0280
www.continental.com

Delta Air Lines
☎ 800/221-1212
www.delta.com

Frontier Airlines
☎ 800/432-1359
www.frontierairlines.com

JetBlue Airways
☎ 800/538-2583
www.jetblue.com

Midwest Express
☎ 800/452-2022
www.midwestexpress.com

Northwest Airlines
☎ 800/225-2525
www.nwa.com

Quantas
☎ 800/227-4500 in the US
☎ 612/9691-3636 in Australia
www.quantas.com

Southwest Airlines
☎ 800/435-9792
www.southwest.com

Spirit Airlines
☎ 800/772-7117
www.spiritair.com

United Airlines
☎ 800/241-6522
www.united.com

US Airways
℃ 800/428-4322
www.usairways.com

Virgin Atlantic Airways
℃ 800/862-8621 in the continental U.S.
℃ 0293/747-747 in the U.K.
www.virgin-atlantic.com

CAR-RENTAL AGENCIES

Alamo
℃ 800/327-9633
www.goalamo.com

Avis
℃ 800/331-1212 in the continental U.S.
℃ 800/TRY-AVIS in Canada
www.avis.com

Budget
℃ 800/527-0700
https://rent.drivebudget.com/Home.jsp

Dollar
℃ 800/800-4000
www.dollar.com

Enterprise
℃ 800/325-8007
www.enterprise.com

Hertz
℃ 800/654-3131
www.hertz.com

Luxury Rental Cars of Orlando
℃ 888/641-9221
℃ 407/41-9221
www.luxrentals.com

National
℃ 800/CAR-RENT
www.nationalcar.com

Payless
℃ 800/PAYLESS
www.paylesscarrental.com

Thrifty
℃ 800/367-2277
www.thrifty.com

SHUTTLE SERVICES

Mears Transportation Services
℃ 407/423-5566
www.mearstransportation.com

Quick Silver Tours and Transportation
℃ 888/GO-To-WDW

℃ 407/299-1431
www.quicksilver-tours.com

Tiffany Towncar Service
℃ 888/838/2161
℃ 407/251-5431
www.tiffanytowncar.com

MAJOR HOTEL & MOTEL CHAINS

Amerisuites
℃ 800/833-1516
www.amerisuites.com

Baymont Inns & Suites
℃ 800/301-0200
www.baymontinns.com

Best Western International
℃ 800/528-1234
www.bestwestern.com

Clarion Hotels
℃ 800/CLARION
www.clarionhotel.com

Comfort Inns
℃ 800/228-5150
www.hotelchoice.com

Courtyard by Marriott
℃ 800/321-2211
www.courtyard.com

Crowne Plaza
℃ 877/239-1222
www.crowneplaza.com

Days Inn
℃ 800/325-2525
www.daysinn.com

DoubleTree Hotels
☎ 800/222-TREE
www.doubletree.com

Econo Lodges
☎ 800/55-ECONO
www.hotelchoice.com

Embassy Suites
☎ 800/362-2779
www.embassy-suites.com

Fairfield Inn by Marriott
☎ 800/228-2800
www.fairfieldinn.com

Hampton Inn
☎ 800/HAMPTON
www.hampton-inn.com

Hilton Hotels
☎ 800/HILTONS
www.hilton.com

Holiday Inn
☎ 800/HOLIDAY
www.basshotels.com

Homewood Suites
☎ 800/225-5446
www.Homewood-suites.com

Howard Johnson
☎ 800/654-2000
www.hojo.com

Hyatt Hotels & Resorts
☎ 800/228-9000
www.hyatt.com

Inter-Continental Hotels & Resorts
☎ 888/567-8725
www.interconti.com

ITT Sheraton
☎ 800/325-3535
www.starwood.com

La Quinta Motor Inns
☎ 800/531-5900
www.laquinta.com

Loews Hotels
☎ 800/23-LOEWS
www.loewshotels.com

Marriott Hotels
☎ 800/228-9290
www.marriott.com

Motel 6
☎ 800/4-MOTEL6
www.motel6.com

Quality Inns
☎ 800/228-5151
www.hotelchoice.com

Radisson Hotels International
☎ 800/333-3333
www.radisson.com

Ramada Inns
☎ 800/2-RAMADA
www.ramada.com

Red Carpet Inns
☎ 800/251-1962
www.reservahost.com

Red Roof Inns
☎ 800/843-7663
www.redroof.com

Renaissance Hotels
☎ 800/228-9290
www.renaissancehotels.com

Residence Inn by Marriott
☎ 800/331-3131
www.residenceinn.com

Rodeway Inns
☎ 800/228-2000
www.hotelchoice.com

Sheraton Hotels & Resorts
☎ 800/325-3535
www.sheraton.com

Sleep Inn
☎ 800/753-3746
www.sleepinn.com

Springhill Suites
☎ 800/287-9400
www.springhillsuites.com

Staybridge Suites
☎ 800/238-8000
www.statbridge.com

Super 8 Motels
℃ 800/800-8000
www.super8.com

Travelodge
℃ 800/255-3050
www.travelodge.com

Westin Hotels & Resorts
℃ 800/937-8461
www.westin.com

Wyndham Hotels and Resorts
℃ 800/822-4200 in the continental U.S.
and Canada
www.wyndham.com

Index

See also Accommodations and Restaurant indexes, below.